Here lies one whose name is writ on ivory! might be the epigraph of every great pianist's life, and the ivory is about as perdurable stuff as the water in which is written the epitaph of John Keats. Despite cunning reproductive contrivances the executive musician has no more chance of lasting fame than the actor. The career of both is brief, but brilliant. Glory, then, is largely a question of memory, and when contemporaries of a tonal artist pass away then he has no existence except in the biographical dictionaries.

—James Gibbons Huneker in *Unicorns,* 1921

[H]e is a true Chopinist, and I do not care if he stands on his head, for he plays Chopin as does no other living human. The touch, the delicacy, the absolute *finesse* are overshadowed by something mysterious and temperamental; but there—I have been writing about Pachmann for ten years! Other virtuosi display more health, are less neurotic in their interpretations; but what have Chopin and a roast beef sandwich in common!

—James Gibbons Huneker, *Musical Courier*, June 11, 1902

It is true that his playing became more and more eccentric and distorted, like the fantastical character of the man, as the years gathered upon him. Almost certainly personal affairs, peculiarities, tragedies, had to do with this. A romancer or biographer with an appetite for the exceptional would find a rich field in the personality of this singular man, who laughed at the public, at himself, and sometimes at music.

—From Pachmann's obituary in the *New York Times*, January 15, 1933, by Olin Downes

Chopin's Prophet

The Life of Pianist Vladimir de Pachmann

Edward Blickstein and Gregor Benko

The Scarecrow Press, Inc.
Lanham • Toronto • Plymouth, UK
2013

Published by Scarecrow Press, Inc.
A wholly owned subsidary of The Rowman & Littlefield Publishing Group, Inc.
4501 Forbes Boulevard, Suite 200, Lanham, Maryland 20706
www.rowman.com

10 Thornbury Road, Plymouth PL6 7PP, United Kingdom

British Cataloging in Publication Information Available

Library of Congress Cataloging-in-Publication Data
Benko, Gregor.
  Chopin's profit : the life of pianist Vladimir de Pachmann / Gregor Benko & Edward Blickstein.
      pages cm
  Includes bibliographical references.
  ISBN 978-0-8108-8496-0 (cloth : alk. paper) — ISBN 978-0-8108-8497-7 (electronic) 1. Pachmann, Vladimir de, 1848–1933. 2. Pianists—Biography. I. Blickstein, Edward. II. Title.
  ML417.P17B46 2013
  786.2092—dc23
  [B]

                                                          2013010941

∞[TM] The paper used in this publication meets the minimum requirements of American National Standard for Information Sciences—Permanence of Paper for Printed Library Materials, ANSI / NISO Z39.48-1992.

Printed in the United States of America

Contents

Acknowledgments

We would like to thank the following for their help:

Carl Abbott

Mark Arnest

The Bagby
  Foundation

Roald Baumann

Robert Baxter

Robert Bernstein

Otto Biba

Michael Burford

Martin Campbell-
  White

Ken Caswell

Rob Cohen

Frank Cooper

Francis Crociata

Giulio Draghi

David Dubal

Lewis Eastlick

Bill Ecker

Ray Edwards

John Farmer

Christopher Fifield

Howard Fink

Natalya Firsova

Carsten Fischer

Carl Fudge

Andre Gauthier

Geno Gemmato

Tanya Gerasimchuck

Tim Gilligan

Margarita Glebov

Leopold Godowsky III

Mary Milton
  Godowsky

Peter Greenleaf

Roger Gross

Robert C. Harris

Wil Hilbers

Albert Hubay

Rosario Iancale

Christian Johansen

Sergey Kuznetsov

Francesco Libetta

Vasily Lopatin

Ernst Lumpe

Farhan Malik

John Maltese, Jr.

Donald Manildi

Ward Marston

David Mason

Greg Mason

John Mazzarella

Peter Miller

Frank-Thomas
  Mitschke

James Mixter

The Musicians
  Foundation

Derek Oppen

Horace Peek

Ed Plotkin

Stephan Puille

Rick Robertson

Francis Romano

Arnold Schwab

Stephen Siek

Bob Smith

Roland Söderholm

Victoria Solyanaya

Jonathan Summers	Reid von Borstel	Lyuda Zadayanchuk
Teri Noel Towe	Alan Walker	Richard Zimdars
Iris Türke	Harry Weintraub	Georg Zollner

Especial thanks to Nigel Nettheim, dedicated Pachmann researcher and proprietor of a Pachmann website, which makes available some of the documents on which this book is based:

http://nettheim.com/pachmann/

Preface

Gregor Benko

The United States has produced two notable music critics whose specialty was romantic piano playing. One, James Gibbons Huneker who died in 1921, was Vladimir de Pachmann's prophet. The other professed he was not enamored of de Pachmann's recordings. This was Harold C. Schonberg, the chief music critic of the *New York Times* when I came to New York City in late 1965 with the fledgling International Piano Library. Schonberg proved to be very interested in the work of I.P.L., was enormously helpful, and eventually became my mentor and friend. I learned that he was an admirer of critic W. J. Henderson, a predecessor at the *New York Times*. Henderson had been an ardent detractor of de Pachmann. Harold had never heard de Pachmann in person, and only knew some of the pianist's late recordings. Few then had access to all of de Pachmann's recordings, and at the time I didn't know enough to argue with him.

No one else then was concerning themselves with salvaging the heritage of recordings of great pianists of the past and making the material available to the public, and I had the joy of discovering a whole world of piano playing. I can never forget first hearing Josef Hofmann in Chopin's F minor Concerto, nor the people who waited at the I.P.L. doorway for many hours beginning one Sunday night in December 1966 after that day's *New York Times* reported we would be making that recording available on Monday morning.

As a result a number of very colorful people came by to visit I.P.L. obsessive collectors, forgotten minor pianists, pedagogues with dubious teaching methods to push, a few young artists interested in the styles of the past, as well as some fans of particular dead pianists. Among the latter was Edward Blickstein, who had produced a manuscript biography of de

Pachmann. I read it and was fascinated; then Blickstein played some of the pianist's rare, early recordings for me, and I was "hooked."

Blickstein's manuscript had much that was admirable—a poetic voice, great knowledge, and the gift of sympathy and even affection for a subject who was often decidedly unsympathetic. His research was extensive but still inadequate. An editor was needed badly, and I agreed to help in that capacity. We met and worked on the project periodically, a vast task that grew to something more than editing. It was necessary to ferret out much new material, as well as to try to make sense of much that was contradictory. Pachmann himself exaggerated and made up stories for the press, loving to *épater la bourgeoisie*. His son Leonide was given to sentimentalizing the legend his father had become, smoothing over the rough parts and omitting or lying about things like Pachmann's Jewish antecedents and the extent of his homosexuality. And the pianist's companion/secretary, Cesco Pallottelli, had a lot to hide and to cover over as well. Blickstein and I continued this work off and on for more than three decades, cleaning up problems and gathering much new material.

Here at last is the book. It is a fantastic story that would be unbelievable, were it not so well documented. At the same time a brief for romantic piano playing combined with the neat trick in presenting the conflicted personality of a contradictory artist, it is also one of the histories of a homosexual classical musician of the past. I am sorry Harold Schonberg is not alive to read it, and perhaps change his mind about de Pachmann's playing. Perhaps it will serve to change some other minds.

About the nature of my participation: it is probably true that over the years I spent as much time on research and the actual writing as Edward Blickstein, but it is he who has the greater lyrical gift, and we have striven to maintain his voice as narrator, so in the narrative "the author" and "I" refer to Edward Blickstein.

Many older articles about Pachmann capitalized the "D" in "De Pachmann." We have chosen to use the lower case "d" except in cases where we are directly quoting a printed source that used the upper case.

Introduction

Edward Blickstein

Books about celebrated instrumentalists are not numerous. Unlike composers whose great music prompts biographies, and singers whose lives are told with a combination of fact intertwined with make-believe which the public seems to find so fascinating, most instrumentalists dedicate too many of their working hours to the perfection of their art, and in most cases, lead too uneventful lives (interesting perhaps only to their admirers) to warrant detailed biographies.

Vladimir de Pachmann's life was not typical of most instrumentalists. It was filled with colorful and dramatic incidents, some controversial and some humorous, while his personality was so exotic, so colorful and like his art such a mixture of contradictions—a charlatan with the manners of a mountebank and an artist with the message of a poet—that there is very little else about him or his life that could be called typical in any way. Certainly his perverse behavior, at once whimsical, willful and, later, senile and even unhinged, could serve as the source for a fascinating psychological study, since he was probably the most eccentric of all the great pianists of history.

I learned about de Pachmann in 1950 from George Halprin (1890–1966), a piano teacher to whom I had gone after leaving the Juilliard School. He originally studied with Ferruccio Busoni in Berlin, and then Rafael Joseffy at the National Conservatory sometime before 1910. George never spoke of technique. It never interested him. He was more intent on awakening my musical feeling. My individuality and "inner vision" were more important. "Technicians are a dime a dozen," he would say, "but to cast a spell . . ."

One day I was particularly inspired, and George embraced me with the words, "You have really improved." A few days later I received a card from him inscribed "to the gifted ghost of de Pachmann." My interest was fatally aroused. Did I really sound like de Pachmann? How could I play like someone I had never heard? At my next lesson George told me "You're developing a beauty of touch and a love of tone. He was famous for that." Then he played de Pachmann's Victor recording of Chopin's E minor Nocturne. "You see," said George, "how he casts a spell. It is soft yet penetrating. 'Hot pearls on velvet.' I think Huneker said that."

The playing was beautiful, soft and refined; the musings of a very old man. George smiled. "You want to know about de Pachmann? Go to the library and get his clippings. You'll have a good laugh. Though I was poor, I used to follow de Pachmann on his tours to hear him play some works he hadn't performed in New York. I remember I went to Philadelphia just to hear him play the Chopin F minor Fantasy. I've never forgotten how he played certain passages, the melody that begins the doppio movemiento section."

George's memories of de Pachmann's hypnotic effects and his uproarious behavior intrigued me. Eventually I decided to write a book combining my own feelings about Chopin's music, the ideals that I feel de Pachmann's art represented, with a biography of the man himself.

The *New York Times* book review section printed my November 17, 1957, letter requesting any personal memories for a biography of Vladimir de Pachmann. Among the answers I received was one from John Majewski, then publisher of *Musical America* and a close friend of Cesco Pallottelli, de Pachmann's old secretary, who was still alive in Rome. Majewski furnished me with his address and I immediately wrote to Pallottelli. Two weeks later I received his reply: "I have lived with the Maestro for over thirty-five years . . . I am sure no other person can help you on this matter as I can. If you can come to Rome, I will be glad to see you."

Pallottelli proved to be a smiling, affable, red-cheeked old man full of stories about his former employer. He had once planned to write a book about the pianist but the war had intervened. All the material he had collected was stored in the basement of the villa, which had been built originally for the great pianist in Rome.

It was an enormous collection of memorabilia, piled up in tall stacks in no particular order. In some boxes were recordings with white labels, which caught my eye immediately, for the unusual labels meant they might be unissued performances. Included in the group were indeed unique, unissued recordings of Chopin's Nocturne, Op. 55, No. 1, the first part of the A-flat Ballade and various performances of Etudes, Mazurkas, Preludes and the C-sharp minor Polonaise as well as a real oddity, Liszt's *Mazurka Brillante*. On Pachmann's piano and the walls there were autographed photographs of Franz Liszt, Adolf von Henselt, Karl Klindworth and other great musicians. When I started going through the piles in the basement I discovered autographed letters to Pachmann from Ferruccio Busoni, Giovanni Sgambati, Francis Planté, Leopold Godowsky and one letter from his wife Maggie, but there were none from Pachmann to Pallottelli, nor any personal correspondence at all, for that matter.

Lionel de Pachmann, the son of the pianist (he preferred to be called "Leonide") lived in Paris in a studio covered with photos of his mother, and proved to be even more communicative than Signor Pallottelli. He wrote:

> As regards my father's daily life I can tell you much about it and give you authentic and picturesque information in that way, as I have lived quite enough with him, at times to be able even to imitate his way of talking and joking; also to tell you exactly how he used to employ his time, hour by hour

Leonide told me of his father's extreme nervousness before playing. Particularly vivid was his memory of his father's hands:

> You must speak in your book about his beautiful hands. They were fleshy but quite firm and strong. He could move his fingers along the back of one's own hand with such power that it really hurt. Though they were powerful, he could caress the piano with a delicacy and lightness that was absolutely unique. It was as if they were made of both steel and India rubber—at the same time strong and extraordinarily supple.

I spent months in Europe with both. As the research continued, I wrote to George discussing the style I should employ. He felt it was essential that I emphasize de Pachmann's Chopin interpretations:

> He played Chopin as only a woman of genius could play Chopin. And perhaps only a homosexual man could have played him so exquisitely." Although not homosexual himself, George had no prejudice about the subject and did not doubt that de Pachmann was overtly homosexual. "Even Joseffy, great as he was, never revealed the innermost secrets of Chopin. Why? Because Chopin was a man with a woman's genius. De Pachmann's essence," George wrote, "was *charm*. Yes, out of de Pachmann's repertoire of colors emerged poignant charm, anguished charm, melancholy charm. Even tragic charm was not a paradox under de Pachmann's hands.

In a taped reminiscence, George added:

> No one except a man of his genius could have gotten away with it—you can't imagine Pachmann being any other way than the way he was. To be as unconventional as he was, one had to be irrational, to defy the mannerisms of the concert hall. For an artist to have the courage to do this he would have to be a little unbalanced, but there was a method to his madness.

In Pachmann's day artists were allowed great freedom in both their lives and their art. Accepting this, what we know of Pachmann's life and career still seems so fantastic that a biographer could be accused of making it up. Fortunately much of it can be documented. Pachmann was a character out of the pages of E. T. A. Hoffmann come to life, the answer to a press agent's dreams, and his eccentricities at least equaled any publicist's wildest imaginings. He lived his life to the fullest, relishing the admiration he received for his artistry as well as his notoriety. Despite his behavior, Pachmann never lost the respect of the world's greatest musicians, critics and the general public, and was considered one of the greatest pianists of all time.

Chapter 1

Colored Pebbles and Madame Slepouchkine, 1848–1868

Abruptly at the end of the Russian steppes, between the two great rivers Dniester and Dnieper, high on a plateau facing the expansive Black Sea, lies Odessa, a city of almost oriental splendor and squalor. Built by decree of Catherine the Great on the ruins of an ancient Tartar fortress in 1794, three years younger than Washington, D.C., Odessa was, with its wide, tree-lined and newly paved avenues of elegant palaces and stately public buildings, the jewel of the Ukraine in the middle of the nineteenth century. But the glittering facade could barely mask the wooden shacks and hovels not far behind.

Pride of the city and focal point of the boulevards was Odessa's most remarkable feature, a unique flight of steps, which leads from the esplanade to the shore below. On any beautiful autumn evening hundreds of pedestrians filled the boulevards and overflowed onto the steps to enjoy the refreshing air and panorama of the sea. This peaceful and serene idyll contrasted with the noisy crowds that lined the boulevard and the wagons and carts of the peddlers which scurried up and down the steps. The population was an incredible mixture of clashing nationalities—Jews, Italians, Germans, Greeks and even exotic Turks—"most of them wearing the costume appropriate to each and speaking different tongues" according to Charles King's history of the city—all making Odessa the most cosmopolitan city of the empire, with "a style of music . . . that involved both libertine abandon and controlled experimentation."

The owners of most of the major houses of trade were Italians, who dominated life in the city, and the Italian language, not Russian, was most commonly encountered in the city. Street signs identified places in both Russian and Italian. Jews, not welcome in most of the rest of Russia,

1

were accepted in Odessa. The Black Sea littoral was within the "pale of settlement," south of the *Cherta osedlosti,* the line drawn by Catherine the Great demarcating where Jews were permitted to live. In 1812 there was a plague epidemic in Odessa, and the Jews, unusually, were *not* blamed.

The many brightly colored buildings with their flat roofs and the volatility of the people who inhabited them gave the city a distinctly southern Italian appearance. This impression was dampened by the sultry climate, for much of the year Odessa was blanketed by a haze of limestone particles blown from the steppes, covering palaces and hovels with a fine, gray film. Somehow the visual beauty of the city, its humidity and the intellectual restlessness of its inhabitants, were conducive to the development of the arts. Most Russians called their third-largest city the "Florence of Russia." There was no question then for Odessa's inhabitants that they were "Russian," but today people born there are Ukrainian.

Odessa over the years gave birth to many celebrated musicians, especially pianists: Simon Barere, Shura Cherkassy, Ania Dorfmann, Samuil Feinberg, Emil Gilels, Tina Lerner, Pierre Luboshutz, Evgeny Mogilevsky, Benno Moiseiwitsch, Heinrich Neuhaus, Leff Pouishnoff, Vasily Sapellnikov, Yakov Zak and a score of lesser lights, while Sviatoslav Richter grew up there. Vladimir de Pachmann was the first and, in his day, the most famous of the virtuoso pianists to come from this southern Russian (now southern Ukraine) metropolis.

He was born on July 15, 1848 (old style),[1] the youngest of thirteen children. His forty-five year old mother Anastasia nursed him for a year herself. There is a popular folk belief that the thirteenth child has unusual psychic abilities, and he almost certainly grew up sensitive to fantasy and superstition.

Vladimir's father Vikentiy was born on January 25, 1793 (old style), in Prague, and he must have been a remarkable man. The son of military officer Philip Pachmann (1761–1835), Vikentiy entered the Prague University in 1807, where for five years he studied languages, history, mathematics, physics, philosophy, and law. But he was as interested in music, and in 1812 he began three years of study at the Prague Conservatory. He came to Odessa in 1815 and a year later accepted a job as music teacher at the Odessa Charitable Institution, a school for boys.

In 1818 he moved to a position as music teacher at the Richelieu Lycée, an institution of higher learning founded just a year earlier and named for Armand du Plessis, the French duc de Richelieu, who had been appointed Odessa city administrator by Czar Alexander I in 1803. Soon the school enjoyed the reputation as the most prestigious in Odessa, and eventually it served as the foundation for the Novossiya University. When the Lycée was reorganized Vikentiy began to teach Latin as well as bookkeeping for ten years, and later he was appointed head of the department of Roman

Jurisprudence, the field in which he became celebrated. He published a work entitled "The Book of the Steersman" ("Kormchaya Kniga") written in Latin in 1844, outlining the debt of Roman law to Byzantine law. All sources state he was respected as an authority in his field, Roman Law.[2]

Starting in 1833 he also served as an Odessa censor, a prestigious position awarded to trusted professors and others with fluency in many languages. The Odessa publishing house published works in several languages, and all had to be overseen by an official state censor. He retired in 1853, the year he received an award from the government for his services in the position.

Vikentiy Pachmann was by nature a cold and aloof person. Thorough, precise and methodical, the man's one great passion in life was music. Vikentiy published a treatise on harmony he had written in German. As a young man he had learned to play the violin and 'cello, and cultivated many friendships with musicians. Vladimir later claimed that his father said he had played as a teenager in Franz Joseph Haydn's orchestra on the Esterhazy estate, and in 1809 was one of the pallbearers at Haydn's funeral. It is impossible to know how much of this is exaggeration, and how much is truth; Vladimir, in any case, always remembered stories his father told him when he was a very young boy about the great composer. Vikentiy had apparently lived for two years in the same house where Carl Maria von Weber had an apartment, and supposedly remembered seeing sketches for the manuscript of Weber's A-flat Piano Sonata, completed in Prague in 1816. According to Vladimir, Vikentiy also said that "Beethoven stayed in these apartments with Weber."

The only source for these stories attributed to Vikentiy, connecting the family to Beethoven and Weber, was Vladimir; the stories might well be apocryphal, part of Vladimir's "family romance." But it is also possible Vikentiy Pachmann was actually in Weber's circle as he was composing the A flat Sonata in Prague, and even heard the composer play parts of it. Vikentiy's supposed association with Weber and Beethoven was accepted as fact by one of the distinguished early writers on Pachmann, J.A. Fuller-Maitland, in his articles carried in several editions of *Grove's Dictionary*.

The earliest interview we have found with Vladimir's version of these stories was first published in the *New York Advertiser*, and quoted in *Freund's Weekly* on February 14, 1894:

> My father was twenty-four then, and he was a well-known musical dilettante. He lived for many years in the same house with Von Weber and Beethoven, and . . . he taught me to play Beethoven.

According to the most recent research, Beethoven and Weber met only once, in 1823, and it is impossible that the two composers ever lived under the same roof. A likely explanation for the discrepancy is that Vladimir, unquestioning, simply accepted what his father told him.

There has been much speculation about the Pachmann family origins. Within the family there was a tradition that the name had derived from an ancient Frankish family known as "Pachomme," one member of which had made himself useful to Charlemagne and had been granted aristocratic rank along with the right to use the nobilary particle "de" (or "von" in German) as a sign of nobility. There seems to be no evidence to verify this story of nobility. Contemporary references to Vikentiy and his eminent son Semyon, in Russian sources regarding legal matters, refer to both as simply "Pachmann," and the "de" in Vladimir Pachmann's name originated no earlier than 1879, and only with Vladimir. More problematic is the question of Vikentiy's national and ethnic origins. Russian reference books state he was of Bohemian origin; Vladimir's contemporaries assumed he stemmed from Jewish stock and to the end of his life the pianist was labeled a Jew by almost everyone, partially because he was born in the section of Russia permitted to Jews, also because he "looked Jewish." But all evidence shows the family to have been Christian.

Pachmann and other members of his family denied that they were Jewish and pointed out that they had been brought up in the Russian Orthodox religion. When the author asked Cesco Pallottelli and Leonide de Pachmann point blank if Pachmann was Jewish, they said "the family was Russian Orthodox." The question is clouded by the fact that Pallottelli himself had recently emerged from a Fascist scandal, as well as the fact that father Vikentiy emigrated specifically to Odessa, known for its unusual hospitality to Jews. On the other hand, Vladimir's brother Semyon became a functionary of Alexander III, a position impossible for a Jew. It seems that in mid-nineteenth century Russia, Judaism was considered a religion, not a race. Converting presumably allowed one to become accepted as a Christian, with all the benefits attached. One did not even need to change one's name (most didn't). Pianist/composer Anton Rubinstein is the most celebrated example. Most likely, Vikentiy was originally Jewish, but hid those origins.[3]

Vikentiy met a young woman, Anastasia, supposedly the aristocratic daughter of an ancient family who, in one of Russia's innumerable wars with Turkey, had been captured and taken to Russia at the age of six. Born circa 1803 in Roustchouk (then part of the Ottoman empire, now in Bulgaria and called "Russe") she was not quite fourteen when they met. Pachmann always told interviewers that she was Turkish, but her maiden name was "Lovchinsky"—Anastasia Emanuelovna Lovchinsky—which indicates that she was Slavic, the daughter of a man named Emanuel, probably Jewish, and it is very doubtful that she was an aristocrat. Pachmann said that she was a pupil at the school for aristocratic girls where his father taught, but this could not be true, since the school was for boys. Perhaps the idea that she was an aristocrat was another part of Vladimir's family romance.

More a child than a woman, dainty and very small, Anastasia possessed a quiet femininity that must have captivated Vikentiy. They were married on July 26, 1817 (old style), and she proved to be a dutiful and submissive wife. Nine of their thirteen children, four boys and five girls, survived infancy: Varvara born in 1821, Alexander in 1823, Semyon in 1825, Elizaveta in 1827, Grigory in 1834, Adrian in 1836, Katarina in 1838, Nikolai in 1841, and finally, Vladimir, the youngest, born on July 27, 1848 (old style).

Though fertile, the marriage was not happy for Anastasia. Vikentiy was a stern and demanding husband, rigid and authoritarian, and the family was large. The hardships must have been great. The same interview quoted in *Freund's Weekly* carried the pianist's fond memory of his mother:

'Only this tall,' he said, laughing, and measuring with his outstretched hand about four feet from the floor. 'She was a Turkish girl and her father was a Count and a Governor-General of Russo-Turkey.'

Vladimir adored his mother, "I could hold her entirely in my arms," he remembered fondly. A loving woman, she had protected and watched over him. Once when he fell and cut his finger, she sealed the cut with candle wax to stop the bleeding and the scar never left. He was devastated when she died. Later, on all of his concert tours, he carried with him a gift she had left him, a wooden triptych of the Virgin and Child. It was his only tangible tie with her memory and his childhood.

He also loved his brother Semyon, and an 1860 letter from twelve year old Vladimir addressed to Semyon and his wife Alexandra, and their son Leonide, was penned in some of the most astonishingly artistic Cyrillic writing imaginable:

Beloved and esteemed brother Semyon, Allow me to join in the general family congratulations on your upcoming Saint's name day, to wish you all the best in the world, and to tell you how much I love and respect you . . . convey to Alexandra Kasimirovna my earnest congratulations and kiss her hands. I also kiss Leonide. Impatiently waiting for our soonest possible meeting, your loving brother Vladimir.[4]

A large part of the responsibility for Vladimir's upbringing fell on his sister Elizaveta. She was like a second mother to her younger brothers and sisters, with Vladimir her favorite. He called her Lizenka. He was shy and sensitive and was much affected by the family's modest circumstances. Elizaveta spoiled him, feeding him Russian delicacies which she would hoard for him, and for which he developed an inordinate fondness. Later this fondness grew into a gourmet's passion for the finest in food.

Brother Semyon, twenty-three years older than Vladimir, was his father's favorite. He had inherited Vikentiy's intellectual and musical gifts but, unlike his father, he was clever and worldly. Semyon wanted to study law and Vikentiy helped prepare the boy, eventually obtaining a position for him at the Richelieu Lycée, laying the foundation for Semyon's own later brilliant career as a teacher (he eventually developed a theory of Russian civil law, linking precedence to the experience of other countries, which was expounded in his several books). Semyon also wrote a dictionary of the colloquial words of the province of Tula. After moving to St. Petersburg he rose in positions as jurist, becoming a senator of the Russian Empire and finally, a counselor to Czar Alexander III. When Semyon Pachmann died in 1910 at the age of eighty-five, he left a fortune of more than two million rubles as well as an estate consisting of art treasures, books, and perhaps most precious of all, a fine violin reputed to have been a Stradivarius, for Semyon was also an excellent amateur violinist.

Another of Vladimir's brothers, Grigory, a ranking soldier, was a brawling alcoholic, and often came home drunk. Horrible scenes would follow and quarrels so violent that Vladimir, small and easily frightened, would run to the most protected corner of the house, under the steps, and hide. These scenes were a terrible torture for him and he never forgot them. "My heart still trembles when I remember the sound of his boots on the stairs," Pachmann remarked later to Cesco Pallottelli, adding, shaking with emotion, "Paura, paura" (fear, fear).

After Anastasia's death Vikentiy became even more stern and severe. He developed a neurotic miserliness and would hide money inside the walls. One day Vladimir noticed that a servant girl was spending a long time with his father behind the closed door of his room. Curious, he began to watch her. Once he saw her leaving the room with some ruble notes visible in the bodice of her dress. Telling no one, he brooded about it. He was too young to understand why the servant girl was given rubles.

Amid these depressing surroundings, one of Vikentiy's prized possessions was a spinet piano. When Vladimir was almost six years old the British bombarded the city during the Crimean War on April 22, 1854. Vikentiy carried the piano on his back down to the house's cellar to protect the instrument. There the family gathered amid the ominous rumble of cannons and the flickering light from an oil lamp and stayed for hours, making music together in a scene reminiscent of Dostoyevsky.

It was about this time that Vikentiy discovered his youngest son's musical talent, and started the lad on the violin. As might be expected, he was a strict and severe master who demanded hard work. His method of instruction however, was so successful that Pachmann would often say later that it was his father who had bequeathed him a system of discipline and thoroughness that developed into the art that made him celebrated throughout the world. After a period of study Vikentiy felt Vladimir was ready to participate in the family musicales. They would gather around the spinet, Vikentiy playing the 'cello, one of the daughters at the piano and Vladimir with his violin.

He was a diligent if not inspired student and soon mastered all of the Karol Lipinski studies. Vladimir remained a competent performer and retained some ability on the violin even into old age. In 1915 when he was sixty-seven and was giving some joint recitals with the great Belgian violinist Eugene Ysaÿe, Pachmann surprised those at a rehearsal when he picked up a violin and played a melody. He told no one of his experience with the violin sixty years earlier, but played well enough that Ysaÿe knew immediately that he had once studied the instrument.

"Beautiful instrument," he is supposed to have said to Ysaÿe. He put the violin down and held up his fingers. "But no good for ze velvet finger tips."

But by the time he was ten, Vladimir's four years of violin studies were becoming increasingly wearisome. He was finding it hard to concentrate, for the sounds of the piano fascinated him, and he begged his father to give him piano lessons. He obviously had begun playing piano on his own for, in 1855, a letter to Vladimir from his nephew, his brother Semyon's son Leonide (a missive from a twelve year old boy to his seven year old uncle!) stated, "You now play very well on the piano and the violin, and I can still do nothing!"

Three years later, on his tenth birthday, Vladimir received his first piano lesson from his father. After a few sessions at the keyboard, the violin was forgotten. In a 1927 interview Pachmann told Stanley Markham: "Gott made me a pianist . . . I had to be; nothing else was possible." All time was effaced by enchantment with the spinet. He would spend hours, ceaselessly trying out combinations of touch and tone. The sound of the instrument soon became an obsession and while he was at the keyboard nothing else mattered.

There was an hour lesson every day. It was soon apparent that Vladimir had an extraordinary gift for the piano. Very Teutonic in his musical tastes and distrusting Russian musicians, Vikentiy decided there was no other teacher for the boy than himself. Vladimir was given a solid foundation in harmony and theory. By the time he reached twelve, he was analyzing complicated fugues.

Vikentiy was not interested in the piano per se but only in the elements of music. As Pachmann told an interviewer in the *Etude* magazine in December 1923:

> My father was too much concerned in teaching me music to take any time with the niceties of touch or technique. Of hand position I knew nothing, my texts at the beginning were the ordinary instruction books. If I remember rightly, they were those of Mueller or Adams. My father was a critic but not a pianist. He merely advised me but could not show me how. I studied everything that came my way. How long did I practice? It would be easier to find out how long I didn't. I was at work at it all the time. Good health permitted me to work enormously. I felt that either you play or you don't.

At this time Vladimir heard something he never forgot. He related this event in an article that appeared in the December 1926 issue of *Cassell's* magazine:

> There is one sweet picture of long, long ago that I remember ardently. It is the picture of my mother playing a Chopin mazurka! Oh! The melody was divine, entrancing, superb! And my mother was sixty years old. I was fifteen. I danced for joy. I had never heard Chopin played like that. . . . My father was beside himself with happiness.

The boy's introduction into the musical world outside his home was sudden and unexpected. It seems a passer-by, a certain Dr. Morgan, chanced to hear him playing a Handel fugue[5] through an open window, and was so impressed on discovering that the pianist was a mere boy that, shaking the lad's hand, he predicted a brilliant future for Vladimir and ran off to spread the word about the prodigy to his friends. Soon stories of Vladimir's abilities were included among the important topics of musical conversation. Odessa, like many European cities of the time, fostered a musical public that marveled at the idea of a prodigy in its midst, and many wanted to hear him play. Vladimir became a frequent performer at soirées arranged by Princess Vorontsova, the local patroness of the arts, and was apparently presented at several recitals sponsored by various members of the Odessa aristocracy.[6]

The pianist later claimed that it was at one of these childhood performances that he met the fantastic old lady whose memory was to haunt him for the rest of his life. This was the curious Madame Slepouchkine, supposedly the widow of a general, a friend with one of his sisters. In later years everyone who knew the old pianist was familiar with her name, for he never tired of describing her. But in fact, there is no proof that she ever existed, and she well might have been entirely an invented alter ego, much like Sairy Gamp's imaginary muse, Mrs. Harris, in Dickens's *Martin Chuzzlewit*. As Pachmann described her, she had a perverse and childlike nature that intrigued him. Her artless eccentricities, whether real or imagined, greatly influenced the development of his own personality. She was still alive for him well after Pachmann had passed the age of seventy and he would have a place set for her at his dinner table (much as pianist Alexander Siloti would have a place set for his long-dead teacher Franz Liszt), and he would have his guests toast her health. "She is the Satan of negation—a Mephistopheles in the guise of a talkative old woman. I am her Faust and she turns into laughter and whimsical foolery, every attitude of mine towards life!" he explained later to Pallottelli.[7]

According to Pachmann, Madame Slepouchkine had a palatial home in Odessa. Lonely in her old age, she would invite young Vladimir to dine with her and later to play. If it was winter she would complain of the heat and put on the lightest of garments, and if it was summer, during the most oppressive heat, she would sit huddled by her samovar, swathed in furs. During dinner she would attempt to eat her soup with a fork and declare that it was delicious, and after dinner when they retired to the music room, this redoubtable lady might announce that she wished to play the piano. Casually sitting down, she would say, "Ah, Vladimir, is not this Beethoven Sonata beautiful?" and then proceed to murder the "Maiden's Prayer" (by Tekla Badarzewska-Baranowska, one of the most banal pieces ever written and one on which Pachmann later "improvised" variations for a Welte piano roll). She always carried a pack of cards rather than a missal when she went to church. If someone chanced to visit her unannounced, she would receive him with profuse compliments while audibly remarking to a servant, "What a bore he is to waste my time."

Madame Slepouchkine was irascible but lovable, so there is something strangely appealing about young Pachmann's invention, or at least exaggeration, of her eccentricities. The two seemed to understand each other despite the difference in their ages. She would do anything for her young friend, such as let him use her splendid grand piano any hour he liked, and feed him watermelon. Vladimir adored the fruit all his life and when he was eighty, the most important item on the menu at the party honoring him was watermelon.

Sometimes he took advantage of her. Once while she was away he went to her home and practiced for hours, helping himself to the sweets in the process. A few days later when they chanced to meet, she greeted him: "Ah, Vladimir," she cried, "we have the rats again. They have been into the pantry and eaten all the sweets."

Already introspective and apparently deeply obsessed with the piano, his relationship with her was the closest thing he had to woman's friendship. She was his only intimate contact, a possibly imaginary confidante with a complex personality. It is not unusual for children to create imaginary friends, even whole universes, which in today's psychology are called paracosms. The phenomenon is seen as a healthy sign that a youth's personality has enough confidence to organize his or her experiences into stories.

Vladimir was a solitary and impressionable lad whose loneliness needed an outlet. The boy developed an unusual pastime. While other children were enjoying games, he would spend hours searching for brightly colored pebbles which he brought home and polished until they gleamed. His make-believe gems and his music had been the only solace in a bleak and miserable existence. Madame Slepouchkine appeared and filled a void in the desolate years of his early life.

As he grew into young manhood, Vladimir became even more obsessed by the sounds of his piano. Not even the meanness of his surroundings could deter him from what was turning into a compulsion—a quest for the most perfect, the most beautiful and jewel-like of piano tones. Eventually the eccentricities represented by Madame Slepouchkine and the art he strove so hard to perfect were to be fused into a unique, exotic, personality.

When Vladimir reached nineteen, Vikentiy decided to send him to a professional conservatory. He would not even consider those recently founded in Moscow and St. Petersburg by the Rubinstein brothers. Only Vienna, with its ghosts of Mozart, Beethoven and Schubert, could provide the boy with a thorough musical culture. A subscription was raised by Princess Vorontsova and perhaps other aristocrats to send him to Vienna to study for two years at the Conservatory. It was to be the only professional training he would ever have.

Chapter 2

The Awakening, 1868–1879

Vienna must have presented a bewildering sight to a traveler arriving for the first time in 1867. The heart of the city seemed to be a mass of scaffolding, wooden planks, mounds of brick and mortar, half-finished plastered walls and ditches filled with refuse. It was the time of Vienna's rebuilding and an atmosphere of feverish activity pervaded. Ten years earlier Emperor Franz Joseph decreed the demolition of the walls which separated the old city from the suburbs and he filled in the moat and fields around it. In its place was to be a grand boulevard in the shape of a horseshoe—the Ringstrasse—which was eventually to become the symbol of the new prosperity, the triumph of the enlightened liberal bourgeoisie over the radical revolutionaries of 1848. Around the Ringstrasse would rise the great palaces and public buildings which, though a melange of pseudo-classic, Gothic and Renaissance styles, blended together into an ornate nineteenth-century grandeur. To many it was the essence of Imperial Vienna.

When Vladimir arrived in late 1867, only the Opera House, that huge, Romanticized Renaissance confection with a splendor that evokes the gaudy opulence of an over-stuffed era, stood nearly complete. But he knew nothing of that affluent world, arriving with only a little money, and ill-prepared to take care of himself in the cosmopolitan atmosphere of a world capitol. He managed to find quarters with a family named Lukcsh, people of modest means with whom he lived for almost two years.[1]

Somehow he managed to stay alive while he pursued his studies at the Conservatory, desperately poor with barely enough money at times to eat. Impoverished artists traditionally bear this as the price they must pay for "artistic freedom," but food already represented more than a mere necessity. Vladimir, spoiled by his mother first, then his sister and finally (in his mind) by Madame Slepouchkine, craved rich food by nature. Apparently he particularly loved the Ukrainian hors d'oeuvres called zakusky. Once he was so hungry he traded a gold watch his father had given him for a meal.

An air of gloom surrounded the old music school on Tuchlauben Street. The new Musikverein, a severe structure in the Renaissance style, was under construction on the Ringstrasse and there were plans to move the Conservatory to those new quarters. Seventeen years had passed since Joseph Hellmesberger had been appointed director of the school. Being a man of conservative nature (those were the days when Wagner's and Bruckner's music was hissed at Philharmonic concerts) Hellmesberger surrounded himself with as many colleagues as he could who were also conservative and pedantic. One of these was Joseph Dachs (1825–1896), Vladimir's professor of piano.

Years later Pachmann would tell interviewers several different versions of the story of his initial audition with Dachs, each version replete with flamboyant exaggerations and characteristic embellishments. In each he told that he had showed up without any scores. Not noticing this breach, Dachs bid him to play anything he wanted from the music he brought. Proudly Vladimir informed his prospective teacher, "I'll play anything you want from memory." At that the professor scowled in rage and told him off. Music was a serious profession, the Conservatory was no place for a provincial like him to be making jokes and he was never to come without sheet music again. When his anger subsided, he bade Vladimir to play something. He played Liszt's Rigoletto Paraphrase and Dachs commented favorably on his touch, but assured him he was on the wrong track, that he should study Bach's Well-Tempered Clavier, for "No musical education was complete without an intimate knowledge of Bach's fugues."

One version of the story is contained in an "interview" published in October 1911 by James Francis Cooke in the *Etude*. Cooke wrote up the interview from notes he had taken during conversations with the pianist, but in his editing he changed Pachmann's diction and elevated his speech considerably. According to Cooke, Pachmann remembered:

Consequently I secured a copy of the fugues and commenced work upon them. Dachs had told me to prepare the first prelude and fugue for the following lesson. But Dachs was not acquainted with my method of study. He did not know that I had mastered the art of concentration so that I could obliterate every suggestion of any other thought from my mind except that upon which I was working. He had no estimate of my youthful zeal and intensity. He did not know that I could not be satisfied unless I spent the entire day working with my artistic might and main. Soon I saw the wonderful design of the great master of Eisenach. The architecture of the fugues became plainer and plainer. Each subject became a friend and each answer likewise. It was a great joy to observe with what marvelous craftsmanship he had built up the wonderful structures. I could not stop when I had memorized the first fugue, so I went to the next and the next and the next. At the following lesson I went with my book under my arm. I requested him to name a fugue. He did, and I placed the closed book on the rack before me. After I had finished playing he was dumfounded. He said, "You come to me to take lessons. You already know the great fugues and I have taught you nothing."

Cooke published another version twelve years later in the same magazine (December 1923; he was the magazine's editor). There he quotes Pachmann giving a different story about his first acquaintance with that Bach volume, "When I was twelve years old my brother made me a birthday present of the Forty-eight Fugues of the 'Well Tempered Clavichord' of Bach. I adored them as student material." This probably stems from a subsequent and more realistic interview with the pianist, and is likely closer to the truth. It helps explain how Pachmann was able to play "all the fugues" at his second lesson . . . he had been familiar with them already.

Pachmann told many versions of the audition story; another in much in the same vein and based on a late interview was written by Stanley Markham and printed in a 1927 volume entitled *Music of All Nations*:

> I sat down and played Liszt's selection from Verdi's "Rigoletto." After a few notes the professor began to take serious notice, and by the time I had finished he had run off to bring the Director of the Conservatoire. I thought at first that I was going to get into trouble for something but I was asked to play again, and then the two men heaped congratulations upon me. How relieved I was. Well, they ended by requesting me to prepare for the following day two studies of Chopin. I kept the appointment punctually—Pachmann is always punctual—and then informed the professor that I was ready to play any of the twenty-four studies of Chopin in any key and without music.

In the 1923 *Etude* interview Pachmann claimed he played Chopin's third Sonata in addition to the Bach Fugues. Some of these accounts, rendered by Pachmann in his later years, are definitely exaggerated. It is difficult to believe that an almost self-taught nineteen year old could have mastered most of Bach's Preludes and Fugues, or the Chopin Etudes. But he had already spent nine years in intense study and was an incredible talent, so there is certainly a kernel of truth in the stories. No doubt Dachs recognized the youth's ability and was impressed by what he heard, even if Vladimir had, in reality, played perhaps only the Rigoletto Paraphrase and a few works of Bach and/or Chopin.

The youth's un-academic methods must have shocked Dachs, a pupil of Czerny, who was a pupil of Beethoven. But Dachs didn't play with

Beethoven's impetuousness, for similarly to Pachmann's father, he was unimaginative, strict and pedantic. He soon gave his new pupil a thorough schooling in the old-fashioned Viennese manner and, before long, Pachmann acquired a complete mastery of the keyboard: scales were even and clean; arpeggios "rolled;" octaves elastic, from the wrist; thirds and sixths were legato and gliding, and so forth. By the end of his first year with Dachs, he had developed into an example of the well-trained, correct Viennese pianist of the time, his playing characterized by immaculate finger work and sparing use of the forearm in cantabile, but with little other utilization of the body. That mass was supposed to remain perfectly still. The pedal was used to create a euphonious and beautiful sound but all excessive fortes, and drama, were to be avoided. Used on the quick action, silvery, wooden-framed French and Viennese pianos of the 1830s and 1840s, this elegant and aristocratic approach perfectly suited the music of Hummel and Thalberg (even some Chopin), but was not really adequate for most of the Romantic literature, which needs the fuller tone of the heavier, steel-framed pianos of the mid-nineteenth century. By 1867 and 1868, the years Pachmann studied with Dachs, this style was already outmoded. Dachs turned him into a perfect mechanism but gave him no soul.

A requirement of the conservatory was that students also concentrate on theoretical studies, and Pachmann enrolled in Anton Bruckner's fugue and counterpoint class. The composer had just begun teaching there; among Vladimir's classmates was Felix Mottl, later to become a celebrated Wagnerian conductor. Bruckner was one of the most whimsical and naive men who ever taught at a conservatory. His personality, a cross between a peasant and a man of God, was well known to musical Vienna, as was his fanatical Catholic faith. According to some pupils, whenever a church bell chanced to toll, he would stop in the midst of the lesson and fall on his knees to pray, or even rush out of the building to a nearby church.

Bruckner was an excellent teacher despite this. He insisted students master rules before breaking them—everything must go according to the rules, and one was not allowed to write one single forbidden note. But then he added: "If later, somebody would come and show me something similar to what we made in school, I would throw him out." Pachmann received a thorough foundation in counterpoint and fugue. The result of these studies was his composition of a piano concerto in F minor, supposedly written after a year's study with Bruckner. If this composition was ever more than a rumor, it is now lost. It was a rare attempt at composition, for he soon realized he had little gift for it.

After less than two years of study Pachmann was awarded a prize medal, and the prestigious opportunity of performing Liszt's Concerto in E flat at a concert honoring the composer on April 13, 1869, at which

Liszt was present. In later years, publicity material often stated Pachmann had won first prize with its requisite gold medal, but this was not true; it was another Dachs pupil, sixteen year old Laura Kahrer, who won the gold, for unlike Pachmann, she excelled as both pianist and composer.[2] Pachmann had won second place with a silver medal. Kahrer performed Liszt's first Mephisto Waltz at the same concert.

It was on this occasion, Pachmann said, that he first met Liszt, who happened to be in Vienna to attend performances of his oratorio "St. Elizabeth" in the Redoutensaal on April 4 and 11 conducted by Johann Herbeck. The *Neues Fremden-Blatt* mentioned Pachmann's performance of the Liszt Concerto, stating:

> We have found a strong and developed pianist, a follower of the Liszt school, in Mr. Pachmann. His performance was distinguished by calmness, confidence and elegance. He performed the very difficult concerto excellently.[3]

Thirty-five years later, Pachmann played that Liszt concerto once more in Boston, and soon again in Philadelphia. In a December 4, 1904, interview for the *Boston Herald,* Pachmann told a reporter that he had "studied Liszt's Concerto in E flat with the composer" who insisted that the last section should be taken with a certain dignity, maestoso, not as it is hurried usually.

Just six months after the event, an unidentified reporter for the Odessa paper *Novorosijsky Telegraph* wrote on October 12, 1869 (old style): "The pianist learned the piece under the direction of the composer himself."[4] An article in the October 1, 1926, issue of *Radio Times* quotes Pachmann:

> I met Brahms in Vienna too, but my most intimate friend was Liszt. And in spite of his enormous, powerful hands, he was really full of tenderness . . . this wonderful man gave me much encouragement, although I was only a youngster.

Pachmann remembered (*Cassell's* magazine, December 1926): "What a marvelous man was Liszt! And handsome!"

Musicians were everywhere, for Vienna and Berlin were the musical capitals of Europe, and for the first time Pachmann had an opportunity to hear the celebrated virtuosi of the day. He also performed at least once in public at this time, for an undated review from the *Neues Fremden-Blatt* compares his performance of Rubinstein's Fourth Piano Concerto favorably with the composer's own performance, heard in Vienna two years earlier.[5]

The innocent boy from Russia was becoming a sophisticate. Winning a prize at the conservatory had made Pachmann a local celebrity himself and he was asked by many socialites to play at their homes. At one of Pachmann's private concerts he met a charming, flirtatious-but-married-woman, the kind for which sophisticated, old-world cities like Vienna are famous, and he had an affair, probably his first. One night during a tête-a-tête, they were startled by a loud noise. Fearing it was her husband, the lady implored him to leave as quickly as possible. What could be more romantic than a paramour's escape through the garden window in old Vienna? The lady, alarmed that they might be caught before he could get away, told him, "Not the window, not the door, but the chimney!" Pachmann was a very small man, scarcely five feet one when fully grown, and so he exited, unromantically, up the chimney. Much to his embarrassment he suddenly found himself in someone else's apartment. Soon the neighbors realized what was transpiring and were more amused than angry at the pathetic figure, covered with black soot. This typical story was told much later in the maturity of Pachmann's fantasy. All that is missing is the frothy music from a Viennese operetta.

Pachmann wrote no memoir of those student days in Vienna, but Laura Kahrer did, and it is not unreasonable to assume Pachmann attended many of the same concerts as she:

> the greatest artists appeared repeatedly . . . Clara Schumann, Julius Stockhausen, Anton Rubinstein, Johannes Brahms, who occasionally conducted, David Popper, Sofie [sic] Menter, Josef Hellmesberger, the one armed piano player Graf Zichy, Ignaz Brüll, Mary Krebs, Carl Reinecke, the singers Albert Niemann, Frederieke Materna, Bettelheim, Josef Erl, the violin virtuoso Emil Sauret as a 14 year old boy, the world renowned Florentine string quartet and many more. The major impression was Anton Bruckner, as organist! . . . the monumental power and greatness of his conception and inspiration, the inventive richness of his improvisations, the virtuoso treatment of all stops and not the least, the rich stream of all the melodies that flooded these sound edifices.[6]

After graduation, Laura Kahrer's parents aggressively launched her on a concert career. She wrote:

> For my first concert tour I traveled to Prague in 1870 with my parents . . . one weird feature of concert life of that time . . . as an artist you had to personally drive to all the gentry of each town by coach and personally invite them.

Furnished with letters of recommendation, Laura Kahrer accepted an 1870 invitation from Liszt to come to Weimar. But Pachmann had no parents eager to help launch a career, nor any money to finance studies with Liszt, and if he was invited to do so, details have not survived. So after completion of the second year of his studies at the Conservatory, now twenty-one, he went back to Odessa. There was no money for him to remain in Vienna.

The earliest-known photograph of him, age about twenty, shows a pale, round-faced youth with a mop of black hair as smooth as his cheeks. The eyes seem both playful and poetic. His personality, with its mixture of mischievous play and piercing shrewdness, was already formed.

The October 12, 1869, article from Odessa's *Novorossijsky Telegraph* had reported:

> The reader will understand the joy which filled us when we heard of an able and serious artist coming to Odessa . . . V. Pachmann arrived here recently, and should more than anyone else justify our hopes. Two and a half years ago he gave a concert in our city and brilliantly showed his worth. . . . Having entered the Vienna Conservatory, he diligently studied harmony, counterpoint and piano . . . . A few rumors of Pachmann's success reached us. . . . We have had an opportunity to hear Mr. Pachmann and we can say without any exaggeration that such pianists do not often come to Odessa. It is especially pleasant to know that Mr. Pachmann is planning to stay in our city in order to teach music theory and piano. We however cannot agree . . . that Mr. Pachmann is a follower of the Liszt school. We think that his unique playing is more like that of Mr. Ritter . . . but he is better than Ritter in technique. Mr. Pachmann is going to give a concert at the end of October.[7]

The anonymous writer had perhaps been correct in thinking Pachmann's playing similar to that of the French pianist Theodore Ritter (teacher of the American critic and writer, James Gibbons Huneker), but Ritter, who died in 1886 at the age of forty-five, was a Liszt pupil himself.

On November 13, 1869 (old style), Pachmann gave a joint recital at the Harmonia Club in conjunction with the opera singers Mlle. Teresa Brambilla and a certain Mme. A. Abarinoff. The concert opened with Pachmann playing the Mendelssohn Fantasie in F sharp minor, Op. 28, after which the women sang a duet from Mercadante's opera *Il Giuramento*. Each woman also sang a solo, the proceedings interspersed with Pachmann playing Chopin, Schumann and a Schubert Impromptu. It was all very high class, with the program printed in western characters and in French., but nothing much came of it.

Pachmann continued to play in miscellaneous concerts in Odessa. The *Novorossijsky Telegraph* reported on February 3, 1870 (old style):

> The third evening of chamber music was a little triumph for Vladimir Pachmann, which many people envied. The concert hall was terribly cold, with devotees of music sitting in their fur coats and hats, but this didn't prevent Mr. Pachmann from reproducing the quintet of Schumann in its majestic beauty. . . In our times, virtuosity in playing the piano has reached extreme limits, because of the new mechanical improvements in the instrument, in

the power of its tone, its quality and compass. A pianist needs to have some special feature, a brilliant aspect to his talent to be distinguished from the numbers of other talented pianists. We want to add that this kind of virtuosity is losing its prestige, and is beginning to appear boring for even the least exacting of musicians. . . . Today sensitive and intelligent people are absurdly looking to apply almost any means of penetrating the outer elements of the art, but with this they can have only temporary success. As a result, a few of the smartest ones aspire to investigate and analyze the situation, checking what has been accomplished until now. And in these researches art doesn't always take the last place . . . Mr. Pachmann, as a student of this new school, aided by his great talent, has very quickly learned these new ideas of musical technique. We especially liked in his performances his resilient and confident voicing of chords and scales, in consequence of his correct mechanism. We don't know of many such pianists on this level in Odessa, who can boast of this skill or ability. In corroboration of our words we refer to his performance of Schumann's quintet, in which Pachmann played legato and staccato; he played the difficult passages, consisting of sixths and octaves, with vividness and purity. Energy and life were heard in every note of this quintet. The success of Pachmann's performance was admitted, even by those people who have never done so before. Our wish for the young pianist: don't be content to dazzle with this success, but continue even more assiduously to study the art of music. Quartets of Spohr & Mozart were played while there was five degrees of frost in the hall. It was very piteous to see the frozen performers.[8]

The statement: "The success of Pachmann's performance was admitted, even by those people who have never done so before" apparently meant that there had been people in Odessa who did *not* admit Pachmann was a successful pianist and musician before this concert, but were now converted. Odessa was a provincial city, in many ways a small town, and word of his arrogance and cockiness, a local who had been to the big city of Vienna and returned with a patronizing attitude, must have passed from music lover to music lover.

That presenting concerts in Odessa was then a rough business is revealed by another review from the *Novorossijsky Telegraph* of a few weeks later (March 21, 1870, old style). Pachmann's concentration was disturbed by the rudeness of noisy boors in the audience, and he obviously was unused to the unnamed American piano; because he couldn't concentrate, he wasn't inspired. The reviewer took pains to point this out:

The opening of the Odessa concert hall on March 1st was marked by a brilliant performance given by Vladimir Pachmann for the elect of society. This gave the evening an air of solemnity, and the center and prime mover of it was the Princess K.E. Vorontsova. The artistic soul of Her Highness, sympathetic to everything beautiful, is always ready to encourage talent, and in the face of the whole music circle we consider it our duty to express to her our true thankfulness. We pin our hopes in music on her, and we hope that the poor muse will not die in Odessa under her patronage. Mister Pachmann played very well, especially excellently while performing a duo concertant from the Huguenots to the accompaniment of a violin. But to be honest, knowing how well he can play, we have to say that the pianist didn't show himself in his true light, and he can play better. The Caprice of Mendelssohn, Op. 33 [unknown which of three from this opus], was just satisfactory. It fell short of the necessary élan needed to be made lively. The Scherzo of Chopin, Op. 31 [B flat minor], also was played as if by fixed routine. Mr. Pachmann has to pay more attention to the melodic side of his playing, and develop his left hand. We repeat, we state such conclusions because we know how Pachmann can play, and he has all the makings of a good pianist who can leave other ordinary pianists far behind. But there were some extenuating circumstances, which have to be known: one had to notice that troublemakers tried to make everyone happy by their presence, where extreme silence was necessary. By the way, nothing can spoil the good mood of a musician like the noise of a public which doesn't pay attention. 1) The excellent American piano on which Pachmann played differs from ordinary pianos by its full, rich tone, elastic when compared with other pianos; this attribute insures that the player must be responsible to use the pedal very skillfully and carefully. Mr. Pachmann hadn't had enough time to get to know this, so he couldn't use the tonal riches of this instrument, which was appearing for the first time in Odessa. 2) Many people from the garland of the finest flowers of society allowed themselves to lapse from the silence which is needed for the performance of musical compositions. They not only did not just listen themselves, but didn't give other people a chance to listen: they moved chairs and talked aloud. These people have an ability to talk that is unstoppable. Once the famous Henselt noticed two ladies talking while he was playing. He suddenly stopped the performance, and spoke to the public with these words 'I must ask, does the public want to listen to me, or not?' Everybody started shouting 'Yes, yes!' 'In that case,' said Henselt, 'I am going to wait until the end of the conversation of these two ladies.' All of the public turned to stare at the offenders against silence, who felt very uncomfortable. Definitely, such an attitude influenced the playing of the participants of the music evening on the 1st of March.[9]

It was at this time that Pachmann first perpetrated a prank that he enjoyed enormously, and repeated later. Inspired perhaps by a desire for whimsy, and under the pretense that he was an amateur music lover who wished to learn the piano, he paid a visit to an elderly piano teacher in Odessa, a lady so deaf that she needed an ear trumpet. After some discussion during which details of the fee were arranged, she bid him play a scale. Delighted, he sat down and proceeded to bungle a simple scale. Immediately the old lady stopped him, protesting that he had not the slightest idea of music and that she would have to start him with the most elementary rules. After explaining some of them, as a special favor she allowed him to hear her in a performance of "The Maiden's Prayer" by way of example, demonstrating how one would play after one had mastered all such rules. We can only imagine the effect this deaf and pedantic old lady's playing had on Pachmann. By the time she had finished he could barely contain himself, begging her to resume her ear trumpet. He excitedly told her that he had learned so much from hearing her play only once "according to the rules," that he wished now to repeat the piece for her. He then played the work at a breathless pace, adding all sorts of flourishes, variations, ornamentations and technical difficulties, whereupon the old lady dropped her ear trumpet and nearly fainted. Roaring with good-natured laughter, he apologized for his deception and told her of his success at the Vienna Conservatory, and of his plans to be a great pianist. Afterwards he took her out for tea and sweets. This charade became the template for a pattern of foolery Pachmann would repeat throughout his life, sometimes as we shall see with comical embellishments.

Pachmann could hardly wait to show off those pearly runs and rolling arpeggios, his professor's pride and joy. Spoiled, petted, and praised by so many, and flushed with his own importance, he persuaded his father to finance a joint concert with a friend named Herbeck in the town of Kherson, five hours away (this was probably the 'cello student Emil Herbeck from St. Petersburg). Inexperience triumphed over exuberance, and the concert was such a fiasco that aged Vikentiy Pachmann had to come and fetch the youths, who had no money left. This momentary setback, however, did not stifle the young pianist's spirit, for soon afterward he managed with the influence and help of his patroness, Princess Vorontsova, and that of an equally important personage, a member of the all-powerful Strogonoff family, to give more concerts, this time in Odessa and Kiev.

Cesco said the name of the Strogonoff patron was "Maximillian von Leutenberg." He was, correctly, a member of the family "von Leuchtenberg," probably one of the three stepsons of Count Grigorii Alexandrovitch Strogonoff. These three were offspring of the first marriage of the Count's wife, Grand Duchess Maria Nikolaevna. All of these stepsons had "Maximillian" for a middle name. Their natural father was a grandson of Josephine de Beauharnais, the offspring of Napoleon's stepson, while their mother was the eldest and favorite daughter of Czar Nicholas I! Grigorii Alexandrovich's father was Count Alexander Grigorievitch Strogonoff, one of the richest men in all of Russia. Strogonoff was one of the most powerful men of the century, rich enough to do what he wanted, but known for his eccentricity. In the Russian culture of anti-Semitism he became notorious when it was revealed that his most intimate, confidential companion and friend was a Jew from the merchant class. Strogonoff lived like a king to age ninety-six (1795–1891.) His visiting card read simply, "First Citizen of Odessa."[10]

Through von Leuchtenberg Pachmann met Karl Tausig and heard him play, in 1870, on what was to be Tausig's final Russian tour. He would die a year later at age thirty. Pachmann had never heard such sounds before: crescendos that built to a tremendous roar, then died in whispering pianissimo, terrific, passionate, driving virtuosity, all under unearthly control. Tausig seemed incapable of playing a wrong note. Pachmann was both overwhelmed and inspired. Were these the sounds that were missing in his own playing? He would try and capture them, and set about preparing for his debut with a program that Tausig might have played. A year went by. The concerts that he had given earlier in Odessa were decidedly more successful than the debacle in Kerson, but 1871 saw a smallpox and cholera epidemic in Russia, and worse, a pogrom in Odessa's Jewish quarter, a three day rampage with several murders. The young pianist soured on the city; he decided it was time for him to "escape" Odessa and make a St. Petersburg debut. In late January 1872 Pachmann wrote to his brother Semyon, now a well-known teacher and jurist in St. Petersburg:

> My dear brother Senya,
> You have probably heard from father concerning my return from Vienna. It has now been two and a half years where I've been frittering away in this wretched Odessa. During this period of time, I've been giving music lessons and thus making a living.
> In December, [Polish violinist Henryk] Wieniawski came to Odessa and gave several concerts. I met with him and upon hearing my playing he invited me to participate in his concert, which made me very happy so I agreed. At the concert, we played Beethoven's Sonata, dedicated to Kreutzer; the audience and Wieniawski himself were ecstatic. If you see him, ask him about my playing; he will tell you everything and this will serve as the best endorsement for me. Following the concert, Wieniawski came to me and asked why I'm destroying my talent in this ungrateful Odessa. He also recommended that I go to Petersburg and Moscow, which is precisely where I can find true music enthusiasts.
> Following Wieniawski's advice, I quickly decided to go to Petersburg; I'm leaving Odessa on February 24th with sister Lizenka. Thus, I ask you, my dear brother, to send to the editor of St. Petersburg *Vedomosti* a short announcement saying that I am planning to give one or two concerts in Petersburg as I pass through there. I believe that this announcement will prove useful if we can let the Petersburg public know about me in advance. This will make me very much obliged to the brother I love.
>
> Vladimir[11]

Semyon saw to it that *Vedomosti* published the notice, and the St. Petersburg recital took place on March 31, 1872 (old style). It was an ambitious program, opening with Beethoven's "Waldstein" Sonata, continuing with a Rubinstein Barcarolle, a Henselt Impromptu, Mendelssohn's Scherzo a Capriccio, Chopin's G minor Ballade, a Schumann Novellette followed by a Bach Gavotte, ending with Liszt's super-virtuosic Don Juan Fantasy.

If Pachmann thought the audience would be overwhelmed as if Tausig had been playing, he was bitterly disappointed. No managers came to see him afterwards. No tours were arranged. The brilliant career he had envisioned vanished with those roaring crescendos he tried to imitate.

Chapter 3

The Struggle to Find His Own Voice

Karl Tausig, one of Liszt's earlier students, performed in the grand style that originated with Liszt. He was probably the most finished of those early pupils, while he also made the piano sound more like an orchestra. Although Tausig could "freeze one's blood" as Oskar Beringer wrote, and send "bursts of passion like molten fire" to the furthest reaches of the hall, it was his fantastic control and marvelous composure while playing bravura passages, such as the roaring octaves in the middle of the Chopin A flat major Polonaise (an effect which he introduced that pianists have copied ever since) that amazed audiences and colleagues. He was the most accurate pianist in an age not known for note perfection. The nobility of his conceptions, his strength, and the refined beauty of his tone, all combined to suggest the playing of his master, Liszt. While his repertoire was all-inclusive, he was the first pianist (after the composer) to feature recitals consisting entirely of the works of Chopin, for which he had a great affinity.

Chopin pupil Wilhelm von Lenz in his important book *Great Piano Virtuosos of Our Time* wrote of his playing of the E flat major and C minor Nocturnes:

> Tausig played me both Nocturnes in the most finished manner, in fact, just as Chopin played them. . . . His command of all musical resources was so great, that in this command resided the poetry of a conqueror holding sovereign sway over material and machinery, a poetry peculiar and apart.

With all these qualities went a subtle mystery that defied analysis. Liszt said he was "all bronze and diamonds." In the last years of his short life Tausig's playing, however, underwent a change. While retaining the accuracy and thunder, he had begun to explore an entirely new aspect of his art, just when Pachmann heard him—unexpectedly soft playing. This is revealed in a review, written by composer/critic Caesar Cui, of a recital Tausig gave in St. Petersburg on March 6, 1870 (old style):

> His playing is highly smooth, his pianissimo fantastic; we have never heard such gentle and even, soft playing before . . . he is simple, delivering what is being played with complete understanding, with taste, not overly emotional, even a little bit dry, very willingly resorting to his incomparable soft playing. . . . In his hands Chopin was transformed and emerged in a very unusual form for us: the composer's ultra sensitivity, sentimentality, eternal sorrowfulness and whining had disappeared, and playfulness, flirtatiousness and vivacity came to the foreground. I have to admit, such a new and piquant way of interpreting Chopin affected me refreshingly and nicely, for in the Mazurkas I think such interpretations absolutely correct . . . The last piece on the program was Liszt's fantasy on 'Don Juan'. . . . It was Mr. Tausig's triumph: it let him open all his wonderful qualities, and his power appeared; and taste, understanding and self-control were kept until the very end, all completed with wonderful effect.[1]

After his unsuccessful 1872 St. Petersburg debut in which he tried to imitate Tausig, speaking to no one, Pachmann locked himself in his room to ponder what had gone wrong. Because of the lack of enthusiasm for his playing in St. Petersburg, he realized that Tausig's heroic approach was not the answer. He never had the ferocious energy and drive for that type of music. Still, in Tausig, he heard not only heroic aspects, but tonal beauty, and depth of tone. His own tone was beautiful, but superficial. He concluded that he had to combine the finesse of his Viennese training with this new style he had heard from Tausig. He resolved not to rest until he acquired depth of tone, something far greater than mere prettiness. He became obsessed with achieving this, and remained so for the rest of his life. He idealized sensuous, beautiful piano sound as no other pianist in history. He was haunted forever after by a search for the most penetrating cantabile.

His youthful arrogance and confidence had been shaken. In agony, he could not escape the conclusion that his playing, though facile and skillful, was too imitative, and not expressive of his own true talent. He had to return to the beginning and try and capture the beauty he heard with his inner ear but could not express at the piano. He had been imprisoned by Dachs's teaching. He would never free himself from the tyranny of the bar line and develop his own style until he worked deeply and intensely so that his own inner voice was liberated.

Pachmann gave no further concerts, living at the piano in his father's house in Odessa for the next seven years. He appears to have done little else than obsessively practice, and omnivorously devour volumes of French literature. By this time he spoke several languages with varying degrees of proficiency: his native Russian, as well as German in which he was fluent; Viennese dialect also, and polished French, supposedly without a trace of Slavic accent. French was the language of cultured Russians of the day, and Pachmann already considered himself an expert on French literature, starting with Rabelais and Madame de La Fayette, ultimately all the way up to Anatole France. His life consisted of little else than reading French books and practicing, practicing, practicing. It was a habit that never left him. He told an interviewer for the *Musician* magazine in October 1913, that when he wasn't giving concerts, "I spend my time wearing out pianos."

There are no other details of his life during this extraordinary retirement. Vikentiy was old, retired and probably home all day, driven to distraction by the constant practicing, and must have provided (whether willingly or grudgingly we know not) the funds that enabled his withdrawn son to spend further years studying. Perhaps some monetary help came from brother Semyon.

Just how Pachmann went about teaching himself is a mystery. Although later in life he was never reticent to talk about his great mastery, he was conspicuously silent about how he had achieved it, except to emphasize that he practiced each piece thousands of times. Like Wanda Landowska and other great artists, he was jealous of his mastery and eager to preserve the illusion of necromancy in his art. He guarded his unique approach to the piano and later, only to his wife and son did he confide the details of his pianistic genius.

If we do not know how he accomplished his ends, we know from his son Leonide what those ends were. Pachmann was not satisfied to have his scales "purling," he wanted them to murmur, to roar. Double thirds and sixths must not be merely legato, but must sound like a suave duet between a violin and a viola. The tone quality he wanted was of a soft, sweet roundness then heard only in his imagination. In those seven years he spent more time on touch and tone than on mechanical technique. He already had the facility, but not the *sound* he wanted.

The recently introduced iron-framed pianos had allowed Liszt's orchestral style of playing to quickly proliferate all over the world. Pachmann's training in the older, intimate style had to be updated. More overtones were now possible, but one could not play on a modern instrument the same way as Chopin played on a wooden framed one; the touch was heavier and the instrument less responsive to extreme delicacy. Pachmann's genius found a way to achieve his vision of Chopin's sound through manipulations of touch.

The touch he wanted had to be of such quality and purity that the fullest overtones of the strings were audible, always giving the sound a golden roundness, not unlike a perfectly placed vocal tone. He discovered that touching the keys so that they depressed, not suddenly, but gradually to the base of the keyboard, in three different levels, gave the tone a chance to "bathe in its own sound" (*un bain de son*). The roundness of tone in both the loudest and softest passages is what he most wanted. He worked particularly to acquire an exquisite pianissimo that paradoxically was fragile and piercing—later celebrated as the Pachmann sound, the "Pachmannissimo," which made his playing among the most immediately recognizable of players of his day. In his prime Pachmann was able to produce tones of such incredible sensitivity and beauty that a tonal gulf grew between him and all other pianists. That most other pianists of the time envied his tone is documented, and its quality and purity became the standard by which others were judged.

We can deduce that this very special sound he labored to summon from the piano actually determined his conceptions of the various works he played. All else—the wonderful lilt of his rhythm as well as his overt emotionalism—was subordinate to the central idea, the conception derived from unique, exquisite sounds. A simple Chopin Mazurka, for instance, was conceived as purely abstract: "Little to do with drama, nothing to do with philosophy or romance, everything to do with aesthetic proportion and sensuous charm," as described by critic Olin Downes on January 15, 1933, in his obituary for the pianist.

Pachmann was not completely glued to his piano bench. He needed to hear and absorb all the great piano playing he could, to feed and shape his own art. He told Arthur Symons in an interview published in *Vanity Fair* in December 1915, that he heard Liszt perform at a charity concert when Liszt was 63, and that "he was incomparable." That would put the concert in 1874, during the period when Pachmann was apparently shut up in Odessa, obsessively restudying his art. It is likely Pachmann was thinking about Liszt and Liszt's compositions during his self-imposed exile, trying to broaden his art and find the best pieces by the master to suit his own repertoire. He would have jumped at the opportunity to hear Liszt play a recital, so rare now that Liszt had retired from the concert stage. Liszt did not visit Russia in 1874, but did play a benefit concert in Vienna on April 6, 1874; the program included, besides several of his own compositions like the Legend of St. Francis Walking on the Water, many improvised works. This was probably the charity concert Pachmann heard, and we can only speculate about the circumstances that would put Pachmann back in Vienna in the middle of his retirement.

In Russia Pachmann often had the opportunity to hear Liszt's only real rival as a pianist, Anton Rubinstein. While Tausig was famous for his inhuman accuracy, Rubinstein was well-known for his wrong notes. He himself said that he could have made another recital from the notes which fell on the floor. But all was forgotten in the onrush of his emotional outpourings, and in the wake of his magnificent technique, monumental style and miraculous tonal color. Rafael Joseffy wrote that Rubinstein's touch was like the sound of a French horn, and Rachmaninoff declared, "One listened entranced, so unique was the beauty of his tone." Renowned for his loud playing which, despite its power, never lost its beauty, Rubinstein's quiet playing was just as miraculous. Towering above it all was his marvelous personality, "the lion of the keyboard," who hypnotized audiences. His famous first entrances were terrifying and overpowering, when he attacked the piano with his "grand accent." However his performances, like those of many very emotional people, were uneven, "sometimes playing like a god, other times like a barbarian," according to Oskar Beringer. In those moments he was truly awesome, like a mad man drunk with his own power, raving over the keyboard.

In an interview in the *New York Times* printed on October 30, 1911, Pachmann said:

> Rubinstein played Chopin perhaps better than Liszt, but he was not so great. He knew it and said so himself. I heard Rubinstein play hundreds of times. For thirty years I went to his concerts whenever I could. He was wonderful. He had force and power, the big tone that one associates with Caruso.

Rubinstein's unparalleled symphony of colors opened new vistas for Pachmann, who had never heard such ravishing sounds, not even from Tausig. Here on the concert platform was the round tone he had heard in his imagination and was coming close to actualizing on his own playing. Like many others hearing the great thunderer Rubinstein for the first time, he was shaken to his very core. Eventually the beauty of Pachmann's own quieter playing probably surpassed even the fabled tone of Rubinstein. Leonide de Pachmann told the author that his father once went backstage to compliment Rubinstein, saying "Your loudest tone doesn't hurt our ears!" According to Pachmann, Rubinstein replied, "Ah, my dear fellow, but I don't have your touch."

⤳

In July 1878 Vikentiy Pachmann died. His father's passing merely strengthened Pachmann's attachment to his sister Elizaveta, his beloved "Lizenka." His relationship with his father must have been complicated, if not loving. When he was older he professed to hate the sound of the 'cello. When acting up or threatening not to appear for a concert, managers were able to bring him into line quickly by telling him, "Oh, very well, we have an excellent 'cellist who can substitute." It always worked. Vikentiy had played the 'cello as well as the violin.

Elizaveta, who apparently never married, now watched over him. When he would become depressed and discouraged, her faith in his talent sustained him. After he became famous he sent her all the newspaper clippings so she could follow in her old age the successful progress of the career she had fostered and for which he was grateful.

Vikentiy's will left a total of 22,000 rubles, divided among various family members. Elizaveta was left 5,000 rubles, and Vladimir received 4,000. Pachmann, thirty years old, now had the means to go to Leipzig and at last again present some concerts, perhaps even play with the orchestra and, with luck, attract the attention of an enterprising impresario. Elizaveta accompanied him, the couple probably arriving in late 1878.

They found that the city was saturated with music. Since Mendelssohn had founded the Conservatory, Leipzig had been one of Europe's music centers. There was the splendid Gewandhaus Orchestra under Carl Reinecke, whose concerts students attended without cost. There were innumerable small orchestras that specialized in modern works and where seats were always available for nine or ten pence. Even more important, all the great artists visited and one could hear on successive nights the violinist Pablo de Sarasate and the pianist Sophie Menter.

In the spring of 1879 Pachmann played a private matinee at the Leipzig showroom of the Blüthner piano company for invited members of the press and the city's musical elite. His remarkable playing was immediately recognized, and he attracted the attention of composer/pianist/conductor Reinecke. Pachmann then presented a solo recital in the hall of the Gewandhaus on October 31, 1879. Cannily, he programmed Reinecke's transcription for solo piano of the slow movement of Chopin's E minor Concerto. It was his first public concert as a mature artist, and the first occasion on which he attached the nobilary particle to his name (in this case "von," later "de") to suggest nobility.[2]

The review by musicologist Eduard Bernsdorf in *Signale für die musikalische Welt* (No. 58-1879) was one of the first in a lifelong succession of raves:

No piano virtuoso in a long time has given us so much pleasure and enjoyment as Herr von Pachmann, and he . . . will soon be counted as one of the Optimati of today's piano players. The brilliance and perfection of his technique is obvious beyond any doubt; in addition, he possesses the most delightful touch that could be imagined, and in this respect it should be emphasized that he produces his pianos and pianissimos, not only with mechanical shifting (una corda pedal), but also without this (in our time unfortunately excessively overused) mechanical aid, exclusively by free reign of—so to speak—natural piano sound, he is capable of producing the necessary tenderness of sound. His performances in the end show finesse and elegance, and his playing is less marred by mannered and affected effects as with most of today's pianists. Herr Pachmann accomplished the program with roaring applause.[3]

The strategy of playing Reinecke's transcription worked, and Reinecke asked Pachmann to play his third Concerto in C major with the Gewandhaus Orchestra on December 4, 1879. The C major is certainly the best of Reinecke's piano concertos, a skillful example of compositional ability, but the absolute poverty of melodic invention sabotages all the skill Reinecke brought to bear on the work. Nevertheless, it did offer Pachmann the opportunity to show off his pearly scale passages and ethereal pianissimos. Bernsdorf reviewed the performance for *Signale* (No. 67-1879):

> Herr von Pachmann reconfirmed through his performance in the most perfect way possible the most favorable opinion, which he had allowed us to form of him as a pianist after his previous appearances and which we have expressed in this paper already. If the Reinecke concerto tainted a little the great pleasure . . . perhaps through a temporary (perhaps caused by nervousness) rushing of the passages, then the Bach-Tausig Toccata and Fugue, as well as the Henselt Etude were perfect in every way, and especially in the latter piece, the truly rare beauty of Herr von Pachmann's touch was proven in the most delicious manner.[4]

He played another solo recital at Leipzig's Blüthner Saal on April 11, 1880. It was during those months in Leipzig that Pachmann first heard Liszt's great pupil Hans von Bülow play, and Bülow's art also had an effect on his own pianism.

Nothing could be greater than the contrast between the passionate and sometimes unruly surgings of Anton Rubinstein, and the careful, intellectual conceptualizing of Hans von Bülow. There was little tonal magic in his art, for he was an entirely different kind of pianist, one for whom effects meant nothing. He was interested only in the clearest outlines in black and white. Even in the most involved contrapuntal passages, his etched phrases made the separate voices stand out clearly, and this was justly admired, as was his intellectual grasp of Beethoven, where according to critic James Huneker, "his meticulous approach exposed the composer's minutest meanings."

Bülow was almost as famous for his nasty personality as for his insightful playing. Rudeness accompanied his appearances and no one could count on escaping it. He treated audiences like a despot by insulting them, and was notorious for his angry "ssshh" to the Kaiser at a moment when the German Emperor chose to whisper while he was playing.

Once, in a temperamental outburst, he threw a music stand at someone who displeased him. His evil wit was proverbial, and his remark that a rival conductor should have been a bus driver "because he was always behind" was characteristic. A well-wisher once approached him with the words, "I'll bet you don't remember me." Bülow replied, "You've won your bet!" as he turned away. At one recital Bülow stopped abruptly and ordered the ushers to turn the piano around when a woman in the audience annoyed him by fanning herself out of time. Another occasion at a benefit recital he noticed some important but ugly women in the first row. He stormed off the stage and told his manager: "You do not expect me to play with those ugly witches gazing at me. . . . Until those women are removed I will not play a single note."[5]

Pachmann was deeply impressed with the sincerity and probity of Bülow's performances. He particularly admired Bülow's masterly phrasing, and had a high regard for his edition of the Chopin Etudes.[6] The Puck in Pachmann delighted in the German's public temper tantrums. Bülow was a noted wit, once describing a critic known to be susceptible to accepting small bribes: "He takes so little that he is almost honest." With his "puckish sense of humor," according to his biographer Alan Walker, he was not above posing for whimsical and humorous photographs: "there was that bright red Turkish Fez with the tassels that he wore while sitting on the front row of a concert in Edinburgh, in which Alexander Mackenzie conducted his own overture to 'Cervantes'—a humorous reminder to the audience of the five years that Cervantes had spent as a prisoner of the Turks in Algiers," wrote Walker.[7]

There is little doubt that Bülow's outrageous and sometimes disgraceful platform behavior influenced Pachmann's mannerisms, though even in his wildest moments Pachmann's antics never exhibited the nastiness of "Irritable Hans's" outbursts. Pachmann once told conductor Wilhelm Ganz that Bülow had been his "beau ideal," but it is likely he meant the Bülow personality as much as the sober musician.

Pachmann's Leipzig concerts were financially successful, and with the money he earned he went to Berlin and presented a recital at the Architectural Hall. It was enthusiastically received but not the triumph for which he hoped. Apparently Pachmann also appeared in concerts about 1879 in Florence and Milan, Italy.[8] No documentation for this has been found, and these months are the dark ages in Pachmann's story. His career was stalled. He had little money left and no prospective engagements. Worse, he was no longer a student but not yet an artist. He returned to Vienna. He was 32.

Chapter 4

Alone on a Mountaintop, Early 1880s

The Vienna to which Pachmann returned was the Vienna of the Imperial Golden Age. Around the now-completed Ringstrasse could be seen the daily parade of high society in its opulent finery. Mixed in this panorama were Vienna's great composers, the soul of the city—Brahms, Bruckner, Wolf, Goldmark and young Mahler. Only Johann Strauss kept aloof. He never walked, but preferred an open carriage on the bridle path where, with his dyed hair and mustache, this young old man could be found surrounded by his aristocratic admirers. Underneath the blithe exterior, his worldly pose and lifelong pursuit of sensuality (reflected in his music) had an undercurrent of sadness suggesting the impermanence of worldly pleasures. He, more than any other composer, epitomized the gilded, glittering facade of the Ringstrasse—a world in which Pachmann now found himself.

Daily he visited the opulent Bösendorfer piano store where he would practice. Although he had spent eight years in intensive practice and had appeared in a few concerts, he was still dissatisfied with his playing and not ready to appear in concert in Vienna again quite yet. He allowed no one to hear him and kept the doors of the salon closed as he worked. Herr Ludwig Bösendorfer, son of the founder, had heard many pianists in his time, but he was especially impressed with the playing of the strange young Russian who came to practice in his salon. Pachmann had made him promise not to speak to anyone about what he heard, but once among friends, Bösendorfer couldn't keep his promise. Vienna was a city of gossip; to keep an ordinary secret was difficult enough—a musical one, impossible. Rumors spread, fanned by Bösendorfer's story of the remarkable playing that he was hearing daily. Soon, much to Pachmann's chagrin, impresarios began to wander in and out during his practice sessions. Leonide de Pachmann vividly remembered his father telling him of the ensuing dialogue:

"Mind that no one comes too close," he told Bösendorfer, "for I am not ready to be heard. Let us say I have arrived at the letter 'C' in the alphabet. You see the distance I have to go before I reach 'Z.' And even when I get there, who knows? I may have to begin all over again."

A new friend, a prince from the Hohenlohe dynasty who was himself an accomplished pianist, tried to use his influence to persuade Pachmann to appear in public, but he refused. When an impresario gingerly mentioned possible plans for a concert, he flew into a rage. Nothing could persuade him that he was already prepared well enough for a solo recital debut and a career. Nine months passed in this fashion.

His confidence slowly began to build, and occasionally Pachmann agreed to appear, assisting in private salon concerts and in public as a subsidiary artist to established musical figures. These appearances were much discussed, and soon he was the best-known "unknown pianist" in Vienna. One day he was overheard by a certain Herr Waltmann,[1] a music lover who was starting a career as a manager, and had been traveling with Liszt's pupil Sophie Menter. Waltmann considered himself a connoisseur of piano playing. After listening to Pachmann play Chopin's G minor Ballade he was so impressed he spoke to others about this amazing pianist.

Pachmann was slowly feeling his way. Exasperated, Waltmann finally asked him point-blank to make his debut and play a solo recital.

"What, you want me to play in public? I tell you, I am not yet ready." With a wave of his hand, he dismissed poor Waltmann.

"Come back in a year."

"A year?"

"Well, perhaps six months."

Waltmann was not a man to be dismissed lightly by an unknown pianist. He lost no time in pointing out the difficulties most young musicians had in just finding an impresario who would agree to hear them audition. He undoubtedly if subtly alluded to Pachmann's already "advanced" age. He spoke so persuasively that Pachmann's fears and self-doubts were dispelled. He agreed to play in a fortnight. But a few days before the event, a very nervous pianist visited Waltmann, shaking all over. "I'm ill, I'm ill, it must be postponed."

At first Waltmann tried to talk him out of it, but the more he talked, the more nervous Pachmann became. The concert had to be canceled, but Waltmann was a clever man. Unknown to the pianist, he had submitted notices in the *Neue Freie Presse* and other Viennese journals, and while Pachmann vacillated his name was kept before the public, which was even more tantalizing. A second time Waltmann prevailed upon him to name a date. But as the day approached, Pachmann again became nervous. "You can't expect me to play. What are you thinking of?"

Waltmann told him of the notices and of the public's mounting curiosity. Bösendorfer had promised to provide any piano he wanted "an easy one," if he wanted it. But to no avail. Stubborn Pachmann was adamant.

"No, no," he said, "I cannot . . . I will not play. Now leave me alone!" Waltmann thought he was being made to seem ridiculous before the public, and he was losing prestige and money as well, for the unpredictable and fickle Viennese public was beginning to think the whole affair a hoax. His reputation was at stake. Pachmann must play, there was no alternative. The program for the concert was already printed and dated January 9, 1882, but the date passed and there was no debut.

Something else besides Pachmann's nervousness would have contributed to the postponement. On December 8, 1881, a fire in Vienna's Ring Theatre had broken out, minutes before the start of an opera, the house completely packed with the city's most prominent residents. As the Royal family arrived, Crown Prince Rudolf cried in horror when he saw the bodies of the dead. It is believed 850 people died in the carnage, the theatre was destroyed and life in Vienna sadly disrupted for weeks.

〜

Eventually Pachmann returned to Waltmann.
"Mon cher, I tell you, I will play in a fortnight."
"Will you honestly?"
"This time, I'll try."

On January 17 Pachmann appeared again as an assisting artist, this time to the great lieder singer Gustav Walter in the Bösendorfersaal. Leipzig's *Neue Zeitschrift für Musik* had their reporter L. Schrottenbach attend the concert, and he wrote (March 10, 1882) "Herr von Pachmann demonstrated a technically significant achievement in Liszt's Concert Etude in D flat and several pieces by Chopin."[2] The debut recital was finally to take place the next day, with the date "January 18" superimposed over the old "January 9." But when the time came, in the artist's room just before it was to begin, Pachmann was as nervous as before, if not more so. He complained of headaches and stomach pains. Prepared for such emergencies, astute Waltmann had a doctor waiting in the wings. This fine gentleman, it appears, was as proficient at psychology as at medicine, for he said to the pianist:

"Ah, you are nervous? You must be a great artist then."

Pachmann looked up at him.

"Do you really think great artists are as nervous as I am?"

"Undoubtedly."

It was enough for Pachmann who quickly prepared himself for the performance. Just in time, too, for he had kept the audience waiting so long that they had begun to hoot and stamp.

"Quiet them or I won't play!" he cried.

"But you must play," replied Waltmann soothingly as he gently led him by the elbow to the stage door, saying, "Look at all the people who have come to hear you play."

The pianist stood on his tiptoes. "Let me look."

As he peeped out at the house, Waltmann seized the opportunity, gave him a push and hissed, "Sink or swim!" Suddenly Pachmann found himself on the platform, in full view of the audience. There was no turning back, no choice but to swim—the concert was a great success.

Eduard Hanslick, one of the most esteemed of all music critics, mentioned the debut recital in passing in the January 24, 1882, issue of the *Neue Freie Presse*: "The well-known and widely-acclaimed pianist Woldemar von Pachmann again proved his remarkable virtuosity in his own concert."[3]

A few days later an extended critique of the recital appeared that was probably the most important review of Pachmann's career:

> The recent concert by the pianist Mr. Woldemar von Pachmann in the Bösendorfer Hall was an unusual occasion. With one stroke Mr. von Pachmann has advanced to the ranks of first class artists. He combines an incredible technique with a highly artistic understanding, blending into an extraordinary entity. Beethoven's Sonata in A major, Op. 101 was the highlight of the concert. At this point it is not uninteresting to draw a comparison between Pachmann and Bülow, who in the preceding year had performed this Sonata in the Bösendorfer Hall. Although Bülow is considered the foremost interpreter of Beethoven, we have to admit that Pachmann's performance was definitely more lively and interesting. Although Pachmann does not have the scholarly attitude of Bülow, he amply makes up for this with the greater warmth of touch, and more soul and heart in his interpretation. Bülow says: 'This is Beethoven.' Pachmann, on the other hand, 'This is how I perceive Beethoven.' Pachmann is completely unique in the interpretation of Chopin. To play Beethoven and Chopin equally well is the unusual force in Pachmann. In his veins flow German and Russian blood; Beethoven drives the German root, while Chopin follows from the artist's Slavic blood mixture. A rare effect was achieved as we have never heard before, by his amazing ability to beautifully evoke nuances of touch, as complete as the piano's octaves can produce. Added to this is a bravura which leaves the listener breathless. This was especially notable in Chopin's Etude in Thirds. Mr. Pachmann also played Liszt's charming and oh so emotional composition, 'Benediction de Dieu dans la solitude' wonderfully. If one closed one's eyes one could really

believe that the Old master Liszt himself sat at the grand piano. We are looking forward to Mr. Pachmann's next concert in the near future.[4]

This review appeared in the February 1, 1882, issue of the *Vienna Abendpost*. Reviews were not signed in those days so it is impossible to identify
the writer at this point, although some feel it was Hanslick himself, since
the *Neue Freie Presse* had recently purchased the *Abendpost*. The rave review heralded Pachmann's pianistic genius, comparing him favorably to
Liszt. It was a harbinger of a great career.

Pachmann's daring seven year retirement was not easily understood by
many, but he was vindicated. Twenty-three years afterwards the distinguished American composer, Edward Burlingame Hill, wrote about it in
the June 1905 issue of the *Musician*:

> What was the magic that drove the young de Pachmann into retirement.
> . . . Nothing but the keen recognition that still greater success would reward
> his unsatisfied ambition . . . his unquenchable love of perfection would not
> permit him a respite . . . he devoted himself to work once more. . . . The
> reason for this unexampled disciplining of himself was that every triumph
> revealed his capacity in a new light; it showed new depths of achievement
> which could only be realized by a longer and more arduous abnegation of
> cheaply won success. . . . One has . . . to be grateful for the high ideal which
> demanded so much.

Some who may know of Pachmann's reputation as a glib old man whose
easy platform manner never seemed to betray any sign of nervousness
may be surprised by the most unusual details of his Vienna debut and
extreme self doubts. But it is a fact that intense anxiety seems to have
plagued him throughout his early career, and one reads in many early reviews of memory lapses. To minimize or conceal these, he would gesticu-
late to the audience, making them think his hands were cold. Sometimes
he would even make a great show of borrowing a muff from someone in
the hall. All this made the audience forget his nervous memory lapses.[5]

These slips profoundly disturbed his sense of perfection and it did not
take Pachmann long to discover the antidote. He found that if he talked
to the audience, took them into his confidence, much of the anxiety would
dissipate. At first this behavior was purely therapeutic, growing out of a
desire to soothe his frayed nerves. When managers in different cities realized that audiences seemed to enjoy these "unconventionalities," they
encouraged the pianist to even more outrageous acts, and he obliged.

At first these antics were limited to a kind of pantomimic expression
of the difficulties of the concert artist. In mime he would let the audience
know that the music he was playing was very difficult; that he really was
tired; that the piano in this hall was wretched, and of all the many other

irritations which interfere with an artist's desire for perfection. Facial contortions and grimaces accompanied hand gesticulations. Of course he would soon become notorious in most of the Western world for this, but the days when his mannerisms deteriorated to the point where he would slip one page from a telephone book under his piano bench saying "you'd be surprised the difference an inch makes!" were still in the future.

Pachmann's debut was so successful that he was asked to play two further solo recitals in Vienna on February 9 and March 6 and he continued to appear as assisting artist in concerts by others. He elicited an unambiguous Hanslick review, printed in the February 21 *Neue Freie Presse*, of the earlier joint recital:

> We heard Pachmann during [Gustav] Walter's second "Liederabend" which gave the virtuoso an opportunity to demonstrate his musical skills before the largest and most sophisticated audience of Vienna. Herr von Pachmann was most successful in this. Yet he lacked the necessary style and even the physical strength, especially in his left hand, to play Bach's Toccata and Fugues, which we imagine to be cast in iron. On the other hand we were impressed with his delicate, melodic touch, his soft pearly playing of passages in an Etude by Liszt and two by Chopin which earned Herr von Pachmann stormy applause.[6]

This was the first appearance of a leitmotiv which was to appear in reviews of Pachmann's concerts throughout his career—the lack of power and energy in certain works that demanded them. But the recitals were generally greatly acclaimed and after one he had to play eight encores. Later he was engaged for the Mozart D minor Concerto with the Vienna Philharmonic under the baton of Wilhelm Jahn on November 26, but it was his Chopin which conquered Vienna. The city's discriminating music lovers felt something important was happening, namely that not since Chopin himself had visited had such exquisite performances of his music been heard.

Pachmann's career was finally launched. Next came Paris. On April 29, 1882, he played on an Érard piano at the firm's Salle Érard, and the May 4 issue of *L'Art Musical* reported:

> M. de Pachmann extends the mechanism of the piano toward perfection . . . so powerful is his touch, but it is never hard; so full of detail that his playing is never dry. He deliciously played the masterpiece of Schubert, the Impromptu Op. 90 No. 4, as well as a Polonaise of Chopin, and 'La melancolie' of Rubinstein, which begins like a Romance Without Words of Mendelssohn, finishing grandly with a beautiful Etude of Liszt."[7]

Waltmann was advertising him as a "pupil of Liszt," exaggerating the pointers Liszt had given him when he played the E flat Concerto as a student into a false claim of a teacher/pupil relationship.

〜

Pachmann forgot Tausig's, Rubinstein's and von Bülow's playing when Franz Liszt touched the keys. He was, as Pachmann was to say later, "alone on a mountaintop." Liszt was nearly seventy and had been retired from the concert stage for over thirty years. In his youth Liszt had played and had heard Chopin play on low-tension, wood frame pianos, with their intimate sound. His genius was to translate that kind of playing into something appropriate for the modern steel framed pianos.[8] In his old age his playing, if we are to believe those who heard him, was even more beautiful, more spiritual than his playing in his prime. It seems that although he no longer practiced, his technique had mellowed, and the thunder and lightning that had catapulted him across the continent like a brilliant meteor had now dissolved, leaving only exquisite traceries.[9] According to his pupil Felix Weingartner, his touch was now "a thing of glory to dream about" and had "pearled" and melted into something quite idealized, while his tone, no longer vibrant, had a piercing delicacy and sweetness that transported his hearers into dreams. Perhaps most remarkable of all was the extraordinary way he perceived each composer's meaning and delineated it before his audience so that they felt they were hearing the music for the first time. "It wasn't an interpretation but a recreation" wrote Richard Wagner. Although Tausig surpassed him in accuracy, Bülow in intellect and Rubinstein in tone and volume, all agreed with Rubinstein's remark, "Next to Liszt, we are all nothing."

There was even more to Liszt than his remarkable playing. It was his personality that people remembered the most. He had the most extraordinary effect on those who saw or heard him. His marvelous manner, a cross between a *grand seigneur*, a worldly courtier and a diabolical wizard, fascinated all. Amy Fay, one of his American pupils, wrote, "It was this quality, this *diablerie*, which made Liszt so unforgettable—and his playing so magical."

He had an immense effect on Pachmann, particularly his playing of Chopin. In a reminiscence in the *New York Sun* printed on December 15, 1911, Pachmann wrote "I was a young man of nineteen when I heard him play Chopin's Nocturne . . . he was a master." This probably occurred at the Vienna Conservatory when the composer played for the students. Liszt loved Chopin and as an old man played many of Chopin's shorter pieces, supposedly with an authentic quality not unlike Chopin's own playing. It was Liszt's Chopin style, with its ideal touch, hazy poetic atmosphere, its personality, exquisiteness and absolute freedom of interpretation, that influenced the whole school of Romantic Chopin players of the late nineteenth and early twentieth centuries. Pianists like Moriz Rosenthal, Rafael Joseffy and Pachmann apparently remembered every detail of performances of Chopin they heard from Liszt for the rest of their lives. Pachmann said he couldn't play for two days after hearing him. In a March 17, 1912, interview in the *Cleveland Leader* Pachmann was quoted speaking about Liszt:

> I believe he was the most sublime example of the genius that ever lived. He was more than a musician, more than a composer, and more than a poet—he was all three, and then the story was not half told.

When he was seventy-five, he was still in thrall to the memory and told a reporter for the *New York Herald* (August 30, 1923) "How Liszt could improvise!"

It wasn't any Chopin pupil who shaped Pachmann's approach to playing the music of Chopin—it was Liszt. Although Pachmann himself never spoke about the so-called "Chopin school" of playing, Franz Liszt did leave us an opinion—he found it distasteful, and in 1880 told the Reverend Hugh Haweis, an English curate passionately interested in music:

> Chopin had no life, properly speaking; his was an exclusive, self-centered personality. He lived inwardly—he was silent and reserved, never said much, and people were often deceived about him, and he never undeceived them. People talk of the *style* of Chopin, the *touch* of Chopin, and of playing like Chopin. When he played himself, he played admirably well, and especially his own compositions; but he was supposed to have formed a school of Chopinites, who had the Tradition—and you heard that Mr. *This* and Madame *That*—they alone could play like Chopin—he had formed them—people danced round them, and they affected to have the true Chopin secret. Yes . . . it was absurd enough; and Chopin looked on, and said nothing; he was very diplomatic—he never troubled himself to stop this cant, and to this day there may be those who play "like Chopin"—who have received the sacred "Tradition." C'était comme cela du commencement, ce n'était pas *l'école*, c'était plutôt *l'église* de Chopin! . . . [It was like that from the start—it wasn't the *school*, it was rather the *church* of Chopin!]

In her memoirs, Laura Kahrer wrote:

> I have heard only a few pupils of Chopin play: Madame Mouchanoff, née Kalergis; Wilhelm von Lenz, and a few others. But only ONE could create a fabulous, mirror image of Chopin's playing, and that was Franz Liszt![10]

According to Pachmann Liszt showed him many secrets—nuances and pedal effects—that Chopin had used himself. Liszt's understanding of tempo rubato was consummate. Bettina Walker, an English Liszt pupil, wrote that the Master used to illustrate how Chopin, having wandered from a first thought, seemed to be groping and swaying. This he pictured in his playing most wonderfully, for while not losing the rhythmic pulse, he'd have the music waver and sway as if in uncertainty, while saying as he continued, "He has not found it yet but it's coming . . . it's near . . . Now!" With a note of triumph he would sweep into the main idea. This expressive way of using rubato to give emotional tension to the music, yet never losing the basic rhythmic pulse, gave Pachmann many ideas for the expressive use of rubato in his performances of Chopin. He learned some of the divine secrets of pianism from Liszt, who had a unique way of making the piano sound human.

⸌⸍

No part of Pachmann study is more difficult than attempts to unravel fact from fantasy concerning specific details of the pianist's relationship to Franz Liszt. Early biographers relied heavily on Pachmann's own exaggerated claims, especially stories he told in his last years that were almost completely unreliable.[11] Solid historical evidence links the two, and one must bear in mind that there was always a substantial basis in truth, a historical starting point, from which the elder Pachmann's romantic stories were elaborated. But we must discount the details from certain interviews Pachmann gave that are just unbelievable. These consisted of Liszt's supposed praise for his playing, which increasingly reflected the state of the old Pachmann's mind: "He, the great master, said that some day I should be one of the greatest pianists in the world . . . Liszt told me I was the first piano genius in the world . . . Liszt . . . attended one of my recitals and remarked to a friend, 'Pachmann's execution is such that I have never been so moved before' . . . Ah, my friend Liszt, you used to say that it was a pity that Chopin died before he could hear the tear-laden sweetness of a nocturne played by Pachmann . . . " et cetera.

Another progression of unreality consisted of increasingly fantastic stories told of Liszt taking him to play for Wagner. Pachmann elaborated many versions of this story, and in later years he would constantly speak of it, further embroidering the tale each time. The earliest the author has found dates from thirty years after the fact, if it was fact, in the *New York Sun* of December 15, 1911:

No one except Liszt had everything. Liszt was a great man. He was proud like a king, like a God . . . It was in Rome, in a house in Via Del Barbarian [*sic*]. He had taken me there to see Wagner. Wagner and Liszt, what a couple! Wagner was not always arrogant, he was not then. He played something from the Niebelungenlied. Liszt played Chopin. I must have divined Chopin's execution. I could not have heard him for I was only a year old when he died. I played Chopin's Ballade in G minor. When I finished, Wagner said to Papa Liszt, 'Have you heard such a tone like that?' Liszt said, '*Charmant,*

charmant.' Afterwards he wrote some musical friends of mine in London saying that Rubinstein was next to me. The letter is still in existence.[12]

In later versions, Pachmann claimed that Wagner had kissed his hands
after he had finished playing. Those came when Pachmann was more than
seventy years old, by which time his conceit had assumed monumental
proportions, and each has a fair share of Pachmannesque extravagance.
Here's the London *Evening Mail* quoting Pachmann on June 4, 1925:

> Only a year before he died Liszt took me to Wagner . . . Liszt asked me to
> play a Ballade of Chopin's for the great man. I played, and I played with
> all my heart and soul, and when I had finished, the great Wagner took my
> young hand and kissed it. 'One day, my child,' he said to me, 'you will be the
> greatest pianist in the world.' I was amazed that so great a man should kiss
> my hand and I cried, 'Master, master, it is I who should kneel at your feet.'
> But Wagner would not listen to me and he spoke very kindly to me.

Knowing Wagner's disposition, we can doubt if the composer of *Sieg-
fried* would have kissed the pianist's hands. A final version, from 1926,
has Wagner kissing Pachmann on the lips!

There is no mention of Pachmann in any of the voluminous Wagner
literature examined so far. That does not mean the meeting did not take
place, for the Wagner literature, vast as it is, is yet incomplete, and there
are many individual days in Wagner's later life for which there are no
specific details. If the *Evening Mail* reminiscence is correct, the meeting
would seem to have occurred in 1882.

Liszt inscribed and autographed a photo of himself to Pachmann,
which he cherished all his life. This photo had a place of honor on his
piano, framed and matted in between two others inscribed to him from
Klindworth and Henselt. The dedication in Liszt's hand in German with
the word "Pachmann" is clearly visible—unfortunately some of Liszt's
signature was hidden by the matting in this snapshot of the frame taken
by the author. That photo (and the rest of Pachmann's memorabilia) was
dispersed after Cesco Pallottelli's death, but it eventually found its way
into the stock of an Italian autograph dealer who offered it for sale in the
1980s. Its present whereabouts is unknown.

In 1884 Pachmann performed Chopin's F minor Concerto with Liszt's
Au bord d'une source as an encore in Budapest at the Philharmonic Hall
on March 5. Liszt made a special effort to attend, not letting Pachmann
know he was in the audience until afterwards. Pachmann played a series
of solo recitals in the following days, and Liszt attended the second one

on March 17. At the first recital on the 14th Pachmann played works by Liszt (including a Russian Galop after Bulakhov), but the composer chose to attend the other program, the one without any of his own compositions. Pachmann played Chopin's Third Sonata, and it was immediately after that performance that Liszt apparently stood and made a glowing comment to the audience: "Those who have not heard Chopin before are hearing him today." That is the version Pachmann told his son Leonide.

However, according to F. Foster Buffen's *Musical Celebrities*, Pachmann played Liszt's D flat Etude as an encore, after which Liszt exclaimed "This is what I have always required." Buffen states that the pianist then spent three days with Liszt, and after supper together one night Pachmann "played for upwards of two hours to the *maestro* who christened him 'the poet of the piano.'" Buffen's account was written about ten years after the event, and seems to be derived from conversations with Pachmann or his wife, or both.

It seems the old Mephisto of the piano found something of his own younger self in Pachmann, and cherished it. More than forty years later Pachmann remembered to interviewer Herbert Greenhalgh (*Strand* magazine July–December 1925):

And his sense of humor! He roared with laughter when I told him how I had surprised the professors at the Vienna Conservatoire. "Like me," he said. "Exactly like me. When the great Czerny first heard me play (I was a boy then) he nearly fell over with astonishment. What a joke!"

Liszt had written (quoted in the Boston *Musical Herald* in January 1885):

When I as very young, I often amused myself with playing school-boy tricks, of which my auditors never failed to become dupes. I would play the same pieces at one time as of Beethoven, at another as Czerny, and lastly as my own. The occasion on which I passed myself off for the author, I received both protection and encouragement—"It really was not bad for my age." The day I played it under the name of Czerny, I was not listened to; but, when I played it as being the composition of Beethoven, I made certain of the bravos of the whole assembly.

A few lines later Liszt writes about deliberately interchanging trios by Pixis and Beethoven at a concert he arranged at the Paris Conservatoire; the audience cheered the "Beethoven" trio, really by Pixis, and found the real Beethoven trio, listed as composed by Pixis, "cold, mediocre and even tiresome." These pranks suggest the same spirit of slyly initiating pranks to come later from Pachmann.[13]

⌒

The American Liszt pupil Amy Fay recounted one lesson with her master: a rapid run was to be followed by two staccato chords.

> "No, no," said Liszt. "After you make a run, you must wait a minute before you strike the chords, as if in admiration of your performance. You must pause as if to say, 'How nicely I did that.'" Then he sat down and made the run himself, waited a second and then struck the two chords in the treble, saying as he did so, "Bra-vo," and then he played again, struck the other chord, and said again, "Bra-vo," and positively, it was as if the piano had softly applauded! That is the way he plays everything. It seems as if the piano was speaking with a *human* tongue.

It is only one year after his long encounter with Liszt in Budapest that we have the first press report of Pachmann's audibly congratulating himself after a particularly exquisite performance and exclaiming, "Bravo de Pachmann!" to the audience. Another piece of evidence showing Liszt's influence on Pachmann appeared in an April 6, 1884, review by Hugo Wolf for the *Wiener Salonblatt*, of a concert by Liszt pupil Arthur Friedheim. Wolf wrote:

> Like Rubinstein, he [Friedheim] never for an instant allows the piano out of his gaze, but eyes it greedily. That is how tigers and panthers are with their prey. Liszt and his imitator de Pachmann, on the other hand, seem rather to go strolling during a performance, letting their gaze wander where it will, anywhere but up and down the keyboard. That is how lions toy with their victims.

Pachmann was invited by Liszt to Weimar where he lived like an uncrowned king, which indeed he was. It was Liszt's habit to invite guests to hear student performances at master classes. On these occasions, to save the pupils embarrassment in front of the visitors, Liszt often would walk to a window through which he gazed out to the grounds of the palace complex. Thus the identity of the student then performing could be said to remain a mystery to the old maestro.

This peculiar mannerism was repeated during a class Pachmann said he attended. Perhaps only childlike Vladimir de Pachmann of all the musicians in the world would have thought to play a practical joke on the great Liszt. He enlisted the aid of a student. When it was this pupil's turn to play for the Master, he performed an exceedingly difficult Liszt transcription with which he struggled until he arrived at a momentary pause, before even further complications began. Then Pachmann sprang to the piano and began to play the music written for the right hand alone with his two hands, while the pupil took care of the left hand in the same manner. The difficulties of the music were lessened by half, and together the two brought it off with unbelievable speed and brilliancy. The others present must have been stunned at the pair's audacity.

There was not a sound in the room, for every eye was on Liszt's back. He was still gazing out the window and had not moved in the slightest. Without turning, he said softly, almost as if to himself, "Marvelous improvement, perfectly astounding. The right hand part sounded exactly like my friend Pachmann's playing. No one else in the world plays like him and I thought I could tell his touch from among a million pianists, and yet how is it possible that my pupil could imitate him so wonderfully? If I did not know my friend Pachmann would never stoop to play such a wicked joke on his old admirer, I should have said that during the pause in the piece, he jumped in and helped out my perspiring pupil with the right hand part."

With that a roar of laughter swept the room. Pachmann not only survived the occasion, he rose to it. "I consider it an honor, my dear Master, that you recognized my touch . . . with your back turned." This amusing and fantastic story was told by Pachmann years later to a friend, Arnold Somlyo, who typed it up with others like it; it was never published and the original typescript is in the New York Public Library. It may be true.

More believable, perhaps, was the fact that Liszt was so charmed by Pachmann's playing that he would often ask him to play for friends. Pachmann told his friend and promoter Arnold Somlyo that once, while he played a Chopin Etude, Liszt listened as if lost in meditation. Then he walked over to the piano and said in front of everyone, "Play it again," and Pachmann played it a second time. Then Liszt whispered, "Again," and he did as he asked. Liszt stood, raised his hands over Pachmann, and murmured "Divine!" The pianist cherished the memory and often said it was the greatest compliment he ever received.

Encouraged by Liszt's acceptance and advocacy, Pachmann became more confident about himself and his abilities. He had always cultivated his personality as much as his art, for they were irrevocably entwined. No longer plagued by intense doubts, or fears that audiences would laugh at him or ridicule his platform behavior, he could now give full rein to both his music and his eccentricities . . . until they fused. Meeting Liszt was the turning point in his career. Liszt opened the gate by giving him permission to be Pachmann: success flooded in.

Chapter 5

Paris to London on a Bridge of Applause, 1882–1883 and Later

Pachmann's appearance in Vienna created so much enthusiasm that echoes reached Paris where *Le Ménéstrel* chronicled on March 26, 1882, "He has excited the enthusiasm of the musical world. His talent made a sensation in the salons where he has already been asked to play."[1]

Liszt had provided him with a letter of introduction to Camille Saint-Saëns, and he performed at one of the composer's Monday night soirées. Arthur Friedheim reported that Saint-Saëns told Pachmann, "I have some technique myself, also a 'touch'; but you are simply astonishing [*épatant*]!" Friedheim, a passionate disciple of Liszt, was present at this musicale and told Saint-Saëns afterwards, "If he [Pachmann] would apply energy to his dynamic range instead of the exact opposite, he would probably be *the* pianist after Liszt." Friedheim astutely identified the unique aspect of Pachmann's art, for he explored the avenues of quietness, of pianissimo and even further, "Pachmannissimo," in a direction no one else had ever gone.

Pachmann was drawn into the social whirl of Paris as he had been in Vienna. He was besieged with invitations to play at salons as he was the ideal salon player, perhaps the greatest since Chopin. His art transcended the stuffy formality of drawing rooms and the impersonal atmosphere of concert halls. Just as he brought the great intimacy of the salon into the concert hall, he brought the great art of the concert hall into the salon.

Adelina Patti's sister, Carlotta, hosted "evenings" during one of which Pachmann met two young sisters, Jeanne and Louise Douste, teenage prodigies (each as both pianist and singer) who had recently returned from successful tours of Europe and America. After they became friends, Pachmann was a constant visitor to the Douste's small flat where he

45

would amuse them with tales of his student days, or of Madame Slepouchkine. He was still, in the curious manner of so many grown-up musical prodigies, an overgrown adolescent, so we can imagine his child-like
intimacy with these very young girls. He played for them by the hour, going through whole concert programs. Louise wrote in her diary (quoted
in the book written about the sisters by Garceau):

> He plays admirably; his style is correct and pure, beautifully sonorous. I am
> enchanted . . . De Pachmann came to lunch and then afterwards played Po-
> lonaises, Ballades, Valses of Chopin, Polacca of Weber, Fugue of Bach. That
> is because the artist thoroughly enjoys good cooking.

Madam Douste was one of those celebrated French *mamans* whose savory
cooking was the pride of her family. As soon as its odor wafted through
to the drawing room, Pachmann would leave the girls, quietly creep up
behind Madame Douste, and lift the lids of the simmering saucepans one
by one to slowly inhale the aromas. He'd glide back to the piano and surpass himself "in a nocturne of Liszt or a Sonata of Chopin."

Pachmann's formal concert debut in Paris took place at the Salle Erard
on the 22nd and 29th of April, 1882, and the concerts were new triumphs.
Le Ménéstrel wrote:

> We heard last Monday an interesting piano recital given in Salle Erard by
> Vladimir de Pachmann, a virtuoso of much merit to whom the public gave a
> good reception. M. de Pachmann was applauded warmly in different works
> of Beethoven, Weber, Schumann, Mendelssohn, Chopin and Liszt; and for
> our part we particularly appreciated the way he played the Chopin Etude
> in G-sharp minor [double thirds Etude], the transcription by Liszt of a Men-
> delssohn Romance and Etudes Symphoniques of Schumann. He is a pianist
> of good training who has earned in Paris all the success he had in Vienna,
> which is just.[2]

Another friend the pianist made in Paris was Frederic Hymen Cowen
(not yet Sir Frederic), then a prominent English composer and pianist
originally from Jamaica who had studied with Tausig. In his memoirs, he
presented this picture of Pachmann, "He was quite a young man in those
days, just beginning his career, but had already made a sensation by the
playing of Chopin's music, notably the Etude in double thirds [Op. 25,
No. 6] which was the most perfect thing of its kind I have ever heard."

The double thirds Etude was apparently considered one of Pachmann's
most perfect conceptions. Years later pianist Edwin Hughes copied into
his notebook his teacher Rafael Joseffy's comments about some Chopin
Etudes, among which we find "The G-sharp minor Chopin Etude is de
Pachmann's biggest etude. All the smaller etudes he plays beautifully." It
was, as he played it, a poetic fantasy. According to his son Leonide, the

rising and falling of the right hand double notes were like sparks of color, whirling along in half tints of pianissimi, while a delicious fragment of the melody from the left hand darted in and out of the delicate fabric. He made audiences gasp with a magical cascade of pianissimi in bars thirty-one through thirty-four. Cowen also wrote, "He was, even then, full of those quaint little personal ways and mannerisms which have always delighted his audiences as much as his great pianistic gifts, and which made him then, as now, a very entertaining person in private life."

Pachmann's eccentricities were still in their formative stage, but were apparent enough to audiences and friends. To him audience members were friends. He needed to feel that his hearers—whether in an intimate salon or a vast concert hall, be it while recounting a highly embellished and amusing anecdote or simply playing Chopin—loved his performance and loved him. In his mind there was no difference between the two. "You like it," he would tell them, 'that is enough.'

While in Paris in 1882 and 1883 Pachmann met another extraordinary British man, fifty-two year old Campbell Clarke, at whose home he played several times, as on May 1, 1882, when he appeared at a musicale there along with American soprano Emma Thursby. An ideal Victorian gentleman, he was cultivated and scholarly, with a deep interest in literature, drama, art and music, all of which he wrote about in a sympathetic manner, with "insight and feeling," according to his 1902 obituary in London's the *Times*. Clarke had been secretary to the Philharmonic Society of London, then in 1866 succeeded Henry Chorley as music critic of the *Athenaeum*. Widely known and popular, he had moved to Paris where he mixed easily in French society, and where apparently he also served in several secret diplomatic ventures for his government. Clarke, as Paris correspondent for London's *The Daily Telegraph*, wielded considerable influence. Eventually awarded the Legion of Honor, he was also knighted by Queen Victoria in 1897. Clarke seems to have used his power to foster Pachmann's career.

Pachmann's subsequent concerts in Paris created a "furor," the actual word used in several biographical dictionaries of the time to describe the event. An unnamed critic for *Le Figaro* wrote on May 17, 1882, of Pachmann's final performance at his first visit to Paris:

> Pachmann didn't appear before us until the very last hour of the season. We regret it because . . . of his wonderful instinct for the style of the German masters.[3]

Ultimately more important to Pachmann's career was a restrained mention (compared to the extravagant French reviews) of Henri-George Blowitz, who was the Paris political correspondent for London's *Times*, in an article printed there on May 2, 1882. Interrupting his usual dour discussion of political matters, he declared:

> Wladimir de Pachmann, one of the greatest living pianists, and a pupil of Liszt [*sic*], gave his second concert in Salle Erard yesterday [April 29]. His performance of selections from Chopin, Schumann, Rubinstein and Liszt was a great success. He is about to visit London.

Blowitz's unusual, sudden interjection of enthusiasm for a musician awakened substantial interest in England to hear Pachmann. Conductor Wilhelm Ganz, needing someone to substitute for the indisposed pianist Fanny Montigny-Rémaury, invited Pachmann to make a British debut with his orchestra. It had taken just five months for him to go from being totally unknown to performing with a prestigious orchestra in London.[4]

The concerto at Pachmann's British debut on May 20, 1882, was his favorite, the Chopin F minor. Of greater delicacy and limpidity than its companion Concerto in E minor, it showcased Pachmann's unique pianism. Throughout his long career, he took the F minor Concerto around the world and played it with many of the great orchestras. Like the E minor Concerto which he also played but not as frequently, he treated the passage work in which the work abounds, the trills, double notes and cantabile melodies, with an inexhaustible variety of delicate shades and poetic fantasy. Critic James Gibbons Huneker wrote that in his performance of the F minor, Pachmann made the piano sound like "a miraculously tuned Aeolian harp."

The Larghetto movement was one of the great triumphs of his art. His veiled, almost ghostly tone, the sinister shading of the declamatory sections, the poignant inflections he gave to the reprise of the melody, his "breathing out" the ornamental passages with great tenderness—these were not easily forgotten. His performance of the Finale was a feat of grace and charm, stressing the mazurka-like rhythm as he "pearled" up and down the keyboard with an almost insouciant fantasy, finished with rubato touches that had not been heard before.

Besides the Concerto Pachmann also played three solos: a Haydn Fantasy in C, a John Field Rondo in E, and Liszt's *Waldesrauschen*. The impact of his playing on the English public was profound. Familiar with Clara Schumann's cozy musicality, brought up on Sir Charles Hallé's cold, meticulous style, as well as Arabella Godard's equally frozen manner (and in recent months, Rubinstein's miraculous thunder), London had heard nothing quite like him before, and his playing created a sensation. Francis Hueffer wrote in the *Times*:

One may learn to play Beethoven or Mendelssohn, they appeal to all artists of high intellect and aim; but to play Chopin is almost a matter of idiosyncrasy. The pianist here must be able to read between the lines; the printed music does little more than hint at what the composer meant; the essence of his genius was too volatile, too airy to be fixed in written signs and symbols. There is, for instance, the so-called *tempo rubato*—that transition from the most striking rhythm to no rhythm at all, which only the few can render whose mind is in absolute harmony with the composer's own. M. de Pachmann is among these few. His touch is of the utmost delicacy; the subtlest gradations of time and strength are to him as natural as they were to the composer when he wrote; there is, indeed, about his playing that charm of dreamy poetry of which those speak with enthusiasm who heard Chopin himself. Nothing more perfect in its way could, indeed, be imagined than the slow movement of the Concerto as rendered by M. de Pachmann.

Applause swept the hall with the men in the orchestra as enthusiastic as those in the audience. On May 22 the *Glasgow Herald* wrote: "The young artiste fairly astonished his hearers by the beauty of his touch, the reserve of his manner, and by the neatness and facility of his execution." One newspaper noted: "The applause was unstinted and unqualified and the Royal Party took part in the demonstration." The Royal Party consisted of the Prince and Princess of Wales, whose friendship with the pianist began after that concert (but did not include the Queen, Victoria). The Prince in particular was so enthusiastic that he sent Pachmann a box of cigars. Forty-two years later when he was in his dotage, the old pianist told an interviewer (Deborah Beirne in the September 1924 issue of the *Human* magazine):

I felt sad that the Queen had not come to my concert, the Prince of Wales . . . winked and said, "We're a bit unusual, de Pachmann, and she doesn't understand us"—and he went off laughing. Very soon after that I was commanded by the Queen to play before her majesty—of course it was the Prince who persuaded her to do it.[5] After the program was over, the Prince offered me one of his own cigars. I could not refuse to accept it, but I told him I would not smoke it—for after smoking one of his I would never be able to return to my own cheaper brand—and that I was too poor to encourage a desire for tobacco de luxe. But he insisted that I smoke the cigar. Then the very next day a Chamberlain or Chancellor—I forget the rank now, but he was someone very important, brought me a box of cigars—of the same brand as the one I had smoked the night before—with all the formality and dignity of the British royal etiquette. A few of them I smoked, but I saved one for each of my dearest friends. For the Grosse Meister [Liszt] I saved four, but he wouldn't take them. "I will buy my own cigars" he said. "I cannot be annoyed having my thoughts interrupted with new tastes." You see Liszt had temperament.

Pachmann's career in England was secure. Only the one concert was necessary, after which his reputation as a great Chopin interpreter was made. His fee for that concert was fifteen pounds and fifteen shillings.

One may wonder, however, whether the excitement was due entirely to his beautiful playing. The advocacy of the Royal Family must have played a part as well. The Duchess of Edinburgh was present and enjoyed it so much, she spoke to Ganz, who was persuaded to hire Pachmann for a second concert. Reviews suggest some mannerisms on Pachmann's part might have contributed, as this (unfortunately unidentified) clipping suggests:

> Then came a M. Pachmann, who in consequence of his long hair and bulkiness about the waist and coat tails (suggestive of concealed fish bowls to be presently produced from under a handkerchief) I first set down as a conjurer. He wasn't however, being a pianist of considerable skill, with an overpowering propensity for getting the most out of every note and listening in rapt admiration to its dying away in the distance, and then slowly raising his left hand as though pronouncing a blessing on the instrument as he went along.

Pachmann's mannerisms, mostly pantomimic and still in their formative stage, were apparent enough. It is entirely wrong to suppose, as some have, that the pianist's eccentricities were conceived later, by both the artist and his scheming managers, as a clever enticement for popular appeal.

Once more he was besieged by hostesses. There were more of the endless invitations to perform in the salons of London as there had been in Vienna and Paris. If he could play a practical joke on Liszt, who knows what amusing *bon mot* he might utter at a soirée? His innocent conceit (if not his originality) was already well established. When asked by one admirer at one of these affairs what he thought of London, he replied, "Madame, it is not what Pachmann thinks of London, but what London thinks of Pachmann!"

London thought so much of Pachmann that another concert had to be arranged immediately. Some papers suggested that while his playing was very beautiful, it was rather "special," and to judge his talents better he would have to be heard in the classics.

The *Musical Times* June 1882 issue reported, "M. de Pachmann made a decidedly favorable impression, and justified the honors he has recently enjoyed in Paris . . . but we must, of course, hear him in a leading pianoforte classic before venturing to give a precise estimate of his powers." Ganz suggested Beethoven and one month later on June 17th Pachmann was soloist in Beethoven's Fourth Concerto at the Ganz concerts, also playing some Chopin solos "most beautifully," according to Ganz, and as well, a remarkable piano duet composed by Mendelssohn and Moscheles together, on themes from Weber's "Preciosa," with Ganz at the other piano.

This single performance was the only time he ever played the Beethoven in public. *The Musical Standard* thought the first movement rather tame; the second, lugubrious; the third, "excellent, all grace and fairy lightness." Another critic, while finding his playing "neat", felt he didn't grasp Beethoven's essential style, while still another went so far as to call his handling of the opening passages in the first movement, "tiny little chirpings." Ganz himself liked the performance, telling his daughter Georgina that Pachmann "observed the traditions of tempi derived from his father—a great friend of Beethoven," as she wrote to the *Daily Telegraph* on January 21, 1933.

On June 22, 1882, he gave his first London solo recital at St. James's Hall. The program was much the same as his concerts in Vienna and Paris, a varied selection including Bach's Prelude and Fugue in B flat from Book One of the Well-Tempered Clavier, Beethoven's Sonata Op. 101 and a Bagatelle, and shorter works by Mendelssohn, Schumann, Rubinstein, Liszt and the inevitable Chopin group, ending with three Liszt transcriptions—a Chopin song, Mendelssohn's *Auf Flügeln des Gesanges* and Weber's Polacca Brilliante. Joseph Bennett wrote a typical review of the recital in the June 24 issue of the *Daily Telegraph:*

> At any time the exercise of such talents as his would be acceptable, but now, when energy and force pass too readily for true art, it is more than ever desirable that execution characterized by refinement and grace should be heard . . . In all the pieces by Chopin the executant appeared to great advantage.

On June 24 *The Pall Mall Gazette* reported on both the recital and the concerto with Ganz, slamming the conductor in a way quite unusual in the British press at the time:

> Beethoven's sonata . . . the immense difficulties of which were overcome with a power that had not before been conspicuous in M. de Pachmann's playing . . . he played Beethoven's G major concerto finely, though scarcely with sufficient force. In the finale a breakdown very nearly occurred, the conductor completely losing his control over the orchestra—unless, indeed, that phrase be considered inaccurate, as seeming to accredit him with a power he has never possessed.

Pachmann was featured in several concerts in London in the next weeks. In a "roundup" review of these that appeared in the *Academy* (July/December 1882), the pianist J. S. Shedlock (who is today remembered as a translator of Beethoven's letters) wrote:

> We remember once hearing Rossini say, "Pianists, and even good ones, are plentiful as peas." And the saying is also true at the present moment. Herr Pachmann, however, is something more than a good player: he is a great one.

For delicacy of touch and beauty of tone he reminds one of Rubinstein, but indeed excels him in general correctness and (so far as Chopin is concerned) in purity of style . . . The performance of Beethoven's grand trio in B flat (op. 97) [the "Archduke"] by Messrs. Pachmann, Joachim and Piatti was very fine indeed; and the pianist gave ample proof that, although Chopin's music seems to be his specialty, he can understand and worthily interpret the works of the great masters . . . It is to be hoped that one day the pianist will favour us with a 'Chopin' recital; for a portion of the spirit of that illustrious Polish composer certainly seems to have fallen on him . . . The program included . . . Mozart's pianoforte quartet in G minor performed by Messrs. Pachmann, Joachim, Strauss and Piatti.

Pachmann's London recital programs were typical of the concerts he gave in the 1880's during the first decade of his career, and reflect the emphasis Dachs had placed on developing a large repertoire, ranging from Bach through contemporary Russian composers. On December 10, 1883, he performed C. P. E. Bach's Sonata in G (No. 6 from the first collection). He was criticized for not specifying in the printed program that he played Bülow's arrangement of the Sonata, rather than the original. His repertoire then—some Bach and Mozart, much Beethoven, much Weber, a little Field and Schubert, some Grieg and Brahms, a lot of Mendelssohn and Schumann, as well as much Henselt and Liszt, with the all the large works of Chopin and many of the smaller ones, some rare Chopin works like the Trio and the *Allegro de concert*, with forays into the Russia of Tchaikovsky and Rubinstein and the salon composers of Victorian England—was not unlike that of other virtuoso pianists of the day.

This catholicity rested on a bedrock of Viennese classicism, one which presupposed the superiority of the German masters, especially Beethoven. In these first years Pachmann's concerts stressed this bias, and he placed the works of Beethoven in the more important first half of his recitals, and the works of Chopin, Henselt and Liszt in the "lighter" second half. Considering himself a direct successor to Liszt and Rubinstein and possessing a sovereign technique, it seemed appropriate and natural for Pachmann to play works from the Classic period through the Romantics and moderns. Liszt and Rubinstein were noted for their performances of Beethoven and Chopin, and he thought of himself as cut from their mold. Some of the critics reinforced and encouraged this idea, for there were several reviews similar to what the *Sunday Times* wrote on November 15, 1885, "There are many reciting pianists, but there is only one Pachmann, as there is only one Liszt, one Rubinstein, one Clara Schumann and one Hans von Bülow." But nature and art conspired to prevent Pachmann's success as a player of the classics. At first it seemed as if he would succeed in the traditional way of Liszt and Rubinstein, and Clara and Hans—he had become very popular in Paris and London; the *Times* of December 11, 1883, wrote that:

> His popularity, unequaled at the moment by that of any other artist, was proved by the crowded state of the hall and the warm applause which followed after every piece of the long and interesting program.

Some critics suggested that his audiences may not have been overly sophisticated. The *Sunday Times* of December 23, 1883, reported that St. James's Hall was filled (it held 2,000 people) and the audience:

> Consisting as usual for the greater part of the fairer sex—genuine amateurs every one of them; as was clearly proved by the breathless attention with which they hung upon every note played by the now favourite Russian pianist.

That review appears to be the earliest notice we have calling attention to the attraction Pachmann's playing had for "the fairer sex." This was to become a dominant theme of his career in both England and later in America.

One woman wrote to him, a completely unknown lady, saying in a touching way how much she would love to attend his concert, but couldn't, for she had for a long time been bedridden, "and it is impossible for me to reach this highest goal of mine." Half an hour after receiving the letter Pachmann was in her home, and he played the entire concert for her.

But he was a great pianist as well as a curiosity and his audiences always included musicians who were equally attentive. On February 7, 1886, an anonymous *Sunday Times* critic wrote:

> There was quite a large sprinkling of Professors of the pianoforte—larger, indeed, than I have ever observed at any recital, other than Rubinstein's. This fact should be taken as a distinct compliment. Professors do not as a rule run away from their lessons in the afternoon unless they want to take a lesson themselves; and that, I imagine, was their object on the present occasion . . . amateurs and professors vied with each other in the endeavour to give vent to their enthusiasm.

Australian soprano Nellie Melba had just moved to London when she wrote to the tenor Rudolph Himmer on May 10, 1882:

> Last Saturday I heard . . . a pianist Vladimir de Pachmann who is a true artist; I never heard such playing in my life, it was simply beautiful.

A few weeks later she was still extolling Pachmann in a letter to her teacher, Pietro Cecchi, in June. She had heard concerts by Sir Charles

Hallé, one of Anton Rubinstein's legendary historical recitals, and Pachmann. Trained as a pianist, Melba wrote that it was Pachmann who impressed her, "a wonderful pianist."

The praise was not unanimous, and one critic was vicious. The earliest instance so far discovered of a rabid Pachmann hater—the first in a string of Pachmanophobes that persisted his entire career—was one Felix Remo, a visitor in England who published a book in French in 1885 of his sharp opinions of *Music in the Land of Fogs*. He thought Pachmann was a charlatan imitating Liszt:

> A word about Abbé Pachmann; pardon, I mean to say, Herr Pachmann . . . is a star pianist who has understood his public and has taken London by acclaim . . . Rubinstein can rest tranquilly. Personally the Abbé, oh I mean Herr Pachmann, is a short, fat man, badly built, who walks like a duck, and who, after cleaning the keys . . . looks alternately while playing at his hearers, one after the other. He fixes his gaze on them with effrontery, even grossly . . . he has studied all the tricks of charlatans, and the Abbé lifts his eyes to heaven and makes noble hand gestures consisting of raising his palm slowly when he strikes a chord . . . As an artist he is a Chopin machine. One accords him a certain ability in his interpretations of this master. Apart from this, the public knows that in general he massacres Beethoven without pity, and is not a bad wrecker of other music too.[6]

If Pachmann knew this about Remo's report he ignored it, and encouraged by his general popularity, went right ahead with his "Classical" programs. We can only imagine his chagrin and surprise as it became clear that he was being acclaimed for his Chopin and Henselt in the lighter, second parts of his recitals—and receiving only disdain and even dismissal for the works he considered the highlights of the events, his Beethoven and Mozart. The *Sunday Times* of December 23, 1883, declared:

> He was not at his best in these works, and their rendering quite failed to evoke the expressions of delight that came subsequently when the lighter section of the recital was reached.

When he returned to London after an extended tour of the continent, the *Sunday Times* critic was explicit (November 15, 1885):

> Why will he attempt Beethoven? No one wants him to. He cannot approach a realization of the spirit and meaning of the Bonn master. Yet the sonata Op. 31 No. 2 came first in Wednesday's programme, and pleased none but those who had come prepared to be pleased with everything.

He persisted and the reviews got even worse. The *Sunday Times*, January 24, 1886:

His interpretation of the sonata in D minor, Op. 31 No. 2, was as unlike Beethoven as anything could well be. However perfect in a mechanical sense, it was completely lacking in the breadth of phrasing, and sentiment, the masculine power, the nobility of style for which musicians look. M. de Pachmann's pretty little touches, his delicate *nuances*, his frequent *ritardandos* and use of the *tempo rubato* were completely out of place . . . His failure to interpret, even if he grasped, the composer's meaning was only too evident.

But Pachmann would not stop playing Beethoven; in fact, he felt he was one of the few who had the true Beethoven style. He was quoted in *Freund's Weekly* (February 14, 1894):

"[W]hen he[his father] taught me to play Beethoven it was as the real Beethoven had played it, not as it is played now. That is why, when I played the 'Moonlight Sonata' in Boston recently the people rose in their seats and called 'Again! again!' They had never heard it played just as Beethoven meant it should be played. Now, see —" and with a hop, skip and jump the eccentric pianist rushed to the piano, and leaning tenderly over the keys, his head on one side, his eyes screwed up half closed and his lips drawn into a most extraordinary grimace, he played the soft, sweet prelude of the sonata. "It is played much quicker now and not pianissimo as it should be,' he cried; 'now these three notes should be soft and sweet, the middle one even sweeter than the others. What shall I call it—a charming little rose between two thorns?"

He ignored the critics and the following month played two Beethoven works in one recital—the 32 C minor Variations and the "Appassionata" Sonata. The *Times* review of February 3, 1886, declared:

The idea has grown in the popular mind of his being unable to do justice to Beethoven . . . if he wished to show that Beethoven is, or ever could be, his specialty in the sense that Chopin and, in a minor degree, Mozart are, then his thesis was too large for his argument. M. de Pachmann is a great and a versatile artist, and whatever such an artist undertakes he does well . . . his rendering of the 32 Variations in C minor . . . Nothing could have been finer than the delicacy of tone and discrimination of thought and feeling which each little piece stood forth in its separate character, and at the same time was made to fit in the vast frame of the entire conception . . . the Sonata in F minor, op. 57, which followed, was less satisfactory . . . the grandeur of Beethoven's intention seemed occasionally marred by a want of breadth and repose . . . one observed certain effects of phrasing which seemed to belong to M. de Pachmann rather than Beethoven . . . it cannot be denied that subtleties of reading which are allowable in Chopin or in Schumann, somehow seem to pervert the perspective of Beethoven's vast design.

He seemed immune to the criticism. Two months later, he played the Sonata Op. 101 once again, the same sonata that had been so highly praised at his Vienna debut. The *Sunday Times* curtly dismissed his efforts (May 9, 1886):

> How the Beethoven Sonata, Op. 101, was played I can hardly describe—à la Pachmann is the nearest definition that occurs to me.

It seemed the more Chopin Pachmann played—audiences couldn't get enough—the worse his Beethoven became. His ears had become "Chopinized," exquisite detail, vivid coloration, and minute nuances played with rhythmic freedom predominating, wreaking havoc with his Beethoven. He desperately wanted to succeed with the German classical composers, to live up to the ideal he inherited from Dachs and his father. Had not an important Viennese critic stated that both German and Slavic blood coursed through his veins? His efforts were rebuffed by both critical complaints and audience displeasure. He found he had to devote increasing attention to Chopin and Henselt and less to Beethoven and the other classical masters. Eventually, when he was fifty years old and at the peak of his art (just at the turn of the twentieth century), he was forced to put much of his large repertoire on hold—audiences didn't want to hear it from him. By then he was resigned, and there was a truce. The English forgave him if he was expert in Chopin and inexpert in Beethoven, and appreciated him for what he was.

Chapter 6

Pachmania, 1884–1885

Returning to Paris from London the next year, Pachmann took the city by storm with his playing of Chopin's E minor Concerto in January 1883, with Jules-Etienne Pasdeloup conducting his orchestra. On January 23 *National* published a review making the extravagant claim that he "interpreted Chopin as well as Chopin himself" while *Gauloise* wrote on the 28th that he deserved "to be placed beside Liszt and Rubinstein."

But because his London successes were even greater, Pachmann decided to find a permanent home there, a place to which he could return after his travels. London soon became his home city, despite the fact that he had been specifically warned about England by friends on the continent. According to them, it was second only to Siberia. In fact, to some, after a continuous ordeal of inedible food and "Victorian Sundays," Siberia might have seemed a blessing. When not performing and being charming at soirées, Pachmann spent his spare time looking for a decent place that served delicious food, and after a while found a small Georgian hotel at Number Two Golden Square, named The Ronveau. He hated the deluxe hotels so beloved by the Edwardians and Victorians. Even a few years later when he could well afford more opulent accommodations, he remained faithful to The Ronveau. It was small, elegant and somewhat genteel, affordable but not cheap, but most important of all, it boasted a marvelous kitchen, and even more, was discreet. Whenever he was in London he always reserved the same suite, a group of rooms near the entrance with a view of Golden Square. Guests could receive visitors without raising eyebrows, and it was just a short walk to Piccadilly Square (where, incidentally, men went to meet other men).

Pachmann in large part was responsible for the hotel's being adopted by many musical artists from all over the world. He stayed there from his first visit in 1882 until the hotel was closed in 1914, after a hundred years of service; he was the first celebrated artist to patronize The Ronveau. Subsequently it became a well-known oasis for other visiting continental musicians. In its heyday one could often find Fritz Kreisler, Leopold Godowsky and Ossip Gabrilowitsch there.

The hotel had been in business for decades; Dickens had a character in his 1839 novel *Nicholas Nickleby* stay there. In Pachmann's time it was owned by a certain Madame Peter and her husband, and the pianist became particularly fond of the redoubtable proprietress, who remained his friend for more than thirty years. Her Alsatian vivacity always amused him and kept him in good humor, even when he was cross or tired. She loved a certain Chopin Mazurka and, after a particularly good meal, perhaps his favorite dish, *bœuf à la mode*, he would lead her and a few friends into the drawing room where he would play it for her. Sometimes if he saw her in the audience during a recital, he might dedicate an encore to her, as he did once in the Albert Hall when he announced, "This is Madame Peter's Mazurka."

The parents of local talented piano pupils implored Pachmann to hear their prodigies. One of these was a true prodigy, the teenaged Frederick Dawson, born in Leeds in 1868. Dawson had already memorized the entire Well-Tempered Clavier and had attracted the attention of Sir Charles Hallé. In 1883 he played for Anton Rubinstein, who told him that he must practice, despite the fact that he already had a wonderful technique. Pachmann also recognized the boy's talent, and gave him some lessons. So smitten was Pachmann that he offered to become Dawson's mentor, if his parents would permit him to travel with Pachmann on his tours. In an interview (*Topical Times*, September 9, 1893) Dawson was quoted: "I date everything from that meeting. He took the greatest interest in me." Dawson was indeed a talented artist, as his acoustic recordings reveal. He was also as handsome as Paderewski. But he was not allowed to travel with Pachmann. "My parents did not consider me strong enough," according to the interview.

In the audience at Pachmann's debut in London had been another talented pupil, a seventeen year old Australian pianist named Margaret (Maggie) Okey (born December 14, 1864). Her family had moved to London in 1869 and she played two solos at a London concert as a prodigy in October 1872 (the press was told she was only six). The *West End News* then described her (October 16) as a "clever little wonder." Later she became a pupil of Dr. Henry Wylde at the London Academy of Music. Under his guidance she developed into one of the leading female pianists in England, and had just recently been appointed his assistant at the Academy. Like many pianists, she had read Blowitz's account of Pachmann's Paris success. In the run on tickets for his first British concert which followed in its wake, she had barely managed to secure a seat. She had never heard the piano sing like that. Completely astonished by the performance, she naively wrote to Pachmann asking him to give her lessons. When there was no reply she went on with her studies, feeling disappointed and mediocre.

After Pachmann's death she wrote an article that was published in installments in the French newspaper *Candide* beginning August 31, 1933 (and published in England in her own translation in the *Daily Telegraph* that November), in which she wrote of how chance intervened and changed her life:

> A certain piano-maker[1] wished Pachmann to use his instruments. Pachmann liked them, but wanted to know how they sounded in a large hall. He was told, "Miss Maggie Okey (myself) is playing one to-morrow at her recital at St. James's Hall.[2] Come and hear her!" At the end of my concert, while friends were pouring out the usual compliments, Pachmann—who in the meantime had become the lion of the season—came up to me and, speaking in French, before all the company, made this extraordinary speech: "Young lady, you know nothing, nothing, nothing at all, but"— happily there was a "but"—"there is feeling in your touch and you have musical sense. Will you be my one and only pupil? I warn you—you will have to begin all over again; for four years you will not play in public; and you must not show my method to anyone else." Without hesitation I said "Yes." Friends and relations thought me mad, but I realized the luck that had come my way and soon I made them realize it too.

We can only wonder whether something other than music may have prompted Pachmann to make that extraordinary speech. Maggie Okey was a handsome woman, a typical English beauty with auburn hair, a clear complexion and chiseled features softened by the loveliest, deep-set, expressive eyes. She bore such a strong resemblance to that famous beauty of the day, Lily Langtry, that she had come to be known as "The Lily Langtry of the Piano," and young men in her audiences would stand as she played, to see her graceful and elegant movements. When she gently crossed her left hand over her right in performances of Liszt's *Au Bord d'une Source*, a murmur of delight would sweep the hall—all of which conjures up the most Victorian picture.

Pachmann had to leave to fulfill further engagements in Paris, and did not know when he would be returning to London. He asked her to come with him. As one might expect, Maggie's parents objected, as well they might, what with her youth and his much discussed peculiarities. Pachmann paid a visit to Mr. and Mrs. Okey, telling them candidly, "You must accept me as I am." He tried to persuade them to change their minds. He spoke of her great talent and the tremendous musical gifts he saw in her. ("She played beau-ti-ful-ly," he reminisced in old age.) For whatever reason, eventually they gave their consent and the two left for Paris with Waltmann. She lived with friends of her family at one end of the city and he at the other, in a small apartment in which the tiny rooms made the piano sound enormous. Maggie had to commute for the lessons.

Great as he was as a Chopin player, as a teacher Pachmann was very irregular. When she arrived for a lesson he might say, "I have a splitting headache," or "I must prepare for a concert, come back tomorrow." Maggie would commute back across half of Paris, and when she returned the following day, he might make her wait hours, only to tell her, "I'm too busy now; come back tonight." When she would return at night, he would keep her so late that she had no time to eat. Often she went home exhausted from the traveling, hungry and nearly in tears, for he was nearly as severe as he was unpredictable.

He would assign her exercises that took hours of practicing each day, designed to change the position of her hands on the keys and improve her touch. He wanted her to be able to play any single note with a myriad of sonorities, like "a string of pearls." He placed great emphasis on a beautiful hand position; the hands should never flop about but should present a certain elegant and beautiful appearance. "Never forget the dignity of the hands," he told her. He invented exercises for her with special fingerings which helped keep her hands in certain positions when playing. These, supplemented by Cramer Etudes, were all that she played for six months. He refused to teach her a single composition until she had mastered this method and had acquired a solid technique his way. After a while, Maggie forgot her old repertoire and was again a beginner.

At the end of six months of study, Pachmann took her to Vienna where he had received a command from the emperor to play Mozart's D minor Concerto with the Vienna Philharmonic on November 26, 1882. Waltmann had reserved two widely-separated rooms for the pair, so they wouldn't be disturbed by each other's playing. Both were hard at work, he on the Mozart and she on his method. Unknown to him, she would arise at six a.m. and practice finger exercises until noon. After lunch she would, for diversion, go into the garden and study German which she was lately trying to master. Then promptly at two, she went back to the piano until seven, when she met Pachmann for dinner. In this way she studied ten hours a day.

Pachmann sensed that she was working too hard and forbade her to study more than five hours, which he felt was sufficient. In her desire to master his method, she disobeyed and after a while developed such pains in her wrists that she was unable to continue. A doctor had to be called. Leonide recalled the incident for the author:

"How many hours do you play?" he asked.

She looked at Pachmann who commanded, "Tell the truth! I told her to play five hours. Let us say, she plays more?"

"Seven hours?" asked the doctor.

Maggie looked at them both. "Sometimes even more," she murmured.

"What!" exclaimed Pachmann.

And then the whole story came out.

The doctor ordered her to stop at once, or she may never play again. She had developed inflammation of the nerves and cysts had formed. To treat the condition Maggie was forced to wear a bracelet of live ants which stung terribly! Somehow, after a few days treatment with ant venom, the cysts disappeared and the inflammation was gone. She was cured.[3]

It was a great honor for Pachmann to receive an invitation from the emperor himself to perform with the Vienna Philharmonic. Afterwards he was presented at Court and Emperor Franz Joseph gave him a ring.

Before he left Vienna, he visited a coffee house, one that he had frequented earlier during student days. Then he had often seen Johannes Brahms and Eduard Hanslick together but had been too shy to speak to them, but now he considered himself an artist and could meet them on his own terms. Hanslick apparently did not review the performance of the Mozart concerto; the legend is that, seeing Brahms again now, Pachmann went up to the composer and upbraided him for not having brought Hanslick to his concert!

For the next year or so Pachmann and Maggie traveled over Europe together, he giving concerts, she studying his method. She had yet to appear in public again. During those eighteen months of travel, Pachmann fell in love with his beautiful pupil. When they returned to London in early 1884, they played a joint recital, their first appearance together, on January 14. The *Times* said she had "considerable promise," while the *Musical Times* wrote that she had "a musical touch but not much power." Later that month Pachmann was scheduled to play at a "Ballad Concert" but didn't arrive from Scotland in time, and Maggie got up from the audience and played in his stead. On February 13 the two played together again, and she was billed as "his pupil." On March 5 Maggie accompanied several singers and the renowned violinist Madame Norman-Neruda (wife of the august pianist/conductor Charles Hallé), but Pachmann did not yet allow her to play another solo recital.

Maggie was very young and very beautiful; some people must have thought she was Pachmann's mistress. It would be fascinating to have more details, to know whether people were talking because the unmarried couple were traveling together, to know what Maggie's family thought and if they exerted pressure, and especially to know when Maggie found out about Pachmann's interest in men. But all we know is that propriety trumped everything, that he proposed and she accepted.

Perhaps only Maggie could have unraveled some of the mysteries surrounding this extraordinary relationship, and we are left only with speculation. It is almost inconceivable that Maggie's relatives in Paris, charged by her parents with her care, would have, at the height of the Victorian era, allowed a beautiful girl not yet twenty to travel throughout Europe with a highly exotic artist and his manager.

They must have made inquiries, and it is tempting to conclude that they were told that "Monsieur de Pachmann posed no problems." There is ample evidence from later in his life that women held little attraction for Pachmann, but the only evidence of an attachment to a man at this early period is a photo of a handsome Russian youth dating from the time of Pachmann's adolescence. This mysterious photo, which the author saw when it was in the possession of Leonide de Pachmann, was kept by his father in a most treasured album, along with pictures of his early musical life.

For whatever reason Maggie had been allowed to travel with Pachmann. She most probably was over-protected in the manner of Victorian girls, and had no experience of worldly affairs. Pachmann, already in his mid-thirties and fast becoming a famous concert artist, was in many ways more provincial and innocent than Maggie. First, there was his overly sensitive nature and his own over-protected upbringing. Then there were the years he spent in seclusion developing his art, years when young men usually learn of the world and its responsibilities. Lastly there was Pachmann's artistic temperament, which determined his personality more than any other trait and kept him, like so many other famous concert prodigies, an adolescent beyond his years. Somehow during their travels, Maggie and Pachmann found a common ground on which they could communicate as each could with no one else.

After his death, in the *Australian Musical News* (April 1935) Maggie described the man she married:

> All those originalities which astonished one were the outcome of his natural self and were not, as some thought, charlatanism . . . He was, with all his genius, a child.

And although she was sixteen years younger, it is probable that she protected and mothered him as had his mother, his sister Elizaveta, his friend

Madame Slepouchkine and recently, Madame Peter. These were probably the only women with whom Vladimir had emotional relationships during his entire life.

Maggie may have been innocent of sexual matters, but she certainly knew exactly what she wanted: a career in music. She knew that Pachmann was a great pianist, perhaps the greatest she had heard, and that by teaching her, he might instill something of that greatness into her "mediocrity." It would be the only chance of her whole life. This desire was so overwhelming that somehow she overcame all parental opposition. She had a very strong will, and her parents must have loved her deeply. An obsession to make her mark as a pianist was at Maggie's core, and when her wish was magically granted, love followed. She could not possibly have known what a fantastic and difficult relationship she was entering.

On Pachmann's side, he heard something promising in her playing. A very narcissistic artist who jealously guarded the secrets of his art, he normally kept these wholly to himself. He never would have shared, let alone taught any of these "secrets" to any other being, but in this beautiful young girl he sensed talent that could be unearthed, a beauty he could develop. He took time to teach her, and had the pleasure of seeing her evolve. Of course, he also may have been attracted to her, but he was probably more attracted to the beauty he was creating in her playing. Maggie was quoted later (the *New York Sun*, April 9, 1890) saying:

> For two years . . . I think my husband did not know how I looked—whether I was dark or fair, and he was terribly strict. I found it very difficult to please him but at last he awoke to the fact that I suited him and then we were married.

In the end, like Pygmalion, he fell in love with his own creation—a beautiful woman transformed into a beautiful pianist.

Pachmann played a "Farewell Recital" in St. James's Hall on February 29, 1884. Perhaps he was inspired by love, for he outdid himself and received rhapsodic notices. The *Times'* review of the next day sums up his career in England to that time and also gives a picture of his playing and his popularity:

> The Farewell Recital which M. de Pachmann, previous to his departure for the continent, gave in St. James's Hall yesterday afternoon makes it desirable to say a few words of recapitulation with regard to the remarkable career of this artist in England. The name of the Russian pianist at that time was barely known in this country and his success on that occasion at once placed him among the first living representatives of his instrument and that position he has continued to hold ever since. Whenever he plays, whether in London or Birmingham, his name has the same attraction everywhere—to a degree

unknown in England. Indeed, he is among the few virtuosi who are able to fill St. James's Hall by unaided effort . . . He is, in fact, unique when he deals with Chopin. Every turn of the phrase, every modulation, the very shakes and grupettos and fioriture are in Chopin marked by a distinctive individuality. All this M. de Pachmann renders with a perfection of style and with a degree of insight which can only spring from the most absolute harmony between composer and interpreter which fully justifies the unanimous opinion that M. de Pachmann's manner resembles in the minutest detail, that of the master himself.

The author never found anyone other than Franz Liszt who actually heard both Chopin and Pachmann, and claimed that Pachmann's playing resembled that of the great Polish composer. However critics and public alike were so swept up with the Pachmann fervor that few noticed the outrageous nature of the insupportable claims being made. Because he was a "pianissimist" (by choice, not by necessity as in the case of the composer), and because, like Chopin, he stressed finesse, elegance and beauty of tone, all with an intuitive mastery of rubato, his playing was thought by contemporaries to closely resemble that of the composer. In the minds of many this was enough, he was the greatest Chopin interpreter of his time. It was the birth of Pachmania.

❧

The couple moved on to Vienna at the beginning of 1884. Eighteen year old Ferruccio Busoni was living there and, eager to make a living, agreed to write some articles on music for the radical Trieste newspaper *L'Indipendente* early that year. He reviewed a Pachmann recital. He called the pianist "tragicomic" and wrote:

His pantomime as he plays has reached such a degree of perfection and is so characteristic that even an institution for the deaf and dumb is able to understand the music he is playing. It is enough to just look at his facial expressions: every little trill, mordent or grupetto has its own relative smile, and a kind of indescribable arching of the eyebrows. Upon executing a trill, Pachmann turns toward the audience with an expression on his face that says, 'How about that trill! Hah! What do you think of that?' Pachmann has a predilection for the miniature; his playing is a thing of filigree. It delights for the moment but lacks deeper artistic content. However extravagant or clever he appears to be, Pachmann remains a highly refined performer, irreproachable in balancing the dynamic and the agogic.[4]

They made a quick sojourn to Budapest, where he played the Chopin F minor Concerto on March 5, 1884, and Liszt attended the performance and a solo recital, mentioned earlier. Then Pachmann and Maggie were married in London on April 30, 1884, in a Russian Orthodox ceremony, and again, for her parents' sake, in an Anglican ceremony. A reception took place at the beloved Hotel Ronveau. In a few days they left for the continent on their honeymoon, during which Maggie, a girl of nineteen, met many of the greatest musicians of the day. For all its benefits, she soon discovered that being a great pianist's wife was quite different and infinitely more difficult than being his pupil. And by October she was pregnant.

Chapter 7

Bearded and a Father, 1885–1888

There were difficulties on this "honeymoon" almost immediately. Pachmann got into a dispute with a fellow train traveler—something about whether a window should be open or not; a little thing, but for him these things were important. The dispute became so heated that the two might have come to blows had Maggie not separated them. It was a bad omen.

He was a child who had to be pampered and coaxed; Maggie had been brought up in the strict Anglican tradition, and the clash made for endless argument. He might wake her up in the middle of the night excitedly to show her some new fingerings he had devised for a troublesome passage, yet if she would ask for advice concerning her own pianistic problems when he was preoccupied, he would bark at her, "Go away! Can't you see I'm practicing?"

Vienna was the first stop. While there they paid a visit to the most celebrated piano teacher in Europe, Theodore Leschetizky, and his pupil/wife, Annette Essipoff. Pachmann had Maggie play some Cramer Etudes for the famous pair, each of whom complimented her, and Pachmann for his skills as a teacher. Years later Leschetizky told a pupil, Serge Krish, "He'd be better if he didn't talk so much."[1]

Pachmann played a recital in Vienna at which his mannerisms were annoyingly apparent. Ludwig Speidel reported in the *Fremden-Blatt* (April 11, 1884):

After the leonine paw of Rubinstein came the feline foot of Pachmann . . . He does not pose at the piano as others do, gazing abstractedly forward in complete absorption; no, he turns his face to the public, fixing them with his glowing black eyes and holding them in complete control. Let one address but a syllable to his neighbor during the playing, he calls him to order with a sibilant "Bst!"[2]

The review described Pachmann refusing to play an encore, pointing to his watch to show he had no time for encores. Speidel, who was born in 1830 and had probably heard Thalberg, continued:

> With his soft, sweet tone, with his caressing hand he reminds one of Sigismund Thalberg, only his technique and his musical taste are more universal . . . nothing is more charming then when he plays Chopin's dance pieces (one wants to say, when he improvises them)—when he revives little Henselt trifles with soul, when in Liszt's minor piano scenes—where Ferenc is the little Franzie—he lets the woods murmur or the cool lake water drop like pearls from the oar. There his playing is at the same time sensual and sensitive.[3]

These unconventionalities did not go unnoticed in staid England, as when *Punch* reviewed his May 3, 1886, recital:

> St. James's Hall was crowded with his admirers, and with some in whom the performance excited less admiration than amusement. Why *will* these pianists be so affected?

People came to his recitals to hear his beautiful piano playing and good naturedly tolerated the eccentricities. Somehow, despite the prevalent attitude, a certain amount of Bohemianism was expected of artists. After a few initial and uncomfortable minutes, audiences couldn't help being amused by his spontaneous outbursts, shrewd observations and innocent pranks. No other pianist in history had treated audiences quite that way; with each concert Pachmann's personality was developing further into that strange amalgam of creative silliness, artless naiveté, and willfulness; the mixture was to become notorious in just a few years. Unlike many performers who, once on stage, forget their audience, Pachmann was always acutely aware of the mood of his hearers as well as his own mood. In this way he was both subjective, spontaneously inspired by the music, and objective, in the awareness of the effect of his playing and mannerisms on the audience.

Spontaneity had its price, as in February 1886, when he had a memory lapse in the last movement of the Chopin F minor Concerto at the Crystal Palace under August Manns, and the *Musical Times* severely criticized him for not using the score during the performance. Such lapses were rare but happened to Pachmann periodically, and they didn't seem to bother him. He passed over the incidents smoothly. In Berlin in March of 1896 he got completely lost in Schumann's Carnaval, and couldn't find his way back. The *Etude* reported (April 1896) "After trying three times in vain, Pachmann suddenly jumped to his feet and shouted, 'Never mind, never mind; bravo, Pachmann, you played lovely anyhow!'" Later he had a terrible slip while playing one of Liszt's Legendes. According to the manager Alfred Vert (*Etude*, January 1898) he stopped abruptly, "and not until he had performed some mysterious gyrations with arms and legs did he recommence."

Cracow was the next stop on the tour where, backstage while preparing for a concert, he was approached by a flamboyant looking youth with a mop of red hair who had some music he had composed, and who wanted to ask his opinion. The scene amused Pachmann, who took the manuscript and looked it over carefully, complimenting the youth on his beautiful handwriting and the fine quality of the music paper, but ending with the malicious remark, "It is a pity to waste this fine paper on such music" and abruptly handed it back. The young man, understandably offended, left in a rage. Only when Maggie reproached him for his unkindness did Pachmann realize that he had done something that hurt someone very much. He became so upset that he ordered: "Have someone fetch him back!" but it was too late, for the youth had departed. Later they would find out that the youth's name was Ignace Jan Paderewski.

The same young man was soon to become the most successful pianist of all time, and one who made Pachmann forever jealous. Eventually the world seemed too small a place to contain them both. After the incident in Cracow they met publicly only one other time, many years later when by chance they found themselves on the staircase of the Congress Hotel in Chicago shortly after each had given a concert there. Pachmann knew that Paderewski had drawn a larger audience, and as they were shaking hands, he turned to a companion and loudly exclaimed, "I make zee music and he make zee money." Paderewski smiled. Being the world's most celebrated pianist, he could afford to forgive almost anything. But as we shall see, he never forgot the Cracow incident.

In December 1884 Pachmann appeared in at least two concerts in Finland. The program for a huge solo recital there included Bach's Chromatic Fantasy and Fugue, Beethoven's Op. 101 Sonata, Chopin's B minor Sonata plus the three Etudes that were his specialties and the *Tarantella*, as well as Rubinstein's fourth Barcarolle and pieces by Brahms, Schumann, Raff and Henselt. The program for an orchestral concert at which he played both the Mozart D minor and the Chopin F minor concertos also contained Liszt's *Au bord d'une source* and other solos by Raff, Brahms, and Bach.

The tour continued to St. Petersburg where the newlyweds took a suite in the Hôtel de l'Europe on the Nevsky Prospect. The venerable Adolf von Henselt visited them each day. Though old, he still played exquisitely. In his youth Pachmann had heard Henselt play in Russia, and almost certainly, it was Henselt who first inspired Pachmann's quest for the most beautiful and pure piano tone. Henselt was renowned for his penetrating, full-toned pianissimo that carried and resonated throughout any hall, despite its softness. His touch was regarded as unique. Wilhelm von Lenz wrote of him: "Never, never have I heard such a magical 'cantilena' flow from the pianoforte." According to his pupil Bettina Walker, Henselt's touch and tone suggested:

> Flawless beauty and purity . . . the exhalation of an essence—so concentrated, so intense that the whole being of the man seemed to have passed for the moment into his finger-tips, from which the sound seemed to well out.

There are several similarities between Henselt and Pachmann. Each had to struggle to find their individual tone. When Henselt heard Liszt's rival Thalberg, he was so overwhelmed that he had to make a fresh start. He retired to restudy his whole repertoire, listening intensively to the sounds he produced until he found that perfect tone. Like Pachmann he had small hands and worked on stretching his fingers with fan-like lateral movements until he was able to master wide stretches. These stretches became the most characteristic feature of his own compositions. His Etudes are pianistically interesting, particularly valuable for the development of beautiful tone and sonority. *Si oiseau j'étais*, perhaps his most famous composition (recorded by Rachmaninoff) is an etude in alternating double-sixths in both hands that depends exclusively on a soft, even and resonant touch, and might as well have been written specifically for Pachmann. But on the whole Henselt's music has aged badly. Almost a hundred years ago Huneker condescendingly wrote (in his 1915 introduction to Joseffy's edition of Chopin's Waltzes): "Henselt is only a German who fell asleep and dreamed of Chopin."

Maggie was quite proud when, playing a Henselt Etude for its composer, he stopped her and asked how she fingered a certain passage. They both loved the composer, whose own eccentricities delighted them. He conducted his lessons with a flyswatter, which he brandished at the student like a rifle. He had rheumatism and always kept his fingers wrapped in little bandages which somehow did not stop him from playing. His way of dressing with a white suit and red fez, covered with six overcoats, one on top of another, was really comic. When he arrived at their hotel suite he would invariably exclaim, "How hot it is!" and then discard one garment after another.

In January 1885 Hans von Bülow was in St. Petersburg. Apparently Anton Rubinstein had been scheduled to conduct a concert there for the Russian Music Society during which Pachmann was to play the Chopin F minor Concerto. At the last minute Rubinstein opted instead to go to Moscow and conduct some concerts there, allowing Bülow to conduct the concert, including the world premiere of Tchaikovsky's Third Suite, thus avoiding comparisons at home with his old rival Bülow, as well as the music of his student Tchaikovsky, which he hated. It was Bülow who conducted the St. Petersburg orchestra, but for unknown reasons, without Pachmann.

Another musician with whom they spent time in St. Petersburg was the celebrated editor of Chopin's music, the Liszt pupil Karl Klindworth. Pachmann already had the highest regard for Klindworth's edition of Chopin and preferred it almost exclusively. He was not alone in this preference—many musicians of the late nineteenth and early twentieth century were brought up on Klindworth, which was considered *the* edition of Chopin. Klindworth grafted the Lisztian aesthetic, with free interpretation of the notes and virtuoso fingerings, onto Chopin's pristine text. His elaborate editing, with almost no phrase left untouched, expressed perfectly the Victorian attitude to Chopin. Today it is heresy to suggest, as we do, that Klindworth's edition has any merit whatsoever.

While in St. Petersburg Pachmann visited his brother Semyon, who now held the exalted position of Counselor to the Czar. Through Semyon, Pachmann was able to secure an invitation to play at the court of Alexander III. The opulence and medieval splendor of the court created an impression which he never forgot. The jewels worn by the emperor and empress—particularly the famous blue diamond—haunted him for years until eventually he possessed one like it. His efforts to buy a blue diamond provided the impetus that began his collection of uncut gems.

Later in 1885 the couple were in Denmark to continue Pachmann's only tour of Scandinavia. Waltmann mounted a publicity campaign, plastering the cities where he had engagements to play—Copenhagen, Stockholm and Christiana (Oslo), as well as several smaller towns—with posters depicting the pianist, and providing the newspapers with copies of a 227 page volume in three languages entitled *Revue critique des concerts du pianiste Vladimir de Pachmann*.[4] The first concert in Copenhagen on April 9 was a tremendous success, and the critics wrote that no other artist had ever had such a success in Denmark. Echoing colleagues in Vienna, Paris and London, their comments—"Pachmann is the Chopin player par excellence . . . nothing can compare with the beauty and delicacy of his touch . . . he is inimitable . . . "—had already become commonplaces. The *Nationtidende* went so far as to write, "Bülow is nothing compared with Pachmann as far as musical freedom is concerned." Pachmann's fame in Denmark grew so great that he played to absolutely packed houses, with tickets selling for as much as two or three Crowns apiece—an unheard of price for provincial concerts in Odense, Aarhus, Randers and Aalborg. Returning to Copenhagen on the first anniversary of their marriage, the couple performed together in a joint recital on April 30. The concert was Pachmann's seventh appearance in the city, and probably the first ever appearance in public of Maggie playing jointly with her husband. They played the Schumann Variations Op. 46, Chopin's Rondo and Henselt's *Si oiseau j'étais*, the last work a solo piece they played in unison. Maggie's playing was criticized for "lack of warmth."

On May 2 and 3 Pachmann played the Chopin F minor Concerto yet again—he couldn't resist the invitation from the Royal Danish Orchestra and its conductor Johann Svendsen, and the ovations he knew it would bring. Before they continued on to Sweden, Danish king Christian IX invited both of them to perform at court. After the concert the king presented Pachmann with a breast pin and Maggie with a bracelet. From that day on Pachmann was a favorite of the Danish royal family.

Later Pachmann used to tell a story about a luncheon to which he had been invited by King Christian. Supposedly the king himself had come to Pachmann's hotel and knocked on his door to present the invitation in person. Pachmann asked if he could bring the young pianist Eugen d'Albert, who was visiting him, and permission was granted. Pachmann deliberately omitted to tell d'Albert that he had already spoken to the king, and wickedly insisted a formal invitation wasn't really necessary for d'Albert to accompany him to the royal party. D'Albert had serious misgivings about attending without an invitation, but was relieved when the royal couple received him and Pachmann with equal graciousness.

On May 9, 1885, Maggie (who was now acting as her husband's secretary) wrote from Stockholm to The Philharmonic Society of London, which had requested him to play with them again:

> He can't accept as he is giving recitals every second day until the middle of June . . . he has four more here to give, then to Norway and then Copenhagen for three—he already gave five there.

It was a breathless pace.[5] We have a reminiscence of these concerts written by one of the pair of Pachmann's Scandinavian concert promoters who were Danish, and who most likely were recruited by Waltmann. Pachmann's behavior was much like Liszt's during the days of his great virtuoso career:

> His interest in things didn't extend further than his art, and precious stones. He used to wear a ring with a rare, beautiful cut diamond, and it was one of his greatest pleasures to contemplate it and see it throw its rays of sunlight . . . After the concerts in Copenhagen Pachmann had to leave for Stockholm, where he had an engagement (we were taking the same risk) for twenty concerts for the net sum of 16,000 crowns. Some days previous my partner and I went to the Swedish capital to make arrangements for the concert; later my partner went to Christiania where he was also to perform, to make the same arrangements. We—my colleague and I—decided that it would be

better first to invite the press and musical authorities for a private concert, which we arranged to take place in the "Grand Hotel" hall, while the actual concert was to take place some days later in the great hall of the Royal Musical Academy. Enthusiasm at the invitational concert was even greater than in Copenhagen, and the artist was much praised. Pachmann himself was comfortable among strangers, as though amidst family and friends; he went among the listeners, spoke with them, nodded smiling to one and another, played a little and was soon after in animated conversation again, which was always about music. "Mr. Pachmann, could I kindly ask you to play Chopin's . . ." you heard from one of the guests. "Yes, with great pleasure" answered Pachmann and just played. "Ah, Mr. Pachmann, would you please . . ." "With pleasure," and so it went. They always wanted more, and Pachmann was indefatigable. People surely thought this introduction to be quite peculiar, but amusing at the same time. They admired him, and they laughed and when you saw people leaving the concert hall, you found, as always happened after one of Pachmann's concerts, only happy faces. The next day you could read in practically all the Stockholm newspapers that Pachmann really was an artistic glory, and at the concert a few days later in the Royal Music Academy, the big hall was almost full. The enthusiasm was overwhelming and Pachmann was applauded in a way he wasn't quite used to. In fact people didn't limit themselves to claps and cries of Bravo, but stood up on chairs and waved their handkerchiefs . . . Pachmann himself seemed to consider this homage as the most natural thing in the world; he just played one encore after the other, while smiling to the audience. I have never seen any bigger success, any more real triumph for an artist than Pachmann had . . . Before he left the North he had a last concert in Copenhagen after which he was made a Knight of the Dannebrog. His joy at receiving this decoration is inexplicable and I am convinced his interest in precious stones was temporarily decreased; surely he looked as often to his Cross as to the brilliance of his ring.[6]

The Danish press report had spoken of a brilliant ring that Pachmann wore and which he could often be seen admiring during his concerts. Now he was frequently observed admiring his bejeweled medal of the Order of the Dannebrog as well. Although he was decorated many times during his long career, he was particularly proud of this honor and was buried with the cross of the order.

The czarina of Russia, the younger sister of Princess Alexandra of England, had heard of Pachmann's Scandinavian triumphs and he was once more invited to St. Petersburg to play at Court. After the performance there were presentations of a ring by the czar, and by the czarina of "a handsome Etruscan vase, which she had bought at the Moscow exhibition," as one writer reported. Alexander III also gave him a special passport, which Pachmann used for the rest of his life. Maggie was not present, for she delivered their first child, a son named Victor, that very night.

Later Pachmann visited Odessa for the first time in a decade. He took Maggie to meet his sister Elizaveta, but the occasion was not happy, for soon after arriving they received an urgent wire from St. Petersburg. Their son Victor, who had been left behind with a nurse, was dangerously ill. By the time they were able to return to the capital the baby was dead. Now the glamour, the excitement and the triumphs seemed insignificant. The ovations and critical acclaim were no compensation for the death of her child. There were monotonous months of traveling in overcrowded, uncomfortable railway cars. Maggie longed for England and her family. To please her, Pachmann abandoned the tour, and after two years of traveling and interminable triumphs, their protracted honeymoon came to an abrupt end.

Maggie became pregnant again after their return to England, and she gave birth in August 1886 to their second son, Adrian. A year later a third son, Leonide, was born. Perhaps as a sign of his virility, Pachmann had grown a long, black, silky beard. Later he tried varying the style, assuming the mustache and goatee known as the "Imperial."

Like many eccentric artists Pachmann was absent-minded, so much so that he sometimes didn't know where he was. Princess Alexandra, hearing of the extraordinary pianist from her sister the czarina, expressed the desire to hear him and invited him to Buckingham Palace. He didn't want to go, claiming he was a true believer in anarchy and would not visit royalty (although this was not many months after he was willingly feted by Scandinavian royalty). Friends pleaded with him for hours, at last persuading him not to commit an impertinence that would never be forgiven by the English. At last he was dispatched to the palace in a taxicab. After many hours he had still not returned and Maggie began to worry. By morning he had still not returned and she was frantic, enlisting the aid of friends who tried to help find him. At last the taxicab drove up to the house and Pachmann came out. What happened was that as he was leaving the palace, he couldn't remember where he lived, and could only tell the driver that it was "in a square with a church on it." The driver had spent the entire night with his famous passenger making the rounds of the innumerable squares of London.

He completely disregarded the practical side of life. He could be strict and precise about the details of contracts and business matters, but he never knew the value and meaning of, nor cared for, money. When Maggie or Waltmann offered him some he would recoil, pantomiming horror, and shout, "*Cochonnerie!*" Maggie found living with him a series of complete surprises.

They were staying with Maggie's family in Hampton and the pianist could sometimes be seen in the garden polishing the few precious stones he had somehow acquired and kept in his pocket—his collection of jewels was evolving.

◡◠

On March 18, 1886, Pachmann again played the Mozart Concerto in D minor with the Philharmonic Society; Sir Arthur Sullivan was indisposed so George Mount conducted. Correspondence in the orchestra's archive in the British Library reveals that Pachmann also was to play the Mendelssohn Concerto in G minor on the same program, but eventually claimed he wasn't ready to play the Mendelssohn. Francesco Berger, the Philharmonic's secretary, was most annoyed, and wrote to Pachmann's manager, Narciso Vert, on January 30: "I must remind M. de Pachmann that from October to March is ample time for an artist." The concert took place but Pachmann played only the Mozart. The next day the *Times* reported: "His delicate touch and intelligent phrasing appear almost to as great advantage as they do in his favorite Chopin, the result being little if not all short of perfection." Unexpectedly the most sensational feature of the concert was Italian double-bass virtuoso Giovanni Bottesini (1821–1889) who played some inconsequential variations of his own, apparently filling in at the last minute for the missing Mendelssohn concerto. Pachmann was delighted and for once did not begrudge a fellow performer the limelight. He was astonished that a man could make the unwieldy double bass sound so beautiful.

1886 was a great year for London's music lovers. Liszt visited in April, Rubinstein in May and June, and the couple spent time with both. Liszt had come over for a performance of his oratorio "The Legend of St. Elizabeth." He hadn't visited England in more than forty years and now here he was, with gray hair flowing to his shoulders, a living relic of a lost era. The old Maestro was received like a conquering hero and in the two weeks he stayed he was covered with honors and almost killed by social and musical duties heaped on him by his hosts. From literally the first minute he arrived, he was shepherded around and presented to most of the great people of the day; he dined with Henry Irving at the Beefsteak Club, visited Queen Victoria at Windsor Castle and was received by Cardinal Manning, as well as played several times to very select audiences. Pachmann managed to see Liszt at Sydenham and took Maggie with him. The great man was still as fascinating as ever and there still glowed in his faded eyes a faint glimmer of *diablerie*. He was always at his best when he was with beautiful women and his charming manner put Maggie at ease at once. He asked her to play and she couldn't refuse. She played a whole series of pieces to him, mostly from his own works and those of Chopin. When Maggie played Chopin's Etude in double sixths, he remarked to Pachmann that the consecutive fifths didn't sound so bad after all. After that he sat and played for them. Maggie was lost in wonderment. Liszt was seventy-four at the time, yet still his flame glowed.

On April 8 Pachmann was among the guests at the Grosvenor Gallery, where a reception and concert honoring Liszt had been arranged. After Liszt's pupil and advocate Walter Bache had played the *Bénédiction de Dieu dans la solitude* and other artists further Liszt works, in the words of Constance Bache "came *the* event of the evening." Liszt played his own transcription of the Schubert Hungarian Divertissement, and the Allegro section from his 13th Hungarian Rhapsody. Others noted that his touch seemed to have lost some of its vigor. Sir George Grove was astonished that the playing was "so entirely unlike the style of the so-called Liszt School." Pachmann, remembering the concert in a December 1915 *Vanity Fair* interview, said "it was only an old, sleepy, music, beautiful indeed, but pathetic." No wonder, for the British were overtaxing the poor, old, exhausted and ill composer with their festive efforts.

The next day Pachmann was among several artists who played for Liszt and the Prince of Wales at a small gathering. He played Liszt's 8th Hungarian Rhapsody and a work by Henselt. According to Francis Hueffer, Liszt smiled, hearing the artistry of his old friend Pachmann again, which had "especially delighted" him.

In May Pachmann played his last London recitals of the year, for the following month Rubinstein was coming to present his famous series of Historical Recitals, seven enormous programs played from memory. The June 1886 *Musical Times* wrote:

> Very sensibly, this gifted pianist decided to bring his season to a close before the arrival of his greater compatriot, Anton Rubinstein. While the sun is shining, even stars of the first magnitude cannot be seen.

Pachmann and Maggie had lunch with Rubinstein before the fourth of these concerts. Rubinstein was nervous and twice dropped a plate, but during that recital on May 27, he played so magnificently Maggie and Pachmann were both in tears. Later Maggie wrote:

> Never shall I forget the feeling he stirred in me with the opening phrases of Schumann's Fantasy [in C major, Op. 17] which opened the concert. The gradations of his tone in that divine phrase were so marvelous that I felt my throat swell with emotion.[7]

This was, of course, Rubinstein's famous "grand accent" which gripped one and, once heard, apparently was never forgotten.

After the recital the couple went backstage where the mighty Anton showed them his hands which were bleeding. But blood had not prevented him from playing the last encore, Schumann's *Traumeswirren*, with a delicacy and clarity which Pachmann described as miraculous.

Josef Hofmann told an interviewer for the *Literary Digest* (February 10, 1912) as well as writer Carl Van Vechten, about another incident involving

Pachmann attending these Rubinstein recitals. Apparently, at one point Pachmann laughed out loud as Rubinstein played, and exclaimed "He used the fourth instead of the third finger in that run—isn't that funny?"

At the fifth Historical Recital on June 1, 1886, Rubinstein played thirty-one works, beginning with Clementi and Field, making his way through Hummel, Moscheles, Henselt, Thalberg and Liszt. Gustave Ernst was there and wrote about it for the *Etude* magazine's September, 1940, issue:

Vladimir de Pachmann, then at the height of his fame, attended the concert. One of his show pieces was Henselt's If I Were a Bird, his playing of which had been called unsurpassable. He had played it the day before at the home of a friend. In response to rapturous applause of the audience, he said with a gesture, "Now I am ready for Rubinstein." On the afternoon of the concert, de Pachmann stood with me and some other pianists. He was enthusiastic over the program. When it came to the Henselt etude, however, he put on his hat and stood in the corner with a Napoleonic look of triumphant defiance. Rubinstein began the difficult composition at a speed that seemed impossible to maintain. He played it with that feathery lightness of touch which so impressed Schumann . . . marked by those wonderful shadings from *p* to *pp* to *ppp*, of which Rubinstein alone seemed to hold the secret. When it was over and the audience broke out into thundering applause, I looked around for de Pachmann. He had disappeared. All that was left was his hat upon the floor, which he had forgotten to take with him. De Pachmann again started to study the piece, which he once told me he had played at least ten thousand times before he dared to play it for Henselt in St. Petersburg.

It was surely Pachmann's competitive personality that caused him to flee; he had already achieved a reputation as an inspired interpreter of Henselt's music, particularly that war-horse etude, *Si oiseau j'étais*.[8] Now he needed to study it ten thousand times more, to be able to surpass Rubinstein. Perhaps he succeeded, for in 1899 the American critic James Gibbons Huneker effused in his book, *Mezzotints in Modern Music*:

I have heard pianists play this étude as if the bird were a roc, and they were throttling it Sinbad fashion for its fabulous egg. Ah, Vladimir Pachmann, how that little bird did sing under your coaxing touch! and how tenderly you put it away into its silvery cage when it had trilled its sweet pipe! You triple locked the cage, too, black bearded Pashaw that you were, by playing three chords in F sharp, mounting an octave each time!

As a young man Pachmann had heard Henselt play the piece. He told Arthur Abel, the German correspondent about it; Abel reported this in a private letter to Harold C. Schonberg (August 13, 1951):

Vladimir de Pachmann told me nearly sixty years ago that he had heard Henselt play 'Bird Study' as a young man and he was so enamored of it that he added it to his repertoir [*sic*] . . . I never heard anyone play it with such speed, clarity, lightness and charm as Pachmann. The author [Henselt] was the greatest Chopin interpreter I ever heard.

In the fall of 1888 Novello, Ewer and Company in London issued a volume entitled *Seven Pieces for Pianoforte Composed by Adolphe Henselt, Edited and Fingered by Wladimir de Pachmann* (this was distributed in the United States by the Schirmer company). Besides *Si oiseau j'étais*, it contains a Toccatina, the Fourth Impromptu, *Wiegenlied* and three other works with poetic titles. The "contents" page carries the following paragraph:

The fingering in this Edition is made with regard to the position of the hands; that which at first sight appears awkward will be found calculated to give a fluent rendering of the technical difficulties and at the same time a tranquil movement of the hands. Any alteration in the Notes is made with the approval of the Composer, and by his wish published. W. de P

Today this is a rare volume indeed.

The Pachmann family had been living with Maggie's sister in Hampton, and now that there were two babies to care for, Maggie felt they needed larger quarters and a place of their own. She persuaded Pachmann to lease an apartment in Paris, where they settled into a life of domesticity that lasted almost three years. Vlady, as Maggie and almost everyone else was now calling him, was as inimitable as a father as Pachmann the virtuoso. It was rumored that once he fed his children champagne and caviar while amusing them at the piano. Knowing his eccentricities, people expected anything outrageous from him. In reality, he was extremely conscientious of his paternal duties. Perhaps remembering the deprivations of his own childhood, he used to insist that their cradles be covered with netting to protect against vermin. He adored his children and would let them pull his beard while they bounced on his knees. Then the rooms of the little apartment sounded with laughter.

Maggie continued studying with him in Paris. Five years had elapsed since her last solo appearance in public and finally early in 1887 Pachmann felt she was ready to resume her career. They went to Germany, where Hermann Wolff was then managing the Berlin Philharmonic as well as his own concert agency. He presented both Vladimir and Maggie with the orchestra in Berlin. On January 6, 1887, Pachmann played under Joseph Joachim's baton. The next day the *Vossische Zeitung* reported:

Besides Chopin's F minor Concerto, Herr von Pachmann brought piano pieces by Raff and Henselt, executed with a beautiful, perfected touch, one which combined the powerful with the delicate and the euphonic in rare artistry; with exemplary technique in passagework and fioriture, there was something clear, rounded and flowing, and equally quiet and noble, while at the same time with intelligent, vivid understanding. With the massing of so many concerts happening this winter, Herr von Pachmann has not succeeded yet in coming into prominence to the measure he would deserve[9]

The concert was not well attended. The Monday recital on January 10 was also reviewed in the *Vossische Zeitung* the next day, which again mentions poor attendance:

A demonstration of masterful technique, with regard to beauty and variety of attack, as well as evenness and pleasing roundness of passage work that was almost unsurpassed . . . pieces like Rubinstein's G major Barcarolle or Mendelssohn's Rondo Capriccioso could not possibly be played in a more perfected manner . . . one novelty was found on the program, a set of enticing Variations by Marguerite von Pachmann. Unfortunately, the overabundance of concerts this season has prevented the public from a more vivid participation in Herr von Pachmann's concerts, as his talents merit. Nevertheless he cannot fail to have noticed how excellently he has been accepted by the unmusical Berlin public.

Maggie's turn with the orchestra came on January 21, when Karl Klindworth conducted for her in Chopin's *Andante Spianato e Grande Polonaise*, Op. 22. She also played Beethoven's Rondo, "Rage Over the Loss of a Penny," a Gigue by Bach, and Henselt's *Danklied nach Sturm*. Again a *Vossische Zeitung* review appeared the next day:

With her clear and deliberate attack, the clean, perlé technique and her musical agility, the artiste brought vivid satisfaction. If however she was not able to touch the audience deeply, this was because of a certain reserve in expression, which led up to a dryness of tone, especially noticeable in the Beethoven rondo.

Shortly after these concerts Hans von Bülow was named conductor of the Berlin Philharmonic. He and Wolff had an agreement—he would accept any soloist Wolff suggested, if Wolff gave him complete autonomy to program whatever works he wanted. But Pachmann's poor draw at the box office made him hesitate when Wolff suggested a return engagement for Pachmann, and Bülow, who thought of most other pianists as "vermin," wrote to Wolff on July 7, 1888:

Herr W V Pachmann is, among the UNmusical pianists, perhaps the most interesting one—at least more poetic than the other vermin—but whether he fits in the surroundings of the Berlin Philharmonic, that I leave to your insight to decide. Or would you not remember (and hide from me) how his

performance of the Chopin Piano Concerto under Joachim's baton went, two
or three years back?

Pachmann was not re-engaged with the Berlin Philharmonic, and did
not play again in Germany for a few years.

Soon after these concerts Maggie gave a recital in the Salle Erard in
Paris. She was an instantaneous success there and the critics were jubilant.
Pachmann sat in the first row exultant with joy. "I couldn't have played
it better," he declared loudly. After the concert, Pachmann chanced to
overhear one of the directors of the Salle Erard complimenting Maggie.
Leonide de Pachmann reported that his father shouted: "Marvelous? She
plays *genius-ly*! You don't know anything about music!" and then added
under his breath an even less complimentary phrase. The director was
deeply offended and never spoke to the pianist again. Pachmann had
probably not intended to insult the man, he simply wanted everyone to
like Maggie's playing and in his exuberance did not weigh his words.
Childlike as ever, he could not restrain his feelings and though he might
say, "we must be 'politic,'" in music he never paid false compliments.
"Who is your teacher?" he once asked a French girl after she had played
some Chopin to him. "Why, he is M.— of the Conservatoire," she replied.
"Tell him, he's a donkey!"

The couple shuttled back and forth across the channel, both giving
concerts individually and sometimes together; occasionally in London,
occasionally in Paris—always with success. Maggie's playing was praised
everywhere, and her position as one of the leading British pianists of her
day was re-established. Maggie fancied herself a composer as well, and
occasionally included some of her own pieces on her programs. At the
February 6 recital she played her two best-known works, the "Theme and
Variations" (which Pachmann had played in Berlin) and *Rêverie du Lac*, a
slender salon piece reminiscent of Chaminade, which her husband also
played a few times in public. The *Musical Times* writer dismissed it as
"an elegant trifle" but thought the Variations were written "with a large
amount of musicianly skill, and left a very favourable impression."

Pachmann, now performing regularly in London, had his customary
triumphs and was often giving all-Chopin recitals. But he played more
than just Chopin, and his performance of Liszt's E major Polonaise was
singled out for praise by Francis Hueffer in the *Times* in January 1888:
"Liszt's magnificent Polonaise in E, which in addition to much that is
impetuous and wild, contains some music fit for the revels of Oberon
and his fairies. Here the pianist was at his best." Hueffer undoubtedly
was referring to the work's cadenza, and his words perfectly describe
Pachmann's 1915 recording of the cadenza.

Pachmann's mannerisms were soon evolved from gesticulations and
pantomime to spoken "asides," which later became typical of his recit-

als. He had discovered that the encouragement and acceptance of the audience seemed to free his spirit. This freedom permitted him to communicate his vision. Without the antics it was impossible for him to play as only Pachmann could play when he was inspired—there was a relationship between his eccentricities and his nervousness. It seems the more nervous he was, the more he talked; and the more he talked, the more eccentric his behavior became.

With the maturing of his art Pachmann was able to regulate the eccentricities, which relaxed the audience as well, and provided the freedom necessary for inspiration. They did not affect his musical performances adversely. It was a very thin line he trod and even in his prime, there was always the temptation to overdo mannerisms to the detriment of his art. But on the whole, he managed to preserve this delicate balance until the years just preceding the First World War, when his art deteriorated and the equilibrium was destroyed.

However, from the beginning there were some music lovers, critics and other well-known performers who could never accept his performances. They felt his eccentric behavior destroyed the sanctity of the concert hall, and with it went any respect as a serious artist. Even when his playing had undeniable merit, they would disparage it. He could only play small works, his performances lacked power and manliness, he was too limited. One of those who was not amused was a young man with a bright red beard who sat angrily mumbling to himself, amid the applause and laughter. He was a self-declared music critic who originally wrote under the pen name of Corni di Bassetto. His real name of course was George Bernard Shaw, and he had first heard Pachmann shortly after the pianist's debut in London. Pianist Harold Bauer, whose own delicate, refined and finished playing was sometimes compared to Pachmann's, happened to be sitting next to Shaw at one Pachmann recital, and wrote in his autobiography:

> I heard him once utter the word "monkey" when Vladimir de Pachmann was making antics at the piano, and I was deeply shocked. De Pachmann, in my estimation, was a genius to whom everything was permitted, and I could not bear to have him ridiculed.

According to journalist and critic Charles Osborne, Shaw thought music criticism in general in England "was then refined and academic to the point of being unreadable and often nonsensical," and he set out deliberately to vulgarize it. On August 19, 1889, Shaw reviewed a Pachmann recital for the *Star*:

> M. Vladimir de Pachmann gave his well known pantomimic performance with accompaniments by Chopin, a composer who I could listen to M. de

Pachmann play for ever, if the works were first carefully removed from the pianoforte.

This is one of the best-known quotes about Pachmann, and one of the most misunderstood. It does not mean that Shaw hated Pachmann's music; it refers to the pianist's mimicry and pantomime, the fact that you could almost appreciate the music from gestures alone—that is what Shaw hated.[10] Shaw heard an otherwise unknown young woman named de Llana play the Chopin third Ballade, and wrote in the *Star* on March 7, 1890:

> At one complicated passage her memory and her fingers failed her for a moment; and she had to pause for breath. Unlike M. de Pachmann, who passes off mishaps of this sort so effectively that he has been suspected by evil-minded persons of bringing them about on purpose, Mlle de Llana looked very angry with herself.

In the *World*, reviewing a Crystal Palace performance Pachmann gave of the Beethoven Third Concerto, Shaw wrote on October 19, 1892:

> De Pachmann is unquestionably a very able pianist, and by no means an insincere one; but now that I have seen, in La Statue du Commandeur, a lady sing a song in dumb show, I want to see a pianoforte concerto played in the same way; and I think there can be no doubt that de Pachmann is the player for that feat.

⤶

Pachmann's nervousness before the joint recitals he played with Maggie made her tremble with fear. She was irritated by his increasing mannerisms, and for a while she tried to temper them. A few days after a recital in which Maggie had played decidedly better than her husband, the couple visited J. A. Fuller-Maitland, the critic of the *Manchester Guardian*, whose severe review of their concert had appeared the day before (he later wrote about it in his memoirs). "Did not Madame play like an angel and did not I play like a pig?" Pachmann asked him.

Fuller-Maitland admitted that Maggie had done herself more justice than he had. Their conversation according to the critic "dwelt on the corruptness of continental criticism and the ease with which it was possible to buy [favorable] opinions abroad." While they were talking Pachmann suddenly fell on his knees before the critic:

"But ven I zee creeticism like yours, I . . . I . . ." he stuttered. His manner, with his bearded face in an ecstatic grimace, was too much and Fuller-Maitland almost burst out laughing.

Here Maggie took the situation in hand and said to the critic: "Now Mr. Fuller-Maitland, you have often said in print that his affectations are to be regretted, tell him so in person." While Pachmann crouched before the two, they joined in reproaching him. "I promise, I promise," he shouted. "Yes, yes, you zee at my next recital, I vil play for *you alone*." And here he turned to Fuller-Maitland and smiled. "At his next recital, he performed a whole Chopin sonata without as much as a glance to the audience" according to Fuller-Maitland, and "he never played more beautifully."

It seems that Pachmann *could* give of his very best without the grimaces, pantomimic accompaniments and other accouterments when he was playing solely for one individual whom he wished to please greatly, and whose appreciation of his art he knew would be dampened by eccentric behavior.

On the verge of becoming an international star, his career in full flower, Pachmann suddenly faced a new problem. Apparently an argument with Waltmann erupted about some minor details, and he and the man who had introduced him to the world separated.[11] It is said the great pianist became so angry that he bit his old impresario on the neck. (Waltmann wasn't the only impresario Pachmann was to bite.)

No sooner had Waltmann departed than a replacement appeared. An American named Frederick A. Schwab, in Europe for a summer vacation, heard the pianist in London. Schwab was a most unusual fellow, a critic and an impresario at the same time. He had been the manager of the soprano and actress Adelaide Neilson (who eventually became his lover) while acting as the drama critic of the *New York Times*, gaining a reputation for corruption for writing favorable reviews of La Neilson. A group of theatre owners and managers threatened to withdraw their advertising if he weren't removed. He countered by suing the *Musical Courier* magazine when it printed an article that suggested he had been fired from the *New York Times*. The fracas was settled when *Musical Courier* hired him to write opera criticism, and the suit was dropped. In 1875 he then became a music critic for the *New York Times*, a position he left before managing the last American tour of Hans von Bülow in 1889, and then a few months later, the next tour of Pachmann.[12] The April 12, 1890, *American Musician* printed the story of how he happened to become Waltmann's successor:

> I had no more thought of engaging M. de Pachmann than I have now of signing a contract with General Boulanger[13] . . . we have so many pianists in America . . . I thought it judicious to go hear him, at any rate. I went, intending to remain ten minutes—and I stayed an hour and a half. That same night I wrote to him and asked him to confer with me on the subject of an American *tournée*, and simultaneously I wrote to Chickering & Sons. I met M. and Mme. De Pachmann a few days later in Paris, where, by the way, they have one of the prettiest *interieurs* imaginable . . . It required no end of

eloquence and imaginative imagery to induce M. de Pachmann to cross the Atlantic, for he suffered terribly from sea sickness (unkind souls called him 'Mal de Mer' de Pachmann).

In 1890 Pachmann was forty-two. Vienna, Paris, Budapest, London and Scandinavia had been conquered, yet somehow the picture was not complete, for across the desert of the Atlantic lay the oasis of America. European pianists remembered the tremendous successes that Thalberg had there in the sixties, and Rubinstein and Bülow later. The great Rafael Joseffy emigrated in 1879 and established himself as probably the most important pianist in the New World. Franz Rummel had made his second American tour in 1886 and stayed. Many other pianists of great renown were crossing the ocean—Eugen d'Albert and von Bülow were coming (they played some concerts together), Carl Ansorge was giving concerts in New York, Xavier Scharwenka was coming to open an American branch of his own conservatory, and apart from Joseffy there was much other local pianistic talent that could regularly be heard in New York.

In London Pachmann played two concerts in one day, March 1, 1890. In the afternoon he played an all-Chopin recital in St. James's Hall. The *Academy* reported (January/June 1890):

> The pianist on mounting the platform tried by gesture to let the audience know that his hands were cold . . . soon the player warmed to his work, and surpassed himself. During the performance of the Funeral March one could have heard a pin drop, so rapt were the listeners . . . The D flat Valse was given with numerous *arabesques*, somewhat after the style of Tausig's treatment of Weber's 'Invitation.' . . . Not only in the Valse, but in one or two of the other pieces, there were readings not according to the text.

That evening he appeared again at a "Popular Concert," playing Mendelssohn's *Variations sérieuses* on a program that included performances by violinist Joachim and 'cellist Piatti. He was beloved in England, but despite seasickness and pianistic competition, the lure of America was too enticing. Pachmann sailed.

Chapter 8

Chronicle of the Chopinzee, Part One: American Debut, 1890

The ring into which Frederic Schwab was throwing Pachmann's hat was indeed crowded, so crowded that the American critic Henry Krehbiel wrote: "there was enough pianoforte music in the [1889/90] season to make one . . . wish that the instrument had never been invented."

When Pachmann arrived in America in April 1890 he found that his enormous English reputation had not preceded him. In fact, the *Chicago Daily Tribune* had published an article on July 21, 1889, that actually demolished him:

Mr. Otto Florsheim of the New York Musical Courier writes as follows concerning De Pachmann, the pianist, whom he has just heard in London: Rarely before have I been so disappointed as I was in the case of Pachmann. I had always heard that he was a fine pianist, and especially a great Chopin interpreter. This reputation he has almost entirely earned in England, or rather in London, where he is a great favorite; but it seemed to me that if ever there was a case of mundus vult decipi, ergo decipister [sic][1] it is this cult of a man who is much more of an actor or clown than he is a pianist. Not that he had no technic, for without that he could not undertake Chopin in the sometimes ludicrously fast tempos he chooses; and even his touch was acceptable, although he operated on a poor Broadwood concert grand, the upper half of which, when Pachmann used the damper pedal, sounded as if he were performing on cracked tumblers. But the agile, black bearded and piercing-eyed little virtuoso made his deepest impression upon the musically rather unimpressionable English maidens chiefly by the art of mimicry. When he plays Chopin's funeral march he literally sheds tears all around; when he interprets the B flat minor scherzo his face is wreathed in smiles; when he toys with the great A flat waltz his face becomes as gentle and seraphic as becomes a man who is enjoying an [sic] scene of bliss; when by some unfortunate chance he lands on some other note than the one written by the composer or intended by the player he contorts his face into such folds of genuinely disgusted and yet good-humored astonishment that you forget and forgive the mishap, and all through the performance he casts such loving glances at the best looking young ladies, and sometimes even at the somewhat advanced ones in age, that everybody seems delighted, grows most enthusiastic, and thinks he, or rather she, has enjoyed a great treat—a genuine Chopin interpretation—while in reality it was nothing but a Chopin caricature, entirely on the outside and surface of the composition, no depth, no true feeling, and no genuine sentiment, but in its stead only sickly sentimentality.[2]

This negative impression was repudiated and forgotten completely soon after Pachmann's debut at Chickering Hall in New York on April 7. It was the first in a series of three "Chopin cycles" on three successive afternoons that included Chopin's greatest works: three Ballades and three Scherzi, the F minor Fantasy, the two great Sonatas, the Barcarolle, Berceuse and various Etudes, Mazurkas, Preludes, Nocturnes and Waltzes. In a fourth concert on April 11 he played the F minor Concerto with conductor Frank van der Stucken and the New York Philharmonic. Maggie made her American debut at the same orchestral concert in the Liszt E flat Concerto.

It was Schwab who hit upon the idea of presenting the pianist to America in three programs consisting entirely of works by Chopin, the composer for whom Pachmann had become most renowned. There had never been such all-Chopin concerts in New York before. The novelty of the programs was eclipsed by the public's delight with the playing, which again created a sensation. His exquisite touch, subtle phrasing and velvety tone were so appealing that once again success was achieved after just one recital, and he was established in America. The next day the reviews were positively ecstatic. The *Herald* headlined:

Vladimir de Pachmann The Noted Russian Pianist Creates a Sensation in Chickering Hall

It is not often that the verdict upon a pianist is so unanimous as that pronounced yesterday afternoon in Chickering Hall by an audience made up largely of experts . . . as a Chopin player he stands alone . . . this is saying a great deal . . . many persons expected to hear an interpretation suggestive of an idealized music box—runs so perfect that nothing short of machinery could produce them, and taken at a pace beyond that of human fingers. We have had so much of that kind of playing in New York in the last few years . . . There is nothing of the music box about Mr. De Pachmann. His playing is marvelous in accuracy but it leaves one more impressed with the beauty of the music itself than with the perfection of the means employed to bring out that beauty . . .

every note of the recital was listened to with literally breathless interest . . . It is possible that in works requiring great breadth and power the pianist may fall short. For the present it may be said that his playing of the first Chopin program was a rare treat . . . people refused to leave the hall and an impromptu reception was held . . . many noted music lovers among the distinguished New Yorkers crowding upon the stage to congratulate the pianist.

The *Tribune*:

One is transported into another musical atmosphere . . . where . . . nobility and genuine poetic feeling predominate . . . Pachmann's pianissimo appears to begin where other pianists end theirs.

The *World*:

The Russian Pianist M. de Pachmann Astonishes Music Lovers

The New York public is not willing to take the judgment of London or any European capital upon matters musical . . . There can be but one opinion in regard to M. de Pachmann as an interpreter of Chopin's works. He has a perfect knowledge of the Polish composer's meaning and the fullest ability to give poetic and faultless technical interpretation of that meaning . . . He does not astonish his hearers by his brilliancy or dramatic intensity, yet he not only astonishes but charms . . . by the marvelous delicacy and smoothness of execution and his fairy-like pianissimo effects.

W. J. Henderson, considered by some connoisseurs to be the greatest music critic America has ever produced, was then the critic for the *New York Times*. He found much to admire:

He possesses a very clean and smooth legato, which never loses its distinctness nor approaches a staccato in the most rapid passages, but which makes his runs positively beautiful in their ease and intelligibility. His tone color is very soft and agreeable, and there is at no time the slightest hardness in his touch. His playing is full of nuances, which are never forgotten even in the most rapid passages. His cantabile is sweet and well sustained and his octave playing is neat. On the other hand, his range of dynamic effects is not large. His limits appear to lie between an extremely delicate pianissimo and a fairly sonorous forte . . . His use of the two pedals at once, evidently for the purpose of obtaining a soft and sustained tone, frequently leads to obscurity in broken arpeggios and irregular successions of chords. But on the whole M. de Pachmann's playing of those numbers which represent the feminine side of Chopin's character was delightful . . . the D flat Waltz we have never heard so beautifully performed . . . Mr. de Pachmann's demeanor at the piano is, perhaps, not a matter for consideration here, except in so far as smiles, nods and grimaces tend to distract the attention of his hearers from the music.

Henderson did not review the second recital in the series, but of the third wrote:

> Within his limits he is a remarkably fine performer. His distinguishing characteristics are grace, delicacy and extreme finish. He has unquestionably made a close study, measure by measure, of the Chopin works, and his playing of them is very instructive. He does not achieve nearly such good results in the broader Chopin compositions as he does in the small ones. The polonaise . . . has been more impressively played by other pianists . . . but the etudes, the fantasie impromptu and the valse have never been given here with such beautiful finish

But Henderson seemed offended by the pianist's obvious lack of masculinity. That first review contained another sentence, one which presaged years of considerable hostility to come:

> It is pretty well established, however, that there was a masculine side to Chopin's nature, and so far as yesterday's performance indicated, the new comer will not teach his American hearers much about that.

The first recital had not been sold out, but the succeeding recitals were filled to capacity. The *Sun*'s review of the second recital hit on a formula, calling him the Meissonier of the piano, a metaphor much used thereafter:

> Repeated hearings of M. de Pachmann in his interesting Chopin cyclus reveal him fully as the Meissonier of the pianoforte . . . extreme delicacy . . . overlaid by the most ornate, but microscopic adornments, and the whole musical picture is a wonderful bit of cunning handiwork.

Pachmann's performance of his signature concerto, the Chopin F minor at the fourth concert on April 11, did not make the expected effect on everyone. Apparently there was insufficient rehearsal time and the Philharmonic played poorly. The *Herald*'s critic wrote:

> Chickering Hall was packed to the doors, something almost unprecedented in the history of piano concerts, and if the engagements already made for Boston did not prevent, it could be filled again every afternoon next week . . . Mr. de Pachmann gave a smooth and effective, but not astonishing, interpretation of the Chopin F minor concerto. The pianist has been ill for several days and was evidently not yet himself. Moreover the accompaniment . . . was anything but helpful . . . Mr. de Pachmann was presented with a wreath tied with ribbons of the Russian colors, and bearing the motto, "To Chopin Redivivus."

Henderson in the *Times* was beginning to get exasperated with Pachmann:

His rendering of the second movement . . . of Chopin's concerto in F minor
. . . was a lovely piece of singing on the piano, but he was not uncommonly
successful with the first and third movements . . . none of our resident pianists could have won as much applause with a similar performance. Famil-
iarity breeds contempt . . . we are prone to look through magnifying glasses
at those who come from afar.

When Pachmann played the concerto in Cincinnati under the baton of
Frank van der Stucken, "the audience simply made a child of itself in
almost refusing to allow Mr. van der Stucken to proceed with the other
numbers on the program," according to the May 1890 *Musician*.

At that time the musical press in America was far livelier than today,
and far more daring. One of the best music journals to ever appear was
America's *Musical Courier*, from which we will draw copiously in succeeding paragraphs and chapters, and identify as "*MC*."

James Gibbons Huneker, writing in an ornate style about all the arts,
was considered by many at the time to be the greatest all-around American critic. He wrote regularly for *MC*, including a column entitled "Raconteur." Two months before Pachmann's debut in New York Huneker
had written a blurb in his "Raconteur" column (*MC*, February 12, 1890):

Some people don't know when they are well off. Pachmann, the Chopinist,
has had great success in London, but not on the continent. He is now going
to risk the United States, according to a late rumor. I doubt if he will make
a hit; he is too effeminate and his style is stilted. His wife, Maggie Okey, is
in reality a better pianist than her husband, who is as mad as a March hare
when it is chased by the shadow of the festive ground hog.

These were words the critic later forgot he had written, with opinions
that he would soon reverse. He shared a box for Pachmann's debut with
Rafael Joseffy, "the Patti of the Piano," then the leading pianist resident
in America. In his *Unicorns* Huneker wrote:

In the same school as Joseffy is the capricious De Pachmann; with Joseffy I
sat at the first recital of this extraordinary Russian in Chickering Hall (1890).
Joseffy . . . at once recognized the artistic worth of Vladimir de Pachmann.
This last representative of a school that included the names Hummel, Cramer, Field, Thalberg, Chopin, the little De Pachmann (he was then bearded
like a pirate) captivated us.

The imperious Joseffy was Huneker's own revered teacher, and the only
other pianist in the world whose idealized playing was like Pachmann's,
for he was also a "pianissimist." Today Rafael Joseffy (1852–1915) is almost completely forgotten. Only those who consult his Chopin and Liszt

editions published by Schirmer will know his name as an editor. In his heyday he was considered one of the world's greatest pianists. Indeed, Huneker off and on thought him the greatest of all. A pupil of Tausig and Liszt, Joseffy had mastered the rhetorical splendors of the orchestral style of piano playing, with its *éclat* of power and virtuosity. But his playing was tempered with aristocratic restraint, unique among the Lisztianers. Moriz Rosenthal, first Joseffy's pupil and later his colleague and friend, said of him (*Etude,* November 1938): "He was very young at the time—barely twenty-two—but I have never heard a more elegant, aristocratic performer." Rosenthal was certainly aware that his readers would be thinking of his other teacher, Franz Liszt, when reading this description.

Added to this was Joseffy's exquisite touch, with a "mastery of pianissimo" that rivaled Pachmann. Most of all, it was the beauty of Joseffy's touch that George Halprin remembered. "It was just like Pachmann," he told the author.

This judgment is confirmed by the historical record. Joseffy's American debut was in late 1879. The first issues of one of the pioneer American music journals, the *Musical Review,* chronicled the success of his concerts (November 6, 1879, writing of a Boston performance of the Chopin E minor Concerto):

> His pianissimo is something absolutely wonderful with its delicacy, purity of tone and sweetness . . . Of his touch it must be allowed that it possesses a veiled sensuousness peculiar to itself. It is difficult to imagine the composer himself imparting a more perfect elegance, a purer sentiment to the Adagio [Romanza] or a more elfin delicacy to the finale with its charming arabesques of ornamentation.

On Christmas Day the *Musical Review* wrote: "Joseffy's style is analogous to the paintings of Meissonier . . . " But his art was not found perfect, and on October 23 the *Musical Review* wrote: "The trouble is that he sometimes shows this delicacy where it is out of place and to the exclusion of the requisite breadth and depth . . . " And on November 6 "If he has a blemish it is a tendency to overindulge himself in pianissimo effects which in serious compositions becomes . . . monotonous after a while." These familiar sounding reviews describe Joseffy's playing ten years before Pachmann's American debut. Had Joseffy been able to maintain a career, he and not Paderewski would certainly have become Pachmann's competitor for public affection.

Joseffy once told his pupil Edwin Hughes:

> [Pachmann] does not need a fireworks piece to end with . . . he played the Mendelssohn Rondo Capriccioso most exquisitely. For an encore he came back and repeated the octaves [the piece's ending measures].[3]

Huneker reported that Joseffy had called Pachmann "The Hero of the Double-Thirds." But Joseffy was none too fond of Pachmann's behavior, and found his overweening egoism abrasive and his eccentricities trying, and even at times, repellent.

Unlike Pachmann, Joseffy was not a miniaturist, and played large scale works with "a soft but very deep tone," according to Halprin. He was one of the earliest to perform Brahms's works in America, playing the B flat Concerto and other works when they were unknown. He was also greatly admired for his elegant but sensuous performances of Liszt's A major Concerto. But it was in playing the works of Chopin that he made the greatest impression, particularly the E minor Concerto and F minor Ballade, the latter which served particularly to display his combined delicacy and strength.

However, despite his unique combination of pianistic talent and musical gifts, Joseffy's career sputtered after dazzling early successes, undermined by emotional problems associated with a nervous condition that necessitated his hospitalization when he was in his forties. After he returned to the concert platform, his career never regained momentum. He was a perfectionist and had perhaps unreasonably high standards, inflexible and haunted by the idea that his art was deteriorating as he aged. In Joseffy's obituary, Huneker wrote: "Nothing in life had significance for him but artistic perfection so he was doomed to disappointments." His nervousness increased with time and quickly reached such a level of intensity that by 1906 he was forced to withdraw from further public performances.

In his later years Joseffy was almost a recluse; in 1906 he also gave up teaching at the National Conservatory to devote himself to his magnum opus, the "School of Advanced Piano Playing," a killer "method," a book of daily exercises encompassing the entire range of piano technique. He never made any recordings. It is for this method, and not his piano playing, that he is now remembered.

⌇

For whatever reason, the unsigned review of Pachmann's American debut that appeared in *MC* (April 9, 1890) was not written by James Huneker, despite the fact that he was the magazine's star piano specialist:

> Pachmann is *sui generis* . . . there is method in his madness, which one instantly discovers after listening . . . Pachmann's touch is most musical and almost too luscious . . . his management of rubato effects is all that can be desired . . . Pachmann commands a somewhat limited range of tone but commands it to perfection.

But Huneker subsequently wrote a lot about Pachmann, always fascinated by him but often hostile for several months before eventually changing his critical stance. The next year Huneker happened to be in Chicago, and running into Pachmann at a restaurant, wrote an article about the meeting for a Chicago newspaper, which he reprinted in *MC* on December 16, 1891:

I sauntered into that attractive Rathskeller a day or two ago in company with Mr. Hall, the excellent Chicago representative of the New York Musical Courier and Adolph Carpe, the pianist.[4] We had all been critical auditors of Vladimir de Pachmann at his recital . . . and an hour and a half of classical music is quite enough to make one both hungry and thirsty. We had been talking about de Pachmann, his unsatisfactory performance of the Chopin left hand etude, the Chopin scherzo and the Schumann "Carnival," [*sic*] and one of us had just expressed the opinion that Mr. De Pachmann had not a big enough intellect to properly play the great Schumann composition, when lo and behold ! the famous pianist walked into the Rathskeller, also in search of something to eat and drink. He was not alone. Arthur Bissell, the manager . . . Mr. Mittleschultze, or something like it, an organist who has lately come here from Berlin,[5] and another gentleman, who was said to be De Pachmann's bodyguard, were with him. The pianist knew Mr. Hall and stopped to chat with him, while the other gentlemen sat down at a convenient table and ordered their beer and dinner. De Pachmann joined them in a minute or two and gave the most elaborate instructions to the diminutive waiter as to what he wanted and how it should be served. It may be remarked here by way of introduction that De Pachmann is the same personality off the concert platform that he is on the concert platform. He never speaks a word that he does not accompany it with a gesture, and nearly every gesture that he makes is either picturesque or grotesque. There is nothing conventional about the gentleman. He is undoubtedly a great artist at the piano, but that does not prevent him from being very funny in his individuality as a man. When he is pleased he rolls his eyes, lifts his hands and smacks his lips . . . There is more in De Pachmann's gestures than there is in his talk. He says not much, but what he lacks in words is ten times made up in these effective and eloquent pantomimic signs. One cannot conceive his fertility in gestures until one sees him at work . . . De Pachmann returned to our table. He did not sit down . . . He stood there and talked, gesturing in a hundred different ways, with hands, fingers, eyes and mouth. Naturally, he was the center of attention in the room, and everyone stopped eating to hear him talk and see him gesture. He speaks English so as to be understood. But when he found that Mr. Carpe was a German he gave up all other tongues and stuck to that. I cannot say that I was powerfully impressed with his neatness. He had just come from his recital and his collar was considerably soiled . . . Naturally the chat was confined to pianists. Mr. Carpe asked him who were his great exemplars in music. He raised his hands and eyes. "Liszt, ah! Rubinstein, ah! Paderewski, ah! Those are the three greatest pianists. First comes Liszt, then"——and Mr.

Carpe, laying his fingers on Pachmann's breast—said, "Then Pachmann." "No, no, no don't say that. I am not counting myself,'" replied Pachmann. Then he advanced towards Mr. Carpe, put his arm about his neck and said, confidentially and sotto voce: "You see, Liszt and I are a good deal alike, and I think that Liszt is really in all things the only one that can stand with me. Then, after Liszt and me"—I cannot truthfully write that Pachmann said "me and Liszt," although his whole air conveyed the same idea—"after Liszt and me came Rubinstein and Paderewski. Von Bülow—ah! He is a great player! I like Von Bülow. Ah, Friedheim is a fine player! I like Friedheim, but he is too modest, too modest. I feel sorry for him. How did the people like him here? Yes, yes, yes, he is a good, a very good, pianist." These opinions were delivered not as the ordinary man would deliver them. De Pachmann, it must be borne in mind, is an extraordinary man. They were given out in staccato installments, and every word was accompanied by a dozen funny gestures and grimaces. He seemed, after unbosoming himself to Mr. Carpe, highly satisfied with himself, and the sundry glances he gave to the mirror, in the front of which he stood as he talked, convinced me that he was not without vanity and affectation. Then someone of the three ventured to ask him what he thought of Rosenthal. He puckered up his mouth, shook his head and went through the motion of moving a crank. How about Grünfeld? Again the face was contorted and again he went through the crank movement. And how about Rummel? He smiled, laid his head on one side, screwed up his nose and turned the imaginary crank. "Ah!" he ejaculated. "There are only three great pianists: Liszt, Rubinstein, Paderewski . . . " "and Pachmann" interjected Mr. Carpe. Pachmann smiled beatifically, hugged Carpe, who is about three times the size of Pachmann, and patted him lovingly on the back. "Ah, I see you have ze appreciation. But Rosenthal, Grünfeld, who is a charming gentleman, and Rummel"–again he turned the crank—"all machines." All of which will be good news to the three piano players mentioned. "Did you like my playing of ze Weber Rondo?" he inquired. "Oh yes," we all answered, "very much." "Ah!" Again the hands and eyes went up. "Joseffy can't play that. But I must not talk about music while my soup is getting cold," and he tripped away and in a moment or two was doing his level best to get on the inside of a dunkel beer.

Today someone accompanied by a paramour would most likely introduce them as a personal trainer; there is no evidence that Pachmann ever actually engaged the services of a bodyguard. This was the first of several articles Huneker was to write that slyly included details about Pachmann's men friends.

As for Maggie, just like her earlier performances in England before she studied with Pachmann, in New York it was her physical attributes that primarily attracted male press attention; descriptions of her actual playing in the reviews were almost off-handed. *The World* reported:

> She is a beautiful woman, lithe and graceful in form and extremely picturesque . . . lovely to look upon. She has a beautiful head, well poised, soft brown hair which is worn in a hose coil low down on the neck.
>
> The *Tribune*: "A slight, girlish figure and a young, but serious face."
>
> The *Sun*: "Handsome and graceful . . . sits well at the piano."
>
> The *Herald*: "A very beautiful woman, whose cause on this account is more than half won before she touches the keys."

Henderson in the *Times* tried to confine himself to reporting the musical news, stating:

> Being . . . a pupil of her husband, it is not strange that her playing was distinguished by grace, delicacy and finesse rather than breadth, brilliancy and power. She has acquired a good deal of Mr. de Pachmann's mastery of cantilena and not a little of his phenomenally smooth and beautiful scale playing.

He did manage to slip in the fact that Maggie had a "delicate physique."

The *Chicago Daily Tribune*'s correspondent reported on the Boston concerts (May 11):

> She is by no means so great a pianist as is her famous husband . . . an odd little incident marked the first appearance of the wife here. She is, it may be remarked in passing, an exceedingly pretty woman, a trait which is by no means characteristic of woman pianists. On sitting down to play Madame Pachmann took off her wedding-ring, a circlet of gold of a heaviness perfectly barbaric, and deposited it on the piano in her handkerchief. When she rose to leave the stage she picked up the handkerchief with an absent-minded start that sent her ring rolling off the stage and down the aisle.

And as for her playing, the *World* (April 13) said it was:

> Marked by elegance, fine finish, great accuracy and brilliancy. Her execution was beautiful and smooth and at times sparkling in its daintiness. Her style is good. She has a beautiful and elastic touch. Her phrasing is artistic and her technique is correct and finished.

These sentiments were echoed by the other papers, but the *Sun* critic was less impressed (April 12):

> Her touch is lacking in inspiration and magnetism, while her interpretations are formal and cold. One of the hardest tests she was undoubtedly put to was performing immediately after Mr. de Pachmann.

Pachmann naturally was quite proud of Maggie's playing and apparently basked in the praise that her appearances evoked. H. C. Lahee recounted:

> De Pachmann made himself amusing by sitting amongst the audience and applauding vigorously, also exclaiming *"Charmant! Magnifique!"* and in English "Bravo Madame, Bravo."

A year later Huneker wrote (*MC*, March 11, 1891):

> Pachmann is a whole team in himself when it comes to applauding his artistic spouse's piano playing . . . he was the best part of the performance, acting as a sort of Greek chorus to every piece—in fact, every passage his wife—who is a clever pianist, played.

Critics reported that the two flirted with each other while he was playing and she was in the audience. But sometimes Pachmann was unbearably cruel. In his autobiography *Steeplejack*, Huneker wrote of one recital Maggie gave in Chickering Hall. Pachmann had applauded "uproariously," but after she had difficulty in the Henselt Etude entitled "Thanksgiving After the Storm," the audience was startled to hear a sibilant hiss cut through the applause. It was Pachmann ungallantly showing his displeasure.

⌒

Pachmann's cycle of three Chopin recitals was repeated in Boston's Chickering Hall starting on April 14, 1890. The response of the critics was mixed. The pianist came onto the stage mopping his forehead with a white handkerchief, and casually informed the audience in French that it was warm. He toyed with the piano's keys in between numbers, interspersed the playing with comments in both French and German about how well he had played particularly difficult passages, and smiled at his hearers as if they were dear and long lost friends. Boston didn't know what to make of this. Then there was the playing, which included musical liberties sure to offend some puritans. The unsigned review in the *Evening Transcript* on the 15th revealed that the writer had derived some pleasure from Pachmann's unique effects, and this apparently made him feel uncomfortable. The review began: "Mr. de Pachmann is so unusual a pianist in many respects that one does not quite know how to foot him up artistically after but a single recital."

It went on to grant him a wonderful technique, but took away the compliment by reminding that all the great pianists had great techniques; it then granted him a "pure and beautiful tone. He never pounds, nor strikes through his tone . . . however, he makes one curious impression" then went on at length expounding the theory that perhaps Pachmann was deliberately doing exactly the opposite of what other Chopin specialists did, rather like a Victorian Glenn Gould. The reviewer ended:

> Yet with and in spite of all this, the man has great magnetism and an indescribable charm. It is a very sophisticated, artificial, hot-house sort of fascination, if you will; we could find no touch of genuine, wholesome Nature in it . . . we have rarely heard a pianist take the art of being charming so seriously; he seemed to be playing to all the pretty women in the audience. At moments he made Chopin sound absolutely coquettish. But . . . the invariable beauty of his tone, the exquisite effects he produces, still remain. We have seldom heard a player in such complete sympathy with the nature of his instrument.

On the 17th the same reviewer published his opinions of the second recital of the day before. The playing of Chopin's Etude in thirds was "simply astounding, and as bewitching as it was astounding" however, several of the performances "were produced at the expense of utterly effacing the original character of the music." By the next day the reviewer had decided that Pachmann was not sincere, and let him have it full blast: of all Chopin's many wonderful qualities, Pachmann has only one— "piquancy." His rhythm is defective: "in some of his very rapid playing you cannot, for the life of you, tell whether he is playing in even or triple time." He played

> With a certain over-strained and premeditated expressiveness . . . very suspicious, self-conscious and skin-deep sort of romanticism, devoid of all true poetic feeling . . . flat . . . ineffective . . . cloying . . . impudent . . . shallow, superficial . . . far-fetched, mincing graces . . . meretricious . . . there is something in us which rebels . . . he perverts the character of the music . . . murmuring and cooing with the most seductive sweetness.

The reviewer, after pointing out the mincing and perversion, ended by reporting that Pachmann had spoken to the audience, saying that Liszt had told him that the "Revolutionary" Etude was poetic, not dramatic; he suggested Pachmann really played it that way because it was easier to play poetically than dramatically.

The conflicted and negative opinions of this unknown reviewer were not shared by Philip Hale, the distinguished annotator for the Boston Symphony programs and the doyen of Boston critics, who wrote a long, purple review for the *Boston Journal* on April 19, a few words from which suffice here:

> How he sings a melody; as though the dead keys were a voice coming from human throat, rich with warm blood . . . He is one of the very few pianists who has what is so lost sight of today, a true *cantabile*, full of soul, full of

color. His technique is such that he is absolutely free of the keyboard, and so he is able to hear himself, to be one of the audience, as it were . . . it is as though he listened to himself, and sitting close to the hearer, by personal contact, by the magnetism of the body, the two become one in spirit . . . when a man like Pachmann plays, we see that the art of piano playing is not wholly lost . . . would that there were more pianists like him . . . His use of the pedal, that difficult point in piano playing, calls for comment. In *cantabile* playing it is most remarkable; one sees that he almost never pedals on the beat . . . in the terrific scale passage in the A flat Polonaise, a passage generally smeared by pianists, [he] used the pedal so little that the notes were clear as crystal.

The *Chicago Daily Tribune*'s correspondent reported on April 27 that a staid Boston concertgoer had told him:

> "If a man has a European reputation . . . .He still has to run the gauntlet in Boston, where every school-girl thinks she is competent to judge him, and condemn" . . . .now there is not a school-girl in town, or a bank clerk, or a saleswoman, who is not prepared to express positive and, of course, original views of his playing.

Ultimately Boston was a complete triumph, and the general consensus was that Pachmann was a pianistic genius whose odd behavior was somehow just the natural consequence of his genius. Additional concerts had to be scheduled and Maggie and Pachmann stayed in the city for several weeks. On May 15 they gave a farewell recital together, playing separate solo groups, but no works together. Pachmann was angry when a piano stool proved inadequate and had to be replaced with an ordinary chair, and left the stage in a rage. Hale's review from the 17th gently takes Pachmann to task for his mannerisms but then seems to immediately forgive him and segues into a description of Maggie's inadequacies compared to her husband:

> His love of pantomimic display was more provoking than ever . . . De Pachmann should abstain from such tricks, for they reflect upon the sincerity of his art . . . the greater the technique the more zealously should the owner of it strive after apparent simplicity . . . On the other hand the repose of Mrs. De Pachmann was akin to coldness . . . there is an absence of real emotion . . . So she apparently plays from preference compositions which call for but little sentiment or passion. When her husband plays an Etude, the Etude is no longer merely an exhibition of technique . . . the Etude becomes a study of a passing passion or caprice.

The joint "farewell" recital was not sufficient for Boston could not get enough of Pachmann, and on May 26 he gave another recital. Two days later Maggie played a recital that included Schubert's "Fantasie Sonata" in G major, a most adventuresome choice for the day,[6] but it was Pachmann who fascinated the critic. Hale wrote on the 30th:

> In Pachmann's playing there are so many contradictions. When you hear him play the Barcarolle you would swear that he was wanting in rhythmical sense, and then he confounds you with the swing of the Mazurkas and the rare perfection of his waltz-bass. His delicacy and sentiment tremble upon the verge of sentimentalism, and he will suddenly be grandly simple. He will play passages of extreme difficulty so quietly that they escape notice, and he will then give molehills the shape of mountains.

Hale could not have known of Mme. Slepouchkine, but had inadvertently described her influence on Pachmann's playing. A few lines later he seems to tie up the contradictions by stating: "Music should appeal more to the senses than the head." As for Maggie, Hale was bored by her performances, writing that she ultimately lacked magnetism.

Boston became Pachmann's favorite city in the new world, for no other American city so took him to its heart. His popularity there eventually surpassed Paderewski's! This réclame among the aristocratic Boston Brahmins, who soon were giving him ovations rivaled only by those given by English admirers, was due to the influence of Philip Hale. He wrote that it was the greatest Chopin playing he had ever heard, and he had heard Rubinstein and Joseffy. Both critics Hale and Huneker soon became Pachmann's most fervent American admirers.

Chapter 9

Chronicle of the Chopinzee, Part Two: An Immortal Epithet is Born, 1891

Maggie was uncertain about whether to remain in the United States for the summer. She had what was described in the May 18, 1890, *Chicago Daily Tribune* as a "tempting offer to appear in London," so she sailed for Europe at the beginning of June.

Chickering was so delighted with her husband's success that they offered him a contract for the next season guaranteeing fifty concerts. He went to the Catskill Mountains alone, where according to the *Chicago Daily Tribune* of June 15, he would spend the summer "exercising his talents as a mineralogist." In a few months Maggie returned and the couple went to Chicago where the ovations for his playing were repeated. All agreed that America had not heard such great Chopin playing since Anton Rubinstein's tour of 1872.

Occasionally they gave joint recitals—really groups of alternating solos (Pachmann always beginning and ending the programs), interspersed with some duo-piano work. While a few genuine duo-piano works would appear, the most interesting feature was the unison playing. This art form disappeared before World War I with the enlargement of the two-piano repertoire, but in its time this was a popular feature of duo piano recitals. The idea was to select a celebrated solo (usually an etude or sometimes even a lyric work) and play it in unison. It presupposed a balance between the two players so exact, so precise and absolute, with no rough or uneven notes and perfect unanimity in dynamics, that the music suggested a tonal enlargement of a solo performance. Among the couple's specialties was Mendelssohn's Spinning Song—a tricky enough piece on one piano. They had great success with it, but were surpassed a decade or so later when Joseffy and Moriz Rosenthal gave some two-piano recitals in which they featured Chopin's Black Key Etude—the last word in unison playing.

From Chicago the couple swept through the Midwest, to St. Louis, Kansas City, Cincinnati and down to New Orleans. Detail work for the tour was handled for Schwab by James V. Gottschalk, who later was manager of Madison Square Garden and associated with John Phillip Sousa.[1] Pachmann was particularly amazed by Negro porters, attendants and stewards, for he had never seen a black man before. He was delighted. As it was his exuberant Slavic nature to kiss people he liked, he showered them with kisses, according to pianist George Copeland, who told the author the story in 1960. Copeland eventually wrote an unpublished memoir with the following glimpse of Pachmann, showing that Mme. Slepouchkine was always with him:

> He had all sorts of amusing ideas about food, and he would go into the diner and start dinner at dessert and go backwards ending with soup. The entire staff of waiters was aghast not knowing what was going to happen next.

As one might expect, the pianist's behavior throughout the tour was extremely unpredictable. If he didn't feel like playing or wasn't in the mood, Maggie would have to substitute. Once in a midwestern town, he walked out on stage and announced: "Couldn't put on my tie right . . . You see it still isn't straight . . . My wife had to help me. Anyway, I von't play today. She's consented to play instead." Without warning or preparation, Maggie would have to run on stage and play before an audience that could hardly have been happy at this sudden change.

In San Francisco Pachmann might have thought he was in Boston, for the reviews were equally enthusiastic. The critic for the *San Francisco Chronicle* thought him more powerful than d'Albert and wrote (December 16, 1890):

> Vladimir de Pachmann's first recital in San Francisco was given last night in Odd Fellows Hall . . . He has many mannerisms, some of which are almost comical, but he has a wonderful touch, which seems to put a sort of spell upon the keys and get[s] a new kind of music out of them . . . De Pachmann's playing does not lack variety. His hands and their action are like D'Albert's, but he has more power than D'Albert . . . the most remarkable thing about his work is its emotionalism. His manner re-enforces this, and the effect upon his audience last night was as disquieting as it was inspiring . . . No one else has had so much warmth or magnetism perhaps, but no one else has gone so near to music madness.

Chickering had him write an extravagant endorsement which was widely reproduced and advertised. According to James Huneker, when he appeared in one town in the Midwest he found that the local agent of the firm had hung an enormous sign with the word "Chickering" on the side of the piano. When he appeared on stage and first saw the sign, he tore it from the instrument and jumped on it till it had broken into pieces. Then he played. Later that night he wrote a letter to Frank C. Chickering in which he said that he was proud to play the Chickering piano but, in his words, "would not be ticketed as an employee of the piano firm." Mr. Chickering, a gentleman of the old school whose sympathies were always with the artists, replied in a kind letter that he appreciated Pachmann's attitude but thank God he had jumped on the sign instead of the piano!

Very soon Huneker changed his mind about Pachmann. On February 4, 1891, he wrote his first extended assessment of Pachmann's playing in *MC* (conveniently forgetting the very negative things he had written just months earlier):

> Americans . . . are rapidly becoming *fin de siècle*—that is, New Yorkers are; we enjoy all that is fine, keen, nervous, subtle, and hate the reverse. That is why we go to listen to Pachmann play Chopin, tolerate his grimaces and whimsicalities, for his mere touch is pleasure; a chord from his velvet fingers is like molten music. I for one have always boldly espoused Pachmann. I did it before he came to the country (I heard him on the continent) and I do it still, and I have been ridiculed for it by some. There is I admit, an unhealthy magnetism about the little bearded bundle of affectations. But when he is serious it is very great piano playing he gives us, not alone from the technical point of view, but because of its suggestiveness, ever poetical, ever sensuous. He played some Chopin Nocturnes . . . and the air smelt of tuberoses, but poisoned ones . . . it is like a new sin, one returns to it for its novelty perfectly aware of the danger . . . Pachmann is unapproachable in the preludes, etudes, valses, mazurkas and nocturnes. He is a miniature painter. It is Meissonier's art, but a Meissonier who has attained to a richer, riper and perhaps more morbid art . . . Pachmann is a humorist, he has just that touch of dainty satire that makes the Chopin mazurka a veritable Heine epigram under his fingers—sweetness and bitterness, honey and gall . . . He is not intellectual in the sense of giving great readings. I'm glad he isn't. I am a bit tired of intellectual artists . . . But don't mistake me; the little Russian's work is from the linear view absolutely pure, but I wouldn't care to hear him play Beethoven or Schumann . . . He plays on the sensibilities of his audiences, mostly women.

Huneker's mature assessment of Pachmann's playing was printed in his book *Unicorns* just before the critic died in 1921:

> It was all miniature, without passion or pathos or the grand manner, but in its genre his playing was perfection; the polished perfection of an intricately carved ivory ornament. De Pachmann played certain sides of Chopin incomparably; capriciously, even perversely. In a small hall, sitting on a chair that precisely suited his fidgety spirit, then, if in the mood, a recital by him was something unforgettable.

Like most in the audience, Huneker couldn't help noticing the pianist's droll, simian-like gesticulations and grimaces. Because of these mannerisms, as well as the pianist's predilection for Chopin, in an inspired moment Huneker coined an immortal epithet. Initially he declined to take personal credit for something so cruel but accurate in *MC* on March 18, 1891, the first appearance of the epithet, "Some wag in Boston calls Pachmann a *Chopinzee."*

Discussing the pianist two years later (*MC*, July 26, 1893), Huneker owned up to coining the term: "the imp, the sprite, the only Pachmann, whom I christened the 'Chopinzee' . . . " The epithet stuck, so apt that it was seized by all the other metropolitan papers, and eventually, all writers on Pachmann.[2] The comparison with a monkey was to follow Pachmann beyond the grave. James Francis Cooke, editor of the *Etude*, wrote there just after the pianist's death ("The Strange Case of Vladimir de Pachmann," April 1933):

> His monkey-like behavior at his recitals, his squat, grotesque figure, and his simian antics at home, all these were emphasized now and then by peculiar guttural noises and snorts which the writer has only heard duplicated in close hand studies of anthropoid apes here and in the famous collection of Mme. Abreu in Havana.[3]

Pachmann actually enjoyed being called the "Chopinzee," and later would sign personal notes with its Italian equivalent, "Sciammotto," (little monkey).

⤺

Pianist Edwin Hughes's diary of his lessons with Rafael Joseffy in New York has Pachmann's name darting in and out of the various entries:

> Once at a banquet de Pachmann was asked to make a speech. He said to Joseffy, "I want to shake hands with you. You are my greatest colleague since Liszt. I'm the greatest pianist in the world and you are my greatest colleague." . . . Once after a concert, Joseffy went with Alexander Lambert[4] and some others to speak to him. He was sitting in the basement of Chickering Hall, "Oh," said de Pachmann, "I didn't know you were coming to hear me today. I played so badly." "You played like a little god," said Joseffy. "And who are you, the great god?" said de Pachmann . . . One day when de Pachmann was in Schuberth's music store, someone asked him why he did not play something of Liszt instead of all Chopin, that he did not give an all-Liszt afternoon? "Oh," he said, "people do not want anything but Chopin, why should I play anything else. Have you some Liszt music here?" They brought a copy of the "Dante Sonata." He sat down to the piano and pretended to read it over and study it there for the first time. He said, "I have

never studied this, but you let me take it home. I will bring it tomorrow and play it." He did so the next day. He said "I have studied it and memorized it since yesterday and played it all by heart." I afterwards found a program of a Vienna concert where he played the Dante Sonata years ago.

Hughes also noted one incident when Joseffy related that he had told his son Karl, "'I pity de Pachmann, he's a little off.' Karl said, 'What is the matter with him?' Oh, he had a bad boy (with a smile looking at Karl) . . . "

⤙

In Chicago it had been noticed that Pachmann altered Chopin's text in one place, but he was extravagantly praised nevertheless. *Chicago Daily Tribune*, November 26, 1890):

The Polonaise Op. 53 afforded another example of the player's splendid mastery of the keyboard, though some would probably object to his manner of treating the crescendos and diminuendos in octave passages for the left hand . . . he played the Berceuse with a refinement and delicacy of tone perhaps never before heard. It was listened to in breathless silence.

On November 28 that paper summed up the general impression Chicago had of Pachmann, "Probably no player has ever been able to put his public into such a state of good humor and enjoyment. Even his eccentricities seem to draw the player and the listener into closer sympathy."
This was amplified in the same paper on March 11, 1891:

Probably no pianist ever heard in Chicago has possessed the gift of making his auditors forget rules and standards of criticism, and, delighted, yield themselves to the sensuous enjoyment of exquisite tones and harmonies to the degree that Pachmann does. He is a player who stands alone, unique, his work almost defying analysis or criticism.

But on March 14, 1891, Pachmann played the Liszt Sonata in Chicago, then a rarely heard work. The critics were not amused. *Chicago Daily Tribune* (March 15):

Musically considered, it is a veritable nightmare, void of melodic beauty or harmonic reason . . . its ideas are disconnected, distorted, and illogical . . . the oblivion into which the sonata has sunk is the best place for it to remain.

Pachmann's first appearance in Toronto, Canada, on December 30, 1891, was at a concert taking place as the closing event at the convention of the Canadian Society of Musicians, where he had to share the stage. In between his playing there was a performance of "Annie Laurie" sung by the Mehan Ladies Quartette of Detroit, which apparently was uninspiring, followed by the Quartette's encore, a "darky song." Also, a Miss Julie L. Wyman sang some salon songs. At first he was greeted warmly, but the audience soon expressed its irritation with his platform mannerisms as he played a group by Chopin. The *Globe* reported:

> His habit of looking around the hall while he plays causes the impression that his playing is often rather mechanical than magnetic . . . his selections were largely trifles by Chopin . . . displayed considerable power in Liszt's Etude de Concert, as well as in the fantasia on Rigoletto by the same composer, the efforts of which, however, were lost on account of the departure of the audience while it was being played.

Three months later in Toronto things were even worse. This time he shared the stage on April 11, 1892, with the very famous Canadian soprano Emma Albani, who had not appeared in her native land for two years. Also on the bill was a blind Canadian violinist named Ernest Willett. Albani was the draw at the concert and three hundred seats had to be added to accommodate her fans. Again the audience's pleasure was diminished by his platform mannerisms. According to the *Evening News*:

> De Pachmann with all his fame and ability did not seem to please the greater number of the audience. Perhaps his manner had something to do with this. He moves like a jumping-jack—as when the string is pulled. Then he throws up his hands while playing and seems to stroke his moustache between notes. He looks half indifferently half pityingly over the audience as though to say, "Isn't that fine?" He received only mild applause, and large numbers of people left the hall before his last appearance, which concluded the program.

The reporter for another journal, *Saturday Night*, explained why people left early:

> The programme was late in opening, and was too long with too much piano playing for a general audience. People like to get away a little after 10 o'clock unless the programme is of more variety and interest and many of the audience on Monday found seven more piano pieces after Albani's last song at 10:25 too much for their money and went home. And I went with them.

It was not the perfect atmosphere for a Pachmann concert, the wrong audience (fans of vocal divas rarely are tolerant of instrumentalists on the same bill with their idols), and the pianist was scarcely at his best when sharing the concert platform. But he had to agree to this maladroit arrangement for he was unknown in Canada.

Suddenly, out of Europe, came a phenomenon. A young piano student named Alfred Cortot described it as "that flash of lightening, that dazzling irruption into our hearts and minds of the magnetic personality of this grand seigneur drawn from legend."

On November 17, 1891, Ignace Jan Paderewski appeared in his first concert in America, at which he played two concertos. Within the week his sponsors, the Steinways, presented him in four other concertos; it was a spectacular debut. Not to discount his considerable pianistic talent, the almost unbelievable adulation that accompanied Paderewski's debut was perhaps due as much to his physical attributes, including his halo of billowing red/gold hair, the dreamy, poetic expression in his eyes while playing Chopin, his lean, muscular body, but most of all, his grand, princely and virile manner. These all combined to turn Paderewski into a legend almost overnight. He captured America's imagination like no other pianist before or since, and everyone—shop girls, school boys, businessmen and especially romantic women (even renowned critics who should have known better)—fell under his spell. W. J. Henderson saw nothing effeminate in Paderewski and wrote in the *New York Times* (November 22):

> Let us sound the loud timbrel of praise o'er Egypt's dark sea. . . . Great is Paderewski and thank heaven for it. If Paderewski has shortcomings, he is a man and not a God.

Huneker fell completely and forever under Paderewski's spell. In a letter to critic Henry J. Finck he wrote, excusing Paderewski of committing pianistic sin: "If he pounds occasionally—is it not, after all, Paderewski pounding? He is becoming a Rubinstein and Liszt rolled into one." Poet Will Moody described him as "that auroral head uttering gold."

Pity almost all the poor pianists who were unfortunate enough to be playing in the early 1890's; they were thrown into the shade. Except for Pachmann. His thunder was being eroded, but he still offered something beyond compare. Huneker had called him "Vladimir the unique de Pachmann." Ultimately the Paderewski craze did not appreciably diminish Pachmann's popularity—there were enough lovers of Chopin for both of them. Eventually they became the two most popular romantic pianists of their time in England and America.

Chapter 10

Chronicle of the Chopinzee, Part Three: Friends and Foes, 1891–1892

More than a music critic, James Gibbons Huneker was a restless thinker as well, and he left a huge body of far-ranging prose, as well as some simply awful fiction. His reputation has diminished considerably since the days when he was thought to be one of the immortals, and the depth of his penetration into non-musical spheres and the value of his literary style are now seen in a considerably less rosy glow. His purely musical contribution, however, will stand as his important legacy.[1] Huneker wrote about his philosophy of music criticism in his autobiography *Steeplejack*. This is one of the things he had to say about interpreters:

> Great artists are secretly contemptuous of what amateurs—meaning critics— may say of them . . . Criticism is an inverted form of love. The chief thing to the public performer . . . is neither blame nor praise, but the mention of their names in print. The mud or the treacle is soon forgotten. The name sticks. There is a large element of charlatanism in everyone who earns his living before the footlights of life.

Huneker fraternized freely with some of the musicians he reviewed—at the time no one thought anything about it. It was a different world, a different galaxy even. In the *London Musical Courier* on May 12, 1898, he had written: "I know nearly all the artists, and have seldom allowed friendship to weigh for much in a criticism." He was attracted by Pachmann's playing but suspicious of his personality. Perhaps he needed to assure himself that the pianist was sincere, that his personality was real and not some invention. He and Pachmann gradually became close personal friends. According to Huneker's biographer Arnold Schwab, by 1891 the critic had softened his initial disdain for Tchaikovsky, and homosexuality "a subject that fascinated him more and more as he became better acquainted, through reading and personal encounters, with artists of all kinds." However this didn't prevent him at first from printing veiled references to Pachmann's perceived effeminacy. In an article in *Musical Quarterly* (Spring 2006) Schwab wrote:

> Huneker was far more interested in and knowledgeable about the sex life of artists than most Americans were . . . as *Musical Courier*'s "Raconteur" . . . he had probably retailed in his column more scandals about musicians than any other man in America.

Like others, Huneker seemed amazed that flouncy Pachmann wore a beard, then the emblem of masculinity. On December 16, 1891, Huneker published the following in *MC*:

> [T]he man is as funny as a jabberwock with whiskers. In company with many others at Chickering Hall last week I enjoyed the spectacle of the little imp vigorously applauding after the Volkmann 'cello concerto [at a Boston Symphony Concert in New York with 'cellist Alwin Schroeder]. 'Bravo l'orchestre!' called out Vlad, for the accompaniment was beautifully played. He does not admire personally Arthur Nikisch, and he took this extremely subtle manner of showing it. The orchestra appreciated it anyhow. I can't exactly remember the details of the story, but it happened in Baltimore at Mr. Knabe's house. Mr. Nikisch made a remark to the effect that 'a little more pepper and salt' would improve Mr. de Pachmann's playing. Mr. de Pachmann suggested in a roundabout way that Mr. Nikisch's terpsichorean abilities would shine to better advantage in the ballroom than before the conductor's stand—all of which was very unkind and unladylike. I'm going to christen de Pachmann the 'Klavierfee' or *anglice*, the 'Fairy of the piano,' for he has a gossamer personality which, with his diaphanous intellect, gives the man a zephyrish coloring (not on his beard, however) which renders him quite unique.

For his part, such comments never affected Pachmann. He admired Huneker, especially after he found that the critic had studied piano with Joseffy, and after he heard him play. In the December 10, 1890, *MC* Huneker wrote that "a little pianist, a friend of mine" had remarked, "For a man that can't play, you are one of the best pianists I know." H. L. Mencken, a great admirer of Huneker, wrote in his *Book of Prefaces* that Huneker really knew what he was writing about when he wrote about Chopin:

> Pachmann, that king of all Chopin players, once bore characteristic testimony to the fact—I think it was in London. The program was heavy with the etudes and ballades, and Huneker sat in the front row of fanatics. After a storm of applause de Pachmann rose from the piano stool, leveled a bony claw at Huneker, and pronounced his dictum: "*He* knows more than *all of you*."

Schwab tells of an occasion when Pachmann tested the critic:

[W]hen he was about to begin a recital, Pachmann, looking at the audience and waiting for complete silence, spied Huneker slipping into his seat. "Ah," he said gleefully, "I see you Huneker. Now I play this just for you." The Chopin he played was beautiful but rather unfamiliar. When he finished he looked at Huneker and said, "How you like?" "I never like any composition played backwards, especially Chopin," the critic replied, refusing to be caught in the trap. "Now stop fooling around and let's have it as written." Pachmann laughed and clapped his hands. "You are very bright man, Huneker," he said. "Now I play it right for you." And he played it exquisitely.[2]

In Boston, reviews of a different kind now began to appear in the *Evening Transcript*, obviously written by someone who adored Pachmann. The 1890 reviews had showed a writer who could not accept Pachmann's unique style, while the 1891 notices reveal someone who was enraptured by it. The February 4, 1891, review of the first recital in the series pointed out that he played some dynamics backwards:

What matter if, as yesterday, he played the great Op. 40 Polonaise backwards, as it were, or just inverted its dynamics, explaining, as he proceeded to take the *fortissimo* in *pianissimo*, 'It is my conception'? . . . De Pachmann is enough of a personage to be allowed to insist on his own conception if he will have it so, and it does not lie in the pale and prim aesthetics of Boston to say that the Russian is not nearer the Polish composer's real thought and passion than the most cultured of Teutonic students of piano poesy. The true way to listen to de Pachmann is to enjoy him, not with the eyes shut—for to see his countenance express his own enjoyment of his playing is delightfully contagious and infects the coldest listener with some of his sentiment, gaiety, passion or what not, but with the book shut . . . He is earnest, undoubtedly, in this unconventionality . . . Where other players seem content to excite admiration for technique and execution, he openly scorns all that, save as the means to his end, which is to get out the musical contents of the composition . . . Indeed, yesterday afternoon after the 'Impromptu' he declared that it was the piano, the Chickering, and not he who deserved the applause . . . In short, De Pachmann is a treat, an exquisite banquet, with plenty of flowers on the table, and the rarest of sweet wines and confections. Go to! Because Boston is virtuous in music shall it have no De Pachmann?

Pachmann was now the darling of musical Boston and his popularity was almost unbounded. Huneker wrote as the "Raconteur" in the February 18, 1891, *MC* that the pianist, scheduled to play in a few days in Boston, was: "So delighted with America that—well of course you know. Any man that can play to a $1,000 house on a rainy day *must* be a friend of the Yankees."

It seems that it was on this second year of his American tour that all the elements that characterized the pianist's mannerisms and antics for decades to come had coalesced. The concert would invariably start late. He would appear, and start to relieve his tension by deliberately fiddling with the piano bench. Then, in his playing of the first number on the program, he seldom did himself justice. He would look out at the audience as he played and say, "This is not Pachmann!" But soon he could feel the tension release and that tone would emerge, and he smiled and didn't have to say more. "He turns his face to the public, fixing them with his glowing black eyes, and holding them in complete control," wrote J. Cuthbert Hadden.

His series of recitals in Boston was preceded by the same series in New York in January, and the review of the first New York recital, printed the next day on January 27 in the *Sun*, was the first to contain references to all the following:

1) His show of adjusting the piano bench
2) His playing resembling strings of pearls[3]
3) His rude handling of audience members who disturbed him
4) His complimenting his own playing with bravos
5) His sincerity and great playing excusing his antics

All the elements which were to become Pachmann clichés were in place:

The first thing Mr. de Pachmann did when he stepped out upon the stage yesterday afternoon was to make a profound obeisance to the large audience . . . Having placed himself at the piano with rather a weary air, he discovered that his seat was too low. A motion brought the efficient stage manager . . . and the bench being screwed to the proper altitude, M. de Pachmann again took his position at the piano and ran his fingers over the keys in liquid arpeggios and scales. The sweet tones rippled like pearls dropping from a broken string. De Pachmann gave an inarticulate sound of satisfaction, and then said, in a voice loud enough to be heard at the furthest point of the room, '*Ein schönes Clavier*'—which indeed it proved itself. Then the pianist struck the first note of Chopin's 'Allegro de Concerto,' but as conversation was not yet quite hushed among the inhabitants of the parquet, he stopped short, folded his arms and looked sternly into the audience. Instantly a dead silence fell upon the house . . . He certainly never played better than on this occasion . . . Of the last [Chopin Polonaise in A major] he gave an entirely new rendering . . . transformed under his hands into an elegant and refined picture of ladies and gentlemen in stately procession, which, passing by, gradually vanishes out of sight and hearing. To indicate to his listeners the idea he had wished to convey, M. de Pachmann waved his hands from one side to the other, on the conclusion of the *morceau* nodding his head violently, this illustrating by clear and simple pantomime his original conception so cleverly carried out.

At another time after a beautiful but intricate passage, so exquisitely played that it came like finest filigree work from under his fingers, De Pachmann the man called out to De Pachmann the pianist 'Bravo! Bravo!' Still later, at the end of the Etude Op. 25 in F minor . . . De Pachmann turned to the audience and stretching forth his right hand with fingers outspread, explained loudly 'Charming, charming' and thereupon proceeded smilingly to repeat the number. There is no doubt that carried to a certain extent, his audiences enjoy the friendliness . . . If the dignity of his pianistic method did not antidote in large measure the apparent tendency to charlatanry in his manner, he might deserve censure for his eccentric behavior. As it is, De Pachmann calls forth pure admiration for his wonderful execution no less than his noble and just musical conceptions. He plays again in Chickering Hall this afternoon.

ॐ

On February 21, 1891, Pachmann played the Chopin F minor Concerto with the Boston Symphony under the baton of Arthur Nikisch, who was undoubtedly one of the greatest orchestral conductors of all time. The performance was received with wild enthusiasm and Pachmann was recalled six times and obliged to play three encores. It was a great compliment as no encores were permitted by the severe Boston Symphony Society. It was both the climax and the nadir of Pachmann's American tour, his performance divine, his behavior despicable.

At that time many of the greatest pianists used the printed notes for performances of concertos (Myra Hess seems to have been the very last famous pianist to regularly do this, continuing until the end of her career in the 1950s), and Pachmann invariably had the score propped on the music desk since his memory lapse in 1886 at the Crystal Palace under Manns, and the *Musical Times* had severely criticized him for *not* using the notes: "sympathy for the performer is mingled with annoyance at the cause of his misfortune—namely, the compliance with the prevailing fashion of dispensing with the notes."

His reliance on the score in Boston led to an almost unbelievable series of incidents with Nikisch. An uncredited writer for *MC* reported the story (March 4):

I hear that in Boston he actually had the man who turned over for him to place the concerto (Chopin, I think) upside down so that he might smile and shrug his shoulders at the audience . . . not only does he get the best tone I ever heard from his piano but attracts audiences by these self same eccentricities.

Years later at a party in Cincinnati, Ohio, Nikisch (perhaps lubricated by good cheer) told a certain Dr. Nicholas J. Eisenheimer about the performance. This account was published in the December 1924 *Musical Observer*:

> "One evening," said the great conductor, "just before De Pachmann's number, a Chopin concerto, the librarian came to me in great consternation and said: 'Mr. Nikisch, I am ordered by Mr. De Pachmann to place the music upside down on the piano.' I simply answered: 'Go and do as he requests!' With unmistakable reluctance the librarian did as he was told. After the usual applause which greeted the entrance of the artist, all was in readiness, and we started the rather lengthy introduction to the concerto.
>
> "De Pachmann was quietly fanning himself with his handkerchief, when suddenly he stopped and glared at the music with the greatest astonishment. Then he began laughing and gesticulating, first to the page turner, then to the audience as he turned the music right side up. His pantomime showed clearly what he thought of the librarian, but his mirthful hilarity began to grow and grow, and finally reached such proportions that he was unable to start the solo part at the time of entrance. The audience was enjoying the situation immensely, and showed their pleasure with laughter and applause, de Pachmann rising repeatedly to acknowledge same. Then, turning to me, he said: 'You see, I receive applause before I have even played a single tone.'"

Unashamed Pachmann was proud that he had a sense of humor, and in an interview for the *Strand Magazine* (July–December 1925) he told Herbert S. Greenhalgh: "At Boston . . . I pretended I was nervous . . . the audience roared when they found out . . . I have a sense of humor."

This was a trick Pachmann probably had elaborated from Liszt. Astonishingly, Liszt enjoyed taking a quick glance at any new manuscript a supplicant composer would bring for his inspection, snatching the music from the composer's hand and putting it on the piano's music rack upside down; he would play the work faultlessly, pointing up his remarkable musical memory and sight reading ability.[4] Almost unbelievable to us today, Pachmann's behavior was excused by most of the critics, orchestra members and the public, and the performance considered a work of genius. The unsigned February 23 review in the *Boston Evening Transcript* stated:

> The singularity of the concert was that the middle number, the piano virtuoso element, like Aaron's rod, devoured the rest . . . Pachmann was all himself in his fantastic ways, his smiles, grimaces, amiable appeals for sympathy, frequent remarks and ejaculations addressed during the most exquisite moments of performance to the person who turned the leaves for him. To many . . . these childish ways of the man took off attention from the musical artistic side of him, or at least disturbed and spoiled the poor enjoyment of it. We are more than ever convinced that there is no affectation in it; that it is all natural, frank and simple; that it is the irrepressible, involuntary, almost unconscious acting out of his peculiar nature; that he so intensely, dearly

loves . . . all the music he plays so *con amore*, as to crave sympathy and feel unhappy unless all enjoy it with him. Take this for the secret of his strange behavior and for a condition to be accepted, and you will surely find an artist in him . . . Did Boston ever listen to a performance of the piano part which approached in exquisite finish and delicacy, in sympathetic truth to the composer, in beauty, in vitality of touch, in reproduction of the spirit of the work, this rendering by Pachmann? . . . it was like a dream, a magical realization of the impossible. Such piano-playing, such interpretation, one cannot afford to lose on account of a few personal mannerisms wholly outside the music.

The same day the *Boston Journal* printed a very descriptive review by Philip Hale:

The seventeenth Symphony concert . . . might justly be described as a pianoforte recital given by Mr. Vladimir de Pachmann with the kind assistance of the Boston Symphony. He was the lodestone which drew the many who lined the walls of Music Hall. He was applauded to the echo as soon as he appeared upon the stage. He was cheered after each movement . . . at the end the great audience was wildly enthusiastic. It was the wish, or rather the demand, of the hearers that he should play again, and so the excellent rule which has prevailed was broken . . . and upon this occasion it was broken thrice. For after the superb performance of the Rigoletto Fantasie tumult was at its height; a Chopin Waltz was no more effectual in appeasing the clamor than the empty tub which seamen fling out to the pursuing whale. It was only after he had given a remarkable exhibition of his prowess by playing a Moscheles study that he was allowed to depart in peace. Nor was it Mr. de Pachmann who was greedy. It was the Symphony audience, and the members of the orchestra joined actively in the demonstration. Music Hall has seldom witnessed such an event . . . It was a rare and complete triumph of legitimate pianoforte playing. Here was a man who has been dubbed by the admirers of the athletic school as Monsieur de Pianissimo; he was in Music Hall with an orchestra at his back, and yet, such is the 'carrying' quality of his tone, every note of a melodic phrase, the most delicate run, the gossamer-like arabesque—these were all distinct and beautiful even in the remotest corner . . . He has been called the incarnation of effeminacy. Was there any lack of virility in the Rigoletto Fantasie? An astonishing individual, this Mr. de Pachmann, as player and man . . . at times he eyes curiously his audience, as though wondering at their toleration or approval of his antics. For, unfortunately, even the presence of that august body, a symphony audience, has no chastening effect upon his mad spirits. He is a man of emotions; are they real, or feigned, or a mixture? . . . has he eaten of the insane root? Who can tell? Last Saturday he tripped gaily across the stage; he was, in fact, hilarious, and the hilarity became contagious. Our symphony concerts are, as a rule, conducted with decorum, as a religious rite. The proper enjoyment of them demands a preparation of meditation, if not absolute purification. But de Pachmann, who breaks all precedents, was the master of the house, and pleasure brightened the faces of his guests. He carries his mannerisms with him; they go with his playing. Though they may be disagreeable, though they may be offensive, they can easily be pardoned; for he is more than a pianist of great talent, he is a pianist of genius. And in the display of genius, the observance of conventionalities is a secondary matter. And after all, could he act otherwise and be his natural self?

An anonymous dissenter seemed to feel guilty for liking the musical part of the performance. He or she wrote in the *Boston Musical Herald*, quoted in the May 13, 1891, *MC*:

Success which was almost phenomenal. Playing . . . in a wonderful manner . . . Ordinarily such a triumph would have given the critic delight, but there was a large proportion of gall mingled with the honey in this case, for this great artist mingled with his work a degree of grimacing, of sensational flirtation with the audience, that one could not but ask if musicianship led to such monkey tricks . . . To turn to a constant expression of emotion merely, to leave the intellectual part of the art altogether out of one's work, is to lower the entire mission of music. That is what Pachmann does . . . the thoughtful musician . . . can point to him and say: "See the affectation, the simian antics, the display of overweening conceit of the player; that is what one is apt to become if one allows technique and sentiment to rule unchecked in music; that is the result of altogether discarding the intellectual side of the art."

Three days later (February 24) Pachmann had his second occasion to cross swords with Nikisch, when he and the Boston Symphony performed in New York, this time in a work particularly unsuited to the pianist's peculiar talents—the Mozart Concerto No. 20 in D minor. Huneker missed the performance but was able to arrive in time for the encores, and his comments appeared in his column in *MC* on March 4:

He played technically wonderful, but a screen really would have been a wise intervention of his manager. Behind a screen Pachmann's playing would have sounded lovely and his odious mannerisms would not have annoyed the audience.

The same issue carried an unsigned review of the concerto performance itself:

To play Mozart well takes the nicest of technique, the finest of finish, the best of touch, and, above all, the purest, cleanest, most straightforward of interpretation. Who has these qualities nowadays? Certainly not that actor pianist Vladimir de Pachmann, who force of circumstance had foisted as soloist upon the program . . . he could not refrain from indulging in those grimaces at the audience and other peculiarities of his own which he tries and succeeds in diverting the attention of the listener from the performance and drawing it to his own impish little personality. That the audience last Tuesday night dropped into this pitfall was shown by the double encore they tendered to the little wretch, and of which he was by no means slow to avail himself . . . If the piano movers had not then stepped forward and taken the instrument away, De Pachmann would in all probability be still playing encores on it. What we cannot understand, however, is why Mr. Nikisch allowed such nonsensical and undignified proceedings . . . It was probably on account of his being riled at this undeserved and incongruous compliment paid by the undiscriminating audience to the clown . . . that Mr. Nikisch allowed himself to be carried away by the applause and to still further increase the length of the program by repeating the 'Waldweben' excerpt.

Nikisch and many of his men wanted to get even with the "player of pranks," as the conductor called him, but the Mozart Concerto wasn't the right "accompaniment" for the prank they soon planned for their revenge. On February 25, the Boston men under Nikisch and Pachmann were to play the Chopin F minor Concerto again in Philadelphia, which gave them their chance. The *Philadelphia Inquirer* wrote the next day that the audience was probably larger than for any other symphony concert ever given there: "It was a Pachmann night, and this may in some measure account for the extraordinary audience." The unnamed critic loved Pachmann's playing, but hated his antics, and the audience came in for a drubbing as well:

Mr. Pachmann is a queer mixture of charlatan and artist. He is a magnificent performer, but his mannerisms—not to use a harsher word—are in exceeding bad taste and it is to be regretted that his audiences are not dignified enough to pass them by unnoticed.

The *Musical Observer* article quoted earlier continued with Nikisch describing how he and the men got their retaliation in Philadelphia:

One of my cellists had the amusing ability to imitate the Chinese language extremely well. So this clever pseudo-linguist was delegated to turn the pages of the artist's copy and instructed to answer De Pachmann in his mock Chinese, whenever that eccentric personage said anything to him. I did not deem it advisable, as was my usual custom, to face the pianist, as I did not trust my own power to control my feelings. Matters proceeded smoothly until the virtuoso began to intersperse his playing with his familiar sayings. As he was each time promptly answered in Chinese he began to express surprise, then he became vexed, and finally alarmed and excited to such an extent that he had great difficulty in finishing the movement. The laugh being decidedly on him, he indignantly demanded the removal of the "Chinaman" page turner. This being promptly done we had, for once, a dignified performance of at least the last two movements of the concerto.

〜

In March 1891 Pachmann played three recitals in Chicago, the third on the 14th an amazing program for any pianistic Hercules, much less a "pianissimist": Schumann Fantasy in C major, four shorter Schumann works, Chopin Funeral March, Liszt Sonata in B minor, Etude in F minor *La Leggierezza*, Thirteenth Hungarian Rhapsody and *Waldesrauschen*.

Later when he returned to New York Pachmann had a run-in with Frederick Schwab, accusing him of withholding money. He created a terrible scene. A few days later, he chanced to meet Schwab in Schuberth's Music Store on Union Square. "Ah", he shouted when he saw him. "I love you so much I must kees you."

James Huneker happened to be in the store when this incident occurred, and in *Steeplejack* wrote that when the pianist went to kiss Schwab on the neck, it turned out to be not a kiss of peace, but a bite so nasty that the manager had to wear a silk scarf to hide the teeth marks. This simian outburst was characteristic and prompted Huneker to remark of Pachmann: "His Bach was worse than his bite." Huneker first wrote about the altercation in successive *MC* articles on April 29 and May 6, 1891, suggesting that Schwab had precipitated the affair by calling Pachmann a bitch:

> Inspector Byrnes has issued an order of search for a pianist who last week in a piano wareroom on Fifth Avenue showed decided hydrophobic symptoms. The mad manipulator of ivory took an affectionate bite out of the neck of his manager, and is now secluded in his home playing the 'Katzenfuge' of Scarlatti. The affair . . . began in banter, the aforesaid manager jocularly remarking that the great Chopinzee was a great artist, but personally—well, not a human being. The great pianist politely returned the compliment . . . but insinuated that he personally was a—cat. This badinage concluded with the little pianist giving the Judas kiss to his manager and biting him severely on the neck. He then coolly remarked, "So bites a dog" and went to Boston and wove dreamy Chopinesque for the bean eaters . . . perhaps the following special may be out in a day:
>
> **Beware of a Mad Chopinzee**
>
> A dangerous pianistic Ripper . . . is abroad. He shows decided symptoms of madness, such as piano playing, biting and barking violently . . . General appearance—A tiny, black bearded prelude in the key of the chromatic scale . . . It appears, after all, that it was a question of money . . . and a very small sum of money it was too. Who was to pay the trip of the pianist one way across the Atlantic—he or the other. Such was the momentous question. In his effort to convince De Pachmann that such an expense was not to come from the managerial coffers the real little Suabian used terms of reproach that indicated his devotion and attention to the canine race (we believe he cultivates a couple) and the Chopinist resented the insult as any man would.

Huneker made clear that he took Pachmann's side:

> He would not touch the Suabian kennel owner with the same fingers with which he interprets Chopin, and that accounts for his not using his hands or his fists. In the excitement of the moment de Pachmann forgot that he could use his boots, but they certainly were the weapons he should have used.

Schwab apparently called the police, but used his position as a bargaining tool, and dropped the matter after compelling Pachmann to sign a new contract. Thirty years later in *Steeplejack,* Huneker explained how the wily manager profited by the affair:

> He did not have de Pachmann arrested for mayhem—surely a Chopinzee then—but, so it was whispered, made an iron-clad contract for the next season, by the terms of which the manager would not altogether be the loser.

Pachmann had other problems in America as well. Except for the more sophisticated East Coast cities with European culture, he was stunned by the smoke, the noise, the confusion and above all, the dreadful food and the puritanical attitude about alcohol. Charles Santley, the eminent English baritone, wrote in his memoirs of the answer he got when he ran into the pianist on a ferry crossing the Hudson:

" . . . How are you?"

"Oh, vat a horrible country!"

"Hush! The people will hear you and may retaliate!"

"I don't care, it is horrible, nossing to eat, nossing to drink, except very dear vine, I cannot sleep, I get no rest. Oh, it is horrible!"

"Well, be patient, you are going to leave soon."

"Thank God! I suffer with my liver, oh, I cannot tell you how awful! Ah! You remember ven I was in London, I was nice pink and vite, and now I am green, oh, it is horrible, I never come no more!"

Huneker made reference to Pachmann's problems with American puritans in *Steeplejack*:

> He was not a drinking man ever, but he was accustomed to his 'petit verre' after dining, and was ill-tempered when deprived of it. Such is human nature, something that puritans, prohibitionists, and other pernicious busybodies will never understand.

The pianist also had to contend with the smug attitude of some provincial piano teachers. One prim woman attended his recital in Louisville,

Kentucky, on October 30, 1891. A correspondent for *MC* reported on November 25:

> De Pachmann was, for the hour, the reflex existence of the composer [Chopin] . . . Is it Chopin or de Pachmann who guides the fingers on the piano? The player's own wits are busy with pretty girls in the front row, to whom he nods, smiles, talks and winks . . . More Chopinesque than ever . . . he Chopinized everything he played . . . Here is the immense program . . . Think what a memory the man must have! Pure intellect cannot account for it. Just hear him play with all the soul of an idealist, at the same time look about the room winking and blinking and jabbering like Blind Tom[5] . . . Leaving the concert, a lady teacher who has lately been extensively advertised in the daily journals said to me: 'That man can't play Chopin, he just stumbled through that waltz—didn't keep no time—he ain't got no soul in it. I play it myself by note and he don't play it as I do no how."

The writer asked the woman if she would be interested to give Pachmann lessons on correct Chopin interpretation.

Leonide de Pachmann said that the constant traveling with scant sleep between engagements was beginning to tell on his father. The frantic pace of the tour and the strange American customs strained Pachmann's nerves. He became irritable and would flare up into anger at the slightest provocation. Disputes arose constantly; Maggie's life must have been almost unbearable. The American tour had been a great success, but it was destroying their marriage.

Maggie left for the second time on March 18, 1891, while Pachmann remained in the new world to fulfill his contract. When Maggie did eventually return to America, it was under entirely different circumstances.

The marriage had been deteriorating for some time. Once after a concert in London one of the constant disputes about money arose. Pachmann was furious, oblivious to the fact that they were in a taxicab on the way home. "Five hundred pounds is not enough!" he screamed. The more Maggie tried to soothe him, the more angry he became. He was completely unmanageable by the time they reached Hampton, where they were staying with her sister Carrie. "No, no, this egg isn't cooked well, send it back again." Three times he sent it back and finally worked himself into a fury. Refusing to eat, he got up from the table and shouted "I'll scratch you and burn you all in ze fire!" and left the room screaming.

There were days when, after such an outburst, he might come back in tears, asking on his knees for her to forgive him. "I can't help it, it's the vay I am." But his repentance made things no less difficult, for the outbursts continued. After another quarrel, he raved like a madman, threatening to kill everyone. He was so beside himself with rage that he had to be locked in a cabinet until the police were called.

On another occasion a discussion arose, carried on in German, concerning an Etude by Henselt. Little Leonide laughed at the funny language his parents were speaking. Soon however their voices rose and the discussion turned into an argument, and as things became more heated, the child started to cry and was sent out of the room. Screams became louder and more furious. At last they stopped and there was silence.[6] It will probably never be known exactly what was the decisive reason for their separation, but a good guess can be formulated courtesy of Huneker, who wrote in New York's *Morning Telegraph* on February 19, 1898 (and almost immediately reprinted in *MC* on March 2):

> He played Chopin as a poet would and had a weird admiration for waiters. No hotel harbored him for longer than a month, and finally he left town between two days. De Pachmann brought a wife with him on his second trip, and set musical circles gossiping, for she was very handsome, very reserved and played the piano in a glacial fashion. She was her husband's pupil and bore him several children, but it is evident that Marguerite and Vladimir did not live happily. He had a habit of screaming in a frenzied manner if his wife used incorrect fingering in a Chopin study, and he was given to clawing and biting when enraged . . . It was then that I christened him Chopinzee . . . a fresh scandal drove his wife to the law; she got a divorce . . . His friends should have locked him out of harm's way years ago.

Never passing up an opportunity to hint at Pachmann's sexuality, Huneker wrote later (*MC*, October 1902): "The cause of the separation has been conjectured and slyly hinted at, but never fully explained." Most likely, this is what happened: Maggie had caught the pianist *in flagrante delicto* with a waiter or another male. She was stunned, told Schwab the story, and left the United States precipitously. Huneker learned of it from Schwab. Most likely the scandal described by Huneker was the last straw—not only was he impossible to live with, and a very inconstant father, but now he was shameless—probably unfaithful with men, and sometimes in a very public manner. Maggie asked for a divorce. She must have been unaware of his homosexuality when they married, but it was obvious now.

⌒

Pachmann played a series of five recitals in New York's Chickering Hall, the last consisting entirely of very weighty works of Liszt, with no transcriptions. The pianist had told Huneker that he was an "ardent Lisztianer" (*MC*, February 18, 1891), an homage to the great maestro who had inspired him just a few years earlier to use his own individuality and fuse it with his playing. As a "prelude" he played the Dante Sonata in the first recital, four big Liszt works in the second, skipped Liszt for the third recital and included only *Waldesrauschen* in the fourth. He got unexpectedly good reviews. *MC*, February 18:

> In the Liszt number [Dante Sonata] he, so to speak, let himself out and played with no little fire and intelligence. What he lacks in actual physical strength he more than balances by his diverse shading and perfect knowledge of his pianos and fortes.

The program for the fifth, all-Liszt recital on April 21 was gigantic: the B minor Sonata, *Harmonies du Soir*, Second Legende, First Polonaise, *Mazurka Brilliante*, the etude *La Leggierezza*, *Eglogue*, *Cantique d'Amour*, and the Tarantella from *Venezia e Napoli*. The *MC* review (May 11) was obviously by Huneker:

> The concert began with his sonata, which is so rarely played as to be almost unknown. I, for my part, only recall two performances of it in this country, of which the remarkably fine one given by Friedheim last season was one . . . the sonata belongs to the very most advanced musical thought and deals with subjects above this world, ending in a sort of apotheosis, or, as De Pachmann reverently puts it, "God." . . . De Pachmann adores and appreciates Liszt, and he brought all his powers to bear to give a faithful and loving interpretation of the sonata, and it was indeed an interpretation. He had evidently studied it in the closest and most analytical manner and had fully mastered it. In the beginning of the first movement he was perhaps a little dry, owing to his intense determination to keep cool and not let his nervous temperament get the better of him. Also in the adagio his pianissimos were a little too exaggerated, and at times one could not hear them at all. These were, however, but momentary defects in what was otherwise a splendid performance . . . The "Mazurka Brilliante" charmed the audience, and . . . the etude de concert in F minor was like fine lace work, it was so fine. Technical finish could no farther go than De Pachmann's in this piece. His fingers just rippled over the keys in a manner that forcibly recalled those of Liszt . . . De Pachmann never played more superbly than throughout this entire concert, and he covered himself with glory.

Chapter 11

Chronicle of the Chopinzee, Part Four: Sobering Reality, 1893

Leaving the glory behind, Pachmann returned to England after fulfilling his American engagements in 1892. Maggie stayed at their Paris apartment while he toured England, giving concerts in the provinces. He returned to playing regularly in the land of fogs where he was a fixture of concert life, but he had to face the reality of his deteriorating marriage.

Maggie remembered a handsome young lawyer she once had met in London; he had been four years older than her sixteen years, named Fernand Labori. He was later to gain fame as the great advocate for Dreyfus and Col. Picquart in their infamous trials, as well as Emile Zola in his trial for taking Dreyfus's part. She had never forgotten him, for she thought he was the handsomest man in the world. According to Huneker's article in *MC* (March 2, 1898), Labori "secured" the divorce for her.

Tall, manly and dignified, he was everything Pachmann was not. Maggie had gotten to know him slightly when he stayed with her parents as a boarder, before she met Pachmann. They had even gone to balls and the theater together. All the memories of those bygone days were revived and they fell in love. Maggie sent Pachmann a kind letter, supposedly as follows:

Dear Vlady,
　You must not be sad or feel lonely. Go if you like and stay with my sister Carrie. She will be, I am sure, very kind to you.

Maggie

We will never know many of the details for Maggie destroyed their letters. We do know that he never fully recovered from the grief of losing her, and though he might talk whimsically, almost facetiously of it, those closest to him knew how he felt. "She divorced me," he said later, "because I played the Etude in double thirds of Chopin better than she." The fact was, while they were married, he used to play the etude considerably slower than usual so that critics might say Maggie played the same etude faster than her husband.

Decades later Leonide de Pachmann supplied the text of Maggie's letter quoted above. He also said that his father was always suspicious about the birth of his half-sister Violette, the first daughter of Maggie and Labori. "When was your sister born?" Pachmann asked Leonide repeatedly through the years, never certain but suspecting something. In fact the Pachmann divorce was not final until August 3, 1895, many months after Maggie and Labori had started to live together as man and wife, and Violette was born before Maggie had divorced Pachmann and married Labori.

As for his successor, Pachmann always regarded Labori with the greatest respect. Many years later he took an apartment in Paris with Cesco Pallottelli. His sons came to visit and he would sometimes give them a box of cigars to carry back to their stepfather. He often told people: "*Père* Labori is an admirable man. They say he is quite handsome." Then he would add slyly, "but I played zee first violin and he, zee second." Pachmann always referred to him as "*Père* Labori," even in front of his sons.

He never forgot Maggie. Once Madame Labori telephoned to speak with Leonide, who was visiting his father. Her son spoke to her for a while and then Pachmann asked to be put on, but as soon as he took up the receiver and heard Maggie's voice, he was unable to speak, standing there with the receiver dangling from his hand. Finally Pallottelli removed it and Pachmann slumped in a chair and wept.

He was lost without her and the recitals in the British provinces were unfulfilling. At Warrington, one woman in the audience called out during the performance: "Play summit we all know, mate." Pachmann stamped on the stage and after the concert, railed about the town's "depraved musical taste." He shouted: "I speet on Varrington!"

Fortunately he had some friends, the Defries, wealthy patrons of the arts, with whom he spent some days at their country place in Overstrand on the East Coast. At one party they had pianists Pachmann and Leopold Godowsky, and the violinists Fritz Kreisler and Jacques Thibaud. Godowsky wrote to his wife on May 25, 1902:

> Overstrand, where we are, has not more than a few hundred fishermen. The house stands on a high cliff right at the sea. From any window of the house one can see the ocean, and at night the roaring of the waves puts one to rest. The air is invigorating and mild.

Pachmann especially liked Mrs. Defries because of her marvelous kitchen, and he would spend hours with the family playing the piano. It was Mrs. Defries who convinced him that it would be the best thing to return to America for more concerts. Despite his earlier oath never to return, circumstances dictated otherwise. Pachmann had contracted to return to America in October to fulfill his agreement with Chickering for forty more concerts, but he unexpectedly arrived very early on a French steamer on July 15. According to *Freund's Weekly* (July 26, 1893), no one recognized him until he signed his name on the hotel register:

> He no longer wore the beard . . . and the change . . . made a great alteration in his personal appearance. He looks younger than before, and on the whole better . . . De Pachmann's arrival took the Chickering people entirely by surprise . . . said a representative of the firm . . . "We have no idea why he came so soon. He came too, very quietly without giving us any notice of his intention." De Pachmann says himself that he is going to devote his time at present to active practice, for he has scarcely touched the piano for this purpose for the past six months.

Why did he return three months early without telling anyone, and why had he not practiced for six months? One might suppose there were scenes with Maggie, that he implored her to change her mind, that he begged and was distraught when he saw it was futile, and that he was too shattered to work.

Huneker reported (*MC*, July 19, 1893):

> Vladimir de Pachmann, the possessor of the most highly burnished technic on the habitable globe, arrived in the city last Saturday night. He is at the Gilsey House, and is driving the guests of that excellent hostelry mad, with his performances of Czerny's velocity studies. Vlad believes in getting ready for the fall season quite early. He won't allow any other pianistic bird to catch the public worm, that is if he can help it.

A week later (*MC*, July 26, 1893) Huneker wrote about the newly shaved Pachmann:

> Suddenly I saw a little man whose gait seemed familiar. His face was not, however, and I remarked to my inner man that a wraith of Pachmann, the pianist, was in town, but a wraith with a shaved face . . . And so it was: the imp, the sprite, the only Pachmann, whom I christened the "Chopinzee" and who plays Chopin as no other pianist on the globe . . . without a beard looks ten years younger and a cross between an actor and a Catholic priest. He has gained immensely by discarding his whiskers, and now looks no longer like a "Chopinzee," but the actor pianist he certainly is. He told me that he is to play forty concerts and perhaps more. Certainly he will be

the crack virtuoso of next season unless Paderewski should return . . . The little man has magical fingers, and I am sure his success will be enormous. He plays into your affections, captivates your heart, but never storms it. That he leaves to pianists like Paderewski and Rummel, who conquer one by sheer power. His soft touch is like red hot velvet at times, and then he is as capricious as an imp and as perverse as a woman. He has met with great success in London and the provinces, and of course he had to make a speech in one of the smaller English towns. He remarked, in that winning, confidential tone of his, that "I am the most unmodest man in the world, except Hans von Bülow; he is a more unmodest man as I, but after him, I am a very unmodest man. I play very, very beautiful." Unmodest is good. De Pachmann has had private troubles recently, and, like all such things, the public will benefit for such emotional temperaments as his greatly transmute all subjective sensations in their art. The one note of passion is absent from de Pachmann's playing. Let us hope that sorrow has intensified and deepened his mercurial, Puck-like nature . . . He will go to the mountains for the next four months to study, for he has not had a piano, that is, to practice on, for the last six months, so he says. At Chickering Hall, however, yesterday afternoon . . . he . . . sounded very much like the old de Pachmann who enchanted us . . . As Joseffy once said of him, his playing is "inhuman," meaning, probably, superhuman.

The column continues in a different vein, telling the world that Pachmann:

Ran up against the great American watermelon on Tuesday, and of course was knocked out after the first rind, or round. He scared the whole Gilsey House staff by announcing long after midnight that he had Asiatic cholera with a soupcon of leprosy, but it was only old-fashioned every day Gotham colic. He was well enough to study with his left hand alone. De Pachmann is an amateur geologist, and is never so happy as when, tiny hammer in hand, he taps a nice fresh vein of quartz. He will summer in the Catskills.

At this time the proponents of a silent piano keyboard known as the "Virgil Practice Clavier" began pushing their product strenuously, and Pachmann was intrigued. Rather than produce piano tone, the contraption produced mechanical "clicks." Hearing these made him decide that his playing of double notes was not precisely simultaneous. In the Catskills he obsessively spent several months working with the Virgil Clavier until he succeeded in playing the Chopin Etude in thirds "more evenly and rapidly than anyone else in the world." He kept one of the Virgil Claviers for a few years and traveled with it.

In one respect the second American tour was different. Earlier he had Maggie, and later he had a secretary/companions to accompany him, but on this tour he crossed alone. Perhaps to assuage his loneliness, according to an unsigned note in the August 23, 1893, *MC*, quoting a blurb from the *Idler*, Pachmann occupied the ocean liner's bridal suite costing $600. The writer suggested the gesture was to keep up appearances, probably because of that inverted humor of his. He was recently divorced. Perhaps he had booked the bridal suite in a desperate attempt to convince Maggie that they could have a second honeymoon and a new beginning if only she would return to him. It is also possible Schwab's contract had guaranteed passage of his choice and in spite, Pachmann chose the most expensive option.

Freund's Weekly (August 2) reported:

> De Pachmann will again be under the management of Mr. Fred. Schwab. It is to be hoped that this lion and this lamb will lie down in peace together and not renew their combats.

It was back to what had become an American routine—several recitals in Boston and New York, then touring the country. W. J. Henderson's reviews in the *New York Times* remained vitriolic (October 18, 1893):

> Unfortunately, M. de Pachmann appears to believe that his performances of the music of the famous composer [Chopin] are interpretations . . . He coaxes from the piano its sweetest and most delicate tones, while his runs are the very essence of smoothness and limpidity. If his intellectual equipment were as large as his technical mastery of the keyboard, he would be a great pianist, but it takes brains to make an artist . . . as long as M. de Pachmann persists in treating his art as a mountebank would, he cannot expect much commendation in these columns.

An unnamed critic reviewed the Boston recital of October 19 for *MC* on October 25, and as so often happened, found much fault, but ultimately was won over to Pachmann's musical world:

> Within the scope of his powers Vladimir de Pachmann is the greatest pianist alive. As an interpreter of sundry moods of Chopin he has no equal, and fails in any music which requires breadth, nobility of conception and sustained fire. Yet the audience . . . could not help remarking that the "eerie" little Russian has grown musically, grown technically . . . his tone is more wondrous, his attack stronger and his rhythms surer, truer. There is about the man something more commanding, and certainly more dignified . . . Such fingers this artist has! Can they be duplicated? . . . Mr. de Pachmann's fortes are usually blurred by the pedal, a curious fault in so great an artist . . . But despite the usual abuse of the rubato and a tendency to over-sentimentalize, the recital was a revelation of the possibilities of the instrument. Pachmann is still unique. Pachmann and his morbid magnetism [are] as potent as of yore.

Huneker agreed that Pachmann had gotten better and reported on the New York recitals (*MC*, November 1, 1893):

> The Pachmann boom is rapidly growing . . . all three concerts were crowded to the doors and the little artist was rapturously applauded. I assure you sincerely that he plays very much better than he formerly did. He handles the instrument with more authority and sincerity. On the technical side too he has grown. His scales are marvels and his tone better . . . in the G flat etude last week his fingers sang like tiny, tender flutes. In the F major study, the concert previous, I heard the prancing velvety hoofs of a miniature pony. Yet what tricks doth he not indulge in—tricks which bring tears to your eyes . . . The Berceuse was delightful and oh what a tender, tranquil eyed infant he rocked to sleep! Most pianists fancy that they have to spank the baby before putting it to rest . . . squalls in chromatic thirds. Pachmann proved a delightful nurse, and it was an "ideal" lullabye . . . Pachmann's art was born under a bureau. It is that which makes his phrasing so short-legged at times. But what an artist he is in his own genre! He has no equal and I fancy he will leave no followers. His is an unique gift, and that singular face, with its veiled glances and desperately wicked expression, is part of the show.

Apparently news of Pachmann's separation from Maggie was spreading; several reviews mentioned "problems" and many assumed they had divorced, and that Maggie had remarried. In the same review Huneker tempered the sad news with humor:

> Mr. Schwab told him of the remarriage of his divorced wife, the pretty, graceful woman who froze the keyboard when she touched it. Pachmann was really fond of her, and when he heard of her marriage to a French lawyer he broke down completely. It was after his first recital and his nerves were very shaky. Finally he dried his eyes and plucking his manager by the arm he murmured in a husky voice, "Lieber Schwab, how much money vas in the house to-day?"

There is no question that the pianist was a chastened man—*Freund's Weekly* (October 25) noticed at his first New York recital that "he no longer indulges in those mannerisms which formerly marred his performances." And in Boston it was noted (*MC*, November 1) that:

> Mr. de Pachmann gave a recital at [Boston's] Chickering Hall on October 26 . . . On this occasion the eminent pianist was the quintessence of dignity. His composure was painful, for everyone expected a volcanic explosion at any moment, but the explosion that they looked for never came. He bowed to the audience almost severely, something after the fashion in which Malvolio proposed to treat Sir Toby Belch, quenching his familiar smile with an austere regard of control.

Usually Pachmann played poorly on those occasions when he was forced by managers to omit his mannerisms and pantomimes; now he was depressed and sad, and the mannerisms were absent for other reasons. Sadness apparently broadened and improved his playing. The same review in *MC* reported: "He was in excellent vein and he played delightfully."

Huneker reviewed two New York recitals in one short piece (*MC*, November 8, 1893), again referring to the separation and a Pachmann "boom":

> The opening number [of the October 31 recital] was the "Allegro de Concert," op. 46, of Chopin . . . Its possibilities were revealed by de Pachmann, as the famous biographer of Chopin, Frederick Niecks, testifies in his very important volumes. Pachmann played it exquisitely.[1] He also gave the Barcarolle, the Fantasy-Impromptu, the D flat nocturne, this last named with several additions of his own and thereby spoiling the poetic close of the original. The F minor fantasy, B flat minor scherzo, D flat prelude, B flat minor prelude, and D minor prelude—the latter a noble fragment, colossal in idea—were played with more breadth than the concert giver usually invests Chopin's music. The de Pachmann boom is growing I think, and it deserves to. The best things . . . last Saturday [November 4] were the F minor etude of Liszt and the interpretation of the Liszt legende . . . Schumann . . . was represented by his "Carnaval," a work which taxes a player's fantasy more than his technic. Some of the numbers were delightfully spoken, but the "Valse Noble" was not noble and the "Chiarina" was actually pounded. It seems as if de Pachmann was venting his hatred of the sex upon poor Clara in F minor. But he gave the "Paganini" in a most remarkable fashion, not a skip missed and the tricky rhythms of the bass exceedingly clear . . . I wish the "Sphynxes" could have been omitted.

This review is interesting not only because of Huneker's bold if veiled reference to the pianist's homosexuality (then commonly misunderstood as hatred of women), but also because it is the only reference and occasion in the huge Pachmann literature which even hints that the pianist ever pounded the piano. Apparently it did happen at least the one time, presumably a result of the emotions engendered by his wife's leaving.

Pachmann tried to mitigate his loneliness with some socializing, on at least one occasion with a young man. The gossipy "Newark Letter" column written for *MC* by one Mabel Lindley Thompson, reported (November 23, 1893):

> Vladimir de Pachmann recently entertained Mr. Tonzo Sauvage, son of James Sauvage, and pupil of E. M. Bowman at dinner at the Savoy Hotel, New York, after which the two went to Pachmann's residence and had a tete-a-tete musicale, each playing alternately.

Ms. Thompson probably wrote this in entire innocence.

Two months later Huneker wrote his last words on the separation and its effect on Pachmann. In a column (*MC*, January 17, 1894), he tells a story of a society affair "on a grand scale, nearly half a hundred people" to which Pachmann and other artists had been invited. The hostess had wanted Pachmann to play for the remaining guests after the supper, but he refused.

> Artists should not have to play for food. Then a young society woman approached him, and reminding him that she knew him well, pleaded with him. The answer was, "I would not play if the Emperor of Russia asked me." "But you will play for me?" and the virtuoso was so overcome at her cleverness that he assented and was led to the piano, subdued but not conquered. Here, however, the trouble began. De Pachmann insisted, like the great spoiled child he is, that she should sit near the keyboard so that he could look at her . . . she . . . had the pleasure of being stared at during the performance which followed, which by the way was said to be exquisite. Mind you, there was no note of disrespect in all this, but simply the vagaries of an enfant-gâté. When he finished he asked the fair lady if he might kiss her hand, first requesting that she must remove her glove. This of course was promptly refused, and she deftly turned the conversation by sweetly saying, "How is Mrs. de Pachmann?" The effect was electrical. Instantly the pianist's eyes blazed with wrath, and he cried out, "There is no Mrs. de Pachmann! There is no Mrs. de Pachmann. She's married to another." The lady then withdrew and the curtain fell with a crash. Evidently the news of the de Pachmann divorce and subsequent marriage of the fair Marguerite has not penetrated into the inner circle. But it had now.

〜

Pachmann's concerto for New York this time was a most unusual choice, the Hummel B minor, a work he had studied with Dachs. At one time the early Romantic Hummel was considered the *ne plus ultra* of flawless finger technique combined with ease and elegance. By this time Pachmann was firmly associated in the public's mind with the freer Chopin rubato style, which he had grafted onto his Viennese Dachs method. Everyone was completely surprised that he had also mastered the earlier style, which to them seemed completely alien. A review, unsigned but unquestionably by Huneker, of the Hummel performance under the baton of Walter Damrosch with "The Symphony Orchestra" as listed on the program[2] appeared in *MC* on December 13, 1893:

> De Pachmann played the work beautifully from start to finish. He read it in a perfectly legitimate fashion, but with a variety of coloring that could have surprised old Johann Nepomuk if he had been at the concert Saturday night or Friday afternoon. Mr. de Pachmann's 'rhythmus" has improved greatly

since last season. His technique almost bordered on the fabulous and he fairly outdid himself . . . The florid runs, trills, all written to cover up the deficiencies of the piano of a hundred years ago, were delivered with a purity of style and finesse of which de Pachmann alone seems to know the secret . . . The last movement was taken at a breakneck pace. All was clear and understandable. There is probably only one pianist alive to-day who could have played the concerto as well as did Mr. de Pachmann. His name is Carl Heyman [*sic*] and he is immured in an insane asylum in Germany.[3]

In January 1894 the pianist gave another series of three recitals in New York, successive Tuesday afternoons in Chickering Hall, making a special effort to include works which he had not yet played before—Beethoven's "Apassionata" Sonata, Schumann's *Waldscenen* and *Etudes Symphoniques*, Weber's A flat Sonata, and others. The third concert on January 16 had a gigantic program starting with the Schumann Fantasy in C, the "Moonlight" Sonata, a Chopin group, and ending with a Liszt group—*Harmonies du Soir, Sonnetto del Petrarca No. 104*, the B minor Ballade, and the *Mazurka Brilliante*. Pachmann played the same program in a recital in Boston's Chickering Hall (both cities had Chickering Halls) two days later, an unsigned review of which was carried in *MC* on January 24. It found "indescribably beautiful effects of color" in the Fantasy, and in the Liszt, "Mr. de Pachmann achieved great things in these pieces . . . his hands were like unto the lightening and the thunder. The most difficult passages were played with jaunty ease." Yet the reviewer intensely disliked the Liszt works, calling them "colossal and bombastic bores." It was probably Philip Hale, who hated Liszt.

~

In Utica, New York, there was a blizzard and his Chickering piano never arrived. Pachmann had nothing else to do but pass the time in the small city, where he was befriended by a violinist named Louis Lombard. He played for a small group in Lombard's music room each evening during the days they were snowbound. Lombard[4] and Pachmann exchanged instruments, perhaps after the wine had flowed, and attempted to fiddle through Braga's "Angel's Serenade." A man who was there reported "de Pachmann's violin tone resembled the screech of a tight cork drawn slowly from a bottle of beer."

He continued playing in America through May. The *Chicago Daily Tribune* reported (May 6, 1894) that Pachmann was cancelling the rest of his season because of "lameness." There seems to be no evidence that he suffered any accident or illness that could have resulted in lameness and cancellations. Whatever caused the cancellation, it did not prevent him from meeting a new young man.

Pachmann decided to spend the summer in the Catskills again; only this time he was not alone. An article entitled "Catskills Hotels Well Filled" that appeared in the *New York Times* (June 17, 1894) listed the names of prominent people staying in these hotels, including, "Vladimir de Pachmann and W. McKay at the Ackerly House in Margaretville already." This young man was to become Pachmann's first private secretary / companion. McKay traveled with the pianist to Europe.

~

Pachmann became mysteriously ill. Cesco Pallottelli later said the pianist had contracted hepatitis in America, and a photo taken in Berlin some months later seems to show him with jaundice. It was the only serious illness Pachmann ever suffered until he was very old. It probably was not contracted from food; for Pachmann fine food and the compulsive rituals he associated with dining were obsessions. He was fastidious about what he ate, the places at which it was served, and the cleanliness of his crockery. It would not be stretching the imagination to suppose the pianist had contracted a sexually-transmitted disease—from another man. What is known is that the forty-six year old Pachmann, accompanied by McKay, went to Berlin to seek a specialist.

Chapter 12

Berlin Days, 1894–1899

In Berlin, exhausted and depressed, Pachmann consulted medical specialists. He presented a sad figure, his once-dark hair now streaked with gray. Never particularly fastidious about his dress, he was now a pathetic figure with a threadbare coat and baggy trousers. The spark that Maggie had kindled was extinguished. His beautiful collection of leather bound volumes of French literature had lost its attraction, and on impulse he sold it. Even those precious charmers of happier days, his small collection of gems, could not give pleasure. He was depressed as well as very tired, lonely and bored. He was too ill to work, and didn't play or teach for many months.

He realized that he had to change certain aspects of his life. A personal secretary would solve many problems. Pachmann was a man and artist with an intense sex drive. It made sense to hire a man who could regularly function both as a secretary and sexual partner. We know that he had found young McKay in America and brought him to Europe. McKay traveled with Pachmann for a few years and functioned as his amanuensis, staying with him at least until 1905. There were other men, among them an Austrian named Günther. Later Pachmann claimed he was a "horrid" man: "I do not like Austrians," he would say. "They are an insincere lot." This bit of prejudice should not be misconstrued, for Pachmann was to say the same thing to various interviewers about the French, the Italians and the Jews. Only the English escaped his wrath: "I love the English, they are so profound."

It seems that Pachmann was in need of funds. Not playing in public, money did not flow from that source. He sought pupils. A pretty American girl who lived in Germany, Marguerite Stilwell, asked him for lessons, and volunteered that she would even pay for four or five lessons in advance. At first he refused but was persuaded soon enough, and began what must have been a most unusual series of lessons. Teaching helped him forget his grief, allowing him to lose himself in his world of eccentricities. At some lessons he would take a candle and place it under the piano, making the poor girl lie on her back under the instrument to observe his pedaling.

In a reminiscence that was published just after Pachmann died (The *British Musician and Musical News*, February 1933) she wrote:

> He always stressed the point of playing to the man in the back row of the gallery. In a certain Nocturne, where the theme enters pianissimo, I was made to play the first bars again and again, until the tone quality, though of great delicacy, still penetrated to the back of the hall. Pachmann may have talked to those in the stalls, but his mind was ever with the man in the gallery, and this all-embracing sympathy was the great secret of his personal magnetism.

Miss Stillwell seemed to enjoy the lessons as much as her teacher, who was forever after indebted to her. She had helped him through a very difficult period and he never forgot her kindness. Later she married an orchestral player in Liverpool and Pachmann occasionally took the time to visit her.

After nearly six months of silence and rest in Berlin in the company of McKay he recovered enough to resume his career, finally emerging and socializing again. He appeared in an all-Chopin recital in Berlin in January 1895. The notices were sensational (*Berliner Tageblatt*, January 15):

> Wladimir von Pachmann's Chopin evening in Bechstein Hall presented the most exquisite delights. The elegant and ingratiating playing of this first-rate pianist showed itself particularly in the two Etudes Op. 25 and the three Ecossaises with brilliant effect, which unleashed veritable storms of enthusiasm.[1]

There were marked differences from the reviews he was used to receiving in England. German critics tended to speak first about his playing, about which they were very perceptive, and then only slightly about his eccentricities. They had after all calmly accepted the antics of von Bülow with little comment. In contrast, English critics usually wrote in generalities, for readers who knew the music only superficially, and while praising his playing, invariably dealt at greatest length with his behavior. Perhaps unwittingly those pretentious English critics had actually encouraged his mannerisms and antics.

It was at one of Godowsky's famous Berlin Sunday afternoon gatherings in 1895 that Pachmann heard the sensational young pianist Joseph Lhevinne for the first time. Lhevinne had just won the Anton Rubinstein

Prize and played at Godowsky's apartment for a formidable group that also included Moriz Rosenthal, Josef Hofmann, Mark Hambourg and Leonard Liebling, who wrote about the incident years later in an obituary for Lhevinne in *Musical America*:

> He unloosed marvelous brilliancies of technic in . . . Chopin's Etude in thirds . . . Charm was one of the chief factors of Lhevinne's art, for he never ranted or thundered on the keys . . . Everyone was enthusiastic, except monkeyish little De Pachmann, who whispered to me, "I play the Etude even faster, and with much more charm."

A much more physically attractive pianist whom Pachmann met earlier in Berlin was Harold Bauer, who was making his debut in the city. Bauer described Pachmann's flirtatious behavior in his autobiography:

> One day, as I sat at Bechstein's large warerooms, trying the concert grand on which I was to play, I heard a stealthy footstep behind me and suddenly felt my eyes covered with two hands. "Who is it?" said an unknown voice in German. The hands were removed. I turned in great surprise, and there stood a little bearded gentleman dressed in a very tight frock coat. He bowed. "De Pachmann," he said.

The November 1896 issue of the *Pianist and Organist* reported:

> Vladimir de Pachmann, the Chopin specialist, has established himself in Berlin where he will teach piano.

A more advanced pupil turned up in Germany: Frederick Dawson, who had become a well-known concert artist himself since Pachmann had given him lessons as a teenager in England. In the interim Dawson had studied with Klindworth and Grieg, and gained some renown for introducing the new piano concertos of Grieg, Brahms, and Tchaikovsky. He had become a favorite in England and, like Pachmann, was especially admired for his Chopin performances. He spent a month with Pachmann in Berlin. Dawson told H. Orsmond Anderton (*Musical Opinion*, August 1921) that Pachmann "played the whole of Chopin to him, not once but many times, and some of the pieces scores of times." In the November 1925 issue of the *Gramophone*, Sydney Grew, who knew Dawson, reported that "when Mr. Dawson called upon him in a German town he found Pachmann in quite low water, and full of bitterness."

Grew wrote that Dawson indicated Pachmann's bitterness and depression were the result of some rupture that had destroyed his relationship with his former concert management in Germany and England. Certainly the core reason was Maggie's abandoning him, but given Pachmann's personality and his record of feuding with Waltmann and Schwab, it is not hard to imagine another rupture with his English manager Narciso Vert, although no specifics have emerged. In the same article Grew wrote:

> Mr. John Eshelby, the assistant manager of Steinway and Sons, who for some years "managed" him in England, told me recently that Pachmann was as difficult to control as a child and that he was incalculably touchy. It was this touchiness of his which some thirty years ago brought about a temporary, but very serious, decline in his fortunes.

Grew wrote that Dawson was somehow instrumental in resolving this management problem: "It would be a good thing if Mr. Dawson were persuaded to write of his former acquaintance with Pachmann, for this episode in not generally known."

Dawson's scrapbook resides in the British Library and contains many interviews and reviews. It is a curious fact that, after the one *Topical Times* interview of 1893, Dawson seems to have gone out of his way to avoid any mention of, or connection with, Pachmann. Perhaps there was a personal dimension to their relationship about which history will never know.

⤶

On November 5, 1897, Pachmann played a recital in Berlin's Singakademie that received more than the usual press for several reasons, including the fact that he played the double thirds Etude of Chopin twice, the second time in a different key much harder to play. *Norddeutsche Allgemeine*, November 8:

> One has to be indulgent, because Herr v. Pachmann does not always follow the composer's markings exactly. He especially likes to change the dynamic order of things once in a while, and the character of a passage, yes even of an entire piece . . . Equally, one can't be pedantic at all concerning his rhythmic sense. On the other hand this artist possesses a genuine individuality, whose particularity is so strong, that it puts even the most narrow-minded and resistant listener under its spell.[2]

Vossische Zeitung, November 6:

> He cultivates a small garden, but he raises fruits so precious that no one else is his equal . . . At the end of last night's concert he was, at first, in no mood to grant the fervent wishes of an excited audience for an encore. When he finally played a Chopin Etude, with purling clarity and the most sensual shadings, he stood up, pointed under the piano and spoke with a slight bow: "All without pedal; that is art." . . . It is indeed art to create such charming piano effects full of perfume and tonal charm, without making use of the una

corda, which makes the sound brittle. Josef Hofmann . . . could learn from Wladimir de Pachmann in this respect.

National Zeitung, November 11:

> A difference between the white and black keys no longer exists for him. He repeated the G sharp minor Etude in A minor, and his fingers glided lightly over them in their passages in thirds. The keys are not a foreign body for him, and are linked to him organically. But the greatest wonder, though, is the abundance of beautiful tonal colors that he got out of the Bechstein grand . . . Chopin indeed remains under the Slavic masters still the Great One, and Pachmann is the anointed prophet of his glory.[3]

∽

The committee for a group of music educators selected Pachmann to represent piano virtuosi at a congress in Berlin. It featured Richard Strauss, Joseph Joachim, Max Bruch, Camille Saint-Saëns and many other great musicians. He worked hard and prepared a thoughtful, interesting discourse. Standing on the platform, he couldn't begin because the long-winded chairman droned on and on, taking up most of the time allotted for Pachmann's speech. It was almost midnight when the chairman announced that "Pachmann will now honor us with his address." Speaking calmly, Pachmann said: "My address is Hotel Deutscher Hof, on the Königgrätzer Strasse, city of Berlin, I now wish you all good night, for I am far from home."

∽

Hermann Wolff was one of the most important impresarios in the world, the world's first "superstar" among classical managers. He managed Hans von Bülow's and Anton Rubinstein's careers, as well as a host of others, while managing the Berlin Philharmonic as a sideline. His wife Edith Stargardt Wolff kept a diary, excerpts of which were published eventually in a book edited by their daughter Louise:

> But how does this energetic man [Pachmann] look? A dwarf, a gnome, in person. Someone of overwhelming conceit. In his madness and vanity, he is really funny. One is tempted to laugh at his extravagant mannerisms at the piano. When he talks to himself his whole face lights up. His whole person is inflated. He talks likes a lover to his beloved, like a priest in divine inspiration: "I played like a God." "Nobody plays like me. My superb playing . . . " etc. etc. are really common with him and one gets used to this. But it is really funny. After a concert, he goes to a mirror and caresses himself, or if he is

not satisfied, he slaps himself. The whole person is a caricature, something impossible. Not an individual, but a godly automaton.[4]

Louise Wolff added the following to her mother's comments:

His touch was fabulous. His Chopin playing was of such fascinating beauty and finesse that it wasn't really necessary for him to act eccentrically, but he could not prevent it. For example, after executing a difficult passage, he would blow kisses to his audience, or say aloud, "Bravo de Pachmann!" and if he was dissatisfied with himself in the middle of the concert, he would hit his hand, saying, "Now you blundered, Pachmann." Naturally the sensation seeking public waited for such exclamations and bizarre behavior, and as a result often didn't take him very seriously.[5]

⌒

Discussing the months of depression the pianist suffered in Germany, the *Chicago Daily Tribune* (May 14, 1899) wrote:

He has not been especially prosperous during the last few years and when his affairs were at their worst, a well-known singer engaged him for a concert tour in Germany, as he was said to be in real need . . . when the audience applauded him only slightly he was furious and said that nothing would ever induce him to appear again in public with a singer. "Rubinstein and Von Bülow would never do it," he said, "and they were right." He was at that time in great need but he kept his word and returned to Berlin.

The well-known singer was Polish soprano Marcella Sembrich. Throughout his career Pachmann was occasionally paired with other musicians in joint recitals, both singers and instrumentalists, sometimes accompanying instrumental partners—but never accompanying singers. Later managers knew of his high-strung temperament with its streak of competitiveness, and were able to prevent mayhem when they paired him with other stars like violinist Eugene Ysaÿe (whom Pachmann admired) or other artists, most of whom it seems would good-naturedly accept his peculiarities with equanimity. Sembrich did not know what she was fomenting when she arranged a joint recital in Breslau through her manager Hermann Wolff. With Sembrich Pachmann faced an artist as temperamentally exacting as he. They were both divas and there was bound to be friction. Louise Wolff quotes Sembrich from a letter she sent her mother about the joint recital:

It was a scream! The piano was placed incorrectly. The audience could not see enough of his fingers. After the first piece he was furious with the audience: "To do this to an artist of my stature." After the second piece, he scolded that he did not get an encore; he had expected to play a certain etude as an encore. At the end of the concert he said, "It's not right for her to accompany me. I am an artist at the same level as Sembrich, Patti, Liszt, Rubinstein, Sarasate and would only have to play my concert—but not like here only to play one number!" Such singers as me he couldn't surpass. "Not long ago I ruined two singers," Pachmann said, "but you I cannot kill!" And so it went the whole evening. The poor man is beside his senses.[6]

$$\backsim$$

Many have suggested that Pachmann manufactured his antics as a way of insuring full houses. Mark Hambourg wrote in *The Eighth Octave*: "he once told my father that when he talked to the public his concerts were full, and when he did not they were empty!" The quote proves only that the pianist was aware that his behavior drew crowds, not that it was his motivation for behaving peculiarly. In the 1880s when he had played in Germany, he had superb notices but the hall was half empty. Now there was a difference—it seems likely that it was the managers who had learned that antics equaled ticket sales, and that they actually encouraged him.

For his part, Pachmann could do little else than what came naturally. His art as well as his personality had grown steadily through the years and each had now reached its fullest development. Many started to attend Pachmann's concerts because of the outlandish stories they had heard. It was in Berlin in the mid-1890s (some say at the Singakademie, while others identify the location as the Beethovensaal) that the most notorious of all Pachmann eccentricities took place—the "socks incident."

This is probably the most accurate of many versions of the story: It was an all-Chopin recital. Pachmann appeared holding a pair of socks and announced: "Meine damen und herren, Ich veel ein speech gemacht. Dies sind die Söckchen George Sand hat für Chopin geknitted." He placed the socks on the piano for all to see, and played an inspired concert. The next day a celebrated critic visited Pachmann and asked to see the sacred socks, which the pianist presented. The critic proceeded to cover them with kisses. "Wasn't that funny?" Pachmann told critic Olin Downes later. "They weren't Chopin's socks—they were my own!"

The story of the socks which George Sand knitted for Chopin became common comedic property, repeated endlessly with variations. Although it may seem too fantastic even for Pachmann, it was substantiated by Olin Downes in the pianist's *New York Times* obituary. One of Pachmann's managers, an eyewitness, confirmed the story that Pachmann had told Downes. Pachmann now had a reputation forever as a clown associated with the music of Chopin. Like Oscar Wilde and his blue china, he spent the rest of his life living up to it.

⤳

Critics occasionally compared Pachmann to the other well-known, eccentric musicians of the day. The German composer/writer Walter Niemann compared the Hungarian Liszt pupil, Josef Weiss (also known as Weisz—1864–1945) to Pachmann:

> It is lamentable that this great artist . . . is regarded as something of a sideshow attraction because of his affected gestures and neurotic, pathological tendencies towards the eccentric and the bizarre. Surely he deserves to be the object of scorn and laughter for indulging, like Pachmann, in this curse of an otherwise great artist.[7]

Many of Weiss's outrageous traits were comparable to Pachmann's, but his eccentricities had a sadistic core very different and far from Pachmann's spontaneous, often child-like behavior. Audiences came to love Pachmann for his antics, while Weiss's nasty, offensive outbursts outraged everyone. Mahler had tried to help him but regretted it, for on January 29, 1910, at a New York Philharmonic rehearsal Weiss threw a score at Mahler, when the great conductor/composer said "good" and Weiss chose to take offense; the orchestra players restrained Weiss and the rehearsal had to be canceled.[8]

Another pianist whose platform behavior included Pachmanesque asides and commentary was Liszt's good friend Francis Planté, the doyen of French pianists. A few years earlier Maggie and Pachmann had met him just before he was to play Mendelssohn's G minor Concerto with the Berlin Philharmonic, a performance that was an extraordinary success. Planté resembled Pachmann in many ways, also specializing in miniatures. His playing apparently combined the finesse of the French school with the sumptuous tone of the Russian. He was perhaps the greatest French pianist of his time, particularly famous for the ethereal beauty of his "floating tone."[9] The two pianists remained friends for decades. In the late 1960s Planté's American disciple, Irving Schwerke, wrote a record liner note for an LP of the recordings of Planté issued by the International Piano Library:

> People noted that, while he was performing, he often had a way of talking to his hands, telling them how beautiful they were, praising them for their response to every wish, thanking them for their obedience. "You surely have heard of De Pachmann?" he asked me. "Eh, bien, did you know that Vladimir, who was quite notorious for that sort of thing, learned it from me?" Later, when I was visiting with De Pachmann, I asked him, "Is it true?" Nodding affirmation, he said, "ich muss admit that c'est vrai." De Pachmann may never have mixed his Chopinesque metaphors, but, oh how he mixed his languages!

Darius Milhaud wrote about Planté in his *Notes Without Music*:

> He would comment . . . while he played; "Pretty modulation . . . lovely passage . . . Bravo! Bravo! Bravo! Chopin!" He talked of Liszt, and "young Wagner" whom he had known. When he had completed his programme, he still kept on playing, murmuring "Bravo! Bravo! What do you think of this tune? Adorable!"

⌣

There was another pianist who was aware of the value of associating himself with the great Berlin manager Hermann Wolff: Ignace Jan Paderewski. In his autobiography the Polish pianist wrote:

> Wolff's agency was the most powerful in Europe—a medium of the utmost importance. To appear under the Wolff banner meant assured success for an artist.

Amazingly Wolff had refused to add Paderewski to his roster when Paderewski asked, before he became an international phenomenon. A year later, in December 1890, Wolff engaged him to play his own piano concerto during four successive concerts with the Berlin Philharmonic with von Bülow conducting. The initial matinee concert was well-received, and Wolff came backstage to congratulate Paderewski and finally invite him to become a Wolff artist. Paderewski haughtily refused. According to Paderewski, Wolff threatened that he would regret it. Later Wolff groveled in front of Paderewski but the Pole never forgot. He may have forgiven, but he never joined the Wolff roster.

The Paderewski phenomenon was a bitter pill for the Chopinzee to swallow. Pachmann had reached his fullest development and was hailed as the greatest Chopin player of his day, but there was always the acclaimed Paderewski whose followers, he perceived, were trying to usurp his Chopin crown. The two shadowed each other all over the world; when one left, the other appeared, and sometimes their tours overlapped. Everywhere he went, it seemed all Pachmann heard was "Paderewski this" and "Paderewski that." Soon everything about the man was anathema to him. He would avoid restaurants where the Pole had eaten, for fear of being poisoned by "Polish patriots." If service in a hotel was poor, it was because "Paderewski had stayed there." If concerts were poorly attended, it was because his rival had played there previously. On learning that Paderewski was to play an all-Chopin recital in the same city where he had just played, he commented, "There ought to be a law against this!" And if critics raved about Paderewski's performances, he rationalized the situation by exclaiming: "Let Paderewski pay critics, not me!"

Paderewski very soon was as famous as Pachmann for Chopin—and he had something which Pachmann never had: like the composer, he was born Polish, a fact which was exploited by managers. He was touted as "the living embodiment of Poland." They had to divide the world of Chopin.

Many felt Pachmann could never approach Paderewski in performances of Chopin's largest works like the Polonaises, which we are told he played with stately majesty.[10] However when Pachmann played a mazurka or a nocturne with his "morbid witchery," he shut the door, "locked and bolted" as one critic said, on any other interpretation. These two utterly dissimilar artists were constantly discussed, and the difference in their playing of Chopin—a world apart—was the subject of much comment.

An unnamed writer for the British newspaper the *Referee* devoted an entire column to the subject (September 24, 1916), citing several historical references to Chopin's own playing:

> Briefly, Mr. Pachmann gives you the personality of this man; Mr. Paderewski regards him as the mouthpiece of his nation. It is probable that Chopin would approve of Mr. Pachmann's interpretations and be astonished at Mr. Paderewski's . . . Mr. Paderewski gives predominance to the surgings of human emotion which permeate the best of Chopin's works. The music becomes epic in its significance. The Funeral March thrills thousands when played in memoriam. It seems appropriate homage to heroes. When Mr. Pachmann plays it we think of a personal loss.

After the Cracow incident in 1884, Pachmann and Paderewski met only once in public. However they did meet privately twice, each time in the green room after each other's respective concerts. There are two versions of each meeting. In the case of Pachmann's concert, the first version was described by a witness, the 'cellist Carl Fuchs, in his memoirs; the second version was related by Josefy, who heard it from Paderewski. Both concern Pachmann's performance of one of Paderewski's warhorses, Chopin's A flat Polonaise. When Pachmann saw Paderewski backstage he asked if he had liked his performance of the Polonaise. Paderewski said he did, but Pachmann wasn't satisfied and became more insistent. "I played as well as Rubinstein, didn't I?" he asked. When Paderewski nodded, Pachmann prodded, "How many times better did I play it?" Paderewski, starting to feel embarrassed but blessed with sangfroid, replied "Three times as well as Rubinstein." Pachmann looked at him in astonishment: "Let's say, seven times as well?" In the Josefy version, Paderewski was studying with Leschetizky at the time when he went to hear Pachmann. He went backstage afterwards to tell him how much he liked his playing of the Polonaise. "I liked it just as much as Rubinstein's, technically." "Heh? Not musically, though?" asked Pachmann. "But technically you admit it was as good as Rubinstein's?" There were many standing around, and Paderewski had to admit, yes, it was.

As for the story of Pachmann at Paderewski's concert, Pachmann told Cesco Pallottelli one version, while the second is from Leonide de Pachmann. "Ah, cher Maestro, how you played tonight!" "Did you like it?" asked Paderewski. "Five pieces you played." He enumerated them. "Not even Liszt could have played them better." Paderewski smiled. "Do you really think so?" "You see," Pachmann continued, "I'm crying. I had to listen with my eyes closed, for I did not want to see your fingerings to distract me." He grabbed Paderewski's hands and kissed them. "You are the most magnificent player of all. When I play those five pieces I will always think of your beautiful playing. With your fine hands on the keyboard . . . and your fine Polish nose pointed at the ceiling!" Leonide de Pachmann remembered having been told the incident somewhat differently: Pachmann (after the concert) to Paderewski: "Dear Ignace, there are five pieces which no other pianist on earth can play as well as you do." He enumerated them with much comment . . . and added "But I—there are SEVEN pieces I play better than anyone else!"

But Pachmann was capable of magnanimity, and quite disagreed with a bad review Paderewski received at the hands of a Boston critic, telling a visitor who came backstage to greet him in Denver (this was reported in *MC* on February 25, 1900) that he had heard Paderewski once in Chicago play a "little fantasie" of Liszt which he had heard the composer play twenty years earlier and, when he shut his eyes as Paderewski played, he thought it was Liszt playing again. He was quoted: "You hear zat? I de Pachmann of Paderewski say zat. See how good I am!" But he was forever jealous of Paderewski's fame, and remained so to the end. At the age of seventy-seven, weakened by his last American tour, he heard talk of Paderewski's latest triumphs. He snapped, "I'm ill and tired, but not so tired that I could not play a thousand times better than he!"

Paderewski conscientiously strove to appear the grand seigneur. His self-created image was that of a great man who by nature would not condescend to professional jealousy; he was above such things and could forgive de Pachmann anything. The appearance that Paderewski wished to create, either by desire or conditioned by his own public image, could never have allowed any pettiness. Still . . . when he gave a charity concert in Paris before World War One for the Gürzenich Cologne Orchestra, Maggie was present and went backstage and introduced herself. "Do you remember Mme. de Pachmann?" she inquired. "Ah, yes," he replied acidly. "I remember Cracow." And when Maggie told him she was now Mme. Labori, Paderewski said, "At last you have married a great man."

The two were perhaps the greatest actors among all pianists. After Paderewski's death, Leonard Liebling wrote in *Musical America* (November 15, 1940):

> The best acting the concert stage has known was Paderewski's ceremonial miming, and the comedy antics of the impish de Pachmann.

When Pachmann died the always magnanimous Pole sent the following telegram to Cesco Pallottelli: "I AM SORRY TO LEARN OF PACHMANN'S DEATH; HE WAS A GREAT MUSICIAN AND A GENIUS."

Chapter 13

Vlady and Lepp: The Chopinzee and the Buddah

Huneker had immortalized Pachmann as the "Chopinzee," and later paid a similar compliment to Leopold Godowsky, dubbing him the "Buddah."[1] Amazingly, the two pianists were friends and confidants, although one couldn't imagine a more unlikely pair. Godowsky, serious of purpose, profound, intellectual, and afflicted at times with the Slavic version of "Weltschmerz," had a round, oriental face and large ears. With his serene, god-like approach to the keyboard, he seemed as Buddah-like as his friend Pachmann appeared simian. They were dissimilar in so many ways, but Godowsky shared an impish sense of humor with Pachmann, whom he called "Vlady," as almost everyone else was calling Pachmann by now. Pachmann in turn called Godowsky "Lepp." Lepp's world-weariness was kept at bay by Vlady's *joie de vivre*. Godowsky was noted for his caustic and sarcastic personality, and rarely had a good word for anyone. Pachmann was vain, narcissistic and jealous, especially of other pianists. Each specialized in an extremely refined way of playing. But Lepp took Vlady's art seriously, and the meeting of these two atomic elements did not create an explosion, rather an unbelievable attraction. The admiration each had for the other's art made them lifelong friends.

Each was obsessed with the idea of pianistic perfection. Though Pachmann's playing was voluptuous and Godowsky's austere, both were striving to achieve an art of ideal purity. Godowsky's playing was sometimes thought to be remote and aloof. In Pachmann's case, it was glorious tonal beauty that seduced audiences, but in reality Pachmann's art resulted from the same obsession as did Godowsky's. Both were consumed with the pursuit of an abstract ideal of piano sound, their playing stemming from branches of the same tree. Godowsky intellectualized the abstraction, while Pachmann sensualized it.

Pachmann first heard "The Buddah" play in 1893 in Chicago where Godowsky was the head of the piano department of the Chicago Conservatory, but the two did not become intimate friends until the turn of the century. It is difficult to know whether Pachmann was more impressed with Godowsky's perfectly-finished performances, or his lush, contrapuntal compositions. Later he became more enthusiastic about Godowsky's music than any other composer's, putting it on a plane with the music of the great master composers of all time, equating him with his idol, Liszt. In the August 25, 1917, interview printed in *Musical America* Pachmann was quoted saying: "I have known, adored and idolized Liszt and Godowsky." Later, with typical, exaggerated enthusiasm, he was not reticent to proclaim: "He is the greatest composer who ever lived . . . greater than Bach!" And toward the end of his career, on his last American tour, he went even further:

> I don't care what they say about me. But they must understand him. I will live to place him besides Beethoven. . . . Godowsky a Jew and I, both adore Jesus Christ. And I tell Godowsky, Jesus would adore us.

In California he was heard to say "If God played the piano, He couldn't play much better than I do."[2]

∽

In Chicago during several months of 1899 and 1900 Leopold Godowsky was experiencing a white-hot spate of creativity, composing many of his transcriptions of Chopin Etudes. Pachmann was in the city to play two recitals, and spent most of the three or four days he was there with Godowsky, fascinated and soon obsessed with Godowsky's transcriptions. "Nothing was more beautiful than to see the enthusiastic cordiality with which the older artist admired the beautiful versions of the Chopin studies" reported the December 1899 issue of *Music* magazine. A year later Godowsky, in Europe, promised to send him copies of several. Pachmann was impatient. He wrote to Godowsky from Vienna on January 7, 1901:

> I am very anxious to learn the reason why I do not hear from you. . . . I am quite at a loss to understand why you have not forwarded the compositions you promised.

Copies of Godowsky's manuscripts arrived shortly, prompting another, more interesting letter:

Hotel Oesterreichischer Hof
Rathenthurmstrasse
Vienna Jan. 28.01
Dear Friend Godowsky,

I received the music you sent me and for which I thank you with all my heart, which is a very small compensation for your kindness and the trouble and expense I have put you to. I intend to leave Vienna for Berlin about the 11th of Feb. and if you have not left for America I shall have the pleasure of thanking you personally. Yesterday (Sunday) I had the pleasure of seeing Mr. Moriz Rosenthal, he having favored me with a visit. We had quite a conversation over the merrit [*sic*] of your compositions, at first he told me, he did not value them much, (having never seen half of them) but after I had shown him the beauties that were combined with the technical difficulties, he opened his eyes and shouted entzückend [enchanting]. Before leaving me he asked me (the next time I wrote you) to be kindly remembered with 'alle Achtung' ['all respect'] and to say he found the compositions 'wunderbar.' You may think me unreasonable for annoying you the way I do, but I shall not be content until I have all the compositions I have selected in my possession. If you have a copy of the Etude op. *25 No. 6* * (in the edition you approve of) to spare, you would greatly favour me by letting me have it.

Mit herzlichen Grüsse an Sie und Ihre Frau Gemahlen in auch von Herrn McKay [Cordial greetings to you and your wife, also from Mr. McKay Your friend]

Ihr freund
Wladimir v Pachmann

P.S. * op. 25 No. 6, gis moll (g# minor) nur fehlt mir noch diese Etude; dann habe ich alles was ich brauche V. de Pachmann [op. 25 No. 6, g sharp minor is the only one of these Etudes I lack; then I will have all that I require].

The January 28 letter, with all its mistakes, was handwritten by Pachmann's secretary McKay, who probably did not speak German, the common language in which both Godowsky and Pachmann were most fluent. The postscript in German was actually penned by Pachmann himself, highlighting his interest in Godowsky's masterful elaboration on Chopin's double-thirds Etude, the one for which he was famous. (The originals of these rare examples of letters from Pachmann are held by the International Piano Archives at the University of Maryland, in the collection of Leopold Godowsky's papers).

Godowsky had been tinkering with the Chopin Etudes for some time, and the transcriptions fascinated Pachmann. Eventually there were to be a total of fifty-three published Godowsky transcriptions of all but one of Chopin's twenty-seven Etudes, and Pachmann played the world premieres of several. Godowsky wrote to his friend W. S. B. Matthews on

June 26, 1902: "He played three of my Chopin paraphrases at his second recital [in London's St. James's Hall] and made an appropriate speech on this most important occasion." Arthur Abel, the Berlin correspondent for *MC*, wrote (June 14, 1905) that both Godowsky's and Pachmann's performances of the famous "Badinage," a combination of the "Black Key" and "Butterfly" Etudes, "astounded the whole musical world." The thirtieth in Godowsky's set, a transcription of Chopin's Op. 25, No. 2, is dedicated to Pachmann. In 1911 Pachmann recorded the twenty-sixth, the "Revolutionary" Etude for the left hand alone—the first recording of any of the Etude transcriptions and probably the first recording of any work of Godowsky, apart from piano rolls.

One work of Godowsky's which Pachmann particularly admired was his complex Sonata, the labyrinthine first movement of which takes sixteen minutes to perform (with repeats). Once in London, a young student named Serge Krish was visiting and happened to play the first bars of the work. Pachmann rushed into the room and asked, "You know this sonata?" "A little," Krish began to reply, but Pachmann interrupted him, announcing: "This Sonata will never be a success!" Krish mollified, "Oh, no, it's much too difficult." "No, it's not that it's so difficult," said Pachmann. "It's the dedication. If Godowsky had dedicated it to me, the whole world would know it. What did he do? He dedicated it to his wife! Never a success!"[3] It turned out that Pachmann was correct that the Sonata would not enter the repertoire.

In an October 19, 1900, letter to his friend and student, the *Chicago Daily Tribune* critic Will Hubbard, Godowsky wrote, "Pachmann is coming tonight to play the Brahms and Tchaikovsky concertos with me."[4] Pachmann was playing the orchestral part of each concerto on the second piano, helping Godowsky prepare for his Berlin debut, a concert that became a legend.

Godowsky gave that sensational concert in Berlin's Beethovensaal on December 6, 1900. It could be considered the most astonishing debut of any pianist in history, and included the Brahms B flat and Tchaikovsky B flat minor concertos, as well as several of Godowsky's transcriptions of Chopin Etudes, and his fabulous version of Weber's Invitation to the Dance. As encores he played more Etude transcriptions, the Scherzo movement from Saint-Saëns' G minor Concerto, ending with his transcription of Chopin's Black Key Etude for the left hand alone.

Godowsky described the event in a letter to the Chicago music editor W. S. B. Matthews, on December 24, 1900:

> The success was greater than anything I have ever witnessed, not excepting a Paderewski enthusiasm. . . . Pianists like Pachmann, Josef Weiss, Ham-

bourg, Antun Foerster and the entire audience actually went mad. They were screaming like wild beasts, waving handkerchiefs etc.[5]

Six months after Godowsky's Berlin debut, in June 1901 at his London debut, Pachmann sat in the front row. The audience was stunned after Godowsky played one of his Chopin Etude paraphrases for the left hand; some were shocked and a few hissed. Pachmann jumped up from his seat. Instantly recognized, he gave the audience a withering glance and walked up to his friend and whispered something from the footlights. Godowsky went back to the piano and played the work again.[6] After the concert he went backstage to the artist's room. Many wellwishers were waiting in a line to congratulate Godowsky, but when some of them saw Pachmann they deserted Godowsky and surrounded Pachmann. "No, ladies," he exclaimed, according to Krish. "No autographs tonight. You come to my concert first."[7]

The June 1901 *Musical Record* printed a review comparing the two:

> The playing of the great Chopin pianists who have appeared during the month has been full of interest. One may divide it into two schools. The first school is that of M. de Pachmann and Mr. Leopold Godowsky. These artists give us all the absolute musical beauty of Chopin's music. Madame Carreño and Paderewski stress on the emotional side. . . . Pachmann is unapproachable in the smaller Chopin, and I think the composer himself, with his delicacy of technique, must have played his own music in much the same way. Godowsky has the same delicate perfection, but then he does not possess Pachmann's lyrical sense.

～◯

Delia [Cordelia] Porthan Defries was a young girl when she met Pachmann, who was visiting her family's summer home. Later she wrote a reminiscence for the *Godowsky Society Bulletin*:

> I was with my mother walking down Regent Street when we ran into Vlady (as everyone called Pachmann) and he began to enthuse about the then-unknown Godowsky. I can see the scene, the excitable little man shrieking down my mother's ear trumpet (she was very deaf and carried an ear trumpet swathed in black lace) to the amusement of passerbys. Vlady was screaming in his funny English about Godowsky. "I bring you ze second greatest pianist, first myself but second is Godowsky."

The Defries family soon adopted Godowsky as they had Pachmann, and they began to cater to and spoil the Buddah of the piano as they did the Chopinzee. Godowsky stayed with them often at both their London and country houses. On May 25, 1902, Godowsky wrote to his wife: "Mrs. Defries is all the time worrying what she could do for me or give me to make me happy. They all study my whims and wishes and satisfy them before I have a chance to wish for anything."

By 1900 Pachmann was an international star commanding enormous fees, renowned as one of the greatest pianists of the day, while Godowsky was still at the verge of what was to be a somewhat smaller career. Even with his Olympian detachment, his modern insistence on textual fidelity in which every note must be justified, every rest and dotted note played exactly, Godowsky still felt that Pachmann's Chopin playing was authentic, and that his rubato was "genius." Godowsky had written to Will Hubbard from Paris (August 16, 1900):

> Of all the pianists I have heard during the past winter I liked Pachmann the most and Hambourg the least. Pachmann's playing is like a delicate and exquisitely scented perfume—evaporating, volatile, refined, suggestive, enchanting. . . . Pachmann was so impressed with my work that he acted like a maniac. He is studying a good many of my things and intends to play them everywhere next season.[8]

Often Vlady's enthusiasm was an embarrassment for Lepp, who was as shy and retiring in public as Pachmann was outgoing and ingenuous. Godowsky was absolutely horrified if Pachmann spied him in the audience at a concert, for he might do something outrageous—but he couldn't stay away from Pachmann's recitals. At one he was spotted and Pachmann declared to the audience: "There's Godowsky. He can play the next encore." After another recital Godowsky told Pachmann: "I envy your touch!" Pachmann, with typical lack of modesty, answered, "Ah, well you may." Another time, according to Godowsky's son-in-law David Saperton, Pachmann saw him and covered his hands, exclaiming "I don't want him to see my fingering!" In *MC* (February 11, 1933), Leonard Liebling wrote about another time when Pachmann was in the front row of the audience for a joint recital Godowsky was giving with Ysaÿe. When Lepp played an A major chord for the violinist to tune, he was horrified to hear Vlady yelling "Bravo."

At a Berlin recital Pachmann began by making a few false starts, and interrupted the performance that had hardly begun. He got up from the piano and peered out into the darkened hall, calling out while gesticulating with his finger "Godowsky? Godowsky!" He knew Lepp was there but couldn't see him. Lepp had hidden. "Godowsky? Godowsky? Is he here?" asked Pachmann. Many in the audience recognized Godowsky but no one betrayed him. Once again Pachmann called out, "Godowsky . . . is he *here*?" Still silence . . . no one breathed. There was a pause. Pachmann reflected a moment, peered out into the hall once more, and said "Surely my friend Godowsky is here." Shutting the lid of the piano, he told the uncooperative audience, "No Godowsky, no concert!" Becoming impatient and restless, they took up Pachmann's cry and began chanting: "Go-dow-sky, Go-dow-sky." Poor Lepp, what could he do but toddle unhappily up to the platform, where Vlady, beaming radiantly, greeted him publicly. "Ah, Lepp, my friend Lepp." To Godowsky's mortification, he kissed him at the top of his bald head. Laughter swept the hall but his ordeal was not yet over. "Ladies and Gentlemen, here is Godowsky, the greatest pianist of our day. Yes, he is even greater than Pachmann." Here he paused and smiled beatifically at Godowsky "but Pachmann plays more *beautifully.*"

Godowsky wrote to his wife on January 20, 1902:

> Pachmann was invited yesterday by Mr. Baird, but he would not go because he shaved the day before and would not shave again on the following day and he did not want to put on full dress! Lindler [co-owner of the Bechstein piano firm] *never* invited him to the house and never will, though he plays the B. piano for many years. He is as eccentric and sometimes as unbearable as ever before.

On more than one occasion when Pachmann spied Godowsky in the audience at one of his recitals, he tried to get his friend to come up and play an encore. On August 15, 1908, the *Wiltshire Times* published an article Godowsky had written, mentioning an incident that occurred at Pachmann's last recital a year earlier in the Queen's Hall:

> I was in the artiste's room, and after he had been recalled several times, he rushed behind me, seizing me by the coat, told me that he absolutely insisted upon my playing. . . . I was obliged . . . to slip out of my coat and take flight.

Pachmann took Godowsky's coat and triumphantly showed it to his audience: "I couldn't bring Godowsky, but here's his coat!"

Outwardly so different, Godowsky reserved, Pachmann unbuttoned and flamboyant, perhaps their personalities were more similar than people realized, and few today realize that Godowsky's temperament was at times as eccentric as Pachmann's. Once in the 1920s Godowsky was performing Chopin's E minor Concerto. Mrs. Godowsky was sitting next to one of her husband's pupils and they were startled when, in the first movement, Godowsky suddenly got up and shook his fist at the piano. There followed the long process of getting the tuner on stage to fix the problem; everyone, the orchestra, conductor, audience, had to wait. The pupil asked Mrs. Godowsky what it was; she had no idea. Much later, days, weeks after, he asked her again. She laughed: apparently Godowsky had hit a wrong note. He didn't want anyone to know, and had deliberately created a big diversion.[9]

&

Pachmann was one of the earliest famous pianists to play Godowsky's music in public. A fearsome jungle of pianistic difficulties, few pianists conquered it until recently. He learned several Godowsky works including six pieces from the *Walzermasken,* five of the Chopin Etude transcriptions and the most difficult of all, the "Symphonic Metamorphosis" on Weber's "Invitation to the Dance," which is one of the most formidable compositions ever written for the piano.

Godowsky had transcribed "Invitation to the Dance" as a trump card when he made his Berlin debut. At that time the reigning favorite was Busoni, and this fantastically complicated work was designed to be *the* piece with which he would triumph over Busoni, with whom he began playing alternate, dueling recitals in the city. In a sly gesture Godowsky dedicated the work to Busoni when it was published in 1905. However, Godowsky privately dedicated the work to Pachmann on an album page, and the dedication was accepted.

Huneker wrote about it in *MC* on April 25, 1900:

last week, in private, Vladimir de Pachmann played it from the Godowsky manuscript. . . . It is purely a contrapuntal, and therefore a musicianly arrangement, and only formidable in the formidable volleys of double notes, thirds, fourths, sixths, whenever the scale runs occur, is there a suggestion of virtuosity. It is naturally enough virtuosity, but on an ideal plane. Few will dare its orchestral and "pianistic" difficulties. And how it sounds! How rich in odor and texture! Godowsky plays it phenomenally, and De Pachmann rivals him in brilliancy and finger distinction in this particular piece. No one has the Pachmann finger velocity, delicacy and clarity. It is a muscular gift; it is simian, perhaps, yet there it is, and it sometimes steals away its owner's brains.

The occasion Huneker speaks of was at his own home. Twenty years later in his autobiography *Steeplejack* Huneker wrote an extended description of the evening:

After eating a duck, a kotchka, cooked Polish fashion, and borsch, beet soup, with numerous Slavic side dishes, preceded by the inevitable zakushka . . . de Pachmann fiercely demanded cognac. . . . I was embarrassed. Not drinking spirits, I had inconsiderately forgotten the taste of others. De Pachmann, who is a child at heart, too often a naughty child, cried to heaven that I was a hell of a host! He said this in Russian, then in French, Italian, German, Polish, Spanish, English, and wound up with a hearty Hebrew "Raca!" which may mean hatred, or revenge, certainly something not endearing. But the worst was to come. There stood my big Steinway concert grand piano, and he circled about the instrument as if it were a dangerous monster. Finally he sniffed and snapped: "My contract does not permit me to play a Steinway."[10] I hadn't thought of asking him. . . . And then this wizard lifted the fallboard of my piano, and quite forgetful about that "contract," began playing. And how he did play! Ye Gods! Bacchus, Apollo, and Venus, and all other pleasant celestial persons, how you must have reveled when de Pachmann played! In the more intimate atmosphere of my apartment his music was of a gossamer web, iridescent, aerial, an Aeolian harp doubled by a diabolic subtlety. Albert Ross Parsons, one of the few living pupils of Tausig, in reply to my query: How did Joseffy compare with Tausig? Answered: "Joseffy was like the multi-colored mist that encircled a mighty mountain; but beautiful." So Pachmann's weaving enchantments seemed in comparison to Godowsky's profounder playing. And what did Vladimir, hero of double-notes, play? Nothing but Godowsky, then new to me. Liszt had been his god, but Godowsky was becoming his living deity. He had studied, mastered, and memorized all those transcendental variations on Chopin studies, the most significant variations since the Brahms-Paganini scaling of the heights of Parnassus; and I heard for the first time the paraphrase of Weber's "Invitation to the Valse," a much more viable arrangement than Tausig's; also thrice as difficult. However, technique, as sheer technique, does not enter into the musical zone of Godowsky. He has restored polyphony to its central position, thus bettering in that respect Chopin, Schumann, and Liszt. . . . De Pachmann delighted his two auditors that night from 10 P.M. to 3 A.M. . . . When he left, happy over his triumph—I was actually flabbergasted by the new music—he whispered: "Hein! What you think! You think I can play this wonderful music? You are mistaken? You are mistaken. Wait till you hear Leopold Godowsky play. We are all woodchoppers, compared with him." Curiously enough, the last is the identical phrase uttered by Anton Rubinstein in regard to Franz Liszt. Perhaps it was a quotation, but de Pachmann meant it. It was the sincerest sentiment I had heard from his often insincere lips.

⌣⌐

Godowsky's music was ahead of its time, like most music by master composers. Pachmann's attempts to win the public over to an appreciation of Godowsky's works were almost always failures, the critics praising his playing but condemning the compositions, although Leonard Liebling wrote in *MC* on December 7, 1904:

And why did the willful Wladimir not give us Weber's Rondo [the "Perpetual Motion" movement from the Sonata Op. 24] in the excellent Godowsky version. . . . And lastly, why was de Pachmann's trump card omitted—the transcendental Godowsky arrangement of Weber's "Invitation to the Dance?" All these things de Pachmann plays marvelously in private. . . . Pianists are strange folk. They all admire Godowsky's work but they do not play him. Can anyone explain the connection?

Pachmann knew better. He tried to sneak some Godowsky into his recitals, but it didn't work, and the response was usually negative. The Chopinzee had no greater advocate than the English writer Arthur Symons, who reviewed Pachmann's all-Chopin recital at London's St. James's Hall about 1902, incorporating part of the review in an essay on Pachmann: "There were encores, interspersed with conversation, and there was the horrible tour de force of playing two pieces at the same time."[11]

On August 16, 1900, Godowsky also wrote to his disciple Maurice Aronson:

Pachmann is studying hard on my version of "Invitation to the Dance." And hopes to play it in his second recital. He goes as much, if not more, in extasies [sic] over my work, and advertizes me wherever he goes. Manager Wolff says that Pachmann is 'Godowsky-mad!

But within a few months it seems de Pachmann had temporarily given up trying to master the work, for Godowsky wrote to his wife on April 21, 1901: "Pachmann now disliking my 'Invitation' is a case of sour grapes. He can't play it!" We know this can't be absolutely correct, for we have Huneker's rhapsodical description of Pachmann playing the work in private a year earlier. Perhaps Godowsky meant that "He can't play it in public!"

Pachmann secretly continued trying to master Godowsky's "Invitation to the Dance." The March 20, 1905, *Chicago Daily Tribune* reported that he had played a recital the day before, selling out Chicago's Studebaker Hall. The program stated simply "Weber: Invitation to the Dance." The reviewer knew he was hearing a transcription when Pachmann played the work, but he incorrectly thought it was Pachmann's own:

he added his own transcription of the Weber "Invitation to the Dance." It proved an overelaborated and, as played by him yesterday, a distorted and inartistic perversion of the work.

The review ended by pointing out that Pachmann, quite unusually, had made mistakes. Pachmann probably never played the transcription in public again.

In a letter to his wife dated London, June 17, 1906, Busoni wrote:

Yesterday I heard part of M. Hambourg's concert and then went for a moment to Pachmann's. He had just finished "Invitation to the Dance" [Weber's original]. As the public applauded, he showed with his hands that he wished to speak. "Mr. Godowsky," he said—"has made an arrangement of this piece—*very* difficult—he can't play it himself—he he. I—he—he—don't play it yet before the public-must be careful—careful—careful—he—he—he" and went on laughing and shrugging his shoulders.

Busoni's letter captured Pachmann's typically spontaneous and unbuttoned speech accurately, while five years later the *New York Times* carried a much more edited, if less colorful interview with Pachmann about Godowsky's transcriptions (October 30, 1911):

I only have learned a few of Godowsky's transcriptions of Chopin . . . but I have played over by myself all of Godowsky's work in this direction and I can scarcely tell how great I believe it to be. His original work may not be so fine, but his transcriptions are wonderful and very difficult. Who can play them? Only a few. They demand a special technique of their own. Godowsky himself perhaps does not bring to them all the supreme qualities they need. He has written an arrangement of Weber's "Invitation to the Dance" and dedicated it to Busoni, but Busoni has never yet played it in public. I, too, play it in my own room and leave public performances of it to Godowsky. What an astounding thing it is—three of Weber's themes played against each other in the most marvelously brilliant manner. There is but one Godowsky.

Pachmann's fascination with Godowsky's music lasted his lifetime and he continued playing the music until the end, when it became a kind of new lease on life. When he was seventy-six years old he told an interviewer (*MC*, June 26, 1924):

I have lived for the last seven years on the Godowsky Walzermasken. When I got to be seventy years I thought it was time to stop. But then I invented my new method of playing, and just about the same time discovered that marvelous set of compositions by Godowsky, the twenty-four Walzermasken. I made a selection from them and every day since then—this is literally— I have practiced them religiously. The method and the compositions revived my interest in life and art. If I had not found them, I am sure I should be nothing but a doddering old man.

An undated, holograph manuscript found among Godowsky's papers outlines his opinions of several of the great pianists he heard:

Often I was asked by intelligent persons which pianist I considered the greatest I had ever heard. This is a question to which I cannot conscientiously reply. Each great artist has an individuality, technique, purpose, influence of his own, differing materially from his colleagues. . . . The most unique pianist I have ever heard was de Pachmann. His playing had such irresistible charm that he could put all logic aside and turn the composition topsy-turvy and still remain most fascinating. He was a necromancer.

His touch was feline. He addressed me once when we were alone while he was in a confidential mood thus: Lepp, you know so much more than I do, tell me what are my shortcomings and what is wrong with my playing. I replied: Vladi, everything you are doing at the piano is against logic and style, and would be impossible for anyone else to get away with; but when you indulge in your extravagances the result is inimitably delightful—sublime. I could correct every phase of your art, but the consequence would be the loss of your unique personality.[12]

When Pachmann died, Godowsky told a reporter for the *New York Times* (January 9, 1933):

The world has lost its most unique artist. His field was limited, but within its narrow range he was supreme and inimitable. Although he was a miniaturist, his art was one of the greatest and the impression he made upon me is unforgettable. I do not believe his eccentricities were affectations. His own art affected him so strongly and he was so wrapped up in it that he forgot the conventionalities and took his audiences into his confidence. There will never be another de Pachmann.

Chapter 14

The Voluptuary

Beneath Pachmann's childlike and often perverse personality was a very sensitive and sensual man. The beauty and sensuousness of his piano sound was reflected by his other great passions: fine food, the pleasures of Havana cigars and a passion for gemstones, which inspired the exquisiteness of the actual sounds he made.

Spoiled early by his sister and Madame Slepouchkine, he developed a love of rich, savory food, but it was not until he started to earn huge sums that he was he able to indulge this passion to the fullest. After that his life resembled a gastronomic road map. Wherever he traveled, whether at London's Pagani's or the Café Royale, or in Paris at Marguery's or Henri's, or in New York at Café Martin, not forgetting Rome's Ranieri's, he always ate well. Late in life he was quoted by journalist Kurt Welling in the October 1923 issue of the *Musician*:

> "There are for me two things in the world," he is reported to have said, "First and ever my music. When I sit down to play I am Pachmann, the musician. But when I sit down to the table to eat I am Pachmann, the gourmet, Pachmann, the man. Gastronomy is the other part of my life and I pay attention to the homage it deserves. All my life I have eaten and drunk as I willed and for the rest of my life I intend to do the same. On my deathbed if I have the strength I hope to be able to eat a last good hearty meal."

Leonide de Pachmann told of a memory of his youth—his father took him and his brother Adrian to dine at Henri's. After a magnificent meal, Pachmann insisted on congratulating the staff. He sat at a wheezy old piano and all the chefs were lined up in their toques and listened as Pachmann inappropriately played the first movement of the "Moonlight" Sonata.

Food was so important that even a car wreck couldn't keep him from a good meal. The legendary executive of His Master's Voice who recorded Pachmann for the last two decades of his career, Fred Gaisberg, wrote in his *The Music Goes Round*:

> One rainy evening, after a recital in Cincinnati, a car was carrying him and his secretary to a supper party to be given in his honor, when it overturned. As the little pianist was extricated from the wreckage more dead than alive, he is said to have remarked pettishly: "Now we will be late for supper and they will have eaten all the food."

As one can imagine, he was very difficult to please, for food had to be cooked to his precise specifications, and it was sent back if the slightest detail of preparation or presentation was considered wrong. Over the years Pachmann had developed a paranoid fear of being poisoned, which progressed to a neurotic mania—everyone was familiar with it. The great restaurateurs of the day kept special plates and silverware set aside for his use. Pachmann dreaded microbes as well, and always ordered the special service cleaned anew until everything was spotless.

One of manager Lionel Powell's favorite Pachmann stories concerned an invitation from Queen Alexandra to play for her at Marlborough House. Afterwards they were to have tea when Pachmann wiped out his tea cup with the linen napkin. In horror, Powell began to whisper words of excuse to the Queen, who interrupted, "I love it!"

Another time when he was seated next to Godowsky at a formal dinner, he kept switching the plates—putting his food in front of Leopold and placing Godowsky's in front of himself. At first Godowsky smiled indulgently, but when Pachmann accidentally spilled some soup on him, it was too much: "What is wrong Vlady, what is the matter? Look what you've done!" Pachmann looked up with surprise and consternation: "It is the vaiter, Lepp. I'm sure he's one of Paderewski's Polish patriots, who have come to poison me!" Pachmann behaved this way even in front of people he hardly knew. When he felt his life was in danger, it mattered not whether his companion was a mere acquaintance or his closest friend. "They are jealous of Pachmann's fingers," he whispered.

He wouldn't eat the whites of eggs, and if he felt that the waiter had looked at him strangely or the atmosphere was not congenial, he would even refuse to touch a restaurant's silver. He wouldn't drink anything from a metal container. Composer Dmitri Tiomkin remembered seeing Pachmann at lunch in the 1920s, so afraid of contamination that he was pouring his soup through a spaghetti strainer to filter out the germs. This fastidiousness could be a problem for companions. Arthur Friedheim wrote in his *Life and Liszt*:

There was the time in Vienna when Vladimir de Pachmann asked me to dine with him one noon. It was summer, and I arrived in a suit of immaculate white. Steaks had been ordered. The waiter set them down. A look of exaggerated fastidiousness spread across de Pachmann's face. He took his fork, lifted his whole steak to his nose and shuddered with distaste. "This steak!" he complained. "I cannot eat it! It stinks!" And he held it out at arm's length—over my white coat and trousers—and the dripping juices of that rare steak settled one costume for good and all. One day in London I ran into him on the street. "How long are you going to stay in the city?" I asked. "Why?" inquired de Pachmann in the peevish tone he liked to affect sometimes, a whine like that of a spoiled child. "Because you have not been to our house for ages. Will you come?" "Of course. Make a date." A time was settled upon. "As I recall it," I continued, "You are difficult to please in the matter of food. What would you like to have to eat?" De Pachmann seemed offended. "Why do you say that?" "Because I remember so well our last meal together in Vienna when the steak did not seem to please you." De Pachmann's face broke into a grin. "Oh, don't bother about me. I eat everything now. Cat's meat is good enough for me at your house." He referred, of course, to the skewers of horsemeat commonly sold in London for the feeding of cats and not the flesh of cats.

Often Pachmann's humor was not without wit. Friedheim tells of a large dinner party in Montreal which he and Pachmann attended:

A clergyman was seated opposite de Pachmann, and he seemed to know the pianist's reputation for drollery without fully understanding the form it usually took. Throughout the meal he lost no opportunity of teasing the all too temperamental artist. What the clergyman did not know, of course, was that, while de Pachmann likes his pranks, he likes them most when they are at the expense of others. I could tell by the way the blood was rushing to his face that de Pachmann was about to explode. Before the dinner was over, de Pachmann's opportunity came. "Wonderful turkey," he cooed, turning to our hostess. "Never had such wonderful turkey in my life. God himself has cooked!" "But Mr. de Pachmann," objected the clergyman, "that is most decidedly a blasphemy!" "Blasphemy?" de Pachmann's tone was scornful, his look withering. "I say God made that turkey, and He cooked it too. And that is not blasphemy. But you say God made *you*, and that IS blasphemy!"

Fastidiousness and obsession with details, the perfect and flawless way of doing things, was even more apparent if possible in another of Pachmann's great passions—his love of Havana cigars. At age nineteen he had starting smoking cigars, and later he developed a liking for the rich, heavy aroma of a good Havana. In his prime he smoked up to twenty-five a day, and all who met him were aware of the characteristic pungent odor that permeated his rooms and clothing. The minute details that went into the preparation and smoking of the cigar were almost awesome.

In Vienna he bought a filter made of turkey feathers which he always used thereafter. He would take some sterilized cotton, place it carefully in the filter, and precisely place the filter in the cigar holder. Then came the most important part of the ritual. He would open the cigar box and with the gentlest love caress each cigar one by one, all the while inhaling the heavy aroma with true sybaritic pleasure. Taking the box to the window, he chose the cigar whose shape and color appealed to him at that moment, and, using a special knife, carefully placed it in the holder. Bringing it to his lips, he slowly lit the cigar and with the greatest dignity began to smoke.[1]

The third and greatest of his passions outside his art was his love of jewels. He told a reporter for the *Indianapolis News* (October 2, 1907):

> You know that is why other pianists cannot play with Pachmann's colors—they do not know the great science and art of mineralogy. I absorb the colors and the sparkling of my gems and then I reproduce these nuances and tints in my music. That is my secret!

He had been interested in mineralogy from early childhood and gems became another obsession. He bought all the books he could on the subject and made copious notes on the colors, shapes and hardness of various stones. Soon he began to collect jewels. It was still early in his career and his income was not equal to the price of such fabulous rarities as blue diamonds, so he began with pearls (much more expensive then than now), iridescent little charmers he carried with him wherever he went. When he was living with Maggie in Paris, he would tease her by going onto the balcony and tossing them into the air. If he had dropped one, it would have meant the loss of considerable earnings.

As his success increased, he progressed from pearls to opals, then to rubies, and on to emeralds, and finally to diamonds. He bought them unset and would sit for hours with his eyes bathed in their colors. Ordinary stones held no interest for him. He craved only the rarest and most unusual, and for these he searched all over the world until he amassed a fantastic, legendary collection of red and blue diamonds, pink, purplish sapphires, mauve rubies, sea-green emeralds, topazes of innumerable shades, and black opals. His collection became almost as famous as his eccentricities, and he spent vast sums on the hobby. In 1914 the collection was valued at one million, two hundred thousand dollars (at least twenty million 2012 dollars).

Lest one think he collected these stones as a teenager collects charms for her bracelet, a reporter for the Edmonton, Alberta *Capital* (December 28, 1911) reprinted an interview about gems that Pachmann gave, showing the pianist was as serious about the subject as he was about the piano. In this interview the writer did not emphasize Pachmann's exotic speech for comic effect, as almost every other interview had done. It shows that he could be erudite about a subject in which he was deeply interested, and that he was not merely the clown he so often exhibited to the press, and that he indeed so often enjoyed playing. Pachmann was quoted:

> Will the supply ever give out? That is hardly likely. Borneo supplies about 3,000 carats annually, but 98 per cent of the total product used every year comes from the De Beers Consolidated mines in South Africa. Since the discovery of diamonds there in 1867, the De Beers output up to 1897 was over 33,000,000 carats or 7 ½ tons, valued after cutting at $450,000,000. The Brazilian diamonds are purer than those of South Africa, but too few of them are found to make their mining exceptionally profitable. Rubies—that is, the right kind—are more valuable than diamonds because they seldom weigh much or run very large. The "pigeonblood" ruby, or deep red wine color, is the kind most sought after. It is found only in Mandalay, and made famous by Kipling's poems of the same name. The largest ruby ever known is in Thibet [*sic*] and weighs 2,000 carats, but it contains numerous flaws and has no great value. The largest two perfect rubies weigh 50 ¾ and 17 ½ carats, respectively, and belong to the King of Bishenpur in India. Lovers of sapphires seek principally those of a corn flower hue. Lovely specimens are in the museum of the Jardin des Plants, Paris, but the finest example ever known was owned by the King of Ava, in 1827. It weighed 951 carats, but it is believed to have been stolen and cut up into smaller stones. The emerald is the most historical gem of all and was known to the first ancients of whom we have any trace. They valued it for its occult properties and its marvelous healing of diseases of the eye. Pliny tells of a life-size figure of a lion in Cyprus with large emeral[d] eyes which were so brilliant when the sun shone upon them that fish were frightened away by them. The Emperor Nero had an eye glass of emerald. The emerald ring taken from the tomb of Charlemange and used by him as a talisman, was worn by Napoleon on the battle fields of Austerliz and Wagram, and was given by him afterwards to Queen Hortense. The finest emeralds come from Siberia but it is practically impossible to get flawless ones. An emerald without a flaw signifies unattainable perfection.

Occasionally he wore a favorite red diamond set in a ring, and sometimes a brown diamond ring. One photo shows him wearing both, probably especially for the camera, but he rarely wore any of his stones, carrying them in his pockets when they weren't stored in vaults. He named his most precious ones after his favorite composers.

When he wasn't giving concerts, he could be found in the expensive jewelers' showrooms on London's Regent Street or at the stalls in the more raffish neighborhood near Covent Garden where the merchants would hum, "Tra-la-la, here comes Pachmann." Everyone knew him and placed trays aside for his personal inspection. Kunz of Tiffany's autographed a book on precious stones to him. Pachmann would often say, characteristically, that if he hadn't been the greatest pianist in the world he would have been the world's greatest mineralogist.

Sometimes in his world-wide quest he would run into other collectors, as once in London he went to see a fabulous abalone pearl. Louis Kornitzer, a dealer and collector, wrote:

> Only once did I see an abalone pearl of remarkable beauty. I remember every detail of her perfectly. She was fair sized as pearls go, about as big as a pea, geometrically round without a blemish and her translucent medium olivine. . . . Although I had no immediate idea of parting with her, suddenly a whole train of memories long forgotten, unbidden, came into my mind.

At this point Mr. Kornitzer's daydream of this perfect pearl was interrupted by a memory even more unforgettable:

> I saw before me the figure of a man short and squat, no longer in his prime. His face, large and expressive, was framed in graying locks coming well down over his ears and neck. His speech was full of animation, but as though speech was not enough, every muscle of his hand and face sought also to express his thoughts. I had met this strange personage many years before at the office of a well known lapidary in London, to who I had gone to consult about the recutting of a noble emerald. But this little man, client, like myself, had presumed to break in on our private conversation continually, had taken up my emerald and criticized and assessed it, and had altogether made himself a bit of a nuisance. I had, in fact, come near to being rude. But the lapidary smiled, had taken it all in good part. Finally, I had left the stone to be repolished and had hurried away. Within a moment of having reached the street, someone tapped me on the shoulder. There stood the little man. He took my arm as though we had known each other years and straight away plunged into a discourse on gems. I could not get a word in edgewise. . . . Presently, he spoke of his own wonderful collection of green diamonds, and pink and purple sapphires, mauve rubies, fiery amethysts, and black opals. All, so he said, had been presented to him by some King, Prince, Sultan or Rajah. "Nothing but the best, the rarest, the most perfect, do I admit into my collection. If by chance you come across something out of the way, something wonderful and like nothing anyone else possesses, bring it to me, price no object."

The funny man handed Kornitzer his card, which he put in his pocket. Of course later, on the bus when he pulled it out, he saw that it read "Vladimir de Pachmann."

Like his repertoire, Pachmann varied the gems in his collection to suit his moods. One year he collected only emeralds; another year sapphires intrigued him. For a while he even took a liking to zircons, those strange stones that illuminate when heated. He would buy them near Covent Garden at a second-hand jeweler's stall. Then, returning to his hotel, he would place them in an oven in Madame Peter's kitchen. His vexation knew no bounds when the gems cooled and lost their illumination. He returned to the jeweler in a fury: "*Cochonnerie!*" he shouted. But most of all he loved to tell people about his gems. When Pachmann dined with his fellow artists, he invariably emptied his pockets and a shower of diamonds, sapphires, and emeralds fell onto the table. "Aren't you afraid that someone will steal them?" Joseffy once asked."But everyone knows me," he replied innocently. "No one vould steal *my* stones."[2]

The sensuous delight and pleasure he received from jewels and the fine things in life inspired his music. Beverly Nichols in his book *Twenty-five* remembered Pachmann remarking on bubbles in the champagne they were drinking, and then going to piano and illustrating with the cascades in the D flat trio of Chopin's third Scherzo.

The detailed, jewel-like perfection of the sounds he created, in turn spurred him to collect jewels. The one fed the other.

"*Quelle couleur!*" he exclaimed to an American reporter, noticing an emerald ring she wore. He drew it off her finger and slid it as far as it could go onto his own. Then with great exuberance he spoke of his own collection and told her that his deepest desire was to translate this loveliness into sound—a sound as gem-like and as flawless as her beautiful stone.

> "You come to my concert tonight," he said, as he returned her ring with a flourish, "and I vill play for you alone. . . . I play Chopin so," and his fingers ran up an imaginary scale while his eyes glowed. "I play so sweetly that all the people stare and applaud. But you, you alone know that I am playing a living sparkle, a little fountain of green flames, the very color of your emerald stone."[3]

Chapter 15

VladyFlappers and Floppers, 1899–1900

When Pachmann was in his early fifties critics noticed a change, writing that his playing had deepened with the passing of time, broadening and gaining in repose. His rubato which sometimes had seemed capricious was now matured into an inspired expressive device. His tone took on an even richer hue but lost none of its delicacy, its beauty setting him apart. As the Debussy pupil George Copeland told the author in 1958: "There was a gulf between him and all the other pianists of his time." Olin Downes described his playing of the Chopin Berceuse in a 1908 *Boston Post* review of a recital in Boston (quoted in the March 28, 1908, *Musial America*):

A piano that was first piano, then pianissimo, then doubly pianissimo and so on into infinite gradations, until it seemed as if a piano struck by mortal fingers could not be the origin of such tones.

This control over the piano's palette of colors and softest end of the dynamic range would create such a stillness in the hall, with the audience's nerves stretched to breaking, that it is not surprising some hearers were left stunned and drained by the experience. In New York after one recital a woman sent the pianist a parcel containing a pair of shredded gloves, accompanied by a note explaining that she had torn them to shreds because of the tension during his performances of Chopin. She wrote that she felt sure that "every woman present went home in the same state."

There were the usual crowds and demonstrations, only more so. As usual, Pachmann made a special effort to play to the women in the audience. At one New York concert women almost started a riot. They waved their handkerchiefs, kissed their programs and applauded in frenzied rapture. It was a phenomenon the author has named "VladyFlappers."

In his all-Chopin concerts around the U.S.A., as he played Chopin Nocturnes evoking moods of the most tender intimacy, he would glance at the ladies in the front rows (who were holding their handkerchiefs and murmuring, "Beautiful! . . . Perfectly exquisite! . . .") and give them a sly wink.

A typical description of the phenomenon was written by the anonymous critic for New York's *Musical Age,* describing Pachmann's Carnegie Hall concert of April 19, 1900:

> The crowds of enthusiastic women present gave to De Pachmann quite an hysterical ovation, crowding up to the platform after the performance, demanding further evidence of the pianist's skill, to which he generously responded.

Women in England as well as America were subjugated by his art. They were also fascinated by the man and some actually became frantic when he played, for it seemed he was making love to them. "The look in some of the ladies' faces" wrote the *Times* [London] in 1901 "reflected not merely admiration, but adoration." They beseeched him for encores, and one woman in New York cried out "I hope he injures his thumb like darling Paderewski. I'd give him twenty-five dollars if he'd wrap it in my handkerchief."

Fred Gaisberg wrote in his autobiography:

> During his regular visits to London over the last thirty-five years of his career, Pachmann collected a loyal coterie of ladies who attended all of his concerts and sat as near the piano as he would permit. Some of them were genuine survivors of the Victorian Age. When the concert was over these elderly adherents stormed the platform and even invaded the artist's dressing room. I suspect that more than one of them imagined that he cherished a secret regard for them.

Non-flappers as well formed a large and noisy part of his audience and often mobbed him in the green room, demanding autographs. Not satisfied, they would pester him with gifts of flowers, handkerchiefs or scarves, and bad poetry, becoming such a nuisance that Pachmann once exclaimed "It is always like that—they give me no peace!" The phenomenon lasted and grew old with him, the women sharing all his memories, and towards the end of his life when adoration was necessary, even crucial for him, he told the writer Konrad Bercovici "Anybody is young once. Genius is eternal. That's why women, who alone know the meaning of eternity, prefer genius to youth."[1]

Huneker found the phenomenon quite amusing, and in 1893 wrote a deliberately purple parody for *MC* of these fanatic women fans of pianists and their obsessions, entitled "The Woman Who Loves Chopin" (a slightly changed version of the same story was published in *MC* on November 15, 1899). The teller of the story, a pianist, competes with another pianist named Jubbs for the affection of a certain woman named Juno, by performing continually more difficult Chopin pieces for her, but in the end all is in vain, for she deserts them both for Pachmann:

> Then I listened . . . Chopin's F minor Etude, the one in Op. 25 was being played as I had never before heard it, and Juno's whole soul went out in her glance. I had seen enough. She loved the newcomer and I was forgotten. So was Jubbs. I rushed away muttering "It must be Pachmann or the _____!"
> Yes; it is true. She no longer loves me. She loves another; another Chopin player. I will not acknowledge him my superior, for am I also not a pianist? She loves him. Juno loves Vladimir of the pearly-tipped fingers. Oh, misery! Oh, mockery! Oh, paradox incarnate! But I shall be revenged. To-morrow I shall consult with Carroll Chilton, and in forty-eight hours I am equipped with an instrument of virtuosity that not even Rosenthal, De Pachmann or that octave thunderbolt Mark Hambourg may dare emulate. A pianola is the thing to win Juno back; a Pianola, my kingdom for a Pianola![2]

Huneker's parody wasn't far from reality. The VladyFlappers began attending Pachmann's concerts early in his career, but their presence reached a veritable crescendo around 1900, and remained until the end. Pachmann's seductive playing represented a Victorian ideal of refinement to these women that was culturally acceptable, a sensuous model they could safely and morally embrace. This "love of the beautiful" of course masked prurient fascination with the morbid sensuousness of the pianist's peculiarly feminine performances.

The VladyFlapping bordered on hysteria during Pachmann's third and fourth American tours in 1899/1900 and 1904/1905, just as another equally potent force almost overshadowed it, reaching a crescendo not of delight, but of contempt bordering on hatred. A contrary group that the author has named VladyFloppers, a largely male contingent of pianists, critics, teachers and concertgoers, flowered in America as nowhere else, finding something to despise in Pachmann.[3]

The end of the Romantic era in Europe and particularly England had allowed artists freedom of behavior and in styles of living, encouraging the "artistic temperament" with its sensitivity, refinement and delicacy of feeling. America was barren of such artistic tradition, a vast and raw country with little in the way of sensibility. Decades earlier this had been portrayed particularly viciously by Dickens in his novel *Martin Chuzzlewit*. Things had improved since, but in the United States maleness still thrived. Power, energy, aggression, competition—all hallmarks of mercenary free enterprise—were the prized qualities in men. Artistic temperament and all its manifestations were never desirable traits in a "real man." The femininity of Pachmann's playing, with its all-embracing sensitivity and seductive tone used indiscriminately on both sexes—even his jewel collecting—could only offend these men.

There had been murmurs of discontent on his earlier visits; we remember "there was a masculine side to Chopin's nature . . . the new comer will not teach his American hearers much about that" (W. J. Henderson in the *New York Times*, April 1890), but now Pachmann, fifty-one years old and at the height of his artistry, generated disgust and contempt among the Floppers, who found his style of playing cloying and enervating, and longed for music of a masculine cast, powerful and manly.

A writer for New York's *Commercial Advertiser*, reviewing Pachmann's all-Chopin concert on March 12, 1899, pointed out that the large audience consisted mainly of "palpitating ladies," and continued:

> Too many sugar plums and lollipops are good for no one; neither is too much Chopin, especially when played by a pianist whose fingers drip with honeyed sweetness. No man can woo from the piano a sweeter tone. . . . But sooner or later it is certain to become tiresome, and one is moved to ask for bread and cheese and beer in place of sugared biscuit and Tokay. All that de Pachmann did was exquisitely soft and gentle and full of that sensuous beauty of which he is such a great master; but there was no virility, no manliness, no genuine force.

The same critic continued in a similar vein when writing of the pianist's performance of the Chopin F minor Concerto with the Philharmonic under Emil Pauer in October 1899:

> In its own peculiar way it is masterly with its smooth, velvety tone, its exquisite, even runs, its crispness, its feminine softness and gentleness—and its deadly monotony. How one yearns . . . even for a young Hambourg . . . with a little, yes, a little pounding! . . . De Pachmann . . . his work irritates more often than it charms.

And the critic for the *New York World* added on October 18, 1899, "In his interpretations the man has not changed. He continues to exaggerate his pianissimo effects, extracting from his Chopin all virility. He still feminizes the great composer."

The Floppers perceived distortions in his playing of the German masters as well, finding it superficial and filled with mere pianistics, the pianist only interested in effects. There was no brain working. This became a running corollary to the femininity. Today some would call Pachmann's playing "girlie music."

The *Commercial Advertiser* didn't like Pachmann's performances of Beethoven's "Waldstein" Sonata and Schumann's G minor Sonata in the recital of October 21.

It is impossible to speak seriously of a man that twists and distorts Beethoven and Schumann as he did, simply that he might get what he thought were pretty effects. In one way he did attain to his end, but the soft silkiness of his tone, the exquisite evenness of his runs and the general brilliance of his technique would have shown to quite as great advantage in variations on "Johnny get your gun" as in a sonata by Beethoven or Schumann and the susceptibilities of those who really cared for the music would not have been hurt.

These reviews were outclassed by the anger and hostility that arose from the red hot pen of the Floppers's leader, the distinguished critic of the *New York Times* (later of the *New York Sun*), William James Henderson. His opinion of Pachmann had hardened considerably since the '90's, and now extended to both the artist and his admirers. His reputation has survived as perhaps the greatest of American music critics, although Mark N. Grant in his *Maestros of the Pen* concluded that Henderson's "art of epigrammatic cruelty" had left a negative stamp on American criticism. Winthrop Sargeant recalled him as "a dry, salty lean old Yankee, who looked and acted more like a prosperous New England farmer than an aesthete." Henderson had two passions, yachting and music. Colleague Henry Finck wrote: "Much of his wit was of the cruel kind . . . debutantes dreaded [him] as a leopard ready to tear them to pieces."

What really inflamed Henderson's ire was what he perceived as an atmosphere of pruriency at Pachmann's concerts, with its hypocrisy of worshipping, adoring women, as well as the piano playing which encouraged it. In a private letter to Walter Damrosch dated December 19, 1908, he wrote: "to-day a pack of frittering, pin-headed—and in some cases disreputable—women go about among people who ought to have some intelligence and by their cackling and malicious stories make some people believe that I am both ignorant and dishonest." He wrote in his Sunday *New York Times* column of October 22, 1899:

There is no heart in Pachmann's playing. There is something more than sentimental in the mood which prevails in it. The feeling which flows out from his instrumental song is sometimes not quite clean. But perhaps this very element of his work is what makes it so influential at the present time. . . . There seems to be a vast appetite for pruriency. Those who cannot find it in the music of the intellect, as provided by Bach and Beethoven and Brahms, like to think that they find it in that of Chopin, and when they hear the music played by Pachmann they dream of "la vie intime" and George Sand. Some of these lovers of the Pachmanesque reading of Chopin (his reading of Chopin, by the way, is no more sensual than his reading of Weber) like to pretend that they are engaged in an act of reverential and holy worship. . . . The Prurient Prude loves to languish under the strokes of Pachmann's fingers and imagine that he is worshipping Chopin in his holy of holies. The truth is that there is much of the Polish composer's music which is in itself sentimental and languorous, and this lends itself to the treatment of the Pachmann technic so effectively that the net result is really fascinating, if not always quite moral. Surely if Tolstoy had ever heard Pachmann play the nocturnes of the Pole, he would never have written the "Kreutzer Sonata."

One can only imagine what Henderson's reaction might have been if he later read psychiatrist Immanuel Velikovsky's essay "Tolsoy's *Kreutzer Sonata* and Unconscious Homosexuality." It wasn't that Henderson didn't appreciate the pianist's great gifts. For the *New York Times* of November 18, 1899, he wrote:

> He still has the most wonderful finger technic and a velvety delicacy of touch . . . his tonal palette is rich with a variety of tints which give his performances endless fascination. His . . . mezzo-forte playing is in itself something so delicious that no music lovers can ever tire of it. . . . But it is useless to seek intellectual depth in M. de Pachmann's playing. His readings are eccentric and sometimes offensive, but their technical language revels in Swinburgian tone-tints and the bewitched ear lulls the brain.

Three weeks later on December 3 he wrote:

> It is undeniable that Pachmann has the finest touch that can be imagined. No one can play so gently as he can. . . . It is an immeasurable pity that a pianist so gifted otherwise is so deficient in the intellectual department of his art.

And a few weeks later he wrote in *Musical Age* on January 18, 1900:

> His finger technic is unsurpassed, and with it goes a delicate feeling for tone color that he always enchants the ear, even when he disappoints the mind. One must give himself very fully to the sensuous side of musical art in order to be satisfied with his playing.

Obviously Mr. Henderson was not a man to be seduced by sensuousness.

Over the years James Huneker had changed not only from an enemy into a friend of the Chopinzee, in recent days his columns in *MC* had begun to function almost as a personal press bureau for the pianist. In the November 1, 1899, issue of *MC* he published an article entitled "The De Pachmann Case":

> Vladimir de Pachmann plays the piano and Vladimir de Pachmann is excessively eccentric. He is a nervous little body, and does things that to sane, well-balanced persons seem nothing short of madness . . . is there something to

be said in his defense? . . . Pachmann without his Pachmann-ish ways would not be himself. Not a master of the thunderbolt that fulminates, he wins by his magical presentiment of a gentle euphony. He is furnished with very rhythmical springs, and the least over excitement throws them out of gear. . . . To be natural, even offensively, effusively natural, is better than the labored academic *pose* of some other artists. Besides, no matter how he behaves, no matter how he upsets traditional *tempi*, and phrase-architecture, this Russian pianist, with Turkish-Polish blood, is ever interesting. He has the Asiatic temperament, with its morbid, excitable side, and we would rather hear him play with all his absurdities of conduct than the well-bred pianist of no talent. De Pachmann not only plays Chopin; he acts Chopin. To see him is to hear him.

Huneker often filled his weekly column with laudatory excerpts from Pachmann reviews from various American cities. He finally decided it was time to defend his friend's reputation directly, and wrote in the February 21, 1900, *MC*, aiming some barbs directly at Henderson:

While admitting that Vladimir de Pachmann has the greatest finger technic in the world, that he plays beautifully a not very extensive repertory, certain persons qualify their praise by saying that De Pachmann is no artist, has no sense of rhythm and other stuff of the sort. . . . Now in the name of the prophet what fig is this we must swallow? Jealousy, I have made up my mind, is the sign manual of the musician, the successful professional as well as the timid amateur. Drive any one of these into a corner and the nasty meanness of human nature is uncovered. . . . De Pachmann is one of the greatest living players *of the pianoforte* . . . within his sharply defined limitations. Let us enjoy him and not make ourselves miserable by pointing out that if he had Rosenthal's wrists, Hambourg's mouth, Breitner's[4] beard and the pedals of Joseph Weiss, he might be greater than he is. All composites are monstrous, and I suspect all your eclectic players. They are frauds, intellectual and digital. Eugen d'Albert plays Beethoven and Brahms as no one else on the globe. With Schumann and Chopin he is on terms of coolness. Busoni plays Bach and Liszt. His Schumann and Chopin are not convincing. . . . De Pachmann is in familiar country when he plays Chopin, Henselt and Liszt, for he is a romantic artist. His touch in delicacy, absolute beauty and refinement is unique, and it is idle to talk of his mechanical attainments. Seeing the marvelous haze, the atmosphere with which he is able to invest his music, some fancy that his art is . . . volatile, impressionistic. . . . Solid has been the training, severe the schooling of this pianist. . . . I know men who play the F minor Concerto of Chopin with more breadth. Let them play it as big as the side of a house, but De Pachmann's version stands alone. *He knows his forte*, and that is the great secret of his magical dynamics. I acknowledge that his readings are feminine, perverse, morbid, if you will have these handy though little understood words thrown in; yet no woman has ever exhibited such feminine or poetic qualities, no woman has displayed such delicacy. . . . De Pachmanns do not grow on bushes. . . . And he reads everything of Chopin with such intimate feeling. I defy you to prove his interpretations incorrect. They may not suit you—or the Boers—but they are musical and I can't say the same thing for most German piano playing. A plague on this critical condescension! De Pachmann often sports with his music as a magician would sport with his demon, but he can be serious and in a small hall and with a sympathetic audience—he has not his equal.

Henderson responded on March 4, 1900, in the *New York Times* with a sarcastic reference to Huneker as well as an absurd, new idea—Pachmann's success in Chopin stemmed from the fact that the music played itself:

> All these features of his playing are so congenial to these compositions that he creates the illusion of interpretation where he is really concerned about nothing but his technic. Pachmann's success with the music of Chopin is only another case of good music performing itself. . . . Chopin's music is of such a peculiar kind that . . . as Pachmann brings it, it does its work upon the emotions. . . . But let us wait. Mr. Huneker is about to launch a book on this topic . . . after the volume is published we shall know a good deal more about Chopin.

Henderson's conflicted feelings continued to be expressed in print: the *New York Times* of March 29, 1900:

> Probably as long as the public continues to applaud his pretty playing, in spite of his whimsies he will be the same Pachmann. And even at that he will always be worth hearing.

Then on April 20, 1900:

> The recital was less to M. de Pachmann's credit than almost any other he has given . . . gross impositions practiced by the technical trickster. . . . The spectacle was not an encouraging one. . . . He was pleased yesterday to play tricks with the rhythms, and in some instances, as in one of the mazurkas, with the written notes of the music . . . the familiar A flat waltz, Op. 42, was simply wicked . . . transformed into a lilting six-eighth movement, and he played pranks with bass notes not intended to be emphasized . . . the elemental force of tumultuous rhythm in the great C minor etude was utterly buried under a mawkish and pulling effeminacy, which was an insult to the memory of Chopin and the intelligence of the audience. . . . The voice parts in the Op. 25 No. 3 were obscured by bad pedaling. The No. 7 of this opus was sickly enough to please the most morbid of feminine Chopinists.

Two days later in his Sunday *New York Times* column of April 22 came the climax of all Henderson had written in the vein, a think piece filled with bitterness and hate:

> At the close of the entertainment there was a rush of ecstatics to the altar rail, and the pianist's nostrils were refreshed with the perfume of the intimate

worship which is so dear to the interpreter of music. All this took place at a concert devoted to the performance of the music of Chopin after one of the most culpable displays of a lack of respect for the intent of the composer. Mr. de Pachmann had distorted the music of the master whose disciple he is said to be in a manner simply maddening to real lovers of the wonderful Pole. No one in that vast audience seemed to care for poor Chopin. All were present to worship Pachmann, and for what? For an exhibition of cheap trickery of the most vulgar and unmusical kind. The personality of the performer had some sort of hypnotic influence on these people, and they paid the tribute to de Pachmann which was denied to Chopin. The newspapers of the following day found fault with the pianist, and the result was the usual freight of complaining letters to the editor. No one cared that Chopin had been butchered to make a Pachmann holiday; every one was concerned that the sacred personality had been subjected to the rude buffets of honest and intelligent criticism. I trust it may joy these good people to know that, so far as I am concerned, what I have written of M. de Pachmann's Chopin "interpretations" is but a very faint replica of what I really think of them.

At this time Henderson was in his mid forties, a bachelor who was especially close to his mother (later he married). His smoldering feelings were obviously so filled with contempt he couldn't print the words needed to describe them. What were these words Henderson could not write? The reader must not think Henderson's contempt sprang from a lofty desire to protect composers from performers who altered dynamics, highlighted inner voices, added octaves and otherwise changed the composers' marked intentions, although he did regularly point out Pachmann's "sins" in this respect. Pachmann wasn't the only guilty pianist whose Romantic style encompassed such liberties—Hambourg, Busoni, Rummel, Joseffy, Hofmann—almost all the pianists Henderson reviewed regularly then played in that style, to varying degrees. Something more insidious inflamed this upholder of masculinity.

A homo-erotic undercurrent at Pachmann's concerts was by then a strong element of the proceedings, and his audiences included not only women, but also handsome, well dressed young men sitting among them. And as with the ladies, Pachmann often would single one out, playing and sometimes addressing him. Many in the audience took this as just another instance of his eccentricity, and surely a large percentage of audiences in 1900 was ignorant of the particulars of male homosexuality. However, not everyone was so naïve, especially the more knowing members of the musical profession. Pachmann was incapable of masking his true nature and never hid his homosexuality on or off the platform. Family members and his friends were well acquainted with it. Both Colin Defries and Vanita Godowsky (elder daughter of Leopold) discussed it with the author. It was one of the first things about Pachmann that George

Halprin described. Among colleagues and the public, there were many who detested him for it. Vanita Godowsky disparaged him to the author, saying Pachmann was "like a woman, so feminine, with all those jewels."

Josef Hofmann unapologetically told his pupil Abram Chasins that Pachmann was "frequently a poet, always an ass f . . . .r. But a truly great pianist? Never!"[5]

Some of those who detested Pachmann were colleagues who were angered by his antics, and considered them a disgrace to the concert profession. This was bad enough, but adding femininity and homosexuality to the mix doomed him. Since Pachmann seemed oblivious to taunts and happily continued to luxuriate in his behavior, their fury turned to hate. Attitudes and understanding of homosexuality were different from today, with the public generally uninformed, but there was at the time in America a rampant and pervasive anti-feminine atmosphere (which in some circles persists today). What with his free approach to the text, his eccentricities and especially the overriding femininity of his playing, it is amazing Pachmann had an American career. Any one of these factors was enough to destroy a lesser performer, and it is because he was a pianistic genius that he survived. Viewed in this light Pachmann's American success can be seen to be even greater than had been supposed. Pages could be filled with descriptions of the crowds and the enthusiastic ovations, but underneath all was a swirling controversy that never let up. At the heart of the controversy was the homo-erotic element.

Chapter 16

The World's Greatest Pianist, 1899–1900

Pachmann visited his sons in Paris in late summer 1899 before embarking for his third tour of the United States. The *Chicago Daily Tribune* reported (November 8) that he saw Maggie as well. The *Boston Globe* reported (September 10):

> There is a strong friendship existing between the two, due no doubt to their frequent meetings at the school in Paris, where De Pachmann's two children are being educated.

He took the boys to the shipping office when he booked passage. Leonide was eleven at the time, but remembered for the rest of his life the scene his father made, shouting in a loud voice, "No, not *that* cabin, it will stink badly!" Pachmann had used the verb "puer" (to stink) instead of the more polite "sentir" (to smell). People who were booking expensive first class passages were hardly expected to speak that way, and all present, including Adrian and Leonide, started laughing. "Don't laugh," he said sharply "your father is going to America all alone!" Something must have happened suddenly that prevented Pachmann's secretary McKay from accompanying him.

In America, executives of the Wolfsohn Musical Bureau soon discovered the extent of what they had to manage and cope with in a Pachmann without Maggie, and they assigned an unsuspecting novice to personally accompany the Chopinzee across the country and keep him out of trouble. This was Richard Copley, a handsome twenty-two year old who much later started his own musical management company and was the sole agent for years for Josef Hofmann. In later days Copley liked to tell the story of a particular Pachmann concert—alone in the greenroom afterward, he vigorously brushed his hair and set the hairbrush down on a table. As he was leaving, a distraught VladyFlapper rushed in, looking for her idol. Copley recognized her as a pushy woman who had earlier handed the pianist an autograph album to sign—a custom the pianist abhorred. The woman had been disappointed when she was refused, but was relentless. Desperate for a memento and not noticing Copley at the other end of the room, her eyes darted about and came to rest on the hairbrush. Quickly she scooped up some hairs in a handkerchief and with a triumphant smile, rushed out.

Pachmann deserted the Chickering piano for Steinway on this tour. Frank Chickering died in 1891 during the pianist's first American tour and he had played Beethoven's funeral march from the Sonata in A flat, Op. 26 in his memory. After his death the Chickering firm tried to reorganize, but it lost prestige and was never able to recapture the success it had held earlier for several decades. Chickering Hall in New York, which had opened in 1875 with a concert by Hans von Bülow, saw its last concert on April 12, 1900, and was demolished.

The Wolfsohn Bureau, one of the largest and most influential management agencies in the country, persuaded Steinway to underwrite the expenses of Pachmann's tour. This was to be the only time he officially played their magisterial instruments. Of course they needed a flowery endorsement, which they took from an interview in the *Worcester Spy*, a Massachusetts paper, printed on September 28, 1899, in connection with his appearances at the Worcester Festival. He arrived in Worcester with both Henry Wolfsohn and Paul C. Fischer, representing Steinway.

"I fear I cannot speak English well enough for you. I have forgotten it since I was here six years ago. But I will practice on you. . . . I am not very well. . . . I am not very strong. Ever since I crossed the water this last time my digestion has been weak. On shipboard bread and grapes were all the nourishment I could take. . . . A sea trip is to me miserable and monstrous. It is for that reason I always cross in June or July; I speak English well, don't I?" The reporter assured him most truthfully that he did, and asked him where and how he had passed the summer. "In the Catskills, at a little place in the backwoods. Did I play? Not very much; it was too hot. All your America is very hot in summer, I think. But I had a Steinway grand, and how could I help play with such an instrument in the room? . . . Ah, the Steinway. What a piano! Write this down—it is divine; it is the finest in the world—I could not leave it. I can remember the pianos of 25 years ago; but what a development since. There is nothing so beautiful in touch, so beautiful in tone. Ach! that touch and tone. Mozart and Beethoven, could they hear their compositions performed on a modern piano, would not know them for theirs. The tears would flow from their eyes and run down their cheeks to hear them."

Steinway continued to reprint this part of the interview (apparently a spontaneous testimonial) in promotional material for years, despite the fact that Pachmann played their piano for hardly more than a year. But there was more of interest to us in the interview:

"I am perfectly Russian," continued the foremost interpreter of Chopin, "but (mysteriously) do you know what country I prefer? It is this country, America the most honorable, free country: its feelings are good. O, this wonderful, wonderful country! There is none to be compared with it. Put that down. I am not a true cosmopolitan, for I prefer this country. It is so sympathetic, honest, superior, advanced in nearly every respect. I have no home, for I am everywhere at home." Mr. Pachmann pointed gravely to the ceiling. "Wherever the creation is, there I am at home. I cannot disappear. I am beyond all material things. I am a virtuoso and a philosopher. For goodness sake don't say I am an agnostic. I am not. I am like [Count Leo] Tolstoi. I believe in the same things. But don't say that . . . I shall not go to the festival tonight. I have not been to a concert for years. Too many mediocre artists. When I hear poor artists perform, I cannot think" (he rose, and turning his eyes upward, pointed solemnly in the direction of the sky) "of the words of Jesus Christ: Father, forgive them, for they know not what they do."[1]

His reception at the Festival was ecstatic. The *Boston Globe* reported (October 30, 1899):

Notwithstanding the excellence of the orchestra, it was made clear that de Pachmann was a great feature of the evening, for the aisles were literally packed by standers, largely young students of both sexes, who listened to the marvelous playing of the great star with an intensity expressive of idolatry . . . men cheered and shouted en masse, while women waved their handkerchiefs and joined in every conceivable mode of expressing feminine enthusiasm.

It was just a few years earlier that Pachmann had complained bitterly about the United States and the treatment he received there. Now he found the country sympathetic, but the sympathy was not always returned. The same *Worcester Spy* two days later printed a short blurb, complaining about Pachmann's penchant for kissing women and men:

If he were a woman, people would call him a chatterbox. De Pachmann knows that he talks too much, but he cannot control his tongue, and apparently says everything that comes into his head, like a vivacious, spoiled little boy. His feelings are constantly being hurt, and he does not read the papers much, because they jolly him so awfully. If you happen to please him or confer ever so trifling a favor, he expresses his satisfaction by jumping up and kissing your hand, a sufficiently embarrassing for the average American woman, but the man who travels with him to take care of him and the piano, is contented if he does not request a kiss in the name of friendship of a 15 minutes' acquaintance. To say that the people who ran the Bay State were relieved to see the last of him is almost a matter of course. He is fussy to a degree, and finds fault with everything, particularly American prices, which strike him as positive swindles.

After Worcester the pianist began a protracted American tour. In Chicago he was found to still be a marvel. *Chicago Daily Tribune*, November 9:

> The playing has lost none of its charm. It is the same wonderful, satisfying playing as of old. The sonorous tone, resonant even in the softest pianissimo; the expressive phrasing, the eloquent inner-voice leadings, the faultless technique, and the rich but delicate musical perception—all are still there.

His two scheduled recitals had to be augmented with two additional ones, but after all the glory he came close to creating a scene as he checked out of the Auditorium Hotel. He claimed he was being overcharged for meals he hadn't eaten. The desk clerk explained to him that rooms there were rented "on the American plan," under which people were charged a set fee per day no matter how much or how little they consumed. According to the *Chicago Tribune* for December 17, 1899:

> M. de Pachmann could not see the justice of this and exclaimed excitedly, "It is ridiculous that I should be charged so much for eating. Why, sir, I eat just like one bird. I just pick a little here and a little there. I take a little sip of this, a little bite of that, a bit of fruit, and I am done. . ." Nevertheless the pianist paid his bill with a shrug and grimace of protest and an under remark in French that there were some strange and barbaric customs among the Americans.

Pachmann was now firmly established as an international star, considered one of the greatest pianists of his day on both sides of the Atlantic. But only in America was he hyped, and in short order he was being advertised in the United States as "The World's Greatest Pianist" (as were Anton Rubinstein and Hans von Bülow before him). Such exaggeration was not uncommon in the United States, serving as an enticement for less-sophisticated folk to attend recitals.

In certain ways Pachmann *was* "the world's greatest pianist;" but so was Rosenthal and so was d'Albert. And Teresa Carreño, to mention just three others. It was always "in certain ways." The only pianist who transcended those "certain ways" was Franz Liszt, but he never toured the United States.

〜

Pachmann's recital programs had evolved to a usual formula, typically a parade of smaller works surrounding two or three large-scale pieces. Such programs showed him at his best. He invested the smaller works with character and charm, apparently creating a unique momentum that swept audiences away. He brought out of storage certain non-Chopin material, such as Beethoven's "Waldstein" Sonata, Schumann's G minor Sonata, Weber's Chopinesque A flat Sonata (a work almost never played today and already deemed old-fashioned in the year 1900) and Schumann's *Davidsbündlertänze*, a work popular neither then nor now, despite its many beauties.

His managers had told him that it was imperative to impress America with sober greatness as an artist and pianist, and that he had to omit gesticulations and other eccentricities. Their efforts worked for the first New York concert on October 17, after which it was noted in several papers that Pachmann's manner seemed to be more serious.

Huneker attended Pachmann's first New York recital, and wrote magnificently of his performance of the Weber Sonata in *MC* (October 18, 1899), a vivid and detailed description that almost evokes the very sound of Pachmann's playing:

The Weber Sonata, Liszt's favorite, has been delivered here in a more sensational, more brilliant manner, but never so beautifully. First, the opening *tempo* was a surprise. It was *allegro moderato*, as marked by the composer, and in the charming fresco decorations, in which peeps forth "Der Freischütz"— but a moment's flashing mask—no effort was made at technical display. Euphony at all hazards was secured, even with a slight loss of power and pride of Weber's martial spirit. A most sensuous tonal coloring and a flowing *legato*, beyond the dreams of the most avaricious of pianists resulted, and with the Henselt harmonic amplifications—bass figures changed and octaves introduced—the whole composition gained in richness, in massiveness. Very beautiful, indeed, was M. De Pachmann's singing—there is no other word—of the F minor episode. He has gained in power, nervous rather than muscular, and so the working out section was sonorous, if not orchestral. In the C minor *andante* the soprano voice was *ben tenuto* to a remarkable degree. It is an old-fashioned device to give single tones such prominence, and without pedal help. Here the inner voices were finely differentiated. The octaves in the major section were models of accompaniment figures. There were octaves too in the right hand, in the diminished chord, just before the sixths; this is an innovation. The movement was most romantically read ("I confide to you the sum of my experiences, my sorrows, my joys," Pachmann said of the andante). Another surprise was the *menuetto capriccioso*, which was capricious but not *presto*. The top tones in the Trio were taken languishingly and not at all electrically. But again Weber was faithfully followed and not the dictates of the virtuoso. The Rondo was a true Rondo, purling, exquisite in feeling and *molto grazioso*. Astonishing variety of touch and the right historical feeling characterized the entire performance. The last few bars were lovely, the *morendo* a genuine sight.[2]

Of this same performance, W. J. Henderson wrote in the *New York Times* (October 18, 1899): "He emasculated the gracious and gallant A flat Sonata. " In New York they hated his performance of Schumann's *Davidsbündlertänze*, while of his Boston performance Philip Hale wrote (*Boston Journal*, November 3):

> And then that last movement . . . Pachmann has done many wonderful things, but he will never excel the poetic interpretation of that one page— music that is too intimate to please an audience coming together from the four corners at a fixed hour in the afternoon—music that might be thought between lovers far from the curious crowd.

Mendelssohn Hall, an elegant building on New York's 40th Street, had replaced Chickering Hall as the preferred concert venue for visiting virtuosi. The most unusual of Pachmann's many all-Chopin recitals throughout the country occurred there on March 7, 1900 (then repeated in Boston). It consisted almost entirely of Preludes and Etudes, with three Mazurkas. Annette Essipoff had played the Op. 10 and Op. 25 Etudes at one recital in the United States in 1876, and more recently Arthur Friedheim had played all the Op. 28 Preludes as a group. Pachmann never played these sets complete, always programming just a few interspersed with other works. By the 1920s pianists were often performing the Preludes as a group, and today it is usually the only way one hears the Preludes. It took longer for pianists to get to the point of playing all the Etudes at one sitting, but today it is not uncommon. Pachmann knew that he could only play some of the Etudes well and his mixture of these works was apparently musically satisfying. In truth almost all pianists who attempt performing the complete Etudes fail to do justice to some of them, bringing off a stunt of endurance rather than presenting an artistic experience. Josef Hofmann said: "A lifetime isn't enough to play them all!"

In his diary/notebooks Edwin Hughes described another Pachmann recital there that his teacher Joseffy attended:

> de Pachmann was playing the Chopin Barcarolle beautifully. His runs were like little pearls but he played the last page slower and slower. Before the last two chords, he placed his hands on the chords to play, then took them up

and looked around at the audience. Then he turned and finished. The people all laughed. It was awful.[3]

In Chicago he programmed the Schumann work at his second recital on December 16; his friend Leopold Godowsky happened to be in the audience, and Pachmann asked him to act as page turner, for he intended to use the printed score during the performance. *Musician* magazine (June 1900) reported it was: "a division of labor concerning which important differences of opinion might justly be held, Schumann playing being particularly in Godowsky's line."

The unnamed writer for the Chicago-based *Musician* was Will Hubbard, who reviewed Pachmann's two concerts there in the December 1899 issue:

No other pianist before the public has so beautiful a touch and so clean and exquisitely neat execution. Mr. Pachmann uses the pedal very little. . . . It is easy to underrate the technic of this artist owing to the extreme facility and rapidity of his playing and his preference for smaller works . . . there was a very interesting association between him and Mr. Godowsky. During the three or four days that Mr. de Pachmann was in Chicago the two artists spent much time together, and nothing was more beautiful than to see the enthusiastic cordiality with which the older artist admired the beautiful versions of the Chopin studies for the left hand which Mr. Godowsky has been working at during the last summer. De Pachmann declares them to be inimitable, and says that next year in Europe he means to play some recitals composed entirely of Chopin and Chopin-Godowsky paraphrases. . . . It is extremely rare that an artist already at the top of the ladder has the amiability and sagacity to take this view of such innovative work of a composer and pianist twenty-one years younger.

In Oberlin, Ohio, he stayed at the Oberlin Inn, about a block away from the concert hall. When Pachmann did not appear at the appointed time for the recital, a porter eventually appeared and mumbled some distressing news to William K. Breckenridge, the piano teacher at the Oberlin Conservatory who handled arrangements. According to Breckenridge's student, organist Walter Blodgett:

The visiting artist had had a misadventure with the Inn's plumbing which somehow reversed its usual flow and the artist's clothing was immediately if temporarily beyond use. Professor Breck supplied the necessary garments so the concert might take place though they were "too beeg." The concert was further delayed because the piano pedals were out of line with the cracks in the stage flooring. Also de Pachmann spied a young fellow in the audience to whom he dedicated the program. It was a great success and de Pachmann was invited back another season. My teacher met him at the train, which was the only way to get to Oberlin other than ox cart. De Pachmann cheerfully got off the train and displayed a chamber pot which he had brought along for reasons of security.[4]

Pachmann again brought Chopin's F minor Concerto, this time playing it across the entire country. But when he came to Boston, the trustees of the Symphony had not forgotten his foolishness nine years earlier with Arthur Nikisch. They refused to let him play with the Symphony, and the Boston correspondent for *MC* complained (November 8, 1899):

> Why do we not hear de Pachmann with the Boston Symphony? Master that he is, at the head of pianism, why should he not be heard with an orchestra whose art is commensurate with his own? When omissions like this happen, they give rise to each one imagining a different colored gentleman in the woodpile.

He did play the Chopin Concerto again in Boston. Mayor Quincy had decided to organize a series of concerts to benefit the City Hospital, and a pick-up orchestra of fifty men was formed for the occasion. Pachmann was invited to play the Mendelssohn G minor Concerto on November 20, and the Chopin F minor on November 26, 1899. The Music Hall was packed with admirers, his performance (conducted by Emil Mollenhauer) greeted with near-hysteria. He played it again with Mollenhauer and the pick-up orchestra on April 21, 1900. William K. Breckenridge told Walter Blodgett that it was the last time he heard Pachmann, and Blodgett wrote:

> The performance was so beautiful that my old professor stumbled out after the second movement for fear something might happen. He stumbled because he was weeping.[5]

The tour was a huge success. Copley told *MC* that "the tour was a triumph from the day de Pachmann started from New York City."

Covering much of the interior, the West Coast and stops in Canada, Wolfsohn was delighted and extended the tour until June 1. *MC* reported (November 29, 1899):

> Mr. Wolfsohn says that he has never managed an artist who so completely wins his audiences as De Pachmann captures them. Whenever he has played a return engagement he has been greeted by a much larger audience.

Pachmann was scheduled to play thirty-five concerts in eighty days, from Albany to Colorado Springs, and that was only half of the tour. A report concerning his upcoming concert in Atlanta gives a glimpse of the success he was expected to enjoy there. The *Atlanta Constitution* wrote with anticipation (October 24, 1899):

Besides the immense audience that will completely fill the body of the house and the boxes, there will be 300 music teachers seated on the stage, and the fact that they and the entire audience will appear in evening clothes describes a beautiful scene.

MC reported (November 1) that the Atlanta concert was such a great success there were no encores. Pachmann's playing so satisfied everyone that they were "soothed, and under such a spell."

When he returned to Canada his concert in Toronto, after an eight years' absence, received a markedly different reception than before, and everyone stayed until the end. *Toronto Saturday Night* reported (January 30, 1900):

His program consisted altogether of seventeen numbers, but as the majority of them were short pieces, the recital left his hearers almost reluctant to bid him farewell. . . . He has so marvelous a finger technique, so exquisite a tone and so great sensitiveness for color, that his power over those who do not demand depth and intellectuality of interpretation is supreme . . . he abandons himself to the impulse of the moment, and as his emotional moods are ever-varying, he seldom renders the same composition twice alike. Thus the public are always enchanted with new effects and new flights of fancy.

~⁌

In Europe Pachmann had often performed in concerts along with other musicians, in chamber music and joint recitals with famous singers and violinists. Such pairing was rare in the United States, where management felt his personality to be too dominant and his playing too free and spontaneous to be reined in by the good musical manners required in chamber music. The cult of the superstar, if not invented in America, was perfected there.

Nevertheless Wolfsohn had an idea for an added attraction, and paired Pachmann for some joint concerts with the respected French violinist Henri Marteau (1874 –1934), who had appeared in America several times before. His reasoning in doing so can only be wondered at today— perhaps he had guaranteed the violinist a certain number of concerts, found he wasn't filling halls, and solved the problem by sticking him with the guaranteed ticket-seller pianist. The juxtaposition of the two musical personalities brought out extremely divergent critical opinion about Pachmann. To the VladyFloppers, he was still his simian self, the Chopinzee (New York *Commercial Advertiser*, March 29, 1900):

The hall was completely filled with enthusiastic listeners, most of them women. The audience was well-paid for its pains, because it had the benefit of Mr. Marteau's solid musicianship on the one hand, and Mr. de Pachmann's kittenish antics on the other. If the concert suffered in musical merit from the latter, the audience seemed to be more than content with the fun it got out of the Russian pianist. Mr. de Pachmann was in one of his most extreme moods and it was impossible to take his work seriously. In his solos he took all manner of liberties with the music, liberties even for him, but the results were pretty and that is what he is usually after. . . . In both sonatas . . . [Marteau's] work was distinguished by a sobriety and continence and by a true musicianly feeling that was greatly in contrast with his colleague. De Pachmann was quite unable to sink himself in ensemble playing and continually did his best to distract the attention of his auditors by his monkey shines.

But other reviewers found nothing amiss. *Brooklyn Eagle*, March 29, 1900:

The man who combined De Pachmann and Marteau . . . is a genius for whetting the public appetite. At first thought the combination seems impossible, but the two diverse temperaments blended at Mendelssohn Hall yesterday afternoon as well as oil and vinegar in a salad dressing. The violinist was the oil and he took the acid edge from the antics with which De Pachmann decorates his performances and, in the "Kreutzer Sonata," he considerably modified the style of the Russian. . . . It was a performance which increased one's respect for the pianist, though it lacked some of his usual smoothness and finish. Both artists fairly reveled in Mozart's sonata in E flat.

The different pictures presented by these reviews are hard to reconcile, the *Brooklyn Eagle* critic seeing a Dr. Jekyll, and the *Advertiser's* seeing a musical Mr. Hyde. It is puzzling—the positive review so normal, not mentioning anything unusual about Pachmann's behavior or performance, while the negative review is so dismissive. The pair had two recitals planned for in Boston, but the second didn't come off and Pachmann played the date solo, to huge acclaim. Philip Hale couldn't help making some fun of New York critics who didn't like Pachmann (*Boston Journal*, March 25, 1900):

Of Mr. de Pachmann there is nothing new to be said. Even in New York the critics are beginning to realize that he is a pianist of serious claims and genuine importance, and for this concession we should be duly grateful; for it is a step, as the Cambridge woman said when she learned that the Australian savages ate their prisoners cooked, and not raw.

Chapter 17

Ruckus in a Rathskeller, 1899–1900

Towards the end of 1899 Willa Cather, journalist and later a famous novelist, was living in Pittsburgh, where she attended a Pachmann recital in the company of a young man who had studied with the pianist. She reviewed the concert for MC's December 30, 1899, issue (it was reprinted in *The World and the Parish, Volume Two*, a collection of her articles and reviews). She wrote:

Although he no longer affects the long black hair and beard . . . there is no mistaking the Russian pianist's vocation. He wears his hair brushed straight back now . . . and his heavy body and broad, powerful shoulders look queer enough on the absurdly short legs which toddle them about. His feet are small and he is very vain of them. "But then," remarked the Pachmann pupil, "he is vain of everything: he is the vainest man I ever knew, and when I was with him I was almost as vain of him as he was of himself. One falls under the enchantment of the man and Pachmannism becomes a mystic cult, an intellectual religion, a new sort of theosophy. His pupils usually copy his walk, his gestures, I think I used even to wish I had his nose and his little slits of Tartar eyes. But listen!" . . . It was not until he began playing the third prelude of Chopin that the Pachmann pupil utterly collapsed and murmured, "The tone—the singing tone! His own tone!" And singing tones they were: living things that lived a glorious instant of life and died under his fingers. . . . The Pachmann pupil assured me that no one else had ever been able to produce a tone just like that, and he remarked that the peculiar bird-like tone would die with Vladimir de Pachmann, and then he told me a funny story of this quaint Russian egoist. . . . When he was in Pittsburgh on his last American tour, he was playing . . . to a crowd of musicians in a wholesale music store here. He played even better than usual, and when he had finished, he looked up and said with a sigh and a gesture of ineffable regret, "Ah, who will play like that when Pachmann is no more!" There were actually tears in his eyes, for he was overcome with the sense of the great loss which the world must some day suffer.

Unfortunately Cather did not name this pupil. In America as elsewhere Pachmann was approached often by aspiring pupils, usually young men, either by themselves or with their teachers. He was famous and people were always approaching him. He might be interested if they were talented; certainly if they were handsome. One such approach resulted in a relationship with a young man named Jean de Chauvenet. Pachmann's infatuation with the young man, as well as the acolyte's adoration of Pachmann, was chronicled by a Denver *Evening Post* reporter who happened to interview Pachmann while he was entertaining de Chauvenet. The interview went on for too long and laboriously tried to capture Pachmann's weird English, but it showed the exotic environment of Pachmann's hotel room, with the pianist and a willing male protégé. It was also interesting for its mention of Paderewski, then also touring the United States. Huneker, continuing with his unusual dual purpose of using the journal as a de facto press bureau for his favorite pianist, as well as an outlet for his fascination with Pachmann's exotic behavior, reprinted the long Denver piece in *MC* (February 25, 1900), preceded with a short introduction:

I offer no apology for the reproduction here of an article called "The Human Nature of a Great Piano Virtuoso; De Pachmann will not hear of his friend Paderewski spoken of slightingly." It was in the Denver Evening Post and is a joy.

The De Pachmann piano recital was over, but the great pianist was here . . . devoting himself to a caller and making him at home in his apartment at the Brown Hotel, and his whole joyous, volatile soul was in the task. [The article continues with Pachmann introducing the young man to the reporter.] A young man with a fine face and a shine of diffident pleasure in his eyes was now urged forward by De Pachmann from the semi-obscurity of a corner. "You moost meet heem," said De Pachmann with enthusiasm. "Shake him by ze hand. He ees, een our great art, my saun, my brozzer almost I could say, eh?" And then behind his hand in a hoarse aside, "He is r-remarkable! A chenius, truly, indeed, yes. He haf ze speer-rit, ah-h-h! And ze totch so fine, so tainder! He weel someday be ze De Pachmann. Zat ees, w'en I shall no more toch ze keys. Zen he will coam ze gr-reat Jean de Chauvenet—Oh, r-r-rascal! You leesten?" And he turned on the young pianist and embraced him, to De Chauvenet's great delight. "Show him the newspaper clipping," said Mr. Chauvenet to De Pachmann.

"No, no, zat weel nevair do." Said the great Russian. "Eet ees not honorable. First I am, look, ze zhentleman," said he, squaring off and smiting himself on the chest, "zen after I am ze musician."

The clipping was from the *Boston Herald*. It was a very clever piece of sarcasm aimed at Paderewski. It was in the form of a critical review of a Paderewski performance, but it was a discriminating technical "roast" of the man of unmanageable hair. There was also a paragraph of high praise of De Pachmann. Young De Chauvenet, proud of his great master, was anxious to show this, but De Pachmann demurred through motives of professional courtesy... "Let me show it," insisted De Pachmann's protégé.... His guest began reading the clipping, read to where Paderewski's performance was called "monotonous and anemic," and there he paused to say that the criticism was eminently correct. "You seenk so?" said De Pachmann. "Bot zat ees so tarraible—'monotonous and anemic!'—so har-rd, no?" "No harder that it should be," said the Denver man in a tone of confidence. De Pachmann was on his feet again. He grasped De Chauvenet by the shoulder, turned him round and then reached over and tapped his visitor's breast:

Leesten, my saun, my Chauvenet, leesten! See how zey coincide, sees spaindeed Denver creeteeck and see gr-r-reat Vulff. Ees eet not seengulair? Moast zere not somesing zat ees true be een eet? Bot stop! Zees ees not for me to say. Ze courtessee profassianal—I moast r-r-rai-maimber.

The supposed critic read on to where a great wad of disapproval was thrown at Paderewski's rubato.... He said: "Now there's where Wulff[1] has struck the nail on the head again. Ah, what a difference between Paderewski's rubato and yours, Mr. de Pachmann."

"And mine you seenk—you like eet?" cried out the Russian.

"It is the only one in the world."

"Oh, so goo-o-ood, so, swe-e-ed of you to say zat! I kees your hand. Bot I moost say for Paderewski that in some seengs—ah-h-h, he ees grand. Een Chicago I hear heem once play von leetle fantaisie of Liszt—ze same weech I hear Liszt heemself twainty years ago—and my eyes I shot zem and I seenk eet ees again Liszt playeeng ze fantaisie. You hear zat? I, De Pachmann, of Paderewski, say zat. See how good I am! I weel be honist, I weel be joast-bot, mong deeuh, how zat Paderewski ze poor piano hammair and bang and jomp on!"

The relationship apparently did not last. In 1916 de Chauvenet was billing himself in Los Angeles as a "famous organist and composer." A short biography appearing in a California recital program of March 26 of that year stated that he had already been the head of the music departments in three state universities, that he had recently established the de Chauvenet Conservatory of Music at 845 South Figuroa Street, and quotes de Pachmann: "A genius truly." The Los Angeles concert consisted of organ solos, a duet for clarinet and trumpet, a violinist named Reher in a piece by Vieuxtemps and his own "The Mocking Bird," Mme. Helene de Chauvenet singing David's *Charmant Oiseau* and other works, Jean playing his own piano work, "Spring Inspiration," and Margaret Gray McKee, the star attraction of the concert, "Queen on Whistlers," whistling "The Nightingale and the Rose . . . as the curtain rises of the dawn of 'Springtime'" and "Beautiful Isle of Somewhere" as an encore.

Another interesting Pachmann pupil was the American John Adams Warner, a prodigy born in Rochester, New York, in 1886 who graduated from Harvard University in 1906. He studied first with Carlo Buonamici in Boston, with further lessons in Florence, Italy, with Carlo's father Giuseppe, a Liszt and von Bülow student. In Europe he also studied with Harold Bauer and Pachmann, finishing with Godowsky in Vienna. In the late 1930s and early 1940s Warner performed concertos with the Works Progress Administration Orchestra and the Tri-City Orchestra (Albany, Troy and Schenectady, New York). The program booklet for one performance stated that "he had a few lessons in Chopin with the master interpreter of that composer's work, Vladimir de Pachmann." His career took a sharp turn when he married the daughter of New York State governor Alfred E. Smith, and then became a New York state policeman. By 1923 he had become the state superintendent of police. In 1943 he left the police and was called to active duty in the army as a major. He died twenty years later.

Though Pachmann had taught, to one extent or another, some young women and several young men, except for his wife he had no real pupils. It is true that there had been Marguerite Stilwell in Berlin, Frederick Dawson in England and Berlin, de Chauvenet in America, and later John Warner, Allan Bier and Anton Bilotti in the pianist's old age. There may have been others. (In one interview towards the end of his life Pachmann claimed Eugen d'Albert had been studying Bach with him when they visited King Christian IX of Denmark together in 1885.) All of these people had a few lessons, but none studied intensely as had Maggie. His temperament was not suited for teaching. He was too eccentric and high-strung, with a competitive and jealous streak. He was also a perfectionist with very high standards. Even the most gifted would have found lessons with him unpredictable and trying. Besides, he was too preoccupied with himself and his own career. When it ended, he was too old and his mind was too fragmented to ever give lessons of any value. Some, like Aldo Mantia, claimed lessons when Pachmann was in his dotage, but there is no evidence to support the claims (see notes for chapter four). And in most cases, the lessons with young men seem to have involved more complicated relationships.

⟿

Lüchow's restaurant, an eatery on New York's East 14th Street that opened in 1882, was just a few steps from Steinway Hall and the Academy of Music. It soon became famous for its enormous menu centered on German cuisine, as well as the many musical artists who congregated there. It was also a favorite watering hole for numerous journalists who regularly wrote about the same artists. When he was in New York Pachmann liked to eat at Lüchow's, where also often could be found James Gibbons Huneker, sometimes accompanied by his friend Rafael Joseffy. Full of smoke, noise and male conviviality, it was the perfect place to relax and have a good beer.

Being friendly with Pachmann was difficult. He wasn't able to separate his private and public selves, and anyone who didn't like Pachmann's playing was, to him, someone who didn't like him. He had come to expect love and devotion from audiences—it was a large part of the personal rapport he had with them. But from friends he expected even more. From them the admiration and loyalty had to be unqualified and unstinting. He took the slightest divergence as a personal affront and would be furious. In his memoir *Steeplejack*, Huneker wrote of an incident that occurred at Lüchow's that has taken on the aura of a legend:

> One night at Lüchow's, sitting with Ed Ziegler,[2] August–Himself[3]—Joseffy and De Pachmann, an argument was started. De Pachmann, who had been especially irritable, turned vicious and spitting out his rage—he was a feline person—he called Joseffy an unprintable name. Before Joseffy could answer the villainous attack, I, with a recklessness unusual for me, let the Chopinzee have the contents of my glass full in the face. If I had been sitting closer I would have slapped his mouth; as it was, wetting might cleanse it. Sputtering, he was led away by a waiter and presently returned, smiling as if nothing had happened. Joseffy was disgusted with me, as well he might be. It was unpardonable, my conduct, and I promptly apologized. Then De Pachmann explained it was jealousy, as I had mentioned Joseffy's name seven times more—he gave the exact figure—than his in my Chopin book. It sounded childish but it dissolved the disagreeable business into laughter. After all had gone away except Ziegler, Joseffy turned to me and severely reproached me but ended his sermon thus: "And you, of all men, wasted such a lot of good beer!" I can recall the diabolical twinkle in his eye yet.

Josephine Huneker, the critic's widow, later wrote a letter to the *New York Times* denying that her husband ever threw the beer. Arthur Friedheim, the Liszt pupil whom Pachmann had thought "too modest" in 1891 but had become a friend, related a somewhat wilder version of the story in his memoirs:

There was his unforgettable encounter with James Huneker many years ago in Lüchow's famous restaurant. I was not there, but I know others who were, and the tale is true, alright. Huneker had been outspoken in some of his criticism of de Pachmann's playing and de Pachmann felt he had a personal grievance against the critic, else he welcomed the opportunity to do some clowning in public. Huneker was sitting at a table with Harry Rowe Shelley[4] when de Pachmann stepped up to him and snarled: "Now I know why you always criticize my playing!" and mouthed a couple of dreadful phrases. Huneker said never a word, but picked up a stein of beer and calmly poured it over his tormentor's dress shirt. De Pachmann stamped madly up and down the aisles, in full view of the guests, shouting: "Skunk Huneker has insulted great Pachmann! Skunk Huneker has insulted great Pachmann!" The manager came to him and said, "I happened to witness the beginning of this trouble, Mr. de Pachmann, and I think your were entirely in the wrong. I shall have to ask you either to apologize to Mr. Huneker or else leave the premises and not return!" Lüchow's happened to be the restaurant most frequented by musical celebrities and the manager's suggestion had not appealed at all to de Pachmann. He agreed to apologize and he did apologize. He stepped back to the table and, at the top of his voice, shouted at poor, unoffending Huneker: "I apologze you skunk! I apologize you skunk!"

This incident almost certainly took place in 1900, just after Huneker's book on Chopin was issued. There are other versions as well.[5] Huneker claims that it was he, not Pachmann, who apologized, but Friedheim's report of Pachmann shouting "I apologize, you skunk!" has the ring of truth. On the other hand, Friedheim claims that Pachmann came over and said something offensive about Huneker, while the critic wrote that Pachmann was sitting with them and said something offensive about Joseffy, whom Huneker revered. It seems most likely it would have been offensive comments about Joseffy that caused Huneker's anger, whether he actually threw a glass of beer or not.

Today musical ethics would not allow relationships between critics and performers. Then, Huneker was only one of many musical journalists whose admiration for the artistry of particular artists led them to become intimates of the famous performers they were asked to review. In those days it was generally felt that such friendships between critics and artists gave the former a profounder understanding of the latter's abilities. The propriety of it was rarely questioned. The First World War destroyed the Victorian code of honor and ushered in a more cynical approach, which is still with us.

Maggie's name still turned up occasionally in the papers—it was the height of the sensation resulting from the Dreyfus trial, and Labori found himself rocketed to fame as Dreyfus's, and then Zola's, defender. Maggie was sharing that fame, but also retained some of her own as the former wife of Pachmann.

Pachmann earned a small footnote in the Dreyfus story. In August 1899 Labori was shot by an unknown assassin. He survived and went on to defend Dreyfus and Col. Picquart. All France was asking, "Who shot Labori?" Some (obviously anti-Dreyfusards trying to cover their tracks) suggested it might have been Maggie's jealous, former husband. The *Chicago Tribune* reported on August 20, 1899:

Labori's father . . . sends a . . . message . . . "I shall be glad if you will deny the absurd theories of the Paris press that the attack on my son could in any way be associated with M. Vladimir de Pachmann, the former husband of Mme. Labori. M. Pachmann has been in America for a long period. There is no ground whatever for the foolish and malicious reports in this regard."

The *Boston Globe* reported (September 24, 1899):

Yesterday a Globe correspondent asked him [Pachmann] to talk of Labori. "Labori! Labori!" he replied. "I like Labori. He is such a good father to my children. When I heard that because of his defense of Dreyfus he had been shot, I felt as if an iron hand had caught my heart and pressed it. We are good friends. Does that astonish you? His wife—my former wife—is angelic. He makes her happy. She has the attitudes of a living legend. She has only to come to the piano and sing or play the Cavatina from 'Semiramide' to make melody agitate with its wings [into] incomparable jewels. In her youthful voice it is music that [en]chants. Art is not all her life. She has the domestic virtues. And I—and I—have no other charm, no other aim, no other reason for being than my piano. It is my tyrant. It is jealous. It tolerates only one caprice in me—cigars."

All this was sure advertisement for his tour. Pachmann relaxed after he had discharged his engagements, attending the New York recital debut of composer/pianist Ernö Dohnanyi at Mendelssohn Hall on April 3, 1900. He nearly made a scene, calling out while Dohnanyi was playing, "Er spielt sehr schön, aber er sitz zu hoch!" ("He plays beautifully, but sits too high!") and walking out while Dohnanyi played the Brahms Handel Variations, exaggeratedly shaking his head, holding his hands over his ears and muttering "He shouldn't play that terrible Brahms!" He went backstage to the green room at intermission, but not to congratulate Dohnanyi, whose first wife remembered the incident in her memoirs:

"Soo-blime!" he cried ecstatically in his heavy Polish [*sic*] accent. "Soo-blime. Only you sit too high young man! And why, why do you play Brahms? You play Brahms so wonderful as Brahms is not worth to be played!"

On April 11 *MC* reported that Pachmann had yelled bravo when Dohnanyi played Chopin's C sharp minor Valse, and then gave a little recital without piano of his own, in the audience. A week later *MC* was still writing about this incident, reporting that the self-styled Pachmann had explained, "Ah! These titled pianists!" Later Huneker, who was at the recital, agreed that Dohnanyi sat too high (*Etude*, March 1905):

> It was true. Dohnanyi's touch is as hard as steel. He sat over the keyboard and played *down* on the keys, thus striking them heavily, instead of pressing and moulding the tone. De Pachmann's playing is a notable example of plastic beauty.

None of this stopped Pachmann from taking Dohnanyi's showpiece, his transcription of the Waltz from Delibes's "Naila," one of the great piano transcriptions of the Romantic era, to use as an encore piece. Sacheverell Sitwell thought Pachmann's performances of the work surpassed his playing of Chopin, calling them "perfection . . . the nuances and delicacies of his touch can never have been approached by any other pianist."

Pachmann admired Dohnanyi's playing. In the August 27, 1902, issue of *MC* Huneker wrote:

> Pachmann, Dohnanyi, Busoni and Rosenthal foregathered in London, and after the accustomed cloudy coquetries of all piano players when they meet, Dohnanyi began the evening with Beethoven. Busoni followed with Bach, then Rosenthal thundered and lightened, and the little Vladimir ended with a Liszt study marvelous in its finesse. When asked his opinion of the various performances his reply was brief to the point of epigram. "Dohnanyi plays like a youth, healthy, broad; Busoni plays Bach like a man, intellectually; Rosenthal plays swiftly ___" "And Pachmann?" interpolated a foolish one. "And Pachmann, he is more youthful than Dohnanyi, more intellectual than Busoni, plays swifter than Rosenthal, and—he also plays like Pachmann."[6]

When Pachmann played his final New York recital, something unusual occurred at the *New York Times*; someone at the drama desk thwarted critic W. J. Henderson a bit by slipping a favorable notice in between reviews of plays (March 2, 1900):

> The audience was plainly delighted with his work, and he might have gone on playing for another hour without wearying his hearers. What more could the spirit of a mortal desire? That Pachmann will come to us again seems now to be a certainty. That he will be welcomed like a visitor to a provincial town, by "a large circle of friends and admirers," is equally beyond doubt.

∽

When the tour ended Pachmann left the New World with pockets bulging. In the *MC* (July 4, 1900) Huneker wrote:

> The little pianist carries away a sum that ten years ago would have been considered very large . . . being a generous, forgiving man [he] sent 15,000 francs to his two children, who are with their mother Madame Labori. This money was sent through Morgan and Co., bankers, for I saw the draft. De Pachmann is on good terms with the Laboris, and seems to entertain a profound regard for his former wife and her handsome husband. And the French barrister, who is to visit us next fall on a lecturing tour, is a great admirer of the former teacher of his pretty wife. I have heard that the money M. de Pachmann so generously provided did not come amiss in the Labori household. *Bon voyage et au revoir*, Vladimir of the Velvet Hand!

There was enough money left over for Pachmann to buy a farm in New Jersey, which prompted a correspondent for the *Musical Age* (July 12, 1900) to write: "Of course, De Pachmann will soon be heard again in this country. A man who owns a Jersey farm must come over at intervals to see how the turnips grow."

Chapter 18

A Symbol for the Symbolists, 1900–1904

Pachmann had been appearing before the British public for eighteen years. Admirers there were habituated to a set routine—three or four recitals in London, at first in the old St. James's Hall, capacity 2,000, then after it was demolished he moved to Queen's Hall, capacity 3,000, and the Bechstein Hall, capacity 550, which he helped inaugurate, along with Busoni and Ysaÿe, when it opened in 1901. (It is now called Wigmore Hall, the name changed in 1914 out of anti-German sentiment.) In 1903 he gave one of the earliest solo recitals in the huge Albert Hall, capacity 5,500! In addition, several "popular concerts" (the "Pops" where he was the star attraction) were also necessary to satisfy the fans. At these he occasionally played the piano in celebrated quintets like Schubert's "Trout" and the Schumann E flat. Pachmann gamely accepted these assignments at the insistence of his management, but one wonders—he was completely unsuited for chamber music. The violinist Carl Fuchs contributed an anecdote to the *Manchester Guardian*, quoted in the *British Musician and Musical News* (February 1933) shortly after the pianist died:

> On another occasion we played with Pachmann. The programme was long, and at rehearsal we agreed not to repeat the variations in Schubert's Trout Quintet. "But I may repeat my solo-variation?" he asked, like a child. We let him. When at the concert he had repeated his variation a gleam of delight appeared on his face.

After much exposure in the capital, he would venture into the provinces, where he was particularly popular in Manchester and Birmingham. In a few years he extended these tours to include Scotland and Northern Ireland. When he was to tour America rather than Germany, and presented a London "farewell" recital, the critics wrote affectionate words of *bon voyage*. London's *Musical Standard* wrote (May 21, 1904) of his farewell recital a week earlier: "A large wreath with silk ribands depending and two fragrant bouquets were handed to the pianist, who will sail this week for America and be absent a year." This schedule, England and America with periodic visits to Germany and much later Italy (but no concerts elsewhere) sustained his career for the next two decades.

Sometimes this routine continued with the pianist traveling to Germany, which he liked to visit in the wintertime. In the winter of 1902/3 Cordelia Defries was visiting the Godowsky family, and she and Leopold's wife Frieda, along with an American pupil of Godowsky's named Rosa Habermann, called on Pachmann at his Berlin hotel. Cleveland's *Plain Dealer* published Ms. Habermann's recollections of their visit on October 30, 1904:

> He received us with a broad grin, in a torn wrapper or tea gown a la Japan, with many excuses concerning his attire, his forgetfulness, etc. He had just been reading some German philosophy. I asked him what it was and he answered more candidly than politely. "It is Schopenhauer but you don't understand it." I did not dare protest. . . . Then he began his tale of woe: how very sick he had been, and that he had not touched the piano for three weeks, and that he had thought of canceling his concert. I expressed my candid sorrow at all these misfortunes, but Mrs. Godowsky and Cordelia merely smiled and did not say a word; evidently they knew all these stories from A to Z, and also knew that they were not meant. I then rose and looked about the rooms and found many things of interest; letters of Sarasate, pictures of Rubinstein with dedications to Pachmann; books, mostly of a philosophical nature with remarks from Pachmann's own hand in all languages and the queerest orthography I ever saw.

Pachmann had one recital scheduled for Berlin's Philharmonie hall. Trying "an experiment," he would not allow the concert to be announced until two days before the event, telling friends that he wanted to see how many tickets could be sold at the last moment. The hall was sold out, the audience packed with members of the nobility and diplomatic corps, with "everyone who pretends to know anything at all about art and music in attendance," in Rosa Habermann's words. The recital was so successful that two more had to be scheduled soon after.

After Germany Pachmann would return to home base in London for the spring seasons. His programs rarely contained any new works, but at his Berlin Philharmonie recital on February 13, 1903, he included several pieces by a living composer named Ernst Eduard Taubert. By this time Pachmann's recitals had also evolved into a habit—his programs consisted mainly of small works. He still played large-scale works mostly

from Chopin, besides a few by other composers, but compared to other
famous pianists of his day, far less often. As a result his style of playing
evolved to its final form, and he became a complete miniaturist. Most
likely he didn't plan to become one, just as he never intended to be a Chopin specialist, but it came on him from playing so many small works. Of
course he always had a particular mastery of infinite shades of pianissimi,
but now he became even more obsessed with pianissimo, filing down his
dynamics to a *quasi niente* and rarely rising to fortissimo. It was a distilla-
tion of his earlier style, the ultimate refinement of his playing.

Some thought that his intensity and concentration flagged when he
played a work longer than a few pages, losing inspiration, the music dis-
integrating. Otto Florsheim, the Berlin correspondent for *MC,* was of this
opinion. In his review of a Pachmann recital in Berlin (*MC,* December 31,
1902), he wrote:

> His pianistic reproduction can be gauged by the number of pages the piece
> he plays consumes in print. Pieces of one page in length he performs most
> admirably, most exquisitely, most ravishingly, or anything else you choose to
> designate. Pieces of two pages are interpreted very beautifully still; with three
> pages he loses his musical grasp to some extent; with four pages he grows in-
> different, and in works of five or more pages he waxes proportionally reckless.

There probably was some truth to this, but Florsheim exaggerated. According to other critics, Pachmann's performances of Chopin's Berceuse
(six pages), Barcarolle (ten pages) as well as the Third Ballade (twelve
pages) were equally "unforgettable."

It seems that often Pachmann, somewhat like Godowsky, was capable
of playing most magnificently in the intimacy of a home setting. Just a few
weeks earlier Florsheim's colleague in Berlin, Arthur Abell, had written in
the same journal (*MC,* October 29, 1902):

> The other day I enjoyed a rare musical treat. . . . Vladimir de Pachmann
> honored me with a call at 3 o'clock one afternoon last week. Without any
> preliminaries he at once sat down to the piano—something he rarely does
> outside of his own rooms and the concert hall—and began to play to an
> audience of three—a friend who happened to be present, Mrs. Abell and
> myself. First he played Godowsky's wonderful study of the A minor study
> for the left hand. As he played it, it sounded rather like four hands than
> one. Then followed the united G flat studies, then others, for Pachmann
> thinks the world of Godowsky as a man, musician and virtuoso. Then
> he branched off to the original Chopin with a marvelous performance of
> the study in thirds. Such clearness, crispness, velocity and Klangzauber
> [magical sound]! Then followed the A flat Ballade, preludes, impromptus,
> nocturnes, and thus he played on for hours and hours. Twilight came on,
> but he allowed us no light, neither would he allow his audience of three to

move about or speak, but made us sit at his right side in silence, although he himself kept up a running fire of commentary on his playing that was most amusing. After about three hours of Chopin, during which we were in heaven, he changed to Weber, giving a most brilliant performance of "Invitation to the Dance," which he plays as no one else on earth can. Then followed snatches of Liszt, Schumann, Mozart, he ever and anon returning to his chief love Chopin. Words fail me to describe the magic of his playing. I have often heard Pachmann in public, but he is a man of moods, and I never heard him before in such a glorious mood, nor did I ever before realize what he could do in the way of technic. A fit of virtuosity suddenly seized him and for half an hour he reveled in his most dazzling feats of the keyboard. He played scales in thirds first with the right hand from the top to the bottom of the keyboard, then with the left hand from the bottom to the top, in the same rapid tempo in which he played single scales. Then he did the same in sixths and octaves, it seemingly making no difference to him, the double all coming out with the same speed and clearness as the single ones. Then he played chromatic scales in thirds, glissando, the same in sixths, and other tricks. He did the incredible in the way of lightening skips, in single notes and chords and other feats of virtuosity until we were completely awed by the skill of the man. Then he began to prelude, to improvise the most wonderful little cadenzas, runs, variations, &c., until it seemed as if the devil himself were let loose. . . . I was never in my life so impressed by piano playing—and I have heard a vast amount of it. The wonderful technical skill, the poetry, the soul, the magic of it, so affected me, hardened concertgoer though I am, that I could not sleep one minute that night. We all know what a great artist Pachmann is, but such a mood as he was in that day comes to him but rarely. It was both angelic and satanic. He played for fully five hours. My piano is only an upright, and not a good one even at that, but under Pachmann's hands it sounded like a superb grand. There is something extraordinary about his touch; he gets a quality of tone from a piano quite different from that of any other pianist.

While in Berlin Pachmann had a visit from Moriz Rosenthal, who had heard nothing but praise for Pachmann's playing of Chopin's Mazurkas, but had never himself heard him play any. Rosenthal fancied himself a superb Mazurka player, and vowed to find out about Pachmann's Mazurkas. Early in 1902 he knocked on Pachmann's Berlin door unannounced. Rosenthal told Leonard Liebling about the meeting, and Liebling couldn't wait to tell Huneker when he got back to New York. Some details about the visit were printed in Huneker's "Raconteur" column (*MC*, July 30, 1902)—Huneker didn't refrain from including a jibe:

So unbidden he went to Pachmann's flat and was lucky enough to catch the little wonder worker at home. He was probably embroidering, but that was not in the tale. . . . Rosenthal, so Liebling says, tells the story with gusto.

As reported in Huneker's book, *Variations*, Rosenthal asked Pachmann to play some Mazurkas for him so he could learn. The Chopinzee wasn't about to give up any secrets to a rival, and deliberately but exquisitely misplayed for his guest:

> Pachmann did not greet Rosenthal too sympathetically. "Ah!" he exclaimed when Moriz, the octave-thunderbolt, explained the reason for his unexpected appearance. "Ah! but I play the Mazurkas so badly. Now, if I had your technique"—his eyes fairly sparkled with malicious irony—"I might be able to play them!" However, he was persuaded, and once seated at the piano he didn't leave it till he had almost finished the entire collection. . . . How did he play them, this perverse magical artist? Rosenthal told me that he had never heard such beautiful, subtle, and treacherous playing; the treachery was the manner in which he interpreted the music. Not an accent was correct, the phrasing was falsified, though the precise notation was adhered to, and all delivered with a variety of touches positively exquisite. "There!" cried De Pachmann, as he finished, "that is the only was to play the Mazurkas." And he smiled with his eyes. "Not!" thought Rosenthal, who thanked his colleague and hurried into the open air where he could explode. Talk about camouflage! The joke was later when Rosenthal teased De Pachmann about his trickery and the Chopinzee absolutely grinned with joy.[1]

What is undeniable is that Pachmann found his extremely intimate approach difficult when playing with an orchestra. In September 1899 he told the interviewer for the *Worcester Spy*:

> I shall give recitals everywhere . . . but seldom with the orchestra, for I like to get the tone of the piano, its faintest color, and the effect is lost when I play with the orchestra.

Successful concerto performances with Pachmann depended heavily on the conductor. A sympathetic one could allow the pianist freedom while not overpowering the pianissimi, something difficult to achieve in the standardized inflation of Chopin's classical, "thin" orchestration. When Pachmann employed his subtle rubato colorations in works of an entirely different stamp such as Liszt's E flat Concerto, he was doomed to fail, as he did when he played that work with the Boston and Philadelphia orchestras in 1904:

"There are more poetry and beauty and artistic values in Liszt's E flat Concerto than he with his microscopic methods [and] dilettante ideals was able to elicit" complained a reviewer in the *Philadelphia Inquirer* on December 4, 1904. ". . . it seems Mr. de Pachmann's ambition is to rival the delicacy, the brilliancy, the precision and the soullessness of the music box and he appears to be in a fair way to attain his end."

By the end of the nineteenth century Pachmann's constant parade of so many little pieces adversely affected his platform behavior. When he played large-scale works he had to restrain his mannerisms to remain involved in the musical thread. Now with programs consisting entirely of small works he was freed from this restraint. Here is his program for March 14, 1904, in Bechstein Hall:

Mozart: Fantasy, C minor, K. 457
Beethoven: Rondo Capriccioso ("Rage Over a Lost Penny")
Mendelssohn: Two *Lieder Ohne Wörter*
Schumann: *Vogel als Prophet*
Schumann: *Warum?*
Schubert: Moment Musicale, Op. 94, No.3, F minor
Schubert-Liszt: Hark! Hark! The Lark
Chopin: Etudes, Op. 25, No.'s 1, 2, 3, 4, 6 and 8
Chopin: Ballade No 3, A flat, Op. 47
Chopin: Mazurkas, Op. 33, No. 4, B minor, and Op. 59, No 3, F sharp minor
Chopin: Valse, Op. 42, A flat

One of his typical all-Chopin programs of the time (Boston, November 1, 1904) was composed mostly of small works but began and ended with large ones:

Sonata No. 2, B flat minor
Nocturne, G major, Op. 37, No. 2
Four Preludes, Op. 28, Nos. 20, 19, 12 and 16
Valse, C sharp minor, Op. 64, No. 2
Valse, A flat, Op. 64, No. 3
Impromptu, A flat, Op. 29
Impromptu, F sharp major, Op. 36
Polonaise, C sharp minor, Op. 26, No. 1
Mazurka, D flat major, Op. 30, No. 3
Mazurka, A minor, Op. 67, No. 4
Scherzo, E major, Op. 54

This format naturally encouraged Pachmann's mannerisms, inviting him to talk to his audiences, before and after he played as well as sometimes while he was playing. There were gesticulations and grimaces accompanied by very audible comments, behavior that was now habitual. On May 24, 1902, Pachmann played at London's St. James's Hall. *MC* reported (June 18, 1902):

He opened well by getting into difficulties with his piano, which was not, apparently, by any means firm enough upon its legs to suit his exacting taste. However, when several programs had been commandeered to fill the gap between one of the casters and the floor, he requested his audience to "be serious" and set to work upon Weber's Sonata in A flat. The sonata suits his style well, and he played it charmingly. He was evidently in the best of spirits, and no member of the audience appreciated the music more than the pianist himself. He nodded, smiled, sighed and here and there even hummed a bar or two. In short, he drew his hearers' attention to the more beautiful passages by all the thousand and one artifices which de Pachmann has made peculiarly his own. His readings really seem to lose nothing by these little tricks and, indeed, the more he indulges in them the better he seems to play. His gestures are the natural outcome of his emotions, and the more deeply he feels the poetry of the music the more exaggerated do they become.

Apparently it was not alright for the audience to make audible comments. A reviewer for the *Washington Post* had written (March 15, 1900):

He expresses the music with his eyes, shoulders and hands in a way that is marvelous in itself. Most of his audiences are fit to regard him as a curiosity. They go to his recitals in the same spirit in which they would . . . take a trip to the zoo. He is treated as a rare animal, whose every movement is followed with lorgnettes and opera glasses. They would love to poke straws at him, judging from the way they act . . . yesterday Mr. De Pachmann, who is a fine and sensitive artist, was forced to remark that he could not continue unless the audible remarks should cease.

This expansion of his odd platform demeanor had started in Germany, but really gathered momentum in England, where the national heritage was sympathetic to eccentric behavior. The composer John Francis Barnett wrote:

Pachmann, as we know, had a habit of nodding his head in time with the rhythm of the piece he was performing. I observed . . . as did several other persons round about me, that there was an old lady sitting in the orchestra quite near the piano, who was enjoying the music so much that she was nodding her head. . . . The result was, when Pachmann turned round with his face towards the orchestra and indulged in the habit I have quoted, his head nodded perfectly in time with that of the old lady. . . . The effect was just like that of two porcelain mandarins placed opposite one another whose heads had been set in motion. Some young girls sitting in front of me were so intensely amused that they were laughing quite loudly. I almost forgave them, for the situation was too comical for words. It is really wonderful the way Pachmann can play the most difficult passages without ever looking at the keys, for his head is nearly always in a sympathetic manner towards the audience. I feel sure that few pianists could imitate him in this respect with success.

〜

After his extended stay in Berlin, Pachmann returned to England in the spring of 1898. His first recital was at St. James's Hall on May 14; the *Times* reported on May 16: "M. de Pachmann's playing is so meritorious that all the more regret must be felt for the absurd affectations of manner which seem to have grown upon him even more strongly of late." Many people were now coming to his recitals only to witness the antics. A third recital in the same hall on June 18 elicited this from the *Times*:

> A large audience, a goodly portion of which, to judge by their behaviour, regarded the concert merely as a source of amusement. The inevitable result of his many mannerisms has already come about, and it is to be feared that all his hearers, except a small minority, miss the many fine points in his performances in their anxiety to enjoy to the full the facial contortions which seem inseparable from them.

But his actual playing was still receiving rave reviews. The September 11, 1898, *Los Angeles Times* reported:

> Vladimir de Pachmann's reading of Chopin's B minor Sonata has been accepted in London as superior to that of either Eugen d'Albert or Herr [George] Liebling. It is said of him that he surpassed himself in its interpretation and rendition.

The good press and the notorious mannerisms worked to sell tickets, and as London's *Times* reported on October 17, 1898:

> Whatever the cause may have been, an enormous audience attended the Russian pianist's recital . . . when there was not an available seat nor any standing room worth mentioning.

Some critics were disconcerted that eccentricity was appearing in the concert hall, rather than the music hall where it belonged. A notice in the *Times* on June 7, 1901, was typical:

> The entertainment went with almost as much spirit and created almost as much hilarity as a performance of Mr. Chevalier's.[2] M. de Pachmann no longer contents himself with making faces and throwing his hands about; his comments on his own playing are often audible, and when they are so are understood to be laudatory. Considering how much of his attention must needs be given to this side of his entertainment, it is rather to his credit that he should be able to give good interpretations of so many pieces. . . . There would be no objection to the buffooneries in which the performer chooses to indulge if he only did not play so well; it is melancholy to think of the position he might have taken except for his tricks, in which he is of course encouraged by the hardly-suppressed laughter of his hearers.

The same paper wrote the following on November 30, 1903:

Bechstein Hall was crowded for the entertainment provided under the guise of a pianoforte recital by M. de Pachmann, who is now almost universally accepted as an intentionally humorous performer. As we have often said before, blind or very short-sighted hearers are the only ones who can form a really just opinion as to the artist's playing, and even these, though fortunately guarded from the temptation to watch what new grimace will be introduced, are disturbed by the audible remarks with which the player now thinks fit to interlard his manual performances.

A new feature of his outrageous platform behavior was that he now sometimes danced a bit on stage. On June 26, 1902, Leopold Godowsky wrote from Berlin to his American friend, W. S. B. Matthews, describing concerts he had attended:

I forgot to mention Pachmann. He gave two recitals, made extensive speeches, dansed [*sic*] on one occasion a Mazurka on the stage of St. James's Hall, before his entire audience to make his public appreciate the beauties of the Mazurkas of Chopin.[3]

All this was accepted at the time by most critics and members of the public as sincere expressions of Pachmann's art. A reporter for the *Dallas Morning News* wrote (January 12, 1905, quoting a report that appeared earlier in the Milwaukee *Evening Wisconsin*):

As for de Pachmann's mannerisms, one has only to meet him in private to realize that they are not affectations, but an integral part of his fascinating personality. He moves about with a restless activity that reminds one of a bird on a twig—like Adelina Patti, he is always "up and doing." It is not a "pernicious activity" either; on the contrary, much of it comes from a continuous flow of ideas, and an inherent desire to please—quite an unusual trait in a man. . . . Pachmann can not help giving expression to each flitting emotion. Had he not been a pianist he would have been an actor. It must not be supposed that de Pachmann is in any way light or frivolous. Underneath all his effervescent exterior there appears to be a very serious vein, and intermingled are droll humor and keen sarcasm, which make one feel that, after all, he may be slyly laughing at everybody.

Most critics on both sides of the Atlantic realized that it didn't matter, as long as the playing triumphed. The reviewer for London's *Times* concurred on May 24, 1902:

There is so much seriousness—not to say solemnity—in concert-rooms nowadays, that preliminary frivol does little harm; and after all, there is no reason why a great pianist should not enjoy the music he plays as well as the audience to whom he plays it.

The enthusiasm of audiences, the mixture of applause and laughter following this new format encouraged Pachmann, and inspired him to outdo himself in the freedom of his playing and his behavior. That is the famous Pachmann remembered by many who heard him just before World War One.

But even worse was to come later!

$$\backsim$$

William Armstrong interviewed Pachmann at the Hotel Ronveau. The pianist was obviously in a foul mood for the interview, which was published in the *Saturday Review* on October 17, 1903:

His greeting was scarcely an assurance of success. "You want me to tell you how I make my effects in playing Chopin. I should be paid for interviews, and I should not tell you that even then. I am sixty [in fact, he was fifty-five] and I shall soon be dead, and it will be well." This was a cheerful beginning . . . "What have you there?" he asked, eyeing my notebook. "The questions I wanted to ask you." "What are they?" "Why should I bother you with them if you have no intention of answering?" "Tell me the first? . . ." "It is about Beethoven." "Beethoven and Brahms I would throw into the chimney as far as their piano compositions are concerned . . ." . . . If this was not Chopin it was at least interesting. His meaning was perfectly clear. He was judging the piano compositions of Beethoven from the point of the purely pianistic as compared with Chopin, the composer of all others who wrote for the piano as the piano. . . . "Come up to my sitting-room and I will show you how I play Chopin." . . . De Pachmann took his place at the piano, I seated myself in a chair by the window. . . . Nocturne followed nocturne, then came the Cradle Song and the Polonaise in C Sharp minor. . . . De Pachmann played on for nearly an hour without interruption, going from one thing to another. The soft, insinuating, liquid quality of tone, the delicate embellishments, wonderfully soft but vibrant, kept steadily on. De Pachmann was another man; temper, curiosity, childish naïveté had been left for the moment below stairs. . . . "In playing Chopin all lies in the fingering," said De Pachmann presently, talking as he played. "How many have cunningly watched me do these same things to find out how I did them. Did they find out? Scarcely; they would not have kept on playing with such a hard tone afterward if they had. It has taken me thirty years to study out these things for myself. Let them do the same. Why should I give away my bread? . . . But in Chopin all lies in the fingering. In playing his music pianists get hard, brilliant effects, when they should have the singing, velvety delicacy that Chopin requires. They use the wrong fingers. The fingered editions of his works are full of errors in this direction. I very early found out that if I played Chopin as he demanded to be played I must study out my own fingering. Hour after hour I have tried first one way then another, until I got the quality of tone and the legato that I wished . . . The true artist can give such variety of tone to a simple five-finger exercise that he can make it beautiful. But how many play five-finger exercises over and over like machines until they have taken their daily allowance of mechanism. Listen to every tone that you play, and above all, listen if you would play Chopin. What an artist [Anton] Rubinstein was in the study of tone! The first theme of Schumann's Fantaisie, opus 17, is only five notes, but how he played those five notes! But Rubinstein is dead. I am the greatest living pianist, Godowsky is next, Rosenthal is perhaps the third, and Paderewski fourth. I am the greatest, but Godowsky is next. Don't forget to print that; it would please him to know that I said so." I promised.

෴

Another writer of the time who was fascinated with Pachmann was the English memoirist Gerald Cumberland (real name Charles Frederick Kenyon), who a few years later described his encounter with the great pianist in *Musical Opinion* (August 1918):

What a strange, exotic personality he flings in the face of the public. There is something faun-like in it; something that reminds me of an enchantingly repulsive orchid I saw in Paris in 1913. I once stood by de Pachmann as he played Chopin and, as he almost invariably does at his public recitals, talked, looked and smiled as he played. But he was not talking to me. He was talking to an invisible something that had its existence about midway between his right shoulder and the near leg of the piano. His eyes were focused on an unseen object a yard away from his face; it was at *this* he looked, at *this* he talked. . . . His playing was so exquisitely fragile that it can be compared with nothing material. We lavished compliments upon him and he gave a gesture of weary acceptance, implying "Yes, yes. But what is your praise to me who has been praised by all the great ones of the earth?" Yet it was evident that our compliments pleased him, for the more we praised him, the more rapturous did his playing become.

Cumberland's memoir *Set Down in Malice*, published in 1919, includes a "fantastic" appraisal of Pachmann and a description of his "plant-like" personality, as well as a glimpse of the atmosphere at his concerts:

Perhaps the most exquisite and the most fragile thing in the world at the present is the Chopin playing of Vladimir de Pachmann. For more than a quarter of a century writers have been attempting to reproduce his coloured music in coloured words. They have all failed. De Pachmann is an exotic, a hothouse plant. Not a hot house plant among many other plants, but a plant living luxuriously and solitarily and with exaggerated self consciousness in its own hothouse. In thinking of him one feels that he belongs to the very last minute of civilisation's progress. . . . It is strange that so exotic a personality should have a firm and unrelaxing hold on the public. He is not caviare to the general. Villiers de l'Isle-Adam[4] is worshipped by the few; Walter Pater cannot have more than a thousand sincere disciples, but de Pachmann is adored by millions. "Millions" is no exaggeration. People are taken out of themselves whilst he plays. You remember, don't you? the Paderewski craze in America fifteen years ago, when the platform was stormed and taken by assault night after night by society ladies. I witnessed pretty much the same kind of thing at a de Pachmann recital in a Lancashire town; but the latter pianist was stormed, not by society ladies, but by unemotional bank clerks, stockbrokers, merchants, working men and women. At the end of the concert, they flowed on to the platform in hundreds, and surrounded the pianist whilst he played encore after encore, smiling vacantly the while and enjoying himself immensely, pausing between each piece only to motion his ring of worshippers a little farther from the piano. An enigmatic creature, this; a creature who will never give up his secret; perhaps, even, a creature who is not aware that he possesses a secret.

This is quaint reading today, but Cumberland's was not the most colorful example of prose of its kind; he had a friend, a poet who wrote in a bizarre style, who was to become the leading English spokesman on Pachmann's behalf. This was Arthur Symons, one of the leaders of the decadent movement at the turn of the twentieth century. Symons's writing matched the enthusiasm (if not the musical acuity) of Huneker and Hale on the other side of the Atlantic and even surpassed the purple of their prose. Symons became obsessed with Pachmann after he reviewed some of his concerts in 1900, just at the time he published a book of poems entitled *Images of Good and Evil* and another book entitled *The Symbolist Movement in Literature*. Pachmann's concerts inspired him to write poems and short stories and, in 1902, a long, detailed assessment of his art, "Pachmann and the Piano." (This essay first appeared in the magazine *Academy and Literature* in early 1902, and subsequently was included with another essay touching on Pachmann in Symons's book *Plays, Acting and Music* published in 1903, and again in a revised version in 1907.) The article created quite a stir at the time, but a century later the prose appears fussy, and the style pretentious and precious, with an awful aroma of artiness:

> His fingers have in them a cold magic, as of soulless elves who have sold their souls for beauty. And this beauty, which is not of the soul, is not of the flesh; it is a sea-change, the life of the foam on the edge of the depths, or it transports him into some mid-region of the air, between hell and heaven, where he hangs listening. He listens with all his senses. The dew, as well as the raindrop, has a sound for him.

Symons was institutionalized on several occasions and officially declared insane just at the time he wrote the expanded version of this essay. There are passages where, perhaps, this shows through, giving the knowledge-able reader an uncomfortable feeling that this hyper-sensitivity touches on some hidden truth:

> He seems to touch the notes with a kind of agony of delight; his face twitches with the actual muscular contraction of the fingers as they suspend them-selves in the very act of touch. . . . The notes . . . mean for him just the sound and nothing else. You see his fingers feeling after it, his face calling to it, his whole body imploring it. Sometimes it comes upon him in such a burst of light that he has to cry aloud, in order that he may endure the ecstasy. You see him speaking to the music.

Symon's literary achievements are debatable, but at the time he had an enormous reputation as a serious and subtle writer. The essay persuaded many who were repelled by Pachmann's increasing platform manner-isms to rethink their opinions. Symons never forgot Pachmann's playing, remaining the pianist's prophet to his end. Cumberland published his memoir *Written in Friendship* in 1923 after the decadent movement had died, buried in the mud and trenches of the First World War. He quoted Symons remembering the halcyon early years of the new century, and gave readers a glimpse of Symons's madness:

> But listen. Arthur Symons speaks. "Yes it was wonderful, like distant music: like Pachmann playing. Those deft, magic hands of Pachmann's—yes, yes! Nothing in our present art-world is so mysteriously beautiful as Pachmann's music. He plays for me. When he sees me, he embraces me: he recognizes in me the genius he himself possesses!"

Cumberland continued:

> Is there something in Pachmann that recalls to Symons the old days when youth itself was an intoxicant and life a vision, and art the gateway to Heaven? I think there is. . . . Exotic—that is the word. Beardsley was exotic. The *Yellow Book* swam in a sultry haze.

Perhaps it was the voluptuous side of Pachmann's art with its hint of over-ripeness and rancid sweetness that attracted the symbolist writers, and one might add Huneker too: "The air smelt of tuberoses, but poi-soned ones. It is like a new sin one returns to for its novelty, perfectly aware of its danger."

To these writers, Pachmann embodied the decayed and rarified atmo-sphere of the *fin de siècle*. But it is wrong to think that the pianist shared their sensibility, or that because of his exotic personality and fragrant (sometimes too fragrant) art, he somehow was part of the decadent literary movement. Pachmann was no aesthete. He had no visual sensitivity, and later when Cesco Pallottelli took him to see the Sistine Chapel, he said, "Very fine, Cesco, let's go to the Campo de' Fiori" (Rome's flea market). Unlike Dorian Gray, opulent surroundings meant nothing to him. Nor was his collection of gems anything like that of Des Essients, the aesthete-hero of Huysmans's novel *À rebours* (thought by many to be the supreme expression of *l'esprit décadent*), who had a jeweler encrust his pet tortoise's shell with gems when he became disturbed by the clash of colors the unadorned shell presented against the tint of his carpet.

Symons was mistaken in thinking of the pianist as a fellow artist, living in an enchanted world far above the mundane, perfecting his art and ennobled by it. This mistaken idealization left out the man of flesh and blood.

Chapter 19

Captured by Baldwin, 1904–1905

We can guess what Richard Copley and his bosses at the Wolfsohn Musical Bureau had endured in managing Pachmann. Perhaps the guaranteed huge income he produced for them was not sufficient for all things. We do know that in July 1904 an obscure American manager named Loudon C. Charlton made the pianist an attractive management proposal, and he soon replaced Wolfsohn. Pachmann in all likelihood made inquiries about Charlton to his English managers, Schulz-Curtius, and received satisfactory answers. Pachmann had many eccentricities and extravagant ways, but when it came to managing his career, he was very hard-headed, and demanded to know the exact details of fees, contracts and percentages. Perfectly aware of his own worth, he knew his popularity sold out concerts, and he could set his own terms.

Charlton was a novice who had opened his first concert bureau just four years earlier in America's Midwest, managing minor artists. Most likely he offered Pachmann a more lucrative deal than Wolfsohn, probably willing to take a smaller percentage to land a celebrity whose success was guaranteed. Pachmann was in fact his first artist of international stature; later his bureau grew and became quite successful, and he soon managed other stars such as sopranos Nellie Melba and Marcella Sembrich, plus important orchestras including the New York Philharmonic. Apparently Charlton was somewhat flamboyant—later when he managed pianist Josef Lhevinne, he insisted Lhevinne wear a green felt hat "so he would be recognized in small-town railway stations." With Pachmann he met his match in flamboyance and eccentricity.

Charlton played it safe and duplicated the itinerary that Wolfsohn had mapped out for Pachmann's previous tour. Pachmann made Charlton's task easier, suppressing his distaste for playing with conductors and agreeing to perform Chopin's F minor Concerto in most of the cities in which he had played triumphant recitals on the previous tour. This fourth, 1904/1905 American tour took him as before through the Midwest to Texas, swerved up to Canada, then down the Pacific coast before returning east, but there were some surprises. The most immediate and important was the change of pianos. He probably would never have left Steinway if it weren't for a friend, Arnold Somlyo, whom Pachmann had known since his Vienna student days. Somlyo, now manager of the artists department of the Baldwin Piano Company, somehow persuaded Pachmann to play Baldwin pianos.

It was a daring decision, for the Baldwin piano was hardly a worthy competitor for Steinway. Pachmann was the first artist of international renown to use the Baldwin piano at his concerts, founding a distinguished line of artists that any piano manufacturer could envy, one that later included Claudio Arrau, Wilhelm Backhaus, Jorge Bolet, Ossip Gabrilowitsch, Walter Gieseking, Josef Lhevinne, and Moriz Rosenthal. It was a great coup and stroke of luck for Baldwin to have Pachmann as their leading artist, and in ensuing years the company would make a fortune from the sale of pianos which were first exhibited to the public with the unique tonal colors of the famous "Pachmannissimo."

The inferiority of the instrument, at least when compared to the Steinway, did not go unnoticed. Richard Aldrich of the *New York Times* mentioned it in his review of the New York performance of the Chopin Concerto. Pachmann, however, mostly avoided displaying the harsh and shallow tone of inferior instruments because he rarely played loudly. Apparently his caressing touch brought out the best of the instruments he used, from Steinways on down to the lowly English piano Chappell, which the pianist was once obliged to play at a concert, and announced: "Ladies and Gentlemen, I will now play on the world's worst piano!" Chappell was making a major effort, vigorously pursuing a concert artist bureau; by the end of 1903 the company was rumored to have become the owner of both Queen's and St. James's halls.

Amazingly, he was allowed back within the sacrosanct walls of Boston's Symphony Hall to play the concerto again with the Boston Symphony. Thirteen years had gone by since the Nikisch incident, and the city had been divided in its opinion of Pachmann in the interim, the larger camp (headed by the *Herald*'s critic Philip Hale) idolizing him, with the smaller faction deploring him at best, not forgiving his antics. It was assumed by the management that there had been time enough for him to feel contrition, and that he would be on his best behavior—so the trustees of the Symphony must have thought. But Pachmann had other thoughts, and he did it again. By now he knew he could do no wrong in the eyes of his Boston fans, and he remembered his performance with Nikisch as one of his greatest successes in the city. What harm could there be in repeating it—both the playing, and the play acting? The young Olin Downes attended this second, October 29, 1904, performance and reminisced about it in the *Boston Post* nineteen years later (September 30, 1923, reprinted from H. Earle Johnson's 1950 book, *Symphony Hall, Boston*):

> One recalled his performance of the F minor concerto of Chopin here in Symphony Hall, years ago, a performance remembered in dreams. A performance of troubling beauty, because it was so perfect and would be so very soon and forever past. . . . At that time he had complained of nervousness. He had insisted on having his music with him—a rare proceeding by pianists of sufficient experience and reputation to appear with leading orchestras. He had brought on his secretary . . . on the stage to turn pages. The music was before him, the conductor had lifted his baton, the worshipful secretary assiduously turned the pages. Only after the performance was it observed that de Pachmann, who peered earnestly at the notes as he played, had carefully put the music on the rack—upside down. The conductor was Gericke,[1] who obviously thought de Pachmann's behavior atrocious, and who showed no signs of cordiality when the pianist rose to bow, as is the custom, first to the audience, then to conductor and orchestra. De Pachmann was quick. Turning to salute Gericke and his men, he must have seen the latent snub in the leader's eyes. He turned a quarter, not a half of the circle. He bowed three times, very solemnly, to the piano.

Gericke was furious. Pachmann was already contracted to play the Chopin Concerto again with the Boston orchestra on their annual visit to New York. He also agreed to participate in a benefit fund concert on November 28, 1904, playing Liszt's E flat Concerto in Boston, and again in Philadelphia, but the year turned out to be Pachmann's final season with the Boston Symphony, as the trustees angrily terminated any further dealings with the Chopinzee. Fanatic Boston fans would have to travel to other cities to hear him play with an orchestra for his remaining American tours.

Despite the admiration for his playing, Pachmann's Boston fans never really fathomed who he was as a person, but who could fault them for that? A few days after the benefit, Philip Hale printed an interview with the pianist in the *Boston Herald* (December 4, 1904). The printed interview is as much a transcription, or even a translation, as it is a report of a conversation with Pachmann. This was Boston. Pachmann's eccentric, colorful and earthy dialect would never do. In Hale's filtered report, the pianist is made to resemble the polished and sophisticated artist that Hale's readers wanted or imagined him to be. The critic was obviously intent on stressing Pachmann's intellectual ability, perhaps to silence those, like the New York critics, who constantly complained about his intellectual deficiencies, as reflected in both his playing and his platform demeanor:

Vladimir de Pachmann talked . . . last week . . . not only affably . . . but with gusto. He had finished Ribot's "La Logique des Sentiments," a book published recently in Paris . . . Mr. de Pachmann delights in metaphysics, philosophy, psychology. He is an enthusiastic admirer of Ribot and Nietzsche. Schopenhauer appeals to him in less degree. The pianist, Rosenthal, a man of wide reading, is also a disciple of Nietzsche, and Mr. de Pachmann is an admirer of Rosenthal, as he is of Godowsky and Joseffy. Mr. de Pachmann was, in fact, much more inclined to talk about Ribot than about music. He was eager to talk about mineralogy, especially about precious stones, of which he is a passionate collector. His knowledge, his friends say, would put the most expert gemmary to confusion. There is a blue diamond in London longed for by the interpreter of Chopin. Like all men who truly love gems, he does not wear them. He is as simple in his dress as in his eating and drinking. When he did talk about musicians, especially about pianists, his conversation was free from malice. He praised warmly some of the Chopin arrangements by Godowsky. He hopes to play some of them in public. He has been practising one for three years, and it is almost mastered—so he said, but he probably can even now play it backwards. . . . Mr. de Pachmann is discriminative. [Edouard] Risler is a sound, solid pianist, but he has not the grace and the poetry in interpretation that Mr. de Pachmann demands. [Francis] Planté has been overrated; Saint Saens [*sic*] had inimitable chic and elegance; Tausig was dry; Josef Hofmann is really musical—his apparent indifference is in his face, his mask, not in his soul. And how about Liszt? . . . Pachmann described in admirably chosen words, the romanticism of Liszt's interpretations, his poetic touch and his lace-like arabesques, but he did not hesitate to say that his technique, in these days when technique runs in the streets, would not be considered extraordinary; as a matter of fact, some would find it inadequate. . . . When he was asked about modern Russian music for the piano, he had little to say; the music evidently is not to his taste. Yet he is a good Russian. This reporter remembered that some years ago Mr. de Pachmann told him in New York that he wished before he retired to go throughout Russia playing Chopin's music to the peasants. He still likes Henselt's Concerto and he told a story. Once in England he played the Concerto and by accident or intention the composer's name did not appear on the programme. When he struck the last chord there was a storm of applause. After the concert many complimented him on the beauty of the composition and told him, he need not be ashamed to acknowledge it as his; that the composer of such a work had no right to be modest. Furthermore the reviews praised the 'new' concerto to the skies and prophesized wisely that it would be played throughout the world and enlarge the fame of de Pachmann. The pianist, when he told the story was a marvel of mobile glee. . . . "My managers told me in New York a little while ago to be 'dignified' and 'reserved.' For nearly an hour I sat like a good boy, but I could not play. I played only notes. After the concert they said, 'The next time do as you please.' I feel the music when it is beautiful.

I feel it to such a degree that I cannot keep still." Nor is he at all disquieted when any one remonstrates with him for his "perversion" of, say, a study by Moscheles. "But it is impossible to play it the way it is written. It is so stiff, so dry. I make it at least sound beautiful." . . . The pianist may not visit America again. He dreads the voyage, and he does not wish to lag superfluous on the concert stage. "I hear my own music and when it does not sound so that it pleases my ears, I shall stop. Then I shall have Rosenthal and Godowsky visit me and play to me, but if anyone invites me to play, the piano will be locked." He looks forward to peaceful days in some villa in Italy, in the country. Let us hope that he will impart to some pianist the secret of his inimitable touch, his sense of rhythm, his art of mixing colors. But can these things be taught?

Knowing that some readers might wonder why he didn't simply copy down what Pachmann said, with or without dialect, Hale continued:

Any attempt to reproduce his conversation is in vain, for it is impossible to describe in words the illuminative facial play, the wealth of expressive gesture, swiftness of his speech, the use he makes of three languages. They that are disquieted by an occasional remark or bit of pantomime while he is playing should talk with him. Mr. de Pachmann is something more than a virtuoso of singular individuality, a pianist-interpreter; he is a man of reading, and reflection, a wit, a thinker, a philosopher. And in his address, in his quickly shifting moods, in his caprices he has the fantastical irregularity of genius.

⟳

Critic Will Hubbard in Chicago loved Pachmann's performance of the Chopin F minor Concerto with the orchestra and conductor Frederick Stock. *Chicago Daily Tribune*, March 11, 1905:

He played the concerto with the printed page before him, but he was nowise bound to it either musically or histrionically. He wove a spell of tonal beauty which held every hearer entranced, and he indulged in his quaint by play with all his accustomed freedom and liberality. It is futile to attempt to criticize Pachmann. He is a law unto himself, and what in other public players would be reprehensible from a musical and artistic viewpoint becomes with him liberties so captivating that the listener would not have one of them changed or omitted.

Hubbard ended his report:

Ignace Paderewski . . . arrived in Chicago yesterday afternoon. The eminent Polish pianist will give his recital in Orchestra hall this afternoon . . . completely sold out save for a few seats on the stage.

The 1905 tours of the two pianists overlapped, and Pachmann was goaded by the press to comment. An interviewer for the February 10 *Oregonian* wrote: "De Pachmann had somewhere learned the good American slang word 'bluff' and he intimated that he thought that was what Paderewski is—a huge bluff." A career-threatening accident occurred while Paderewski was riding a train that stopped short, awakening him in the middle of the night, hurting him and causing severe pain in his neck and back. He had to cancel further appearances and abandon his tour. He had been scheduled to play at a benefit concert at the Metropolitan Opera House for the Polish actress Helena Modjeska on May 2, 1905. It was Modjeska who had given Paderewski his start when he was young and unknown, and now she was in need, having made bad investments. The theatrical agent Daniel Frohman, arranger of the affair, suddenly found himself without a star attraction. Only one pianist could substitute for Paderewski in America—Pachmann. He agreed and played several Chopin works in the first half of the concert. Modjeska enacted the Macbeth sleepwalking scene and several other celebrities participated. But the biggest star was still Paderewski, who was on prominent display in a box.

Pachmann may have enjoyed replacing his rival, secretly hoping he could replace him elsewhere—even replace him from the face of the earth! We know he had a professional regard for the Pole, but that didn't stop him from feeling jealous. After the benefit there was a dinner—Pachmann probably sat with his friend, American baritone David Bispham, who had sung at the benefit. Bispham stayed at the Hotel Belvedere when he was in New York, and in his memoirs mentions running into Pachmann:

> I came down to a hotel breakfast once and found him finishing his own meal. As I went to shake hands with him, for I had not seen him in some time, he looked up at me as though I had been a stranger. Realizing that he was in one of his moods, I introduced myself by name; but, apparently annoyed, he shook his head violently as he consumed the last of his egg, saying: "Bismarck! Bismarck! I don't know Bismarck." Much amused, I sat at another table to see what was going to happen. When the waiter handed him his bill, he rose and made a deep bow, dismissing him at last with a large fee and an exaggerated flourish, immediately after which he came over, sat down with me, and began to talk in the most natural manner in the world.

Edwin Hughes's diary/notebook chronicled the story of other visitors at the Belvedere:

> Joseffy once said at the Hotel Belvedere he sent up his cards with Dr. William Mason's name also written on it. De Pachmann sent down by the bellboy that he could not read it. Joseffy said, "All right, let's go," but Mason said, "No, now that we have gone so far let's see it through." So he wrote both

names very plainly and sent them up again. De Pachmann sent word back downstairs saying "I haven't slept for two days and if you two come up here now I shall go crazy." Afterwards about 2 p.m. Joseffy met him in the dining room where de Pachmann had gone in his slippers. He was very profuse in his wishes to have Joseffy to come up but Joseffy would not do so then. Joseffy asked de Pachmann what he thought of Rosenthal. He said: "Oh, he is technically the greatest pianist in the world and he has improved so much musically recently" and ten minutes later after the conversation had drifted to something else, Joseffy asked de Pachmann if he had heard Rosenthal play lately. "Oh yes," said de Pachmann, "he pounds worse than ever." . . . After lunch at the hotel, de Pachmann said "Now I have a nice Baldwin piano in my room. I want you to telephone your studio that you will not give any lessons this afternoon. You and I will go up to my room and you will sit there and I will sit there and we will practice together." Joseffy said, "No!"[2]

◡◠

Pachmann's fourth tour of the United States was even more successful than the former ones. Audiences and critics both reached a pitch of appreciation previously unmatched, and couldn't get enough of him. In Chicago he appeared seven times. Orchestral Hall was newly opened and host to concerts by all the world's greatest artists, but the *Chicago Daily News* wrote on March 11, 1905, that Pachmann's performance of the Chopin Concerto elicited "the most pronounced demonstration of enthusiasm Orchestral Hall has witnessed." Will Hubbard, critic for the *Chicago Daily Tribune*, wrote some of the most intense paeans to Pachmann's art (November 9, 1904):

There are some things in the realm of art so beautiful so ideally perfect, that all thought of technical difficulties involved in their accomplishment vanish before the charm of their finished beauty. To this class belongs the piano playing of Vladimir de Pachmann.

And on December 19, 1904, Hubbard continued:

As I came out of Music Hall yesterday afternoon I passed one dried up specimen of the musical masculine—a man to whom the exact value of a dot placed after a thirty-second note is of more importance than is the whole poetic content of a Chopin nocturne—and he was just saying to his companion that "Pachmann so seriously detracts from the dignity of musical art by his antics." And "dignity" and "musical art," as he mouthed them, should be spelled with capitals large, fat and black. He was of the type to whom the letter of music is everything; the spirit nothing save as "tradition" and "proper reading" constitute it. . . . They have forgotten, if they ever knew, that music is a spirit of joy and radiant loveliness.

But then, there was New York, with the hostility of some critics unabated. W. J. Henderson, now moved to the *Sun*, was still leader of the VladyFloppers. With scurrilous similes, he created a picture that suggested there was nothing behind Pachmann's vaunted originality but superficiality, narcissism and meaningless vulgarity. By 1904 he felt that Pachmann's concerts should not be praised, but ridiculed. He wrote in the *Sun* on November 15, 1904:

Mr. de Pachmann was in a highly good humor with himself yesterday afternoon and he played battledove and shuttlecock with the notes set down by the composers in a most gleeful manner. He had heaps of fun with the little bird that undertook to prophesize [Schumann's *Vogel als Prophet*]. No birds that ever lived could have prophesized what the pianist was going to do next, and the sport was to try to guess it. "Warum," the unique person turned into a flowing river of innocent merriment. It was a new conception, entirely Pachmann's own and it will probably always remain so. However, it may never occur to this pianist again. He may have a different conception before 2 o'clock this afternoon and another one after dinner. "Hark, Hark, the Lark" is supposed to be a song transcribed into a piano lyric by Liszt. This is all a mistake. Pachmann disclosed yesterday that it was a full report of the Princeton-Yale football game with the cheers thrown in. Weber's E flat Rondo was found to be an instrumental description of the mud in which the players struggled! At any rate the number was just one swift, rattling smear of the entire keyboard, without rhythm, without outline and without meaning.

Excepting *Warum?*, these pieces were lightweight showpieces. What really drew the critic's ire to the boiling point was Pachmann's performance of the Chopin Concerto. On November 6 Henderson demolished Pachmann's New York performance with the Boston Symphony under Wilhelm Gericke in the *Sun*:

The solo feature of the concert deserves to be dismissed without consideration. It was unworthy of the dignity of criticism. . . . Let it stand then, as the record of the hour that yesterday's performance of the F minor concerto was in its general conception and in most of the particulars false not only to the spirit, but to the letter of the composer. Scarcely a single page of it was not falsely read, and the entire interpretation was marred by freakish eccentricities of tempos, dynamics, accentuation and coloring. It was simply another of those disclosures of the personal idiosyncrasies of this pianist which thoroughly informed students of piano literature have become quite weary in the course of years . . . he apparently has no settle[d] convictions to the reading of any of the master's works but plays according to the fancy of the moment. This is not the method of an artist.

We've heard from critics Henderson, Hale and Hubbard. The fourth "H" among American critics, Huneker, had left the *Musical Courier* in

1902 as a result of a dispute with the publisher, Marc Blumenberg, concerning a lawsuit brought against the magazine by composer/cellist Victor Herbert. The *Courier* had become a battleground with the two hacking at each other in print. Huneker finally had enough and resigned. He was replaced by Leonard Liebling, a pianist who had studied with Godowsky, Theodore Kullak and Karl Barth, brother of soprano Estelle Liebling and nephew of the brother pianists Emil and Georg Liebling, both Liszt pupils. He knew almost as much about piano playing as Huneker, and proved to be as supportive of Pachmann as Huneker had been, rising to the Chopinzee's defense in *MC* three days after Henderson's poisonous screed about the Concerto performance. Liebling began by noting that some New York critics were engaged in "their usual fault-finding pursuit," continued by pointing out that few of these fault-finders knew enough about piano playing to play a simple scale on the piano, and stressed that Pachmann really knew something about Chopin's music:

> He has been a Chopin player and investigator for probably thirty-five years and he not only knows intimately the whole Chopin repertory and literature, but he has made microscopic studies, as it were, of Chopin phrasing, fingering, passage work, dynamics, interpretation; in short, he is an authority of the first water on Chopin. . . . When he plays Chopin I must, of necessity, accept him. . . . As between him and a New York music critic on the subject I could not afford to hesitate. . . . I would really like to hear the F minor now played by New York daily paper music critics to ascertain . . . how they would play the concerto. The one critic who does play the piano could play the orchestra part on a second piano to help the others out. It is a fair proposition. What object is there in announcing any theory unless one is prepared practically to prove it. . . . Why should I prefer a music critic's opinion on Pachmann's piano playing when that critic cannot prove his criticism by practical illustration showing how he believes it should be done? If he has not done it, and cannot do it, I must accept Pachmann and I do, and so does the public and all this proves the hopeless inutility of music criticism. As these critics who cannot play piano express views, certainly I can express views also. I never heard a more wonderful performance of Chopin than Pachmann's on the Baldwin grand piano last Saturday.

Liebling reviewed Pachmann's next recital in *MC* (December 14, 1904), concluding the enthusiastic notice with a sarcastic fantasy:

> Those daily newspaper critics who did not like de Pachmann's playing are said to be exceedingly fine interpreters of the "Polish tone poet," as they call him, and they will give a Chopin recital as soon as de Pachmann has left town. The critics have engaged themselves as program annotators for the recital, and will write the criticism for the dailies. Tickets for the recital are in great demand.

Pachmann was certainly aware of the recurring controversy swirling around him. The noisy demonstrations by his admirers after his concerts served as a buffer. What really mattered to him was the praise from the great of the world: Liszt, Saint-Saëns, Anton Rubinstein and of course, the acclaim of most critics on both sides of the Atlantic. The others he dismissed as "cochonnerie" and went on being Pachmann.

*George Halprin in 1940 with his prize
pupil, 13-year-old Teresa Sterne*
Photo from *Musical America*

Cesco Pallottelli in 1959
Photographer unknown

Leonide de Pachmann in 1960
Photographer unknown

Pachmann in his twenties
Photographer unknown

Pachmann's sister Elizaveta in old age
Photographer unknown

Joseph Dachs, ca. 1869
Photo by Löwy, Vienna

"To V Pachmann, Most Faithfully F[Liszt]"

LEIPZIG, den 31. October 1879

im

SAALE DES GEWANDHAUSES

CONCERT

von

Woldemar von Pachmann

Pianist aus Odessa

unter gefälliger Mitwirkung des Herrn Carl Schröder (Violoncello).

PROGRAMM.

Toccata und **Fuge** (D-moll) für die Orgel (Pedal und Manual) von Joh. Sebastian Bach, zum Concertvortrag für Clavier bearbeitet von	**Carl Tausig.**
Romanze. (Larghetto aus op. 11.)	**Chopin-Reinecke.**
Etude de Concert. (Des-dur.)	**Liszt.**
Menuett op. 17	**Moszkowski.**
Nocturne (für Violoncello)	**Chopin.**
Fantasie op. 28. (Moscheles gewidmet.)	**Mendelssohn.**
Musette (für Violoncello)	**Perrin.**
Etude op. 10. Nr. 3	**Chopin.**
La cloche des agonisants	**Schubert-Liszt.**
Militair-Marsch	**Schubert-Tausig.**

Das Accompagnement der Cello-Vorträge hat Herr **Muck** zu übernehmen die Güte gehabt.

Anfang 7 Uhr.

Concertflügel Blüthner.

The first appearance of the nobilary particle: "von" Pachmann

Fifteen Guineas for a Debut

At the time of his London debut
London Stereoscope Co. photo

Madame Peter and her daughter in the garden of the Ronveau, circa 1912
Cesco snapshot

Maggie Okey, the "Lily Langtry of the Piano"
Photographer unknown

Confident Pachmann, ca. 1882
Photo by Paul Gericke, Berlin

The marriage photo of manager Waltmann with monsieur and madame de Pachmann
Photographer unknown

Sweden in 1885
Photo by Florman

With an "Imperial"
From November 26, 1892, issue of *The Illustrated Sporting and Dramatic News*

Chickering Publicity Photo

In 1890
Photo by Sarony, New York

Fernand Labori
Photographer unknown

Beardless again and resembling a priest
Photo by Sarony, New York

In Berlin 1895, at age 47, depressed and deflated
Photo by Müller

Paderewski, ca. 1895
Photo by Elliot and Fry, London

Godowsky, ca. 1893
Photo by Dupont, New York

Godowsky's admiration for Pachmann
Photo by Dupont, New York

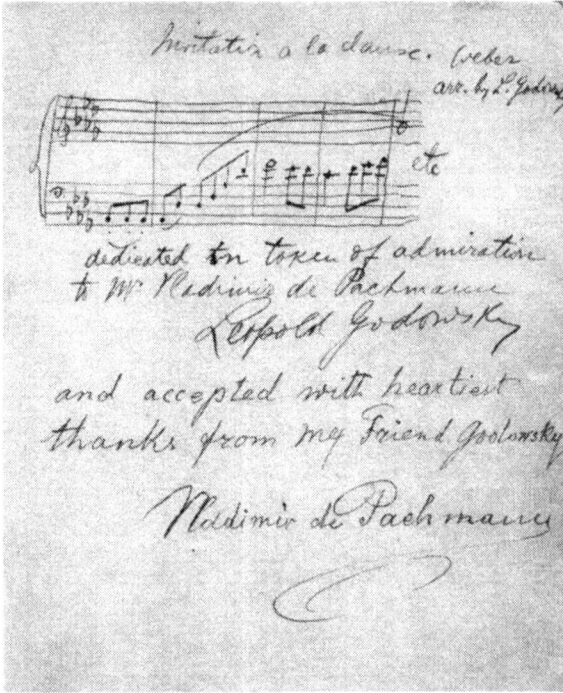

Godowsky dedicated his "Invitation to the Dance" to Pachmann

Pachmann, year unknown
Photographer Unknown

"Vladyflapper" in the front row
From a 1908 Cincinnati caricature

"De Pachmann Con Amore"
by Gianni Viafora

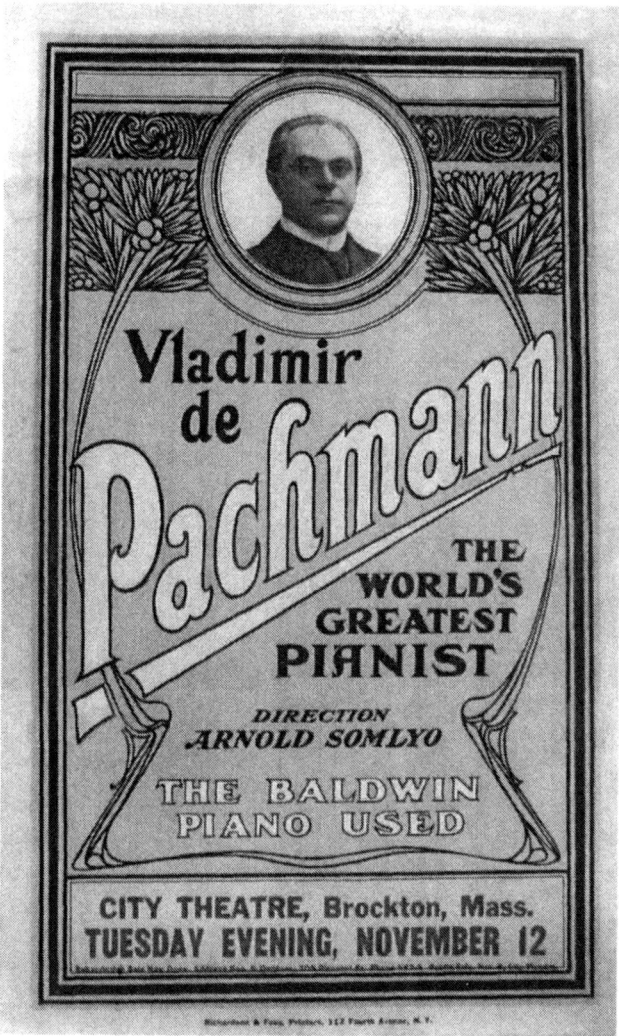

Poster, 1907

Symbolist Pachmann, 1900
caricature by C. de Fornaro

PACHMANN'S

♪ GRAMOPHONE RECORDS

10-inch, 3 6 each.

G.C. 5566.
Octave Study and Waltz
(*Chopin*)

G.C. 5567.
La Fileuse (*Raff*)

G C. 5568.
Waltz (No. 7) (*Chopin*)

12-inch, 5 6 each.

05502.
Barcarolle, Op. 6 (*Chopin*)

05500.
Two Preludes and
Mazurka (*Chopin*)

05501.
Nocturne, Op. 37, No. 2
(*Chopin*)

We have great pleasure in announcing that this great Artiste has just made a new series of records, which will be issued shortly.

Call and hear these splendid Records at :—

THE WEST END GRAMOPHONE SUPPLY Co., 94 Regent Street, W.
HAYS, 26 Old Bond Street, W., and 4 Royal Exchange Bdgs, E.C.
HARRODS, Ltd., Brompton Road, S.W.
IMHOF & MUKLE, 110, New Oxford Street, W.C.
BAYSWATER PHOTO Co., Queen's Road, W.
WHITELEY'S, Ltd., Westbourne Grove, W.

The GRAMOPHONE COMPANY, LTD., 21 City Road, London.

Advertisement for his first records, 1907

Pachmann with Arnold Somlyo
Published in *MC* on June 26, 1907 as "Andante con Moto(r)"

Cesco's first snapshot of Pachmann

Pachmann enjoying one of his own records
Cesco Snapshot

Pachmann with Cesco outside the Hotel Ronveau, early 1911
Photographer unknown

London 1911, with his hair like Franz Liszt's
Photographer unknown

Pachmann with Cesco, left, arriving in Canada, 1911; others unknown
Photographer unknown

Cesco, the secretary, with Pachmann, 1911
Photographer unknown

Pachmann, 1913
Photo by Cesco Pallottelli

Barbizon in 1910 displaying a newly-acquired $14,000 blue sapphire to Arnold Somlyo
Photographer unknown

Private performance under a portrait of Paderewski. Harold Holt on left, man on right unknown.
Cesco Snapshot

Maggie in 1913, still attractive at 49, taken while visiting Canada
Photographer unknown

Pachmann with his sons Leonide and Adrian in 1914
Cesco Snapshot

Pachmann as the center of attention at a garden party
Cesco Snapshot

Mrs. Ysaÿe far left, Ysaÿe at wheel, Pachmann next to him wearing box hat, Harold Holt standing, Lionel Powell in tie sitting on hood, and Cesco at far right. Others unidentified.
From Cesco's snapshots of a party at Lionel Powell's estate in Shropshire in 1915

Harold Holt, Cesco, Pachmann, unknown woman, Lionel Powell with wife and child, Ysaÿe and wife standing

Pachmann with Alichika
Cesco Snapshot

"If Chopin Himself Could Only Hear Me!": a
1916 London Bystander caricature
By Allinson

Caricature of Pachmann (1916)
By Tom Titt

Pachmann looking unkempt
Photographer unknown

Pachmann with Virgilio in 1924
Cesco Snapshot

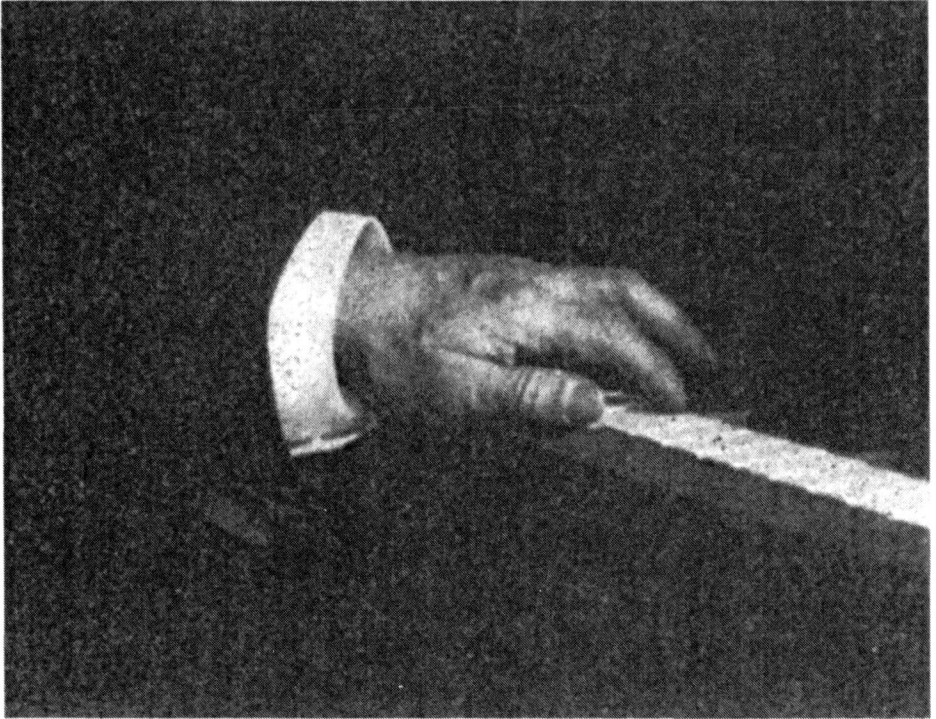

Pachmann's hand muscles
From the October 1913 *Musician*

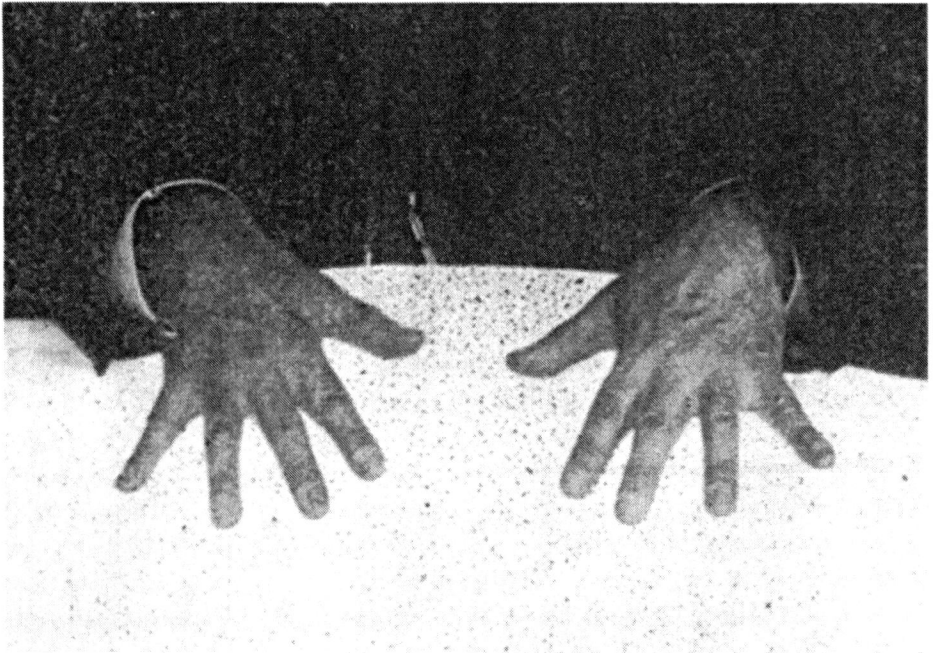

Pachmann's hands
From the October 1913 *Musician*

Villa Gioia
Cesco Snapshot

To my dear, very kind Friend
m... Hilda Day. in Remem
brance of our Long Friend
-ship, —
V. de Pachmann

3/10/22

Inscribed to Lionel Powell's secretary, Hilda Day
Photographer unknown

Baldwin representatives with Virgilio, Alice, Pachmann and Cesco in Fabri
Snapshot from Cesco's Scrapbook

"Framed in a Famous Mane of Hair Which Gianni Viafora Has Somewhat Exaggerated for the Sake of Artistic Effect"

Frederick Dawson, Pachmann's pupil
Photographer unknown

Young Harold Bauer
Photographer unknown

Playing for Godowsky and Anton Bilotti, 1924
Kadel and Herbert photo

Pachmann showing F.C. Coppicus his new method
Photographer unknown

Pachmann and the inviting air of San Diego
Cesco Snapshot

Pachmann in front of, and Cesco inside, a biplane
Photographer unknown

Cesco turns pages
Underwood and Underwood photo

"Breakfast with De Pachmann... The veteran virtuoso is shown here at breakfast with the Pallottellis, his friends with whom he lives.(Left to right) F. Pallottelli, De Pachmann's secretary; Signora Alicia Pallottelli, friend of Mussolini, called Italy's Joan of Arc; Master Virgilio Pallottelli, De Pachmann's only piano pupil; and the maestro himself. On the table can be seen the bowl and strainer with which he carefully cleans each piece of silverware before eating, following his life-long habit..."
Musical Courier, April 24, 1924 (showing interior of leased Heifetz apartment)

1924 Catskills
Photographer unknown

*Pachmann with Strabismus, Looking Terrible
Despite the Obvious Retouching*
Wide World photo

1924 Catskills
Photographer unknown

Pachmann with Cesco and family in the Catskills
Photographer unknown

Melted in America
Photographer unknown

Pachmann happy to be back in England
Photographer unknown

One of Cambellotti's designs for Pachmann's studio

Pachmann caricature by J. W. Proctor
Yorkshire Herald 1925

Pachmann in his seventies
Photographer unknown

"He Has Lived For His Art Alone"
Manchester Guardian 1925

fame and wealth were magnets. The process that seemed to work so successfully in his career wasn't as successful in his private life. It is highly probable that infidelity with a man had destroyed his marriage, and a serious illness (most likely a sexually transmitted disease) brought him to Berlin in 1894.

Hard evidence about this aspect of Pachmann's life is scant from these years—later, as he aged and his mental state deteriorated, he no longer tried to be discreet and didn't care anymore, and there is ample evidence of his homosexual behavior. Information about this behavior from earlier times has to be inferred from the various sources—interviews with his son Leonide, his secretary Cesco Pallottelli and surviving friends and colleagues, as well as oblique and thinly veiled comments found in press reports and letters. One of the richest sources of information was the aged Pallottelli, whose confidence the author gained over a period of months and dozens of interviews in 1959 and 1960.

In those interviews, Pallottelli blithely avoided discussion of many points concerning their history together that could not be easily explained. What Pallottelli didn't say was often more interesting than his direct comments. Son Leonide was more forthcoming about his father's (if not his own) homosexuality. He referred to his father's sexuality in a flippant manner that seemed to deflect direct questions.

Like many career-driven people with a dominant life force, Pachmann needed someone practical to manage the mundane details of his career and daily life. It was a perfectly acceptable custom in the late Victorian and Edwardian era for great artists to travel with paid companions who functioned variously as secretary, interpreter, ticket agent, and gentleman's gentleman. Some artists such as Fritz Kreisler and Sergei Rachmaninoff had their wives to arrange affairs. Others like Paderewski had veritable entourages managing their complicated existences. It seems that Pachmann, since his bout of illness in Berlin, had several managers/ companions who took care of these practical matters, leaving him free to devote himself to his art and his jewels.

Now when he returned to England relations with the most recent secretary soured, and he was looking for a replacement. The pianist most likely had contacts who could suggest the names of healthy young men whose services could be enlisted as secretary and intimate companion. One of these contacts was Lionel Powell, then working for Pachmann's English management firm, the Schulz-Curtius Agency. Later when he was head of his own management firm, Powell regularly catered to the personal needs of Pachmann, Melba, and many other celebrity artists and, eventually, Paderewski.

Through another of these contacts, a certain R. E. Schneider, Pachmann was introduced to a handsome young Italian named Francesco Pallottelli

Maggie, still chic at 64
Otto S. Puon photo

Pachmann, the putter
Cesco snapshot

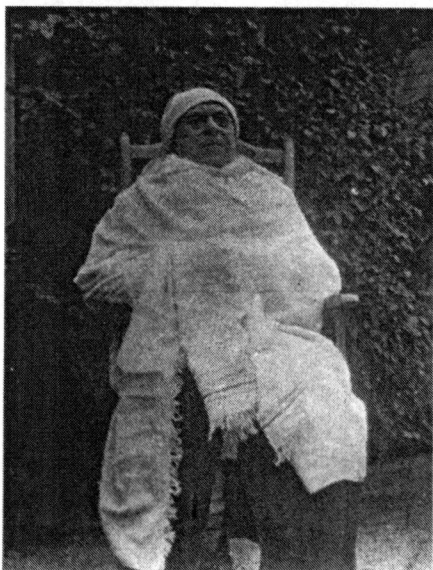

Pachmann in mufti
Cesco snapshot

An impatient Pachmann playing Patience
Cesco snapshot

Pachmann, always the artist
Cesco snapshot

Pachmann en déshabillé
Cesco snapshot

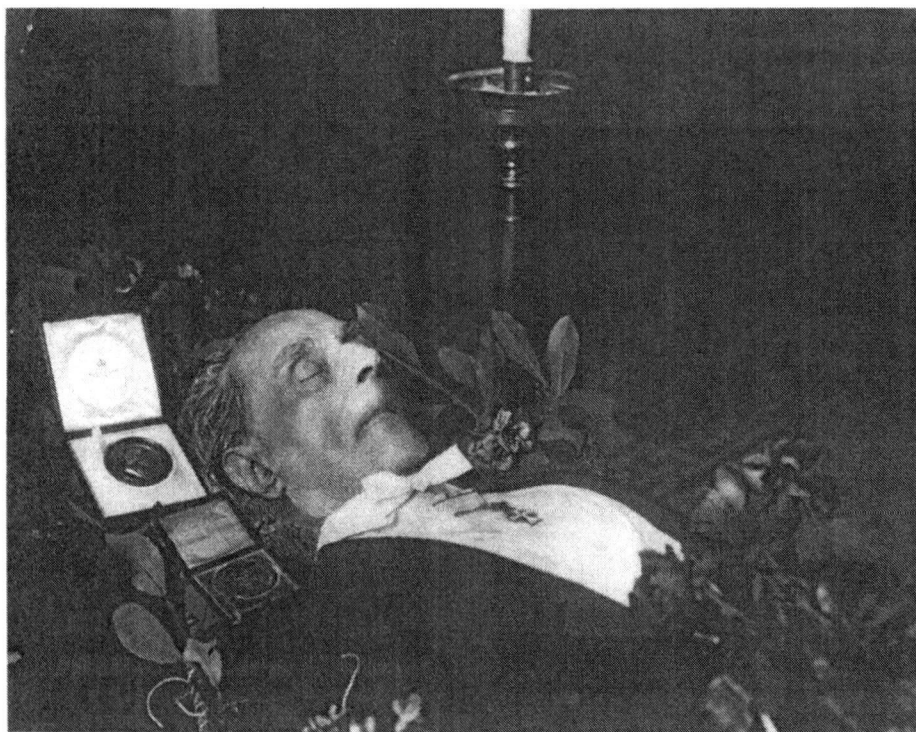

Pachmann lying in state with the order of the Dannebrog and Beethoven Medal displayed
Fotocronaca photo

Chapter 20
CESCO, December 1905
to June 1907

Pachmann was always embracing as well as kissing people—those admired and praised him, those with whose opinions he agreed, most especially, handsome young men. The *Dallas Morning New* ported on January 12, 1905:

> Young people appear to interest him very much, and in the green room he . . . embraced warmly many of the youthful members of the Männercł and obligingly inscribed his name in albums.

Some of these men were embarrassed, but in general Pachmann': havior was written off as "Slavic effusiveness." George Halprin fc himself a recipient in 1907 when he heard Pachmann for the first time was seventeen, a handsome blond, and was amazed by the playing went backstage to congratulate the pianist but never got to, for Pachn grabbed a hold of him, exclaiming, "Preety boy, let me kees you!"[1]

Publicly Pachmann expressed affection to both sexes, but his ¡ erence for his own was obviously dominant, and he did little to] it. The gossip about him that passed behind the scenes of the mu world was apparently no problem for Pachmann. He was as discree he needed to be and, to his fans, his exotic sexuality was just another of his eccentricities. It's not that he was proud of his homosexualit deliberately flaunted it. He was never "out" because he was never " He obviously felt it was just part of him—one of his rights as a g artist, beloved on two continents.

There is no question that at this time he led an active, if discr homosexual life as he toured, indulging in casual sex. He approac some, more approached him, and some were sent to him. Either way, after a recital in Eastbourne, in December 1905. Pachmann knew nothing about Pallottelli, except that he had been told he was "suitable." Pachmann was delighted, for Pallottelli was everything Schneider had said, and more so. Youthful Pallottelli preferred the diminutive name, "Cesco." He had a sweet, affable nature and a smooth, easy manner that was immediately noticeable and made him seem somewhat more mature than his twenty-one years.

Pachmann knew he had found a man who could be his private secretary. Cesco remembered their initial interview: "So, you are a friend of Schneider's? You Italian? Where do you live . . . Rome? Beautiful! . . . You say you work in the hotel business? . . . No good! . . . I'm looking for a private secretary; would you be interested?" Pallottelli was taken completely by surprise. "He was such a funny, strange man. He didn't know anything about me. I could have been a thief, a murderer!" Pallottelli told the author fifty-five years after the event. "Yet he asked me to be his secretary!"

Cesco said he would consider it, but was inclined to turn down the offer. Friends had warned him about the insecurity of a career in the hotel industry starting on the bottom rung; Schneider reminded him of Pachmann's success, fame and wealth, as well as his obvious fondness for him, but Cesco was still hesitant. Eight days after meeting Pachmann, Pallottelli received a letter from Lionel Powell, asking him to come to London to discuss things over lunch. Pachmann was there, but his presence didn't deter Powell from stating "It won't be an easy job, but he's a good-hearted man. . . . You'll never be sorry." Pachmann smiled all the time, but said nothing.

Pallottelli said he wanted to tell them both that he felt he just wasn't suited for the position, but Schneider's remarks kept ringing in his ears . . . he found himself accepting the unusual offer. Cesco stayed in London to serve a short apprenticeship under Powell's tutelage while Pachmann left for concerts in Berlin, retaining for the while his current secretary.

⌒

The Berlin public for the most part adored Pachmann's playing and accepted his eccentricities as part of the package. An American student studying then at the Stern Conservatory was not so accepting. Charles Tomlinson Griffes was twenty-one and studying with Engelbert Humperdinck. After a Pachmann concert that took place on February 16, 1906, the dismayed Griffes wrote home to his mother that Pachmann talked first of all to the piano awhile and made all sorts of motions to the effect that the stool didn't suit him. Then he got up and went off, and some men came on and pretended to do something to the stool, and he finally began. Griffes thought

Pachmann had "played some things absolutely perfectly, according to my taste." Other performances he disliked. Mostly, the future great composer found Pachmann's antics "too disgusting and inartistic for anything. But the audience is still more disgusting. They behave themselves as if in a circus, and the more ridiculous de Pachmann is, the more they like it." Griffes was in the minority. The German magazine *Die Musik* had other ideas, and wrote of the same recital in its March 1906 issue:

> Added to the rarest oddities that are offered on the richly-bedecked table of the Winter season belongs, justly, Vladimir de Pachmann. Severe "greats" hold things against him, and strict critics and other masters crusade against his "antics." Good Heavens! As if this petit-genre artist was striving for great things and was raving like an animal! He doesn't harm anyone, and surely has only one goal with his artistic miniatures: to provide enjoyment for himself, and others. "Bella cosa" is what the papal gourmands call the savory tidbits and the sweet, worldly, forbidden fruits of the fine arts, which of course were dear things, a delight to one's heart. . . . Such "bella cosa" are the enrapturing pieces from Pachmann's enchanting hands. The heart-felt joy, humor and wit, the grace of the hand, the delicious "jeu perlé," the coquettish rhythm allow me to savor the filled and unfilled sweets with pleasure, and let me forget for an hour all critical measuring, and pedantic weighing. I honestly confess to belong to those people to whom a Pachmannific Waltz or Mazurka is dearer than the savage Liszt-hammering of a whole winter.[2]

In 1905 Rudolf Breithaupt published the first version of his book, *Die natürliche Klaviertechnik*, an exhaustive study of piano technique that espoused arm weight over fingers. Breithaupt discussed the individual hands of the great pianists of the day, concluding that Pachmann's hands were "ideal." His description of Pachmann's playing is a gem of artistic concision:

> Equally famous as a Chopin player is Wladimir von Pachmann. The music of this peculiar and richly contradictory artist exerts a mysterious enchantment through his wonderful, velvet-like attack and lightly swinging rhythm. From his artless child-like nature, his sunny delight in everything, where all is beautiful, all sings and sounds, let us deduce a genuine and deep sensitivity. As only a genius is able, he always gives with an overflowing heart. The luscious fullness of his delicate attack, the dreamingly soft perfume through which he undertakes to weave everything, and his loving treatment of small things, even the minuscule, these are the secrets of his greatness. His technique is not grand and his ability is confined within self-chosen limits, but his lyrical nature speaks out in Chopin so purely and sensually that one can, without hesitation, include him among the Great for all these little precious things. This charmer of an eternally-young disposition, totally-lost-in-the-play-and-dreaming of a grown-up child, this enthusiastic loss of self into the

world of ideals, elevates him—at any rate—to one of the most doted upon favorites of our time, and even permits us to forget the mistakes and weaknesses of his comedic persona.

~

Returning to England, Pachmann found Cesco ready to begin his new life. Soon it was clear to him that Lionel Powell's comment, that the job would not be easy, was an enormous understatement. The young Italian discovered that success in the job required a combination of patience, tact and understanding. To his great dismay Cesco learned quickly that the great pianist, having worked so hard and long to be able to play the piano faultlessly, also expected almost-inhuman perfection in everything and everyone else, down to the smallest details of everyday life, and demanded this from others . . . most especially those in his employ.

If a porter was carrying his bags and valises crookedly, if a window in the hotel was drafty or the fire in the fireplace wasn't lit, Pachmann might run into a hotel's hall shouting at top voice for the manager. Cesco would calm him, often by suggesting they go out to eat. But that would cause even more problems to erupt.

"The butter is no good. The meat is too hard. Why aren't the rolls hot?" He complained, not softly but shouting so the whole restaurant could hear. At first Cesco cringed with embarrassment. But worse was to come.

At breakfast he'd shout: "Why aren't my eggs brown? Where is the hot cream for my coffee? No, don't serve it to me in that!" (He hated to have coffee served in a metal pot.) "Take it away!"

A talkative waiter tried to sooth him, telling him of the other great artists who had visited the hotel, and the enthusiasm they exhibited when they praised the establishment and the food. The poor man didn't know what he was saying: "Why, just last week the great Paderewski honored us with a visit!"

"What?! Cesco, did you hear what he said? Don't touch the food!" Cesco was then ordered to go out and buy cooked ham, cheese and wine, and Pachmann refused to eat any more food provided by the hotel that Paderewski had praised.

Cesco soon learned that Pachmann was never well, forever counting his own pulse, complaining 'I've got a pain—here. It's my heart," or "It's my lee-vaire. It's dropped." Eventually Cesco asked him why he was always complaining about his health, despite the fact that he missed very few concerts and, though small, was compactly built and actually blessed with remarkably good health. The reply? "I tell people I'm sick so they will pity me."

While Cesco's official function was to concern himself with the practical side of Pachmann's career, sometimes he found himself involved with its artistic side as well. His services might be needed as a page turner. On those occasions Pachmann's commentary would be directed to Cesco rather than the audience. "Isn't this passage beautiful, Cesco?" or "Listen to this phrase." But as the concert progressed Pachmann became more confiding. "I'm sorry I kept you awake complaining last night. My fourth finger is wonderful today . . . just perfect."

The aging, fifty-nine year old pianist took the twenty-two year old Italian in tow in England in 1906 and America in 1907. Most of his colleagues and friends understood. What they didn't know then was that Cesco would also prove to be a clever and very competent young man who soon realized that running an artist's life was not too different from managing a hotel. Both depended on meticulous mastery of menial details.

Pachmann quickly realized he had a prize, and appreciated Cesco's good nature and talent. Many years later Fred Gaisberg wrote in the *Gramophone* (October 1943):

> Pallotelli [*sic*] was short, thick, voluble, animated and energetic like his master and made for him a good foil that kept the party lively.

As the 1906 season was ending he decided to show his appreciation and told Cesco he would present him with the proceeds from one of his recitals. There were two left to play that season, one at Lowestoft and the other at the Crystal Palace. Cesco chose Lowestoft. It was a mistake for the house was almost empty. Pachmann told Cesco: "Listen, take the Crystal Palace, I'll take this." Then he walked onto the platform and invited the tiny audience to his hotel suite, where he presented them with a delightful, impromptu, and very intimate recital.

Cesco was with Pachmann for only six months when he learned of the magnitude of his employer's hobby. After the tour was over Pachmann went to Amsterdam to supervise the cutting and faceting of a special stone from his collection. Pachmann would go in search of new jewels but tell Cesco he didn't want him to come along "because you will tell me I am paying too much."

Well he might. Pachmann was absolutely obsessed with finding red, green and blue diamonds for his collection. It was rumored that he commissioned agents in the world's capitals to keep tabs on precious stones as they became available. Eventually George Edward Kunz of New York's Tiffany's found him a small green diamond; it would take him another decade to acquire a red one. Two years after he met Cesco he located an equally rare blue diamond. *Musical America* reported (November 3, 1907):

> Vladimir de Pachmann, the famous pianist, has just added to his collection of precious stones, which is one of the finest in the world, a sapphire-blue

diamond, for which he paid a London firm $23,000. It is said to be of a deeper blue than the Hope diamond and to retain its color even under artificial light. De Pachmann's collection of gems includes . . . specimens of every known variety . . . and his fame as a connoisseur of precious stones rivals his fame as an interpreter of Chopin.[3]

⌣

By 1907 Pachmann's popularity in England had increased to the point where Bechstein Hall was no longer sufficient, and he began to play frequently in the larger Queen's Hall. Occasionally a reviewer would point out that Pachmann sometimes actually followed the composer's indications where others did not. The *Cremona* for May 1907 described his playing of Chopin's third Scherzo in Queen's Hall on March 8:

> The middle section of the Scherzo in C sharp minor, Op. 39, marked meno mosso, commences with four bars to be played sostenuto, and the four succeeding bars are usually played in tempo rubato, though only marked leggierissimo. M. de Pachmann, however, did not accelerate the tempo at this place, with the result the music produced quite a different impression.

Most pianists play the eight-note figurations that follow the chorale-like melody in this Scherzo twice as fast as the chorale, despite the fact that Chopin gives no such direction. Pachmann kept the same tempo, eschewing brilliance in favor of nobility.

A few days earlier he revived his signature concerto—London hadn't heard him in the Chopin F minor for several years. Sir Frederic Cowen conducted the Philharmonic Society. The *Sunday Times* wrote on March 3, 1907:

> The persuasive beauty of his tone, the exquisite finish of his style, and the sensitive regard for the true spirit of the piano which was never more delightfully displayed and there was good excuse for the hero worship that followed.

Queen's Hall proved fine for solo recitals, but many more people wanted to hear Pachmann play the Chopin F minor than could fit, and a second performance with the same forces was arranged for the cavernous Albert Hall for March 17. At the earlier venue Pachmann behaved himself, limiting his eccentricity merely to saluting a bust of Beethoven as he walked onstage. But in Albert Hall he eclipsed himself. The event was described by the London critic W. R. Holt in the *Musical Leader*, reprinted on June 22 in *Musical America*:

> The audience sat and waited. Members of Parliament and notabilities in the city who had failed to get reserved seats cramped themselves into the narrow shilling benches. Suddenly a roar of cheering burst from the stalls. At

the head of the steps, bowing this way and that was a little fat man in a frock coat, his face suffused with good humor. He shouted a greeting to the conductor, he patted a fiddler on the back, he greeted like a long-lost brother the modest young instrumentalist who had been deputed to turn over his pages; a wave of the hand to an enthusiastic small boy, a jolly smile to the boxes, an inquisitive inspection of the bassoons to see if he could find anybody he knew, and De Pachmann turned to the music. But only for a moment. As the baton fell and the band played the opening bars of the concerto, he suddenly remembered that it was the day after the boat race and turned to a horn player to tell him all about it, illustrating the story by imitating Stuart's stroke. The stool was too high for aquatic demonstrations, so he lowered it. Then it was too low for piano playing so he raised it. It occurred to him that he had not told the drummer it was a fine day, so he stood up and conveyed the information by signs. Meanwhile the band was developing the splendid allegro . . . "That's a jolly bit!" said De Pachmann—"La–da–da –di–da!" and he beat time with his fat, graceful hands. A red flower and a blue hat caught his eye, and he remarked that it looked as if it would be a season of bright colors. Still the swelling music rose, and the young man turning over the pages looked excessively uncomfortable. What if the master missed his cue? He need not have troubled—De Pachmann knows his Chopin better than most of us know our prayers. The right bar arrived and the hall was filled with rippling melody . . . oboes, clarinets and flutes engaged in musical conversation with the brass . . . over it all, like the singing of birds, trilled the comments of the piano, enriching and decorating every phrase with fanciful traceries of sound . . . the happiest man in the hall was De Pachmann . . . It was all a splendid joke to the master. He puffed out his cheeks, he wagged his head to the rhythm of the music, he played with his left hand and beat time with his right, and he took the page-turner into the secret of every thought that crossed his mind. . . . De Pachmann hummed the phrases and invited the audience to share in his delight. . . . The climax approached and De Pachmann became boisterous in his merriment. Eyebrows, head, body and arms were all keeping time and the player's face showed the delirious appreciation of a child at a Punch and Judy show. A torrent of explanatory discourse overwhelmed the page turner, and when he bowed his head beneath the storm De Pachmann turned to the stalls and told the people there what he thought . . . the piece was over. De Pachmann was so delighted that he ecstatically shook the page turner by the hand, then, to show that he was enjoying himself, he shook hands with all the audience who were near enough. His only regret was that there was not time enough to lecture.

The cumulative buildup of Pachmann's increasing popularity in London, demonstrated by the five thousand fans at Albert Hall, had its effect. They all loved him or why else would they have come? The huge mass of love released something; he exercised no restraint. In the near future this behavior would progress to actual mental unraveling, but for now it was still regarded as an excess of eccentricity.

Pachmann was starting to feel his age and thoughts of retiring were constant, so perhaps he felt a desire to leave a permanent record of his art. Some automatic piano rolls had been taken of his playing by the Welte firm in Leipzig in 1906, but were highly unsatisfactory. He signed a very short endorsement for these rolls on February 19 of that year ["The 'Welte-Mignon' reproduces the living soul of the Artist, and has not its equal."]. Before leaving for another American tour, Pachmann incised his first actual recordings in London for the Gramophone and Typewriter ("G and T") Company in May and June 1907. In 1907 Pachmann was still at his prime. These crudely recorded discs are undoubtedly Pachmann's best, some of them among the greatest piano recordings ever made, capturing his touch more faithfully than any other of his recordings and guaranteeing him immortality. The company executive for these sessions was the transplanted American Pachmann admirer, Fred Gaisberg, who had assured the future fortunes of the company (soon to be known as "His Master's Voice") by recording a young tenor named Enrico Caruso.

Chapter 21

The First Farewell, 1907–1908: The American Tour

By separate mail we are sending you a photo which you may use for advertising purposes. The young man seated with Mr. Pachmann is Mr. Pallottelli, who will accompany him to America. Mr. Pallottelli has already acted as his secretary during the last winter season in England and has proved himself to be a most trustworthy young gentleman in whom Mr. de Pachmann and we place the fullest confidence.[1]

This letter was composed by Lionel Powell and sent to the Baldwin Piano Company to forward to its various agents throughout the United States, introducing Cesco and officially explaining his attachment to their star pianist.

Like newlyweds just after the honeymoon, the two had a terrible row the night before they were to embark and Cesco almost didn't go, refusing to leave until Madame Peter got involved. "He's impossible, he's impossible!" Cesco complained to her, for she had become his confidante. "You can't let him go to America alone!" she exhorted. Apparently she changed Cesco's mind.

Pachmann was still terrified of ocean voyages and, like a monk doing penance, remained in his cabin for the entire journey. He needn't have, for the sea remained calm throughout the crossing. Cesco managed things at the customs counter so smoothly that they were able to have lunch on the very day they arrived at Pachmann's favorite haunt in New York, the Café Martin. New York was in the midst of a nearly unbearable heat wave. Pachmann was interviewed by *Musical America* (July 6, 1907) almost immediately:

"Oh, the heat," he began. "Is it not terrific? I cannot sleep—I sat much of the night in the window trying for breath. I put ice on my head. I gasped for air. I must go from the city quickly before I bake. There are cool drinks in the drug shops. I drink them—the cold water with the ice cream and then I nearly die with my stomach."

The interviewer had met the pair in their hotel, the Prince George on 27th Street, and wrote:

With him seemingly always is his private secretary, G. F. Palatelli [*sic*], a strange, dark young man with a face of singular refined innocence, and hair not very long but of wonderful fineness.

It was Cesco's lot, perhaps even his main function, to remove the difficulties, the banalities and commonplace trivialities that could intrude on Pachmann's idea of a perfect life. Discharging these duties often meant he had to perform the most delicate diplomatic errands which, despite his best efforts, would sometimes backfire in strange ways. It had become the pianist's routine to spend a part of his American summers at a Jewish resort in New York's Catskill Mountains named "The Sussex." Pachmann adored their renowned food service, particularly a certain type of fried chicken. During the years he had been visiting the resort, Pachmann amused himself by responding to flirtatious overtures from a young woman who was also a frequent guest. Through the years the woman's mother encouraged the pianist's attentions to her coquettish but still unmarried daughter. She even had a "cure" for Pachmann's mysterious ailments—the Coué method. Emil Coué, an early self-help guru, had a system that was popular in America before World War One but is all but forgotten today. Whenever Pachmann complained, the daughter would instruct him to repeat Coué's catchphrase, "Every day in every way I am getting better and better."

No!" Pachmann would invariably interrupt. "I am getting worse, worse. Call a doctor!" The woman tired of Pachmann soon enough and found a younger man and wed. But that man died all too soon, leaving her a young widow. She again began to pursue Pachmann relentlessly and shamelessly, abetted by her mother. The two stalkers were making Pachmann's summer more unbearable than the heat. These harpies followed him everywhere and Pachmann couldn't rest, practice or smoke his cigars in peace. He and Cesco fled to Lennox, Massachusetts, but it was hopeless, for somehow the ladies found the address of the new hotel and sent pleading notes accompanied by flowers.

Sensible and clever Cesco knew there was only one way to solve the problem: Pachmann had to see the woman once, and tell her she was mistaken about his intentions. Pachmann was adamant, and refused. "I won't see her, I've had enough of her." But Cesco wore him down, and the pianist relented. Little did Cesco know how Pachmann would actually handle the affair when the meeting was arranged. "What do you want, Madame? I'm an old man. I've been married once and that was enough. Look!" He pointed across the room to his secretary. "There's Cesco. He's young. Take him, not me."

The escapade was reminiscent of a French farce; Cesco somehow managed to lose the women and not kill his employer, and the rest of the summer passed uneventfully back in the Catskills. Other guests knew they had a celebrity in their midst, with Pachmann happily walking among them, chatting benevolently and bathing in his notoriety. All that was left was for him to play a Chopin recital in the wealthy resort of Bar Harbor, Maine, dedicating a new fine arts building on August 3, 1907.

The reader might find it difficult to understand how so many fell under Pachmann's spell, what with the pianist's negative qualities that were all too obvious. One who tried to explain the phenomenon was a young man named Morris Rothenberg. He was visiting friends at the Catskill resort, which was near present-day Kiamesha Lake, New York.[2] He had heard of Pachmann and was fascinated by the tales about him that he heard from everyone there. He got the idea that he could interview the celebrity and write it up. Before long Rothenberg's friends managed to arrange an interview through Cesco. His article about the meeting appeared on September 4th in *MC*:

I confess I was a little taken aback by his appearance as he stretched his hand out to me—a short, corpulent man, with a dark, bronzed face, a light Fedora hat pulled over his head, attired in a gray summer suit, looking nothing of the artist, and impressing me as some Eastern, Oriental merchant. But stranger than his appearance was De Pachmann's manner of speaking and his deportment. Though extremely gallant and genial and being void of any affectation and pretension, the quickness of his speech, his rapid change of conversation, his quick, agile movements and gestures, and his constant running from one person to another, rather amazed me. There seemed to be a strange incoherence about his speech and actions. And though expressing profuse pleasure at meeting me, he didn't know me after an absence of five minutes from my company. Another friend of mine coming over to me at this moment, and seeing De Pachmann standing near me, introduced him to me again. . . . De Pachmann shook me warmly by the hand, saying that he was very glad to meet me. I chatted with him several moments but could not advance with him in conversation, as he would not follow its trend and repeatedly wandered off to irrelevant topics. Thus we parted and I felt very much perplexed. The next day I saw De Pachmann again. He seemed much more composed. . . . I recalled to him that I had met him the night before and he replied that he remembered me very well, though I think this was said more out of politeness than veracity. His head was now uncovered and for the first time I saw his poetic face. I was much struck with his resemblance to Voltaire, though De Pachmann's face is, of course, much fuller . . . beautiful, brown, deep eyes. . . . But meeting the man in an ordinary way you would not take him to be a musician. His large, shaggy eyebrows, his well-shaped head, his wide forehead, and the general expressivness of his face are rather indicative of the thinker. . . . I attempted to engage him in conversation. I touched topic after topic, changing them as quickly as I saw his indifference to each. I asked him his impression of America.

"Very nice country," he replied. "Beautiful women."

Here was a clue. "Do you think them interesting?" I asked.

"All beauty is interesting," he replied.

"Then you do not believe with Tolstoy, that unless beauty is sustained by moral purpose it is valueless?" I asked.

"Ah!" was his reply, "you have read Tolstoy. Do you like him?"

"At times," I answer. He laughed heartily.

"I am too like that. Sometimes I do not like him at all," in pleasantly accented foreign English.

"When is that?" I queried.

"I will show you," he said. "Tolstoy says, 'Love your enemies.' I cannot do it. It is too hard."

"You have enemies? I think a man like you, who is constantly giving the world pleasure with your art, should have no enemies," I answered.

"Then you think I play well?" was his childlike comment. I answered him that I did.

"Ah, you are kind," taking me by the hand and pressing it warmly.

"Do you play much now?" I asked.

"No," he said. "it is too hot. You see, I am not young any more. I am fifty-nine years, but my playing is as good as it was twenty years ago; in fact, better," he said hurriedly, as if to avoid the impression that his art had suffered through his age.

"Yes, I am still young, very young—in spirit. I will always be young. I love youth. Die Jugend ist Gottlisch. You are young."

He looked at me enviously.

The next day I again went to see him. . . . I had now resolved to hear De Pachmann play . . . if I could but gain his confidence and arouse his emotional nature, I would see his powers. For, like many artists, praise and admiration are the staff of his life. I found him in rather gay spirits and receptive mood.

"Who is your favorite pianist?" I asked.

"De Pachmann," he answered laughingly. "In feeling and style, I am in a class alone. But there is one pianist whose technic and musicianship are incomparable; in technic even Liszt, the master of pianists, cannot approach him. That is Godowsky. He is a god. He is the first one since Liszt who has created something new in piano technic. Combinations and arrangements on the piano that were [not] dreamed of Godowsky has shown to us. And compared to his technic we are like little children. He is superhuman."

De Pachmann was growing more and more animated as he spoke of this new master, whom he seems to fairly worship, and in a sudden outburst of ecstasy he exclaimed "Come with me, I will show you!" I followed . . . to a little cottage near the main hotel, into a little room where he kept his piano . . . De Pachmann's face had turned pale and his eyes became strangely dreamy. He walked up the staircase on tiptoe, as if out of reverence for the instrument. . . . He . . . began to run his fingers across the keys, as if musing. Then he suddenly burst forth like a man possessed, in a selection of almost maddening technic. His face was livid and he breathed heavily—almost snorted as he lost himself in the frenzy of his passion. I sat as one entranced.

"That is Godowsky!" he said, "only not played as well."

Then De Pachmann plunged into Liszt's concert etude in F. When he finished it, I was overwhelmed. I implored him to play more, but I did not need to, for he was already intoxicated with his music and could not help playing. Then followed Chopin. . . . In some respects De Pachmann seems to be a reincarnation of Chopin, both as to his wonderful ability to feel his music and Chopin's strange love of colors. As is well known, Chopin associated all music with colors, and was known to speak of blonde and brunette voices, yellow symphonies, etc. Nothing charms De Pachmann more than brilliancies of color. He is ever in search of some new combination of colors, and this passion has developed in him an uncontrollable love for precious stones, roseate diamonds, rubies, sapphires, etc., of which he possesses one of the finest collections in the world. And his secretary (a fine young Italian, De Pachmann's only and constant companion) told me that every morning De Pachmann opens his collection of stones and plays with them for hours at a time; and De Pachmann himself told me that his love for them is far greater than for music. The roseate diamond, which is one of the rarest in existence, he calls his bride. "Some day," he says, "when I am no longer able to play, I will become a dealer in these stones."

Excepting for his collection, and Cesca [*sic*] as he calls his companion, there is very little that De Pachmann cares for, though he has a passionate love of life and is exceedingly careful of his person. He will not permit you to smoke unless you stand several feet away, for fear of burning him, though he himself incessantly puffs big, black cigars. He will not walk any distance in the grass for fear of "sneks," as he calls them. He seems to lead a lonely life with his one companion. . . . Indeed, knowing him closely, one feels a strong sympathy for this great man. For in spite of his genius, in spite of the fact that the world has for years bowed to this consummate master, he is a lonely figure, a solitary man . . . the keynote of this man's existence is love.

~

The tour was again managed by Loudon C. Charlton, sharing responsibilities with Arnold Somlyo, who was photographed with Pachmann in a Porthos automobile. The pianist was whimsically placed behind the wheel, although it is doubtful he ever learned to drive.

Pachmann's recitals were now presented exclusively in Carnegie Hall, his audience having outstripped the confines of Mendelssohn Hall. In late July the pianist visited Somlyo in his studio in Carnegie Hall, where a reporter interviewed him for a piece published in *Musical America* on September 14, 1907:

> I used to say that Mme. Patti gave her famous farewells that name because she fared so well. I am afraid the same reason may prompt the American public to doubt the sincerity of my leave taking, for I also have fared well on all my former tours to the United States. My decision never again to cross the ocean after my present trip is based solely on considerations of health. I am one of those unfortunate land-lubbers for whom the ocean has no respect and a week spent on the sea always means to me several succeeding months of digestive discomfort and kindred ailments. I always say to my American friends that I cannot understand how so attractive a country as theirs can lie on the other side of so vicious a body of water. "America should be in Europe," I tell them, and they laugh and ask me why I do not stay in their land always and avoid the return journey to Europe. Ah! That is a psychological question and one on which I would prefer to have my manager enlighten you. What do I think of critics? That is not the way to put it. I am more interested to know what critics think of me. Broadly speaking, I should divide all critics into two classes—those who write well of me, and those who do not. Of course, the former are the good ones and the latter are the bad. But you must not take me seriously, eh? No one does, except when I am at the piano. It is said that I do things on the stage to make people laugh and sometimes I am scolded by the critics for what they call my "antics." Why should I not be on good terms with my audience, and converse with them if I feel so inclined? Liszt and Chopin used to make veritable receptions of their recitals and mingled freely with their friends in the auditorium before mounting the platform to play. During the intermission the social atmosphere was resumed. Surely one could not pick out better models to follow in the conduct of a piano recital than Liszt and Chopin! So you see, my "antics" are neither so original nor so irreverent as some persons imagine. I am quite a serious person at heart, really I am. What do you suppose I do at home when I am not practicing the piano? I read philosophy and scientific works—Darwin, Spencer, Kant, Schopenhauer, Huxley, Spinoza—all of them I know as well as I do my Chopin, Schumann, Bach, Beethoven, Liszt. The sidereal system interests me as much as a sonata, and I have thought out as many nebular hypotheses as I have played nocturnes. Next to my reading, my other pet hobby is the collecting of precious stones, for which I have a fondness that amounts almost to a mania. . . . I spent the earnings of years to acquire my wonderful stone treasures. No, I never wear any of them as you can perceive for yourself. My love for gems is ideal, abstract. I have named most of them. My most flawless diamond has been christened Bach. A wonderful dusky emerald I own is called Brahms. My best opal, the most poetical of all stones, bears the title Chopin. A brilliant ruby, full of scintillating color, I have dubbed Liszt. Richard Strauss? I have no stone worthy to bear that name. Ah! What a giant! That gives me an idea. My manager tells me my American concerts are all booked and the tour will be the most successful I have ever made. Well, then, when I return to Europe I shall buy a Richard Strauss for my collection.

This interview gives pause. Certainly the uncredited writer edited and cleaned up Pachmann's diction (as did many of Pachmann's other interviewers), and mercifully spared us a literal and phonetic reproduction of the pianist's "dialect" speech. One suspects the interviewer knew his leg was being pulled at certain points and that Pachmann had probably rehearsed the lines about the sidereal system and nebular hypotheses. The reference to Richard Strauss might be a put-on as well; the composer's opera *Salome* had shocked and rocked the musical world just eighteen months earlier. Like most musicians whose training harked back to the mid-nineteenth century, Pachmann despised the modern trend in music, and his comment about a gem "worthy to bear that name" could have been sarcastic.

Arnold Somlyo invited Pachmann to partake of some watermelon and wine. Pachmann brought a new acquaintance, James Francis Cooke (just named editor of the *Etude* magazine) and Mrs. Cooke with him to Somlyo's. After, they all ventured downtown by the still-novel subway. Cooke wrote about the meeting at least twice (*Etude*, November 1921 and April 1933):

> He is as oblivious to surroundings in private life as he is upon the stage. Once he showed . . . a way of his own devising to serve watermelon. You cut the melon in half, cut out the red pulp in cubes, fill the bowl with Rhine wine, let it soak and then drink it with oscillating eyes . . . [we] were returning . . . de Pachmann . . . entered the subway and found seats in the usual jammed car. De Pachmann, five feet or so in height, with a fur collared overcoat, and a quaint top hat perched upon his long hair reached his destination. In taking his leave . . . the pianist, who was quite sober, protested that he had been greatly honored in meeting the writer and backed out with deep bows the entire length of the crowded car, swinging his silk hat and flourishing his long Newmarket coat . . . stooping so low that his hat repeatedly touched the floor. If he had been parting from the Czar he could not have been more obsequious. The passengers roared at the farce, and one whiskey-steeped Manhattanite waked up long enough to ejaculate, "Nut!" Was he? Perhaps the shoe is on the other foot, for no man ever enjoyed the passing panorama better than de Pachmann.

Musical America was now being managed by another Pachmann fanatic, John Freund, and it ran another "interview" with the pianist on October 5, 1907, the copy for which was supplied to the magazine by Somlyo:

> Franz Liszt once said to me: "Great artists have no biographies; their biographies are in their art." I know of no truer word than that spoken by the king of all pianists. When I die I wish my friends only to say: "He was a pianist who used his heart as well as his hands." Could any virtuoso wish for a finer epitaph? . . . Oh, other artists! What do they matter to me or I to them? Each

one of us who feels it his mission to play the piano in public does it in the manner peculiar to himself or herself, and these differences of interpretation constitute what the music sharps call "individuality." It is an influence which regulates the entire life of its possessor. For instance, I know one famous pianist who prefers dabbling in chemistry to giving public recitals, and does the latter only when he needs the money. Another has a penchant for athletics and is prouder of his biceps than he is the way he plays Beethoven. A third is addicted to the flowing bowl, and that probably accounts for his "liquid" tone which I read about. Vegetarians, anti-vivisectionists, Fabianists and some who have a hallucination that they are composers—all those are among my brother artists of the keys.[3]

The tour began in the Midwest in October. Surprises awaited them in Minnesota at the start, where they discovered that the local concert agent, G. W. Walker, had done a miserable job promoting Pachmann. The pianist was supposed to receive $600 each for three appearances, one each in three Minnesota cities, but the box office take in the first city, Duluth, was only $400. That recital took place in a Methodist church, and while he was playing two moving men noisily pushed a dray down the aisle in preparation for moving the piano after the concert. Pachmann had to stop playing until they were done, and then begin again. Manager Walker was heard muttering "My heart is nearly broken" and "I can't stand it." The men who had put posters up around Duluth advertising Pachmann's concert were not paid, got a court order attaching the pianist's luggage, and Pachmann had to travel on to St. Paul, the next city, without his trunks. Then Walker disappeared with all the meager funds, and the recital in St. Paul took place only because the manager of the hall agreed to reduce the rent. The third recital in Minneapolis was cancelled. To top things off, a bank as well as a postal strike were in progress and they found themselves completely without money. There was no way to contact Baldwin in New York, so they were obliged to stay in a local St. Paul hotel until funds could arrive. The hotel management was not impressed with Pachmann's fame and suspicious that perhaps they were being bamboozled, so they ordered a local policeman to accompany the pair when they walked to the train station and back. Local papers quoted Pachmann: "I hate Americk."

Elsewhere Pachmann had his usual successes, but there were exuberant audience demonstrations not seen before. Nineteenth century audiences had been conditioned by the Victorian idealization of music that encouraged artists to play romantic music romantically. Artists had freedom in their interpretations, and audiences, freedom to respond emotionally. In one sense music acted as a release from the constraining manners of daily life (perhaps today rock concerts fulfill this function). Eccentric Pachmann added something new to the late nineteenth and early twentieth century brew. His platform behavior encouraged audiences to loosen their own decorum even more. Even so, even he was unprepared for what happened when he played his first recital in Chicago in early November. By now Pachmann was used to acclaim and expected it, and became angry when he perceived an audience to be cold and unresponsive; but that Chicago audience went from the warmth of acclaim to a heated demonstration that suddenly veered out of control. He had played a seemingly endless string of encores, provoking a mounting hysteria that actually frightened the pianist.

The *Denver Post*, November 4, 1907, quoting a Hearst wire story:

Foolish Women Almost In Riot Over De Pachmann

The most sensational scene ever enacted in a Chicago concert hall occurred in Orchestral Hall yesterday afternoon when Vladimir de Pachmann, the Russian pianist, drove an audience of women into hysteria. The frenzy displayed surpassed anything seen in the Paderewski concerts ten years ago. . . . After the concert de Pachmann gave eight encores, being frantically recalled again and again. Women struggled to get near the platform, hats were wrecked and veils torn. Parasols were broken in the struggle. The pianist appeared and was received with ringing cheers. He played another number from Chopin. Cries of "Bravo" rang out. The audience demanded more. Everyone was standing, and excited throngs were pressing to the front of the hall. . . . Excitement still rose higher. After the sixth encore, someone ran to F. Wright Newmann, manager of the concerts, in the lobby. "The women are getting hysterical," he was told. "Stop those encores. Something might happen." Mr. Newmann hurried back of the stage and sent out a man to lock the piano. He appealed to . . . the manager of Orchestra Hall, to turn the lights down. A man rushed out . . . and locked the piano. "Open the piano!" bellowed a voice in the topmost gallery, and the frantic throng and women took up the cry. An uproar arose. De Pachmann, pale and visibly frightened by the demonstration, advanced to the instrument. "Wait, wait, I will play, I will play," he cried, waving his hands at the audience. He played once more, and the throng of women beseeched him with clasped hands to play again. "Only one more," he replied. . . . He played the eighth encore. Mr. Newmann had made his arrangements, and immediately on the conclusion of the number the piano was locked. Three stage hands pushed it to the back of the stage. At the same time the lights were turned down.

The Chicago hysteria did not impress Pachmann and seems to have frightened and put him in a bad humor. He played a recital in Brockton, Massachusetts, on November 13. The next day a report appeared in a local paper (the dated but otherwise unidentified clipping is found in a Pachmann scrapbook in the Boston Public Library):

Vladimir de Pachmann may never come back to America. "They are too cool, these American people," said the distinguished visitor, shivering and wrapping himself all the tighter in his long coat. "Appreciation? They have none.

Rapture? The word is not in their vocabulary. I shall never play in America again. I am going back to Europe as soon as I can get there. When can I get a boat? America does not appeal to me in any way, shape or manner. It is too bizarre, too indifferent, too cheap." There was nothing cheap about the tickets of admission to de Pachmann's concert last night.

On November 19 his New York audience at Carnegie Hall packed the house. The critics wrote that his playing was "unmistakable"—H. E. Krehbiel, *New-York Tribune*: "There is no escaping the charm of this magician's playing from the purely pianistic point of view." Richard Aldrich, the *New York Times*:

> The Nocturne [D flat, Op. 27 No. 2] floated from his fingers like the breath of a summer wind and the melody in the A flat Etude [Op. 25 No. 1, "Harp"] was as pure and clear in tone as a lambent flame.

After a quick trip to Philadelphia where he played Mendelssohn's G minor Concerto with the city's orchestra under its leader, Carl Pohlig, he went on to his beloved Boston, to repeat the same program he had played in New York. *MC*, December 11:

> Flowers were presented, cries of "De Pachmann" were heard from all over the house, and the stamping and clapping continued long after the pianist had responded with three extra numbers.

Great appreciation, of course, but no hysteria, for this was Boston, not Chicago.

His favorite critic, "Dr. Hale" (in his discourse, Pachmann had rewarded Philip Hale for all his praise with a doctorate), said it all (December 3, 1907, *Boston Herald*):

> There are other great pianists, as there were before him, as there will be after him, but for many years there has been only one de Pachmann. And now he leaves us before his coloring is dim, before his rhythm halts, before his memory fails. A student of the philosophers, he himself is a philosopher. He knows that it will be something for one of the younger generation to say in after years, when there is talk about some meteoric pianist: "But I heard de Pachmann."

Boston would not let him go and he had to schedule three extra recitals. Perhaps it was the sympathy he felt there, for Boston always brought out the best playing in Pachmann. The intensity of the playing was mirrored with increased gesticulations, whispering, asides, as well as increased contentment at being with an audience he loved. The celebrated composer H. T. Parker, also a regular drama critic for Boston's the *Transcript*, wrote (December 14, 1907):

> His own playing was charm itself, yet he whispered to the audience now and then that the particular phrase on the tip of his fingers was also charming. Often he drew the curve of a cadence upon the air. He communed by eye and gesture with his hearers to the right and left of him, before and behind him. And steadily he smiled a half smile of tranquil content upon the piano and upon his audience. He even clowned a little when he put his head through the huge wreath he received

There was always a possibility that something would trigger Pachmann to outrageous, circus-like behavior, and it happened at the next Boston recital. The prominent American pianist George Copeland was there, and decades later described it to the author. After a ravishing performance of Weber's Invitation to the Dance, one of a pair of extremely ugly spinster sisters, pillars of Boston society who attended every Pachmann performance, got up from her stage seat and impulsively handed the pianist a rose she unpinned from her bodice. Pachmann took the rose, held it aloft and put it down several times in succession. Only then did he take a good look at the donor. Miming acknowledgement of the gift with the grandest of gestures, he then made some dreadful grimaces, took the rose, threw it to the floor—and jumped on it.

About this time Cesco obtained a camera and began taking snapshots. The first was of his master, leaning over the balcony of a New Jersey hotel. In the next years he took many of the pianist that are as revealing as any memoir. Back in New York the pair rested and got ready for a change, a series of concerts in Canada. Pachmann thought Cesco, because he was Italian, might enjoy and be amazed by the glamour of the Metropolitan Opera House, where he had played during a Sunday evening concert in 1900. They went to hear Pachmann's former nemesis, the soprano Marcella Sembrich, singing the title role in Verdi's *La Traviata*, in January, 1908. But it was Pachmann who came away amazed. He asked Cesco, "How could she be dying? She sings so beautifully."

On April 26, 1908, Pachmann appeared again at a Met Sunday night concert, a benefit for The United Hebrew Charities, at which the reigning Brunhilde Johanna Gadski sang. They also found time to attend a concert by the Valkyrie of the piano, the Venezuelan Teresa Carreño, on January 10, 1908. According to *Musical America* (January 18):

> There were . . . many of the artist's colleagues, the most conspicuous being Vladimir de Pachmann, who went through a series of ecstatic, facial and bodily contortions and punctuated the program with frequent cries of "Brava."

Pachmann attended the Carnegie Hall concert in a box, along with a party that included Dr. J. C. H. Beaumont, a surgeon who loved music and served as a ship's surgeon for many decades. He and Pachmann had met on several trans-Atlantic crossings. In the September 15, 1925, issue of *Pearson's* magazine Dr. Beaumont remembered:

> At the end of her piece he got up, very excited and cheered loud and long, shouting "Bravo!" In resuming his seat, he stumbled and nearly fell out of the box, but I grabbed him in time to prevent a disastrous fall into the stalls below.

That same evening Pachmann attended a glamorous gilded-age party at Sherry's, given by the great soprano Lillian Nordica. There were several hundred guests drawn from the arts and high society. Pachmann played some Chopin Etudes "in true de Pachmann manner" according to *Musical America*. The French baritone Victor Maurel (creator of Verdi's Falstaff and Iago) sang, and towards the end La Nordica sang and accompanied herself. Still later she began dancing with the conductor Vasily Safonoff to the strains of the new and already immensely popular *Merry Widow Waltz*, while the distinguished guests watched—Gustav Mahler, Mark Twain, Karl Muck, Sembrich, and soprano Emma Eames among them. Pachmann joined in the merriment by partnering Maurel in some informal singing. *Musical America* (January 18) wrote:

> We have always known that Mr. de Pachmann had a delightful singing tone in his playing, but we never heard before that he sang. Possibly the enthusiasm he displayed on Sunday afternoon, when he attended Mme. Carreño's concert at Carnegie Hall, so overcame him that when he was with his good friend, Mme. Nordica, later in the evening, he burst, like a lark in Spring, into song.

Carreño and Pachmann first met in 1901, when he attended one of her London recitals at St. James's Hall. Probably the greatest woman pianist of her day, she never forgot that first meeting with Pachmann, describing it vibrantly to a reporter for the *San Francisco Argonaut* (reprinted in *MC* on January 15, 1908):

> At the time of this adventure I had never heard or seen De Pachmann. I was playing in St. James's Hall, London, and the public was kind enough to be very enthusiastic. But my attention was particularly attracted by a little man who looked like a Protestant minister, and who stood up in his chair and shouted and applauded wildly. Naturally, my curiosity was excited by such a marked display of enthusiasm, and I asked my manager, Mr. Vert, who the demonstrative person might be. "But don't you know?" he answered. "That is de Pachmann." It was the height of the London season, and after the concert the small green room was crowded, for I have many friends there, and Busoni, Godowsky and Rosenthal were also fulfilling engagements in the

city, and with several other artists of equal eminence had been kind enough to attend my recital. Suddenly there was a commotion at the door and De Pachmann entered. Talking in a most excited manner he forced his way to the center of the room, and falling on his knees before me, declared "So, madame, on my knees do I acknowledge your supremacy! Queen of pianists! Most Glorious of artists! Regal woman!" And turning to Godowsky, Busoni, Rosenthal, and the rest, he commanded that they, too, kneel. "Well, it made me sick," Mme. Carreño continued, colloquially, emphatically. "Such extravagance was, to say the least, embarrassing, but though I finally persuaded Mr. de Pachmann to stand, he continued to overwhelm me with compliments. At last, however, Mr. Vert persuaded him to leave. And though most of my friends had left, and those that remained were as sick with long repressed merriment as I was with mortification, we were just beginning to feel comfortable when the door was again opened suddenly and De Pachmann returned, like the Music Master in the 'Barber of Seville,' to add one more word of extravagant compliment." "Your sixth rhapsodie," he cried, "I have heard it from Liszt himself, and not even he could play it so." A year later my daughter, Teresita, met de Pachmann in Berlin. "I know your mother," he said. "A beautiful woman. But she should not try to play the piano!"

Four years later the *Cleveland Leader* printed an interview with Pachmann:

Can a woman be a great pianist? Yes and no. I'd say no as a usual thing. But that is not mentioning Teresa Carreño. She is a great artist as Americans well know. Carreño plays like a man when she plays in a manner she knows is right—but she does not always do that.

Toward the end of January they began the Canadian segment, touring the provinces of Quebec and Ontario. He had been gathering Canadian admirers since the '90s. On April 9 he played another recital in Toronto. The Toronto *Conservatory Bi-Monthly* (May 1908) reported:

The effects produced by his mastery over technique were almost bewildering. Several in the audience thought there was 'something inside the piano,' others declared they heard "echoes."

The weather turned cold and wet during the Canadian visit, and Pachmann fell ill. This was only the second time in his entire career that he was ill for an extended period, and this time it happened while he was actually touring. He was ill for four weeks, but even though he was suffering (this was mentioned in some reviews) he managed to continue playing. After Canada he toured the Midwest and then went to the Pacific Coast and south. In San Francisco he was deemed the best pianist the city had seen (*San Francisco Chronicle*, January 28, 1908):

The interpretations of other men passed in review. . . . The difference lies mainly in the fact that De Pachmann gets a tone that is almost uncanny.

. . . While playing the "Berceuse" De Pachmann could not resist explaining
it to those close to him. His voice traveled until fully one third of the audience heard him say, "Now go to sleep." Again, in the "Troisieme Scherzo"
in C sharp minor, he said just before the finale, "Here's sunshine." And the
Chopin numbers carried the audience by storm.

They returned east for the tour's grand conclusion, his final appearances in New York and Boston. At his first two concerts in Boston (all-
Chopin) he was particularly talkative, apparently going way beyond his
usual "conversations with music." The audience was highly entertained,
but Pachmann's favorite admirer, Philip Hale, was for once not amused.
Extremely irritated, he wrote a review in which one can notice, perhaps
for the first time, a sarcastic, wry humor penetrating the usual ponderous
pages (*Boston Herald*, March 22, 1908):

> This recital might be described as a lecture on Chopin compositions, with
> musical illustrations. The pianist commented on pieces before, during and
> after the performance. He was fantastic with the fantasia; he lulled himself
> with the berceuse; he polonaised, and mazurked and waltzed. The only thing
> that was lacking for complete enjoyment was a stereopticon with views of
> Chopin's portraits, houses where he lived, pianos he played, women that
> he loved, national and salon dances and a series of photographs of Mr. de
> Pachmann from his childhood to the year of his first American tour. Miss
> [Isadora] Duncan and Miss [Maud] Allan dance on the stage with bare legs
> and arms, clad in a garment of thin gauze; they dance poetically in illustra-
> tion of various pieces by Chopin. It is a pity Mr. de Pachmann cannot do this
> and play the piano at the same time.

After mentioning that he would be giving a final concert next Saturday,
Hale cautioned his favorite pianist: "Let us hope that he will be somewhat
chastened in spirit; that he will farewell the audience with the dignity
becoming the rare artist that he is."

Perhaps Cesco read Pachmann the review, for he seems to have taken
Hale's advice to heart. Next Saturday's Boston concert saw a Pachmann
who was a model of the dignified, world-famous artist, and his favorite
critic rewarded him with a short but glowing Farewell (*Boston Herald*,
March 29, 1908):

> Mr. de Pachmann bore himself with dignity, and he was wholly in the vein.
> . . . It seemed as though this incomparable pianist wished to leave the fra-
> grant memory of a concert distinguished by flawless art and a poetic expres-
> sion of the rarest quality.

All was not Chopin on the tour. Among the non-Chopin works, the
most memorable, certainly the most unusual, was Beethoven's C major

Sonata, known as the "Waldstein." As was often noted, if there was one composer Pachmann was ill-suited to play it was fire-storming Ludwig. Apparently, his performance of the "Waldstein," however, was something exceptional and special. George Halprin heard the performance in Carnegie Hall on April 8, 1908, and said the first movement was indeed a caricature, but redeemed by the performance of the last movement, which he called "unbelievable." Pachmann found fantasy behind the music, and he played the haunting horn theme with amazingly beautiful tone, and then fitted the little sixteenth note figurations following into the music's fabric like a delicate undercurrent of filigree, "making the renowned Beethoven players look sick," according to Halprin. The critics thought the conception too much Pachmann and too little Beethoven, but the audiences were enchanted.

One of his last interviews before returning to Europe, with the by-now usual curious mixture of sincerity, leg pulling and ego masquerading as humility, was for the *Toledo Blade* (undated clipping):

Wagner was my dear friend. So was Liszt. So were Renan and Hartmann,[4] my dear philosophers. No longer do you find de Pachmann in the high society of savants and artists. You see, I have learned "ze quiet philosophy." I say to myself, "life is good." This table is good, and this chair. I say this earth is heaven, but I must be in Italy or France to say so. But there is no life to come. I love my philosophers. So I am like Christ in this, that I love all the people to the ends of the world. I like the American people, for they have been good to me. I have given away much of the money they give to me. But now I must keep their money, for else I may have to beg in my old age. I do not like to beg. And I have said this is to be my farewell to America. I am a gentleman, and I will keep my word. In this one way—mind you, in this one way—I am superior to Patti. . . . My audiences I like because they like me. There are about a dozen men living who really understand me. The others only try to understand. . . . Tomorrow I go to Italy, or the south of France, and I start to write operas like my good friend Offenbach.[5]

In New York he still enjoyed dining at Lüchow's restaurant, where total strangers could join one at the table and new friendships were born. In a whimsical column entitled "Fact and Fancy," the *New York Times* (September 13, 1908) reported on one of Pachmann's adventures there. A young man sat at the table with Pachmann, who asked the unmusical youth if he knew who he was. The young man demurred, and this did not go over well. Pachmann was quoted:

I played before the Kaiser of Germany—he adores me . . . the other day I was the soloist with the Boston Symphony Orchestra. The whole orchestra adores me. Oh, my child, it's marvelous. And yet I am perfectly democratic.

I associate with the Kaiser and other rulers, and I'm a Baron myself, yet it doesn't turn my head. I have just as good a time sitting here talking to a plebeian—like you. Marvelous!

Just before leaving the United States Pachmann was asked to write "a few words" for the *Neume*, the year book of the New England Conservatory of Music. Pachmann letters are extraordinarily rare. In more than forty years the author has found less than a dozen—he obviously did not like to write them.

Mr. Darden Ford, Editor of "Neume"
New England Conservatory of Music, Boston, Mass.

Mr dear Sir: — You ask me to write a few words for the "Neume." I am delighted to do so, as it gives me one more opportunity of saying good-bye to my friends in Boston. I shall always treasure in grateful remembrance the concerts I have given in Boston, for I felt that genuine sympathy and musical comprehension of a higher order, which is an inspiration to an artist. New York may spend more money for music than Boston, and yet I consider Boston much more musical and more capable of discrimination between an artist who lives for his art, and an artist who lives for what he can get out of his art. And what applies to Boston audiences applies with equal force to the Boston music critics. I have the greatest admiration for them, for they judge an artist solely by what he plays and how he plays, and judge him fairly— justly, in the true sense of the word. I cannot say that much of the New York critics. Although I have no intentions of ever returning to the United States again, I am frank to say that the opportunity of playing in Boston once more might be a temptation for me to cross the ocean, as much as I dread it. Sincerely, Vladimir de Pachmann

Chapter 22

Peripatetic Pachmann, 1908–1911

Pachmann and Cesco returned to England in 1908. In June he gave a recital in Queen's Hall, and the *Times* reviewer grudgingly wrote:

> It is now many years since M. de Pachmann began his eccentricities of demeanour . . . which delight the unthinking part of his audiences, and it was inevitable that they should grow upon him. . . . At one point . . . the player executed such fantastic movements in his seat that his neighbours in the orchestra (with whom friendly relations had previously been established by gestures through the whole concert) could not resist going into fits of laughter. . . . It is only fair to say that in the "Waldstein" sonata of Beethoven, with which he began, there were no tricks of manner, and a tendency to labour some of the accents was the only blot upon a very fine performance. . . . In former years M. de Pachmann's recitals have been a genuine musical treat varied by some distracting moments; it must be confessed that in the present day they seem rather like a music-hall "turn" relieved by interludes of magically beautiful playing.

They toured the provinces. In Liverpool Pachmann was awakened about midnight by strange sounds. He was terrified that it was mice scratching in the walls and raised himself in bed to a sitting position, but was so afraid he couldn't move further. Unable to strike a match or call out for help from Cesco sleeping in the next room, he remained in that position until daybreak. Cesco found him in a state of nervous exhaustion. He had a high fever and the concert had to be cancelled. A few days later he was recovered and couldn't resist letting his Eastbourne audience know about it, blaming Cesco. In between chords he told them, "My secretary, he eez quite mad. In my room in the hotel, he not block up chimney—mice come down at night!"

Despite the many points of affinity between Pachmann and England, the pianist could never adjust to certain British habits. Afternoon tea both perplexed and amused him, and he couldn't understand how anyone would interrupt their daily work for a cup of tea. He loved to poke fun at this custom and in Bristol he treated the audience to an "English style" performance. During the recital five p.m. came—afternoon tea time—but the audience was respectfully silent. There was no coughing and nary a restless shuffle, only the glorious music. Suddenly in the middle of a Chopin Etude he unexpectedly stopped playing. An attendant came out from the wings bearing a tea tray. The audience gasped in astonishment but remained silent, not knowing how to react. The only sound heard in the hall was that of Pachmann serving and drinking his tea. Returning to the piano, he confided to the audience, "I drink tea!" and then continued with the Etude exactly where he had left off.

Three years passed with Cesco in faithful service, but there were constant crises that tested his resolve. In some strange, illogical and inexplicable way, perhaps something that could only happen in real life, and despite seemingly insurmountable difficulties, Cesco and Vlady (as Pachmann now wanted Cesco to call him) grew very fond of each other, and completely dependent on each other's presence. In important ways Pachmann was a very simple person, pure in heart and childlike. Of course, he was almost impossible to live with, high-strung and moody, infuriating and obsessed about minor details of routine. Cesco eventually understood what was necessary to make him happy, and the great pianist became devoted to him, with the unquestioning devotion of a "child and genius," to borrow Maggie's words. Added to the equation was Cesco's physical attractiveness.

With Cesco of course, things were different. Not being homosexual, it took him much longer to adjust. He enjoyed the excitement and glamour of living with such a flamboyant "exotic" (to use his word). And he certainly liked the challenge of managing the personal aspects of Pachmann's career, and grateful to have it all in the service of art. Of course there was always the attraction of the applause and réclame that surrounded Pachmann's success, the money, the clothes Pachmann bought him, the expensive restaurants, the famous people he met—all the trappings of a world-famous virtuoso's life. Eventually it went even beyond all this. Fifty-nine years later, when Cesco recounted the circumstances of Pachmann's death to me, tears filled his eyes.

Perhaps the wide difference in their ages (in 1908 Pachmann was sixty while Cesco was scarcely twenty-four) contributed to the fatherly feelings Pachmann began to have for his young Italian secretary. Much to Cesco's surprise, he took him aside one day and told him, "Cesco, I want you to call me Papi—it's Russian for 'little papa.'" So Pachmann was no longer Mr. de Pachmann or Vlady for Cesco—he was Papi. Soon the pianist asked all his friends, Lionel Powell, Somlyo, Godowsky, the Defries, Madame Peter to call him by his newly adopted name, which pleased him but really didn't suit him. Except for his gray hair, there was nothing remotely elderly about Pachmann, nothing in his demeanor nor his playing. The world's constant delight with his pianism was still a source of endless satisfaction for him. At sixty he still preserved the feeling and wonderment of a young artist, and every concert was a new experience.

His friendship with Cesco was probably the closest relationship he ever had with a man, and more intimate than his relationships with his sons Adrian and Leonide. While not neglectful of them, he didn't find time to see them very often. He usually managed one or two visits a year while passing through Paris, usually coming from concerts in Germany en route to engagements in England. Adrian became a lawyer, serving first in his stepfather Labori's office, and later on his own, specializing in quick divorces for the many Americans who flocked to Paris in the 1920's. He succumbed to a heart attack in his fifty-first year in 1937. His younger brother Leonide (also known as Lionel, born one year later) inherited some musical gifts from his father, becoming a professor of composition and piano at the Paris Conservatoire. He studied piano with both his parents and eventually founded his own school, known variously as the Lycée, or Ecole, Frederic Chopin, where he presided, remaining active into his nineties. He died in 1981 at age 93.

During the hectic time of the Dreyus affair the lives of the boys were threatened more than once (they were after all Labori's stepsons) and they had to live in seclusion in the country, where Pachmann visited them a few times in secrecy. When not in hiding, Pachmann would take them for a deluxe treat at expensive restaurants, at one of which, Marguerie's, ordering one of the specialties, "Filet de sole Marguerie" (a belle époque concoction of shrimp, mussels, filet of sole, mushrooms and cream). Leonide remembered riding in a car with his father once when traffic was stopped for a funeral procession. When Pachmann found it was his friend Mr. Marguerie's funeral, his first exclamation was "My friend of twenty years? Ah, no more filet de sole!"

Leonide heard his father play in concert only three times, the first time in London in 1909.[1] Being in a particularly good mood, Pachmann introduced Leonide to the audience: "Ladies and Gentlemen," he said. "This is my son Leonide. You see, he is taller than me. He is a musician . . . as a pianist (Pachmann made a nasty face) he is not ready yet. . . . As a composer—maybe. But as a thee-or-a-titian, he is (here he cupped two fingers to form a circle) ah, one of the most learned of musicians. At the Conservatoire he is already a professor 'en attendant [in waiting].'" Leonide told me there were some real professors from the Conservatoire at the concert who were visibly upset by the jest. Leonide was made to sit next to his father as he played the opening work, all the time addressing remarks to him specifically. When the piece was ended, Pachmann abruptly dismissed him with a warning to remember all that he had been told.

In early 1909 Pachmann gave an unusual recital in the Albert Hall. On January 21, 1909, the *Times* reported:

> A novel concert will be given by M. de Pachmann in the Royal Albert Hall. Instead of playing on the orchestral platform at the end of the hall, he will be seated in the center of the arena.

It seems a shell was erected around the piano, in an attempt to focus the sound and dampen the echoes that plagued the hall (these problems were not solved until World War II). Today we can only deplore this innovation. Pachmann could hardly have been heard to best advantage in such a vast amphitheater. His was the art of intimacy, and he was happiest when playing for four or five people around the piano. Nevertheless, Pachmann's concerts in the hall were so successful from a financial standpoint that other famous artists began using the Albert Hall regularly.

In London on October 29, 1909, the *Times* began a review of his recital of the day before:

> **Pretty Fanny's Way.** M. de Pachmann's recitals tend more and more to become a sort of drawing-room entertainment. The asides and gestures which at one time seemed perfectly spontaneous and unaffected, the promptings of a highly emotional nature to express more vividly and fully the thought of the music he was interpreting, have become so extravagant and almost continuous that they often overshadow his actual playing and when, as in repeating the Mazurka in A flat, he repeated also each gesture in full detail, it was difficult to resist the impression that the pantomime had been carefully prepared to tickle the groundlings. Still, it is "pretty Fanny's way," and there is an end on it. Besides, we can always shut our eyes to it, and enjoy without disturbance the otherwise perfect legitimacy of his playing.[2]

June 14 and 22, 1909, were the dates for Pachmann's second set of recording sessions for the Gramophone Company in London. Only four recordings from these sessions were issued (on discs bearing the "pre-dog" label, used just before the company obtained the rights to the picture of the dog, Nipper, listening to "His Master's Voice"). There is a dramatic improvement in the sound quality from the first records of two years earlier, but eleven selections were recorded and not issued, including something listed as "Improvisation on petite Barcarolle" and Liszt's etude, *La Leggierezza*. A great loss that the latter was not issued nor a test pressing preserved, for the pianist was already famous for his performances of the

Etude, and all posterity has is Pachmann's crude Welte "reproducing" piano roll of the work "recorded" in 1906.

The years between 1909 and 1913 saw the last flowering of Pachmann's exotic personality, before his eccentricities became predominant, ultimately overtaking his art. Some of his recitals then were among the greatest of his life. Scottish critic A. Russell Walker told the author of an extraordinary concert he had attended in Scotland in 1909. Some of Pachmann's earlier performances in the country were sparsely attended, as were his concerts in the British provinces, but in 1909 his concerts in Glasgow's intimate Queen's Rooms were tremendously successful, and apparently among the most memorable all-Chopin recitals of his career. Delighted by both the enthusiastic reception and the romantic atmosphere of the old hall, he played as if inspired. Instead of waiting until he completed the recital, he departed almost at once from the printed program and added encore pieces after each scheduled number. The audience sat hypnotized while Pachmann, fired by the spell of his own playing, continued well on into the night. When at last the recital ended (the audience was forced to exit in the dark as the lights had to be turned off to get them to leave), more than thirty Chopin compositions had been heard. Backstage Pachmann was surrounded by fans and admirers. He was heard quoting an Italian proverb: "Chi va piano, va sano"—who goes softly, goes safely. The Scots had been slow to come to his art, but sure.

Pachmann complained incessantly during this tour of being cold. The northern dampness and the endless gray days depressed him and he longed for the sun. Traveling was beginning to tire him and his sixty odd years weighed down on him. At the tour's end Cesco persuaded him to go to Rome, and they spent the winter there, Pachmann's first visit to the enchanting city in many years. They socialized with several musician friends including Liszt's Italian pupil Giovanni Sgambati and the great baritone Mattia Battistini, who invited them to dine at Caffè Greco, a Roman landmark since the early nineteenth century.

These were happy days. Cesco rented an elegant suite of rooms in an old palazzo, where Pachmann relaxed and listened to the test pressings of some recent disc recordings. The atmosphere was carefree, and Pachmann had Cesco pose while wearing a Neapolitan Lazzaroni costume, emphasizing Cesco's good looks. Pachmann was not particularly fastidious about his own personal appearance, but when he noticed his hair turning gray, he began to paint his bushy eyebrows. "Don't you think I look younger, Cesco? I've put on my eyes." We can see this in the snapshot of him listening to test pressings on a horn gramophone, taken in Rome in 1910, and many subsequent photos.

The émigré Russian colony gathered at Ranieri's, a famous Roman restaurant still in existence, and there the two met an old man who claimed to be Modest Tchaikovsky, younger brother of the composer. He told them that in his youth he had been a pupil of Vladimir's brother Semyon. Cesco tried to interest Pachmann in seeing the city's famous landmarks, but when they went to Saint Peter's, he got out of the taxi, looked once at the majestic Bernini columns, then said "Very nice, Cesco—now let's go to the Campo de' Fiori." Rome's flea market interested him more, and he went there every day in search of precious stones, becoming a familiar figure to the merchants. "Tra-la-la" they sang, "Papi è tornato" (Papi has returned).

Pachmann complied with an unusual request. The English royal family had always been sympathetic and he was more than once asked to play for King Edward VII and Queen Alexandra. They had attended his debut, as had the Duchess of York who went to some lengths to assist with his career. Pachmann was in Paris when the king died on May 6, 1910; when he returned to England to finish his season, he was asked to play Chopin's Funeral March in the king's memory. At first he refused, claiming he would suffer too much. But he yielded, and eight days later at a recital in Bournemouth on May 14 he played it in honor of the king's memory.

After his concert in London, Pachmann was greeted with a May 21, 1910, review in the *Times*:

> It has been long agreed that M. de Pachmann must be allowed to do what he likes so long as he will consent to play Chopin; and on Saturday at Queen's Hall it was as usual well worth the while to sit through the peculiarities in order to hear the pianist's exquisite playing.

On June 19, 1910, the *Sunday Times* ended a review of his performance of both Chopin concertos at one concert in honor of the centennial of Chopin's birth, at Queen's Hall on June 15:

> Of course he punctuated his reading with the usual marginal notes of gesture and grimace. They apparently give offence to a good many worthy people, but personally I think this expression of an almost child-like unaffectedness is preferable to the pretentious pose of some of his rivals. And after all, one need not watch his annotations if they offend.

The British musical press occasionally entered into the spirit of fun when reviewing Pachmann. The *Times* for October 13, 1910, concluded a review of his recital of the day before thus:

> Ended with Godowsky's arrangement of the first etude from Op. 25—an arrangement which, in the adapter's words: "is intended to give the illusion of a piece for four hands." Perhaps it does, but if you are going to perform miracles, why draw the line at four?

Three days later the *Sunday Times* referred to the same recital:

M. de Pachmann was . . . more liberal than ever of those marginal notes which are, as the old lady said of Henry VIII's marrying propensities, 'is little 'obby.

On November 13, 1910, the *Sunday Times* reported:

M. de Pachmann was more than usual persnickety about the position of his piano and the exact height of his stool at his recital at Queen's Hall on Thursday afternoon, and it was not till the attendants had made repeated attempts at satisfactory adjustment, and he himself a couple of speeches of comic despair, partly in polyglot and partly in pantomime, that he was able to settle down to his work with the needful admonition, 'Now you must all be quite quiet for seventeen minutes.'

Leonide heard his father in concert for the second time in 1910, again in London, but this time at Albert Hall in a joint recital with the Czech violinist Jan Kubelik. Each was to play solo groups, and together Beethoven's "Kreutzer" Sonata. Pachmann was already ill at ease at the thought of performing jointly with another artist. Hours before leaving for the concert he was seen sitting in the lobby of the Hotel Ronveau, nervously puffing his cigar. An elderly gentleman recognized him and tried to strike up a conversation:

"I understand you are to play a concert this afternoon at the Albert Hall?"

"Are you a musician?" asked Pachmann, looking him over.

"Ah, no, I just play for my own pleasure," he replied, and then in the same breath: "I'm told you will accompany Kubelik?"

Pachmann almost dropped his cigar and looked at the man incredulously.

"I, accompany Kubelik?"

In the nervous state he was in, it was enough to prompt him to a near-violent rage. "The great pianist, accompany?" He was screaming. "No, not the great Pachmann!" Cesco rushed in and quickly led his master away while Pachmann kept shouting "It is finished. I can't play. I'm too nervous. If people like that are in the audience, what kind of concert will it be?! I, Pachmann, accompany? Ouf!"

After he quieted down Cesco went to complete last minute arrangements and left young Leonide to look after his father and bring him to the hall in a taxi. Inside the car, Pachmann said only "Don't talk!" He was in a dreadful mood. As they reached the hall, there was a confusion of taxis, carriages and pedestrians around the huge arena surrounding the hall. The driver was unsure about the many entrances and hesitated for a moment. A policeman quickly approached them.

"You can't stay there," he ordered. "Go farther on!"

"What are we doing?" Pachmann asked the driver, then his son. "Leonide, he doesn't know where the artist's entrance is. Tell him!"

"But Papa, I don't know."

"Oh, you stupid!" yelled Pachmann, as he commanded the driver to stop so he could get out. The policeman had been following the cab's progress like a cat with a mouse, and arrived as Pachmann alighted. The faced each other, the policeman as tall as Pachmann was tiny.

"Are you coming to the Pachmann concert?" asked the constable.

"Whose concert?" said the pianist disingenuously.

"Pachmann concert!" replied the policeman sternly. "Have you a ticket?"

"I . . . a ticket?" Pachmann was uncomprehending. "What is he saying?"

Leonide sensed a storm coming. "But he *is* Pachmann!" There was a long pause.

"But don't you know me? Have you never seen my photograph before? You can't be a musician."

At that moment Cesco arrived and led the disillusioned Pachmann into the artist's entrance, while he mumbled over and over, "I, a ticket . . . A TICKET?"

The simmering upset apparently was purged completely after Pachmann stood at the piano and heard the roar of approval from the packed house and saw many of his old friends applauding wildly. His spirit was uplifted. Leonide said he now appeared radiant, smiling and blowing kisses to admirers. After his solo portion of the program was over the audience demanded many encores, and Pachmann generously provided them—so many that Kubelik, waiting in the wings for his turn to go on, angrily paced the floor, cursing and muttering to himself, "Well, is he going to stay out there all day?"[3]

His performance of both Chopin concertos at one concert (June 16) in Queen's Hall was a highlight of the 1910 London season. The usual problems when Pachmann played concertos surfaced and the festive atmosphere couldn't mask the problems—conductor Landon Ronald, a well-connected figure in London society, succeeded in subduing the orchestra, but at best he was a mechanical time beater, and was either unwilling or unable to allow Pachmann much breadth in the lyrical sections. The *Sunday Times* (June 19) wrote that the pianist's playing of the concertos suggests the man of independent and rather erratic impulses who finds himself compelled to keep up with a personally conducted party of tourists.

But of the solo group between the two concertos it declared:

M de Pachmann found his accustomed freedom and played with loving sentiment, the persuasive grace of phrasing, and the delicate and almost infinite gradations of tone that are so individual to him.

At the end there were two bouquets for Pachmann, each representing one of the concertos, and he flattered Ronald by presenting him one.

After the 1910 season concluded they returned to their apartment in Paris, perhaps seeking a change from the atmosphere of the Ronveau. Leonide also took a separate Paris apartment, his first. His father would come and his visits there were much longer than at Chez Labori. Of course he gave Leonide lessons. On one visit Pachmann gave him some pointers on the Chopin Etudes. Leonide never forgot it and particularly remembered his method in teaching the "Ocean" Etude [Op. 25, No. 12 in C minor]. Pachmann told his son "I remember hearing Rubinstein play it," and then demonstrated at the keyboard just how the great Anton did it. He played with such power and so huge a tone that the sound reverberated in a way Leonide had never heard before. It created a terrifying sound picture of giant waves crashing against a rocky shore. Leonide didn't know his father was capable of such volumes of sound, but before he could say anything his father said "I also heard Liszt play it." Pachmann played it again, this time with tapered arpeggios, sonorous but lacking the mighty roaring and crashing, and now suggesting waves billowing. Finished, Pachmann allowed "But I think I prefer my own approach," and then played it à la Pachmann, with pianissimo runs and piano tones suggesting iridescent foam washing up on shore.

Leonide tried to interest his father in playing some contemporary music. Despite Pachmann's flamboyant behavior, his repertoire was conventional and conservative, and the only "modern music" he played was by his friend Godowsky. He avoided most early twentieth century compositions, and very well might have been unaware of modern music until one Paris visit when Leonide played some Debussy for him, thinking his father's touch would be perfect for the composer. But the unresolved dissonances were too much for Pachmann, who covered his ears, crying in pain for Leonide to stop.

Another incident that took place in Leonide's first apartment was notable—in telling the story to the author, Leonide made the only reference to his father's attraction to younger males that occurred in the dozens of hours together, during our month of interviews in 1960. Over these days Leonide began to feel at ease and look forward to our daily visits. In our last hours together, he took me to a restaurant situated one floor below a homosexual bar upstairs. A steady stream of men went up the stairs. Leonide noticed one of these and said with some delight, "Oh—he smiled at me!" He then told a story that happened fifty years earlier. He had had a young male friend who happened to be visiting when his father came by. Leonide mentioned that the young man was handsome. After the introductions, Pachmann sat down on a sofa next to the young man, and unaffectedly took his hand and held it. He held it and held it and eventually the uncomfortable and embarrassed young man had to leave. Leonide laughed when he recounted this story.

Chapter 23

The Last of the Chopinzee, 1911–1912

Pachmann knew how much he was beginning to resemble Adelina Patti, who he had said earlier had "fared so well" with her constant farewell concerts. He genuinely longed for a less active schedule and the time to pursue something in life besides travel and concerts, and often spoke to interviewers of his desire to live in leisure in Italy, but he couldn't bring himself to leave the concert platform. He talked continuously of retiring, but booked another American tour for 1911/1912, advertised as a "Farewell Tour." It raised some eyebrows since his previous American tour of 1907/8 had also been billed as a Farewell, but the pianist was now sixty-three, and the general feeling was that there would not be a third Farewell.

Again wishing to avoid rough seas, Pachmann and Cesco left England in late June 1911 on the *Mauretania*, filled with revelers returning from the English coronation festivities. The turbulent ocean and the constant tossing were torture for the pianist. They arrived in the intense heat of a hot summer, and when they tried to take his special padded piano stool through customs (Pachmann had carried it tenderly in his own hands off the ship), he was immediately pounced on and asked to pay $2.25 duty for it as an item of trade. His ire flared up at once. "Trade? Trade? I have no trade," he screamed. "I am the gr-r-reat pianist Vladimir de Pachmann. . . . How mean, how petty! To me, a great artist!"

He was in no mood to see the reporters who showed up. "I will not be interviewed. I hate reporters . . . critics . . . New York! What does this city know about music? Nothing! I hate New York!" He avoided a reporter from *Musical America* who requested an interview, but submitted on June 30, and the results were duly printed on July 8:

"And what do I find when I reach this detestable city? Noise, noise, nothing but noise. I cannot sleep, cannot rest. They are building a house opposite my room and the machines are always going—always, always! That house is full of machines, thousands of machines! They pound and pound and hammer. It overcomes my nerves, it drives away my sleep. My head is like the head of an idiot. I went to bed last night at one—alas, no quiet, no rest. . . . I began to fall asleep this morning at six. Then immediately they made the hammering machines begin to work. I am in despair. . . . Oh, how I loathe New York! New York is not America. It is the place where all the humbugs come together. It is the place where foreigners of all nations mingle. The New Yorkers are not Americans. The real Americans are the Yankees from New England. Ah! How different they are and how I love them, one and all! But New York, bah! I should be out of it already if I had a good house in the country. This is my last trip to America. It was not any great love of the country that brought me over. It was not any need for money. I'd not need to travel for money, for I am . . . to inherit a vast fortune. What really brought me here this time was my esteem for the people of the Baldwin Piano Company. What ideal, what good and noble people they are." And the pianist threw kisses at the chandelier. . . . "I always wonder why Americans are so proud of themselves, why they think everything they do is so perfect. It isn't perfect."

Pachmann's brother Semyon had died on November 29, 1910, and he had received notice that he was to share the large inheritance ($300,000 then, a few million in 2012 dollars) with two relatives. Pachmann's estimate of the nobility of the Baldwin piano and the Baldwin staff was helped along by the fact that the piano manufacturer was determined to unseat Steinway as the concert piano of choice, and was paying him a subvention to play their instrument, in all likelihood a sum larger than was offered by any rival.[1]

To add even more certainty that he would have sufficient income when he retired, Pachmann was persuaded to invest a considerable sum in the "coming thing"—the American film industry. Through Arnold Somlyo he bought shares in a film company, but the investment was a disaster, for it turned out that the entire scheme was a fraud.

Cesco found them a "good place" in the country, a hotel in White Sulphur Springs in Sullivan County, and they spent the weeks relaxing. He had grown his hair long. A reporter for the *New York Times* later commented on the resemblance to old Abbé Liszt, and printed his apology for slandering America (October 30):

He has returned to America wearing his hair like Liszt—long and cropped about the neck and pushed back straight from the forehead, and in a sense he suggests the Abbé. . . . When he landed some weeks ago in the Summer he confessed that after a bad voyage he was in a bad mood. "Touring fatigues me," he said, "and that voyage was dreadful. Then when the reporters met me at the dock and asked me if I liked America I told them no. That morning I did not like anything. They printed all I said about America and musical critics and what not, and of course I didn't mean it at all. I was sick and cross. I shall not complete the tour that has been mapped out for me this time. I think I should like to drop out about thirty concerts. It is too much. I am no longer young and it tires me to travel. I love to play and I shall continue to do that, but I do not want to travel any more. I should like to live in Italy, and there I think I shall go to pass my old age, just playing for the people that I love."

The interview was widely quoted and reprinted in other papers:

Just now I am playing better than I have ever played, because my technique is greater. Tone is at the command of an artist's technique, and now I devote all my time to the piano. I am as I was twenty years ago. I had another interest—certain collections of mine—which a year ago I gave up. I think of nothing but music now. I give myself to my music. I am learning the new technique, the technique which enables one to play Godowsky. . . . I have taught a few pupils, but I think I shall never teach again unless I can find someone to whom I can pass on the tradition of my playing. . . . I would take all the pains in the world if such a one existed. It is not my son. My boy will not be a great pianist, I think, but he will be a great composer. . . . Do you know who the greatest teacher of piano is now? It is Rafael Joseffy. He is the greatest teacher anywhere. He has issued a piano method—exercise which I think are invaluable. It is a flawless method, indeed, and now more exercises are coming from his pen.

The tour commenced in Canada, where most of the reviewers were not very musically sophisticated, wallowing in generalities, but delighting in reporting his eccentric behavior. One Montreal paper (unidentified clipping, October 3, 1911) wrote about his last appearance in that city:

The main effect of his playing was difficult to describe, since no mere concrete ebullition of feeling could express what he made people feel. As his fingers seemed to produce the most ethereal effects, he carried the spirit of his audience to almost unthought-of heights of musical exaltation, and with the concluding chords there was almost invariably a general sigh, as of one who had awakened from a wonderful dream. And with it all there was the mixture of inspiration with humanity. De Pachmann was at the outset very much annoyed at the noise made by the audience. He abruptly stopped in the middle of the opening Fantasia, and demanded, first in French and then in English: "What is the matter back there? Keep quiet. We cannot have a concert with all this noise."

While in Canada he visited a friend, the pianist Michael Hambourg[2] (father of the more famous pianist Mark Hambourg). Michael Hambourg had moved to Toronto in 1910, and a year later had founded the Hambourg Conservatory with his other sons, Boris and Jan. At Hambourg's house he played on a Canadian piano. An undated clipping from the *Vancouver World* reported:

> It seems that Professor Hambourg . . . and de Pachmann have been friends since their student days. . . . Several of Toronto's musicians had been honored with an invitation to meet the illustrious de Pachmann, and to hear him play. De Pachmann approached the piano, looking rather dubious, having never met with one of the same make in his career. It was the "New Art" Bell piano. However, he sat down and struck a few chords. In a second he was on his feet looking at the instrument in apparent amazement. Then he walked all around it, taking in its every detail. Again he sat down and this time he played and played as though inspired for over an hour. Finally when the last soft note had died away and he was about to leave, in his enthusiastic foreign way, and almost with reverence, this old man who has swayed vast audiences with his divine music, bent over and kissed the piano goodbye.

The next day Pachmann called the manager of the Bell piano works, invited him to visit at his suite in the Prince Edward Hotel with a few other friends, and after dinner Pachmann toasted the New Art Bell piano.

His first New York recital was in Carnegie Hall on October 20, 1911. *Musical America* reported (October 28):

> The pianist was more reticent than usual in the matter of cabalistical gestures and gyrations, but the immense audience, one of the largest Carnegie Hall has held for a long time, got no little amusement out of the many facial contortions with which he accompanied his performance, while his newly-grown crop of hair was an item not to be overlooked. More important, however, it heard some ravishingly beautiful playing.

Richard Aldrich wrote the next day in the *New York Times*:

> He still commands all his old marvel of "touch," his old magic of delicate, filmy iridescent tone, of sighing pianissimo, of purling, rippling passages, of clear articulation, to transform the piano into a celestial instrument. It is pretty, wonderfully pretty, ravishingly pretty, and it beguiles the senses of the listener in a way that hardly any other piano playing can do.

A feature of the concert was his performance of two numbers from Godowsky's Renaissance Suite, and as the last encore, Godowsky's transcription for the left hand alone of Chopin's "Revolutionary" Etude, the original version of which he had played during the main concert. Pachmann considered the Godowsky work important, and told the audience before playing it that he wanted "silence and no conversations and . . . emphasizing his wish by gestures of admonition," according to *Musical America*. Aldrich had written: "The net result of this seemed to be to establish the fact that it sounded much better as Chopin wrote it," although *Musical America* reported:

> Strange to say he played it better and more dramatically on the whole than he had done previously with two hands.

Olin Downes echoed the general opinion of Pachmann's idolators in Boston in the same issue of *Musical America*, and found something new to say about the pianist:

> When Mr. de Pachmann returned to Boston on Saturday afternoon he was in capital condition. . . . The stage, as well as the auditorium, was filled with seats, and it was not a solemn sight to see Mr. de Pachmann explaining to the gray-haired ladies who sat about him with such earnest regards the intricacies of the music that he was discoursing, and the manner in which he was outrivaling all pianists who ever existed. The climax of this sort of thing came suddenly, when, after finishing the "Revolutionary" étude, and just before beginning the A flat Ballade, de Pachmann turned to his audience, and said: "All the editions mark this passage fortissimo. That is not right. Forte, at the most, is enough. I could play it three times fortissimo if I wanted to, but that would not be music." We may jest at this sort of concert-giving, but at the same time there are very few pianists who could do the sort of thing as soulfully and delightfully as Mr. de Pachmann. He is, in his way, Napoleonic. How few can come on and get off the stage so engagingly! What esprit! May he long continue!

Rafael Joseffy was no longer playing in public and almost all pianists on the world's concert platforms were descendants of Liszt, Leschetizky and Anton Rubinstein. Pachmann was the only one whose art harkened back to earlier schools. He was aging, advertising farewells, and connoisseurs realized that something precious would disappear from piano playing with him. At the time Edwin Hughes was Leschetizky's assistant. He was asked by the Music Teachers National Association to deliver a lecture on piano playing at the group's convention in December 1911, that was published in their proceedings for 1912:

> There is a decided trend in piano-playing today in one well-marked direction, as seen in the work of nearly every prominent virtuoso before the public, and there is just as evident a disappearance of some of the relics of piano playing of former days. The trend . . . is entirely in the direction of the production of a big tone, the seeking of orchestral effects. . . . Of the

type of piano-playing . . . being in the course of disappearance, Vladimir de Pachmann, who may trace his pianistic lineage through Henselt directly to Chopin and Hummel, is the only representative of note on the concert stage at present. The last time I heard him, as I sat listening to the Chopin program, some of the numbers which will ever remain to me among the most precious memories of the concert-room, I felt a thrill of joy at the thought that de Pachmann, although the oldest pianist now before the public, is still preserved to us for an occasional "farewell tour." But, as he himself recently remarked sadly to an interviewer, who is to take up his art after he has left it? The answer is, alas, no one. It will be but a beautiful memory, for there is no further development for piano playing along these lines, piano playing which leaves us cold to all but the lyrical and rhythmic.

Pachmann was obviously playing at the height of his powers, but just as obviously, his personality was becoming more extravagant. On November 18 he played a work he amazingly hadn't played in America before, the Chopin E minor Concerto, with the Metropolitan Opera Orchestra, conducted by Josef Pasternack at a Metropolitan Opera Sunday night concert (his only New York orchestral appearance). The *New York Times* (November 27) wrote:

> Mr. de Pachmann's platform antics were as much in evidence as they ever were, but he played at his best. It is perhaps too bad that his audiences have to see him, but last night his performance of the concerto was so beautiful that what he did besides playing the piano might be forgiven. It is enough to say that his tone quality was on a plane which even he does not often obtain.

At the concert he played three solos as well, one of them the rare Liszt *Mazurka Brilliante.* He had recorded the piece a week earlier during his first recording sessions for the Victor Talking Machine Company, on November 7 and 8. Later a second pair of sessions for Victor took place on April 25 and 26, 1912; together they comprised his most extensive series of recordings up to that time. The playing captured on them is not quite up to the level of the earlier London Gramophone and Typewriter recordings, and somewhat spoiled by the shallow-sounding Baldwin piano used.[3] The harsh Victor acoustical recording process and scratchy shellac surfaces were largely unable to capture the delicacy of the pianist's touch, but despite all this, these Victor recordings preserved some inspired performances, particularly and paradoxically, the numbers that remained unissued by Victor and survived only as unique test pressings.[4]

1911 was the centenary of Liszt's birth. Pachmann's devotion to Liszt verged on mania, and he now revived several Liszt works he hadn't played for years. Apart from the *Mazurka Brilliante,* he played the Tarantella from the Venezia e Napoli suite, the B minor Ballade and other works. His concentration on tone and nuance hadn't robbed him of virtuosity. *Musical America* (November 25, 1912) reported on his recital in Boston's Jordan Hall on November 13:

> He had at his command an unusual amount of reserve strength, and in Liszt's Tarantelle he made a display of force and virtuosity that was simply astounding and exceedingly amusing to behold. The audience gaped, as suddenly, without warning, de Pachmann landed like a load of bricks on the piano—minus the metallic concussion—played the Tarantelle at an amazing pace. Then sang the melody of the middle section as few pianists save himself can sing on the instrument, and finally raised his paws on high and smote the keyboard until it reverberated the true Lisztian thunder. I think that de Pachmann is human like the rest of us . . . even the prince of pianissimists will now and then glory in a red-blooded fortissimo. . . . It was a virtuoso performance of the highest rank, and it was more, de Pachmann never went past the limits of artistic piano playing.

On December 15 and 16 he repeated the Chopin E minor Concerto in Philadelphia with the city's orchestra under Karl Pohlig. To have the acknowledged greatest Chopin interpreter of his time play a Chopin Concerto they hadn't heard before was considered a triumph, and the concert generated a lot of press. *Musical America* (datelined December 18) reported, "The Philadelphia Orchestra . . . played one of its trump cards in the way of a soloist." *MC* reprinted excerpts from a series of reviews of these concerts in its December 27 issue. The encomiums quoted included:

> There occur only once or twice in a generation giants. . . . Such is De Pachmann holding the audience spellbound . . . the "ovation" that is more often heard-about than witnessed, a veritable Doctor Miracle "The Tetrazzini of the piano" "aroused the vast audience to a pitch of enthusiasm which is not often witnessed these days . . . something of a revelation" "miraculous genius" perfect mastery of the piano . . . such poetry, such perfect command of every latent resource of the piano.

Further concerts took him south and west for a few weeks, but friendly Boston was forever beckoning, and he was back in his favorite city at the end of November and in early December. Altogether he presented five recitals in Boston which prompted his favorite critic "Dr." Philip Hale to bestow the most extravagant compliment ever on his favorite pianist (*Boston Herald*, December 10):

> He cannot play here too often. To think that Chopin's music will not be interpreted by him to future generations! Mr. de Pachmann should be immortal.

But he wasn't immortal and his memory began to slip—age might have played one part, the stress and excitement of the tour another. He sometimes forgot pieces and had to substitute another at the last minute. It was all done so casually that few seemed to mind. He was quoted in the *New York Times* (October 30):

> My memory is not as good as it once was, and I find it difficult to remember pieces I have not played for years, and I have no time to restudy them. Now when I am at home I can remember everything without difficulty, but when I get on the platform things make me nervous. The lights especially make me nervous.

Cesco took steps to insure that house lights would be lowered at future concerts. In the already charged atmosphere, his playing in almost completely darkened halls resulted in a nearly supernatural effect, as described by "H. K. M" in the *Boston Transcript* on December 5 concerning his recital there two days earlier:

> The unspeakably rich gentleness of the legato section of the E minor study or of the largo of the B minor Sonata, had a supernatural directness of appeal. . . . It was not until the audience left the hall . . . that it realized how . . . complete had been the focusing of attention under the spell of the pianist on the stage.

The end of the year brought the grueling final segment of the Canadian tour, his only visit to the Northern Territories. A surprise blizzard engulfed them as they traveled north and west. All rail service was suspended and Cesco and Pachmann had to abandon the train and continue by sled to Edmonton. As they huddled together under blankets, Pachmann whispered, "Like Russia, Cesco." After the Edmonton concert they had to wait until rail service to Calgary was resumed. The weather worsened and the wine they had brought with them froze. When they finally arrived for the concert in Calgary, Cesco found the piano had never arrived from Toronto, and the hall held only a worn-out upright rehearsal piano. He somehow found a technician to try to get the instrument in shape; that was easy. The really difficult part was telling Pachmann, and he broke the news as gently as he could. "Never mind, Cesco, it's not your fault. We must do what we can. I have given my word." The pianist's mild response was more surprising than the weather. Wearing a heavy coat while playing (the hall was unheated), this temperamental artist who screamed if an egg were cooked half a minute too long, played Chopin on an upright piano. The final surreal touch was added when a black cat found its way onto the platform as he played, and jumped onto the piano, content to listen. Pachmann interrupted the piece he was playing, and told the audience, "Let's have an encore for our friend on the piano." He played the Scarlatti Sonata known as "The Cat's Fugue" (Longo 499, G minor).

In January the entourage arrived in San Francisco, where de Pachmann played three times. Thomas Nunan of the *San Francisco Examiner* spoke to the pianist and came away convinced that de Pachmann was "wise and shrewd," according to *The History of Music in San Francisco*, which reported: "In conversation with . . . [Nunan] . . . he talked freely and jocularly about the added publicity obtained by the clowning." Nunan brought a shorthand stenographer to the first recital, and the man took down all of Pachmann's remarks from the stage in German and English, but failed to get the remarks in other languages. He reported his findings in the *Examiner* on January 31:

Mozart Sonata, No. 9, in A major—De Pachmann began the first movement, *Tema con Variazioni*, after a tremendously enthusiastic greeting. Smirked and nodded to the audience. Blinked eyes frequently. Whispered something to himself and smiled blandly. Said, 'That's the way!' as if to assure himself. Added "Ja!" Then he complained: "Hands kalt!" Before beginning the minuet he rubbed his hands vigorously to warm them, while he was bowing in response to prolonged applause. As he brought out the grace and courtliness that Mozart had written into the second part, he exclaimed, as a teacher might to a pupil, "See!" He hugely enjoyed himself; that was evident. And as he finished the movement he threw his hands up and laughed at the fun he was having. His fingers were in fine condition at the commencement of the third part of the sonata. "Ha!" he exclaimed. He struck a wrong note and apologized to himself—or perhaps to the piano, or perhaps to Mozart. "Pardon!" was what he said, looking at nobody. Sweeping a glance along the front rows, "You like it?" he inquired in German. "Expression!" a little later, he confided. . . . At the end of the sonata the fifteen hundred cultured listeners broke into applause so long and loud that the pianist was kept amiably walking back and forth between stage and dressing room for several minutes. . . . A big bunch of pink roses was passed to the stage. De Pachmann turned that wonderfully versatile face of his into an expression of ecstatic surprise. "How fine!" he exclaimed as he kissed the roses. And, walking from the stage: "How beautiful they are!" This in German; the rest of the recital provided little more material of this sort, for de Pachmann made no remarks about short pieces by Mendelssohn and Schumann, only "Isn't this fine!" about Moszkowski's Minuet in G, Op. 17 No. 1, and "I like that." And "It's nice!" about Weber-Henselt's Rondo. He announced the titles of his encores, but when he got to Chopin's Nocturne, Op. 27 No. 2:

"Ach Gott!! The nocturne," rapturously exclaimed the pianist, stretching upward his hands and gazing aloft, after he had dusted off the piano keys with his handkerchief. He began to play and we all felt the rapture to which he had given verbal expression. "Alone in the middle of the night—Beautiful!"

Further strange doings at a February 29, 1912, recital in Philadelphia were reported in the *New York Times* (March 1):

He was somewhat late in making his appearance . . . he gave a lingering look at the instrument before him and then backed away from it as though he were in fear of a personal attack from the piano. He then walked around it, and, stooping, looked underneath, the audience meanwhile beginning to titter. Hearing this, de Pachmann spread his hands in a gesture of seeming despair, and addressed his hearers. "If you felt as I do" he said, "you would cry and not laugh." It was all so tragically comic that folks laughed again, and this time, in what must have been feigned anger, the artist reported with a gesture of command: "Sh! If anyone laughs again I will not play at all." Then a stage attaché came forward with a vacant chair, which was placed beside the stool on which de Pachmann took his seat. With a triumphant sweep of the arm, he placed his handkerchief on the chair. This was what he had wanted all along, and he was again all smiles. Then the recital began, with the player taking his auditors into his confidence in quite a drawing room fashion. He made audible comments upon every one of his numbers, calling out: "There's a sob in this; you think it's good, but listen for the finale." And at the conclusion of several selections he said: "Now," as a sort of signal for the applause to begin. Then again he would wave his left arm frantically in the air, while the right was performing some intricate passage. It was altogether most diverting as an exhibition of "temperament."

Pachmann seemed afraid that an assassin might be hiding under the piano. Things seemed to unravel through a series of uncanny episodes. He had been on edge when he first arrived, and had just recovered his bearings when he was given another jolt. A maddening incident occurred next in St. Louis, where he was scheduled to play the Chopin E minor Concerto in a pair of concerts with the local orchestra under conductor Max Zach. The Friday afternoon rehearsal with an invited audience went well, and the audience was aroused to a high pitch of enthusiasm for Pachmann. Things deteriorated at the Saturday night performance, on February 24. The incident was reported in several journals. *MC* (February 28, 1912) wrote, "The Saturday night concert for the first time filled the hall with a very expectant audience; every seat had been sold."

They loved Pachmann's playing of the concerto and several solos, and this spurred him on. According to a report in the *Indianapolis Star* (March 3, 1912):

> He flirted with his audience. He made funny faces. He played . . . with his left hand, waving his right hand in the air, as if to say, "See what I can do with one hand." . . . he bounced up and down in his seat and at the conclusion of a waltz, he danced from the stage. These gymnastics, coupled with his superb art, excited his auditors almost to a frenzy . . . the applause compelled him to return to the stage time after time to bow his thanks. Still the audience insisted, and after the seventh bow, the lid of the piano was closed.

According to *MC*, conductor Zach did not want to allow Pachmann to play encores:

> At this very moment, Max Zach, the conductor, gave the signal to have the piano closed, whereupon the audience became tumultuous beyond bounds,

and two parties seemed to be created at that moment, one for de Pachmann and one against Zach. The conductor attempted to go ahead with the performance, but there was no possibility to overcome the applauding, stamping, whistling and general clamor, and this went to such an extent that Zach put his baton on his desk and left the stage. The orchestra members, unable to decide, gradually followed him. A moment of painful silence ensued, and the public, pushing toward the exits, again assumed its applauding and whistling, and next day there was hardly a family of any consequence in St. Louis in which this matter was not discussed.

The remainder of the concert was cancelled. The *Indianapolis Star* article quoted Pachmann, "From the gallery to the pit, they were all in ecstacy [*sic*]. Sacré bleu! What does Zach think? The people can hear him any day. Me—they can hear me once in a lifetime!"

On March 10 when Pachmann played a recital in Chicago, he did something unusual for even him, described by the tour's manager F. Wright Newmann to a reporter for the *Chicago Examiner*, printed on April 8:

He amazed the audience by moving the stool away from the piano, going down on his hands and knees on the stage and looking under the legs of the piano apparently as if expecting to find some assassin lurking there . . . the theatre was so crowded . . . we had to place 150 chairs on the stage.

The Chicago piece then referred to the Philadelphia recital two weeks earlier:

You can imagine the surprise of those nearest to him when they saw him under the grand piano . . . at a concert in Philadelphia . . . when the audience laughed at him he plunged his hands into his hair, danced up and down and cried, "Beasts! Beasts! Is this the way to treat a pianist? Why do you titter? Stop or I will not play." The audience stopped laughing and he gave the recital.

The idea that there might be an assassin under the piano was not a figment of Pachmann's imagination. Just after the St. Louis concert he had received a threatening letter in Chicago. The police were called in, and news of this was withheld from the public for almost a month. The *Chicago Examiner* article continued quoting the manager of the concert series:

He has been terrified by a black hand, or anarchist letter, sent to him by some one in Chicago. . . . The letter threatened him with death, and, though in all probability it would not be followed by any attempt on his life, he cannot be persuaded that he would be entirely safe.

Pachmann absolutely refused to return to Chicago for a second recital scheduled for April 28, despite the city's police department promise to provide an escort of plainclothes detectives. His manager told the *Chicago*

Examiner reporter, "It is of no use trying to get de Pachmann to change his mind. He will not come to Chicago again. He intends to sail for Europe this month and will not return to America."

The threatening letter, which was signed with the initials "D. C. M.," was filled with obscenities and claims that he would be "blown up." At the time, "Black Hand" threats were very real menaces. At first a manifestation of organized crime, the group consisted of southern Italian immigrants who sent threatening letters demanding extortion money from wealthy and famous people. Some targets were actually killed, and it is impossible to know how many quietly paid the extortion money. Later the insignia "Mano Nero," or Black Hand, was taken up by anarchists having nothing to do with the crime syndicate. Tenors Enrico Caruso and Tito Schipa were targeted, and Paderewski had to cancel an American tour in 1914 because of the threats. Financier J. P. Morgan's Long Island mansion was actually bombed. The "Black Hand" was frightening, but there is something about this episode in Pachmann's story that remains strange and unexplained.

Cesco gave an interview about the situation to a reporter for the Chicago *Record Herald* (April 8) saying that there was no reason why he [Pachmann] should have been frightened.

What did Cesco know that would lead him to this conclusion? Often there were bogus Black Hand letters, sent by copycats and impostors with other agendas. One claim was that the letter signed "D. C. M."—a putative threat from the Black Hand—was really from the father of a young man who had become involved with Pachmann, but no hard evidence for this claim has been found. In this unverified version, the pianist had taken a dangerous fancy to this younger man, and even offered him Cesco's position as his assistant. Of course this would not have sat well with Cesco, as it obviously did not with the man's father who, it is likely, wished to kill the pianist, or at least frighten him enough to break up the relationship. In this the threats succeeded. The threat could have been sent by Cesco, angered that Pachmann had a new male interest. Perhaps such a threat was bound to happen, given Pachmann's irresponsible behavior, and the atmosphere that surrounded it. Everything now was tinged by the deterioration of Pachmann's mental and emotional state.

The pianist cut the tour short and gave his last concert on April 13, 1912, in New York's Carnegie Hall, where he played the Liszt B minor Ballade in his "Last Appearance in New York for All Time," as the program styled it (April 14). *The New York Times*:

> It . . . afforded the doubtful pleasure of an afternoon of music combined with an afternoon at the Zoo. . . . Mr. de Pachmann . . . has seldom been so pantomimic, so full of gestures and grimaces, or so chatty. His playing suffered

from the excess of effort he made in other directions, and was not so enjoy-able or so convincing as that which he gave at his first recital in the Autumn. . . . The most satisfactory . . . the Berceuse . . . could hardly have been of more ravishingly filmy grace and delicacy, of more exquisite iridescence of tone. . . . Mr. de Pachmann is a representative of a school of piano playing now almost extinct. . . . And so, if he has really given his last recital in New York for all time, the art of the pianoforte has lost something that is not likely to be made up to it in kind.

Seven years before, when he was twenty-one, Cesco had replaced an earlier secretary-companion. Now he decided to leave Pachmann. Cesco told the author of the conversation he had with his master as they parted at the end of the tour, in the spring of 1912. The pianist asked Cesco if he were coming back to Europe with him. Cesco responded, "No, my life is ahead of me, not behind." Without another word, Pachmann walked away.

Chapter 24

The Summer before the Storm, 1912–1914

Cesco stayed in America only a month or so after Pachmann left. With his intelligence and experience he might conceivably have remained in the concert field, working for a large management firm, perhaps traveling with other concert artists as Richard Copley did. Cesco had real skill in this, but few besides Lionel Powell would have known it, and to almost everyone else he was simply Pachmann's companion. Cesco did not find other prospects in the United States. He had become spoiled by the luxurious lifestyle he enjoyed during the seven years he had been with Pachmann and missed the fine things Pachmann's money had bought. His future seemed very uncertain.

Pachmann had vanished and Lionel Powell did not hear from him. The next season's concerts had to be booked, plans made and details arranged, and where was Pachmann? When Powell learned that even Cesco did not know where to find the pianist, he cabled Cesco to return to Europe.

Like Powell, Cesco was realistic. He needed Pachmann more than Pachmann needed him. Even though the pianist could be infuriating with his unpredictable behavior, Cesco knew he never held grudges for long. Pachmann probably missed him already. Who knows exactly what Cesco told Lionel Powell about what had happened? While Powell had genuine affection for Pachmann, he was too realistic to let this prize cash cow escape so easily, and he told Cesco to find him.

Pachmann's sons didn't know where their father was. Cesco went to Berlin and spoke to people in the Hermann Wolff management firm, but they didn't know either. He then went to Vienna and asked the people at the Bösendorfer piano firm. "Why of course," they answered, "Mr. Pachmann is in Abbazia at the Hotel Steffanie. You can give him the mail we have been holding for him." Abbazia? Now known as Opatija, it is a sea-side resort in Croatia on the Adriatic Sea. At the time it was a nearly secret place for a handful of Viennese royals, almost unknown to the rest of the world, certainly to any potential assassin from Chicago. The proprietor of the hotel had apparently been a friend from Pachmann's student days in Vienna, and Rosenthal had a place there since the 1890s. Cesco wired Powell that he had found him.

The pianist's life there was calm and routine. Every morning he'd go in search of jewels where he would argue with merchants about this or that stone: *"Cochonnerie!* This one has a flaw!"* (As always, he was forever exchanging one for another.) By midday he was at the tobacconist complaining about the exorbitant price of rare Havanas, which in Abbazia were exceedingly dear. He ended the day by taking coffee with his friend, the hotel proprietor, who usually insisted on discussing financial matters, for it seems Pachmann never then concerned himself with unimportant details—like paying the hotel bill. He seemed content, but was getting bored.

Cesco suddenly appeared in Abbazia (this was probably at the end of June 1912). Pachmann thought he was still in New York and was surprised to see him. "How did you find me?" he asked. He threw his arms around Cesco and took him back, as if nothing had happened. The appearance of Cesco reminded him again of the glories of his career, the excitement of traveling to the world's centers and the adoration of the multitudes. Still strong, with the vitality and personality of a great artist, he could never be satisfied with such a calm, dull life.

Playing concerts was in his blood; before long the charms of retirement began to fade. Cesco had little difficulty in persuading him to return to the concert stage. Pachmann, who had easily retired at twenty, could not retire at sixty-five. Cesco ordered Bösendorfer to send him a concert grand from Vienna, and Pachmann started practicing again. Then one day they were stunned to receive a summons from a court in Vienna—Pachmann was being sued by a Viennese man who claimed that, in his student days, the pianist had borrowed a sum of money which he had never repaid. Pachmann denied it and all the way to Vienna cried: "But Cesco, I don't know this man . . . I don't remember him."

Appearing in court dressed in his best cutaway, Pachmann was the very model of a dignified artist. However, as soon as he stood before the judge, he couldn't restrain himself and started to act as if he were on the concert platform. Cesco said he nodded and smiled during the testimony, and told the judge, "My friend [not "My Lord," or "Your Honor"], I don't know this man." Looking deeply in the accuser's face: "No. I don't know him. It was so many years ago. I was very young and poor . . . just a student." He paused to collect his thoughts and smiled at the judge. "I remember Brahms. He was very tall and handsome. You'd never know he was a Jew. . . . Yes, it's true. And there was Bülow, two great musicians in one—a great conductor and a great pianist." He paused and shook his head. "But *this* man? My friend, the only person I ever borrowed money from was the cook with the family where I lodged, and I repaid her with my watch." This sincere and unusual confession worked, and the case was dismissed. Pachmann was jubilant and shook hands with the judge and everyone else except the plaintiff. He told Cesco "Maybe this man is my enemy and wants to squeeze my hand and injure me!"

They returned to Abbazia. With few details to arrange while sojourning in this resort, Cesco was on his own. Before long there was trouble in paradise. Cesco fell in love with Magda, the beautiful daughter of the hotelier. A flirtation quickly developed into a dalliance, which soon became serious. This Magda was beautiful, but very possessive. She kept asking Cesco, "But what about Pachmann?" Cesco said he hoped Pachmann would understand. Actually the pianist did understand, seeing what was happening. When Cesco told Pachmann that he wanted to spend time alone with Magda, Pachmann answered "All right, Cesco, take me to Tours, where they speak the best French—real Français. There I'll be quite content." Cesco booked a month's stay for himself and Magda at Venice's Hotel Bauer-Grünwald, dropped Pachmann off in Tours, and notified Leonide.

Pachmann seemed happy, but immediately after Cesco left, he turned the atmosphere in the Tours hotel into something less than peaceful. "I am ill!" he screamed. It was the usual turmoil that resulted when something upset or frightened him. The hotel management wired Leonide in Paris to come and do something. "You father is making a big noise, claiming he is ill, but doctors can find nothing." Leonide came and took his father back to Paris, installing him in a hotel on Boulevard St. Germain, not far from his own apartment. Things quieted down.

In Venice things didn't work out as Cesco had hoped, and all was not unrelieved romance. He had hoped to discuss marriage with Magda as well as spend a romantic interlude with her, but she had insisted on bringing her old, widowed sister with them. This woman was an avid opera lover and apparently would burst into arias from Mascagni's *Cavalleria Rusticana* everywhere she went, drawing stares and even crowds. Privacy was impossible. To make matters worse, certain mercenary traits made Magda seem less attractive. She insisted on knowing how much money she would be allowed, and where she would live. And besides, there was Pachmann to be considered. Cesco had vowed to stay with Pachmann, perhaps not only out of selfish motives. He tried to make her understand that things would not be easy. Eventually Cesco mollified Magda enough to temporarily leave her and go to Paris to pick up Pachmann.

Rather than stay in the city, the pianist decided to spend the summer in Barbizon, the little town south of Paris in Ile de France, which at that time still preserved some of the rural charm of bygone days, when it had been a haven for artists. Charles Henry Meltzer, the Paris correspondent for the *New York American*, ran into the pianist there, and his account was published the next day, on September 13, 1912:

> As I was hurrying through the woods today, near Barbizon, to keep an appointment at Fontainbleu, I had the good fortune to meet Vladimir de Pachmann. With the urbanity of which he has the secret, the distinguished pianist lured me back to his hotel, and there for fully an hour he entertained me with a monologue, a rhapsody. The theme—with variations—was de Pachmann.

Meltzer's long interview with Pachmann covered much familiar ground, and broke some new. The catalogue of other pianists was enumerated—Rubinstein was "too brutal—although he had some virtues"; Busoni and Joseffy were also dismissed. Only Chopin and Liszt were worth mentioning in the same category as de Pachmann. Paderewski?

> Once . . . we were both engaged for Chicago. Paderewski gave a recital and I went to hear him. He played this and that with fascinating art. I closed my eyes and almost believed I was hearing Liszt . . . and when he ventured on a concerto [sic] of his own, he did not please. After the concert I expressed the delight with which I had heard his interpretation of Beethoven and Mendelssohn. "Do you really mean it?" he exclaimed. "Let me embrace you." The next night it was my turn to appear. I played Chopin—well, I need not tell you how I played Chopin. And then to oblige my fellow brother-artist, I played his concerto [sic], and this time it charmed the audience. You see, as I explained to Paderewski, I could not bear to see his triumph incomplete.[1]

Pachmann told Meltzer of confronting a critic in New York, one who had denigrated him for decades but had come round to the green room after his performance of the Chopin E minor Concerto at the Metropolitan Opera House to praise him:

> I listened to his praise. But when he had done I turned to him and said these crushing words: "Yes. Very fine. For twenty years and more you have waited. In all that time you have vexed me with your articles. And now you eulogize me. But now, kind sir, I have no need of you. Get out."

Continuing, Pachmann again unwisely told a representative of the American press how much he hated America and New York in particular, again said he was not "like Patti" and would not make another farewell tour there. And Paris? He would not play in Paris, and had turned away millions of francs by not playing there; there were reasons—his former wife lived there, and French critics had to be bought:

> De Pachmann never, never pays a penny for a good opinion. Liszt never paid. I have no need of critics.

Excerpts from this extraordinary interview were widely reprinted. Pachmann was always Pachmann, but now he also seemed to be going into another realm of imagination.

In Barbizon they had a neighbor, the great-granddaughter of George Sand. She showed the two a prize possession, a pair of *petit pantalon*, a genre of short pants which supposedly had belonged to Chopin. Of course Pachmann couldn't resist, and once more produced his famous socks of Chopin, wretched old things, holey as ever. The woman, according to Cesco's story decades later, was so impressed that she begged to have the socks, which she wanted to darn and then send to Nohant for display as authentic *bas* knitted by her illustrious ancestor. She soon also produced an old *paletot*, a coat she claimed had belonged to the great Polish composer. Pachmann somehow acquired the threadbare item. He delighted to wear it while playing Chopin and later modeled it for reporters. American critic Olin Downes had seen the thing and left a description of it in the *Saturday Evening Post* of March 15, 1930:

> The first time we met was at De Pachmann's apartment. He played. Before he played he insisted that he must don "Chopin's *paletot*." This *paletot*, when he had fetched it, proved to be a frightful old, dirty gray coat, hanging in ribbons from the lower hem, torn in the seams, with some fantastic kind of stuffing—cotton or what?—protruding dirtily from between layers of cloth. Truly a fearsome sight. De Pachmann being small, the fringes of the *paletot* of Chopin dragged along the floor, gathering more dirt as he moved.

Downes quoted Pachmann as telling him:

> This *paletot* . . . may not be Chopin's *paletot*. I don't say positively, you understand. For the public, for the newspapers—yes. Between ourselves, one can't tell. One can't be positive that it's Chopin's *paletot*.

This fantastic conceit was not original to Pachmann, for the great conductor Hans Richter had earlier acquired and proudly wore Wagner's dressing gown. In his autobiography Harold Bauer wrote:

> I recall visiting Richter in his home in Vienna and being received by him in a loose dressing gown, so ragged and dirty that I was quite shocked. "I notice your looks, young man," he said. "Learn that this dressing gown was worn by Richard Wagner."

After the summer, Pachmann rented an apartment in Paris in the Parc Monceau neighborhood. No concerts were scheduled, and he stayed in Paris until the end of 1912, his longest period of residence in that city since the 1880s. Pachmann was ambivalent about the French, often saying they were "an insincere lot," and he had bitter memories about his former wife and bygone days. But he had great admiration for French culture, the cuisine and literature especially, as well as France's philosophers. Apparently Pachmann had taught himself to speak French by reading French novels. Besides the many four star restaurants in Paris there was the famous French jeweler Boucheron, where the management always set aside the finest gems for his inspection. And, of course, there were his two sons to visit.

As Pachmann had not played in Paris for over thirty years, many were eager to hear the legendary keyboard wizard, whose Chopin reputation was "made in England." Cesco let it be known that he was giving a party in celebration of Pachmann's return to Paris, and the soirée drew a brilliant and notable group, including composer-pianist (and great wit) Moriz Moszkowski, organist Marcel Dupré and the French pianist Lazare Lévy, among many others. Perhaps it was on this occasion that Pachmann, bragging to Moszkowski about his huge earnings, asked him to guess how much he had earned. Moszkowski is supposed to have answered, "Half."

It would have been presumptuous to have Pachmann play too early, and first there was a dinner to which only a few were invited. Happily Pachmann was in his most light-hearted and talkative mood at the dinner. That night he took extra care of his appearance, and throughout the meal was seen constantly glancing at his own reflection in a nearby mirror. Finally it became too much for him and he couldn't refrain from telling the dinner guests how well he thought he looked, only he did so indirectly. "How old do you think I look?" he asked the woman next to him. "Umm, I'd say, not more than fifty-five," she replied diplomatically. "Oh, really?" replied Pachmann, making a grimace in the mirror. "I think so too." "Oh, no," said the woman sitting opposite. "I would say, fifty!" At that Pachmann jumped up and kissed her. "Mamushka, mamushka, only you understand." She was much younger, but he still called her "little mother."

When the majority of the party guests arrived, Pachmann asked Leonide to make the introductions. He could not refrain from performing in another way to the distinguished guests:

"Pst, Leonide, who is that elderly man there?"

"'Papa, that is my harmony teacher Monsieur Georges Caussade, Professor at the Paris National Conservatory . . . But let me introduce you." And he brought him over.

"This is Monsieur Caussade, my harmony teacher."

There was a pause. Pachmann looked incredulously at his son.

"But Leonide, say more than that about your teacher, the man who taught you all you know about counterpoint and fugue. . . . Why, why, I bow down before this great master."

"Oh, no," replied the other, "it is I who should bow down before you."

And in front of everyone, the two began to bow. Everyone watched the performance. Everyone expected him to play, but the pianist was enjoying himself chatting and circulating among the guests and he didn't seem much inclined. Cesco hit upon the idea of using a decoy. Cesco asked Lazare Lévy, then an unknown young pianist, to play. This was risking the disaster of one of Pachmann's rages, for many evenings had been ruined by similar circumstances. Cesco's gamble won, however, for Pachmann merely told Lévy "Your touch is a little hard. . . . I tell you not only for yourself and for our ears, but for my piano." He walked to the piano. "I let very few people play on it." Lévy vacated his place, and sitting at the piano, Pachmann continued "You must touch the keys like this." He played a few short arpeggios by way of introduction, and the part of the evening that everyone had been waiting for began.

He not only played Chopin's first and third Ballades, the Nocturne in D flat and a couple of Mazurkas and Waltzes, but also Beethoven, Schumann, and Bach. It was two a.m. when Pachmann took out his watch. No guest had made a move to leave, but it was evident that he was tired, and Cesco announced that the concert was over. As the guests were leaving, Pachmann returned to the piano and dashed off Czerny's Etude, Op. 266, No. 1, played pianissimo and prestissimo, ending with a tremendous crescendo from the top of the keyboard to the bass. Flushed with excitement, he jumped up from the piano to shout "Good bye" to the last of the guests. Leonide said that he had never heard his father play better.

By June 1913 the pianist had still not decided to return to the concert platform. A clipping of an undated article from a newspaper identified only as the *Sun* (found in a scrapbook in the Boston Public Library) reported:

London June 13, 1913. Special cable dispatch to the Sun. Pachmann to Retire. Vladimir de Pachmann, Polish [sic] pianist, announced that he is about to retire. "I am sorry to go, but I must rest now," he said today. He is looking forward to spending a peaceful time at his chalet in Switzerland with his piano. It is believed that de Pachmann's fortune is enormous. It is said to be bigger than Paderewski's.

The desire to retire—a refrain that would be heard often in the coming years as he continued playing. There is no evidence that the pianist had ever purchased a chalet in Switzerland; perhaps he planned to buy one and retire there, but such plans were soon abandoned when Cesco and Pachmann returned to England for the 1913/14 concert season. Pachmann hadn't played there since 1911, and was happy to be back among friends, ready to face both the discriminating critics and the somewhat less discriminating public—he couldn't stay away from the stage.

Cesco was still thinking about Magda, and had been corresponding with her during the intervening months. The letters had settled into a kind of sameness: Cesco writing "I doubt if I will be able to afford to support you the way you want," and she replying "I don't care, I will be content to live on bread and water if I can only be with you." Cesco knew this was not true but did not know how to extract himself from the predicament. He didn't want to confide in Pachmann and had no one else to talk to, so he discussed the problem with Madame Peter. A letter came from Budapest. Cesco happened to be out, and Madame Peter, perhaps innocently, brought it to Pachmann, who opened it. It was from the hot tempered Magda. She wrote that she knew Cesco still loved her, but blamed his reluctance on "that old devil who was interfering." Claiming that she was coming to London, she threatened, "When I get my hands on the old man, I'll kill him!" Pachmann fled to his room, and it was only with the greatest perseverance that Cesco and Madame Peter got him to come out. The episode served to allow Cesco to sever his ties to Magda, and thus the affair ended like a comic opera.

Concerts and reviews by now had settled into a kind of routine, with the public clamoring for more and more Chopin, the critics loving it also but always expressing terse dismay for his antics. One exception was a notice in London's *Sunday Times* of June 12, 1913:

> Much in the mood of the American colonel who, at the funeral of his mother-in-law, mingled grave thoughts with refined pleasantries, was M. de Pachmann's treatment of the B flat minor Sonata at his all-Chopin recital at Queen's Hall on Wednesday afternoon. Between the Scherzo and the "Marche Funèbre" we had a characteristic interlude in which the pianist explained, with a wealth of expressive pantomime, that he was troubled with cramp. Of course that part of the audience which was out for 'pretty Fanny's ways' found it excellent entertainment, but it did not frame one's mind for hearing a movement which is fulfilled with the bitterness of death. Still, these whimsies are part of M. de Pachmann's quality and one can readily forgive them for the sake of Chopin interpretations of peculiar intimacy and for the sake, too, of playing of consummate delicacy and finish and perfect legitimacy. He scattered all disturbing thoughts indeed as he gave the Trio with a fine simplicity and gentleness that made it go straight from heart to heart.

On October 4, 1913, Pachmann invited the twenty year old violinist Daisy Kennedy to lunch. She was then being courted by the young pianist Benno Moiseiwitsch, and wrote to her parents on the 10th:

> Went to lunch with Elsa to Vladimir de Pachmann's the famous old pianist he is 65! With long white hair he looks extraordinarily like Liszt at that age. He sent us to a theatre afterwards with his secretary and adopted son Cesco Palotelli [*sic*] and Benno Moiseiwitsch. He says the latter will be very good and he seldom praises anyone at all![2]

There was another occasion when, after one of his recitals, Moiseiwitsch came onto the platform to congratulate the Chopinzee. Pachmann put his arm around Moiseiwitsch's neck and spoke to the others crowding the piano: "Let me introduce you to a great artiste. He possesses the technique of Godowsky and" continuing with his hand on his heart, "the soul of Pachmann."

Pachmann played a "great farewell recital" on October 15. The *Sunday Times* reviewer seems to have developed the same kind of love for Pachmann as some of the American critics: (October 19, 1913):

> On Wednesday he was as prodigal as ever of marginal comments and expressive gesture. To some people his *bizarrerie* is an offence, to others a mere entertainment, but it seems to me the exuberance of a child-like delight in the beauty of the music he is interpreting, and my only disgruntlement is that I catch so few of the piquant 'asides.' And surely it is at worst quite tolerable in association with playing of such incomparable delicacy, finish, and sensibility . . . afterwards the pianist entered into his special domain in a Chopin group. And of this I need only repeat one of his own naïve remarks, made some years ago: "I know that it would not be modest that I say it, but Chopin would be charmed with my interpretation."

Daisy Kennedy wrote to her parents (October 16):

> He is 65 and retiring. I couldn't go on account of rehearsals. Benno M was there and just imagine, after the concert Pachmann beckoned to him—it was in Queen's Hall and shook hands with him from the platform. The only person he did that to, and then in the artist's room in front of numerous artists and friends he said aloud, "Do you see this boy? He has the greatest technique and wonderful soul—and is a great artist—look at him!" Just imagine, poor Benno turned quite white people say. He is coming to tell me all about it. He says Pachmann spoke about me to him. I am very anxious to know what he said. Pachmann is the successor of Liszt, you know.[3]

1913 was the year of Pachmann's final flowering, the sunset before the darkness of decline; as one London reviewer then put it in an unidentified clipping:

> There is in M. de Pachmann's playing something that transcends the usual achievement of gifted pianists—a triumph of interpretation that seems to see something lying beneath the printed page and divine in its significance. This gift makes him in regards to certain works the greatest pianist of his time.

But perhaps intermittent signs of a decline were discernable. His memory was getting worse; in one of his 1913 London concerts his handling of the problem was unusual. Pianist Rosina Lhevinne, who witnessed the incident, told her biographer Robert Wallace:

> In the middle of the sonata he completely forgot where he was in the music. Without any hesitation, instead of going behind the stage, he went forward and up the aisle. He walked like a lunatic, staring straight ahead, and slowly went to the very back of the hall. There he jumped up on a chair, reached up and stopped a clock, and said in a loud voice that the ticking of the clock had disturbed him. Then he returned to the piano and resumed playing.

〜〜

Maggie, who had not been back to America since she left Pachmann in 1891, returned twenty-two years later. In September 1913, the *New York Times* reported that "Maitre Fernand Labori" had come to the new world in grand style. Madame Marguerite Labori and their four daughters (with a governess) accompanied him. They arrived on the *Lusitania*, along with England's Lord High Chancellor, Viscount Haldane. It was the first time in hundreds of years that a Lord High Chancellor had left England's shores. The American Bar Association was meeting in Canada, where Viscount Haldane was the star exhibit. Labori was among those invited to speak at its convention at McGill University in Montreal. Along with Haldane, Senator Elihu Root, ex-president William Howard Taft, and Frank Kellogg, the outgoing Bar Association president. Labori was given an honorary doctorate. In her book about Labori Maggie wrote: " I was especially moved when Mr. Taft, the ex-President of the republic, declared that . . . 'Labori symbolizes the model for all lawyers.'"[4]

The Laboris were treated almost like royalty, and provided with luxury cars to travel everywhere. There was a lot of high level socializing at the homes of the elite, but they managed to visit Maggie's Canadian relatives, and toured the country using a free railroad pass provided by the government. After the festivities were over they went to Boston, where Labori became gravely ill. He had appendicitis, much complicated by a heart lesion. He remained in a hospital there for five weeks—ex-president Taft, now the new president of the Bar Association, sent flowers every day. Just as they were about to leave, an invitation came for Labori to lecture at Harvard University. When they departed it was again on the *Lusitania*. Maggie wrote that the captain upgraded their quarters to the "Royal Suite," but her husband continued to be dangerously careless about his health.

⌒

Audiences were surprised that Pachmann continued to perform Bach's Italian Concerto. He had never lost his admiration for the composer whose name he had lent to his most valuable diamond. But he remained his irrepressible self when playing any of the revered works by the be-wigged Master of Eisenach. In a notice entitled "Pachmann and Bach," London's *Times* (June 25, 1914) wrote:

> We all fully share his outspoken enthusiasm for the Etude in F minor, the Valse in C sharp minor, and the Mazurka in D, which he played with the delicious ease of a breeze stirring amongst grasses. But it was perhaps less easy to be content when the breeze rose to a hurricane of hilarity over Bach's Prelude and Fugue in G major from "Das wohltempierte Klavier," although he enforced his view by telling us that artists and critics were all mistaken in believing that Bach needed to be played seriously. Perhaps perfection lies between the seriousness which M. de Pachmann indicated by a hopeless gesture, and that extreme vivacity which one understood him to say had earned him the name of "very wicked musician."

Pachmann's delight in being a deliberately wicked musician, one who played Bach in a vivacious and unserious way, would be irrelevant four days later, when Archduke Franz Ferdinand was assassinated at Sarajevo, the spark that ignited the First World War.

⌒

In 1914, much to Pachmann's dismay, the Hotel Ronveau lost its lease and was torn down. Mme. Peter had returned to France and Pachmann impulsively decided to visit her. At the end of the season he hired a touring car, a monster of very high horsepower. At the phenomenal rate of forty miles an hour he and Cesco motored through France, where they stayed long enough to visit with Mme. Peter in Troyes and then continued on to Lac d'Annecy in the Haute Savoie.

A vision of canals and painted roofs with a chateau hovering over the town, bordering on a magical mountain lake, with elegant villas strung like a necklace around the lake, all surrounded by rolling mountains, Annecy is one of the treasured spots in France. Pachmann was so enchanted that he had Cesco rent a villa overlooking the lake, where they stayed for the summer. He invited Lionel Powell from London. Cesco asked some of his friends from Rome, and Leonide and Adrian came from Paris for a visit.

During the long summer days there were innumerable garden parties with Pachmann the center of attention. The summer passed uneventfully, though not without some storms of temperament, those little tantrums that Pachmann seemed to throw whenever things became too quiet."I've got a pain," he shouted. "It's my lee-vair, lee-vair. . . . In fact, I'm poisoned!"

At first, no one took him seriously, for his fear of poisoning was a chronic complaint, and everyone was familiar with it. But on this occasion his extravagant gestures and dreadful grimaces were sufficiently alarming to send Leonide hurrying for a doctor across the lake. When he returned and told him that a doctor would be arriving shortly, Pachmann announced:

"Telephone to say I'm all right."

"But, Papa, it's too late, he's already on his way."

When the physician appeared, Pachmann began to dance before him:

Ah, doctor, look how well I am. And you know it's all because I heard you were coming. In fact, I was told that you are so successful (Pachmann had, in fact, never heard of the man before) you could cure everyone at once, and I was cured even before you arrived!

But as soon as the doctor left, Pachmann began to complain: "Oh, I feel ill again. Perhaps you ought to call him back."

One night a party was in progress, when there arose a terrible storm, one of those typical summer showers that come on so suddenly in the mountains. It was so violent that the electricity had to be turned off while everyone sat in candlelight discussing it. But the wind was so strong that it quickly extinguished the candles and the thunder was so intense—it pealed from the heavens in great roars which echoed through the mountains—that soon conversation stopped and everyone sat in silence in the dark, listening in wonder to the majesty of nature.

When the storm subsided and the electricity was restored, Pachmann's guests looked for him. He had taken refuge beneath a table, where, white as can be, he kept repeating over and over again, "Jesu, Maria, Jesu, Maria." He was completely terrified.

But this incident was unusual. Most of the time the weather was sublime, the glorious summer of 1914, with a sky blanketed with stars, and the garden filled with friends, Pachmann entertained visitors with his playing. On one occasion, Leonide remembers his father throwing open the French windows, and as the moonlight flooded onto the piano, playing the "Moonlight" Sonata, while sardonically smiling.

Who could have thought that this beautiful evening's idyll would be interrupted by menacing clouds? In August the First World War broke out.

Chapter 25

I'm Given My Work, and I Must Play, 1914–1918

Annecy was in turmoil; the war had come as a shock, and wild rumors circulated everywhere. "France will go bankrupt." "Our money will be no good." "There will be a food shortage." Pachmann was as confused as everyone else, and believed every word. He made Cesco change all their paper money into silver and "lest we all starve," persuaded him to buy two dozen rabbits which were kept in the garden. Expecting anything, they awaited the fall of France.

Cultural life in Europe came to a standstill, and many celebrated artists fled. Some like violinists Fritz Kreisler and Jacques Thibaud enlisted to serve their respective countries, others like Godowsky emigrated to America, and still others, idealists like Busoni, retired into isolation and remained silent throughout those chaotic years.

After the first weeks of hostilities, the shock diminished for Pachmann, and he began to see things somewhat differently from most of his pessimistic colleagues. This was no time to stop giving the world music; it was the duty of an artist to communicate, and music was a solace for the public, especially in a period beset by misery and confusion. As he told Cesco, "I'm given my work and I must play."

Cesco packed things for England and they arrived in Calais. Pachmann's long hair ("Is that Lloyd George?" asked one customs official) as well as his ridiculous Russian passport, given to him decades ago by the Czar but now old and torn, with so many pages it resembled an epic Russian novel, were regarded with utmost suspicion by the French officials.

"What's the matter?" the pianist asked. "I'm not responsible for the war. I'm Russian; but my sons, they are French, fighting for France!"

His managers took advantage of the fact that Adrian and Leonide had enlisted, and when Pachmann arrived in England, his concerts were advertised as Chopin recitals by Pachmann "Who Has Two Sons Fighting at the Front." Adrian won a *Croix de Guerre* for his bravery at the Battle of Verdun, and Leonide suffered an arm injury, which he later claimed was the decisive factor in destroying his hopes for a career as a concert pianist.

In England Pachmann was now an institution, and his popularity as a concert artist had reached Paderewskian proportions . . . nothing surpasses the sentimental patriotism of the British during war. Images of his grave face were featured on the covers of mass circulation periodicals.

They took an apartment around the corner from Queen's Hall, and it was to there that the English Columbia record company took machinery and recorded him in 1915. These records show a decided decline—the energy and drive of the pianist's playing shown on his Victor recordings have completely disappeared. Even the miniature compositions sound mannered and stale, compared to the earlier performances. How can one account for this sudden decline? While one might expect some weakening after thirty-three years of constant concert giving, this is too precipitous. Possibly he was cross and bored, but this could be evidence of his insecurity and mental state at his changing relationship with Cesco.

Cesco told the author in 1960 that he had been thinking about getting married through all the years he had been with Pachmann. After the pianist reached his mid-sixties, with the possibility of retirement looming, it apparently became an ongoing concern, and Cesco discussed the idea with Pachmann. There was some talk of his marrying one of the Defries sisters. Cesco said "religious differences" quashed that possibility. But when the author discussed the incident later that same year with Colin Defries, the sisters' youngest brother, he was told that there was no possibility for such a marriage—the Defries family was perfectly aware of the nature of Cesco's relationship to Pachmann. It seems Cesco thought people didn't know.

Pachmann could not escape realizing that the years of his living with Cesco as a couple would soon be over. Certainly Pachmann enjoyed the semblance of family life that living with Cesco brought (and this became more important over time), but his sexual needs were still preeminent. He had a driving sexuality that was part of the energy that sustained him on his long career. For Pachmann, the spark that had illuminated their relationship began to dim. It was as if the earth itself had been pulled out from under him. He was no longer Cesco's center of attention.

If there was a decline in his playing due to emotional distress, he soon recovered, for he subsequently received mostly positive reviews from the British critics. Perhaps it was just that he had become an institution that could do little wrong, and then he always played better in concert than in the recording studio—everyone who heard him pointed that out.

The outer features of life continued as before. Pachmann invited Lionel Powell to dinner at his apartment, at which the English sister pianists, Mathilde and Adela Verne (both Clara Schumann disciples) were also to be guests. Apparently Pachmann had expressed some interest to play two piano works with Adela. Mathilde left a reminiscence of the occasion in her autobiography:

Pachmann was an interesting host. To begin with, dinner was kept waiting, because the fancy seized him to turn on his gramophone almost as soon as he had shaken hands with us, and he listened, spellbound, to a record of his own beautiful playing of Liszt's "Liebestraum." He turned to us several times for approval, and said gleefully: "Ah, Liszt could not have played it like this!" Once he laughed heartily at the reproduction of a very difficult run, which he told us *he* always played with one hand, the majority of pianists having to divide it and play it with both hands. Dinner was quite out of the ordinary run of dinners; Pachmann insisted on wiping every plate, every glass, and all the forks and spoons before he allowed us to use them. He also tasted every dish before we partook of it. "For fear lest you are poisoned," he said gravely, but, as we knew that this was only fun, we entered into the spirit of the jest, and dinner became a very lively affair indeed. After dinner, Pachmann asked if I had heard his renderings of Bach, and when I was obliged to confess I had not had that pleasure, I am sure I went down several degrees in his estimation.

This is a pretty picture of Pachmann on his best behavior with Powell and the maiden lady pianists. We have a much rarer picture of him receiving another visitor at about the same time. Cesco had mentioned to the author that Arthur Symons visited Pachmann then, and that "they talked all day." One could imagine the occasion, with brilliant conversation flowing from Symons and inspired music from Pachmann. If the visit started on a high level, at some point it veered to something quite different. Symons described a part of the meeting in very genteel but fragmentary fashion in an article published in *Vanity Fair* in December 1915, "He then played, in his neat little room, in which everything was in faultless order, two other studies by Godowsky." However Symons's biographer, Karl Beckson, paints a more vivid picture of the tea party:

Symons had spent some time with de Pachmann in London and told his friend John Quinn that de Pachmann uttered Rabelaisian words of an unspeakable nature. He: "I love fucking," with an immense chuckle. I: "Yes, I also, Mais fornication simple et extraordinaire." Where upon he actually hugged me in his arms rubbing his cheek on mine—with bursts of Rabelaisian laughter. I veritably imagine his desire was—for me—to sleep with him that night!

The exclamation point seems to indicate that Symons was shocked. He certainly was no stranger to male homosexuality, but apparently had no idea Pachmann had designs on him. In his view, Pachmann's art was subtle, intellectual and on a high level, high-minded Art with a capital "A." He completely missed (or deliberately omitted in his writing on the pianist) the element of Pachmann's art that relied on sensuous seduction.

In 1916 Pachmann received the highest honor bestowed on a musician by the English. On January 31 he played the Chopin first Concerto with the Royal Philharmonic Orchestra under the baton of the very recently knighted Sir Thomas Beecham, who told Neville Cardus about the occasion:

> In the middle of the slow movement, Pachmann stopped dead, stopped playing, and leaning over the keyboard towards me, said "Isn't it lofely?" And I replied, "Indeed it is lovely, M. Pachmann—but would you mind going on?"

At the concert the orchestra members and officials presented him with the Royal Philharmonic Society's gold medal, the Beethoven Medal, in recognition of all the years he had played in England. It was one of his greatest honors and, on this occasion according to the February 1 *Times*, he "for once in his career, seemed to have nothing to say." Like a child accepting his first prize, he expressed his gratitude in pantomime—first his surprise . . . then bewilderment . . . and finally, his utter unworthiness at receiving the honor. He thanked the audience profusely in the best way possible by playing two encores: the favorite Chopin D flat and the C sharp minor Waltzes, much to the delight of the large audience. Later, in the artist's room, according to Beecham, he grabbed the medal from its case and bit it, to make sure it was really gold![1]

In April he played his signature Chopin Concerto in F minor with Beecham; the notices as usual saying that his playing was "radiant," filled with delicacy and sensitiveness. Not long after he played Mendelssohn's G minor Concerto, and then the orchestral version of Chopin's Andante Spianato and Grande Poloniase—it was an outburst of concerto playing for a pianist who had specialized in solo recitals.

Continuous benefit concerts for the Red Cross were arranged, and he began appearing in these in conjunction with other artists. To raise further money for the cause, Cesco became an author. He wrote a short history (in Italian) of Pachmann's childhood and his daily life, ending with a series of anecdotes about his eccentricities. This was badly translated into English, published as a booklet, and the proceeds from its sale at Pachmann's concerts went to the Red Cross. It was an idealistic picture of a rather child-like genius who enjoyed infantile games, had no interest in money and loved the serenity of the evening, when he could practice undisturbed, and stay up late. At least the part about "no interest in money" was absolutely false. The booklet painted a charming picture that Pachmann's British admirers could readily accept. Cesco conveniently omitted any mention of the monumental difficulties of living with Pachmann, or of the pianist's obsessions and mood swings, of his sexual urges, and especially of his own relationship to Pachmann. Reality was a more fantastic picture than admirers could have ever imagined.

Not that Pachmann's eccentricities didn't often have a certain charm. On February 18, 1916, after an Albert Hall benefit concert for the Italian community, the ushers, young women dressed in the traditional Red Cross outfits of hats and capes, shepherded him to the piano and placed one of the hats on his head and a cape around his shoulders. Pachmann of course loved to be surrounded by admirers, particularly young people, and entered into the spirit of the thing and began to play Chopin waltzes. He enjoyed himself so much that it was difficult to get him to stop until someone hit on the idea of removing the pedals of the piano. As this was being done Cesco whispered to him, "Come along, Papi, or the Zeppelins will get us." But before he could be led away he went to the Australian soprano Elsa Stralia and, standing on his tiptoes, kissed her on both cheeks. Later he asked Cesco, "Wasn't that a good effect?!"

The most memorable of these wartime benefit concerts were the duo recitals Pachmann gave with the Belgian violinist Eugen Ysaÿe. Lionel Powell, who managed Ysaÿe as well, had introduced them. Powell invited them to his place in Shropshire, and the two great artists got along very well. Pachmann immediately liked the fiddler, and amid the serene English countryside the two played Beethoven sonatas, particularly Beethoven's "Spring" Sonata, one of Pachmann's favorites.

Pachmann soon expressed the desire to play concerts with Ysaÿe. Powell arranged a few joint recitals around the British Isles that became quite popular. They made an intriguing pair, for Ysaÿe was a huge man, his fiddle seemingly lost in the vast recesses between his shoulder blade and chin. Next to him Pachmann, short and squat, appeared to be a pudgy elderly elf. Beneath Ysaÿe's burly frame, however, dwelt a boyish heart, and his personality perfectly complemented Pachmann, whom he called *Cher Papouchka*. Sometimes they would simply play solo groups at different parts of the programs, but sometimes they played works together. The *Sunday Times* of May 28, 1916, wrote of one of their concerts from one week earlier:

Despite the temptation of the sunny afternoon to take one's pleasure *al fresco*, there was a big audience at the Albert Hall on Sunday for the special concert with the twin attractions of M. Ysaÿe and M. de Pachmann. The famous

Belgian violinist was first heard. . . . A vocal interlude followed, Mme Aileen d'Orme singing . . . and then we had an hour of Chopin with M. de Pachmann. It was fully characteristic in its antic commentary, and also in its full *intimité* and inimitable exquisiteness of expression, and the audience enjoyed it whole-heartedly.

Cesco had flirtations and dalliances with various women—in America during the 1911/1912 tour he had become involved with a socialite, but the relationship ended with the tour. Cesco of course was involved with arrangements for Pachmann to appear in the benefit concert for the Italian community, when some small girls, children of Italian immigrants from the local Dante Alighieri School, sang at the concert's conclusion. In assisting with preparations for this concert Cesco met a young Italian woman named Alice Fonseca, who was teaching the girls at the school. Cesco was thirty-one, and Alice was twenty-three. Cesco liked her so much that he arranged a dinner party at Pachmann's flat in Hampstead to introduce her to the pianist, who was in one of his best moods at the party, and took a great liking to Alice immediately. He ignored everyone else at the dinner, concentrated all his charm on Alice, and said afterwards, prophetically, "Cesco, *there* is a girl for you to marry!"

But when Cesco decided to do just that, Pachmann was less than enthusiastic. He never really objected to the marriage, but everyone sensed a certain unspoken opposition, which expressed itself in little ways. The wedding ceremony took place on June 3, 1916, and was attended by both Lionel Powell and Ysaÿe. Neither the bride nor groom was late, but the best man, Pachmann, kept everyone waiting at the altar until he appeared, shouting, "My God, I was so nervous I couldn't put on my eyes!" There was a reception after at the Hotel Piccadilly and Pachmann, unusually, got drunk. Ysaÿe did also, which probably was not so unusual. The two attempted to play but the violinist could not hold his bow steady, and the poor pianist couldn't even find the piano.

The pianist had always had someone to take care of the complex details of his career and to look after him. The importance of having someone to do this was even greater now as he aged. He was justly concerned that Cesco might not have time for his needs, and voiced his concerns. "Don't worry, Papi, we shall always look after you, and if you feel lonely, you can live near us," Cesco generously offered. "No," Pachmann replied, "I won't live near you. I will live *with* you!" And he did.

Soon it was very apparent to Cesco and Alice (whom Pachmann called "Alichika") that the pianist was not living "with them" because he so shaped and dominated their lives to suit his needs that in reality, they were living with him. Later Cesco did not tell the author of the financial arrangements for this extended family, but it is reasonable to assume that Pachmann was paying all the bills.

Perhaps to ease Alice into her expected role, Cesco took her with them on a brief tour of Scotland, to familiarize her with Pachmann's idiosyncrasies and serve as a short training course for their future life together. Alice must have left her position as a teacher. It was her baptism by fire, and proved to be a devastating experience. Pachmann, perhaps to express his displeasure at the marriage, decided he was going to be, in his words, "a little devil."

In the railroad station he refused to board the train because he claimed the seat was directly over the wheels, and only with the greatest patience was he persuaded to enter the car. Lest they win a victory, though, Pachmann had the last word and remained in the water closet all the way to Scotland, where it took as much persuasion to get him off the train as it had taken to get him on.

The turmoil was just beginning. The hotel service was "r-r-rotten," the food "a nightmare." And the hotel room? He refused to enter it, citing "microbes" as his reason. A frantic ritual began, a chaotic hunt with the hotel staff, Cesco, Alice and Powell looking under beds, on window sills, in the fireplace until Pachmann was satisfied and everyone else exhausted. "Oh, Cesco, I pity you," said Alice. "How could you have had the patience to stand it all these years?" Cesco was furious and told him: "See, Papi, you have been so nasty, so impossible, Alice will not stay. She is returning to London!"

Pachmann was always amazed when people objected to his tantrums. He looked at Cesco, at Lionel Powell and finally at Alice, and with an expression that resembled a child who is caught violating a confidence, burst into tears. He went to Alice and got on his knees and began abasing himself: "Naughty Papi, naughty," he said. "I don't blame Maggie for divorcing me. She understood. But I cannot help it when my nerves give way. I cannot control them."

An interim of calm followed, and there was a period of testing, when Pachmann tried to see if Alice were capable of understanding him. First he spoke to her rather shyly and in a guarded fashion about his jewels, and he told her of the red diamond that he hoped to find some day. Such diamonds with a predominant red color are still considered to be the rarest and most fascinating of all gemstones, the reason for the occurrence of the red color remaining unclear today. When he saw that she did not laugh at him but was truly interested (she was "brainy," in his word), he became less cautious and went on to tell her about his music and memories of Liszt, Henselt and Madame Slepouchkine. Little by little, she too soon entered his private world, and he made an effort to accept her. A very rare letter he wrote to Alice in Italian just before a concert reads: "To you dearest Alice, I wish to tell Madame Slepouchkine that I am displeased at not being able to have dinner with you. Embrace you affectionately, Papi P.S. Compliments for Nora, Little Monkey will play 'Moonlight Sonata' this evening. Let's hope the weather will be clear." [Nora was Cesco and Alice's dog. The translation was made by Cesco.]

Pachmann's popularity in England had reached the apex at which it remained for the rest of his career. His person was catnip for cartoonists and caricaturists, and a plethora of drawings of him trailed the path of his concerts. His eccentric platform behavior could now be said to have entered a "third phase." In the earliest days it had often included pantomime. Then as early as 1900 this was supplemented by occasional talking while he played. This talking gradually developed into "running commentary," heard occasionally in 1911 and 1912, although still rarely interfering with an audience's enjoyment of his great playing. But during the war years as his art weakened, the commentary began to dominate. A fan even timed one of his concerts and found that the music and the talking shared equal prominence. What had once been spontaneous, like the first time he fooled with the height of the seat, had evolved into a routine, even at times into a production, such as some of his later London appearances with retainers, mechanics and movers coming onto the platform with tools, screws and pieces of wood to tame the offending stool. His performances of smaller works could still be enchanting and his tone, while not as luxuriant as it was on his previous tour in 1911/1912, was still lovely. Occasionally one could still hear a really great performance of a larger work as well. There were even times when he didn't talk, save for some short introductory remarks.

The atmosphere had become so informal that the concerts resembled the popular "entertainments" to which some unhappy London critics had been comparing his concerts since he started talking to his audiences. In the 1880s and '90s some critics had been shocked and irritated when he stared out at the audience, but by now no one was shocked at any of his behavior. Audiences expected something special, some secretly hoping he would catch their eye and play to them. Of course, everyone wanted to hear his "asides." Seats on the platform and the front rows were always at a premium. Despite all the years he had played, there were still surprises, and no one could predict what might happen.

Many, including some critics, actually loved this, even his preluding with snatches of well-known works. The unnamed critic for London's *Times* wrote on December 4, 1916:

M. de Pachmann's official concert began at 3 o'clock last Saturday in the Queen's Hall . . . and held a houseful . . . spellbound till 4:40. Then the unofficial part began with the Prelude to Bach's third English Suite, and with some Schumann and some more Chopin lasted for half an hour. It was as if a poet had taken us into his library and was reading to us, one after another, bits out of his "dear and dumpy twelves."[2] The procedure is unusual enough to be dubbed with a short word which for robust minds covers everything from unconventional to bizarre. If it is madness, we could wish that M. de Pachmann would bite some other pianists who could be named. It is, on the contrary, sound sense. There is no doubt the large concert hall has killed the most valuable part of music, its intimacy: and the *obiter dicta*, the little slips made on purpose—a bit of a Czerny exercise before Chopin's Valse in D flat, a bar of Beethoven's Funeral March Sonata before Schubert's Impromptu in A flat—the fragments of which de Pachmann impiously interpolated in the old masters, are unconscionable attempts to get it back. All these are, however, only the adjunct to the feast. What fills the hall and holds it is the certainty that the limits of true pianoforte tone will never be exceeded, the entire absence of "the charm of woven paces and of waving hands" which some players affect, the fingerwork which never fails at a crisis and which makes a new thing of the simplest bit of melody, and the personality which lies behind these.

Decades later, after Harold Schonberg's book *The Great Pianists* was issued in England, a Pachmann admirer named J. A. Harrison sent Schonberg a letter with a long personal reminiscence of a Pachmann recital he had attended in St. George's Hall in Bradford during the war:

Every seat was sold, including fifty or sixty on the platform. My seat was there, on the front row, about five feet from the bass end of the keyboard. He seemed about 5 feet 4 inches[3] and nearly half of him head. He came up the four steps on to the platform, turned to the manager of the hall and said "All se door and ze window, all, all, please shut." Mr. Carter assured him that had been done. Halfway to the piano he stopped and called for his servant to screw up the stool. He tried it, and had it screwed down again. Then he examined the audience both in the hall and on the platform and looked disgusted. After putting his hand on the keys twice and taking them off again he started. The programme, as near as I can remember it was Mozart Fantasia-Sonata in C min.; Schubert Impromptu in F min.; Mendelssohn Rondo Capriccioso; Weber Invitation to the Dance and Chopin about a dozen items of which the 3rd Ballade was the main. I had memorized the Ballade and had learnt the Mozart and several of the Chopin pieces in my teens. I noticed scarcely any alterations of notes from the text, but liberties of timing were great, except in the first three items. The audience was Bradford at its vulgarest, and it applauded at the 'wrong end' of both the Mendelssohn and the Weber. He talked most of the time. We could hear him, but the nearest seat in the hall was 20 feet away and many were obviously annoyed, especially as we kept smiling at his remarks. "Ziz very lovely tune of Mozart (the

transition to D maj.) it sound wrong if not finger like I finger . . . it repeat
. . . watch fingers again." I think everybody knew the Chopin best and had
come to hear that. Of the Black Key study he said "Every leetle girl play zis
like him written, but I play him different, I play ze left hand in ze right hand
and ze right hand in ze left. You zink it cannot do. I show you. How many
times shall I play him, once or twice?" He looked at me and I dare not say a
word but a man on my left said "Twice" and the old man played it twice. The
audience was mystified with that left hand and the chords slapping about in
the right hand. Some of them can only have tumbled to what he was doing
when the double octave scale (as written, not inverted) arrived. No sooner
had he struck the last chord than he played the whole thing again. For me
the treat of the evening was the A flat Ballade. He paused and looked at
the keyboard, and then at his hands, and shook his head. "At 26 I play zis
Ballade. I play him perfect. But at 76,[4] no I cannot." Then he gave the finest
reading I have ever heard. Delicacy, strength, the good earth under the flowers, everything was there. I have never heard the like since, and there is not
another rendering of it I care to remember. Incidentally it was the only item
in which he did *not* talk.

Pianist Mieczyslaw Horszowski's memoirs, published by his widow,
carry a story of a Wigmore Hall Pachmann recital that Horszowski attended during the war. In the middle of the Variations movement of
Mozart's Sonata in A major, K. 331, Pachmann stopped dead and spoke
to a bewildered gentleman in the first row. "Be patient," he said, "this is
the last repeat."

Pachmann had created a fantasy that had become his reality. We are
fortunate to have another wonderful description of one of these concerts,
written by W. N. P. Barbellion in his *Journal of a Disappointed Man* on May
5, 1918, and quoted by Eric Blom in *The Music Lover's Miscellany*:

Arrived at Queen's Hall in time for Pachmann's Recital at 3:15. . . . As usual
he kept us waiting for 10 minutes. Then a short, fat, middle-aged man
strolled casually on to the platform and everyone clapped violently—so it
was Pachmann: a dirty greasy looking fellow with long hair of dirty grey
colour, reaching down to his shoulders and an ugly face. He beamed on
us and then shrugged his shoulders and went on shrugging them until his
eye caught the music stool, which seemed to fill him with amazement. He
stalked it carefully, held out one hand to it caressingly, and finding all was
well, went two steps backwards, clasping his hands before him and always
gazing at the little stool in mute admiration, his eyes sparkling with pleasure,
like Mr. Pickwick's on the discovery of the archaeological treasure. He approached once more, bent down and ever so gently moved it about 7/8ths
of an inch nearer the piano. He gave it a final pat with his right hand
and sat down. . . . At the close we all crowded around the platform and gave
the queer, old-world gentleman an ovation, one man thrusting up his hand
which Pachmann generously shook as desired. As an encore he gave us a

Valse—"Valse, Valse," he exclaimed ecstatically, jumping up and down in his seat in time to the music. It was a truly remarkable sight; on his right the clamorous crowd around the platform; on his left the seat holders of the Orchestra Stalls while at the piano bobbed this grubby little fat man playing divine Chopin divinely well, at the same time rising and falling in his seat, turning a beaming countenance first to the right and then to the left, and crying, "Valse, Valse." He is as entertaining as a tumbler at a variety hall. As soon as he had finished, we clapped and rattled for more, Pachmann meanwhile standing surrounded by his idolaters in affected despair at ever being able to satisfy us. Presently he walked off and a scuffle was half visible behind the scenes between him and his agent who sent him in once more. The applause was wonderful. As soon as he began again it ceased on the instant, and as soon as he left off it started again immediately—nothing boisterous or rapturous, but a steady, determined thunder of applause that came regularly and evenly like the roar from some machine.

$$\backsim$$

In March 1917 Pachmann received a letter from Maggie informing him of the death of her husband Labori, whose health apparently had been deteriorating for a year. Leonide told the author that his mother had taken Labori to hear Pachmann play in 1910 but the pianist never knew this—perhaps the same Albert Hall concert that Leonide had attended. The letter is now apparently lost with the other items in Cesco's possession.

In April America entered the war. Many European artists like Leopold Godowsky were now living in America. Cesco sent Godowsky a copy of his little Red Cross booklet, and Godowsky responded. Lepp and Vlady hadn't seen each other or been in touch for several years. A copy of Godowsky's letter survived:

It was like a ray of sunshine to have received a communication relating to my great and admirable friend, the unique and only de Pachmann. The older I grow, the maturer my thoughts and feelings become, the more I grasp, comprehend, love and adore, the art of this magician of the keyboard, the hypnotizer of musical utterances. His art defies all laws, all conventions, all analytical dissertations. It is the most individual form of artistic expression I have ever encountered. Your booklet does not say one iota in excess of facts. I could have written a long essay on this phenomenon of the ivories, without ever exhausting my vocabulary of adjectives. I wish I could get some definite information regarding de Pachmann and yourself. How are you both in health and spirit? How is the relentless march of time affecting the dean of pianists? What does he say, read or play? Is he approximately happy or do the fearful and fateful events of the past three years cast a deep shadow over the impressionable master? The world catastrophe, the universal cataclysm has affected me to an extent which almost passes human endurance. It has shaken my belief in man's sanity—it has shattered completely my faith in our present day civilization and culture. We are atavistically not far removed from the wild beasts in the primeval forest. I would be glad to hear from you soon.

Most faithfully yours,
Leopold Godowsky,
Lake Placid, New York,
Adirondacks,
June 10, 1917

It is unknown whether Pachmann or Cesco answered this effusive and sad letter from Lepp. No answer has been found among Godowsky's papers.

On October 20, 1917, Godowsky played a recital in Carnegie Hall. A press notice reported that the pianist's daughter Vanita was spotted in the audience sitting next to a handsome French military officer, who turned out to be Adrian de Pachmann. The French high command had sent him to New York as a lobbyist to enlist American sympathy for the French war effort. A Sunday rotogravure newspaper carried photos of the French officer's reception in America.[5]

Cesco was in the Italian military reserves and was called to active duty in early 1917. He was given a plum at the Italian embassy in Paris, a job to act as a kind of secret courier between countries. Whether it was through efforts of influential contacts of his or Pachmann's, or as he later told the author, because he spoke French and German fluently—or a combination of factors—Cesco achieved a much higher position than one might have thought, given his humble background.

It meant their all moving back to the French capital. The apartment on the Parc Monceau which they had occupied since 1912 was unsuitable for the newly constituted family, so they took a larger one in the same area that could accommodate the two as well as Alice, who had become pregnant in late 1916.[6] Food was scarce, and Cesco had to set up a system of rationing meat and butter for their table. It was a calamity for Pachmann, and behind Cesco's back he would implore the cook to use more butter and sugar. A terrible shortage of milk followed, and after Alice gave birth to a son named Virgilio in August, Cesco would have to arise at two a.m. and take a tram to the outskirts of the city to find milk.

Paris turned out to be much less safe than London. Germans advanced closer each month, and Zeppelins bombed the city twice, leaving a trail of destruction. Once as sirens were wailing and bombs falling,

Cesco pleaded with the pianist to come with them into the safety of the building's cellar.

"In the cellar? . . . Never in the cellar!" He was afraid of mice, and when the Zeppelins were overhead, he threw open the windows and went onto the balcony and looked up at the sky: "The Germans know me. They are my friends. They'd never drop a bomb."

Later that evening the Germans scored a direct hit on an adjacent building, and the confusion kept Cesco and Alice awake all night. But Pachmann slept soundly, and when informed about the bombing the following morning, confided, "You see, Cesco, I told you they wouldn't hit us."

Pachmann was quoted about this in the December 1926 issue of *Cassell's* magazine:

> I had to put up with the terrible inconveniences because of the war. Whenever there was any fear of the city being shelled or bombed from aeroplanes they hustled me out of the way as if I were a piece of delicate china. I was often angry and indignant, but it made no difference. They were stronger than I. I had to go wherever they put me.

Cesco's work, he told the author decades later, was "highly confidential" as a courier between the Italian and English governments. Though he avoided service at the front, his job was dangerous, requiring him to travel back and forth across the English Channel in a submarine. Cesco decided to send his wife and son to Rome, and Pachmann to London, where all presumably would be safe while he was away. When Cesco was in London on assignment and had a few moments, he visited Pachmann there, and the two planned for a happy reunion after the war ended.

Cesco was then reassigned to continue the same work in Montenegro, just as his pianist master was growing quite comfortable in this unique family situation. Though temperamental and exceedingly difficult, Pachmann often was capable of repaying his friends with unswerving and touching attachment, and he had emerged a fond grandfatherly figure. The separation threw Pachmann into a profound state of gloom. He lapsed into listlessness and his spirit seemed devitalized.

Lionel Powell's firm had become the number one concert management in England. Besides directing the professional lives of many leading musical artists, Powell was also the director of the London Symphony Orchestra concerts and the Albert Hall Sunday concerts. His legal advisor, a lawyer originally from South Africa, was Harold Holt, who acted more and more as Powell's assistant with the responsibility of looking after Pachmann. The two were unable to cheer him up, and when they went to visit or fetch him, he would appear unkempt, ill-shaven and wearing a dirty old robe.

Pachmann wrote little Virgilio a letter on his first birthday:

> Just a few lines from your dear old grandfatherly Papi who, though miles away, is always thinking and wishing he were nearer to greet his little friend on his first anniversary.

He grew to love the boy.

Chapter 26
Villa Gioia, 1918–1920

Pachmann continued to play in public throughout the war, but separated from Cesco (who doesn't appear in our narrative again for two years), he became withdrawn and introspective. He even tinkered with composing again: "I made up a few pretty preludes and fugues. But there are so many bigger pieces. I am not satisfied . . . I must do something big. So I do not compose. I interpret instead, and sometimes, for my own pleasure, I improvise" he told a reporter four years later (*New York Herald*, August 30, 1923).

He had always been haunted by piano methods, and shortly this preoccupation developed into an actual obsession, all about pedagogical details. The cumulative strain of events combined with the deterioration of age had kindled a pianistic crisis. Being a very small man with small hands, he had to find ways to use them to get the most from them. G. Mark Wilson wrote in the *Musician* (October 1913):

Compared with other famous pianists, his hands are the smallest of any playing at the present time. They are rather odd in shape, the body of the hand being long and narrow, while the fingers are short and thick. He asserts that pianists with short fingers have greater command over the volume of tone, style of touch, rapid execution, etc., on account of the decreased though steadier leverage which they of necessity must adopt. Evidence of great muscular development is at once apparent in the hands. This is particularly noticeable when viewed from the side. The wrists are large and powerful, but like the fingers are as flexible as finely tempered springs; springs that act in perfect harmony with his mind when producing the exquisite tone pictures that delight us now and which we will recall with pleasure many years hence.

Just after Pachmann died, James Francis Cooke wrote a reminiscence (*Etude*, April 1933) showing how Pachmann guarded his hands:

> Once we went with our dear friend, John Luther Long, to visit him behind the scenes of the Philadelphia Academy of Music. We started to introduce him and Mr. Long proffered his hand. De Pachmann ran away in evident panic. "Oh! Oh! Dese precious hands! Dese precious hands! No one can touch dese precious hands!" We then explained to him that Mr. Long was the author of "Madame Butterfly." "Oh!" he smiled, "den I shake his hands and I kiss him." And he did.

Long's short story had provided Puccini the material for his opera.

Throughout his life Pachmann was constantly polishing his technique with daily exercises of his own invention (Leonide showed the author one in double thirds, and Cesco remembered his continuous practicing of exercises: "Dah! Dah! Dah!"). But he was like a sieve, always searching for more material to use. Once he said of Moszkowski's *School of Double Notes*, "If only I had known about them earlier!" and he found Joseffy's *School of Advanced Studies,* a collection of daily exercises, "unsurpassable." Pachmann depended on complicated fingerings to solve difficulties and conquer passages resistant to small hands. He practiced exercises like these, as well as passages taken from his concert repertoire, over and over in between concerts.

This had served him well all through the years, but when he reached the age of seventy-one in 1919, he found it no longer beneficial. His body had lost its spring and resiliency, he no longer had the strength and agility of earlier days, and his small hands were now registering pain. He was facing disaster if he didn't find a way to prevent further deterioration, and he began to look for a pianistic fountain of youth. He could, like many others, continue to play and ignore imperfections, since many of his admirers would not have been too critical. Perhaps in his own way he was too great an artist, too profound a philosopher of pianistic art, to resort to self-deception. He decided to find new principles that would lessen the fatigue of his aging muscles. His search for a "new method" became so strong an obsession that it almost supplanted his quest for new jewels, and he no longer had time for them. At an age when many look forward to retiring, Pachmann spent all his time at the piano, as he had to undo what took him a lifetime to learn. He had to begin all over again: to re-finger, rephrase, reedit, and restudy his entire repertoire.

He could no longer produce a velvety tone or his legendary nuances when his muscles were stiff. Fatigue was becoming so pervasive that it was interfering with his facility, and his spontaneity. His pondering of these problems led him to the conclusion that stiffness and loss of strength were related somehow to the use of excess movement, and that preventing further mechanical deterioration depended on restricting, if not banishing completely, all superfluous body movement. It was a difficult problem but after a year of experimenting he evolved a way of playing that was economical, conserved his strength and was aesthetic in appearance. He called this system his "New Method."

Pachmann had always been interested in the various theories of placement of the arms and hands at the keyboard. Never a showy pianist himself (despite his eccentric behavior), he often ridiculed the excess gestures of some contemporaries in his "running commentaries" during his recitals. Lest audiences miss the point of this ridicule, he would caution them, "Never forget the dignity of the hands." It became the motto of his New Method. Cesco's scrapbook contained an unidentified clipping from this time, quoting the pianist:

> The wrists must be held so, like a rose bush pendant with rose buds that are the fingers. They must not sway to and fro with any gust of passion, but must be immobile, as the placid hush on a windless summer evening.

In essence: when the forearms were placed above the keyboard, the elbows had to be on a level with the chest, and the forearms in a completely horizontal position, while the fingers remained slightly curved. As a result, the forearms, wrists and hands together formed more or less a straight line parallel to the keyboard. No sideways movement was permitted—only the wrists were allowed to move in graceful, billowing motions.

It was not unusual for pianists to obsess about pedagogical methods. But Pachmann's obsession was almost unique in that he was interested in what it might do for his own playing, rather than that of others, such as students and potential purchasers of printed methods. He told the piano journalist Harriet Brower all about it in an interview she published in her book, *Modern Masters of the Keyboard*:

> A revelation; it came to me from Heaven. . . . I can play hours and hours without fatigue. I could play the whole twenty four if I didn't have to eat a little and sleep some. But the pianists of today, especially the younger ones—see with what effort they play, and with what a hard tone! . . . Ah, the poor piano. But *my* piano will yield lovely tones because I treat it in the right way. Why not caress it like this? Listen to the upward passages, how delicate and shadowy! How ethereal they can be made if the heart speaks through them by means of the fingers! And the fingers, doing their part through the right adjustment and correct choice, glide up and down the keyboard with little or no effort or exertion. Do you think all this is easy? Of course it looks perfectly so—and it is easy, for me. But each of these passages has cost me months of study. Some of them I have played thousands of times. And even yet they do not quite suit me; they can still be improved with more labor, till they become superlatively perfect.

Pachmann described how he had refingered passages, and now often played passages that formerly were accomplished with one hand, with both. Works that could not lend themselves to the new approach were dropped. He had little remorse: "You can't play everything!" he declared. Among the discarded repertoire were most of the large scale works he had been playing regularly for years: Chopin's third Sonata, Beethoven's "Waldstein" Sonata, Weber's "Invitation to the Dance" and Perpetual Motion, Liszt's etude *La Leggierezza*, Henselt's *Si oiseau j'étais*, the Chopin Etude arrangements of Godowsky, and even his number one showpiece, Chopin's Etude in double thirds. He told Sir Frederic Cowen that he could no longer play it.

With few exceptions (Liszt's Rigoletto Paraphrase, Raff's *La Fileuse*), what remained were the smaller pieces of Beethoven, Chopin, Schumann and Mendelssohn, plus a few by Schubert and Brahms. He had always played these too, but never with the insistence of his last decade on the platform. He still attempted to play some large-scale works of Chopin, but only the first and third Ballades and fourth Scherzo were managed with some success.

Although the promulgation of this New Method seems to have brought a renewed lease on life for Pachmann, on the face of it, the details of the method hardly merited the pianist's esteem. With its complicated set of rules forbidding certain movements, it was no different, nor more original, than most pedagogical methods. The similarity of all these is in forbidding certain movements, while advocating others. James Francis Cooke, the knowledgeable editor of the *Etude*, spoke of the New Method in his long obituary essay on Pachmann in that magazine:

> Its principles were almost identical with the method advocated by Ehrlich in his notes on Tausig's revision of Clementi's "Gradus ad Parnassum."

After his struggles in evolving the New Method, Pachmann rewarded himself. He had talked of retiring to Italy for years, and now he made the first steps towards that goal. He was eager to see Cesco, Alice and Virgilio again, and had a joyful reunion with them in Rome. They all went to spend the summer together in Fabriano, a picturesque medieval town in central Italy. Cesco had been born in the poor village of Campodonico, fifteen kilometers away. With Pachmann's money Cesco purchased the biggest house in Fabriano, a magnificent villa on the hill that dominates and overlooks the town like an ancient castle. It was a symbol of the poor boy's return home as a rich and successful man.

The property had to be renovated, so they rented a smaller villa nearby where they lived during the alterations. Each day Cesco took Pachmann into the town to introduce him to local dignitaries, including the mayor, the councilmen and the bricklayer who doubled as the leader of the local band that played on holidays. The band played a concert on All Saints Day at the Town Hall, at which Pachmann was the honored guest. As much as this puffed up ceremony pleased Cesco, it pained Pachmann. He thought these local dignitaries were tiresome provincials, and the town itself a dusty and dirty place, and he complained incessantly about "dese mosquitoes." He was glad to go back to England to play concerts, and in the fall of 1920 to be back in Rome.

Eventually the work was completed and the place named "Villa Gioia." Cesco planned for it to be their summer home, but Pachmann refused to go. "But Papi, the country is good for your health; you must come with us," he pleaded. Pachmann thought about this for a while, and replied: "I suppose you're right, Cesco. It is good to go to the country, and we'll see Papa Salvatore!" The pianist had taken a liking to Cesco's father.

Pachmann was seventy-two, and the rigorous life of a touring virtuoso was a great strain. He could play as many concerts as he wanted to in England and elsewhere, but he claimed that constant traveling in unheated railroad cars, then having to sleep in overheated hotels in America and underheated ones in England was ruining his health. He went to spend the summer with his family at the Villa Gioia. Surrounded by the beautiful Italian countryside, he gradually changed his mind and soon grew to love Fabriano. (*Toledo Blade*, 1908, unknown day and month):

> You see, I have learned "ze quiet philosophy." I say to myself, "life is good." This table is good, and this chair. I say this earth is heaven, but I must be in Italy or France to say so. . . . When I reach Italy I say "Life is heaven."

The town's peasants knew that a strange old man had moved into the villa on the hill. While they walked in the fields they heard the unearthly music coming from the villa, for Pachmann often opened the shutters of his studio and the sounds of his piano flooded into the valley. Pachmann remained an aging adolescent and rarely left the villa, but on occasion he might walk into the fields and meet some of the peasants. He would talk to them and even sometimes take them back to his studio, to show them how only he could play.

"Who knows, perhaps one of them is a genius," he told Cesco. Before long he was the town celebrity, and asked to give a benefit concert for the poor. It was in the town hall and everyone came, mostly out of curiosity. They remained to the end, for his personality reached out to the peasants and delighted them.

When Pachmann attained the age of seventy-three on July 27 it was quite natural for the entire town to celebrate. Early in the morning before they went to work the local band, led by the bricklayer, serenaded their maestro beneath his window, their primitive instruments all played out of tune. They started in at five a.m. while Pachmann was still asleep. He awakened and Cesco pleaded with him to acknowledge the villagers, and to appear at the window. Refusing and cupping his hands over his ears in pain, he complained: "Send them away, they're driving me crazy." Finally unable to stand the discord any longer, Pachmann threw open the window, shouted down that they should learn to play in tune, and threw down a vase!

The band members stifled any negative reactions when they learned the entire town was invited into the villa later that day to attend a great celebratory party in Pachmann's honor. Refreshments consisted of Pachmann's favorites—wine to drink, and watermelon to eat. The melon was an expensive delicacy in Italy then, but it was so plentiful in Russia during Pachmann's youth that he told Cesco, "We used to give it to the donkeys." The affair lasted long into the night, and was the first of several successive yearly birthday celebrations there, often attended by visiting celebrities like the composer Ottorino Respighi and pianists Nikolai Orloff and Carlo Zecchi. Another was an attractive young American piano student named Allan Bier, who came and asked for lessons and was given some. He was photographed, seated with his arm around an unidentified male friend, with Pachmann and some townsfolk standing behind.

Villa Gioia became Pachmann's permanent summer home, and each year he stayed there from late June until October, when he would leave for a winter season in England. In early spring he returned to Rome for a few weeks, then back to England for a short spring season, and back to Fabriano at the end of June.

Celebrities sought Pachmann out in Rome during his weeks there, as they did in England. Perhaps the most celebrated to visit him in the Eternal City was the pianist Moriz Rosenthal. They had met in Berlin decades earlier when Pachmann mischievously misplayed mazurkas for Rosenthal rather than give away any secrets. Now the two were in Rome, and Rosenthal gave Pachmann a sly look as he commenced to play Chopin Mazurkas. Pachmann was surprised, expecting something virtuosic from Rosenthal, who he knew only as a thunderer, and his surprise turned to delight; he had never suspected that "The Mighty Moriz" had a sublime, intimate and poetical side to his nature. He became genuinely fond of Rosenthal's playing of the mazurkas and now often referred to him as "my pupil."

He played a few concerts each year during his stays in Rome. At the first of these on January 5, 1920, he played his signature Chopin F minor

Concerto, with the Rome Philharmonic under Bernardo Molinari's baton. This review by Alberto Gasco appeared the next day in the *Rome Tribune*:

The old artist has a shock of gray hair that reminds one of Ernest Renan. It's important to note that Pachmann's originality has something to do with his mimicry—he smiles or furrows his forehead according to the character of the piece that he is playing. He often speaks to his listeners who sit near him, he comments on the music. Basically he calls on the audience's attention, "Now comes a delicious flourish," "Now the orchestra has a sweet ritornello," "Listen to the Cadenza—if you listen to me well you'll be quite satisfied." The audience allowed itself to be transported into his world. In Chopin's Second Concerto Pachmann interpreted the Andante with majesty and delicacy and there was a unanimous consensus of approbation. Apart from the listed program, the concert pianist played a Chopin Ballade, revealing himself far more in poetry and fantasy than in robustness and perfect technique. Tomorrow Tuesday Vladimir de Pachmann will play at the Augusteo Theatre and will play a quantity of music that is not unfamiliar, but that will allow us to make a definitive judgment about this unique and valiant maestro.[1]

As reviewer Gasco indicated, it was Pachmann's solo playing that permitted the Italians to judge him completely, and allowed him to bring forward the full force of his personality. Like England and America, Italy found Pachmann irresistible and succumbed to his spell. Here is part of a review Gasco wrote of a Pachmann recital on December 13, 1921:

We are face to face with Vladimir de Pachmann, the Polish [*sic*] pianist who is filled with tender style and certainly a notable comic actor, as well. If de Pachmann weren't an admirable trained master of the demi-semiquaver and hemi-demi-semiquaver, we could say that he had made a mistake by dedicating himself to the interpretation of Beethoven and Chopin, rather than that of Moliere and Goldoni. He would probably be successful, arousing the jealousy of Coquelin or our own unforgettable Benini.[2] With that refined mastery the witty artist presented himself yesterday on the stage of the Quirino. He seemed to be a comedic character presenting his 1,000th esteemed benefit performance. Mysterious and unrestrained gestures that aimed to propitiate the Muse, smiles and asides to the public before each selection, and then during the actual piece itself, the most eloquent mimicry, he did this all to point out to the public the beauties of this or that melody. What an incomparable man! De Pachmann, deliberately playing astute games, amusing himself with the aim of capturing the soul of the audience. He is an extravagant person but he is sincere, although his curious way of behaving might appear to depend on an abnormal conformation of his brain. If that were the case things would be more interesting. It doesn't happen every day that we find a pianist who continuously astonishes his public this way, who walks about the piano, who raises his arms now and then with burlesque demeanor, seemingly desperate like a noble father filled with woe, and who when he begins to play finds, suddenly, the equilibrium, the seriousness, the good taste to present the Romantic melancholy of the music of Frederick Chopin. It is in the music of Chopin that the sympathetic de Pachmann is victorious. He appears to be pensive, elegant and tender, without any frenzy, eliciting maximum effect from his flowing technique and pianistic touch, filled with that suavity that we know. In the Nocturne Op. 27 No. 1, in an Etude, and the Valse Op. 64 No. 3 and the second Ballade and most especially in the angelic Berceuse, de Pachmann yesterday largely merited the enthusiastic applause of the crowd that filled the Quirino. Chopin closed the program, but first we had Beethoven's Sonata in D minor, op. 31 No. 2, Mendelssohn's eclectic and seductive Songs Without Words—Fileuse, Duetto, Reverie and the Hunting Song, in which de Pachmann had a moment of amnesia—it was a little bad. He turned to the public and said, "J'ai oublié," then continued playing it without error. The public then acclaimed the old man with especial enthusiasm, yelling "Bis," asking for the piece to be encored. This time it was played marvelously—hunters, dogs, deer fleeing past were all depicted in a cloud of golden light. Imagine the overall contentment of the audience . . . another concert has been arranged for next Wednesday.[3]

For the Italians, Pachmann was a character straight out of the Commedia dell'arte and come to life—a pianistic Pulcinello that could not go unnoticed.

Chapter 27

England's Favorite, 1920–1923

Pachmann had submitted to the blandishments of the Welte piano roll interests in Germany in 1906, and then the Aeolian company's Duo-Art piano roll brand in America in 1912, and allowed his name to be used in connection with rolls that were issued that purported to be "exact reproductions" of his playing. Despite the fact that he, like most of the pianists represented on rolls, signed statements endorsing them, the rolls present a grotesque caricature of his playing that cannot in most ways be called "recordings." After the war Pachmann visited each of these two companies for a second time, and further rolls were issued. The main value of these episodes for the pianist was some hefty checks and even further publicity. A unique film made in England in approximately 1923 showed the process by which Pachmann recorded a roll for Duo-Art. There is some question as to whether the film ever had a soundtrack (if so, probably recorded on a separate shellac disc) for it has never been found. The pianist seems reserved, but aware that he was expected to produce some pantomime, and he does that; more importantly, we are shown close up views of his hands as he plays. These demonstrate his very active and precise fingers, and the awareness and importance he put on them as he alternately stares at the camera and talks to the technicians, supposedly just as he would to an audience as he played on a concert platform. When the roll is finished and brought to him, he mocks surprised delight as if he were being presented with a gift. Then with a great flourish he signs the roll. The immense charm of his personality is readily apparent. The piece he was playing is less so, but was most probably Raff's *La Fileuse* in Henselt's transcription.

⤣

On May 5, 1920, pianist Samuel Chotzinoff was in Steinway's London showroom with violinist Jascha Heifetz to select an instrument, which he used to accompany Heifetz at his London debut the next day. His memoirs recount:

> As we walked down one of the corridors, there came the sound of exquisite playing from a room. By the beauty of the tone and the delicate shadings and rippling, pearly scales, I knew the player could be no other than Vladimir de Pachmann. At a pause in the music we knocked, and were told to come in. De Pachmann was sitting at a piano, and near him stood a woman who appeared to be in the very last stage of pregnancy. De Pachmann rose and greeted us affectionately. He was unshaven and unkempt, and his teeth looked quite decayed. He hugged us each in turn. Notwithstanding my great admiration of him as an artist I felt very uncomfortable in his embrace. Then he placed his hand squarely on the woman's abdomen and whispered, as if he were letting us into a secret, "She's *pregnant*. Baby *soon*." He sat down again and began playing Chopin's "Minute" Waltz, talking in a kind of ecstasy with himself as he played, congratulating himself on his beautiful legato and lovely tone. After the final run he threw his arms toward the ceiling and asked the air whether anyone else could have played the scale so faultlessly. We agreed, and asked to be excused. And as we said goodbye to his companion he reiterated *sotto voce*, "Baby soon!"

It seems most likely that the pregnant woman was Alice, but nothing is known of the child she was carrying.

Alice accompanied Cesco and Pachmann on their trips to London, while Virgilio was most likely left behind in Italy with servants. Decades later Alice told the author that she wanted dearly to please the pianist who was, to say the least, difficult to satisfy. She said Pachmann quoted to her a Russian proverb to the effect that, if you love a person dearly, you would want to please him. Finally she discovered the best way to please him. She had learned that Pachmann still pined for a red diamond, despite the fact that he had almost given up his former obsessive pursuit of rare gems. He told her once that he regretted having never found the red gem, that it would have been the crowning jewel of his collection—a stone of perfection, its rarity the summation of a lifetime spent searching for "something wonderful, something rare, of which no one possesses the like."

In 1920 in London Alice began searching for a red diamond for Pachmann. Naively, she went to shops in Piccadilly and Bond Street and to second-hand shops near Covent Garden, telling the shopkeepers that she was seeking a red diamond for the collection of an elderly gentleman who was very dear to her. She was met with polite derision, as well as outright laughter and scoffing. She said she had begun to think herself quite mad for even attempting the quest and was about to abandon it when she met a merchant who did not laugh. She was directed to a society matron who owned such a diamond—the prospect of large sums possibly to be forthcoming from the "elderly gentleman" probably oiling the wheels of commerce. Alice told Pachmann that she had located someone with a red diamond, but that it would be "very expensive." He was overjoyed and arranged almost at once to see the gem.

An interminable period of negotiations ensued—he was delighted to find a red diamond, but not so happy about the price. After months of wrangling, the stone was his, but he scolded Alice: "I know you love me, Alichika, and want to please me, but if you hadn't found the stone, I wouldn't have had to spend so much money!"

He had the large diamond cut and made into two rings. He had rarely worn any of his precious stones, but this was his ultimate, and he wore these rings and posed for photos with them, sometimes wearing one, sometimes both.

Cesco said when Pachmann would wear the rings, it was an inducement for old Mme. Slepouchkine to emerge. Everyone thought the red stones were rubies. He would reply, "Psssst! Madame Slepouchkine: It's NOT a ruby—it's a diamond!" While staying in Eastbourne Pachmann discussed the red diamond with a correspondent for the *New York Sun*, and the interview was printed on September 5, 1922:

> Vladimir de Pachmann, the great pianist and exponent of Chopin, has gone to live in Eastbourne on the south coast of England. . . . The wonderful little old man, who has a curious habit of uttering his thoughts aloud, has decided to spend his last years in the spot he loves best in England—close to Devonshire Park. . . . Beyond his veneration for Chopin and his pianos, Pachmann has few interests. But one mundane thing he loves. It is a red diamond set in a ring—and it cost him $20,000. Holding it to the light so that it scintillates in ruby flashes, he will say, "Diamonds! What do I care for such things? I would walk on them like pebbles on the beach . . . but my red diamond—it is the most adorable jewel in the world. I love it."

England had other lures for Pachmann, and he loved to go to music halls and vaudeville shows. One of his favorite performers was the Scottish comedian Harry Lauder, and a recording of Lauder doing a routine in which he laughed obsessively was one of Pachmann's prized possessions. Cesco told the author that he would play it over and over, laughing along wildly with Lauder. The celebrated Swiss clown known as Grock had an act in which he imitated Pachmann, but it is unknown if the pianist was aware of Grock.[1] There was another comedian named

Barclay Gammon who he came to know, who also imitated him. The two met one day while Gammon was coming out of the Queen's Hall as Pachmann was arriving. The encounter was reported in the December 2, 1916, issue of *Today* magazine:

> Someone said to Pachmann: "This is the man who imitates you." Pachmann went up to Gammon and asked him to imitate him there and then. Gammon asked to be excused, but Pachmann insisted. They went to the artist's room at the Queen's Hall, followed by a few friends, and Pachmann sat by himself while Barclay Gammon went to the piano and imitated the great man. Pachmann was delighted. "But," said he, when Gammon had finished, "you make me smile too much. Sometimes I do not smile. Sometimes I am *triste;* show me when I am *triste.*" And Gammon had to give an encore.

After the Great War, Harold Holt became Lionel Powell's partner, continuing among other things to assist him in looking after Pachmann. Powell was no fool, and while Cesco was unavailable in the Italian army, he had Holt (who was attractive and a year younger than Cesco) accompany Pachmann on his tours in the British provinces. Holt died in 1953, not before he penned several memories of the great pianist, stories of his eccentricities that became increasingly outrageous as he aged:

> I went to Papi's room. He was dressed in his dirty beige dressing gown, far too big for him.
>
> "Harold, did you hear vot happened?"
>
> "Yes, Papi, you want to take a bath. We have come to look after it."
>
> The water was turned on by Cesco. When the bath was full de Pachmann went up to it, then turned to me.
>
> "You tink I vash my body vere hundreds of dirty people vashed in it before? No, Papi vants a clean sheet in dis bath."
>
> We let the water pour out and put down a clean sheet. I don't know whether you have ever tried this particular bath operation, but it is no means easy to keep the sheet down while the water is pouring in. It means we had to tie various weights to the end of the sheet, so that it did not rise to the surface. The task accomplished, we ran the water again. Papi said:
>
> "Vot is de temperature?"
>
> Cesco replied, "Beautiful, just right."
>
> Papi sniffed: "Papi must have a bath thermometer."
>
> It was Sunday morning in Dundee and all the shops were closed. Fortunately, I had noticed a chemist's shop just outside my bedroom window. I crossed the road in my pyjamas and rang the bell of the shop. A bonneted Scotsman opened the upstairs window.

"Have you perhaps a bath thermometer," I shouted.

"Aye," he answered.

A minute later I was on my way back to the hotel with the bath thermometer. By this time the water was cold, so we ran it out and in again to the exact degree wanted. De Pachmann sniffed:

"Vere is de soap?"

"Here," said Cesco, "this is my own special soap; a nice piece of soap."

De Pachmann turned on him: "Ven Papi has a bath he vants a new piece of soap."

"I have only used it once," Cesco implored.

"No good, Papi must have a new piece of soap."

Down I went to the chemist's shop. The Scotsman was pleased to see me. He was doing a roaring business for a Sunday morning. Being wise to old de Pachmann, I bought several pieces, all different colours—pink, green, blue, yellow, ivory and white. Back in Pachmann's bathroom, I held them behind me. Sure enough—

"Vot colours?" asked Papi.

"What colours would you like?" Pachmann deliberated a moment.

"Green," he announced, "only green soap."

Out came the piece of green soap which surprised the old man. By this time the bath water was cold so we ran it out and in once more. Now we had the soap, the bath thermometer, and the hot water. All was set for de Pachmann's bath. But Papi had not finished yet.

"Cesco, vere is de bath towel?"

Fortunately the bath towel was brand new and very large indeed, so there could be no complaint, but de Pachmann rose to the occasion.

"Has it been varmed?"

"No," I said, "it has not been, but we will warm it for you on the radiator."

This was done. But by this time the bath had become cold so we had to start it all over again. It must have been an hour since I entered de Pachmann's bathroom. This time we had everything—the hot water, the thermometer, the right soap, the sheet inside the bath, and the warm towel. I said triumphantly to Cesco: "I leave it to you," and made for the door. But just as I was leaving de Pachmann took hold of me and winking slyly whispered into my ear:

"Harold, Papi has changed his mind, he's not going to have a bath."

I could have murdered him.

❧

Powell arranged for a short tour of the provinces for a double bill including two of his great artists, the thirty-eight year old violinist Bronislaw Huberman, and Pachmann. Just what miracle Powell accomplished to induce Pachmann to agree once again to play joint recitals is unknown, but at the last minute Huberman was taken ill and had to cancel. Powell substituted a sixteen year old Serbian violinist named Milan Bratza, whom he was hoping to promote. Serge Krish[2] served as the violinist's accompanist, and to make certain there were no "incidents," Powell went along himself. Any fears about Pachmann's possible behavior were allayed when Pachmann took a liking to the boy, and proved affable throughout the tour. Krish told the author of many amusing incidents, including that Pachmann even served as a kind of *claqueur*, inciting the audience to applaud the violinist. Before Bratza was to play, Pachmann addressed the audience, saying "I've heard violinists in my time, but this boy is, ah, a great, great talent."

Throughout the tour Pachmann had steadfastly refused to play one of the audience's favorites during his portions of the concerts—the Liszt Rigoletto Paraphrase, one of his usual encores. He had become bored with it, and felt at his age he could play what he wanted. Cesco and Powell pleaded with him. But the old maestro was adamant: "I've played it so often, I'm tired of it." "But you play it so beautifully!" young Krish added. "You want to hear it too?" asked Pachmann. "Well, den," he replied, "you come out with me and I will play it for you." True to his word, at the next concert, during the encores, Pachmann walked out with the young pianist at his side, and addressed the audience: "Ladies and gentlemen, I will now play ze Rigoletto Paraphrase of Liszt, but not for you . . . for him!"

A chair was brought out and Krish made to sit next to Pachmann while he played. The performance was dazzling and so inspired that Pachmann himself was left in a daze when he finished, unaware of where he was, and his young friend had to take hold of him and lead him off the stage. Decades later Krish still remembered Pachmann's performance. "It was unbelievable that a man of his age could play like that . . . too bad they didn't record that performance!"

An unfortunate incident occurred at a London recital at which the composer Alfredo Casella was present. According to Casella's memoirs, Pachmann spied an ugly woman in the front rows. Either she was removed, or he refused to play. Casella didn't know it, but she was Lady Quarrie, and not someone who should be insulted. Cesco was deputized to make some excuse: "Please, Madame, the Maestro is extremely sensitive to the color of your dress," etc. In this instance disaster was averted when the Lady Quarrie graciously agreed to move. One only hopes she did not hear the comment Pachmann whispered to the people seated in the stage seats when he returned: "How happy I am that old horrendous monkey that was in front of me is gone!"[3]

But not everyone was so amenable. On the same tour with Bratza an offending gentleman with a stage seat was asked to move, and refused. "I will not," he said. "I've paid my money and I'm going to stay here." Pachmann stalked offstage to the greenroom, refused to play and a Pachmann-esque tantrum began. The awkward and embarrassing situation lasted for more than twenty minutes, with Cesco going back and forth between the gentleman and Pachmann, imploring the former to accept a different seat, and trying to calm the latter. The audience was getting impatient, and finally the man agreed to move. Pachmann emerged, sat at the piano and tried to compose himself: "Now ve shall see vhat ve can do."

Once more he let his eyes roam over the stage and this time he caught sight of a black man standing in the wings. Getting up, Pachmann grabbed him by the collar as the audience gasped. Would he eject him? But Pachmann led him to the center of the stage and held up his hands. "Dis man I like . . . and for him and him alone, I vill play Chopin's Etude on ze black notes."

The restless audience didn't find this amusing and was irritated with all the strange interruptions. The concert was not a great success. Pachmann sensed something was wrong, and told Krish afterwards: "You know, I felt dere vasn't dat great enthusiasm dat I'm accustomed to having." After this tragi-comedy, Krish didn't know how to reply. But he noticed that at his next concert, Pachmann kept his mannerisms at a minimum, and had a great success.

Pachmann's recital in the Albert Hall in October 1920 drew an enormous audience that filled that barn. According to Clarence Lucas, MC's correspondent for England (October 28, 1920):

> Could any other pianist than De Pachmann draw an audience large enough to fill Albert Hall? I do not know the players who draw best in the other great cities of the world, but I have had the best kind of evidence that De Pachmann is the favored pianist to the London public. Yesterday afternoon the huge hall was filled to hear him. His audience would have crowded all other concert halls of London put together. He was greeted with the warmest enthusiasm and he was evidently in the best of mood.

Prompted by the warmth of the enormous crowd, Pachmann put on a big show before he played a note. Lucas's report continues:

> Having bowed slowly and profoundly to the four points of the compass, he strode to the center of the stage and began a series of pantomimic gestures

which would have done credit to the Russian ballet. He rubbed his hands and smiled, showing that he was in good humor. Then he parted the muscles of his arms and felt of his wrists to show that he was fit for the task ahead of him. Then he raised both hands very high, assumed a tragic expression, and pounded away at the air like Macbeth clutching the imaginary dagger. He shook his head violently that the audience might know that he despised piano pounding. In fact the mere suggestion of banging the keyboard upset him completely and he covered his ears with his hands and shuddered. Recovering himself, he smiled significantly at his spectators, put his hands outstretched in front of him as if playing on an imaginary keyboard, moved his fingers up and down and indicated by his eyes and elbow gestures that he would play in a gentle and undemonstrative manner the compositions set down on the program. These visible and intelligible gestures were accompanied with an inaudible stream of Pachmann polyglot in which a few fragments of English, French, and German syllables were detected floating. Having finally inspected his Steinway and satisfied himself that all the strings and keys were in place, he cast aside, metaphorically, the comic mask of Thalia and took on alternately the masks of Terpsichore, the dancer, and Erato, the muse of amatory poetry. But why say more about the playing of an artist who was famous before most of the readers of the *Musical Courier* were born![4]

$$\backsim$$

In January 1922 the Russian pianist Alexander Siloti, pupil of both Rubinstein brothers and Franz Liszt, experienced some trouble with his Steinway piano bench—it was too low, and he wanted the firm to alter and raise it in time for his performances with Rudolph Ganz and the St. Louis Symphony. Somehow Steinway failed him, and the bench had not been altered. On January 7 he wrote to the company's artist's representative, Ernest Urchs:

> I want to tell you that your representative probably does not comprehend German very well, since he has not taken any measures to make my piano bench higher. I had asked if he could just put a couple scores on top of it, but when I came onto the podium the conductor had to bring me a ream of bound scores, which caused the public to burst out laughing.[5]

The American public had not forgotten Pachmann and his antics. Siloti's first cousin, Sergei Rachmaninoff, makes an appearance in Pachmann's story at this time. We know what Rachnmaninoff thought of Pachmann: he and Benno Moiseiwitsch attended a Pachmann recital at the Albert Hall around 1922. A copy of an undated, unsigned negative review found in a clipping file in the British Library mentioned that they had attended the recital and were as displeased as the reviewer. Daisy Kennedy, the violinist who was once married to Moiseiwitsch, also attended the recital sitting in a box along with Lionel Powell, Rachmaninoff and Landon

Ronald. Rachmaninoff apparently had only agreed to attend after much persuasion by the others. Kennedy remembered in an interview:

> So we all went off to the Albert Hall and sat in Landon's rather prominent box. Pachmann came on and did his stuff. He played a couple of pieces, repeated them—talked to the audience . . . and then repeated them again. Pachmann would talk about everything. He talked about his playing, about them (the audience), about himself, about the piano, about the music. . . . Rachmaninoff—very tall, very dignified, s-l-o-w-l-y rose from his seat and said, "I cannot stay. He is a Charlatan." Landon and I had to persuade him somewhat vigorously not to leave! He had to stay. And I have never seen a more agonised face than Rachmaninoff's listening to Pachmann. He just could not take it. We enjoyed it thoroughly, but were sad to see Rachmaninoff so unhappy.[6]

Lionel Powell persuaded Pachmann to play a joint recital in London on December 17, 1922, with another famous pianist, thirty-eight year old Wilhelm Backhaus. Except for Maggie, this apparently was the only time Pachmann played in public with another pianist. Powell wanted to enlarge the English audiences for Backhaus, featuring him first in a joint concert with Nellie Melba, but this had little effect. A better way was to have him to play in tandem with Pachmann, who had heard Backhaus in 1913 and liked what he heard. The *Saint Louis Post-Dispatch* reported (November 9, 1913) that he said that Backhaus's playing is finer than his, but not as beautiful.

Krish, who attended the recital, said Backhaus acted most deferentially towards the older pianist. Whatever the reasons, the combination worked. The plan was for Pachmann to play a surprisingly small Chopin group, then Backhaus to play his selections, and then for the two to play the Mozart Sonata for two pianos and Schumann's Andante and Variations together. But Pachmann could not stop being Pachmann. He played his Chopin group as planned and retired, but then walked out on stage with Backhaus when it was time for Backhaus's portion, sat on the stage (which was not planned) and made deprecating gestures while Backhaus played a dazzling performance of Brahms's Paganini Variations, one of his specialties. Pachmann's pantomime left no question that he thought that Backhaus's playing was loud and pounding. But in reality, said Krish, Backhaus's terrific performance overwhelmed Pachmann's playing. Somehow Backhaus overlooked Pachmann's boorishness, and never lost his admiration for his older colleague. A. H. Eichmann quoted both Mrs. and Mr. Backhaus in his biographical sketch of Backhaus:

> We were visiting Vladimir de Pachmann. He asked my husband to play. He played Beethoven, Chopin and Brahms. Then Pachmann asked for Mendelssohn's *Spinnerlied*. My husband pretended not to hear and went on with

Chopin. But Pachmann insisted: he desperately wanted the Mendelssohn. Finally Wilhelm gave in and played the *Spinnerlied*. Immediately afterwards Pachmann went to the piano and played the same piece with dazzling brilliance ("a hundred times better than me," Backhaus put in) and then admitted that he had been studying the piece furiously so as to be sure to "outclass" his young colleague! Wilhelm had no hard feelings about the episode as Pachmann was known throughout the world for his eccentricities!

The Baldwin Piano Company wrote to Cesco in 1922, asking whether Pachmann wanted to come to the United States for another tour. Cesco wrote back that Pachmann wasn't interested—he was too old and didn't want to leave his family. They responded that he could bring his family, and suggested they could guarantee the pianist an immense sum. The first inducement changed Pachmann's attitude, and he began to look forward to a new audience to charm, and to play for people who had never heard him. The second inducement interested Cesco, who must have been keenly aware of the huge profits such a tour could generate. He was now known as Pachmann's manager. A Rome correspondent for *MC*, a woman named Dolly Pattison (who obviously was a little out of her depth writing about music), visited Fabriano and wrote a long account published there on September 13, 1923:

> Not alone is he proud of the agility of his fingers, which is prodigious, but also that of his feet and limbs; while conversing on the subject, up he springs like a youth, saying: "Look now," and runs around the terrace of the garden, up the stairs of the veranda and down again, without losing breath or seeming tired. "You see, I can run as though I were eighteen." Pachmann has been spending the early summer at the Pallottelli summer home in the mountains near pretty Fabriano. . . . He confided to me that he possesses two treasures, one the new method. . . . While in the depth of conversation a gentleman, representative of one of the largest piano manufacturers, who was present, interrupted, saying (as they familiarly call him): "Papi, why don't you show the lady how it works on the keyboard?" "Oh yeas, I vill, because the lady she understand; but I must put on my Chopin coat, else I cannot play." So off he went to reappear later after a few moments, in a well worn old brown silk coat, led us to the very appropriate music room and sat down before a magnificent grand piano. He allowed his fingers to glide along the keyboard and it seemed as if the sounds had been transformed into mellow fluidity. He played Liszt's Seventh Etude [*sic*] with the most remarkable brilliancy, overcoming the immense difficulties as though they were child's play, and greatly attributing this enormous facility to his new method which he explained so clearly one could easily follow it as he played. "Now, you see, I am never tired; before, after a big Liszt piece for instance, I was sometimes

tired. Now, oh now! Nothing!" and he laughed and chuckled and pranced about like a child in his happiness. He then played some Brahms waltzes. . . . Godowsky's Carneval[7] he played next, and last, but not least, a Chopin Nocturne[8] hardly known. How he sang, with what intense emotion he played and how he conveyed his emotion to his listeners, is a thing one cannot describe. . . . What a lucky man he is to be able to dedicate himself entirely to his art and to concentrate upon it. This he owes to the charming family of his manager, which thinks of everything and takes care of him in every detail. Thus he has been able to work out the first of his treasures, his new method. During a pause he got up from the piano and whispered to me: "Now you wish to know my other treasure? Vel—it—is—it—is—a rare diamond, one of the greatest exemplars of the red diamond. The Czar of Russia and I alone possess such a diamond. I have mine but the poor Czar—who knows where the Bolsheviki have sold his?" It was getting quite late and Papy [*sic*] was quite sorry to have to stop, as it was dinner time; but those who were far more sorry were the entranced listeners. . . . Dear, young, old Papy promised that on his return we should have more music with the new method—and thanks in advance for that.

All that was left was for seventy-five year old Pachmann to finish preparing for the tour. He had outlasted most of his pianistic contemporaries—Teresa Carreño, Annette Essipoff, Rafael Joseffy, Sophie Menter, Raoul Pugno, Xavier Scharwenka, and his friend James Gibbons Huneker were all gone—and here he was embarking on another transatlantic tour. The day arrived to depart; Pachmann, Cesco, Alice, Virgilio, and Eva (the cook) made the long trip from Rome to Cherbourg, from where they embarked on the *Majestic* in a luxurious suite, which Cesco said cost Baldwin $5,000 (more than $100,000 in 2012 dollars).

Chapter 28

Melted in America:
The First Season, 1923–1924

Pachmann stayed in his cabin for the entire trip over, ill and cross. His friend the ship's surgeon Dr. Beaumont tried to coax him to play for fellow passengers but he would have none of it. Beaumont wrote (*Pearson's* magazine, September 25, 1925):

> Feeling mischievous one morning and wishing to draw him out, I said something about "our great English pianists." The dear old gentleman held up his hands in amazement. "Dear doctor, a great English pianist—I have never heard of one." Nothing daunted, I referred later, casually, to the "great American pianists," which seemed to horrify him, for he exclaimed, "Oh, doctor, which one? There is none. Surely now you are joking."

This was just the prelude to a controversy in which Pachmann became embroiled immediately as he disembarked in the United States. Several journalists were on hand with photographers, and Pachmann was induced to be photographed arm in arm with cantor Joseph Rosenblatt. Then one reporter asked him who was the greatest pianist in the world, and Pachmann's predictably ill-considered answer appeared the next day in the *New York Times* (August 29, 1923):

DE PACHMANN SAYS 'I'M THE GREATEST PIANIST' Russian Artist, 75, Belittles Other Noted Musicians—Proud of His New Method of Playing

Vladimir de Pachmann, the Russian pianist, who is 75 years old, arrived here yesterday from England on the White Star liner Majestic to go on a concert tour which will commence at Carnegie Hall on Oct. 11. This will be the first appearance of the noted pianist in the United States since May, 1912. He said that American audiences were so intelligent and sympathetic he was very glad to get back. Mr. de Pachmann looked very slim and fragile and wore his long, wiry gray hair combed back in the style of Liszt, whom he had known and regarded as the greatest of all pianoforte performers. . . . When he was asked by the reporters who was the greatest pianist in the world, the veteran maestro modestly replied, "I am the great player—the grandest player." After an interval of a minute or so the reporters asked him about the noted pianists who had been performing in America for the past five years, to which query de Pachmann said that he had no wish to say unpleasant things that would hurt other musicians, as musicians are intolerably jealous. Then he proceeded to mention them by name. Some he admitted were good pianists, but not great—that is, not in his class. Others were second class, he said, and others who were mentioned to him did not exist so far as he was concerned. . . . "What about the musical critics?" "The only critics in the world are in Berlin, Rome and Boston." "What about the New York musical critics?" "They are capricious."

Pachmann's opinions of other artists had hardened in recent years, and he now found nothing in anyone else's playing to admire. He had become coldly dismissive of every other pianist, even Godowsky (although he still allowed that Godowsky was the greatest living composer). The next day the paper printed a gratuitous second article, this time giving the specific names of the pianists whose art Pachmann had denigrated. The *New York Times* (August 30):

> Christian charity leads him to admit that Paderewski, Busoni, Rosenthal and Godowsky are "good but not great"; Hofmann was good when he was 9 years old, since when he has been going south fast; but as for Rachmaninoff—"My God!" says Mr. de Pachmann fervently. "No such people exist for me." We draw a veil of antiseptic gauze over the thought of what he might have said if asked for an opinion of Prokofieff or Ornstein. . . . Our critics give no light and leading. They are "capricious." The only critics in the world, says Mr. de Pachmann, are in Berlin, Rome and Boston. So New York audiences can ignore New York critics as they scratch feebly with the inadequate pen their uncomprehending critiques of the Master. We shall have to wait till he goes to Boston.

MC pointed out that this kind of talk was not unusual (September 6, 1923):

> That line of utterance is nothing new for De Pachmann and the authentic anecdotes about his sophisticated vanity stretch over the past thirty-five years or so . . . and are endless in number. Amusing as he is when he speaks, nevertheless De Pachmann is a superb artist.

Despite these calming words, there was a minor uproar. Journalists smelled a good story, and pursued it. The *New Haven Register* sent a reporter to various managers and pianists to ask what they thought, then to interview Pachmann, and the results were printed on September 7:

Rachmaninoff, from his country home at Locust Point, N. J., regretted politely that de Pachmann should have such a low opinion of him. He pointedly refrained from saying what he thought of de Pachmann as a pianist.[1] Leopold Godowsky, recovering from an operation for gallstones and appendicitis in Mount Sinai hospital, chuckled: "I admit that while I am sick in bed anybody can play the piano better than I. What effect the recent removal of my gall bladder will have upon my technique, the critics . . . will have . . . to disagree with the most individual and unique artist of the keyboard, de Pachmann, in his opinion of me as a composer." . . . In his room at the Hotel Majestic de Pachmann was playing Chopin, wearing a 70-year-old brown silk coat of Chopin's . . . and his 42-year-old slippers . . . he reaffirmed his opinion that he, de Pachmann, had no rivals. "I do not care for people," he said, "because I am de Pachmann. I have all peoplts [sic] in me. . . . But I am not a savant," he added modestly. "I am only a great pianist." . . . The greatest pianist has only one fear, the elevator. He walks up seven flights every day to his room in the Hotel.

Hofmann was asked what he thought, and replied with aplomb, in *Musical America*, on October 20, 1923:

When Josef Hofmann arrived from Europe on the Majestic the other day, the reporters, in order to make him feel good, especially as he had had his hair cut very short, told him what Vladimir de Pachmann said about him, namely that he played well at the age of nine but had done nothing of any great account since. Said Josef, "de Pachmann has not heard me play in twenty years, and besides the dear old gentleman has aged considerably in that time. Yes, I agree with him if he says that he is the greatest living pianist. If de Pachmann says so it must be true." Evidently Josef has a very pretty wit.

On October 29, *Musical America*'s columnist "Mephisto" (probably Allan Haughton) reported that he had had lunch with de Pachmann, who named further names:

Here is his latest pronunciamento: "I am a great pianist. There have been few great pianists—Liszt, Chopin. Rubinstein? He was too brutal, though he had some virtues. Busoni? Too hard, too cold, too heavy. Joseffy? He was too reserved. Besides, he had no legato. No one on earth has ever mastered the legato except Chopin, Hummel, Liszt, Leschetizky and—de Pachmann."

Moriz Rosenthal, in characteristic feisty fashion, was ready for a piano duel. *Chicago Daily Tribune* (November 23):

ROSENTHAL HURLS CHALLENGE AT PACHMANN

"Mr. De Pachmann has been putting himself ahead of all living pianists," he said. "He has referred particularly to Paderewski, Rachmaninoff, and me. I am not as old as Mr. De Pachmann, but I am willing to play against him on any stage at any time before a jury of composers, orchestral conductors,

and critics, devote the proceeds to a fund for poor musicians, and see where
we stand."

Composer Kaikhosru Sorabji in far off London was incensed. His letter
to *Musical America* (dated October 10) was published on October 27:

I see "Your mephisto" [sic] mentions some remarks of the egregious de
Pachmann and his comparison of himself with the giants of the piano such
as Rosenthal, Godowsky, Rachmaninoff and Hofmann and the supreme and
incomparable master of them all—Busoni. The kindest thing that one can say
of this sort of thing is that it is the babble of second childhood coupled with
vanity. Critical listeners in London remember his last recital here. Distortion
and sentimentalism were everywhere. Apropos of a group of Chopin Mazurkas, they were rhythmically simply unrecognizable as Mazurkas. Of his grotesque attempts on some bigger works of Liszt's it is difficult to give an idea.

Montague Glass, a now-forgotten humorist who wrote a regular
"race" column for the *New York Herald* featuring the dialogue of two
New Yorkers, Mawruss and Abe, published a long conversation between these imaginary Jews on November 4, discussing the pianist's
motives for slighting his colleagues. The gist was that Pachmann should
be commended for his splendid sense of advertising, and even suggested that he erect a sign:

It Pays To Hear The Best. De Pachmann's Velvet Tone Piano Playing. Graceful, Dignified, Unobtrusive and 22 Carat.

The most infuriated response came from a pianist whom Pachmann
hadn't mentioned, the aggressive and ambitious Ethel Leginska (born
Liggins), whose pretentious letter reached a height of indignation. The
New York Times published a shortened version of her letter on October 21;
the entire letter appeared in *Musical America* on October 27:

Ethel Leginska's Protest

To the Editor of Musical America: The interview given to the New York
papers recently by Vladimir de Pachmann has come to my notice and in the
name of modern pianism and sincere musicianship I protest that such things
should appear without public resentment from the many splendid musicians
in America today. True, they may consider such piffle not worthy of serious
consideration, but then again there is a large body of music students in this
great country, a few of whom might be influenced by such stupid statements.
Having waited in vain for some of my colleagues to answer these assertions,
I have decided to express my own opinion. De Pachmann quite modestly
calls himself "the greatest pianist in the world" and impudently declares that
both Hofmann and Rachmaninoff are "third rate pianists." That de Pach-

mann has made a name for himself as an exquisite performer of small pieces cannot be denied, but where is the big sweep, the gigantic power, the colossal brain of a great pianist such as Liszt (with whom he so discretely (?) compares himself) or of a Rubinstein, of olden days—of a Hofmann, a Busoni, or a Rachmaninoff of today—where the superb musicianship of a Harold Bauer or a Gabrilowitsch? (By the way, the last named can play a Mazurka of Chopin with quite as much charm as de Pachmann.) Typical of de Pachmann's attitude towards his self-asserted "greatness" is a little experience I had with him some years ago. During one of his Queen's Hall concerts in London I was taken into the artist's room to meet him. Upon being introduced as a coming young pianist, de Pachmann lifted his hand to my mouth in order that I might have the honor of kissing it. Being not at all inclined to avail myself of this opportunity, I gave him instead a good British handshake. With a howl of indignation he went hopping about the room, first on one foot, then on the other, exclaiming "She bruk' my wrist! She bruk' my wrist!" while a circle of doting de Pachmann enthusiasts glared at me for my "gross affront to the master." This is only another instance of the overwhelming conceit of the man who considers himself the equal of Liszt. To play the piano in a great way does not mean just a marvelous twittering of the fingers. Nearly every great pianist of the past and present century has composed, conducted and taught, which meant continuous musical development. This was reflected in their playing, making it not just a lovely noise, but something that speaks from the head and heart. De Pachmann in making the public statement he did, spoke as if America were still as musically ignorant as it was twenty-five years ago. On the contrary, probably now there is no other country in the world better able to decide for itself, having had all that is best in music and the world's greatest artists. Assertions that thus reflect upon the intelligence of the musical public here should not go unchallenged.

Ethel Leginska, New York City, Oct. 17, 1923

Pachmann certainly should not have provoked the uproar by specifying the names of pianists he disdained to a reporter, and the *New York Times* probably shouldn't have published them, but neither does Leginska's letter ring true, her indignation seeming forced. The tired old arguments of the VladyFloppers—his own playing was charming, dainty, feminine, but without power or energy or manliness, *no brain*—are dredged up again, the call to American patriotism and the rest probably designed as much to get people to notice Leginska,[2] as to uphold decency among pianists. It worked, up to a point, and Ossip Gabrilowitsch wrote to her privately on November 1, 1923:

Dear Madame Leginska

Good for you! Congratulations on your letter to Musical America. I am delighted with it, not because you say a few complimentary things about my playing but because you "gave it" to De Pachmann as he deserves. I am sure that if I had read his interview I would have felt like writing somewhat as you did but somehow his interview escaped my attention. It would have been a pity indeed if his stupidity and arrogance had remained unchallenged. I feel that you have spoken so well that the rest of us need say no more.[3]

At least two people came to Pachmann's defense—Olin Downes in the *Boston Post*, and a former Busoni pupil, a young pianist named Anton Bilotti[4] whom Pachmann had befriended. Downes wrote (November 4, 1923):

Mr. de Pachmann is possibly unique among pianists in his possession of a sense of humor. How he must prance as he reads the solemn objurations of critics and the self-appointed arbiters of elegance. Miss Leginksa, a brilliant pianist, could profit by two things, a little less serious view of herself and more of that sense of beauty which distinguishes the art of Mr. de Pachmann.

Bilotti's letter was published in *MC* on January 31, 1924. It was a very weak defense, but he wrote "I feel much honored by the fact that De Pachmann has shown a friendly interest in me."

Great artists all have high standards. Pachmann's whole career, with his early retirement for self-appraisal at age twenty, attests to his artistic ideals. His remarks to the reporter were indefensible, the end result of decades of uncontrolled egoism, now colored with the pulsating, not so hidden insecurity of an aging, deteriorating mind.

～

The tour opened out of town, with the first concert in Toronto on October 1st. The initial New York concert was on the 11th, a sweltering autumn night. A huge audience filled Carnegie Hall to suffocation, and a festive atmosphere of welcoming pervaded the hall. Among the audience were celebrated musicians as well. In his book *Speaking of Pianists* Abram Chasins wrote that Godowsky told him: "If he plays for one minute the way he used to, it will be worthwhile being miserable for the rest of it." Stories and legends about the Chopinzee were rife, but no one was quite prepared for what happened. Chasins continued: "I wish that I had never gone . . . a senile, tragic old man." Details of the concert were reported in several papers. Pachmann grinned, laughed and joked, and lived up to expectations. He went further with his running commentary than ever before. Gilbert Gabriel, the subordinate critic for the *New York Sun* and the *Globe*, (his mean-spirited headline, incidentally, read: "De Pachmann Returns With Velvet Touch, Gay Tongue"), took it down as it happened and reported it verbatim in his review the next day.

During Beethoven's "Pathetique" Sonata:

Ah, bravo Pachmann!! Beautiful. C'est Jolie! Bellissima!! . . . This Adagio it is like the Ninth Symphony. It goes so grand, so high . . . it is like singing for the fingers. . . . But not so perfect. Fingers are more velvety than the throat . . . oh yes! And my method. . . . This is the first time you are hearing my new method . . . afterwards in Italy. . . . Ah! that pianissimo! Bravo Pachmann!

During the Chopin group:

Liszt has told me . . . oh, yes, it is true, Liszt has told me. . . . It is of how Chopin is playing and then he is so frightened. . . . Mon Gott, how frightened he is . . . it is someone knocking on the window. . . . Very interesting. . . . Liszt say, "Silly, why you frightened?" But Chopin cried. . . . I hope I shall play it well. I'll try my very best. . . . I am 75 years old, you know. . . . You see . . . there . . . not banal. . . . I change . . . pianissimo . . . not *boom, boom*, like that. . . . No! I pray Gott I shall not forget. . . . But my playing is perfect. . . . Oh, yes, perfect. . . . You see how I play Beethoven . . . and the piano! The piano has a beautiful tone. (Applause) Mr. Mur—It is like a cello, a voice up there in the sky. . . . Very, very, difficult . . . for five months I study this piece . . . you will see. . . . The old merry-go-round players, they play it better than I do, hey? Bah, you will see. . . . Now the cadenza. . . . Ah, bravo, Pachmann, bravo! My next program I will play all Chopin.

Just before playing a Schumann Novelette:

Listen, you will see a new light. I heard Mrs. Schumann play this. Mon Gott, it was terrible!

To top things off, as an encore he played Chopin's "Minute" Waltz in two versions, first in a stumbling manner, explaining that he was showing how a schoolgirl played it, and then again as only he could play it. It was obvious to those who knew him from before that his pianistic powers had declined, and that he had become more garrulous in his platform behavior. At intermission many declared how disappointed they were. But there were still some beautiful moments, especially in the smaller works. Ultimately, the love and admiration of his die-hard fans carried the day, and most everyone left with smiling faces. Many old hands knew how to separate the nonsense from the gold. Leonard Liebling, as the author of the "Variations" column in *MC* wrote on October 18:

The main discussion in the lobbies after the De Pachmann recital seemed to resolve itself into the question: "Does he do it purposely and with deliberation, or is he sincere, and unconscious of it?" Of course he is sincere and he does it because he cannot help it. We asked him about it many years ago and he replied: "Do I do those things at my recitals? Yes, I suppose I do. Why? I don't know. Perhaps it is my form of nervousness." ... De Pachmann and his platform talks are one and inseparable. Take him as he is, or leave him. ... De Pachmann's piano art in itself is unique for he seems like a pianistic apparition from the Parisian days when Herz, Thalberg, Kalbrenner and others were preaching the gospel of a singing tone, a light touch, and elegance of technique. ... De Pachmann, whether through design, or physical limitations, fixes his scale of dynamics at a degree where great volume of sound never is in evidence ... in the smaller pieces come moments sheer irresistible in delicacy, grace and charm. The big and melodramatic Allegro de Concert by Chopin was laid out by De Pachmann mentally in a design meant to be large and impressive but the performance had not enough physical force behind it to carry the intention of the player to success. The tiny trifle, Chopin's Minute waltz, was an unforgettable episode. ... De Pachmann remains in a class by himself. He is eminently worth hearing whenever he plays. And as another great pianist remarked within our hearing at the recital: "One always may learn something from De Pachmann and one is sure to have several good laughs in addition." Godowsky, Lhevinne and Levitzki were among the keyboard heroes who listened intently and laughed heartily last Thursday evening at Carnegie Hall.

None of the newspaper critics were amused. Many of Pachmann's admirers among the critical corps had died, and a new breed had emerged, for whom Pachmann's values were an affront. One even left at the intermission, and what some of them wrote was scathing. The critic H. C. Colles of London's *Times* happened to be in New York, and wrote a guest review for the *New York Times* (October 12, 1923):

> Most of the music of his program contained a deplorably large element of caricature ... we waited ... only catching glimpses of the magic of his hands in a few passages, notably in the Allegro de Concert, Op. 46. But against these glimpses had to be set the garrulous puerility of his Beethoven. ... It was a good sign that the audience, which began by listening breathlessly for Mr. de Pachmann's remarks, took to drowning them with applause.

Henry T. Finck in the *Evening Post*:

> It was shallow, dry, monotonous, boresome. There are thousands of pianists in New York who could have played these pieces as well as he did.

Lawrence Gilman in the *Tribune*:

> Unutterably wearisome and afflicting to those who are aware of his singular genius as a musician, and have passed the time of life when a performance of Beethoven's "Pathetique" Sonata can be enhanced by buffooneries on the part of the interpreter which indicates a mental age of about six and a half.

Composer and critic Deems Taylor was one who had never heard Pachmann before, but knew the stories about his eccentricities. He wrote that they had not prepared him for what he witnessed, and his review in the *New York World* was devastating:

> Three thousand people saw murder done last night in Carnegie Hall . . . the brown curtains parted and out came a chunky little old man . . . put his feet together and clasped his hands, and bowed stiffly from the waist, looking like the frog footman in 'Alice' as he did so. . . . And Beethoven died and went to hell, and everybody was frightfully amused.

The pianist had brought two programs for his final American tour, bolstered by copious encores. The first included Bach's Italian Concerto, Beethoven's "Pathetique" Sonata, the Mozart C minor Fantasy K. 475 and smaller works by Mendelssohn, Schumann, Liszt and Brahms. The other program was all Chopin, and included the Ballades in G minor and A flat, the Scherzos in B flat minor and E major, the Fantasy in F minor, the *Allegro de Concert*, and numerous smaller works. Sometimes he made a program out of a mixture of the two. While he had some success with the miniatures, the large scale works taxed his energy and memory and were really beyond him at this stage.

Some critics thought his great qualities completely gone, while others wrote that some of his playing was exquisite. It is safe to say that his excessive eccentricities were now the driving force of his musical judgments, and this combined with faltering hearing resulted in some dreadful performances. The managers were handling him the way Barnum had hyped Jenny Lind. His mind was becoming fragmented, and certain stylistic devices he used were so exaggerated that his playing at times resembled a parody of his earlier performances. But there was still his touch, and some of the critics pointed this out. Pitts Sanborn in the *New York Evening Mail*:

> The old time Pachmann magic is still there. The touch is as ravishing as of yore. Those "tiny golden mallets," as the late James Huneker called the fingers with which Mr. de Pachmann strikes the keys, have lost none of their necromantic cunning.

Despite kind words, Pachmann received some of the worst reviews New York critics ever gave a world-famous virtuoso. Music critics were not the only critics who attended. Sensing that the best show in town was not on Broadway but in Carnegie Hall, drama critics Heywood Broun and Alexander Woollcott came to the pianist's defense. For a while Pachmann was the center of a lively journalistic controversy.

Heywood Broun in the *New York World* (October 17):

> We have the feeling that Deems Taylor disliked him because he was a little strange, while our feeling is that no art form of any kind amounts to much unless it has in it aspects surprising and curious . . . sometimes he is irritating and distracting, but he is not dull. . . . He is not reverent in the usual fashion. "Beethoven died and went to hell," was among the comments of Deems Taylor about de Pachmann, but we are not at all sure that the phrase carries the full weight of condemnation which Deems Taylor intended. Beethoven probably enjoyed the reversal of the usual process of the concert hall. There are more than enough musicians who play as if Beethoven were in heaven and had never been elsewhere.

Alexander Woollcott of the *New York Herald,* quoted here as reprinted in the *Literary Digest* (November 3):

> That curious contortion of the mouth which Deems Taylor reported as a grin is instead an attempt of the little man to gulp down an overpowering ecstasy. . . . But really weren't they rather the candors of an artless and quite simple person who would have behaved in exactly the same manner had the hall been empty, and who would have had just as good a time alone with the composers? Many of these "monkeyshines" were prayers, for de Pachmann was not talking to A-2, A-4, A-6, A-8. He was talking to God.

Deems Taylor responded in his column in the *New York World* on October 21 with a supposedly humorous parody, a scene from Ibsen's *A Doll's House* as if the part of Nora were played by an actress who performed like Pachmann, with asides in mixed languages commenting on her own performance as she went along:

> NORA: Exactly as before I was your little skylark, your doll—*Alec Woollcott thinks I'm the best actress in the world; dear man!*–which you would in future treat with doubly gentle care, because it was so brittle and fragile. *Mon Gott, what a beautiful speech!*

It wasn't very clever. Taylor's parody was as outrageous as typical de Pachmann dialogue, but Pachmann's interior monologue speeches had an added benefit—his undying fantasy.

Everyone was having a lot of fun with Pachmann. James Francis Cooke joined Heywood Broun and publisher Condé Nast in a visit to Pachmann's hotel room. They asked him to play, and he began the A flat Ballade of Chopin. Cooke described the meeting a decade later in the *Etude* (April 1933):

> He centered his eyes mysteriously upon his guests and then suddenly darted from the keyboard and whispered in my ear "Cet homme, il a une ressem-

blance mystérieuse à George Sand. Je dois l'embrasser." [That man, he bears a mysterious resemblance to George Sand. I must kiss him.]

In Minneapolis Pachmann visited a speakeasy. A cub reporter with the *Minneapolis Journal* named Robert Hardy Andrews asked for an interview, which Pachmann said he would grant only if he could have a glass of vodka in his hand. Andrews wrote about the occasion in his memoirs:

> I obliged, on my expense account . . . in the speakeasy, de Pachmann suddenly produced half a dozen uncut rubies and emeralds and tossed them in the air "to make a rainbow." He lost one, and insisted on having the floorboards torn up while we searched for it. This brought in what de Pachmann insisted on calling the Cossacks: a couple of Prohibition agents who didn't really want to close the joint, but had to under the circumstances. We found the missing ruby in de Pachmann's shoe, which he had taken off to swat a cockroach.

On October 13 he gave an interview to a reporter for the *Chicago Daily News* in anticipation of his recital the next day. He apparently uttered words that couldn't be heard or understood and were represented by asterisks:

> "When I play Chopin it is perhaps a little bit better than any one else in the world can play it—but can I help it? . . . Ah, I am in love with it! I love it all, I tell you!" His arms open in an embrace that would include the world. "Chicago * * * to play * * * it is such youth, this city, such youth! I love it because it is young. Everything young I love, You * * *" He takes the hands of the reporter warmly between his own . . . . "Ah, some of the critics, they do not understand me. I play Beethoven, Chopin, Schubert—these I love. But Bach, Liszt, Grieg—no. For the young I play. Yes, I am myself already old. See, tomorrow, I will shave and put on the eyes"—he indicates the eyebrows—"a little bit of black and I will look younger. Sixty-five years I have been playing. Since 10 years old, yes. And now these critics, they do not understand me."

These eccentricities might have appeared amusing to many, but there were two men to whom they seemed poison—Frederick C. Schang and F. C. Coppicus, Pachmann's American managers. They were worried that further reviews full of stories about his talking and eccentricities would begin to drive people away and kill ticket sales. They had promised the pianist the enormous sum of two million dollars net for two seasons of concerts (a difficult figure to translate into present day terms, but at least forty million 2012 dollars), and money is money. Once again an effort was made to suppress Pachmann's talking during concerts. Schang tried to convince the old man that he would appear "more dignified" if he didn't talk. A futile effort if ever there was one, but perhaps Pachmann was not so eccentric that the threat of lost revenues might have trumped arguments about dignity. Eventually Schang's entreaties worked and Pachmann agreed to play a concert in the Midwest at which he would make an effort to suppress his talking. He was successful and didn't utter a word during the concert, but the ordeal was so terrible for him, it seemed as if he were in a straight jacket. Schang rewarded him with an expensive cigar.

The second New York recital in Carnegie Hall was coming up on November 16th, an all-Chopin program, and Coppicus gave the pianist the same speech. Again it worked, and Pachmann played the Chopin program without speaking. All the critics mentioned that it was the first time he had played in New York in decades and remained silent. But the effort took its toll, and his playing was so lackluster and devitalized that Cesco said he received more than sixty letters from fans, wanting to know what was wrong. On November 22, .MC claimed that the pianist had "double crossed" his audience:

> After his first recital, some of the critics had called upon him to stick to his muttons, and omit the running comment, and he did it, determined to show that he could play the piano without delivering a lecture at the same time. Yes, he did it—and with his silence there went, at least for one hearer, half the attractiveness of his performance.

Coppicus and Schang soon got the bigger picture, realizing that more tickets would be sold with talking than without, and after this they let him do as he wished.

In the seventy-five days between October 6 and December 19 Pachmann played thirty-two concert engagements in Canada and the eastern United States—three concerts a week with much traveling in between—Toronto, New York, Philadelphia, Chicago, Winnipeg, Boston, Detroit, New York. The pace continued with sweeps through the south and on to the West Coast. Reviews continued mixed, with many critics finding his playing appealing, and others the opposite. Chicago *Music News*, October 19:

> Once, long after her good singing days, Adelina Patti gave a concert at the Auditorium, and W. L. Hubbard, then on The Tribune, described in his review of the event the writhings and grimaces of the very furniture on the stage when confronted with this faded out copy of what had once been so admirable. The same feeling was present last Sunday at the same place when Vladimir de Pachmann began his recital . . . the entire impression of the concert was one of regret and, as several people said in my hearing, "It is certainly a pity to make the old man play anymore."

H. T. Parker in the *Boston Transcript* on October 21:

> Mr. de Pachmann is neither the pianist nor the musician of his prime. In flashes but only in flashes, both occasionally return . . . played Beethoven's "Pathetic Sonata" in the veritable manner of the dry, desiccating, meticulous Rakmaninov [sic] whom he professes to abominate.

Everywhere local reporters wanted to interview the curious and talkative pianist—he made colorful news in less colorful locales. Alice developed a habit of clipping these news stories and reviews and pasting
them onto sheets of hotel stationery from the town or city where they
appeared—unfortunately, she did not often identify the date or publication. Pachmann talked and talked and talked to reporters, often saying he
didn't want to talk.

From Detroit:

> At first he seemed shy and withdrawn, and didn't want to speak to reporters.
> But when he saw their young faces, he warmed up considerably. . . . "Fine
> boy," he cried, waving his arms around still another reporter. "Take a kiss to
> mother from de Pachmann."

From Chicago:

> I am seventy-five years old, you know. I have been playing since I was
> twelve—sixty-three years, yet the critics they don't understand . . . yes, even
> the Chicago critics. Maybe they live too near the stockyard—smell very badly.

On a boat going from Oakland to San Francisco:

> "Why are you pointing that camera at me, tell me? Here I came straight from
> the train and they have to take my picture. I have no shave and no sleep.
> In my picture I will look one hundred and sixty and I am only seventy-five
> years old and four months. . . . Only seventy-five and they have to do this
> to me! No, I don't want to talk. I don't love you nor anybody. My heart is
> broken. To make me look one hundred and sixty years old!" (Just then he
> caught sight of a flying seagull): "Ah, the gulls, I love them, Like flowers
> falling from the air. . . . They come here to 'Freesco.' . . . Yes, I know it's bad
> to say 'Freesco,' but I love being bad."

The pace was grueling and took a toll on the old man, but the warmth
and sunshine of the West Coast seemed to revitalize him. A snapshot
taken in San Diego shows him beaming. While Cesco and Pachmann
toured, Alice and Virgilio remained in New York, staying in violinist
Jascha Heifetz's apartment on Central Park West near 59th Street, which
had been sublet. The task of "managing" the pianist and his entourage fell
to Baldwin's new employee, William B. Murray, formerly a music critic
for the *Brooklyn Eagle*. A glimpse of this cozy family group was captured
when they were interviewed there by "Mephisto;" the interview was published in *Musical America* (October 6, 1923):

> William Murry [sic], a bright and handsome young man . . . now director
> of the artists' department of the Baldwin Company . . . has steered you into
> an apartment on the upper West Side that overlooks Central Park. At the

entrance you are met by Francesco Pallottelli Corinaldesi of Rome, Italy, who, in spite of his long name, is rather short. . . . Mme. Corinaldesi, a vivacious and beautiful young Italian woman, who, as she seats herself beside you on the sofa, tells you that she is a devout follower of Mussolini—that's why she wears a black blouse—and is in this country to make propaganda for the fascisti and explain to the American people what they mean. She is full of enthusiasm for her cause and only regrets that an engagement with the Italian consul prevents her being present at the luncheon to which you have been invited by that most distinguished and notable virtuoso, His Royal and Imperial Highness Vladimir de Pachmann. As, unshaven and unshorn, the great one appears and takes you in hand. . . . You immediately land into an excited argument with him when he starts to speak about pianists. . . . When . . . he has exhausted his vocabulary in describing the shortcomings of all pianists except himself . . . the luncheon proceeds, occasionally interrupted when Francesco Pallottelli Corinaldesi . . . or Murry [*sic*], strives for peace by throwing oil on the troubled waters . . . the man is absolutely sincere. Every exulted gesture, every peculiarity, all are an absolutely natural expression of his personality. . . . You are astounded at his vitality, his energy, his tremendous psychic power, which makes him sometimes appear seven feet high, and today I don't think he is quite five feet high. . . . His speech is remarkable, his diction wonderful, consisting, as he shows you, that he has only about two teeth left. This brings an earnest plea from Murry [*sic*] that he should seek an American dentist and be fixed up. "Never!" he replies. Arguments as to the hygienic necessity of such a procedure leave him unmoved. You notice further that he eats with facility and drinks very sparingly.

This quote shows that Cesco had now taken the added name "Corinaldesi" and was becoming grand. Alice came along to America specifically to help publicize her fascist agenda. Apparently a year or so after she married, Alice visited her family in Rome, where her father was a proto-fascist publisher. Perhaps through him she was introduced to Benito Mussolini, who was one year older than Cesco. She became one of his idealistic disciples, devoted to "the movement" from 1917 on. Undoubtedly, her physical attributes played a part. Men considered her a very attractive young woman. (Leopold Godowsky Jr. described her to the author as "a knockout.") She had already been described as the "Joan of Arc of Italy." Sometimes while Pachmann was giving concerts, she would be delivering lectures on the benefits of fascism. She was proud of her involvement, and still unrepentant in her beliefs when the author interviewed her in 1959 and 1960. Eventually those beliefs brought her and her family great unhappiness.

Alice, Virgilio and Eva the cook took the long train trip to the West Coast to meet Cesco and Pachmann in San Francisco. Everybody then traveled together on the return east, Pachmann in splendor in a stateroom, the others in Pullman berths. Surprisingly, Pachmann's behavior was subdued on the trip, even sedate. Perhaps having his entire family accompany him was a balm, and he remained in his stateroom going over his scores. Six year old Virgilio posed more problems than the aged maestro. At a stop in Salt Lake City, they lost him for a while. It seems he had decided to explore the Mormon temple and had gotten locked inside. Another time he came down with whooping cough and had to be quarantined.

Rail travel had greatly improved but there were still inconveniences. Once they had to change trains at four in the morning. Always the earliest one up, Pachmann ran out of his stateroom in his dirty dressing gown into the Pullman car, shouting "Wake up, Cesco, wake up, Alichika!" He woke the entire car. Another time a train was delayed and they were late for a concert. Pachmann insisted on having his usual eggs and tea before the concert and going to the hotel to change into concert dress. Nor could he omit making a speech to the audience and fooling with the piano bench—the concert didn't start until 9:30.

In December 1924 Pachmann began his second series of recordings in Camden, New Jersey, for the Victor Talking Machine Company. Only two selections were issued from these sessions. Raymond Sooy, the Victor Artist and Repertoire man, left this reminiscence:

> Another artist was taken to the Victor Lunch Club for luncheon. This artist found a speck of something in the drinking water and immediately started to rave and accuse someone of trying to poison him, and as each course of the luncheon was served, declared it was the vilest food he had ever put in his mouth. After a few compliments were paid to this artist's ability, he forgot about the food, and when the luncheon was finished, he arose from the table, kissed the colored waitress' hand, complimented her, and told her how he had enjoyed the luncheon.

Cesco was reading the newspaper one day in January 1924. Pachmann recalled the day in an article in *Cassell's* magazine in December 1926:

> It is more than thirty years since I was in Russia, and I don't think I shall ever go again. I am told they have murdered the Czar. It is strange, you may think, but I did not know that, until one day I asked my secretary what he was reading in the paper. He answered, "About the death of Lenin." I did not know who Lenin was. It was the first time I had heard his name. It was the first time I heard the name of Trotsky. For you must know that I never read the papers. I have no time for that. I am still learning to play the piano.

He played a recital in Austin, Texas. A musician with the improbable name of Mint James-Reed, who had studied piano with the American Liszt pupil, Julie Rivé-King, presented the concert. She was disturbed at the way she thought Pachmann was being taken advantage of by Cesco. In her memoirs she wrote: "Of course, his genius earned a fortune for those who 'took care of him.'"

When they reached Cincinnati, home of the Baldwin Piano Company, they stayed nearly two weeks. Pachmann was their leading artist, the first pianist in whom the company invested a large sum, and he was treated accordingly, with visits to the factory, conferences with executives and the like. He was also given two Baldwin concert grands that were shipped to Italy, one to Fabriano and the other to Rome.

He played a concert in nearby Columbus, Ohio. At the time Philip Wyman was vice-president for marketing at Baldwin. Long after Pachmann died Wyman still regularly regaled regional Baldwin sales meetings with a story of his experience with Pachmann. He had been assigned to travel with the pianist in the Midwest and in Columbus he was contacted by a local woman, an arts patron of some standing in the community. She was an amateur pianist and wished to play for Pachmann. Wyman asked Pachmann, who refused to hear her, but eventually was persuaded. As she played, Pachmann blurted out, "That's the worst piano playing I have ever heard!" The woman was crushed and burst into tears. Later when she was alone with Wyman she said that, even though she had been insulted, the meeting had been the greatest event of her life, to have played for the supreme pianist Pachmann! When retelling this story, Wyman would stress for the salesmen the value of associating the Baldwin name with great pianists like Pachmann, saying the woman had probably bought a Baldwin piano because of this association.[5] What Wyman didn't tell the salesmen is just how far Baldwin went in this instance to keep the prominent local music patron happy. To diminish her humiliation, Baldwin persuaded Pachmann to conciliate her (Cesco probably accomplished the trick for them), and the pianist duly sent her a letter that now resides in the Ohio Historical Society, consisting entirely of lies. Pachmann did what he was told when it was necessary. He certainly didn't write the letter, but he did sign it:

56 Central Park West New York City
2 May 1924
[To] Mrs. Grace Hamilton Merrey
99 North Monroe Ave.
Columbus, Ohio

Dear Mrs. Merrey,

Many thanks for your charming letter. I was much interested in hearing you play for me. Yours is indeed a great talent which has been developed through earnest study and pianistic gifts. Your playing moved me exceedingly.

With my best wishes, I am Sincerely yours
Vladimir de Pachmann.

Chapter 29

Melted in America: The Second Season, 1924–1925

Returning east Pachmann developed strabismus in his right eye, a condition in which the eye turns unnaturally and is sometimes known as "wall-eye." It was due to age and stress, and remained with him for the rest of his life. He was nearing seventy-seven years old, and some of the critics wrote that he looked it. "I am weary," he told a Philadelphia audience. "Seventy-six is a long time, isn't it? I do not see well in the eye—poor me. But the other is all right." He smiled sardonically. "I don't have to see."

The Chopinzee was plainly tired. Cesco decided they should all take the usual summer vacation in the Catskills, but late spring 1924 was particularly chilly. They decided to postpone the vacation until things warmed up. For whatever reason, Pachmann decided then that he wanted to spend some time with Harold Bauer.

Bauer wrote a story about the resulting luncheon, the manuscript of which remained unpublished for decades. He obviously had plans to publish the piece, and the memoir is so detailed and specific that one suspects he had arranged beforehand with Cesco to have a shorthand secretary hidden in the apartment. We have added translations of the fragments in other languages in brackets [ ]:

New York, 17 June [1924]
Message from Pachmann through manager: "Why don't I go to see him? Excuses—I don't care to go." Second message through secretary: "Mr. Pachmann would like you to call on him." Excuses—I don't think he can remember me, it is so long ago, etc. Meet Pachmann, who says: "Why did you not come to see me?" I answer laughingly: "I thought you did not like pianists." The old man pats me on the back:
"Oh, you are not a pianist, come and dine with me."

This is irresistible, and I accept. Mr. and Mrs. Pallottelli, beautiful apartment Central Park, house owned by Heifetz. Fearing too much piano-playing, I had bandaged a finger. Hot evening in spite of terrific thunderstorm in the afternoon.

Pachmann comes in, unshaven and dirty, bows to me like a Chinaman for five minutes. "Mr Pauer? no, Bauer Pauer—Ach, it is so long, á Londres, nicht wahr? O yes!" clasping his hands and looking up. "Sie sind der grosse Pauer Bauer je vous ai entendu that wonderful beautiful piece marvellous, the arrangement in octaves of Weber's *Perpetuum Mobile*. Grossartig! I kiss your hands." I answer that I regret it was not I. I never played that piece. "Aber wass! Mais oui, c'était vous, in London that marvellous piece. No? No?? I am very glad because that is a disgusting, disgraceful piece, no artist would play it." I present my rose. "A single flower for the unique artist." "For me! Ah, that was well said: the unique artist (confidentially)—It is true, of course. Pallottelli! you hear what Mr. Bauer says: for the unique artist. Did he not say it? Ach, mein lieber Freund, I went to see Wagner, he kiss my hand. Pallottelli, did he not kiss my hand? Nonsense, you were not born. I am an old man but young again since I discover my méthode. Godowsky tell me (you know Godowsky, ach, my Lep! As composer the greatest. Yes, pianist, polyphonic technique and he make me discover my méthode but I play better) Godowsky tell me (did he not tell me, Pallottelli?), 'Vladi, it is sublime, you play like God.' 'Dear Lep,' I answer, 'God did not discover my méthode.' Wait, Mr. Bauer, I shall show you my fingering. Kolossal! You can only say it is perfect. How do you do? I am glad to see you."

We go in to dinner. He hammers on the table with a spoon. "Mr. Bauer, you do not listen when I speak to you. I tell you I played in St Petersburg, Chopin F minor concerto, and Rubinstein would not conduct, disant que je parlais trop au public [saying that I was speaking too much to the public]. O what a Jewish pig. But happily my von Bülow was there. O my Bülow, the great artist (sein Spiel war doch ein bisschen trocken) [but his playing was still a little dry, indeed] and he conducted while Rubinstein, ah ha! the great Rubinstein, ja! yes, I tell you, he was green, yes, and blue, yes, and yellow, yes, and brown, yes, and black! Yes. Jealousy. Ah Ha!"

"Pappi," says Mrs. Pallottelli, "don't you know those pieces by Godowsky yet? You have played them thousands of times, every day two hours." "Nonsense, not two hours, one hour. An artist must play every piece every day. Mr. Bauer, I ask you, is that too much? One hour with my Godowsky, his polyphonic technique. The lovely waltzes, as great as Beethoven. One hour a day. I am an old man, that is my pleasure in life. Eating is not everything. I cannot love any more. And no teeth." (showing his gums) "O yes, the storm today, I could not shave. I prayed to God. Who knows, it might have been I. Tell me, you are afraid in the storm? You go under the bed, behind the door, and you pray, n'est ce pas? Of course, you are an artist, and one hour a day for yourself (only in the morning when nobody is there) is not too much. You see I am not shaved, but for the public it is different. Il faut, nicht wahr [it must be, no?] ? I make my chin smooth and white, like—like—like this. But today in a hurry, no soap, no hot water, the storm. I have a Gillette, cold water and so quick, just a little you know on the eyebrows, not stiff and white and old. The appearance, aha! Mr. Bauer, you do not drink. We have plenty of wine, but I must strain it for you. What do you know, some flies perhaps. You will play for me later. What do you say, a sore finger? It does not hurt much."

He goes out with a young man and whispers to him, comes back looking very shy. "Tell Mr. Bauer what I say." Young man solemnly says, "Mr. de Pachmann thinks you bandaged your finger because you were afraid to play for him." "So I am," I say, "but if you will play for me I will play with my sore finger." I play Bach Partita.

"Beautiful, sublime, what a touch! Liszt did not have such a touch, nor Tausig nor Thalberg (I never heard him) nor Reisenauer. O how I hate Reisenauer! Dead. Yes. You are a great artist. I kiss your hand. Ach! Adelina Patti when she heard me play, she wipe her eyes. What use to sing wenn man so auf dem Klavier singen kann? [when one can really sing on the piano?] Did she not tell me, Pallottelli! O oui. I teach you my fingering and you will be a good pianist. But I whisper to you: trop de [undecipherable word]. It is a disgusting sound. Since Liszt, no pianist has pleased me like you. Ask Pallottelli if I did not tell him. Ask him." (Pallottelli winks.) "You know, these critics do not understand you. They do not appreciate my genius here. Only two cities in the world—in the world!—where there are good critics. In Rome, great critics. They appreciate my genius. I tell them about you. They know what it means if Pachmann says you play well. Berlin, great critics. They appreciate my genius. Only two cities. O yes, one more—O the lovely beautiful man. Dr. Wolff. Doctor of Music. He is a genius. Only a genius can understand a genius. I used to be modest, but I can say since I discover my méthode I am no longer modest. Dr. Wolff appreciates my genius. I show you his criticism, I only show it to my friends. Where was that place, Pallottelli? Lancaster. Ja. Lancaster.[1] Three cities in the world where there are great critics. Rome, Berlin, Lancaster. All the others are fools and dogs. Jewish swine I call them. No, I cannot play for you. Die Gesellschaft gefällt mir nicht [the company doesn't please me]. She says I play too much. Poor Pachmann! One hour morning, is that too much? Eating is not everything, and I cannot spoil my hands if the music does not suit my méthode. O my méthode! Nothing is perfect, but my méthode, you can only say, that is perfect. And such time to make my fingerings. And new programmes. Only one piece by Mozart—tum-tum tum tum tum tum tum—you know, C minor *Fantasie*. I play the sonata last season, nobody can play it like I, but it is a stupid piece. I put it in the fire. But it suits my méthode. Never tired. Other pianists, ugh! pianists! play two hours, three hours, and they fall down sweating. I play twenty-four hours. Never tired. But practice without cuffs, without sleeves. You must watch the straight wrist. Ach, what fingering! And always wash your hands. Everybody has dirty hands, and you would not touch a lady's face with black fingers. Moi qui vous parle [It is I who is talking to you], I wash my hands three times since dinner. Aber nein [But no], I cannot play to you. It is true that you do not know how I can sing on the piano. Such a pity you cannot hear me play the slow movement of my *Pathétique*. Tum Tum Tum. Paderewski is a good man, a great man. He hates the Jews. I tell him

to his face in Chicago—Pallottelli, did I not tell him to his face?—Five pieces
you have no equal. Five pieces, ja. You play the *Variations sérieuses* and after
the theme I wipe my eyes. Ha Ha! The A-flat polonaise, all the others, stupid,
they lie down their heads on the octaves, you stand on them. Aha! That was
well said. Schumann *Fantasie*, grossartig [magnificent]. La grandezza. Pallottelli, what was the fourth piece? I do not remember, but I do not like it. And
the last Beethoven sonata, Tum, Tum, Tum. Without equal, I tell him to his
face. Grand. Noble. Polish. Yes. Paderewski was honored to hear such words
from me. He tell me so. And the other pianists in the artist room, they were
black and green. Jealousy. I am not jealous. I tell Paderewski to his face. Did I
not tell him to his face, Pallottelli? Five pieces. All the rest I play better. Tout à
fait entre nous, mon cher ami [Just between us, my dear friend], I play better
than Liszt, better than Rubinstein, better than Paderewski, but I whisper you,
one thing Pachmann has not, yes? La grandeur. The grandness. If I must play
for you, I first wash my hands. And I wipe the keys. Pfui! the dirty keys. You
have played on my piano—And you must not smoke cigarettes near my piano. The ashes might fall inside and spoil the action. With cigars is different."

Goes out and returns with a dirty rag.

"I keep this napkin for my piano keys. I wipe them. Excuse me."

Goes out again, comes back with long brown ragged coat and stands
bowing in the doorway. "Chopin's coat. He wore it. I would not sell it for
$100,000. One must have money, n'est-ce pas [isn't that right] but I do not
like to sell. Mr. Bauer, are you not interested in my méthode? You must sit
near me and see my fingerings. The piano is so beautiful. I like Steinway.
What is this piano, I always forget. O yes, Baldwin. But the finest piano in
the world I find in Canada. What was that piano, Pallottelli? Heintzman.
Yes. Heintzman is the finest piano in the world. Imagine, it plays itself when
you blow on it, what it sounded when I play with my méthode! Now you
hear something. Watch my méthode. Tum, Tum Tum. Ach, the memory! I
am old like Beethoven. Time to go. Quelle tragédie quand je ne sérais plus là
[what a tragedy when I will no longer be here]. Singen, das kann niemand
mehr [singing, no one is able to anymore]. Chopin's coat, old too, perhaps I
live so long as that. Old but pratique, comfortable. Tum, Tum, Tum. I cannot
remember. Pallottelli, can I remember my Pathetique?" He says yes. "Well
. . . Tum, Tum, Tum, Tum, Tum, Tum, Tum, you see my thumb? Kolossal, wass? . . . There, you never hear that again like that. I must say: Bravo,
Pachmann! I play E major scherzo by Chopin on my programme of course
the best scherzo, nobody can play it without my fingering. I cannot teach
my fingering, I will not sell, why should I give away? Brahms, yes, I know
Brahms in Vienna. He kiss my hands. Rhapsodic en si mineur I play, they all
try to play it, but they do not know till they hear me."

"There are other rhapsodies by Brahms, Mr. de Pachmann, do you play
them?"

"*One* other. Tum Tum Tum Tum. Not good."

"Pardon me, Mr. de Pachmann, *two* others."

"*One* other. Tum Tum Tum Tum. Not good."

"I assure you, two others. One in E-flat."

"So? Then not in the same collection. I do not know it. It is not good. You know my B major nocturne? Chopin was with Liszt and frightened when they knock at the door. Brrrrr! Frightened. Liszt said, 'Do not be frightened.' Aha! Nobody knows this story. Dramatic, Ah! I wipe the keys, you wipe your eyes when I play—Ha Ha! Tum Tum Tum Tum. Wonderful, yes? Pallottelli, he says I am unique. O what a great artist you are. But too much soft pedal, a disgusting sound. I never play soft pedal."

"Mr. de Pachmann, I thank you for your charming hospitality, and fear I must now leave you. It is late."

"Never late, but I do not play in the evening. I would not play any more. J'avais fini déjà. [I had already finished.] You are great as composer, and I enjoy your conversation, ein hoch gebildeter mann [a highly cultured man]. You are a learned man, a scholar. You understand my genius, like Bach and Beethoven and Chopin. Bach a little old sometimes, like Mozart. Adieu, mon cher maitre, you honor me. I come to the door with you. Liszt came to the door with me in Weimar. Good-bye. O the intelligent conversation not like others. Auf Wiedersehen. Good-bye. I have pleasure to show you my méthode. Unique, perfect, wars? Aha! Next time I play you." Elevator door closes on me.

Bauer's remarkable story shows many things about Pachmann—that he was capable of uttering anti-Semitic epithets in practically the same breath used to accuse Paderewski of anti-Semitism, that he took it very personally when Anton Rubinsein had refused to conduct for his concert in St. Petersburg in 1885, that he was aware that Paderewski's playing had a grandeur that his own lacked—but most of all, that his mind was dissolving, fragmented and cluttered, and not able to keep one thought before going on to another . . . resembling the way he was then playing.

Soon after this bizarre luncheon Pachmann and his party left for their vacation in the town of Dunraven, New York, in the Catskill Mountain country. There were immediate problems because of the food. In past years in these Catskill resorts Pachmann had accepted the simple country cooking offered, and even looked forward to his favorite chicken dish, but it no longer pleased him, and he scowled when it was served now. It is probable that it was now as much the waiters as the food that drew Pachmann to these resorts. It was in Dunraven during that vacation that the most famous of all photos of Pachmann were taken, showing the pianist in his dirty dressing gown amidst cows in the pasture. Harold C. Schonberg included one of these photos in his book, *The Great Pianists*, with a caption explaining that Pachmann considered that milking cows "was better finger exercise than anything devised by the mind of man," but the author has found no information that Pachmann ever actually said that.

Cesco and some friends took Pachmann fishing. After watching Cesco for a while, Pachmann asked for a rod and reel and much to everyone's astonishment, most of all himself, five minutes later hooked a sixteen inch trout on his first attempt. He threw the fish back in. Everyone made a terrific fuss over Pachmann. When he practiced there was always someone standing outside his door listening. This made him angry—he wanted to choose his hearers. Once he swept the door open, prepared to shout, but the person listening was a little girl. He took her by the hand and began explaining his New Method to her. He avoided music lovers and dilettantes, piano students and teachers, and instead played for little Virgilio and his friends. Pachmann had never been fond of children before Virgilio.

After vacation they resumed the tour. The first New York concert at Carnegie Hall was on October 17, 1924. "Mephisto" wrote (*Musical America*, October 25):

> He began to play the Mozart fantasia but something went wrong. He stopped. Holding up his left thumb he murmured, "Hurt!" He regarded his sore thumb dolefully for a moment, then by pantomime informed his audience that he was suffering a little as a result of a slight accident. Then, like a child who has brought his injury to his mother, he was satisfied. Then he resumed playing.

Olin Downes's review in the *New York Times* (October 18) was fantastic:

> It would be possible to exclaim in irritation at the passing eccentricities . . . what is more important, namely, that when Mr. de Pachmann rises to his full height as a musician and pianist—and it is not to be forgotten that underneath his fooling and his "causeries" lies a profound knowledge of his art—he gives performances of a unique poetry and beauty which will die with him, and that often constitutes revelation in single phrase.

Lawrence Gilman in the *New York Herald* on the 18th wrote that Pachmann should be "spanked and sent to bed for his 'vaudeville stunt,'" but concluded his review describing the ending Chopin group:

> Mr. de Pachmann was irresistibly, as he has so often been before, the master of a ravishing and magical art. Hearing him thus at his happiest, what could one do but forgive him all his other sins?

‿

In October 1924 the twenty-five year old writer Vladimir Nabokov was in Berlin, where he wrote a short story entitled "Bachmann." It concerns an eccentric pianist who mixes up three and four languages, fiddles with his piano stool and who inspires the sighs and passion of an older woman who seems very much a VladyFlapper. Despite the obvious similarities,

Nabokov later wrote, disingenuously, "I am told that a pianist existed with some of my invented musician's peculiar traits."

⤷

On December 14, 1924, de Pachmann played the Chopin F minor Concerto at a Metropolitan Opera concert with Giuseppe Bamboschek conducting. The next day the critic for the *New York Sun* wrote:

> His performance was remarkable. The changing, iridescent shades of tone color, the sparkling legato and the exquisite finish of phrasing proclaimed a master hand.

Pachmann particularly liked the accompaniment—the critic for the *New York World-Telegram* wrote that Bamboschek:

> Kept down the orchestra to the vanishing point . . . and somehow got through without casualties. But he perspired visibly and has probably seven or eight newly sprouted gray hairs today as a reward for his valor.

It was Cesco's job to keep him amused, and while in New York he took the pianist to see a silent film, a curious documentary about the process used to manufacture gorgonzola cheese. Pachmann refused to eat any ever again.

⤷

The tour was fast approaching its end. A couple of concerts in Canada, a few in New England, one in New York and then it would be over. In Toronto he found that the locally made Heintzman piano he had to use for his recital now did not meet his demand for a keyboard height of 26 inches, a couple of inches less than standard. Two inches were sawed off the concert grand's legs, but still he wasn't satisfied, for he wanted to play "uphill" towards the treble. A worker shimmed a one inch block under the right leg, Pachmann contentedly smiled, and only then began the recital.

Eight years after the fact, after Pachmann's death, the Sherbrooke (Montreal) *La Tribune* printed a reminiscence of Pachmann's visit there, written originally in French by Arthur Friedheim's amanuensis, Theodore Bullock (January 28, 1933):

> In his last years, he was, I am convinced, really crazy. His manners were impossible, he lived like a pig but played like a God. . . . He came to Montreal in the winter of 1924/25 and I passed a few hours with him at his suite in the Hotel Windsor. Despite his protestations of age, he drank glass after glass of

cognac. "You are an idiot," he cried to his manager. "Go! And return when I demand!" We talked for a long time in French. He understood and spoke English, but he detested the language. . . . More times during our conversation, the little Jew from Odessa who detested Jews rose and advanced in the manner of a cat toward the piano, but then gave me a look of contempt. And each time he would then return to his seat. "This horrible box that they have given me," he complained, "is not worth anything. My little feet are not able to touch the pedals. I wish to play for you, but the price would be distorting my body . . . Bah!" he burst out. "The listeners this evening—they'll never see the difference. They're all pigs and dogs. You, you're intelligent. I'll go and play for you. I will play Bach. Pedals are not necessary for that." He sat before the piano and I took a chair and sat next to him. He explained to me at first his "New Method" which he invented after he was seventy. Then he played—Bach, Schumann, Chopin. Forgetting what he said about the instrument, he played using the pedals like everybody else. At the end he leered at me maliciously: "Tell 'Arty' that I was a friend of Liszt's, he was just his pupil." He couldn't resist the desire to give Friedheim a hit in the teeth. After that he said he would play the Eglogue from the Années de pèlerinage of Liszt. "Liszt would cry from envy if he heard me play it," he assured me. . . . De Pachmann made a pause and suddenly appeared to listen, then he inserted an exquisite passage that Liszt had never written. "Where did you get that?" I demanded when he finished. God had commanded it, he said. He returned to his chair and took new glassfuls of cognac and we spoke again. Suddenly, "I am tired," he groaned. "Embrace me and go. You will never hear again from the God of the piano. I forbid you from going to my concert tonight." I never returned. . . . Under the fingers of Friedheim the piano became an immense, palpitating and sympathetic intellect, expressing in sumptuous, clear and universal tones. Under the fingers of Pachmann the piano was made to be a charming courtesan, attracting men in a maze of breathtaking dreams.[2]

After Pachmann arrived in New York he of course went to see his friend Lepp. He told *Musical America* (September 3, 1923):

My friend Leopold! He is the very greatest of living composers. I have just been to visit him. I said, "Leo, you are the greatest of all!" He threw his arms around my neck and tears fell from his eyes. "Vladdy!" he replied. "I am quite sure you flatter me." But I did not. That is my honest opinion.

Godowsky and his family were living in New York at the Ansonia Hotel, where "Popsy" Godowsky kept a near continuous salon. Pachmann was often the guest there. Many pianists could be found at any moment, some famous, some just emerging. Everyone knew that if Pachmann was there, a certain protocol had to be followed. First, Pachmann would play only at the end of the evening, after everyone else had already played. Even more important, no one else was to play Chopin—ever. One evening an unnamed pianist who didn't know these unwritten rules dared to play a Chopin selection and Pachmann was incensed: "Only when I am dead can you play Chopin like that—not before!" Another time Josef Lhevinne played a salon trifle and Pachmann was not pleased, blurting out "How can a man play like this and still have a career?" The atmosphere became icy cold, but Pachmann wouldn't let off: "How can he do it?" His wife Rosina burst into tears, and she and Josef left.

Chicago's *Musical Leader* published a short unsigned story about one of these occasions on May 10, 1924:

> A rendezvous of the elite of the artistic world is found at the fascinating home of Mr. and Mrs. Leopold Godowsky. Artists delight to gather together with the man who is declared, by no less a light than Vladimir de Pachmann, to be the greatest contrapuntalist of all the ages. At a dinner party last week where the veteran pianist was the cynosure of all eyes (as he is at his recitals) and which included Jascha Heifetz, Mr. and Mrs. Josef Lhevinne, Alexander Lambert, Leon Sametini,[3] and other distinguished persons, Mr. de Pachmann declared that of the world's most famous composers none approached Leopold Godowsky in stupendous knowledge of the science of music. After dinner Mr. Godowsky played his own transcriptions of Bach's Violin and Cello Sonatas and as he listened de Pachmann would exclaim "Marvelous!" "Amazing!" "Magnificent!" "There is only one Godowsky, he is the supreme master of our art!" It was a most extraordinary occasion. About midnight de Pachmann, after declaring it was too late, decided he would play, and never has it been the writer's privilege to hear him to such advantage. It seems as if he were inspired by the presence of his distinguished colleagues, all of whom were in worshipful admiration of the man whose playing was a revelation even to them. An evening, going far beyond the wee sma' hours of the morning, will long be remembered.

One suspects Mr. and Mrs. Josef Lhevinne were not quite as worshipful in their admiration as the others. Ossip Gabrilowitsch, at least, forgave Pachmann. He had lashed out in anger at de Pachmann in his letter to Leginska, but we know that twenty months later he spent an afternoon with the Chopinzee, and then took him along to a dinner party at the home of soprano Alma Gluck and her husband, the violinist Efrem Zimbalist. We can only speculate about why Gabrilowitsch was spending those hours with Pachmann, but given the similarities in their pianism, it is not unreasonable to think he was fascinated by Pachmann's playing, and perhaps even thought he could learn something from it. Gabrilowitsch's own playing had a particularly appealing, soft touch, and like Pachmann, he was supremely lyrical and poetic, exhibiting an intimate, feminine attitude when necessary that was in the same expressive neighborhood as Pachmann.

This dinner party probably took place in connection with the venerable violinist Leopold Auer's eightieth birthday concert at Carnegie Hall on April 28, 1925, at which his pupils Zimbalist and Heifetz, as well as pianists Rachmaninoff, Hofmann and Gabrilowitsch all played. Gabrilowitsch's wife had become ill, and since he was spending the afternoon with Pachmann, he telephoned Alma Gluck to ask if he could bring him instead, and of course it was all right. Others guests included, besides Auer, Mr. and Mrs. Rachmaninoff, and Hofmann accompanied by the fabulously wealthy Mary Louise Curtis Bok. Mrs. Bok had recently started her Curtis Institute of Music, at which Auer headed the violin faculty. Zimbalist never forgot the occasion, the first time he met Mrs. Bok, for she was to become his second wife. Vera Fonaroff, a well-known violin teacher and Abram Chasins's aunt, was also there. She told the author that she was talking with Pachmann and as they were conversing, he noticed an elderly man standing at the other end of the room. He said to Madame Fonaroff: "Can this be Auer? Komm . . ."And he led her by the arm towards the elderly man. As they walked, he repeated "Auer? Auer?" When they got to Auer, Pachmann, who probably had not seen him since they were in Russia together fifty years earlier, looked directly into his face and said, "Auer, Gott, Sie leben noch!" [God, you're still alive!] Auer was only three years older than Pachmann. Other details of the party are recounted by Roy Malan in his biography of Zimbalist:

> Gabrilowitsch and de Pachmann arrived late. . . . As de Pachmann divested himself of coat and gloves, he demanded water. He held the glass he received up to the light and handed it back dramatically: "This glass is dirty!"

Malan describes how Pachmann made a beeline for the piano, oblivious of the fact that a holy trinity—Rachmaninoff, Hofmann, and Gabrilowitsch—were in the room. He made a face when he saw that it was a Steinway, and said to a man standing next to him, "What a terrible instrument the Steinway is. I can't understand why people pay so much money for such rubbish. The *only* piano to play is the Baldwin." Of course the man to whom this was spoken was Frederick Steinway.

This final American tour was a great success financially, but took a dreadful toll on the man. By the fall of 1924 he had become so tired of crowds, reporters, concerts, managers, interviews and travel that signs of physical and mental exhaustion were apparent and shadowed his every move. By the time he arrived on the West Coast in February 1925 he was worn out. His patience and his strength had gone. He refused to be interviewed. He angrily complained, as recounted by one of Alice's [unfortunately unidentified] press clippings:

"Qui est cette jeune fille?" The press, maestro. "La presse, oh. . . . La presse. Oooo—oh, LA PRESSE!" The words rose to a shriek, and the little figure catapulted from the room, disappeared behind some curtains from which there came a monologue sprinkled liberally with several "cochonneries" and "schweins" Finally, he grabbed the curtains and thrust his head through its fold: "Ah, I have a migrain, what you call a headache. Very bad in the head. This city, she go boom, boom, boom. . . . Much loudness. I live in Italy—more quiet than America. I play five hundred concerts a season, sometimes more. . . . I am a genius; I am Pachmann. . . . MAIS LA PRESSE!"

Another of Alice's clippings:

I can say what I wish. . . . For reporters I always say the reverse of what I mean: This tour is torture, I tell them it is fine, great. They are crazy to hear me play . . . well, I'm not so crazy to play. Soon it is over, the twenty-third of May. I'm tired, tired, sick. . . . I'm weary, weary. Seventy-seven is a long time, isn't it?

And another:

I will kill you. . . . I will kill you. You don't know de Pachmann. I don't want to see you nor nobody. Look at these hands. I use them all day and night. I play sometimes six or seven hours at a time and then at night I cannot sleep . . . it's as if they're wounded. What do you want to know? Something about the weather? People like you are dangerous. If you write one word about me I will hold you to it. . . . No, I will kill you and I can do it too. You don't know me—I am God himself.

Because he was so childlike, lacking any adult restraint when angered or irritated, he would blurt out his dreadful thoughts. Such quotes must have alarmed Pachmann's own entourage more than the readers of the provincial papers. He had always been conceited and egotistical, and used to quip, "Rubinstein was the most modest artist I have ever met. I myself am the most un-modest artist, except Hans von Bülow. He was more unmodest than I." With the steady acceleration of acclaim over the decades, this "unmodesty" increased to megalomaniacal proportions. To have known many of the great of the world, to have been decorated by kings and emperors, and adored by hundreds and thousands had finally culminated in a God complex. Pachmann had become convinced that he was the first and senior being on the earth. (Ego raised to the level of a God-complex was not something unique to Pachmann, and other performing artists also suffered this affliction—often sopranos.) Eccentricity, overweening egoism and insecurity combined and culminated in the most bizarre behavior. The scenes intensified as his exhaustion grew. Cesco, Schang and Coppicus now had to deal with an almost impossible situation. Pachmann's mind had started to crumble.

⮌

Olin Downes obviously idolized Pachmann's playing, and the pianist had actually visited him at his home two days after that October 1923 Boston recital. Downes later wrote about the visit in the *Saturday Evening Post* (March 13, 1930):

> It was a joyous occasion. He was as playful as a kitten, except when, toward evening, a dog bayed, and he paled, glancing around in the corners, fearing, as he said, that this portended his death on an early occasion.

Commercial clipping services had been born, and Pachmann now kept track of critics and what they wrote about him. Months later in an interview with a reporter for the Kentucky *Louisville Sunday Herald* (November 30, 1924), he maintained bad critics were "the one big grievance against the musical public on this side of the water," and was quoted:

> But why do they do it? . . . Why must they always talk about the things I do at the piano? Why do they not just talk about my playing?

Downes had publicly stated his regard for the pianist often, and continued in his review for Pachmann's second concert in Boston in the fall of 1923, printed the day after in the *Boston Post* on November 2nd. Extravagant encomiums take up most of the review, but it was not completely unrelieved praise, for it included the observation:

> Mr. de Pachmann himself is sick to death of playing programmes of all Chopin. . . . Sometimes he was supremely eloquent, sometimes perfunctory . . . much of the time bored.

This tiny lapse from total adulation did not go unnoticed, and Downes found that out a few months later. Pachmann's behavior was becoming more unstable daily, and climaxed at Downes's expense in a terrible outburst that occurred before he was to play the Chopin F minor Concerto in Springfield, Massachusetts, for the New England Festival in the spring of 1924, a gala yearly affair in which he had participated several times before. A month earlier Downes had left the *Boston Post* and accepted the prestigious position as music critic of the *New York Times*. One of Pachmann's managers in New York got in touch with Downes and suggested that since he knew Downes was going to be traveling back to Boston that week, why didn't he stop in Springfield to hear Pachmann's renowned rendition of the Chopin Concerto, and on the way they could all visit at Pachmann's hotel and have dinner with him. The party included William B. Murray, director of the artists' department of Baldwin Pianos. Downes described the dinner party in Pachmann's Springfield hotel suite a few months after he wrote that review, in his obituary for the pianist in the *New York Times* (January 15, 1933):

We ascended and rang the bell of his hotel apartment. He himself came to the door and stared with unrecognizing eyes. "How do you do, Maestro. It's such a pleasure to see you again. Do you remember the delightful time we had together last season?" "Yes-s-s," with a hissing intake of breath, and an icy regard. "Yes-s-s, I remember." Nothing more. Presently dinner was served. Nothing seemed to satisfy de Pachmann. He kept bouncing up and down in his seat like a child in the tantrums—which indeed he was. Everything had to be placed differently. All the silver must be changed. The preliminary dishes of the repast were disparaged. He lost his temper with the dark skinned waiter. Very suddenly he shrieked at the top of his voice, so suddenly and violently that every one was startled, "Schwarzer schwein!" It seemed that the waiter, whose eyes began to roll, comprehended, and Mr. William Murray, who will remember this occasion, tactfully took him outside, tipped him, and stated that we would wait on ourselves. We were seated again, but de Pachmann's excitement only increased. Nothing could calm him. Suddenly he whirled about in his chair, glaring malignantly. He thumped the table with his fist and shouted, "As for you, I know you! You are a damned hypocrite. What did you mean by inviting me to your house and then writing what you did about me in the paper? I know every word of it. My secretary's wife translated it for me. I understand you for what you are"—and by this time he was beyond control. Beside himself, in a paroxysm of temper, he was throwing the food, right and left, on the floor. The room was in turmoil. No one could stop him, until, with a violence that matched his master's, "Cieco" [sic] the secretary, also present, leaped to his feet, denounced de Pachmann in fantastical French which included the word "cochon" informing him that he was not ever to bring his wife's name into the conversation, and, slamming a door, rushed out of the room. De Pachmann looked up at the door with a degree of surprise and consternation impossible to indicate, and burst into tears. In a moment he was blindly seeking sympathy. "I did not mean what I said! Nothing! Nothing! I assure you! I have always admired you! You are a magnificent critic! There is only one greater. That is Mr. Hell (Hale) of Boston. It is like Liszt and de Pachmann, he is Liszt and you are de Pachmann. Everywhere that I go I shall tell them about you— in Paris, in London, in Rome. But I am very sad. I could tell you some very sad things. My life is hard. And will you please call Cieco. Tell him he must come. Tell him I must have hot milk for my coffee." Cieco must have been listening, for at the psychological moment he burst in. In no measured terms he called up the restaurant, ordered hot milk for coffee, and disappeared, again slamming the door noisily behind him. Somehow the evening was spoiled. . . . It was deemed best to leave him and go to the movies.

Downes also wrote about Pachmann and Cesco's interplay at that ill-fated dinner in his *Saturday Evening Post* article of 1930:

> He wept audibly, copiously, miserably. He was a poor old man, alone, without a friend. His very bodyguard, protector, and light of his eyes had rejected him in his need.

Everyone was understandably concerned that Pachmann might make a scene the next day at the concert and there would be no concerto performance. The conductor was the stern, no nonsense German Emil Mollenhauer who would not tolerate shenanigans. He had conducted for Pachmann before and knew what to expect. Downes continued the story in the *New York Times* obituary:

> But these fears were groundless. With the morning, his spirit purged and uplifted, apparently by the catharsis of the previous evening's drama, de Pachmann appeared, smiling from ear to ear, beaming upon every one. . . . This was the reward of the pilgrimage. In truth no one did play or ever will play, the Chopin F minor concerto as de Pachmann played it. It had under his fingers an unearthly beauty, and if it is said that when he sang on the keys the ineffable song of the larghetto angels wept over the golden bar of heaven, it is only a little more than the truth. Indeed, the music had a haunting and seraphic melancholy, a freedom from every thralldom of this world, only to be evoked by the supreme artists and the pure at heart. There sat that little fellow, who had the face of a French abbé and connoisseur of the eighteenth century, and the liniments of a monkey, mixed up in one, and he knew that beauty, and was at ease and confident in its company, and brought it down to earth for us.

On April 13, 1925, Pachmann gave his actual farewell concert in Carnegie Hall. Somehow, despite the critics and the grumbling of those who forever dismissed him as a mere showman, a respect, almost reverence for his eccentricities seemed to grow in the vast audience. It was a long and tiring Chopin program, and if he was only in places the great pianissimist, there were still those momentary tones where, as Olin Downes wrote in his review for the *New York Times* (April 14):

> Song floats on air with a delicious grace and waywardness past the telling . . . a virtuoso, at 76, of astonishing qualities, and on occasion a great poet of his instrument, has achieved and forgotten more than many a pianist ever knew.

Even Henderson begrudgingly bestowed praise, as reported in the *Musical Digest* (April 21):

> Attention was called by W. J. Henderson (Sun) in his review to the fact
> that thirteen years ago also Mr. de Pachmann gave an American "farewell"
> concert. He added, "Whatever Mr. de Pachmann's failings in regard to the
> greater Chopin, the velvet quality of his tone, the extreme delicacy of his
> touch, and the sensitive susceptibility and clarity of technic revealed by this
> octogenarian remain talents to marvel at."

Pachmann's final American tour marked the confused entry of this nineteenth century pianist into the twentieth century world of concert business. The conflation of the interests of the Baldwin Piano Company and vicious, cut-throat managers provided a *coup de grâce* to his career and his way of life. If the tour was his most successful financially, the cost to Pachmann personally was incalculable. He had begun it with energy and full of life force, and when it ended he was a shriveled old man resembling, as the *New York Telegraph* described him (April 14, 1925) the "mummified Seti in the British Museum." He never attempted another extended tour, and although he continued playing, his career really ended with this tour. Leonide said that his father had melted in America.

Chapter 30

The Man of a Thousand Farewells, 1925–1928

On May 31, 1925, the Pachmann entourage sailed for Europe, leaving the New World for the last time. Tired and ill, Pachmann almost never left his cabin, but once on his way to join Cesco and the others for a meal, he ran into someone he had known earlier in the United States. This was the writer Konrad Bercovici, an interesting figure now forgotten who was almost as much a character as Pachmann. Part Rumanian, Jewish and Gypsy, he sported long hair and a flowing mustache and looked as exotic as his background. He had worked as a painter at the top of the Eiffel Tower, as a circus wrestler and a blacksmith, won prizes in bicycle and boat races and was a fueler at the first automobile race from Paris to Madrid. In between, he had managed to study the organ with Charles-Marie Widor in Paris, teaching the instrument in the United States when he emigrated there in 1905, and giving recitals. He finally found his true métier as a florid writer shortly before the First World War, and his vignettes published in the *New York Post* were highly esteemed. As a foreign correspondent for that paper he published interviews with Woodrow Wilson, Georges Clemenceau, Kemal Atatürk and Paderewski, among others. Later he was associated with Dorothy Parker and the other members of the fabled Algonquin Round Table. In Hollywood he worked as a screenwriter and even won a settlement from Charles Chaplin, who initially denied Bercovici had assisted in work on the script for the film "The Great Dictator."

In his long essay entitled "Little Stories of Big Men" that was published in *Good Housekeeping* in January 1934, he regaled readers with intimate stories of some of his acquaintances among the great, including Pachmann. The parts about Pachmann range from accurate, to exaggerated, to wildly fanciful. Bercovici was onboard ship with Pachmann and begins the tale as Pachmann is making his last trip back to Europe, exhausted by the tour:

> Only his feverish eyes were alive. His voice had the faraway ring of a man approaching the beyond. The corners of his large, mobile mouth sagged. His hands resting on the coverlet of the bed were still and lifeless. It was difficult to imagine that these same nerveless fingers had played so heavenly, so flaw-lessly; that those ten claws of bone were de Pachmann's "singing fingers." He took it for granted that I had heard every one of his concerts; in New York, in San Francisco, in Chicago, even in Vancouver. "I was great in Los Angeles, wasn't I? I played like a god. I was still better in Chicago. And in Boston I outdid my Chicago success. Why are you smiling? If God played the piano, He wouldn't play it much better than I do. Not much."

Bercovici happened to mention the name of the hotel in Paris where he would be staying when they landed in Europe. Pachmann said he knew the hotel, he had stayed there himself when he was younger, and poor. Was the café Deux Magots still there, the pianist asked?

> I assured him that the Deux Magots was still there and that I, too, had idled away many an hour looking at the moss-covered stones of the gray old church half hidden by the elm and acacia trees. "Still there! Ah, if I could only go there once more. Sit on the terrace and drink coffee and look and look. . . . But I can't." "Why not?" "They'll give me no peace. I'd be recognized in a minute, stared at, pointed at, mobbed by Polish pianists begging me to listen to them and by a thousand fools wanting to speak to me. They'd have to call the police out to hold them at a distance. Don't I know it? It's the penalty of celebrity."

Finally landed in Paris and installed in his room at the hotel, Bercovici received a telephone call from the front desk:

> I was told that an old monsieur was waiting downstairs to see me. "Is he alone?" I inquired. "No. Three or four younger gentlemen are with him." I ran down the stairs. De Pachmann was smiling at me. "Take me to the Deux Magots. We two, just we two." He spoke to his secretaries. The men bowed and left. "There. It's done. Where is your hat?" he asked. "I am all right as I am." . . . To disguise himself he had put on a shining, new corduroy costume, a large-brimmed hat, and a long black cape. When we were on the street, he said gleefully: "Perfect disguise, eh? Nobody has recognized me so far." His suite of secretaries and valets were on the sidewalk following us at a dozen paces. "Look. Will you please tell them to leave us by ourselves," I insisted . . . this time he ordered them sharply to leave us. We sat down at a table on the terrace facing the church and ordered coffee and croissants. De Pach-mann had pulled his hat over his eyes. The muscles of his face had relaxed.

His mouth was no longer shaped ready to grin but to smile. I could see him getting younger. He must have been a handsome fellow in his young days. He was happy to be himself again. . . . He reached for my hand and tapped it lightly. "It's so good to be here alone, free, without being burdened by my celebrity. I will come back again and again. No one stares at me. No one notices me. It is too wonderful to be true. You had a great idea." One after the other the tables were being occupied by men and women, young and old coming alone and in twos and threes. Some glanced in all directions to greet old acquaintances, and others plunged into their morning papers, dunking their croissants in their coffee while they read. It was the typical Parisian morning clientele of the Deux Magots—shopkeepers, clerks, writers, news-papermen artists idling away a half hour before the day's work was begun. Our little, round, three legged iron table received no more attention than any other table. At the second coffee de Pachmann pushed his hat a bit farther back on his forehead, so that his face was fully exposed, and looked around. No one recognized him. He lost his smile. His mouth became set again. He was Vladimir de Pachmann, the great Vladimir de Pachmann. He turned this way and that and fixed with insolent eyes those who casually looked at him. "I'll come back here again," he said. "It's wonderful. I won't even have to disguise myself. They don't know me. I am one of thousand." He said this, but his mouth began to twitch. His fingers tapped nervously on the table. To attract attention, he rose and sat down again. He spoke loudly. The good Parisians paid no attention to the little old man. They went on reading their papers and drinking their cafe in the sweet morning air perfumed by the acacias in full bloom. Suddenly de Pachmann began to scream: "They don't recognize me! They don't know Vladimir de Pachmann is in their midst—The great Vladimir! I won't stay here another minute. I have gone to the trouble of disguising myself, and still they don't recognize me! I will not stay here another minute. No! no, no! I will leave Paris with the first train out, no matter where it goes, and never come back again! I am insulted . . . and it's all your fault!" He snapped his fingers. His four secretaries and two valets appeared from somewhere. A limousine drew up from nowhere. The uniformed chauffeur held the door open. The six men formed a guard of honor, three men or either side, from our table to the car at the curb and held up the passers-by until the great little man had risen majestically from his chair. He turned around, sneered at the people sitting at the tables, and walked slowly across the sidewalk to his automobile. The Parisians looked over their newspapers until the car was gone, smiled, and then continued to dunk croissants in their coffee.

⌒

Alice and Virgilio returned to Italy while Cesco traveled with Pachmann to London, where recording sessions were scheduled at the studios of His Master's Voice. The process of recording electrically had arrived early in 1925. Fred Gaisberg, who had enticed Pachmann to make recordings in 1907, now supervised Pachmann's first electrical sessions in June and December 1925, as the pianist and Cesco were enjoying a leisurely stay in England. Unfortunately Pachmann was in sad shape, still not recovered from the debilitating American tour, with the result that these discs turned out to be his worst. They have been the most readily available and extensively distributed of the pianist's recordings, for he talks during some of them. They are one of the main causes for Pachmann's low reputation among some musicians today, and reinforce the idea that his fame stemmed from his eccentric behavior and not his playing. In a short article for a British publication Pachmann wrote:

> When I made gramophone records not long ago I was particularly requested to talk as I played, expounding the beauties of the passages. In fact, a little audience was provided in the studio to make me feel at home as I played![1]

The executives at the H.M.V. Company unquestionably encouraged his worst traits and as a consequence, unwittingly helped to destroy his reputation through succeeding decades.

⌒⌐

The exhaustion and tension prevalent in the United States, reflected in Pachmann's manic fragmentation revealed in the Harold Bauer dinner story, apparently resolved to a degree after a few months among his English friends. He recaptured much of his equanimity and there was a corresponding return of energy and spirit, though in appearance he remained old.

The London *Evening Standard* asked ten eminent men to tell the reasons for their long life and robust health in 1925 (the article was reprinted in the *New York Times* on January 24, 1926). Pachmann seemed recovered and defying age:

> There are for me two things in the world. First and ever, my music. When I sit down to play I am Pachmann the musician. But when I sit down to the table to eat I am Pachmann the gourmet. . . . All my life I have eaten and drunk as I willed, and for the rest of my life I intend to do the same. On my deathbed, if I have the strength, I hope to be able to eat a last good hearty meal. . . . I eat for enjoyment, for the love of food. I do not over-eat. I am an artist, and to the artist what he loves is something to be treated with respect, something not to be abused. For diets and strict rules of feeding and living I have a monstrous contempt. . . . Consider me today. Seventy-seven, but old age has not yet discovered me. I can play for hours without fatigue . . . though I sleep very little—perhaps four, perhaps five hours—I am full of energy. I cannot remember ever having been seriously ill in my life—certainly I have never had indigestion. Today I eat perhaps less than at one time. . . . For

breakfast, strong coffee and rolls, and two brown-shelled, lightly boiled eggs. Rice or spaghetti, some stewed meat, cooked according to the custom of the country—a white vegetable, fresh fruit, and strawberry jam which I love to eat out of the spoon is a delicious lunch for me when it is accompanied by good red wine. For two years I was in "dry" America, but I always had my red wine. At 4 o'clock I take a cup of tea when I am in England, or a glass of milk fresh from the cow—if I happen to be in the country—near a farm. Then in the evening I am happy to eat, after my soup, two boiled eggs again, some more meat tenderly cooked—my teeth are not as good as once they were, and I refuse to have new ones put in my mouth—a special home-made cake which must only be made by my perfect Italian cook who travels with me everywhere, coffee and wine, and perhaps a liqueur. Before I retire, a little something—chocolate, or a cake or a crust of bread. I never eat before I am to play, but after a concert I will have a fine supper, with champagne and all the things I like. My favorite vegetable is the giant California asparagus, and my favorite fruit a big, juicy watermelon. I am happy to sit alone for an hour with a watermelon. I can eat it all. The doctors will say that the nicotine is bad for you. Well—I still smoke eight cigars every day. The doctors say you must have exercise, walk in the air or play with the ball. Well, I have never taken any exercise in my life unless you count the four hours a day practice at the piano. I have a beautiful little summer house at Fabriano, in Italy, with lovely gardens, but I never walk out in them. All the fresh air I want comes to me through the window. So there is my life. And I am 77. But I do not expect every one to follow my example, for, after all, I am Pachmann the unique. I laugh at your doctors.

Pachmann's success had been so great that he was awash with money, and could spend almost like a king. Australian bass-baritone Peter Dawson witnessed a display that he described in his autobiography:

He was staying at the same hotel as myself, and after his concert he entered the dining-room. To my astonishment I learnt that his food was prepared by his own man. He travelled with his own dinner service of gold. Sure enough he ate off gold plates in my presence. Presently there was a heck of a row, and he was spitting from his mouth—all over the floor—the contents of a glass of champagne that he obviously found distasteful. "Bring the manager!" he cried at the waiter. When the manager arrived, Pachmann asked him whether he had nothing better than that champagne to drink. The manager tasted the wine and, to his credit, was quite firm in his view that the champagne was "Quite good. In fact, Mr. Pachmann, it is very good." "Good! I will show you what it is good for." And he proceeded to empty the bottle into flower vases that were around the room. "Now, sir," he said quietly, "what other wine have you?" The manager suggested a fine old port. This was brought. The manager waited while the *maestro* tried it. To the relief of the manager—and incidentally to all the other diners—Pachmann smacked his lips and with a broad smile said: "Ah, this is indeed the wine good! It is beautiful, beautiful." And silence reigned over the room. When the manager, commenting on the fact that Pachmann had his own chef, carried his own dinner service and drank the most expensive wines, remarked, "You live very well, Mr. Pachmann" . . . replied "Why should I, Pachmann, not live well? Do not kings live well? What are kings but figureheads?"

He played recitals at Queen's Hall on June 15 and 24, 1925, and the *Times* (June 17 and 25) reported that a couple of his performances at the first concert "slipped the leash . . . and made havoc of the rhythm and that at the second recital he kept mumbling about Liszt while he played mostly Chopin. The second review pointed out that he could still play smaller works "with an exquisite shading . . . at the end he paid tribute to his idol by a performance of Liszt's Rigoletto Fantasia, which was an astonishing piece of virtuosity." There were bad reviews, and one writer jumped to his defense:

> Leave de Pachmann alone! There are plenty of other targets for critical errors beside an old man still eager, after seventy-seven years, to tell the world that there is no God but Chopin and that de Pachmann is his prophet.[2]

In November he played in Manchester, where the critics had always been so unstinting in their praise that it would not be remiss to claim it as the "English Boston." Samuel Langford, longtime critic of the *Manchester Guardian*, was the counterpart to the *Boston Herald*'s Philip Hale. His very long, glowing review pictured a great artist in his full powers:

> Pachmann was in good vein for his recital at the Brand Lane Concerts, and played more finely than he has done here for some years . . . at the end there came the B flat minor Scherzo, "the best of all," as Pachmann put it, and in this superb work Pachmann at once rose to greater heights. As a feat of velocity and polished execution it was astonishing. . . . Then came a dazzling performance of the "Black Note" study with the middle section given in a marvelous lyrical manner, and the final octaves taken in contrary motion. It was this piece also, we think, which he enriched in the harmonies by a superbly sustained ninth—a real stroke of genius. . . . We had almost forgotten what we thought was the greatest musical feat of the recital. Few would associate Pachmann with Brahms, yet it was in the composer's rugged "Rhapsody" in B minor that we found him wrestling, and that quite triumphantly, with heroic ideas.

Perhaps Pachmann was playing better than in previous months. Five months had elapsed since his return from the United States, and he had time to rest. He agreed to play a few concerts in the provinces. Fred Gaisberg remembered (in an October 1943 article in *Gramophone* magazine) a story he was told of Pachmann's recital in Bradford:

> The train arrived late at the Bradford station . . . the porter dropped the bags and disappeared. As other porters came along excitedly de Pachmann would say to them, "I am the great de Pachmann, quick, get me a taxi or we will be late for the concert!!" and they would rush off in search of a conveyance. No taxi came and still they waited, while from around the corner swung a noisy steam-roller approaching in their direction. Pallottelli said: "Pappy [*sic*], here's your taxi." De Pachmann angrily turned on him, paused a while and then burst into laughter.

In the Dome in Brighton Colin Defries, the son of his old friends, sat among the stage seats. He told the author: "In the middle of a piece he happened to turn round and spot me. He stopped playing, got up and came and kissed me on both cheeks, telling the audience as he did this: 'I knew him before he was born!'" (Defries later became the first husband of pianist Moura Lympany.)

In Blackburn at King George's Hall, soprano Luisa Tetrazzini had to cancel a concert. Pachmann was asked to allow the soprano to appear at his subsequent recital there, scheduled for three weeks later on November 9, "to compensate for the disappointment" as one article reported. Having played the first half, after the intermission, he walked out leading Tetrazzini by the hand. All 3,500 people in the hall cheered as Pachmann and Tetrazzini glanced at each other, and then embraced repeatedly. Pachmann had even gone to the train station to meet her. Her accompanist Ivor Newton described the event in his memoirs:

> Pachmann . . . had been provided with a large and very expensive bunch of grapes to present to her. Inevitably, he succeeded in dropping them on the grimy station platform.

Newton tells how, during their public embraces, Pachmann, "not content with kissing her hand, kissed the entire length of her arm." The Chopinzee introduced the accompanist to the audience, telling them Newton had ". . . the touch of an angel. And he explained the qualities of my playing, which so far as I know he had never heard, at some length." Newton wrote further. "Pachmann cultivated his eccentricities—no one can say whether consciously or not. . . . Asked to refrain from kissing porters at English railway stations, he declared that to tip them instead would be too expensive." Newton described Pachmann's paranoia backstage, having just read that Paderewski was scheduled to play a Chopin recital, quoting him saying . . . "There ought to be law to stop that sort of thing. . . . No one else was present except Tetrazzini, who was not interested, so that although this was precisely the sort of thing he said to his devoted public, he could hardly have been talking for effect . . ." Newton continued: "Any pianist who listened to his playing would find his bejeweled filigree in Chopin unforgettable."

The warmth of the British public was reciprocated by the pianist. He was now ending his recitals with a florid arrangement of "God Save the King." Sometimes members of the audience were so moved they would cry out, "Thank you! Thank you!"

One unidentified clipping reported him replying:

> I am sorry but I am to play no more, for I have reached a great age and it is best thought that I should live quietly. I have always had a great liking for the British people among whom I have been very happy.

When this short tour of Britain was over, he returned to Italy and what was supposed to be retirement. This time it was not to the Villa Gioia in Fabriano, but to a new home that Cesco had built for them on the outskirts of Rome, using part of his million dollar share of the proceeds from the American tour. The villa was located on the site of an old aspirin factory that was razed—the property had been owned by Alice's father. It had a protected garden where they hoped the old pianist would stroll.

Canny Cesco knew that Pachmann would have to be gently eased into retirement, and he tried to accomplish this by placing that most fantastic of all pianists in an imaginative setting. He commissioned Duilio Cambellotti, a well-known and highly placed interior designer, decorator and stage set designer of the time, to design and decorate Pachmann's private floor in the villa. Dividing a huge studio like a church choir, placing the piano on a platform and seating the listeners below on cushioned benches like church pews, Cambellotti let his fancy roam. He painted a sequence of wild animals around the walls: bears with velvet paws, tigers with glistening eyes, and gazelles with ears aroused, all done in art deco style in frontal views or graceful silhouettes against the foliage, frozen and immobile as if hypnotized by music.

Amid this scene with its exotic fantasy, Pachmann would give little private concerts surrounded by friends. Life was pleasant but dull, and Pachmann broke the monotony by agreeing to play in public again at an all-Chopin benefit concert in Rome on March 27, 1926. That was all it took to rekindle Pachmann's career. It has been suggested that Cesco just could not stop exploiting Pachmann and so more concerts were planned. The author rejects this notion, for Pachmann just could not stop playing, and he required only a small push from Cesco. He played next on December 3, 1926, a recital in the intimate auditorium of Venice's Benvenuto Marcello Conservatory. The *Gazzetta di Venezia* reported (December 4) that he addressed the audience in French:

> "I'm no longer young, I'm 78 years and four months old. Memory goes with time and one loses one's hair, but I hope I have enough gray matter left to give a good performance." He played with great showmanship.[3]

Spending the summer of 1927 in Fabriano, Pachmann was visited by several musicians, including pianist Carlo Zecchi and composer Ottorino Respighi. Soon the "Man of a Thousand Farewells" was back in London at the age of seventy-nine. Some details can be gleaned from an undated, unidentified clipping from a British newspaper:[4]

PLAYING TO LIVE—Pachmann's Return—Pining Away in Retirement

Vladimir de Pachmann, the pianist who is 79, retired two years ago to his villa on the sunny slopes of the Roman hills, but he is back in London, to play again to English audiences. He has returned to the concert platform because he was pining away through inactivity. Gone were the faces of his admirers; gone was the necessity to practise hour after hour at his beloved piano. He became ill. A strange lassitude overcame him. Doctors could find nothing organically wrong with him. Then one day a young Italian physician said to Pachmann's manager "He misses the faces, the applause, the music that enchanted his admirers. He must play again." A woman friend asked him one day if he would not emerge from his retirement to play at her home in commemoration of Chopin. He played, and his strange sickness was banished. Now he hopes to play until he dies.

Another unidentified clipping quoted him: "They say it is wonderful to play when I am nearing eighty. I do not feel eighty. Mostly I feel forty-five. Never shall I stop. I must play if only for myself. . . . When I stop playing, I shall be dead!" He was old, but he couldn't stop playing. Easy venues were found in London. On October 30, 1927, he inaugurated a new series of "supper entertainment" concerts at the elegant Mayfair Hotel with a Chopin recital. The intimate atmosphere was perfect for his unique piano entertainment, with his chatter and small pieces. It's amazing he hadn't played supper concerts before.

The old artist was still capable of occasionally playing beautifully. On November 3, 1927, he visited the smaller hall at Queen's Hall and His Master's Voice recorded him there playing Chopin's Nocturne in E minor, op. 72, and Mendelssohn's Prelude in E minor—his best electrical recording. At last the *morbidezza* sound of his piano tone was successfully captured on recordings, and the two are among his greatest recordings of all. Pachmann reminded Stanley Markham, who interviewed the pianist shortly before he turned eighty, that Busoni had written: "Why should there be any wonder at de Pachmann's death-defying age? He has lived for his art alone, therefore, his art is to him eternally faithful." This appeared in Markham's *Music of All Nations*. Pachmann was quoted in another unidentified clipping:

> There are no people like you Londoners. You are sincere. You do not flatter. You say what you mean in that blunt way you have. Ah London, you are changing, they say. That is a pity for I fell in love with the London I knew, how many years ago? More than forty. I shall never see your new city, for now I do not walk about as I did in those years hour after hour. I spend all my time with my music. . . . But it is happiness for me to be here again.

He was still news. The *Daily Chronicle* interviewed him and induced him to defend his platform behavior; excerpts were printed in the *Literary Digest* on November 19, 1927. He seems to have regained focus, leaving posterity the most insightful analysis of his unique platform behavior of all:

> If I am pleased, I must not smile; if I am angry, I must hide my feelings! Nonsense! One would do better to listen to a concert on an automatic piano! . . . A stockbroker from London once wrote to me asking why I indulged in 'preliminary fuss and adjustments of the piano stool' at my concerts. . . . Ah, my friend, I think you must be one of those who would put a penny in the slot and turn on the music! Art and business are very different. . . . I turn the piano stool this way and that because it is necessary. I can not interpret the music of the great composers until everything is to my liking. If the piano stool is too high, I am distracted all the time I am playing, and my performance falls short of perfection. Often my audiences take me too seriously. I am not always Pachmann the great musician and friend of Liszt and Wagner. Sometimes I am Pachmann the jester. I creep on to the platform and look at the great audience. "What!" I exclaim aloud. "I have been playing in Britain for more than forty years, and you still come to hear me? Marvelous!" Then I turn to the piano and give it a start. "A piano! What is that for? Surely you do not expect an old man like me to play? My fingers are stiff, and I have not practised for six years!" The audience is laughing. I like to hear them laugh, and get angry if they do not respond. I know that they have come, perhaps from a hurried luncheon, and have had to scramble for a bus in the rain. Naturally they are deprest! [*sic*] But when they laugh, then I can take them into my confidence, introduce them to Liszt and Chopin and Beethoven. When people laugh they forget to sit straight up in their seats, and become more human. Most people think that music and humor can not walk hand in hand. Why not? Wagner and many other great giants delighted in a little musical horseplay. So sometimes when I play, I am merry. I hold my right hand high on a rest and when it seems too late, strike the note just in time. Then I turn round and smile at the shade of Liszt, saying

"You dared not do that!" I do not boast when I say that to-day I am the only pianist with a great platform personality. My so-called eccentricities, my little jokes, my whirling of the piano stool, my smiles and my grimaces, they are all the expression of my personality. Paderewski is grand and majestic—but the others are all wooden. They are afraid to be human with music. It is the human touch that binds me to my music and my audiences. I love them, and I want them to love me.

⤳

In 1928 Lionel Powell conceived the idea of celebrating Pachmann's fiftieth anniversary as an artist, a "Jubilee" commemorating the five decades of concerts that began in Leipzig in 1878. It was decided that at age eighty Pachmann would return to many European cities, some of which he had not played in since his youth. . . . Budapest, Leipzig, Berlin, Vienna, London and Paris. In Berlin, Vienna and London he played twice. The first concert was in Budapest on March 4, 1928. He hadn't played there since 1884, when Liszt attended his recital. Pachmann of course compared himself to Liszt in addressing his Hungarian audience in 1928: "Liszt was bigger and stronger but no better, for now I have surpassed him in the technique of my left hand." The *Budapesti Hírlap*'s unidentified correspondent wrote the next day:

A bit of musical history was made Sunday evening on the stage of the Vigadó with the appearance of a short, elderly gentleman: the eighty year old Vladimir Pachmann . . . the spirits of Liszt, Chopin, Bülow and Tausig just seem to emanate from around this tiny little man; his light technique, fresh rhythm, and soft, warm touch are tough competition for any Chopin virtuoso. Only his dynamics were not what they used to be, the piano did not reverberate as it once did. When Maestro Pachmann took the stage, the first thing he did was complain about the lighting . . . he pointed to the piano stool, and then his own bottom, shaking his head in disapproval, whereupon a soft pillow was quickly produced for him. But the real fun was yet to come. As he played, he kept explaining . . . how Bülow or Liszt had played these pieces. . . . When it came time to play a more difficult passage, he would warn the audience ahead of time . . . in effect he talked throughout the entire concert, mimicked even more, and did his utmost to feign terror at having to face the more difficult pieces, in an overt and humorous manner. The audience laughed and cheered, as it could sense an event through the comedic veil . . . the spark of Pachmann's flickering genius bursting into flame . . . one final time.[5]

There was nearly a riot in the hall at the end of the first Berlin recital, on March 15. The audience stormed the platform, eager to get closer to Pachmann, perhaps to be better able to hear his talking. Hugo Leichtentritt, the eminent German scholar and critic whose first book (1905) was on Chopin, sent a report that was published in *MC* on April 12:

> dear old Pachmann . . . was nothing short of sensational. . . . The audience besieged the platform. . . . When finally the police arrived to restore order in the auditorium, Pachmann eloquently pleaded for his admirers, saying they were all his friends, even if they had paid for their tickets! Quite apart from all fun, however, Pachmann must still be rated as a great and unique artist, in spite of his eighty years. His Chopin playing, though lacking in power and passion, still breathes a poetry, an indescribable charm of tenderness, which seems to have almost vanished from the world.

The *Berliner Tageblatt* the next day took pains to point out that the playing redeemed the antics:

> He talked while playing and the immense audience was enraptured, for the commentary was perfectly fitting, even admirable. If this old man . . . were not such a gifted artist, we would rightly feel ashamed at these specimens of cabaret trickery. But despite all this, here was Chopin played in the purest way, with a miraculous touch, with all the sweet, dreamy, nervous charm, which we look forward to, all too often in vain, in concerts of Chopin's music. How many artists strive in vain, with priest-like solemnity, for higher rites of inspiration! And here is a character out of E. Th. A. Hoffmann, who takes neither himself nor the world very seriously, and has been given the grace of mastery. Today he has no rival as a performer of Chopin, and one therefore excuses the talking.[6]

He was not received nearly as kindly in Vienna, where his antics bewildered the audience. In the middle of a piece his memory went, and he stopped dead, telling them "You must excuse me. It is a very long piece and I am a little tired." (This was reported in Olin Downes's March 15, 1930 *Saturday Evening Post* article.)

On May 20, 1928, he played a recital in London, which was reviewed on the 24th in the *Glasgow Herald* by Ernest Newman, who wrote that he "still plays astonishingly well for a man of eighty, and his platform ways are as amusing as ever." Pachmann hadn't played a public concert in Paris since 1883, and he was nervous about a fashionable benefit recital he had agreed to play in the Salle Gaveau on June 4, 1928. A reporter for the Paris edition of the *New York Herald* visited him while he was practicing in his hotel on May 30, and his report was printed the next day:

> "When did you hear me last?" he asked before any question could be put to him. "Ah, in Boston in 1923? I am much better now. You shall hear," he added. "I study every day . . . in Paris I shall not talk when I play. Everybody

expects it, so I shall be like Liszt." He imitated the king of virtuosi, throwing back his head and startling the piano with a ripple from treble to bass. Then he laughed aloud. Before he played the [G minor] Ballade, he pointed to a chord in the second bar. "Chopin did not write that note," he said accusingly. "Once before the war, I was in Vienna and they showed me Chopin's manuscript of this Ballade. It was 10,000 francs. Too dear for me then. Now, I would give 50,000 for it. But (and he laughed once more) I remembered it. Every note of it, and that C was not there. And this is a good edition, too, the Klingsworth [*sic*]." . . . He played the Etude, Op. 25, No. 3 from memory, and then reached for No. 4. "That is the best," he said, "Wagner kissed my hand after I had played that Etude. I was a young man, then, thirty-five years old and Papa Liszt was sitting in the corner. He was jealous. . . . Do not miss the concert. It will be colossal! Divine!"

⤳

Pachmann's obsession with the idea that Wagner had kissed his hand persisted, as did another obsession, with Harold Bauer. They were both in Paris but Pachmann's letter to Bauer somehow got written on stationery from the San Francisco Conservatory. It was a rare day when Pachmann wrote any letter; Bauer included a transcript of the teasing missive, dated June 1, 1928, in his autobiography. The original letter still exists in the Bauer collection at the Library of Congress—it is a rare example of Pachmann's deliberate attempt at florid, "artistic" penmanship:

My dear Mr. Bauer-Pauer (Pauer-Bauer?)
This is only to accompany these pictures and send you my best greetings. I regretted not to see you lately, as I admire you as a good pianist, really *good*, indeed, when you play well it is almost as good as when I play badly and I think how better you could play if you had more opportunity to hear Me and to have My advice once in a while. But, in spite of that, my dear Mr. Bauer-Pauer (Pauer-Bauer?) you certainly are a *good* pianist and I wanted to tell you my sincerest appreciation. I hope you will have a nice vacation and manage some day to come and study with Me and learn to play the Piano, as I do.
Yours Sincerely Vladimir de Pachmann

⤳

The Paris concert, a benefit under the patronage of Marshal Foch and the American ambassador, was an important event of the Paris season. The hall was decorated with roses, and a large contingent of society appeared in evening clothes. The souvenir program for the recital was in the form of a fan with Pachmann's photo on one face and the printed program on the reverse. Someone sent one of these in advance of the concert to Francis Planté, now ninety years old and retired on his estate in southern France. Planté wrote Pachmann:

> It is you who I thank for this lovely souvenir, so cleverly and charmingly composed with your autograph. Henri Etlin wrote me that you still play marvelously. How I should like to have heard in my far away hermitage some echoes of those enchanting moments. I would have thought myself in Berlin again, years ago. . . . I repeat once more my enthusiasm as an artist and my affection as a friend. F. Planté[7]

Many members of the American colony in Paris were there also, including a twenty-five year old soprano named Alice Tully, in town for her own French debut. Leonide attended the recital with his mother, now a sixty-four year old widow, but still chic and attractive. He remembered his father telling the audience, "I promised my manager I wouldn't talk, but I must tell you [and here he made a characteristic gesture with his arms to embrace everyone.] Oh, it's wonderful to play again in Paris. You know why I am so healthy? I've always eaten the best French food and drunk the best Bordeaux. See the strength I have." In the first selection, Chopin's G minor Ballade, he took the opening octave passage in one hand, not divided between the hands as usual. "See?" He shouted, "One hand! . . . Not bad for a man of eighty!"

His playing of the Mazurka, Op. 24, No. 4 elicited an ovation. But not everyone was happy. Nearly hidden in the rear of the hall was Maggie. Monsieur Gaveau, head of the prominent piano manufacturing firm, had invited her to attend the recital as an honored guest, but she declined any show, fearing that Pachmann might see her and become upset. She sat in the back with her son, and her memories. While everyone else was laughing and applauding, she wept. Leonide told the author "And she was not weeping because his playing was so beautiful." Perhaps Maggie's tears were prompted by witnessing the caricature her former husband had become as a man, and from the contrast between the playing she remembered, and what she was hearing now.

A young actress named Hyacinthe Goujon was in the audience and wrote about the experience to author Elliot Paul. She went backstage to congratulate Pachmann afterward, but was struck speechless with fear and admiration. She wrote pages of fevered reminiscence, including:

> He realized what my silence and vertigo meant. . . . What he did was take my hand, and to the consternation of his manager, an offensive little man, and the throng of admirers, he led me into a small room near by and locked the door. There was a piano, a bench and one piano chair. Through the door and the walls I could hear mild clamboring outside. He paid no attention.

... "Which?—For you" he asked. "The nocturne," I said, surprised that my voice was audible. . . . Then he played the nocturne as exquisitely as before.

The author asked Leonide about this supposed incident thirty-three years after the fact. He said he could not remember it having happened. Perhaps this was the very last example of a fantasy of a VladyFlapper, proof that Pachmann could still work his magic on the imagination of certain women even at age eighty.

The Jubilee Tour included a few Italian cities in which Pachmann had never played before—Ancona and Treviso—as well as Venice, where he was remembered from a year earlier. Cesco was worried that no one would attend in the other cities, but he was wrong, and both halls were filled. On October 21st he played his actual farewell concert in London's Albert Hall. The *Times* reported: "His musical programme was diminutive, so as to leave plenty of time for talk. His Chopin can still be exquisite . . . his touch remains perfect." The review faulted him for playing too fast in some pieces and for putting an extra beat in a bar of the E minor Prelude, but ended: "His most exquisite Chopin was heard in the Mazurkas, when to that touch was added the perfectly poised rhythm."

The reader will not be surprised to learn that this was not Pachmann's last concert. There was still one more farewell left. Lionel Powell asked Cesco to persuade the old man to play a charity concert on November 18 in aid of Sir Thomas Beecham's League of Opera, at London's largest theatre, the Coliseum.

There was nothing sad about this last concert, no suggestion of an old artist eulogizing his past. Except that it was his actual final concert, there was nothing different from his other "entertainments." The gales of laughter and applause, his smiles of delight at his own playing, and those beautiful moments, were not unlike his other concerts. The unbridled gaiety in the vast theatre made the applause sound like cannon volleys. Perhaps it affected the old maestro for after he finished playing a Chopin Mazurka, he told the audience: "and this is the way it should be danced!" And he danced a few steps as the audience roared its approval.

When the last encore had been played, the audience rushed to the front, unable to contain themselves. They surged onto the platform and surrounded him. As the *Daily Express* chronicled in its headlines the next day:

PACHMANN DANCES . . . ADMIRERS MOB HIM FROM THE STAGE . . .
PACHMANN BIDS FAREWELL

Chapter 31

A Relic from the Past, 1928–1954

Pachmann retired to Italy to live in opulence and style, spending his remaining years with winters in Rome and summers in Fabriano. Cesco took a number of spontaneous snapshots of the pianist during his retirement, and they provide a revealing and unparalleled documentation of the aging artist.

Often musicians sent pupils to seek his advice, which he hated. He thought his opinions would be misunderstood and they usually were. During his long career he had avoided amateurs and those seeking "professional advice." But in his old age, he had nothing else to do but to listen to them.

Konrad Bercovici's article in *Good Housekeeping* (January 1934) recounted one occasion he witnessed at this time:

While I was visiting with De Pachmann, in his apartment, shortly before his death, a young man came in bearing a letter of introduction from Leopold Godowsky. De Pachmann did not ask his visitor to be seated, but threw the letter at me and said: "You read it to me, please. Can't find my glasses." In that letter Godowsky introduced the young man very warmly to the master and begged his friend to listen to the young pianist-composer. At the bottom of the letter he had set down a postscript, "The young man is very modest." De Pachmann hit the ceiling. He jumped up and threw his hands in the air, twirled his arms as if they were wings of a windmill, and danced like a dervish the while he cursed himself and the world in the choicest curses of a half-dozen languages. The antics of the aged master were amusing, but my heart bled for the poor young victim standing there, pale as a ghost, kneading his hat and not knowing what to do next. He looked at me, looked at the door, and was about to bolt when I said, "Master, that postscript merely said that the young man is very modest." "Shut up!" De Pachmann yelled, and buttonholing the fellow, he grinned into his face and demanded: "What have you already accomplished to be modest about? Ha, tell me! Sit down at the piano and show me what you are so modest about." Whether it was due to the reception De Pachmann had given him or to the fact that Godowsky, who is the kindest of all men, had over praised him, the young man showed less than mediocre talent. When he had gone, De Pachmann drank four glasses of water in succession and said to me: "I am not modest yet, and he is already very modest! The impudence!"

Thus ended the poor young man's chances for studying with Pachmann. Perhaps later he would claim that he had actually studied with the master, based on the one desultory meeting. He would not have been the first to bend the truth in that way. Although he had actually taught a few pupils (apart from Maggie, mostly handsome young men), Pachmann's legacy was not pedagogy. Still he bemoaned the fact that his art was going to disappear with him, that he never found a pupil who would or could carry on his tradition.

In the fall of 1928 Pachmann, now eighty, became ill with an enlarged prostate. The doctors were optimistic and told him that if he had an operation he would live to a very great age, for his whole family had lived long lives. But superstitious and childlike, he felt that it would affect his hands and destroy his playing. He would not submit to it. For the next four years he had to have a male nurse take care of him. This man, a relative of Cesco's, ingratiated himself with the old pianist. Apparently an Iago-like character, he was acting in his own interests as well. He eventually got Pachmann to sign over title to his jewel collection! Later Cesco was able to break this agreement in court.

Although Pachmann did not suffer, the disease was debilitating. Cesco would sooth him: "Don't worry, Papi, you will live to be one hundred." "Do you really think so? My legs are getting thinner." But when he felt better: "Yes, I think I will live to be one hundred . . . and then we go to London and give a concert!"

It became an obsession, and before retiring each night he would murmur, "I have studied the London program. Tomorrow we will write to Powell to arrange a concert." But one tomorrow followed the next, and that one became the following, and thus the months vanished in a sad ceremony. Leonard Liebling reported in the October 19, 1929, *MC*:

De Pachmann . . . is confined to his bed in Rome and spends his time dictating his memoirs. . . . He once said to me: "All pianists may be divided into two divisions, first class and second class. I comprise the first class."

Alice was writing down the pianist's memories, but nothing ever came of the memoirs.

On January 29, 1925, the *Musical Leader* reported that the pianist had said:

> When will I stop playing? Ah, when I cannot play my Godowsky, the most difficult things, the most difficult things . . . then I will quit. Then it is time to stop. . . . When I stop I will wait for death. . . . I came from God. . . . I should not be afraid to return.

When he felt stronger, he would go to the piano and play for friends or Cesco and Alice. In a contemplative mood he would tell them: "Like all men I shall go to another land. What a company of friends I shall find there— Liszt, Wagner, Chopin. Yet they have never really left me. They stand round my piano when I play and although no one can see them, I talk to them. How can I play but marvelously when they are standing at my side?"

A friend of Cesco's known only by the initials "M. G." visited the Villa Gioia at this time and wrote a reminiscence of the occasion for *La Nuova Italia Musicale* (January 1933), an issue of the magazine devoted entirely to Pachmann. It gives a glimpse of the artist in his extreme old age:

> It was at that time that I happened to meet Wladimir de Pachmann. He lived in Fabriano, in Cesco Pallottelli's "Villa Gioia" which did not fail to live up to its inviting name; a beautiful and solid house, built in the ancient style on the top of a hill, it overlooked the hollow in which Fabriano lay, with its dark-colored houses and factories; the villa dominated the landscape like the castles of olden days. De Pachmann had been waiting for us for a long time and was annoyed by the delay. "We have been waiting for you for two hours already" could be heard from the upper floor. "Cesco, what has happened?" A little later, Pallottelli introduced to me an old man, short in stature, frail, slightly bent over, unique in appearance because of his one squinting eye and the long white hair falling almost to his shoulders. Anyone who had not seen him since the times in London and New York when he, prosperous and impressive, wore a top hat with royal dignity and smoked fat Havana cigars, would not have recognized him. The years had changed him completely and although he seemed in excellent health, the ravages of age, one by one, had left their marks on his face and figure. There was almost no affinity between the forty-year old man whom I had seen in numerous photographs and this old man of eighty; one had disappeared forever, the other was practically a stranger to him. 'And the cigars?' he asked. At eighty, just as at forty, still a connoisseur of his excellent cigars, his first thought was of them. When he took them from Pallottelli, one could see a flash of joy, the kind which seems possible only in children and the elderly. Then he started talking, a little to himself, a little with us, about completely disparate subjects. He expressed himself in correct French, practically without any Slavic inflection,

with English terms inserted here and there, constantly returning to one and the same subject: his next concert in London. At eighty he was still preoccupied with thoughts of his art, his piano and his career. The relentless soul of the artist ignored the extreme destruction of the body, overcame it, and at the same time continued to pursue thoughts of beauty and fame. Thus the contrast between that flaming (even though disordered) inner life, and that body which was already weakened by extreme old age, was piteous. "I have studied the London programme. I have to play this piece and this other piece, carefully studying the tonal succession," he spoke in this way. Inserting long discussions, digressions from one subject to another, and then returning to his insistent preoccupation with the London concert. To listen to him was to hear a young artist on the eve of his debut and then it was impossible not to remember that, on the contrary, he had made his debut 60 years ago and that few careers had been as long as his. When, ardently asked by Pallottelli, he sat down at the piano. I immediately saw that he played like he spoke: in spurts. Interrupting himself every minute, jumping from one composition to another, improvising. His hands, however, were still the same as before; delicate and white, these hands, when he rested them on the keys, preserved their lightness of movement. If the thick veins of old age did not protrude on them, one would have thought them the hands of a young girl. They even had that plasticity which would seem to be impossible in an old man. "Do you hear? Do you hear?" he said from time to time, turning either to me or to Pallottelli, or even to his servant. "You'll never again hear anything like it." And he continued to play with vigor, despite his eighty years, tangling one melody with another as if leafing through a large book, reading only a few phrases here or there, without reason. But then, all of a sudden, from this confusion of pieces, there emerged an undulating sweet phrase, supported by the most delicate accompaniment, unrolling like a magnificent ribbon, it seemed suspended in the air, decorated with fine embroidery; it was sad in minor modulation, and revived sweet and serene. The old man once again found the golden thread of art and untangled it wonderfully, reviving with marvelous simplicity the Romanza of Chopin's Concerto in E minor. Our marvel at this miracle was so great that the value of the music almost disappeared; the Romanza revived by the artist caressed and consoled us like the voice of a dear one who had been lost and found again. Chopin, who composed, Constanza Gladowska, who inspired, and de Pachmann who performed, were mixed into one glowing whole which seemed to me to be the very essence of poetry. It is touching to think that the tireless soul of the artist, ignoring the miseries of old age, went on following dreams of beauty and glory.[1]

In his decline, Pachmann remained personally much as he had always been, at least until his last six months when illness overcame him. He relaxed, smoking cigars and looking at his jewels. He played and practiced exercises until dinner. Doctors had forbidden coffee and the cognac he liked with it, and Alice had to hide the Benedictine. He was still vicious about the details of his table, and chased a servant girl around the room with an iron rod, threatening to kill her because the coffee wasn't hot, but told her he loved her when it was to his liking. Once in a restaurant he sent some breakfast eggs back more than a dozen times, going into a fury because they had not been cooked for precisely two minutes. Cesco said eventually the entire staff of the restaurant appeared holding platters of eggs, and he was given his choice of seventeen varieties.

As the disease progressed, he became feebler and soon could play no more. Then, unable to go to Fabriano, Cesco organized gay and festive parties in the villa in Rome and many noted musicians, including Ottorino Respighi, Godowsky and Mme. Tetrazzini visited him in that strange vaulted room, with its paintings of wild animals bathed in an olive dawn.

He was often malicious like a malignant mosquito, for he wanted to play, yet he could not. He would walk among his guests in his little hat and frayed robe, making sarcastic remarks about the incapacity of those who performed. At one of these gatherings, Godowsky was present, as well as the young Russian-Jewish pianist Leff Pouishnoff, who played. Alice Pallottelli told the author that the glib confidence Pouishnoff had exuded riled the old man. While everyone watched, Pachmann took Godowsky by the arm, paced back and forth across the room, all the time muttering, "Listen to that. . . . Listen to that!" Then, so that everyone in the room could hear, he "confided" to Lepp, "Only a Jew could play Chopin like that!" This, despite the fact that Pachmann, Godowsky, and Pouishnoff all had Jewish antecedents. It had not been meant as a compliment.

One evening there appeared in his studio a tall German pianist named Walter Gieseking, then at the beginning of his career. Pachmann noticed him. This incident was recounted by a friend of Cesco's named Frederico Nardelli in his memoir. Pachmann had been told that the young man was a pianist and whispered to the other guests: "That man is going to play and we'll all laugh." When Gieseking went to the piano, Pachmann walked to an armchair near the platform where he could be observed by his guests, as if he wanted to seal an agreement with them: to laugh at the incapacity of this unknown player. But as soon as Gieseking began, Pachmann's face suddenly changed its malicious expression and, forgetting his audience completely, he became immersed in the music. Under its influence, he arose slowly, ever so slowly, from his chair and walked to the piano where he stood erect in his senescence until the performance was over. Then he turned to Gieseking and looking at the floor bowed down in a grand reverence; when he arose, two huge tears had formed in his eyes. "Bien joué, bien joué . . . mais je . . . je." He could no longer compete. At last he realized that he could play no more, that it was for younger men to carry on, and in Gieseking he had recognized a great artist.

Pachmann was no longer in the news, but he was not forgotten. Leonard Liebling, editor of the *Musical Courier,* informed his readers on September 5, 1931, that he had sent a congratulatory telegram to the pianist on his birthday, July 27, addressed to him at Villa Gioia, Fabriano, Italy, but it was returned undelivered.

On Christmas Day 1932, after Alice had given birth to another child, Pachmann walked up to her room and in gestures infinitely more expressive than words, presented her with the little wooden panel of the Madonna, the gift from his mother that he had always carried with him on his journeys through Europe and America. He asked to see the baby, and when they brought the infant before him, he held it in his arms and said, "Cesco, Alichika, it's not for me, it's not for me. . . . What can I do?"

But a week later, on New Year's Day, he said he wanted to present the baby with a gift: he wanted to play the piano, although he had not played in three years. At first they would not let him play, but he wanted to so badly that they carried him with much difficulty to the piano, where he began with Chopin's Nocturne in F Minor, Op. 55, No. 1. He lacked the strength to play it all and improvised a cut in the middle. When he arrived at the familiar coda, with its arpeggios that vanish into air, he executed it with all the grace and prodigious delicacy of his prime. It moved him profoundly.[2]

On January 4, 1933, Pachmann contracted pneumonia. Two days later, the day the baby was being baptized, the eighty-four-year-old maestro neared the end. The same priest, after performing the baptismal ceremony for young Duilio Pallottelli, administered last rites to Pachmann, who died later that day.

Arriving from Paris too late, Adrian and Leonide never saw their father alive again. After the usual open coffin lying in state, burial was in the Roman cemetery at Campo Verano. Pachmann had told Cesco, "If you want to please me, don't spend money on flowers or an expensive funeral, but give it to the home for old musicians in Rome." Cesco told the author that these wishes were observed.

There were hundreds of obituaries around the world, with more than sixty in England alone. Most were suitably respectful and confirmed his reputation as one of the great pianists of his time, but others, especially some English tabloids, carried headlines like "Circus Performer Dead," and emphasized his eccentric behavior, accompanied by a photo of him milking a cow.

James Francis Cooke's "The Extraordinary Case of Vladimir de Pachmann" appeared in the April 1933 issue of the *Etude*:

> Here, then, was one of the queerest, drollest, and also one of the most impressive cases of a dual musical personality. The "Mr. Hyde" Pachmann

might mischievously place a pair of socks upon the piano and dedicate his interpretations to them; but the "Dr. Jekyll" Pachmann was a maker of tonal dreams so poetic and so lovely that they were unforgettable. . . . The ease with which de Pachmann would leap from impish revelry to serious artistic heights was an indication of the abnormal mentality of this queer genius who naturally gave rise to the inquiry, "Does he resort to the various monkey-shines at his recitals because he thinks it is good showmanship, or is he mentally unbalanced?" After many opportunities to observe the performer, when he thought he was alone and did not know he was being studied, we feel certain that de Pachmann was in no sense a fakir but was unbalanced in a measure few people realized. . . . Once the writer saw him unobserved playing alone in a room. At the end of a Chopin Prelude he arose, bowed to an audience of hotel furniture and then applauded himself vociferously. The writer also felt like applauding, for rarely had he heard such Chopin playing. . . . De Pachmann was buried in Rome. A Priest chanted at the graveside. Adieu, cher maestro, impossible and incomparable. We are grateful to you for some of the loveliest musical moments in our experience as well as for some of the most sidesplitting farces.

Since his death, Pachmann has been the subject of controversy, and has been maligned by many writers and critics. In early 1950 there was a flurry of letters to the editor in the London magazine *Radio Times* about Pachmann, some adulatory and others dismissive. On February 17th appeared a letter from Arthur Hedley, at the time a respected Chopin scholar, biographer and editor, who despised everything Pachmann had represented. Hedley's own reputation has declined since (an instance of his scholarship is his claim that Pachmann made "about forty records" when almost twice that number were issued). Hedley believed that Pachmann's departures from Chopin's text utterly destroyed any credibility the pianist might have had. He wrote:

> The phrase about *occasionally adding a note or two* is a curious understatement, when one considers the records made by Pachmann (some nearly fifty years ago) in which Chopin's text is caricatured for the sake of "effect." This positive evidence will stand when mere *memory* has faded—well over a hundred omissions, alterations, etc., in about forty records.

The contrast between the adulation he was accorded in his lifetime and the contemptuous dismissal he has suffered since is one of the ironies of concert history. Pachmann relished his notoriety as much as the acclaim he received as an artist, so this is not surprising. He dared to be different in a field where seriousness and dignity are sacrosanct, and perhaps the obliteration of his reputation as an artist is the price he had to pay for breaking the "sacred canon."

⟿

Memories of Pachmann's antics with piano stools were still vivid in 1956, when author A. J. Liebling described (in his book *The Sweet Science*) the great, surprising upset at the 1954 prizefight between titleholder Archie Moore and underdog contender Harold Johnson:

> Johnson hit him with a beautiful overhand right to the left side of the head and knocked him flat. It was as if Vladimir de Pachmann had been assaulted by a piano stool.

⟿

It was best that Pachmann never lived to see the tragic events that engulfed his family. Alice's ardent fascism placed her close to *Il Duce*. Mussolini lived nearby in his Villa Torlonia. An amateur violinist, he visited the Pallottellis more than once while the great pianist was alive and much was made of the dictator taking out his violin and Pachmann attempting to accompany him. In Cesco's monograph on Pachmann's life, Alice claimed that the pianist was "a great admirer of Italy and Il Duce" but no evidence was given for the dubious second part of the claim.

By 1917 Alice was already known as "The Joan of Arc of Italy." She most likely had met Mussolini around the time of the First World War, when she became part of his coterie. Later in London their relationship progressed to a greater intimacy. According to Gianni Scipione Rossi, in his 2010 book "*Storia di Alice*," the dictator began sharing his company with Alice as well as his acknowledged mistress, Claretta Petacci. Rossi found some letters and documents linking Alice to Mussolini, but his book presents more conjecture than fact. It seems Mussolini enjoyed taunting Petacci with Alice's interest in him. (Petacci, who had begun bombarding the dictator with love letters when she was 14, was ultimately shot with him by Communist partisans in 1945.) She naturally hated the interloper Alice, and in one letter wrote that Alice was "an old viper who has flung herself into my presence with her jealousy and anger." Rossi claims that Alice became the dictator's "*donna*" (mistress). Many people thought that, although we have no evidence that Mussolini thought of her that way. In the early 1960s people in Fabriano were still spreading the gossip that Alice had borne the dictator's child.

After Pachmann's death, Cesco found work in the offices of *Novissimo*, a high-class literary magazine published by Alice's father, Edoardo di Fonseca. It featured the work of well-known Italian authors of the time. Rossi's book reprints part of a 1932 letter from Cesco to Mussolini, in which Cesco, always the opportunist, reminds the dictator that he had been in his faithful service since 1919, and discusses his hopes to publish a commemorative book about the "March on Rome" of October 22 to 29, 1922, the conclusion of which was Mussolini's coming to power in the Kingdom of Italy. Cesco remained at the magazine until it folded in 1938, another result of the serious world-wide economic problems. Desperate, Cesco wrote to Mussolini for help, and *Il Duce* responded by sending him to Ethiopia, to report on conditions there. It seems his duties included scouting opportunities to mine for gold and other precious minerals.

Rossi prints part of another letter from Cesco, describing the Africans he encountered in Lubdo, a town of miners. Cesco explained the difficulty in obtaining the necessary number of native workers to extract the desired quota from the earth. He described a worse impression he received in Addis Ababa, where he witnessed disorder on a wide scale—the blacks did not like the whites, and lived their lives as pariahs against white masters; they were regarded as dangerous to the Nationals. Cesco wrote that "a strong effort at policing is necessary to control these dangerous parasites."

Cesco stayed in Africa until his job was eliminated five years later, and returned to Italy. The war was now going very badly for Italy. With his usual combination of luck and cunning, Cesco somehow was named Podestà (mayor) of Fabriano. But soon he had to deal with the German occupation of the town, the weakening hold of the fascists, the uprising of the partisans, and the general confusion of wartime, with its lack of food and damaged transportation vehicles. As the Allies worked their way up the boot of Italy, bridges and buildings in Fabriano were destroyed.

Cesco was relieved of his duties as Podestà after one year and the Pallottellis returned to Rome. Partisans then broke into the Villa Gioia, "this home of Nazi fascists" as they called it, and in their rage destroyed much of the interior, including Pachmann's piano. In June 1946 Cesco was arrested and convicted as a collaborator with the Germans, both "in intent and design" and imprisoned. Again benefiting from amazing luck, the "Amnesty of Togliatti" was declared a month later, and he was freed.

Just as people knew of her husband's collaboration with the Germans, so Alice's connection to Mussolini was also known. There were rumors that Virgilio, the Pallottelli's first son, was not fathered by Cesco, but by Mussolini. I never thought much about that rumor until I chanced to see Virgilio, while visiting Cesco in the hospital where he was recovering from a prostate operation in 1960. Cesco was short and fair. Virgilio was a tall (probably six feet one or two inches), dark, striking man in his early forties, with something of Alice particularly around the eyes, but no resemblance at all to his younger brother and a sister. I do not know who Virgilio's father was, but it did not seem to be Cesco Pallottelli.

Apparently Mussolini actually treated Virgilio as an adopted son, and he was given the position as a pilot for important assignments, making extensive flights for the fascist government around north Africa. Rossi likens them to the exploits described by Antoine St. Exupéry in his great novel *"Vol de Nuit"* (Night Flight), which Virgilio had read. When he returned to Italy Virgilio was assigned to the staff in Dongo, where his duties seem to have consisted of acting as one of Mussolini's personal chauffeurs. He was with the dictator just before he was captured and killed. Virgilio was also captured but later released.

Rossi's book tries mightily to imply a great connection between the Pallottellis and Mussolini, but offers little proof, concluding that the story remains "an enigma." Rossi's most astonishing claim is that, in 1945, Mussolini invited Cesco, Alice and Virgilio to visit him at a resort on the shores of Lake Garda in northern Italy, hoping that their connections to powerful English friends (Alice was also sometimes called "The English Lady" by her countrymen) would enable him to secretly contact Winston Churchill, to negotiate a deal that would save his life. If that was the purpose of the meeting, it of course failed. Mussolini's fall was also the end for the Pallottellis' connection to politics.

Afterward they lived quietly in the bottom floor flat of their villa in Rome. Pachmann's magnificent studio, with its Art Deco frescos on the floor above, was rented out to a French religious order. Alice was like a shadow, drained and embittered. Despite all this, she remained an unrepentant fascist until the end.

Cesco was more pragmatic. When I visited him in 1959 he was working for the American Fulbright scholarship organization—one has to wonder how he managed to capture that plum of a job, with his reputation as a collaborator with the Germans. But by now it is obvious that Cesco was a supreme opportunist. Details of Cesco's circle of friends and connections are necessarily vague, but among these was John Majeske, publisher of *Musical America*. Like other Nazis and fascists who simply switched sides, he somehow found the right contacts. (While I was visiting them in Italy, the current government fell. Alice's comment to me was: "Mussolini would never have permitted it, and yet they criticize him!")

Cesco died in 1965. Alice then had to leave the villa and take a small apartment under the name "widow Fonseca." Pachmann's second Baldwin concert grand, which had a Welte roll mechanism retrofitted into it at some point, had been damaged, but was restored, now was sold. Of the memorabilia, the important pieces—autograph material of Liszt, Henselt, Klindworth, Busoni and others—disappeared, along with Cesco's photos of Pachmann, the collection of Pachmann's concert programs and reviews, the pianist's scores and manuscripts, and the test pressings of his unissued recordings.[3] The villa was sold, Pachmann's floor divided into apartments. The Cambellotti frescos were whitewashed over.

It is difficult to summon much sympathy for the Pallottellis, for many reasons. From the standpoint of posterity, if they had not been opportunists and fascists, it is conceivable that the villa and all of Pachmann's possessions and memorabilia might have been preserved. After the pianist's death they had been left well-off, all their living coming from Pachmann's earnings. I asked Cesco about what happened to the jewels: "We had to live!" he answered. In the end, Pachmann lost his reputation and every other kind of legacy. This book is an attempt to restore his reputation.

Chapter 32

Pachmann's Vision of Chopin and its Relevancy for the Twenty-first Century

It was wrongly held by many that Pachmann's piano playing more than suggested Chopin's own, that it possessed something intuitive and uncanny that was "authentic." In truth his playing was his vision of Chopin's playing, combining what he had heard about it from Liszt and others with his own fantasy, all woven through his magnetic personality and pianistic genius. Many aspects of Chopin's music were conducive to this vision, which he stressed. It was original, unique playing that fascinated audiences, but equally important, it also pleased critics because it relied on his use of performance practices that were accepted in his own time.

THE FEMININE IN CHOPIN

The great dual nature of Chopin's music is often evident in the tension set up between heroic masculinity and sublime femininity, yet few writers on Chopin have ever discussed this; perhaps, as men, they have found the idea perplexing. Pachmann's stressing of the feminine in Chopin identified him with this aspect of the composer more than any other Chopin specialist in history. In his day, when there were many more great Chopin players than today, the feminine side of the great Polish composer was most often slighted in favor of the more robust Chopin found in larger-scale works. Pachmann reversed this procedure until his stress of the feminine became idiosyncratic. Somehow he had found the key to this side of Chopin: it was the idealized femininity of a sensitive man. Women cannot feel and share this feminine side of a man, while men cannot feel and share the masculine side of women. The two remain eternal opposites. When he played the Chopin B minor Sonata and stretched out those beautiful melodies of the first movement against the flowing bass, with his "lawless rubato," as one critic described it, he seemed to be seducing the audience with the beauty of his touch. And of course one must add, accompanying the melody with smiles and winks in the direction of the most attractive members of the audience, male or female. He really flirted with his audience and apparently had never been afraid of his own feminine nature. But no matter how lush and sensuous he made his tone, the music was feminine but not effeminate, for there was pith to his delicacy. It was the delicate idealism of a man.

Pachmann's love of the beautiful—jewels, fine food, the Italian countryside, even cigars—were all part of a refined and idealized attitude and approach toward all aspects of life. It was natural for him to want to create the most beautiful sounds imaginable. His whole life was an eccentric sublimation towards beauty. This masculine idealization of the feminine dominated his existence, extending even to personal relationships. He was often attacked for luxuriating in femininity, and it is not surprising that some felt any man who expounded the feminine side of his nature must be suspect. To them, an art based on perfect mastery of the intimate could never be as great as the grand, the rhetorical, the heroic. This negative attitude directed toward him was exacerbated by Pachmann's platform behavior, causing many to dismiss him.

Despising man's feminine nature has continued to dominate attitudes in many quarters, even affecting pianists today. Many women in concert history, wanting to gain recognition as serious artists, have felt impelled to "play like a man." But no other man has even wanted to play like a woman. While others conquered with roars, Pachmann dared to seduce with whispers.

INTIMACY AND MINIATURIZATION

Was the greatest Chopin player the heroic player, or was it Pachmann, the most intimate of all Chopin players? There probably has never been an ideal Chopin interpreter. Chopin is a universe. As Anton Rubinstein wrote, he is "tragic, romantic, lyric, heroic, dramatic, fantastic, soulful, tender, dreamy, brilliant, the very spirit and soul of the piano." Perfect as he was in certain works of Chopin, Pachmann's art reflected only the exquisite refinement and sensitivity of the Polish master. He was certainly aware of the other facets of Chopin's music, but his peculiar mastery was so complete in itself that it left no room for anything else.

One of the great writers on music in English was the composer Kaikhosru Shapurji Sorabji. In 1932 he published an essay entitled "Pachmann and Chopin."[1] Sorabji clearly thought his idol Busoni was a greater Chopin player, for Busoni played the heroic works heroically. But he admired Pachmann for what he was, and gave an excellent summary of that part of Pachmann's art he loved:

> Before his extravagances and eccentricities had almost swamped his artistry, that is to say up to within fifteen or even ten years ago, his playing of the smaller nocturnes, waltzes, études and mazurkas was exquisite—the almost unlimited range of his gradations of tone within a *mezzo-forte* to an unbelievable *quasi-niente*, the amazing fluidity and limpid liquidity of his finger work, his delicious dainty staccato; the marvelous cantilena, the exquisite phrasing, and the wonderful delicate fantasy of the whole, all made his playing of these things an enchantment and a delight.

Although Pachmann did regularly play larger compositions, being a miniaturist, he tended to sectionalize those works at the expense of the entire composition, making the sections stand out in relief, so that audiences would remember those beautiful sections within the whole. By doing this he turned a large work into a series of miniatures. The composer's intended architecture was gone, but those beautiful pages, played with a perfection of finished, edgeless phrases and commanding beauty of tone, coming one after the other in graded pianissimi, created a cumulative effect of tension not very unlike the tension created in the conventional playing of his more powerful colleagues. He received ovations, as we have chronicled, that rivaled theirs in intensity. Nothing like this exists today.

Some large-scale Chopin works like the Third Ballade and Fourth Scherzo suited his temperament, and his playing of these was apparently unrivalled. But in those works demanding strength, demonic virility and aggressiveness such as the first two Scherzi, certain Etudes and Preludes, the A flat Polonaise, and the first two movements of the B flat minor Sonata, he was unconvincing, but he redeemed himself in the last movement of the Sonata, which is more about playing fast, without pedal while controlling the touch. In that movement Pachmann showed his pianistic genius. Sculptress Malvina Hoffman, daughter of the great American pianist Richard Hoffman, wrote: "In the concluding movement of the Chopin Sonata that contains the funeral march . . . my father said . . . that only one player, and by that he meant Vladimir de Pachmann, succeeded in giving a perfect rendering of the whistling wind sweeping the hurrying clouds before the face of the moon and lashing the trees in relentless fury, then moaning itself away like a restless spirit."

In his performances of the "Revolutionary Etude" he gave a purling quality to the left hand that was completely inappropriate to the music. While Pachmann's Chopin was never devoid of charm, it was always lacking in heroics. It was not so much that he lacked the physical ability to play powerfully. Though small, he was compactly built, with more than enough strength and energy. It was rather a psychological conditioning that affected him physically. It was almost as if he had early on made up his mind that certain qualities of tone did not exist for him, and because he could not conceive of a world with these undesirable tonal qualities, he could not physically play in a way to produce those tones. It was the reverse of a more common condition prevalent among many virtuosi: the inability to play softly and lyrically. These pianists are ill at ease in intimate and lyrical works, and cannot produce a pianissimo tone of any quality. They happily romp through a Chopin Scherzo, but are baffled by a "simple" Nocturne.

Pachmann was often censured for what he did not accomplish, rather than admired for what he did. Let us not deprecate his greatness—one cannot criticize a cherry tree for not being an oak. That many dismiss his mastery because it was "small and fine," rather than "big and grand," shows a twisted and distorted view of aesthetics, if not a coarsening of musical values. Perhaps today's performers have lost the capacity to experience greatness through sublime intimacy, as well as through heroic grandeur.

LISZT, THE FATHER OF THE CHOPIN TRADITION, AND HIS INFLUENCE ON PACHMANN

Pachmann's freedom of interpretation, his love of expressing himself through Chopin, was really a reflection of an attitude prevalent in the late nineteenth and early twentieth century, when the world expected that each musical artist have a personal statement, a conception that was uniquely their own. This individuality that set an artist apart from colleagues was cultivated to the fullest and colored everything he or she performed. It was thought a sacred duty to use this individuality to interpret the written instructions of the composer, to catch the spirit behind the notes. Chopin and even Beethoven would have been startled if any pianist in their presence would have performed one of their works in the "straight," modern fashion, merely reproducing the printed page.

This philosophy of artistic and spiritual freedom shaped all the older generation of romantic pianists. It was due primarily to the enormous influence of Franz Liszt who, even more than Chopin, defined Pachmann's aesthetic universe. Most of the pianists of his day adopted Liszt's all-embracing approach to music, both in their technical mastery of the modern piano mechanism, and in musical aesthetics. It was he who shaped the tradition of the older generation of pianists, whether it was Bach as played by Busoni, Beethoven as played by d'Albert, or Chopin as played by Pachmann. Pachmann had already fused the Viennese style he learned at the Vienna Conservatory and the Chopinesque feeling dictated by his temperament, with the orchestral, virtuoso style founded by Liszt when he met that great master. Liszt's style of playing had been prevalent for years already when Pachmann was a student, and continued as the major force in piano playing until after World War One, when an aesthetic change altered music.

When Arthur Friedheim, one of Liszt's greatest pupils, first heard Pachmann in Paris in 1881, he felt Pachmann had so mastered Liszt's orchestral style that it was within his grasp to become the greatest pianist after Liszt. Instead, Pachmann went his own way and did something unexpected and unprecedented. He retained some elements of Liszt's style, but in essence turned his back on that pianistic approach and instead began to cultivate the art of intimacy, taking the beautiful touch as far as it could go. It was his concept of Chopin's pianism, contained within a framework of Lisztian aesthetics. For Pachmann, there was no contradiction between the two styles.

Much has been written about the relationship between Chopin and Liszt. That Chopin condemned Liszt's music, disliked his personality and arriviste, parvenu traits, and most of all distrusted his early, monumental insincerity, cannot be denied. But it is wrong to assume, as some modern writers have done, that Liszt's aesthetic outlook was completely foreign to Chopin, or that Liszt did not understand Chopin.

Chopin did not live to hear Liszt's best music and the immature man he knew was not the same man that influenced generations of pianists. After Chopin's death in 1849, Liszt's personality developed and matured, and many of those habits which Chopin had so disliked disappeared. The mature Liszt remembered by Pachmann was a man of infinite warmth and humanity, who seemed to understand life and was ennobled by it. The grandeur and majesty of the man affected all who knew him, particularly his pupils who tried to emulate such traits in their playing. The nobility and freedom that the old Liszt players brought to the master's works was also apparent in their playing of Chopin. Liszt insisted on it. He wanted them to go beyond the notes and encouraged his most talented pupils to play Chopin's music as it appealed to them. He apparently showed Pachmann many little secrets (nuances and pedal effects) he had gained from Chopin. These inspired him, as they did most of his pupils, to transcend himself.

Liszt was a spiritual revelation for Pachmann, who never forgot the old abbé. The inspiration Liszt gave him as a young man lasted a lifetime. Years after Liszt's death he could still remember and illustrate to his son Leonide how the great master played this page or pedaled that phrase, for Pachmann had an enormous memory for pianistic details. As Olin Downes wrote: "He has forgotten more than most pianists ever remembered."

NINETEENTH CENTURY PERFORMANCE PRACTICES

Tempo Rubato

Most composers have always struggled with notation of their music. There always existed a lurking fear that what they wrote down could not encompass their inspiration, and were forever trying to capture in writing the force and spontaneity of their original ideas. It is the interpreter's duty to try to recapture that very elusive inspiration. This is the spirit of music, beyond the printed page, found only within the self.

This improvisational style that Chopin employed and that Pachmann intuitively copied found its fullest expression in tempo rubato, which Josef Hofmann described as "a wavering, a vacillating of time values."[2] Tempo rubato is the life blood of Chopin's music. Chopin certainly tried to help the perplexed pianist understand this when he indicated how rubato was to be played in some of his early Mazurkas. As his music became better known, he abandoned attempts to write out the rubato, leaving its use to the discretion of performers. Liszt in his Chopin edition for Breitkopf and Härtel wrote the following about Chopin and rubato:

> But as the term taught nothing to whomever already knew, and said nothing to those who did not know, understand and feel, Chopin later ceased to add this explanation to his music, persuaded that if one had the sense of the music, it would be impossible not to divine this rule of irregularity. ... He seemed to wish to teach this style of playing to his numerous pupils, especially his compatriots to whom, more than any others, he wanted to communicate the breath of his inspiration.

His pupils became spokesmen for Chopin's style of rubato, which really was almost identical to the traditional way rubato had been used since the Renaissance by polyphonic singers, by violinists in the Baroque era and through the Classical era with Mozart and Beethoven. It was characterized by a steady beat in the accompaniment while the tempo rubato or "robbed time" was employed in the melody. With keyboard players, one kept a steady beat in the bass while employing rubato colorations in the notes of the melody. This was accomplished by either anticipation (where the melody note was played first) or delay (where the bass note was played first). There was only a momentary dislocation of time because the left-hand rhythm remained steady. Another way of playing rubato is found in Chopin's Mazurkas, wherein the first beat is held, then the time caught up before the next downbeat—the time is stretched at the downbeat, then accelerated to catch up by the next downbeat.

Chopin used it in his playing of Mazurkas and Waltzes, where a steady beat is maintained in the left hand, and in the Nocturnes, with their continuous pattern of bass against flowing melodic lines. Chopin also applied it to ornamental, decorative passages, such as the middle section of the A flat Impromptu. However, the more he applied rubato colorations to the melody, even with a steady beat underneath, the more the time was dislocated, until the work sounded "out of time."

This dislocation of time perplexed some musicians like Berlioz, who in his memoirs claimed that Chopin couldn't play in time. This was also the cause of a vicious argument between Chopin and the composer Giacomo Meyerbeer, who claimed that the composer's own playing of his well-known Mazurka in C, Op. 33, No. 3, was not in the 3-4 rhythm of a mazurka, but in 2-4.

That Mazurka was played in an out of time rhythm, which to a person who *hears* in rubato, appears to be in time! If a rubato performance is musically persuasive, the rubato trumps any strict accounting of rhythm, and in fact can suggest the original rhythm, even if one seems not to be playing it.[3] Pachmann seems to have mastered this type of rubato. John Porte, an admirer of Pachmann, in his book (*Chopin the Composer and His Music—An Analytic Critique of Famous Traditions and Interpretations as Exhibited in the Playing of Great Pianists Past and Present*) remembered a recital where the great Chopin player seemed almost too wayward in his playing of a Waltz, only to discover in amazement that his left hand was playing an absolutely steady beat.

But this rubato was not typical of Pachmann's age or, for that matter, how he or other pianists of his time employed it. The development of the heavier, iron framed pianos after 1840, with their deeper, sonorous tone and build up of overtones, gave to Chopin's music a tension and dramatic thrust missing (or not as apparent) on the earlier, wooden framed instruments. It was difficult for pianists to be satisfied with the classic, traditional rubato and there evolved a second type, the romantic or free-style rubato. The steady, restraining rhythm was abandoned, and there was much freer use of agogics (or deviations from tempo). Flexibility of rhythm was everything. Liszt's pupil Valerie Boissier recounted him telling her:

> Music must not be subject to a uniform balance; it must be kindled, or slowed down with judgment and according to the meaning it carries. This goes for all romantic music of the present time. The old fashioned classics must be rendered with greater regularity.[4]

In the romantic, free style of rubato, phrases and even whole pages are played in an asymmetrical manner, in which the performer's unique inner concept causes the music to sound symmetrical. One is guided by one's own intuition when applying it. When studying Chopin, Pachmann would play each hand alone, carefully listening to the beauty of the sound and its natural importance to decide when it was pertinent to employ the rubato. The only rule was that it had a firm musical underpinning. One writer described Pachmann's use of rubato as "the free, spontaneous, myriad-versioned rhythm of nature, as the waving of a field of grain in the breeze."[5]

Chopin stressed the classic rubato with its restraining rhythm, making sure his pupils mastered that style and could control it. But there is evidence that he also used the freer approach. This seems to be confirmed by Karl Mikuli, probably Chopin's most influential pupil, who edited Chopin's works for the Schirmer Company and was the teacher of Moriz Rosenthal, Raoul von Koczalski and other famed Chopin players. "Chopin was far from being a partisan of metric rigor and frequently used rubato in his playing, accelerating or slowing down this or that rhythm. But Chopin's rubato possessed an unshakable emotional logic."[6]

The romantic, free-style rubato became so pervasive that by the early twentieth century a reaction occurred among some musicians that rhythmic license had gone too far and had to be restrained. Articles by Liszt pupil Constantin von Sternberg were widely read and accepted: when one "robs" in one part, one must "pay back" in another.[7]

This idea proved to be demonstrably false. In 1928 John Blackwood Mc-Ewen, measuring the duration of notes in performances of the same work "captured" on reproducing piano rolls by Pachmann, Busoni, and Carreño, found there was never compensation. Paderewski replied to Sternberg's article, saying "What's lost, is lost."[8] He was scientifically correct.

One may well ask then, how can one judge a successful rendition of rubato, if it cannot be scientifically measured. The answer is that rubato must be conceived as Pachmann, Friedman, Rosenthal, Hofmann and other great Chopin players of the past played it—in toto—as part of a complete conception of any given work.

All the great Chopin players were skilled in its use and each employed it in their own way, expressing something of their self with the idiom. To some modern musicians and scholars, the rubato that Pachmann and the others employed did not truly reflect Chopin's usage; the pianists' stopping and starting as they describe it, impeded the flow of the music and was not truly an expressive performance style but a Victorian mannerism.

This is highly questionable. For the author's part, Chopin's lyric works are never more evocative than when played by pianists of the late nineteenth and early twentieth centuries, most of whom seem more imbued with the spirit of romance. One has only to listen to the recordings of Ignaz Friedman playing the Nocturne in E flat, Op. 55, or Pachmann in the E minor Nocturne to hear this style at its best. It is an art that today's pianists have lost.

Breaking the Hands

Perhaps even more important than tempo rubato as an authentic performance practice was a way of playing that affected almost all pianists of the late nineteenth and early twentieth centuries: breaking, or non-synchronization, of the hands. It was an outgrowth of romantic rubato. In the classic rubato the separation of the hands was only momentary, but in romantic rubato, once the rhythm was loosened, the hands were freed from keeping together.

Breaking the hands was one way artists could play more expressively and at the same time show their individuality. Pianists born between 1840 and 1860 were particularly prone to use this device. Fauré, Leschetizky, Michalowski, Pachmann, Reinecke, and Saint-Saëns all used non co-ordination in their playing, as we can hear in their recordings on discs and piano rolls (which are reliable indicators of this aspect of the playing of the artists represented). But pianists born in the 1870s and 1880s, and this includes many of the greatest artists of the older generation—Cortot, Dohnanyi, Godowsky, Hofmann, Lhevinne, and Rachmaninoff among them—used it less, while those that followed, born in the 1890's such as Gieseking, Moiseiwitsch, Novaes and Arthur Rubinstein, used it not at all.[9]

We know when in history the influence of non co-ordination waned, but we do not know how far back use of the device went. The earliest pianist recorded (on rolls) was Carl Reinecke, born in 1824, and his rolls exhibit non co-ordination in his playing. Since it was so prevalent throughout Europe, one wonders if it began with Chopin and Liszt as part of the romantic revolution that overwhelmed music around 1830, with the new double-escapement pianos, and the new music composed for them, with its new transcendental piano technique and romantic style of playing. All this was a complete break from the stultifying classical past as exemplified by Clementi, Cramer, Czerny and Hummel.

But there may not have been a break, but a gradual evolving, which burst forth in the romantic period. Mark Arnest, in his excellent monograph "Why Couldn't They Play Both Their Hands Together," mentions two men who heard Paderewski, "the poster boy of romantic excess," as he calls him, play Bach. They thought his playing reminded them of Moscheles, who was born in 1794! A tantalizing idea—however Paderewski made no recording of Bach.[10]

Pachmann's use of non co-ordination of the hands was extremely imaginative, as if the two were two separate voices. He was extraordinarily skillful in embedding it in the fabric of the music. Only when the musical line was repeatedly broken, in his decline as documented in his later recordings and rolls, does this device become noticeable and really irritating.

It is a legitimate performance style, but we caution anyone from reviving it. It is not suited for today's atmosphere. It takes years to master non co-ordination of hands, and it should never interfere with the musical line. It should be unobtrusive, hardly noticeable. Even when one does notice it as in Pachmann's late recorded performance of Chopin's E minor Nocturne, it doesn't matter because the performance is so memorable. As in tempo rubato, the final estimation of any performance practice should be of its musical persuasiveness. Today, members of other faiths will say: "should be of its faithfulness to the urtext."

THE SIN OF TEXTUAL LIBERTIES

Pachmann's idealized concept of Chopin's pure pianism was influenced by Liszt's aesthetic of freedom and individuality, and he concerned himself more with the spirit than the letter of the music. He was often rather free with the text and, like most of his colleagues, committed what many today look upon as the single greatest sin of the older generation of pianists: he dared to put himself above the composer, thus reflecting (according to them) an arrogance that was unforgivable. This modern approach, which demands the performer leave off as much of the self as possible, is absurd on the face of it; for if it is not through the self that each of us approaches the composer's spirit, then what is a possible approach?

Like all the other great musicians of his day, Pachmann never thought of himself as just a performer. These musicians sought to capture the feelings the composers themselves felt, either consciously or unconsciously, when they created their music, to re-create its freshness and spontaneity as if it were being heard for the first time, and to bring this revelation to audiences. With such an attitude, the score was merely a means to an end. It was each performer's sense of taste that prevented musical anarchy. (In today's scientific world, taste is feared and has been discarded from most musical performances, for how can it be described, measured and logically taught?)

Certainly the free textual approach is suited to the romantic, improvisatory style of Chopin, rather than the classical idiom of Mozart or Beethoven, where textual liberties destroy the rhythmic structure which is often motivic and essential to the logic of the composition. In Chopin's music the rhythmic structure is sometimes decorative rather than motivic and may on occasion be altered without losing the logic of the composition. This free textual approach is part of the whole ethos of romantic composition, and it is just as wrong for modern players to perform the music of Liszt and Chopin in the objective fashion as it was for Pachmann to perform Bach and Mozart in the romantic.

The liberties of the older players can be divided into three categories: dynamic, decorative and rhythmic. Dynamic liberties were most popular. There was frequent arpeggiation of chords. This was partly due to the passion for delaying chords, prompted by a dislike of sudden resolutions, but also was a coloristic device, giving either a richer sound, or clarity to individual voices. Sometimes arpeggiation was indulged for its own sake, reflecting the subjectivity of the performer.

Inspired by the lush sonorities of the pianos of the day, romantic players liked to enrich the text with thirds, sixths and octaves. This was more prevalent among the "grand manner," orchestral style pianists like Busoni, Friedman, Paderewski and Rosenthal, who all wanted the sound to be grander. Pachmann's aim was the opposite; he was more sensitive to the balance of the sound and to preserving its intimacy. He preferred to soften dynamics rather than enlarge them. Sometimes this actually seemed preferable to the original score, as in the ending chord of Chopin's second Impromptu. Other times it appeared inappropriate, capricious and perverse. James Huneker complained that Pachmann's playing of the frenetic coda of Chopin's G minor Ballade at a piano dynamic, then pianissimo prestissimo, was "Strongly irritating to the nerves and reminded me of a tornado seen from the wrong end of an opera glass."

Decorative liberties were particularly popular with Pachmann because they were part of the vocal style of playing Chopin. His diva-like nature searched for the places in the scores where he could imitate a coloratura's trills and roulades. His coloratura double-note trills in his 1907 recording of Chopin's Barcarolle, the trill leading to the return of the main section of the A flat Chopin Impromptu on his Victor disc, his coloratura cadenza (after the middle section) in his 1907 recording of the Minute Waltz, and the fioratura embellishments around the melody in the H.M.V. recording of Chopin's D flat Nocturne—all attest to his love of "vocalizing" on a percussive instrument. These decorative asides did not affect the structure or the melodic content of the music, but still would be condemned today as excesses, and affectations of the romantic style.

Pachmann's rhythmic liberties were similar to those of other pianists of the romantic era. They didn't like quick or sudden resolutions. It was part of the ethos of romanticism, the desire to sustain emotions and not let them go. Like Rosenthal and Paderewski, for instance, Pachmann might play a dotted eighth in a series as a sixteenth, instead of playing even eighth notes, influenced by rubato phrasing. In his prime, these rhythmic irregularities were accomplished with such smoothness, like a stream of unending, edgeless phrases, that the music never sounded restless or convulsive. This dotting of notes was a result of the widespread upbeat consciousness of the time.

Another feature related to this was unique to Pachmann. In playing a descending passage he sometimes liked to lengthen the top note by holding it tenuto, and to hurry the other notes in an accelerando down the keys. He applied this rubato effect not only to Chopin's works, and we can hear it on his Victor recording of Liszt's Rigoletto Paraphrase, where there are passages in double notes played in this manner.

Because his interpretations were thought to carry stylistic authority and insight, critics hardly ever mentioned Pachmann's textual liberties, rarely feeling them completely contrary to the spirit of the music. But sometimes he went too far with a conception which was obviously distorted, changing melodies or harmonies of well-known works. It was then that critics spoke out. The foremost Chopin player of his era was once severely reprimanded for adding baby-blue notes to passages in the F minor Fantasy, and another time for discovering new celestial harmonies in the already heavenly "Aeolian Harp" Etude.

Like Chopin, Pachmann was a man of many moods and occasionally, even in his prime, could play certain works in a way unworthy of him. Perverse, wayward with impossible liberties, his playing at such moments approached the worst excesses of the romantic period.

It is not surprising for a man who was so eccentric and who occasionally played so badly to be dismissed by some as a charlatan. The irony was that his weakness was also his artistic strength. This interpretive freedom, which in his less memorable moments tended to be uncontrolled, gave his playing in his best days an inspirational quality that critic Olin Downes (in his obituary for Pachmann) called "a freedom from every thralldom of this earth."

PACHMANN'S EDITIONS

After Pachmann's death Augener published (1934) a Chopin edition with "Authentic fingering and phrasing of Pachmann transcribed with notes by Marguerite de Pachmann Labori." It included seven Etudes from Opus 10, among them the first, third, "Black Key" and "Revolutionary," as well as eight Etudes from Opus 25 including the first three, the E minor, the double-thirds and double-sixths, the "Butterfly" and the "Winter Wind;" the first and third Ballades, the second Impromptu and Fantasie-Impromptu, the Berceuse, the two Opus 27 Nocturnes and the Opus 55 F minor, the A flat Polonaise, and the Waltzes Opus 34, No. 1 and Opus 64, No. 2.

It is basically an interpretive edition for those who are already familiar with the music. The fingering is complicated and idiosyncratic. For example, in the first Etude of Opus 10, the opening measure is daringly fingered 2, 5, 1, 4 instead of the usual 1, 2, 4, 5. Since Pachmann had very small hands, he tried to avoid the open handed position of a tenth on the first four notes. This increased the use of the wrist in aiding hand movements. (Whether this will help someone studying to play the Chopin Etudes is questionable, since fingering is such a personal matter.)

There are other surprises besides unusual fingerings. The alla breve Opus 25, No. 2 F minor Etude, with its polyrhythmic eighth note triplets in the right hand, against quarter note triplets in the left, is changed to make the polyrhythms more apparent. The right hand is in 12/8, and the left in 6/4. There are also descriptions of how he played certain works, such as the majestic arpeggio ending of the Etude in E minor, Opus 25, No. 5, which she wrote out in four bars showing a diminuendo to pianissimo (Chopin wrote the opposite). As in interpretive editions, there is much editing with stressing of inner voices and bass note melodies.

However there is only so much one can do with fingering and notes in the score. How Pachmann achieved his poetic effects with the subtleties of his touch, his inspired use of tempo rubato, and most of all, the imagination he brought to his playing—these cannot be notated.

It is interesting to compare Pachmann's 1904 edition for Schott of the two Chopin Etudes, in double thirds and double sixths, Op. 25, Nos. 6 and 8, with Maggie's edition, published as taught to her by Pachmann. One immediately notices that, except in the middle part of the double thirds Etude (bars 27 to 34), the fingerings are different. In the beginning of the double note trills, Maggie's edition fingers them 3-2 and 5-1, while in his edition Pachmann fingered them 4-1 and 5-2, a more conventional approach. Generally, Maggie's edition has much more idiosyncratic and tortuous fingerings, while Pachmann's fingerings are more natural, though he has much more use of the same fingers to slide from a black to a white key, rather than changing fingers for this. Sliding, rather than changing fingers, was part of Chopin's original approach, much easier to accomplish on the light action, wooden framed pianos of his time, and much more conducive to a natural legato touch. He may have been able to accomplish this because in 1904 Pachmann was playing on an "easy" piano, but this is just speculation. This may have been one of his accomplishments borne of thousands of hours of practice.

Maggie's edition of the double thirds Etude also has much more fussing with the bass figuration, breaking up Chopin's original long phrases into short ones. Pachmann's edition is more faithful to Chopin's phrases, without punctuating them into shorter phrases. As for the double sixths Etude: in both editions the fingering is similar, with 4-1 and 5-2 for the opening double sixths. In his edition, Pachmann does some sliding with the fifth finger, such as 5-2 to 5-1. Maggie again has some odd fingering, going from 4-1 to 3, 4-1, changing fingers on the second sixth. She does it again, this time from 5-2 to 4, 5-1, or 5-1 to 4, 3-1. She also has some odd fingering in the bass, starting the Etude: 1-5, 2-4, 1-3, 2-4, 1-5 and 4, whereas Pachmann has the more natural: 1-4, 2-5, 1-4, 2-5, 1-4, and 5. Maggie also tends to have shorter phrases again, stopping the flow by emphasizing certain patterns, whereas Pachmann's edition keeps the long phrases.

Leaving aside the differences from these editions and Chopin's originals, we are left to ponder the differences between teacher and pupil. Although Maggie's edition was published in 1934, thirty years after Pachmann's, we can presume it reflects the precepts he taught her fifty years earlier in 1883 and 1884. His edition of 1904 is much less odd than hers. The double-thirds Etude was Pachmann's specialty for most of his career—he played it for several more years after publishing this edition. Would he have published an edition with his "secrets?" This is a question that cannot today be answered authoritatively. What can be said is that Pachmann's edition is much easier to approach for modern pianists, while Maggie's perhaps is too bizarre. But then, every pianist should make his or her own fingerings. And whether any changes from Chopin's indications of tempo, dynamics, phrasing and so forth can be considered is also a personal matter.

Chopin's A minor Prelude, one of his most original and unsettling works, had baffled many musicians in his time, and even today. James Huneker's description of it in his Chopin biography was "desperate, exasperating to the nerves . . . an asymmetrical tune . . . forlorn, despairing, almost grotesque . . . it indicates the deepest depression in its sluggish snake-like progression."[11] This sums up why some find it the least attractive and popular of the Preludes. Pachmann's performances made a strong case for it, and must have truly impressed his friend Godowsky, for he took the time and trouble to actually notate the peculiarities of Pachmann's performance of the Prelude in some printed music that accompanied an article on Pachmann that appeared in *Good Housekeeping* in February 1925. Like Marguerite de Pachmann Labori's edition, Godowsky's notation of the Prelude displays some idiosyncratic fingering. He stresses almost throughout the relentless discordant feeling of the bass notes by emphasizing the top note of the pattern with either the second or first fingers of the right hand. Traditionally only the first two bars were played this way, with the rest to be played with the left hand. Pachmann wanted to avoid the see-sawing of the hand and wrist.

The strange melody is also oddly fingered, mostly using the weak fourth and fifth fingers on the repeated notes in bar six and the F sharps in bar eleven. He must have developed a great cantabile in these most difficult fourth and fifth fingers to use them in sustained, expressive melodic notes as he does in the fourteenth and fifteenth bars. These notes are usually played with the stronger fingers. Since he played so softly, this must have sounded very haunting. Pachmann played this Prelude in Carnegie Hall just before this publication—perhaps Godowsky heard that concert. Reviewing it in the *New York Herald Tribune* (October 18, 1924), Lawrence Gilman wrote:

> It was when he turned to Chopin that Mr. de Pachmann brought us inescapably under his spell . . . in the second Prelude, that baffling, cryptic, haunting, utterly original outpouring of Chopin's melancholy spirit. . . . Mr. de Pachmann was irresistibly, as he has so often been before, the master of a ravishing and magical art

Godowsky's attempt shows us that Pachmann used some very difficult fingerings, but again notation cannot recapture Pachmann's "ravishing and magical art."

L' ENVOI

The musical world that Pachmann inhabited is gone. The romantic spirit that nurtured pianists from the late nineteenth century to the early twentieth century has withered away. The romantic style he epitomized has vanished, replaced by a more objective, clear-eyed approach to the text, which has become sacrosanct—the performer now is considered differently, suspect lest the color of his own personality tinge the composer's message. Performances by artists who left their imprint on every work they played are unimaginable today, when we have a transcendental sameness everywhere. Pinpointing exactly when this change in musical perspective took place is difficult, but after Pachmann's death his reputation plummeted. His name became synonymous with all that was considered bad about pianists of his day—unreliable technique, textual liberties, excessive use of rubato, playing with the hands not together and daring to stress the individuality of the performer. Pachmann's most widely available recordings, made during his decline, encouraged this line of thought.

Indeed classical music itself—more precisely nineteenth century piano music—has become stereotyped—a museum of preservation with the result of audience apathy. This is why the legacy of Pachmann and other artists of his time is so important. Their recordings preserve a glimpse of individuality and personality that has so vanished from the concert stage. Pianists can learn from their best efforts and discard the dated and less attractive features of their playing. But they must have the ears to listen and not be biased by preconceived notions, or historically ignorant musical training. Perhaps Pachmann and other romantic pianists were too free in their playing, but the pendulum has swung too far in the other direction.

When George Halprin was asked about the difference between pianists of his time and those of today, he answered: "In my time they were more poetical. They cast a spell." Perhaps that is what is missing in Chopin playing today. There are enough pianists who can dazzle with an etude, but where are the ones who can cast a spell?

With the arrival of the compact disc in the late twentieth century, rare, earlier Pachmann recordings became available, and today Pachmann's complete recorded output is available on a four CD set from the Marston label (http://www.marstonrecords.com/). Increasing interest in romantic styles of performing and the widespread availability of historic recordings of all kinds has made the style of Pachmann's period more understandable, and his playing is now prized again for its craftsmanship, its tonal beauty and its imagination.

The important point of interest for today's readers and musicians is that, even in his wildest behavior, Pachmann never lost the thread of his unique art. He *was* a great pianist, all the more interesting because he had a unique pianistic viewpoint. Although his playing stemmed from the Liszt-Rubinstein tradition of grand, Romantic virtuosity, he brought to the concert hall a magical Chopinesque intimacy that has not been heard since.

PACHMANN'S RECORDED LEGACY

It is sad to think that the performer's art is as ephemeral as fame. Without mechanical means, it is preserved only in memory. With Pachmann this is particularly poignant since the several attempts to record him were none too successful, although he made over ninety recordings including unissued discs, the first in 1907 when he was fifty-nine, the last in 1927 when he was seventy-nine. As a whole these discs do not reflect his great reputation or the high esteem in which he was held by musicians during his lifetime. Everyone who had heard Pachmann in his prime told the author without exception that his records did not capture his great playing. To these people Pachmann's recordings were shadows of what they had heard in person.

Recording was in its infancy—the early acoustical process could hardly capture the myriad nuances of his touch or the beauty of his tone. His art would have benefited from the improved electrical process—when it came, he was too old. Then he was not always in the vein when he made recordings (unlike at most of his concert appearances), for as with Godowksy and Busoni, and in more modern times Guiomar Novaes, he was ill-at-ease in the recording studio and needed an audience to inspire him. Perhaps the compelling reason for disappointment is that, with some notable exceptions, Pachmann's recorded legacy represents the declining years of his career, when his playing had begun to lose its freshness and mannerisms were replacing spontaneity. Although there were a few unforgettable performances inscribed, Pachmann's recorded output in fact better displays the decline of his playing than illustrates its greatness. Despite this catalogue of complaints, a handful of his discs are among the best recordings ever made of particular compositions, and a few are even immortal performances.

Only recordings that have survived are listed here. The most complete and detailed discography, compiled by Nigel Nettheim of all Pachmann recordings, can be found at:

http://nettheim.com/pachmann/discography.

1907 GRAMOPHONE AND
TYPEWRITER (G AND T) RECORDINGS

Matrix

6001e	Chopin Etude, Op. 25, No. 9 and Valse Op. 64, No. 1
6003e	Chopin Valse, Op. 64, No. 2
6004e	Raff *La Fileuse*
1850f	Chopin Barcarolle (abbreviated)
1851f	Chopin Nocturne, Op. 37, No. 2
1856f	Chopin Preludes, Op. 28, Nos. 22 and 23; Mazurka Op. 50, No. 2

Pachmann was still at the height of his powers in 1907 when he made his first series of six recordings for the Gramophone and Typewriter (G and T) Company, some of the earliest recordings ever made by a world-famous pianist. While undeniably primitive with their rumbling bass and vanishing treble, when each is played at a proper speed Pachmann's G and T discs manage to preserve a semblance of piano tone when compared to the 1903 French piano recordings of Pugno, Grieg and Debussy, with their wavering pitches and calliope sonics. These G and T discs, and the subsequent 1909 H.M.V. records (with one exception), as well as some of the Victor recordings of 1911/12, are among his best discs, and suggest something of his greatness.

The G and T Pachmann discs are his most significant recordings. His fingers danced with a delicate energy in his exquisite performance of a beloved work, Chopin's F major Prelude, which he plays as Chopin is reputed to have played it, in long, non-legato phrases in glistening *jeu perlé*, each note seeming to have a life of its own. This idealization of single notes, making each note iridescent and pearl-like, was characteristic of his playing and is particularly apparent in the G and T series. His performance of the "Butterfly Etude" is an ideal one, and in his "Honor Roll of Recorded Chopin," the indefatigable auteur and encyclopedist Jan Holcman ranked it the greatest recording ever of the piece. George Halprin thought it closely resembled the performance he heard Pachmann give in New York in 1907, played quickly with a dainty, even touch, stressing very slightly the right hand octave melody so that the chord and the octaves almost have the same timbre, ending the work with a magical inspiration: while hastening the double sixths in the treble, he accelerates the octave run down the bass to a pianissimo, as if the butterfly has fluttered away. Mr. Halprin said that when Pachmann finished playing this, his right hand flew and fluttered into the air, imitating a butterfly flying away.

The recording of the D flat Waltz is the first example of coloratura bel canto style for which he was famous. His conception of the Waltz is that of a soprano singing roulades, interspersed with lyrical asides. Carried away by inspiration, he has his imaginary coloratura sing a cadenza at the end of the middle section before the reprise of the first part, and ends the work with great exuberance. It was the fashion at that time for virtuosi to inundate this waltz with pianistic elaborations: both Rosenthal and Joseffy added thirds, Godowsky thirds and contrapuntal melodies and Michalowski, a regular deluge of pianistic bric-a-brac. Against this, Pachmann's tiny cadenza seems harmless enough. But perhaps because there is no other alteration of the original text, it might seem even more disturbing.

The recordings of the C sharp minor Waltz and the Mazurka in A flat are prime examples of both his poetical ability and swinging rhythmic sense. The Waltz is played with great spirit and life, preserving Chopin's "tempo giusto" marking, each time the melody of the Waltz reappears he varies the shape. The beauty of the cantabile playing in the D flat section is vividly recorded, as is his famous diminuendo pianissimo ending. The recording of the Mazurka illustrates these features of his art as well, the first part played as if an idealized refinement of the dance—a fantasy, while the middle part is notable for the brio and bounce of his rhythm. As in the Butterfly Etude, he ends the work with an inspiration: he retards the melody and makes it disappear, as if the dancers had vanished over the horizon, a perfect rendition of Chopin's "morendo" marking.

Many considered Pachmann's playing of the Chopin Nocturnes his greatest achievements. You can hear suggestions of this on his G and T of the Nocturne in G major. The double-sixths have a suave, smooth delicacy and the lush sound he suggests in the "boat song" melody as he floats the song over the water is a rare glimpse of lyrical playing at its best. One can only imagine what this sensuous evocation must have sounded like in person.

Pachmann's abridged recording of the Chopin Barcarolle is the most primitively recorded of the 1907 group. Still the beauty of his touch, the coloratura mastery of double-note passages, the tonal opulence in the piano's middle register and the limpidity and chiaroscuro atmosphere which permeates the music comes through, despite the sonic impediments. The recording seems to illustrate the "bath of sound," as Leonide described it, enveloping his father's playing. Ease and technical mastery are apparent throughout. In listening to this performance, however, one has the feeling that he was racing with time to fit the recording on one side of a record, for the performance surely lacks expansiveness. Even in this abridged version (the opening is omitted as is the A major section), Pachmann probably was forced to play certain sections faster than he would have in concert—the "sfogato" section for example. This somewhat dampens one's pleasure in the performance, which is also compromised by the poor sonics. The Barcarolle was too aurally complex a work to record successfully in 1907.

THE 1909 PRE-DOG H.M.V. RECORDINGS

Matrix

3136f   Chopin Etude, Op. 10, No. 12
3138f   Raff *La Fileuse*
3139f   Mendelssohn Rondo Capriccioso (abbreviated)
3154f   Verdi / Liszt Rigoletto Paraphrase (abbreviated)

Pachmann's next series of recordings was made two years later for the same company, and the recordings appeared on "pre-dog" His Master's Voice discs, before the label adopted the dog, Nipper, as its trademark. The high level of playing of his 1907 recordings is maintained with one exception, and the sound is fuller and richer.

Mendelssohn's chestnut Rondo Capriccioso is among the best performances, demonstrating Pachmann's ability to sensitively mold phrases into a fairy-like scherzo. Once more his lively rhythmic sparkle is in evidence, as is the *jeu perlé* elegance and finesse of the arpeggios and passagework. Particularly admirable at the repeat is his ability to play arpeggios in pianissimo, and at the required presto tempo. The energy and brio of the concluding octave bravura passage is astounding.

This series includes the pianist's first recording of Liszt's Rigoletto Paraphrase. It was one of Pachmann's most beloved encores and he made three recordings of it. This is the most elegant of them, recorded at the age of sixty-one when his articulation in passagework was still preserved. He would often talk to the audience as his unique tone spun out the famous melody in the left hand, stating "This is Caruso," then when arriving at the delicate staccato octave repetitions in the right hand treble, "Here is Patti." His performance becomes both a showpiece for virtuosity and an imaginative, Lisztian operatic recreation. We can hear the sparkle of the chandeliers, even see the red velvet curtains and seats, the bejeweled ladies with their fans and lorgnettes amid the lush operatic melodies. Pachmann suggests all this with his amazing touch. Jan Holcman thought this recording of the piece the best made on 78 r.p.m. discs.

La Fileuse of Raff in Henselt's arrangement was a famous sentimental spinning song, popular in the late nineteenth century with both amateurs and professionals, partly because it illustrated so well the plushness and shimmering resonance of late nineteenth century pianos. It found an inspired spokesman in Pachmann, whose silvery performance has never been equaled. The evenness of his touch, the marvelous scale passages and the ethereal beauty of tone high in the treble, as well as the opulence of the ending arpeggios, made this work *the* Pachmann encore and he recorded it four times. Because of the better sound than the clattery 1907 disc, this 1909 disc may be the preferred recording, though the final Columbia recording with its softer, muted sound seems to suit the music even better.

Finally there is the only unsuccessful recording from this series, the "Revolutionary" Etude. Pachmann's performance of Chopin's heroic and passionate outburst is a total misconception. Performed as a sort of tragic romance, his left hand rolling waves of sound as he enunciates the right hand, not as angry declamations but as nostalgic entreaties! Even the arpeggiated figuration, at the second return of the theme after the middle part, is affected. The left hand figurations, which should be a maelstrom of simmering energy, merely accompany a too inert, lyrically-phrased right hand melody. The final unison descent which should suggest a climax of pent-up rage, here sounds decorative and weightless: a tempest in a teapot.

THE 1911/1912 AMERICAN VICTOR RECORDINGS

Matrix

November 7, 1911, Camden, New Jersey:
  C11198-1 Chopin Nocturne, Op. 15, No. 1
  C11199-1 Raff *La Fileuse*
  C11200-1 Chopin Prelude, Op. 28, No. 24, Etude, Op. 10, No. 5
  C11201-1 Chopin Impromptu, Op. 29, Prelude, Op. 28, No. 23
  C11202-1 Verdi-Liszt Rigoletto Paraphrase (abbreviated)

November 8, 1911, Camden, New Jersey:
  C11204-1 Mendelssohn Songs Without Words, Op. 67, No 7, Schumann
    Prophet Bird, from *Waldscenen*, Op. 82
  C11205-1 Liszt *Mazurka Brilliante*
  C11206-1 Chopin Etudes, Op. 10, No. 1 and Op. 25, No. 2
  C11207-1 Chopin Mazurka, Op. 50, No. 2
  C11208-1 Chopin Mazurkas, Op. 67, No. 4 and Op. 33, No. 3

April 25, 1912 Camden, New Jersey
  C11924-1 Chopin Preludes, Op. 28, Nos. 6, 7 and 10
  C11925-1 Chopin Nocturne, Op. 55, No. 1
  C11928-1 Mendelssohn Songs Without Words, Op. 30, No. 6 and Op.
    67, No. 4
  C11930-1 Chopin Polonaise, Op. 26, No. 1
  B11931-1 Chopin Etude, Op. 10, No. 3
  C11932-1 Chopin Ballade, Op. 47, part one

April 26, 1912 Camden, New Jersey
  C11935-1 Chopin Mazurka, Op. 59, No. 3
  C11936-1 Chopin Nocturne, Op. 37, No. 2
  C11937-1 Chopin Preludes, Op. 28, Nos. 20 and 16
  C11938-1 Chopin Etude, Op. 25, No. 5
  C11940-1 Chopin Ballade, Op. 47, part two
  C11941-1 Chopin Sonata, Op. 35 "Funeral March"
  C11942-1 Chopin-Godowsky Etude, Op. 10, No. 12, for left hand alone

Two more years passed before Pachmann recorded again. He returned to America in 1911 for what was advertised as his "Farewell Tour" and everyone surmised he would retire soon, for he was now sixty-three and older than his years. Amazingly, his tone was undiminished, even richer and fuller . . . but in this series we can hear some loss in articulation and purity of style. Mannerisms had begun to appear, not serious enough to destroy the beauty of his playing, but harbingers of decline.

Admirers, hearing of his imminent retirement, flocked to these concerts and Pachmann's sixth tour of America was the most successful up to then. Capitalizing on this, the Victor Talking Machine Co. offered him a contract for his most extensive series of recordings. He recorded forty works of which nineteen were eventually issued. Proof copies of at least some of the remaining eighteen unissued records went with Pachmann when he left America in June 1912. By the time the author had access to them through Cesco Pallottelli in the late 1950's, only nine remained. Unfortunately Victor somehow furnished Pachmann with inferior sonics compared to the sound given other pianists such as Paderewski and Olga Samaroff. The delicacy of his touch is not as readily apparent because of brittle, too-close sound, while the somewhat shallow Baldwin piano used at the sessions exaggerated this lack of depth. There is also a problem with balance in some places, with improper horn placement resulting in the left hand sometimes sounding almost as loud as the right. In the Chopin Funeral March there is a sudden drop in pitch, as if the engineer was slipshod, and less damagingly, some of the records were mislabeled. Despite all, Pachmann rose above mechanical impediments and carelessness to incise some haunting performances.

The Impromptu in A flat is taken at a very fast tempo, perhaps too fast for the score's "quasi presto" direction. He manages a breathless, crisp touch in the right hand and a whirling "zeffiroso" sound to the left hand triplets. Pachmann's great art here is in the rhapsodic lyricism of the middle section, with its subtle ritard and delightful cadenza "asides" amid the flowering of the melody, all done with ineffable spontaneity, ending with a ravishing Bel Canto-like trill before the return of the first part. This exquisite performance concludes with a typical Pachmann touch: he ends the work slyly, as Chopin wrote, with no ritard.

The issued recording of the Chopin Ballade in A flat contains only half of the work, from bar 116 on—at least Victor didn't issue an abridged version as G and T did with the Barcarolle. He takes the passagework more lyrically than usual, with exquisite rubato colorations, letting the music unfold gradually, building to a majestic climax. The Victor process rumbles badly during the development section but not enough to ruin the performance, which is rich and euphonious, rather than heroic.

Mendelssohn's Venetian Gondola Song is given a poetical interpretation with sensuous trills and double thirds, played with a haunting tone suggestive of watery opulence. Pachmann's extraordinary way of making the trills seems to come from nowhere and then vanish, imbuing the work with a magical spell that is nearly "Chopinesque." His performance of the Spinning Song, the other Mendelssohn work on the same twelve-inch disc, is less satisfying. An extremely fast tempo forces him to rush unevenly through many of the phrases, losing the rhythmic steadiness that the music should have to suggest a spinning wheel. Only the ending with its accelerando diminuendo to a pianissimo ending has the Pachmann touch.

Here Liszt's Rigoletto Paraphrase is a much more passionate and virtuosic. Though there is some loss of articulation and clarity, his *jeu perlé* is as beautiful as ever. The touch seems fuller and richer, and he tosses off the double thirds with a spontaneity and theatrical flair that any modern player could envy, yet the music never sounds harsh or vulgar. As in the 1909 recording, he preserves the feeling of vocal opulence amid Lisztian rhetorical grandeur. It is his ability to project these two contrasting elements in the music that makes the performance so special.

The F major Nocturne is played simply, the left hand figurations with an admirable softness and steadiness, creating a limpid serenity, even though the right hand is not always together with the left. In his subtle use of rhythmic waywardness here he never violates the basic pulse or loses continuity, the rhythm growing out of the music instead of being forced into it. The stormy middle section is played as a disturbing interlude with rushed double sixths, the more lyrical sequences stressed as the music gradually returns to the first theme, becoming more vivid and evocative and permeated with a tense stillness. Unfortunately the spell is ruined at the end because the record runs out, robbing Pachmann of the time to let the music die away . . . Pachmann was famous for his endings, where he would suspend the sound, breathlessly holding it and the audience until the tone vanished. Here, betrayed by the recording process, he simply plays a quick F major arpeggio as the record ends.

Leonide de Pachmann said that his father played the Chopin "Funeral March" at a quicker tempo than was usually taken, apparent on the Victor recording, where the work doesn't sound very heroic. The dotted rhythm is used as an effect of coloration, rushed in a certain phrase (repeated twice) as the pianist shapes the March to its destination. The trio is played with great sensitivity, Pachmann holding back the melody during the repetition as if suspending time with consolation, before returning to the sorrowful march.

The surprising (and rarest) recording in this series is Pachmann's performance of Leopold Godowsky's version for the left hand alone of the "Revolutionary" Etude. Given his poor recording of the original Etude, one would have thought he might have avoided works of this character, and in fact the first few phrases of the Godowsky transcription are played in a bumbling, amateurish manner. But do not discount this record, for after a while he recovers and plays the remaining music with a thrilling abandon and virtuosity unusual for him. From that point on, this is much better than his 1909 recording of the original and (partially) his only truly successful recording of a type of music that was not congenial to his temperament or style.

Other recorded performances from this series contain specific sections which stand out. The beautiful appoggiaturas in the Chopin Etude in E minor are spoiled by the harsh Victor sound, the performance weakened by the rather routine playing of the scherzando sections and the mild, unconvincing ending. But the lyrical E major section receives a suave and graceful performance, with a notable diminuendo before the return of the scherzando theme. The twenty-fourth Chopin Prelude in D minor is ruined by the inappropriate ending, but up to then the performance is intense and concentrated, with a deft, smooth delivery of the left hand figurations, which serve to energize the music.

THE UNISSUED RECORDINGS

Some of Pachmann's best playing on the 1911/1912 Victor series occurs on the nine unissued recordings, unique test pressings of which were preserved by Cesco Pallottelli, who allowed the author to tape the discs some four decades ago. We played them on an acoustic gramophone and I recorded the result using a microphone and portable tape recorder, today a method considered a Paleolithic process. It was all that was available, and since then the discs have disappeared, perhaps gone forever. We are left with less-than-professional sounding tapes, with extraneous noises (Pallottelli coughing, footsteps, etc.). Still the masterly playing comes through, though some indulgence is needed. Let us hope the test pressings survived and will surface someday.

Two Chopin Etudes, in C major and F minor, are among his best recordings. The first Etude, the famous arpeggio study that opens the first book of Etudes like a giant door to a new world, is played as the epitome of *jeu perlé*. He irradiates the notes, gives them an iridescent sheen, sometimes putting air between them, much like a jeweler showing the different pearls on a necklace strand. There is none of the heroic quality usually associated with this Etude. It is more poetical, though not without an intensity of its own. The performance also contains some daring pedal effects, employed to bring out some hidden melodies embedded in the arpeggiated figurations. The F minor Etude is played very evenly with some deft rubato touches in the final repetition of the theme. His legato and legatissimo are exemplary, combining a purling quality of tone with a scintillation uniquely his own.

The E major Etude from Op. 10 is played in an unsentimental manner, not too slowly, with an intensity of feeling and an undercurrent of passion which blazes in the middle section, with an amazing burst of bravura in the cadenza-like passage before the return of the lyrical first part. Leonide de Pachmann, discussing this recording, said his father had the smallest hands of any famous pianist. He said his father would spend hours inventing special fingerings to solve technical problems caused by his small hands. No one would guess, hearing the speed, bravura, accuracy and ease with which he plays these famous passages.

The F minor Nocturne from Op. 55 evolves in a trance-like manner, the oft-repeated melody given very expressively, with the color constantly varied with each repetition. A certain mannered quality in the phrasing tends to spoil the performance's freshness and gives the whole an air of overripeness. Pachmann redeems himself at the end with a tremendous example of pianistic control, as he mounts the arpeggios and lets them vanish in air. No other pianist has so mastered Chopin's "diminuendo morendo" markings as Pachmann, letting the music evaporate in a thread of tone.

The two Mazurkas, Op. 33, No. 3 and Op. 67, No 4 (this latter one he recorded four times) are both played with great charm. There is a daintiness and a fantasy, as if looking out from the chateau, one saw some peasants dancing in the field, closer to the nostalgic mazurka style of Moriz Rosenthal than the more lustily conceived and heavily accented mazurka performances of Ignace Friedman.

As for the group of Preludes, the little C sharp minor Prelude is played like a trickle down the keys, giving the performance enough interest to avoid triviality—a little epigram, no more, no less. The performance of the famous C minor "Funeral March" Prelude, one of Chopin's miniature masterpieces, is remarkable for his control of graded chords, which soften with each repetition of the fatal melody until the final chord, which is louder, suggesting the closing of a tomb. The B flat minor Prelude is given an intense, concentrated performance similar to the issued D minor Prelude recording. The bravura is careful and controlled but not overwhelming. At sixty-three, Pachmann still preserved an impetuous, virtuoso mastery.

The unissued performance of the first part of the A flat Ballade is somewhat faster than usual. He emphasizes the dance-like rhythms of the music, retaining a beautiful flow and smoothness. George Halprin remembered Pachmann playing the broken octaves that introduce the second theme with the most caressing sound, in a pianissimo that you had to strain to hear. The whole performance apparently had a magical, seductive quality that was not captured on either of the two Ballade recordings.

Last there is an oddity, a brilliant, delightful performance of Liszt's rarely heard *Mazurka Brilliante*, the only recording made of the work until the 1960's. He plays it as if it were a masterpiece, with great rhythmic verve and animation. He really believed in this music, and makes the listener believe in it too, despite the fact that this is one of the Master's lesser works.

Of the unissued Victor recordings which are apparently lost, the most valuable would be the great pianist's recording of the Chopin Berceuse, his only recording of the work. Pallottelli said that Pachmann rejected it because of excessive surface noise. One must conclude that his extraordinary pianissimi were beyond the ability of the Victor acoustical process. This is one of the tragedies of the gramophone, for Pachmann's performances of the Berceuse were particularly treasured by his admirers.

COLUMBIA RECORDINGS OF 1915/16

Matrix

December 1915
   6591   Chopin Etude, Op. 25, No. 3 and Prelude, Op. 28, No. 16
   6595   Liszt Polonaise No. 2—cadenza and finale

6596   Chopin Prelude, Op. 28, No. 24
6598   Chopin Impromptu, Op. 29
6616   Chopin Mazurka, Op. 67, No. 4 and Prelude, Op. 28, No. 23
6619   Chopin Nocturne, Op. 9, No. 2

Early 1916
6968   Chopin Nocturne, Op. 27, No. 2 (abbreviated)
6969   Chopin Valse, Op. 70, No. 1 and Ecossaises, Op. 72, No. 3
6971   Schumann *Grillen*, from *Fantasiestücke*, Op. 12
6972   Chopin Sonata, Op. 58 Scherzo
6973   Raff *La Fileuse*
6974   Liszt *Liebestraum* No. 3
6976   Chopin Mazurka, Op. 33, No. 4
6877   Verdi-Liszt Rigoletto Paraphrase (abbreviated)
6978   Brahms Capriccio, Op. 76, No. 5
6979   Chopin Mazurka, Op. 33, No. 3 and Etude, Op. 25, No. 3

Pachmann retired in 1912 and disappeared, but Cesco Pallottelli located him and persuaded him to return to his career. After merely a year's absence, he was back on the concert stage. It turned out to be one of the busiest periods of his career, for his popularity was now at its peak, and he recorded again, this time for British Columbia. The series was made in 1915 when he was sixty-six, under entirely different circumstances from his other recordings.

Knowing the Maestro's aversion to the environment of the recording studio, the management of the Columbia Graphophone Company sent the recording apparatus to his home, around the corner from Queen's Hall, where he could record anything he wanted at his leisure. This resulted in some strange choices, such as a Brahms Capriccio, the Scherzo from the Chopin Third Sonata and two performances of the Chopin Etude in F major, Op. 25. Compared to earlier recordings, the Columbia acoustics are softer, more muted and somewhat fuzzy. The sound is not as focused or close up. Pachmann's touch was better served with this process, but it was prone to very noisy surfaces which frequently obliterate the softest playing.

As he aged, Pachmann's art took on an affected sentimentality, regrettable qualities all too evident on his Columbia recordings. One immediately notices a precipitous decline. There seems to be little energy, and his articulation, somewhat faded in the 1911/12 Victor recordings, is now almost nonexistent. The playing is bereft of sparkle or life, with a corresponding loss of technical prowess, and the musical mannerisms noticeable on some of the Victor discs are now prevalent.

There is a lack of freshness in his interpretations, which is hard to explain since only three years had passed since his previous recordings. There are some beautiful performances in the Columbia series, but the choice items are much scarcer than before. One of the best is the Cadenza from Liszt's fire-eating Polonaise in E major, once a very popular work. Here there is none of the bravura and grandeur to be heard on the recording of Liszt pupil Arthur de Greef—instead we have a performance of breathless, jewel-like delicacy, the notes spun out in graceful and fluid phrases. The polonaise rhythm is not pointed or energetic enough, and the octave scramble at the end doesn't help. Still, the Cadenza (which takes up most of the recording) is unique.

Chopin's C major Mazurka, Op. 33, No. 3, is entrancing, one of Pachmann's great recorded performances. Jan Holcman, once again, singled out this recording as the best ever. The mazurka rhythm is played with a certain fantasy, not rigidly, against a suavely phrased melody that seems to sway. The Mazurka's "stamp," in the middle section, is lively but never heavy, and the unique touch, when the melody returns with an arpeggiated chord, is like an awakening.

The famous B minor Mazurka, Op. 33, No. 4, is given a fantastic (some might say, too fantastic) performance. Again he seems to find a whimsical fantasy behind the rhythm and doesn't keep a steady beat but rushes it, reflecting the different moods of the music. Chopin's pupil Wilhelm von Lenz reported that the composer played it "like a Ballade." It is usually performed either very thoughtfully, even sadly (Rosenthal) or more outgoingly, with a lusty, captivating rhythm (Friedman). Pachmann's performance is somewhere in between, stressing like Friedman the dance rhythm (but with a much lighter touch), at the same time similar to Rosenthal's expressive playing of the lyrical B major section. But in his exuberance, Pachmann adds a chain of double notes in the repeat section following the B major melody. It is done so deftly one might have thought Chopin wrote it. Just a minor thing, yet it can't help but irritate those who find Pachmann's playing already too indulgent.

Perhaps the Columbia of *La Fileuse* is the most attractive of his four recordings. While the earlier versions are more technically adroit, the music suits the softer, muted sound of the Columbia process and the spinning motive is more veiled, allowing the sentimental melody to float. Pachmann plays the final arpeggios in limpid, silvery cascades of sound, well caught by the Columbia process. These are the best of his Columbia discs; all the others suffer from musical or technical deficiencies.

Pachmann frequently played the Etude in F, Op. 25, No. 3, but neither of the Columbia recordings is satisfactory. The first, issued separately only in America, has some poised if mannered phrasing and a lovely, evaporating pianissimo trill at the end, but is played much too slowly to capture the capricious badinage-like feeling required. The second is played faster and livelier, but both suffer from rhythmical inaccuracies and an inability to differentiate the three basic rhythms that give the music its wayward charm.

The increased mannerisms are most apparent in the Columbia recording of the Impromptu in A flat. While not played as fast as the earlier Victor, it has no spontaneity or charm—everything is exaggerated. Even the middle section is stale compared to the earlier version, and the ending sounds affected. The lack of sparkle is particularly apparent in the Scherzo movement from the Chopin B minor Sonata. The piece's thoughtful, enigmatic trio and the delicacy of the Scherzo particularly suited Pachmann in his prime, but now everything is too lifeless and slow, the middle section too mannered and rhythmically uneven. The Columbia recording of the Rigoletto Paraphrase is the least satisfactory, lacking the elegant facility of the 1907 disc and the passion and tonal splendor of his 1911 recording.

The curious Brahms recording is a total loss, Pachmann's most boring disc. This Capriccio, some Waltzes and a Rhapsody were the only works of Brahms he played. There is nothing in the recorded performance to suggest he had any affinity for Brahms's music. The Columbia disc that most obviously shows his great technical decline is the second of his recordings of Chopin's Prelude in B flat minor. A disaster, with the left hand (or what one hears of it through the noisy surface) almost non-existent in a hectic, embarrassing performance.

Finally there are two Columbia recordings of Chopin Nocturnes. The D flat Nocturne was considered one of Pachmann's triumphs when in his prime, on a par with his performances of the Berceuse. Little of the earlier *réclame* is justified by the recording, which is played so slowly (his slowest recorded performance), it would have required a second side had he recorded the complete work. It begins at the second repetition of the melody, vitiating any possibility for the pianist to build a spell and compromising the intensity of the music. The disc is also the noisiest of the Columbias, the surface noise frequently obscuring the sensitive but mannered performance.

But then Pachmann plays the hackneyed E flat Nocturne as if it were the most beautiful music ever written. He colors the familiar melody with an almost unbearable beauty of tone, which becomes more intense with each repetition, ending with a breathless cadenza, letting the music die away as if he were loathe to end it. However the performance is ruined (so Leonide thought) by his constant breaking of the hands. Nowhere else is this very old-fashioned mannerism as obvious or as irritating to modern sensibilities as it is here.

PIANO ROLLS

Like many of his colleagues, Pachmann preferred making piano rolls to incising disc recordings. The effort involved was less stressful, there was no time limit and one could play almost anything one liked, including large-scale works. Best of all, one had real piano sound. While there are a few successful piano rolls by famous performers of the past, Pachmann's are not among them. There is little in most of these rolls to suggest that it was Pachmann who was playing. With all their faults, his disc recordings capture at least at times some of the beauty of his playing, and are infinitely preferable to the rolls.

FINAL RECORDINGS

VICTORS OF 1923/24 AND H.M.V. ELECTRICALS OF 1925/27

Matrix

December 14, 1923, Camden, New Jersey
    C29086-1   Chopin, Impromptu, Op. 36
    C29090-1   Schumann Novelette, Op. 21, No. 1
    C11934-2   Chopin Prelude, Op. 28, No. 15
    C29091-1   Chopin Nocturne, Op. 32, No. 1

May 26, 1924, Camden, New Jersey
    C11934-5   Chopin Prelude, Op. 28, No. 15
    C11934-6   Chopin Prelude, Op. 28, No. 15

September 23, 1924, Camden, New Jersey
    C29090-3   Schumann Novelette, Op. 21, No. 1
    C29090-4   Schumann Novelette, Op. 21, No. 1
    B30934-1   Mendelssohn, Song Without Words, Op. 62, No. 6
    B39035-1   Schumann Prophet Bird, from *Waldscenen*, Op. 82

June 26, 1925, Hayes, London, England
    Cc6253-1   Chopin Nocturne, Op. 27, No. 2
    Cc6255-1   Chopin Mazurka, Op. 24, No. 4
    Cc6256-1   Chopin Mazurka, Op. 50, No. 2
    Bb6258-1   Chopin Prelude, Op. 28, No. 6 and Mazurka, Op. 67, No. 1
    Cc6259-2   Chopin Nocturne, Op. 32, No. 1, with speech
    Cc6260-1   Chopin Valse, Op. 64, No. 1 and Etude, Op. 25, No. 3
    Cc6261-1   Chopin Impromptu, Op. 36

December 15, 1925, Hayes, London, England
    Cc7529-1   Chopin Polonaise, Op. 26, No. 1
    Bb7535-1   Chopin Valse, Op. 64, No. 1, with speech
    Bb7535-2   Chopin Valse, Op. 64, No. 1, with speech
    Bb7537-1   Chopin Valse, Op. 70, No. 1
    Cc7538-1   Chopin Valse, Op. 64, No. 3

November 3, 1927, Small Queen's Hall, London
   Cc11757-2   Chopin Nocturne, Op. 72, No. 1
   Bb11759-1   Chopin Preludes, Op. 28, Nos. 3 and 6
   Cc11760-1   Chopin Prelude, Op. 28, No. 15
   Bb11761-1   Mendelssohn Prelude, Op. 35, No. 1
   Cc11762-1   Chopin Mazurkas, Op. 63, No. 3 and Op. 67, No. 4
   Bb11763-1   Chopin Etude, Op. 10, No. 5, with speech

Pachmann was in his late seventies when he made his final recordings, Victor acoustics recorded during his last American tour of 1923–1925, and electrical recordings made in England for HMV between 1925 and 1927. The decline apparent in the 1915 Columbias has now progressed almost to disintegration. That last American tour went on for three years, the old man giving as many as three concerts a week, immediately an enormous financial success but at an incalculable personal cost. When it ended, Pachmann was played out.

These final American acoustic recordings are preferable to most of the H.M.V. electricals, for they were made before the crushing strain of that grueling last American tour, which exhausted the pianist completely. There is some of his old magic in the second Chopin Impromptu. The late acoustic sound captures his touch better than the earlier Victor discs, and the glistening *jeu perlé* right-hand scale passages, which individualize each note in pianissimo, are well-recorded. Pachmann gives the popular "Raindrop" Prelude a questioning coloration in the D flat melody, with the "raindrops" pulsating underneath, and colors the secondary theme in the middle section to sound like a supplication. Somehow Pachmann seems to get underneath the music, to tune in on Chopin's own "wave length."

Pachmann's pioneer electrical recordings are brittle and tinny, no better at capturing his distinctive touch than many of his acoustic recordings. The vaudeville atmosphere dominating his later appearances, with the pianist talking incessantly while playing is, unhappily, all too well-captured. The frantic tempi, the textural inaccuracies, the headlong rushing of one musical phrase into another, at times making the music almost unrecognizable, were symptoms of the exhaustion and stress the seventy-seven year old pianist was suffering. And as he aged it seems his hearing was affected.

The C sharp minor Waltz sounds like a parody of his 1907 recording; the C sharp minor Polonaise, with its hasty tempi as if he had a train to catch, is comical; the Opus 64 A flat Waltz is given a fitful, petulant reading. Hearing such performances one wishes that the artist would relax if only to let the music breathe. The Nocturne in D flat feels rushed and restless, and sounds like a different pianist from the earlier Columbia disc—the one too fast, the other too slow. The lack of repose and the fast tempo here causes Pachmann some difficulties in the cadenza, which lacks his customary elegance. The hard sound contributes to the tense atmosphere which envelops the performance. There are two extant versions of Chopin's "Minute" Waltz from these sessions, an unissued version having turned up only recently. The performances are almost identical, with a section, he tells us while playing, that is "à la Paganini"—but the talking is different. The unissued version enjoys better sound, but neither version can compare with the pianist's 1907 recorded performance.

These recordings, the most easily found of his discs (except for the unissued "Minute" Waltz), are terrible performances. Sadly they are the best known of Pachmann's recordings and primarily responsible for the low state of his reputation among many musicians. Knowing only this playing, and perhaps only accounts of his eccentric platform behavior, it is easy for some to dismiss him as a mountebank and charlatan—not a serious artist.

After a year's rest in Italy, he returned to England for some concerts in 1927 and made a few more recordings there, which proved to be his last. An inaccurate "Black Key" Etude, with the final octaves in contrary motion "à la Godowsky" (as he says on the record) is both pathetic and laughable. But the electrical recording process had improved in the two years since his previous sessions and both the Mendelssohn Prelude and the Chopin Nocturne, each in E minor, benefit from the more attractive sound. For the first time we can hear Pachmann as he probably sounded before the public.

The Mendelssohn is notable for its admirable vigor. He plays the arpeggios in soft, brush-like waves against a penetrating yet haunting cantabile melody. The tone brightens and the work progresses and ends triumphantly with great zest and verve. As for the Chopin Nocturne in E minor, you can hardly say he plays the work. It floats from his fingers like a beloved memory that can never be recaptured. The matchless beauty of tone brightens with the articulated scale passages only to return even softer, creating a spell that remains long after the record ends. This is his best electric recording, his final testament and a vindication of his art. It is sad to think that of the more than a hundred individual pieces he recorded, only the last two capture the true sound of his playing.

Although Pachmann made recordings that were not worthy of him, particularly most of those from his declining years, there are a few stunning, even unforgettable recorded performances in his discography. If they can never replace the memories of the concert performances that his admirers cherished, for us uninitiated who never heard him, some at least suggest his greatness. Perhaps the pianist was right when he said at the end of his life:

> I shall not be forgotten, I have made some gramophone records. And when your children and your grandchildren ask you who was this de Pachmann? You will be able to show them how he played and understood the works of Chopin. And though they cannot see me, they will hear my voice through my music and they will know why all the world worshipped de Pachmann.

Notes

CHAPTER 1

1. Russia did not adopt the Gregorian calendar of most the rest of the world until after the 1917 Revolution. The difference between the old style (Julian) calendar and the new style (Gregorian) calendar was twelve days in the nineteenth century, thirteen in the twentieth century, the new style calendars having the later dates.

2. Recent research by Michael Kassler has turned up details about a certain Anton Veit Pachmann (1717–1809), a government official in Prague, whose daughter Walburga Pachmann Lackner was employed by Charles, 3rd Earl Stanhope, from 1802 until his death in 1816, and who served as his musical assistant, advising him on his musical inventions. It is unknown if there was a connection to Vladimir Pachmann's family. Kassler's findings appear in his book, *The Music Trade in Georgian England*, Ashgate, Farnham, Surrey, UK, 2011. Information about the Pachmann family's early years is found in material from Semyon Pachmann's estate, located in the State Archive of the Odessa Region. There is a family genealogy, remarkable and unusual for its time, kept by Vikentiy and enlarged by Semyon, as well as programs from concerts that the Pachmann family attended and participated in, letters, wills and so forth. That Semyon left this material to an institution in Odessa, rather than Kazan or St. Petersburg where he became a counselor to the Czar, might show his desire for it to reside in an environment friendlier to Jews than the other cities.

3. This does not mean that converted Jews like Rubinstein did not suffer from anti-Semitism. By the end of the century, in Europe at least, "Jew" had become a racial term, but there is no evidence that Pachmann ever suffered much from anti-Semitic attacks. Later many doubted that Pachmann was even Russian, for his personality became so cosmopolitan, and his playing so "un-Russian." H. Sutherland Edwards visited Anton Rubinstein in the 1890's and left the following in his memoirs: "The Russians are proud of Rubinstein, and, in spite of his

Hebrew origin, look upon him as one of themselves. Pachmann, on the other hand, born in Russia but of the Jewish race, they seem by no means eager to claim. 'Il est Juif, Polonais, Allemand, tous ce que vous voulez,' said Madame Essipoff to me one day; 'seulement, il n'est pas Russe.'"[He is a Jew, Polish, German, whatever you wish, only, he's not Russian.]

4. Translated from Russian by Peter Greenleaf

5. The identity of the Handel work is not certain but most likely it was an arrangement by Ludwig Stark of a movement of the Concerto Grosso in E minor.

6. The exact identity of this patroness is unknown—she may have been Elizaveta Branicka Vorontsova, wife of Count Mikhail Semyonovich, who from 1823 was "Governor-General of New Russia." She had been the lover of Pushkin during his Odessa exile.

7. Madame Slepouchkine is reminiscent of the character "Misrule" in ancient May Day morality plays, a symbolic figure that embodied rudeness as fun, insulting solemn agents of propriety, driving them from the stage with blows and insults, and presiding over a world turned upside down. In Elizabethan England during May Day festivals there were "topsy-turvy days" when the Lord of Misrule presided over such mayhem as boys teaching the masters, women proposing to men, and other similar and at all other times, scandalous and outrageous behavior. A more recent manifestation was Alfred Jarry's 1896 play "Ubu Roi" which featured Père Ubu, for whom "everything is turned upside down." Author Jarry eventually began to think he was Ubu himself, beginning his meals with dessert and ending with the appetizer. Jarry once stated: "Laughter is born out of the discovery of the contradictory."

CHAPTER 2

1. The majority of information concerning Pachmann's earliest years stems from documents in the State Archive of the Odessa Region, and a handful of interviews the pianist gave to Buffen and Saleski, as well as from the specific journals cited, and from Cesco Pallottelli's World War One pamphlet on Pachmann, plus a six page unpublished memoir by Pallottelli entitled "My Thirty Years with Vladimir de Pachmann," the manuscript of which Pallottelli gave the author.

2. Kahrer, after studies with Liszt, went on to lessons with Henselt and Bülow. Although a fiery, passionate player, an international career somehow never evolved for her and she ended up teaching at the Dresden Conservatory.

3. This was quoted in Odessa's *Novorosijsky Telegraph* on October 12, 1869. Translated from Russian by Tanya Gerasimchuck.

4. In recordings of the concerto by Liszt students Emil Sauer and Arthur de Greef, the last movement is played maestoso.

5. From the October 12, 1869, article in *Novorossijsky Telegraph*. Details about the conductor, venue and date for the performance of the Rubinstein concerto are lacking. Translated from Russian by Tanya Gerasimchuck.

6. Translated from German by Carsten Fischer from Kahrer's autobiography.

7. This was quoted in Odessa's *Novorosijsky Telegraph* on October 12, 1869. Translated from Russian by Tanya Gerasimchuck.

8. Translated from Russian by Ludmilla Zadayanchuk.

9. Ibid.

10. When this Jewish merchant lost his fortune through a bad investment, Strogonoff astonished his peers by offering the man a sum equal to his loss; he was refused, but the merchant did accept a sinecure Strogonoff provided. Sadly, all details of his relationship to Pachmann seem to be lost forever.

11. Translated from Russian by Margarita Glebov.

CHAPTER 3

1. Translated from Russian by Victoria Solyanaya.

2. Just at this time a certain Theodor Pachmann (1801–1881) was publishing a series of books in German and Russian on various aspects of Russian law; on the title page of some of these he is listed as "Theodor Ritter von Pachmann." It is unknown whether he was a relative, but not improbable that Vladimir was aware of this Pachmann with the aristocratic "von" in his name.

3. Translated from German by Carsten Fischer.

4. Ibid.

5. Bülow was also unabashedly and proudly anti-Semitic. Adrian Williams has reported that Liszt wrote to Caroline von Sayn-Wittgenstein on June 9, 1881: "he is not given to conciliation, nor to indulgence! . . . His horror of the Jews has not diminished—at every turn he heaps abuse upon them."

6. Bülow's Chopin Etude edition exhibits the worst sins of the Victorian aesthetic towards Chopin, running free over the composer's text, changing key signatures and phrasing. At times the music is almost unrecognizable, a huge distance from the original, so free it is often more Bülow than Chopin.

7. E-mail to Gregor Benko, July 7, 2008.

8. In recent years Allan Evans, an American with ties to Italy, has published claims that Pachmann about 1879 had lessons in Florence with a former Chopin pupil named Vera Rubio, and that "the preparation and style she imparted to Pachmann enabled him to return to performing." These claims are more properly described as rumor and there is no evidence to support them. Vera de Kologrivoff (1816–1880) was a Russian woman who studied with Chopin in Paris, becoming his assistant in 1846. Later she moved to Florence with her husband the painter Luigi Rubio, who had accepted a position at the Academy of Fine Arts. She taught piano privately in Florence. According to what Evans told the author, a century after Rubio died Evans interviewed a piano teacher in Rome, Aldo Mantia (1903–?), who claimed that he, as a young man, had had some lessons with the ancient Pachmann, living in senile retirement in Rome. Mantia's mother, Ida Bosisio Mantia, had been a student of Liszt's Italian pupil Giovanni Sgambati. According to Evans, Aldo Mantia told him that his mother, accompanied by the violinist Teresina Tua, visited Mme. Rubio, who told the pair that Pachmann had been her pupil. Mantia also told Evans that his mother said she had once visited Liszt in Rome, and that Liszt also told her of these lessons. There is no documentary evidence for these supposed lessons, nor Ida Mantia's visit to Liszt, nor Liszt's supposed confirmation of the story, and it is as probable that these claims

rest on exaggeration, misunderstanding and fantasy as much as fact. There is no evidence that Pachmann himself ever spoke of Rubio, or of any lessons with her, and no word about this supposed encounter was ever published until after Evans made his claims. (Since then his claims have been repeated as fact, sadly even finding their way into the recent edition of *Die Musik in Geschichte und Gegenwart*, based solely on Evans's word.) Pachmann had no qualms about trumpeting his associations with other notable pianists, teachers and musical figures, and with his total obsession with Chopin, one would think he would have boasted loudly of a special affinity gained by direct contact with an actual pupil of Chopin. And if not himself, Pachmann's managers would have jumped at any opportunity to publicize such lessons, just as over-eager managers did make exaggerated claims that Pachmann was a pupil of Liszt. But apparently not a word seems to have been mentioned about lessons with Rubio by anyone besides Aldo Mantia and his mother. We do not even know that it was Rubio herself who made such claims, only that Aldo Mantia and perhaps his mother said so. Evans's fantastic assertion that there were lessons which were of "extreme importance" and that Pachmann received any specific style or preparation from Mme. Rubio—or that her teaching enabled him to return to playing (this he had already done) and become an acknowledged Chopin interpreter—is all without a shred of evidence. Evans's claim can be found in his essay included as a liner note to the Dante CD, "Vladimir de Pachmann, Vol. 1"—HPC 056.

CHAPTER 4

1. All attempts to learn Waltmann's full name have proven fruitless. Some sources spell it "Waldmann," some "Wallmann." Sometimes it is spelled with one "n."

2. Translations from German by Carsten Fischer.

3. Ibid.

4. Ibid.

5. Pachmann was already exhibiting signs of hypochondria as well. An August 3, 1882, letter from Moriz Rosenthal to pianist Alfred Grünfeld (in the archives of the Gesellschaft der Musikfreunde in Vienna) begs to postpone a visit because of illness: "It is that I suffer under a little chest pain (not in the sense of Pachmann's)." German original translated by Carsten Fischer.

6. Translations from German by Lottie and Henry Morley.

7. Translation from French by the author.

8. In our day we have pianists who record the works of Chopin on reconstructions of (or even authentic) historic pianos, but using the modern, "bar-by-bar" way of playing which certainly is inappropriate.

9. In an interview in the *Musical Courier* printed on December 14, 1904, Pachmann said "Liszt's technic, in these days when technic runs in the street, would not be considered extraordinary."

10. Translations from German by Carsten Fischer.

11. Huneker's book on Chopin prints a "programme" for Chopin's F minor Fantaisie, Op. 49, that he claims Liszt had received from Chopin himself, and

then passed on to Pachmann. Certainly Pachmann had told him so—the first two bars are an ominous rapping at the front door; George Sand and others want to come in, and soon Sand is at Chopin's feet, begging forgiveness, and so forth. It is absurd, but Huneker seemed to believe that both Pachmann and Liszt himself had embellished the story: "This far from ideal reading is an authoritative one, coming as it does from Chopin by way of Liszt. I console myself for its rather commonplace character with the notion that perhaps in the retelling the story has caught some personal cadenzas of the two historians." Wakeling Dry and E. Markham Lee provided the "Descriptive Notes" for some of Pachmann's Chopin centenary recitals in 1911, and commented: "Various programs, more imaginative than happy, have been attached to it at various times. Surely it is best to let this glorious music tell its own tale."

12. In the December 1915 *Vanity Fair* interview Arthur Symons wrote that Pachmann told him the letter was to "Walter Vache," an obvious misprint for Walter Bache, Liszt's pupil who was instrumental in making the arrangements for the composer's visit to England in 1886. No copy of the letter has surfaced. The Liszt/Bache correspondence is still eagerly being sought by Liszt scholars.

13. The translator is unknown. Liszt was fifteen. Liszt biographer Alan Walker dates the concert in the early weeks of 1837. The original source for Liszt's recounting of these stories is found in volume two of his collected writings: *Essays und Reisebriefe eines Bacalaureus der Tonkunst.*

CHAPTER 5

1. Translation from French by author.

2. Ibid.

3. Ibid.

4. In the spring of 1879 Madame Montigny-Rémaury had simply not shown up for a London performance of Beethoven's "Emperor" Concerto with conductor August Manns at a Crystal Palace concert, and Xavier Scharwenka, sitting in the audience with the other expectant concert goers, stepped up to the piano to play the performance.

5. In *Cassell's* magazine in December, 1926, Pachmann wrote: "Of all the great people I have met I think the one who least liked the piano was the late Queen Victoria." According to Leonard Liebling (*Musical Courier.* December 20, 1943) on one occasion, after a well-known pianist had given a recital of classics at Osborne Castle, Her Majesty asked him as a special favor to play The Maiden's Prayer.

6. Translation from French by author.

CHAPTER 6

1. This was the Ascherberg brand piano.

2. The recital took place on May 31, 1882.

3. Dr. Lewis Eastlick, hand surgeon, wrote in December 2007 in a private communication to Gregor Benko: "There are data from many sources, from ancient

times up to the recent past, which attest to the effects of ant venom on acute rheumatologic conditions (gout being the most effectively treated). This information seems to have been largely forgotten and does not generally appear in modern medical practice. More recently, investigations have been taking place in Miami studying the efficacy of ant venom in rheumatologic disorders. These studies grew out of accounts of remission of rheumatologic disorders, after being stung by jungle ants. Historically formic acid was thought to be the important factor in remission (ants are correctly termed formicids and live in formicaries), but current studies indicate that the actual compounds seem to be a bit more complex and may involve certain proteins or a combination of proteins and other compounds (which may include formic acid). In summary, the story is certainly quite believable from a medical point-of-view, although the exact chemistry is not yet known, nor is ant venom widely used at present (still under investigation)." Dr. Eastlick cited a 1906 article from the *Dublin Journal of Medical Science*.

4. Translation from Italian by Dr. Geno Gemmato.

CHAPTER 7

1. From the author's 1960 London interview with Serge Krish, a Busoni pupil who became a conductor. A private letter to his mother from pianist John Powell, then studying with Leschetizky, recounts how the famous pedagogue was not reticent to show his anti-Semitism towards his Jewish pupils. We can only speculate if this might have colored Leschetizky's opinion of Pachmann, and other Jewish pianists, many his own students.

2. This part of the *Fremden-Blatt* review is taken from Lahee's "Famous Pianists of To-day and Yesterday," where the translation is not credited.

3. Translation from German by Carsten Fischer.

4. This might have been a scrapbook with typed translations of reviews and was probably unique; the author has not been able to locate the volume.

5. The Philharmonic Society did not become "The Royal Philharmonic" until 1912; Maggie's letter is in the collection of the orchestra's correspondence in the British Library.

6. This reminiscence comes from an unidentified Danish publication originally provided by Cesco Pallottelli; English translation by Scandinavian Airline office in Rome.

7. From Maggie's memoirs published in French and English magazines.

8. Pachmann defended his flight from Rubinstein's recital in an interview in *Musical America* on July 6, 1907: "I was in Bechstein Hall, in London . . . Rubinstein was playing. He knew what the English like. He pounded, I could not stand it. I turned to escape, I ran—I ran from the place."

9. Translation from German by Carsten Fischer.

10. Osborne's comments on Shaw were in an article in *Opera* in August, 2006. Some of Shaw's music writing was just this side of insincere. Ferruccio Busoni met him in late October 1919, and wrote to his wife: "he talks too much and he cannot

cloak his vanity." Busoni's biographer, Della Couling, wrote: "Busoni's canny eye saw through a lot of Shaw's bluster . . . he enjoyed . . . twitting him relentlessly on the inconsistencies and shallowness of his pronouncements on music."

11. More than five decades later Cesco Pallottelli was to tell the author that Pachmann said he had found Waltmann with his wife in "suspicious circumstances."

12. Schwab's corruption might seem more obvious than that of some present day managers, but was probably not more venal.

13. General Georges Boulanger (1837–1891) was a French military hero then much in the news.

CHAPTER 8

1. Mr. Florsheim (or his editor), got the Latin wrong. The correct phrase, "mundus vult decipi, ergo decipiatur," translates "The world wants to be deceived, so let it be deceived."

2. Later Florsheim changed his opinion of Pachmann, and was soon including Pachmann's name, along with those of Paderewski and Rosenthal, in his listings of the day's truly great pianists, at the same time railing against Busoni in his *Musical Courier* reports of concerts in Berlin. Some believe that Florsheim's opinions could be purchased.

3. Edwin Hughes (1885–1965), eminent American pianist. His notebooks and diaries were published in 1978 in the *American Music Teacher*, Volume 27, 1978 Nos. 3, 4, and 5.

4. Adolph Carpe (1847–?).

5. Wilhelm Middleschulte (1863–1943), German organist particularly distinguished as a Bach player; the teacher of Virgil Fox.

6. Pachmann himself sometimes programmed only the Minuet movement from this sonata.

CHAPTER 9

1. Considered by many as a superb manager, Gottschalk's career ended in August 1900 when he, along with his wife's two brothers, was killed on a Pennsylvania camping trip as the horse drawn wagon they were riding was struck by a train.

2. Huneker's pun, with its comparison of Pachmann to a chimpanzee, was possibly deliberately reminiscent of a powerfully influential forebear, the English critic Henry Fothergill Chorley, who had died in 1872 at the age of seventy-four. A lifelong bachelor with effeminate manners, Chorley wrote for the *Athenaeum* and today is remembered almost solely for his righteous championing of Gounod's operas as sublime, while dismissing Wagner's *Lohengrin* as "nothingness." According to John Lehmann, Chorley was an embarrassing alcoholic with a squeaky staccato voice and white hair that "stood up straight . . . devious, crabbed and

pompous . . . alternately pathetic and grotesque" an object of both respect and derision, known as "the missing link between the chimpanzee and the cockatoo."

3. Twenty years earlier Cooke apparently thought that Pachmann was actually mentally retarded, and incapable of discussing anything but music. In the September 1913 *Etude* he wrote about the 19th century autistic-savant pianist "Blind Tom" Wiggins (1849–1908), born into slavery in the American South and exhibited like a freak. He could play any music he heard by ear, and composed inconsequential pieces based on non-musical sounds:

> Blind Tom's peculiar ability has led many hasty commentators to conclude that music is a wholly separate mental faculty to be found particularly in a more or less shiftless and irresponsible class of gifted but intellectually limited human beings. The few cases of men and women whose musical talent seems to eclipse their minds so that they remain in utter darkness to everything else in life, should not be taken as a basis for judging other artists of real genius and undisputed mental breadth. I have in mind, however, the case of one pianist who is very widely known and highly lauded, but who is very slightly removed from the class of Blind Tom. A trained alienist, one acquainted with the difference between the eccentricities which frequently accompany greatness and the unconscious physical and psychical evidences of idiocy which agree so clearly with the antics of the chimpanzee of the droll Capuchin monkeys, might find in the performer to whom I refer a subject for some very interesting, not to say startling reflections. Few have ever been successful in inducing this pianist to talk upon any other subject than music for more than a few minutes at a time.

4. Polish born Alexander Lambert (1862–1929) had studied with Liszt before moving to the United States. He gave up playing in 1892 to become a prominent teacher in New York.

CHAPTER 10

1. In recent days Huneker's reputation has begun a process of rehabilitation. Dr. Douglas Hofstadter, in his book, "I Am a Strange Loop" published in 2007, proposed that a unit he coined "the huneker" be used to measure the richness of mental representations, based on Huneker's description of Chopin.

2. We do not know which Chopin work it was that Pachmann played backwards. This stunt is not as improbable as it sounds: in the 1930s, Josef Hofmann played Chopin's fourth Ballade backwards, with the last chord played first and so on, at a party at the Curtis Institute of Music.

3. The earliest use of the simile of pearls for the notes in perfect piano runs was apparently by the composer Mikhail Glinka while describing the playing of John Field:

> It was as if he did not strike the keyboard, but that his fingers, like giant drops of rain, poured over the keys as pearls on velvet.

4. Adrian Williams's book of reminiscences of Liszt relates that the music publisher Albert Gutmann brought the young composer/conductor Felix Mottl

to Liszt in 1879 and witnessed this same upside-down "trick." Gutmann wrote: "a trick, which I had seen him [Liszt] do so on several occasions, even with orchestral scores."

5. Blind Tom Wiggins; see footnotes previous chapter.

6. In 1960 these details were volunteered to the author by Leonide Pachmann, who remembered them vividly.

CHAPTER 11

1. In 1888 Frederick Niecks was not particularly fond of Chopin's "Allegro de Concert" in his two-volume biography of the composer. In a footnote he mentioned a copy he had just obtained of a review from the *Athenaeum* of a recent Pachmann performance of the work, which the reviewer said was "a revelation."

2. It was really the Symphony Society of New York which was having some organizational problems at the time and did not appear under its usual name for the concert.

3. Carl [Karl] Heymann (born 1852), son of a cantor in Posen, was a pupil of Ferdinand Hiller and Friedrich Gernsheim, and has a footnote in history as one of composer Edward MacDowell's piano teachers. He had a nervous disposition and was institutionalized because of it more than once. He had to leave a teaching post at the Hoch Conservatory in Frankfurt in 1880 after only one year and tried to resume his career as a virtuoso, but was soon committed again. He died in a hospital in the Netherlands in 1922.

4. From an unidentified clipping found in the Harry Anderson scrapbooks at International Piano Archives at Maryland. Composer and music educator Louis Lombard was born in France in 1861 and died in Ithaca, New York, in 1927.

CHAPTER 12

1. Translated from German by Carsten Fischer.

2. Ibid.

3. Ibid.

4. Translated from German by Dr. Philip Beard.

5. Ibid.

6. Ibid.

7. Translated from German by Edward Weiss.

8. George Halprin studied at the Hochschule in Berlin with Dohnanyi in 1913, and privately with Busoni. Weiss was there and had descended into homelessness. Halprin told the author that Weiss was a "fantastic" pianist, and that he had allowed Weiss to stay with him.

9. Unfortunately Planté had lost his magical touch by the age of ninety and there is no "floating tone" to be heard on his recordings.

10. See Ernest Hutcheson's *The Literature of the Piano*, p. 195: "Those of us who remember Paderewski will not forget the majesty with which he clothed these gorgeous compositions."

CHAPTER 13

1. This was in an article entitled "A Brahma of the Keyboard" that first appeared in the *New York Times* on April 27, 1919; it was included in Huneker's 1921 volume of essays entitled "Variations."

2. The first quote was taken from an unidentified clipping in Cesco Pallottelli's Pachmann scrapbook and certainly dates from Pachmann's dotage; the second is from Richard Drake Saunder's *Music and Dance in California and the West.*

3. From Serge Krish's interview with the author in London in 1960.

4. Original letter in the collection of Gregor Benko.

5. Antun Foerster (1867–1915) was a pianist who had recently given a recital in Berlin; copies of Godowsky's letters to W. S. B. Matthews and Maurice Aronson are from the Godowsky collection of the International Piano Archives at the University of Maryland.

6. Ibid.

7. From Serge Krish's interview with the author in London in 1960.

8. Original letter in the collection of Gregor Benko.

9. This anecdote was related by pianist William Browning (1924–1997) at a lecture on Godowsky's transcriptions and arrangements presented at London's Goldsmiths College in the early 1980's. Browning had studied with both Will Hubbard and Heniot Levy (1879–1945), a Heinrich Barth pupil who had been an associate of Godowsky's in Chicago.

10. Pachmann had in fact been an exclusive Steinway artist since 1899.

11. This was most likely Godowsky's "Badinage," a combination of the two Chopin G flat Etudes; Godowsky published transcriptions of three sets of Chopin Etudes with two Etudes combined.

12. The manuscript of this unpublished article is also in the Godowsky collection of the International Piano Archives at the University of Maryland.

CHAPTER 14

1. Cesco Pallottelli wrote a six page unpublished memoir entitled "My Thirty Years with Vladimir de Pachmann," the manuscript of which he gave the author; details of Pachmann's rituals with his cigars come from that source.

2. Among the papers Cesco Pallottelli showed the author was a list in Pachmann's handwriting with detailed descriptions of his stones, itemizing their different tints, and with notations next to some listings: "For Cesco" or "For Horvath." The identity and relationship of "Horvath" is unknown. Leonide de Pachmann showed the author one jewel his father had given him.

3. From unidentified clipping in Cesco Pallottelli's scrapbook.

CHAPTER 15

1. This appeared in *Good Housekeeping* in January 1934.

2. The earlier version ends with the protagonist taking up the autoharp. Perhaps the "Paradox Incarnate" stemmed at least in part from the fact that the very desirable woman left him for the well-known homosexual Pachmann. Carroll Brent Chilton was an ardent proponent of piano rolls who had invented a system with musical scores printed on piano rolls, to be read as they unrolled.

3. One of the author's teachers, Dr. Berré, then an elderly member of the Leschetizky Association, had heard Pachmann around 1900 and carried her hated memories of both his playing and antics into the 1970s. So rancid was this hate that it had lasted her lifetime.

4. Louis (Ludwig) Breitner (1854–1933), pupil of Anton Rubinstein and Liszt, played the Liszt E flat Concerto with the Chicago Symphony in March 1902; he began teaching at Baltimore's Peabody Conservatory in 1913.

5. Quoted from the unfinished, unpublished memoirs of Abram Chasins at the International Piano Archives at the University of Maryland. About the same time as he would have confided the quote to Chasins, in 1929 Hofmann's comments on Pachmann to interviewer Keyes Porter were milder:

> Mr. de Pachmann is still playing and playing most delightfully, with a beautiful touch and marvelous fleetness to the enjoyment of his audiences at 80. He has been giving farewells for many years but the public will not let him go.

CHAPTER 16

1. Pachmann was referring to a certain Miss Evangeline Florence, who was scheduled to sing a song by Liza Lehmann and another by Venzano at the last concert of the Festival—on the same program with him!

2. In his book *The Literature of the Piano*, Ernest Hutcheson wrote that Pachmann played the Weber Sonata in twenty-five minutes ("much too fast") while Sir Charles Hallé had taken forty-five minutes ("much too slow").

3. *American Music Teacher*, vol. 27, 1978.

4. From a letter to the author from Walter Blodgett dated July 7, 1969; William K. Breckenridge (1867–1956) had studied piano in Europe and served as accompanist on tours of celebrity artists such as 'cellist Pablo Casals. He taught at Oberlin Conservatory from 1890 to 1935.

5. *American Music Teacher*, vol. 27, 1978.

CHAPTER 17

1. This is Benjamin Woolf, who wrote for both the *Boston Gazette* and *Boston Herald* in the 1890s. He was noted for his rough and uncompromising style. "He

had almost no concession to offer for anyone's shortcomings," wrote American organist Henry Dunham. He left the *Boston Herald* in 1903 and was replaced by Philip Hale, who left the *Boston Journal* to take up the new post at the *Herald*.

2. Edward Ziegler, the journalist who replaced Huneker on the staff of the New York scandal sheet, *Town Topics*.

3. Almost certainly Augustus Brentano, a regular dining companion of Huneker's. He was the eldest brother of the well-known booksellers, whose store was nearby on Union Square.

4. Harry Rowe Shelley (1858–1947), organist and composer.

5. The version contained in the novel *Dvorak in Love* by Josef Škvorecký is completely unreliable, conflating and combining various bits about Huneker and Pachmann from disparate sources and dates into a highly fictionalized tale.

6. The Liszt Etude that was Pachmann's drawing card was *La Leggierezza.* As for Rosenthal's swiftness, Olin Downes reported in the *New York Times* (November 2, 1926) that Pachmann had "wept once when Mr. Rosenthal played the study in thirds at a murderous tempo . . . Pachmann confessed . . . 'He plays it faster than I can.'"

CHAPTER 18

1. The story about Pachmann showing Rosenthal how to play Mazurkas seems to have been a favorite of the Chopinzee, who apparently told it to his friend and associate, Arnold Somlyo of Baldwin Pianos. After he retired Somlyo typed up a group of Pachmann stories drawing on his memories, including an inaccurate and much exaggerated version of the Mazurka story. A copy of Somlyo's typescript can be found at the New York Public Library clipping file; it is unknown whether the exaggerations stem from Pachmann, or Somlyo.

2. Albert Chevalier (1861–1923), a cockney comedian and singer who composed some of the lyrics for the famous song "My Old Dutch."

3. In the same letter Godowsky wrote: "Pachmann was really very ill. He is now in Lucerne. He looks very poorish and I am afraid he will not last long. He is one of the really great pianists, notwithstanding his limitations and eccentricities." Godowsky's fears for Pachmann's life were misplaced, and it is unknown what caused his "poorish" looks, although it very well could have been an emotional state relating to his breakup with McKay, which happened at this time.

4. Auguste Villiers de l'Isle Adam (1838–1889), a French symbolist writer whose work was heavily influenced "by all the *isms* in vogue in his day (occultism, spiritualism and Wagnerism, etc.)" according to the *Oxford Companion to French Literature.*

CHAPTER 19

1. Wilhelm Gericke (1845–1925) was the only conductor of the Boston Symphony to serve two terms as Director: 1884 to 1889 and 1898 to 1906.

2. Published in the *American Music Teacher*, volume 27, 1978. William Mason (1829–1908) was a Boston-born Liszt pupil. His brother Harry Mason was co-founder of the Mason and Hamlin piano firm.

CHAPTER 20

1. A modern day counterpart was the composer/conductor Leonard Bernstein, also noted for kissing indiscriminately. Tapes made in the American White House of President Richard Nixon at the time of the opening of the Kennedy Arts Center in Washington, D.C., reveal that this was a subject much discussed by Nixon and his aides. On a tape from September 7, 1971, H. R. Haldeman is heard telling Nixon about a performance of Bernstein's composition, "Mass," the previous evening, especially Bernstein's embraces of members of the cast and the kisses he bestowed on the men. Six days later, on the 13th, Haldeman again mentions that Bernstein was kissing people on the mouth, "including the big black guy (choreographer Alvin Ailey). Nixon calls this "absolutely sickening."

2. Translation from German by Carsten Fischer.

3. It is almost impossible to adequately translate twenty-three thousand 1907 dollars into today's value, but it would be close to a million dollars. One of history's legendary blue diamonds, the Wittelsbach, once part of the Austrian and Bavarian crown jewels, was sold in London in 2008 for the equivalent of twenty-four million dollars. But the value of the rarest gems has soared even higher since then. The *New York Times* wrote on January 7, 2010 that it probably was "by weight, the most valuable commodity on earth."

CHAPTER 21

1. Unfortunately the author did not obtain a copy of this photo.

2. Once the home of the now abandoned Concord, the largest of the Catskill Mountain resort hotels.

3. Best guesses of which pianists Pachmann refers to here are: Josef Hofmann, Moriz Rosenthal and Alfred Reisenauer.

4. This is undoubtedly Karl Robert Edward von Hartmann (1842–1906), whose two volume *Religionsphilosophie* was published in 1882; it is unknown whether Pachmann actually ever met him.

5. There is no evidence the pianist ever met the composer Offenbach. Comparing himself to Christ now came naturally to Pachmann. Australian bass-baritone Peter Dawson's autobiography quotes Pachmann's response, when Dawson once congratulated him for a particularly fine performance of one of Liszt's works: "I thank you . . . In the last two thousand years there have been three great men . . . Jesus Christ . . . Liszt . . . and Pachmann—Vladimir Pachmann."

CHAPTER 22

1. Leonide remembered that it was at one of his last recitals in Bechstein Hall, but in all likelihood it was the recital at Queen's Hall on May 24, 1909.

2. This refers to Thomas Parnell's 18th century poem, "An Elegy, to an Old Beauty."

3. The pair played at least one other concert together, in Oxford, England, on May 30, 1911.

CHAPTER 23

1. The custom of piano companies paying artists to play and endorse their brand lasted two more decades, but the Great Depression stopped such payments for all but the top few pianists in the world, and by the end of World War Two subventions were not being paid to any pianists by either Baldwin or Steinway.

2. Michael Hambourg (1855–1916) had been a student of Nicholas Rubinstein and graduated from the St. Petersburg Conservatory in 1879. In 1890 he moved his family to London when his eleven year old son Mark made his London debut as a pianist.

3. By request, Baldwin had provided him with specially regulated pianos with a very shallow dip.

4. These survive only because the author was able to have tapes made of the unissued recordings in Rome in 1960; they have been released on compact discs by the Marston label, along with all other existing Pachmann recordings. Perhaps the original pressings are still extant and will someday surface.

CHAPTER 24

1. Music was obviously not Mr. Meltzer's specialty. Pachmann's story about showing up Paderewski is probably an exaggeration, but there is little possibility the Chopinzee himself misidentified the solo work as a "concerto" by Paderewski; it was most likely a "Caprice."

2. It is unknown who gave Kennedy to understand that Cesco had been adopted by Pachmann—no other mention of this possibility has surfaced. From an October 1943 article by Fred Gaisberg in the *Gramophone* we know that Cesco misled Gaisberg, telling him that he "first came to de Pachmann as a pupil." Pachmann's praise for Moiseiwitsch was described by W. S. Meadmore in the March 1940 *Gramophone*.

3. Benno Moiseiwitsch was twenty-three at the time Pachmann became interested in his playing in 1913. Shortly after this Moiseiwitsch and Kennedy were married; they divorced in 1924.

4. Translated from the French by the author.

CHAPTER 25

1. Paderewski was the first pianist to be awarded the Beethoven Medal, in 1897. Emil Sauer got his in 1910, Harold Bauer in 1912 and Alfred Cortot in 1923. Robert Klein's history of Queen's Hall reports that composer/organist Myles Birket Foster "says that Paderewski refused to accept the medal, because his name appeared only on the rim." Klein points out that he was unable to determine whether Paderewski changed his mind, "but his name always appeared on the Society's list of recipients."

2. This locution was coined by English poet and essayist Austin Dobson, referring to certain beloved volumes called duodecimos (abbreviated "12mos"), slightly smaller than octavos ("8vos").

3. Pachmann was closer to five feet one inch tall.

4. Pachmann was closer to seventy.

5. In New York Adrian met an American woman named Edith Sproul, daughter of an antiquarian book dealer, and they married in April 1919. They moved to Paris in September 1919. He also acted as Leopold Godowsky's European legal counsel, dying in December 1937 at the age of fifty-two, a rare early death in the Pachmann family.

6. See Chapter 31 for a discussion of this pregnancy.

CHAPTER 26

1. Translated from Italian by Howard Fink.

2. French actor Benoit-Constant Coquelin (1841–1909), known for his impersonation of Rostand's Cyrano; Ferruccio Benini (1854–1916), the most famous member of a family of Italian comedians and actors who often performed in Venetian dialect.

3. Translated from Italian by Howard Fink.

CHAPTER 27

1. George Grossmith (1847–1912), the English comedian/composer/actor/singer, creator of the roles of Ko-Ko in the premieres of Gilbert and Sullivan's "Mikado" as well as the Major-General in "The Pirates of Penzance," was also probably the world's first piano humorist. One of his acts involved playing "Three Blind Mice" in the styles of various great composers, which he did at his recitals in Brooklyn, New York. At those concerts he also added an imitation of Pachmann, according to the *Brooklyn Eagle* of April 2, 1900.

2. Serge Krish was almost completely unknown until February 2007, when his name appeared in the world press as the teacher of English pianist Joyce Hatto, whose more than one hundred compact disc recordings were later revealed to be sonic forgeries.

3. According to the diaries of Josef Hofmann's first wife, Hofmann once wanted a woman sitting in the first row at a recital of his in Russia ejected, because she was yawning during the performance—it turned out she was deaf. Hofmann told of a similar situation when pianist Alfred Reisenauer refused to continue a recital until a bored looking woman was removed.

4. Ibid.

5. Translated from the German by Carsten Fischer.

6. In Patrick Piggott's biography of Rachmaninoff there appears a story of the Russian composer/pianist hearing Pachmann in concert, and Pachmann

supposedly segueing from the first chords of Rachmaninoff's most famous Prelude into Chopin's Fantasie-Impromptu, after which Rachmaninoff smiled. Mr. Piggott got one important detail wrong. The pianist who was performing and who was the recipient of Rachmaninoff's smile was not Pachmann, who hated Rachmaninoff's music and never played a note of it, but Rachmaninoff's friend, Josef Hofmann. Pianist and scholar Charles Rosen was present at that 1935 Hofmann Carnegie Hall recital and describes the incident in a video documentary about Hofmann scheduled to be issued by the Marston label as "The Complete Josef Hofmann, Volume 9."

7. This is part of Godowsky's *Walzermasken* and properly titled *Karneval*.

8. Probably the B major Nocturne, Op. 32, No. 1.

CHAPTER 28

1. On March 1, 1934, the *New York Times* carried an interview with Rachmaninoff, who answered "Josef Hofmann" when the reporter asked who he thought was the greatest pianist. "Even though Vladimir de Pachmann has said that Hofmann is an amateur?" asked the reporter. "That," replied the artist, "is because de Pachmann himself was an amateur."

2. In 1916 Ethel Leginska had sent out press releases comparing her own playing to Pachmann's, stating that critics had praised her Chopin interpretations, which supposedly were "equaled by only one living artist, the redoubtable Vladimir de Pachmann himself." She seemed to have been indefatigable and to have spent large sums in promoting her own playing and conducting. As a result she garnered a considerable amount of attention in the musical press, and she was no stranger to publicity stunts. In January 1925 she obtained coverage when she failed to show up for a Carnegie Hall recital. She claimed that ". . . the world grew hazy and unsubstantial . . ." (*MC*, February 26, 1925). She said that she had had a nervous breakdown, but had composed a piano concerto during her hazy period. Leginska was most likely aware of the news sensations that had previously ensued when Fannie Bloomfield-Zeisler, and then later Godowsky, had disappeared in a similar fashion.

3. Original letter in the collection of Gregor Benko.

4. Bilotti had some lessons with Pachmann during this final American tour. In *MC* for February 24, 1927, an interviewer asked him if he learned Pachmann's secret: "Nobody ever found out exactly the secret of his tone—at least I have never heard a pianist who sounds like him."

5. Information supplied by James Mixter, who started working for Baldwin in 1940 and succeeded Wyman in the 1970s.

CHAPTER 29

1. Here the pianist was almost certainly trying to recall "Manchester."

2. Translated from the French by the author.

3. Leon Sametini, born 1886, was a violin teacher.

CHAPTER 30

1. The excerpt from Pachmann's interview is quoted in a column defending him for talking while playing, found in an unidentified clipping in the Harry Anderson Pachmann scrapbook at the International Piano Archives at the University of Maryland. There is some evidence in the H.M.V. recording ledgers that Pachmann was enticed into the recording studios many times for these sessions, and that many test recordings were made but never issued, and subsequently destroyed.

2. Ibid.

3. Translated by Roger Gross.

4. This clipping is also among the material collected by piano scholar Harry L. Anderson and can be found in his scrapbooks, now located at the International Piano Archives at Maryland.

5. Translation by Agnes Niemetz.

6. Translation by Carsten Fischer.

7. A copy of this letter, already translated into English, was provided to the author by Leonide de Pachmann. The current location of the original letter and the rest of Leonide's collection of Pachmann memorabilia is unknown. Pianist Henri Etlin (ca. 1889–?) entered the Paris Conservatoire at age 17 and studied with Diémer and Saint-Saëns as well as Planté. He was also talented as an artist and painter.

CHAPTER 31

1. Cesco provided the translation for this article, but certainly did not accomplish it himself; possibly he hired a commercial translating service.

2. This story was told to the author by Cesco, who obviously told it many times to many people, including the writer Paul Landormy, who published a romanticized version in *Le Figaro* in January, 1933: "A supreme effort and a supreme rendering, a supreme joy for himself—which leaves him so profoundly moved that he regains his bed with difficulty and closes his eyes. He has bidden farewell to his piano, to Chopin, to music."

3. In the 1970s an Italian auction house offered the photo of Liszt autographed to Pachmann; it is unknown from where they obtained it, or to whom it was sold. The author fortunately made copies of much of this material while visiting Cesco in 1960.

CHAPTER 32

1. From Sorabji's book, *Around Music*.

2. From Hofmann's book, *Piano Questions*.

3. Chopin's pupil Wilhelm von Lenz witnessed the incident with Meyerbeer, and claimed that Chopin was playing in time. The rhythm had been submerged by the melody.

4. These lessons were transcribed by Valerie's mother Mme. Auguste Boissier in her book *Liszt pédagogue: leçons de piano données par Liszt à Mademoiselle Valérie Boissier à Paris en 1832*, published in Paris in 1927 and in an English translation by Elyse Mach in 1973.

5. Arthur Wilson, in the January 1912 issue of the *Musician*.

6. From Jean Jacques Eigeldinger's book *Chopin, Pianist and Teacher, As Seen By His Pupils*.

7. Sterrnberg's articles appeared in the *Musician* magazine in 1912 and his book *Tempo Rubato and Other Essays*.

8. McEwen published his findings in a book entitled *Tempo Rubato or Time-Variation in Musical Performance* that was quoted in Richard Hudson's *Stolen Time: The History of Tempo Rubato*. Paderewski's ideas were expressed in an article entitled "Paderewski on Tempo Rubato" in Henry T. Finck's book, *Success in Music and How It Is Won*.

9. Ignace Friedman, born in 1880, was an exception. In his freer use of rhythm, he was closer to Pachmann, born in 1848.

10. Available at: www.lib/umd.edu/binaries/content/assets/public/ipam/resources-reviews-and-links/arnest-hands-together-article-pdf-5-15-12.pdf

11. In Huneker's *Chopin*, p. 273.

Bibliography

Andrews, Robert Hardy: *A Corner of Chicago*; Little, Brown, Boston, 1963

Aronson, Maurice: *Forty-Two Years With Godowsky*; unpublished manuscript

Aronson, Rudolph: *Theatrical and Musical Memoirs*; McBride Nast, New York, 1913

Bache, Constance: *Brother Musicians*; Methuen, London, 1901

Barnett, John Francis: *Musical Impressions and Reminiscences*; Hodder and Stoughton, London, 1906

Batten, Joe: *Joe Batten's Book*; Rockliffe, London, 1926

Bauer, Harold: *Harold Bauer, His Book*; Greenwood, New York, 1969

Beatty-Kingston, William: *Men, Cities and Events*; Bliss, Sands & Foster, London, 1895

Beckson, Karl: *Arthur Symons, A Life*; Clarendon, Oxford, 1987

Beringer, Oskar: *Fifty Years of Experience in Pianoforte Playing*; Bosworth, London, 1907

Bispham, David: *A Quaker Singer's Recollections*; Macmillan, New York, 1920

Blom, Eric (Ed.): *Music Lovers' Miscellany*; Gollancz, London, 1935

Boissier, Auguste: *Liszt Studies* (*Liszt pédagogue: Leçons de piano données par Liszt à Mlle. Valérie Boissier en 1832*); translated by Elyse Mach, AMP, 1973

Breithaup, Rudolf: *Die Natürliche Klaviertechnik*; Kahnt, Leipzig, 1905

Brower, Harriette: *Modern Masters of the Keyboard*; Stokes, New York, 1926

Buffen, F. Foster: *Musical Celebrities, Second Series*; Chapman and Hall, London, 1893

Burch, Gladys: *Famous Pianists for Young People*; Barnes, New York, 1943

Burke, Thomas: *Nights in London*; Holt, New York, 1916

Busoni, Ferruccio: *Busoni's Letters to His Wife*; Arnold, London, 1938

Cardus, Neville: *Sir Thomas Beecham, A Memoir*; Collins, London, 1961

Casella, Alfredo: *Il Pianoforte*; Tumminelli, Rome, 1936

Chasins, Abram: *Now That I Think of It*; unpublished manuscript at International Piano Archives at University of Maryland

Chotzinoff, Samuel: *Til Death Do Us Part*—unpublished manuscript at Gottlieb Archives of Boston University

Cooke, James Francis: *Great Men and Famous Musicians on the Art of Music*; Presser, Philadelphia, 1925

———. *Great Pianists on Piano Playing*; Presser, Philadelphia, 1913

Copeland, George: Unpublished manuscript memoir in New York Public Library

Couling, Della: *Ferruccio Busoni, A Musical Ishmael*; Scarecrow Press, Lanham, Maryland, 2005

Cowen, Frederick: *My Art and My Friends*; Arnold, London, 1913

Cumberland, Gerald: *Set Down in Malice*; Brentanos, New York, 1919

Cumberland, Gerald: *Written in Friendship*; Grant Richards, London, 1923

da Motta, Jose Vianna: *Nachtrag zu Studien bei Hans von Bülow*; Luchshardt, Berlin, 1896

Dawson, Peter: *Fifty Years of Song*; Hutchinson, London, 1951

Dent, Edward: *Ferruccio Busoni*; Oxford University Press, London, 1933

Downes, Irene: *Olin Downes on Music*; Simon and Schuster, New York, 1957

Ducat, Eva: *Another Way of Music*; Chapman and Hall, London, 1928

Edwards, H. Sutherland: *Personal Recollections*; Cassell, London, 1900

Eichmann, A. H.: *Wilhelm Backhaus*; Koster, Geneva, 1958

Eigeldinger, Jean Jacques: *Chopin, Pianist and Teacher As Seen By His Pupils*; Cambridge University Press, Cambridge, 1986

Elken, R.: *Queen's Hall 1893-1941*; Rider, London, 1945

Elson, Arthur: *Woman's Work in Music*; Page and Co., Boston, 1903

Fay, Amy: *Music Study in Germany*; DaCapo, New York, 1979

Fifield, Christopher: *Ibbs and Tillett, The Rise and Fall of a Musical Empire*; Ashgate, London, 2005

Finck, Henry T.: *Success In Music and How It Is Won*; Scribners, New York, 1913

Flamant, Alexander: *Das Reich der Tone*; Streit Verlag, Dresden, 1880

Flesch, Carl: *The Memoirs of Carl Flesch*; Rockliffe, London, 1957

Fouquet, Octave: *Glinka d'apres ses memoires et sa Correspondance*; Heugel, Paris, 1880

Friedheim, Arthur: *Life and Liszt*; Taplinger, New York, 1961

Frohman, Daniel: *Daniel Frohman Presents*; Kendall and Sharp, New York, 1935

Fuchs, Carl: *Musical and Other Recollections*; Sherrat and Hughes, Manchester, 1937

Fuller-Maitland, J. A.: *A Door-keeper of Music*; Murray, London, 1929

Funk, Addie: *Vienna's Musical Sites and Landmarks*; Knoch, Vienna, 1927

Gaisberg, Fred: *The Music Goes Round*; Macmillan, New York, 1942

Galafres, Elza: *Lives ... Loves ... Losses*; Versatile, Vancouver, 1973

Ganz, Wilhelm: *Memories of a Musician*; Murray, London, 1913

Garceau, Edouard: *The Little Doustes*; Muller, London, 1935

Gerig, Reginald: *Famous Pianists and Their Technique*, Luce, Washington, D.C., 1974

Gipson, Richard McCandless: *The Life of Emma Thursby*; New York Historical Society, New York, 1940

Godfrey, Sir Dan: *Memories and Music*; Hutchinson, London, 1924

Graf, Max: *Legends of a Musical City*; Allen, London, 1932

Grant, Mark: *Maestros of the Pen*; Northeastern University Press, Boston, 1998.

Graydon, Nell and Sizemore, Margaret: *The Amazing Marriage of Marie Eustis and Josef Hofmann*, University of South Carolina, Columbia, 1965

Grun, Bernard: *Private Lives of the Great Composers*; Library Publishers, New York, 1955

Guerrini, Guido: *Ferruccio Busoni*; Monsalvato, Florence, No Date

Hadden, J. Cuthbert: *Modern Musicians*; Foulis, London, 1913

Hambourg, Mark: *The Eighth Octave*; Williams and Norgate, London, 1951

———. *From Piano to Forte*; Cassell, London, 1931

Hanslick, Eduard: *Vienna's Golden Age of Music*; Simon and Schuster, New York, 1950

Haweis, H. R.: *My Musical Life*; Allen, London, 1880

Henderson, A. M.: *Musical Memories*; Grand Educational Co., London, 1938

Hetherington, John: *Melba*; Farrar, Straus and Giroux, New York, 1967

Hoffman, Malvina: *Yesterday is Tomorrow*; Crown, New York, 1965

Hofmann, Josef: *Piano Questions*; Doubleday, New York, 1909

Hollins, Alfred: *A Blind Musician Looks Back*; Bardon, London, 2002

Horszowski, Bice Costa: *Miecio, Remembrances of Mieczyslaw Horszowski*; Ergo Edizione, Geneva, 2002

Hudson, Richard: *Stolen Time: The History of Tempo Rubato*; Oxford University Press, Oxford, 1995

Hueffer, Francis: *Half a Century of Music in England*; Chapman and Hall, London, 1889

Huneker, James Gibbons: *Chopin—The Man and His Music*; Scribners, New York, 1900

———. *Franz Liszt*; Chapman-Hill, London, 1910

———. *Intimate Letters*; Boni and Liveright, New York, 1924

———. *Letters*; Laurie, London, 1928

———. *Melomaniacs*; Scribners, New York, 1902

———. *Steeplejack*; Scribners, New York, 1920

———. *Unicorns*; Scribners, New York, 1921

———. *Variations*; Scribners, New York, 1921

Hutcheston, Ernest: *The Literature of the Piano*, Revised Edition; Knopf, New York, 1949

Hutschenruyther, Wonter and Kruseman, Philip: *Musicana Anecdotes*; Kruseman, Gravenhagen, Netherlands, 1939

James-Reed, Mint: *Music in Austin 1900–1956*; Von Boeckman-Jones, Austin, 1957

Johnson, H. Earle: *Symphony Hall, Boston*; Little, Brown, Boston, 1950

Kahrer-Rappoldi, Laura: *Memoiren*; von Lepel, Dresden, 1929

Kelly, Wayne: *Downright Upright*; Natural Heritage, Toronto, 1991

Kennedy, Michael: *The Halle Tradition*; Oxford University Press, London, 1960

King, Charles: *Odessa*; W. W. Norton, New York, 2011

Kolodin, Irving: *The Musical Life*; Knopf, New York, 1958

Kornitzer, Louis: *The Pearl Trader*; Sheridan House, New York, 1936

Krehbiel, H. E.: *Review of the New York Musical Season 1889–1890*; Novello, New York and London, 1890

Labori, Marguerite: *Labori, Ses Notes, Manuscrits, Sa Vie*; Attinger, Paris, 1947

Lahee, H. C.: *Famous Pianists of To-day and Yesterday*; Page, Boston, 1901

Landau, Rom: *Paderewski*; Nicholson and Watson, London, 1924

Langford, Samuel: *Musical Criticisms*; Oxford University Press, London, 1929

Legany, Dezso: *Ferenc Liszt and His Country 1874–1886*; Occidental, Budapest,1992

——. *Liszt and His Country 1869–1873*; Corvina Kiado, 1983

Lehmann, John: *Ancestors and Friends*; Eyre and Spottiswoode, London, 1962

Lenz, Wilhelm von: *Great Piano Virtuosos of Our Time*; Schirmer, New York, 1899

Levant, Oscar: *The Unimportance of Being Oscar*; Putnam, New York, 1968

Liebling, A. J.: *The Sweet Science*; Viking Press, New York, 1956

Long, Marguerite: *At the Piano with Debussy*; Dent, London, 1972

Maisel, Edward: *Charles T. Griffes*; Knopf, New York, 1943

Malan, Roy: *Efrem Zimbalist, a Life*; Amadeus, Portland, 2004

Markham, Stanley: *Music of All Nations*; Wavery, London ca. 1927

McEwen, John Blackwood: *Tempo Rubato or Time-Variation in Musical Performance*; Oxford University Press, London, 1928

Mencken, H. L.: *A Book of Prefaces*, Op. 13; Knopf, New York, 1917

Mendl, R. W. S.: *Music Lover's Armchair*; Allen, London, 1926

Milhaud, Darius: *Notes Without Music*; Dobson, London, ca. 1947

Moran, William R.: *Nellie Melba, A Contemporary Review*; Greenwood, Westport, Conn., 1985

Murray, John: *Russia of Today*; Smith, London, 1878

Nabokov, Vladimir: *Tyrants Destroyed and Other Stories*; McGraw-Hill, New York, 1975

Nardelli, Frederico: *Biographie di Dio*; Cosmopolita, Rome, No Date

Neuhaus, Heinrich: *The Art of Piano Playing*; Barrie and Jenkins, London, 1973

Newton, Ivor: *At The Piano*; Hamilton, London, 1966

Nicholas, Jeremy: *Godowsky, The Pianists' Pianist*; Appian, Northumberland, 1989

Nichols, Beverly: *Twenty-five*; Penguin, Harmondsworth, 1926

Niecks, Frederick: *Frederick Chopin as a Man and Musician*; Novello, London, 1888

Niemann, Walter: *Meister des Klaviers*; Schuster und Loeffler, Berlin, 1921

Paderewski, Ignace Jan and Lawton, Mary: *The Paderewski Memoirs*; Scribners, New York, 1938

Pallottelli, Francesco: *Vladimir de Pachmann*; Red Cross, Rome, No Date, ca. 1917

Paul, Elliot: *The Last Time I Saw Paris*; Random House, New York, 1942

Phillips, James H.: *Paderewski Discovers America*; Morris Publishing, Kearney, Nebr., 2006

Piggott, Patrick: *Rachmaninov*; Faber and Faber, London, 1978

Porte, John F.: *Chopin: The Composer and His Music*; Scribners, New York, 1935

Radic, Therese: *Melba, The Voice of Australia*; Macmillan, Melbourne, 1986

Remo, Felix: *La Musique au Pays des Brouillards*; Chex Tous les Libraries, Paris, 1885

Remy, Alfred (Editor): *Baker's Biographical Dictionary of Musicians*, 3rd Revised Edition; Schirmers, New York, 1919

Reuter, Florizel von: *Great People I Have Known*; Freeman, Waukeesha, 1964

Rieseman, Oskar von: *Rachmaninoff's Recollections*; Macmillan, New York, 1934

Roes, Paul: *Essai Sur La Technique Du Piano*; Lemoine, Paris, 1935

Ronald, Landon (Editor): *The Music Lover's Portfolio*; Wavery, London, No Date

Rossi, Gianno Scipione: *Storia di Alice*; Rubberttino Editore, Rome, 2010

Rowland, David (Editor): *The Cambridge Companion to the Piano*; Cambridge University Press, Cambridge, 1998

Rubinstein, Artur: *My Many Years*; Knopf, New York, 1980

Rugoff, Milton: *The Beechers. An American Family in the 19th Century*; Harper and Row, New York, 1981

Saleski, Gdal: *Famous Musicians of Jewish Origin*; Bloch, New York, 1949

———. *Famous Musicians of a Wandering Race*; Bloch, New York, 1927

Santley, Charles: *Reminiscences of My Life*; Brentanos, New York, 1909

Sargeant, Winthrop: *Geniuses, Goddesses and People*; Dutton, New York, 1949

Saunders, Richard Drake: *Music and Dance in California and the West*; Bureau of Music Research, Hollywood 1948

Scharwenka, Xavier: *Sounds from My Life*; Scarecrow, Lanham, Maryland, 2007

Scholes, Percy B.: *The Mirror of Music*; Novello and Oxford University, London, 1934

Schonberg, Harold C.: *The Great Pianists*; Simon and Schuster, New York, 1963

Schwab, Arnold T.: *James Gibbons Huneker: Critic of the Seven Arts*; Stanford University Press, Palo Alto, 1963

Shaw, George Bernard: *Shaw's Music*; Dodd Mead, New York, 1981

Siloti, Alexander: *My Memories of Liszt*; Simpson, Edinburgh, No Date

Sitwell, Sacothereverell: *Franz Liszt*; Dover, New York, 1967

Sitwell, Sacothereverell: *Sacred and Profane Love*; Faber and Faber, London, 1940

Sooy, Raymond: *Memoirs of my Recording and Traveling Experiences for the Victor Talking Machine Company 1898–1925*; www.davidsarnoff.org/soo.html

Sorabji, Kaikhosru Shapurji: *Around Music*; Unicorn Press, London, 1932

Stargardt-Wolff, Edith: *Wegbereiter grosser Musiker*; Bote und Bock, Berlin, 1954

Sternberg, Constantin von: *Tempo Rubato and Other Essays*; Schirmers, New York, 1920

Sutherland-Edwards, H.: *Personal Recollections*; Cassell, London, 1900

Symons, Arthur: Plays, *Acting and Music*; Duckworth, London, 1903

Symons, Arthur: Plays, *Acting and Music (Revised)*; Constable, London, 1909

Temianka, Henry: *Facing the Music*; McKay, New York, 1973

Thomson, Virgil: *The Musical Scene*; Knopf, New York, 1945

Tiomkin, Dimitri and Buranelli, Prosper: *Please Don't Hate Me*; Doubleday, New York, 1959

Turner, W. J.: *Music and Life*; Methuen, London, 1921

Van Vechten, Carl: *Music and Bad Manners*; Knopf, New York, 1916

Verne, Mathilde: *Chords of Remembrance*; Hutchinson, London, 1936

Walker, Alan: *Franz Liszt: The Virtuoso Years*; Cornell University Press, Ithaca, 1983

Walker, Alan: *Franz Liszt: The Final Years*; Knopf, New York, 1996

Walker, Bettina: *My Musical Experiences*; Scribners, New York, 1893

Wallace, Robert K.: *A Century of Music Making*; Indiana University Press, Bloomington, 1976

Watson, Derek: *Liszt*; Dent, London, 1989

Weissmann, Adolf: *Der Virtuose*; Caserer, Berlin, 1920

Whelbourne, Herbert: *Standard Book of Celebrated Musicians*; Laurie, London, 1930

Williams, Adrian: *Portraits of Liszt, by Himself and His Contemporaries*; Clarendon, Oxford, 1990

Wolf, Hugo: *The Music Criticism of Hugo Wolf*; Holmes and Meier, New York, 1979
Wolf, Werner: *Anton Bruckner, Rustic Genius*; Dutton, New York, 1942
Wood, Henry (Editor): *Music of All Nations*; Fleetway, London, no date
Woollcott, Alexander: *Enchanted Aisles*; Putnam, New York, 1924
Wortham, H. E.: *A Musical Odyssey*; Methuen, London, 1924
No author: *The History of Music in San Francisco, Volume Seven, An Anthology of Music Criticism*; Works Progress Administration, San Francisco, 1942

RUSSIAN SOURCES

Entsiklopedicheskij slovar. Izd/ V. IA. Zheilieznova / (Editor) (et al.) Tokyo, Nauka reprint, 1980
Istoričeskij obzor sorokoletija Rešel'evskogo liceja s 1817 po 1857 goda [Historical overview of the 40th anniversary of the Reschel Lyzeum from 1817 to 1858]. Iosif Mixnevič, Odessa. Tipografija L. Ničše [Nietsche], 1857
Russkij biografičeskij slovar' [Russian Biographical Dictionary], Polovcev, Editor, Sankt Petersburg, Publisher: Tipografija I. N. Ckoroxod, 1902
Učebno-vospitatel'nye zavedenija, iz kotoryx obrazovyvalsja Rešel'evskij licey 1804–1817 gg. [Teaching-educational institution, from which the Reschel Lyzeum evolved 1804–1817] N. Lenc [Lenz] Odessa, Ekonomičeskaja tipografija, 1903

Index